REFERENCE

ATLAS of the BABY BOOM GENERATION

Neil A. Hamilton

Jon Keith Brunelle

Beth Scully

Rebecca Sherman

Macmillan Reference USA

an imprint of the Gale Group

Detroit • New York • San Francisco • London • Boston • Woodbridge, CT

Macmillan Library Reference USA
1633 Broaday, 7th Floor
New York, New York 10019

For Macmillan Library Reference
PUBLISHER: Elly Dickason
EDITOR: Tracey Topper
COVER DESIGN: Lisa Chovnick

SEP 2000

For the Moschovitis Group, Inc.
EXECUTIVE EDITOR: Valerie Tomaselli
SENIOR EDITOR: Hilary W. Poole
DESIGN, ICONOGRAPHY, AND LAYOUT: Richard Garratt
EDITORIAL COORDINATOR: Stephanie Schreiber
EDITORIAL ASSISTANT: Renée Miller
PHOTO RESEARCH: Gillian Speeth
"TRENDS" ILLUSTRATIONS: Debra Ziss
ADDITIONAL LAYOUT: Annemarie Redmond
COPYEDITING: Carole Campbell
PROOFREADING: Joseph Reilly and Paul Scaramazza
PRODUCTION ASSISTANT: Yolanda Pluguez
INDEX: AEIOU, Inc.
ADDITIONAL WRITING AND RESEARCH: Aysan Celik, Hilary W. Poole, Stephanie Schreiber, Brian Selfon

Produced by The Moschovitis Group, Inc.
339 Fifth Avenue, New York, New York 10016
www.mosgroup.com

Manufactured in the United States of America

Printing number

ISBN: 0-02-865008-5
Library of Congress Catalog Card Number: 00-101137

This paper meets the requirement of ANSI/NISO Z39.48-1992 (Permanence of Paper).

Contents

Contents

Introduction

"The whole world is watching! The whole world is watching!" So chanted young protesters outside the 1968 Democratic National Convention in Chicago as television cameras took in a riotous scene. If not the whole world, America, at least, was watching . . . and watching much more than the protest. Americans were absorbed in, absorbed by, immersed in, and reshaped by an entire generation of which the protesters were a part—the Baby Boomers.

The nation had never before seen an explosion of births such as those beginning in 1946 and continuing through 1964, an 18-year-long event that clearly separates the Boomer generation from others. Within the generation itself, however, the picture is less clear, filled with contradiction and complexity. Any general picture of the Boomers must confront myriad demographic differences, along with individual qualities that make people unique. Ironically, such a survey threatens to minimize the very individualism that as youths Boomers thought society was ignoring.

Thus we can raise the point of the fairness of lumping together under the rubric "Boomer generation" whites, blacks, Hispanics, and Native Americans; women and men; straights and gays; conservatives, liberals and radicals; or the wealthy, the middle class, and the poor. And notwithstanding the defining 18-year period, we can ask whether it is fair to lump together those born in 1946 with those born in 1964.

That early and late Baby Boomers had different views and expectations shaped by different experiences can be seen in the controversial period from the mid-1960s through early 1970s, when the counterculture thrived. In *The Movement and the Sixties*, Terry H. Anderson describes two waves that swept through this time of political radicals, hippies, feminists, and other protesters against mainstream values and practices. The first wave, those born in the late 1940s (and pre-Boomers born a few years earlier), shook the foundations of the conformist society that had taken root in the 1950s. The second wave, Boomers born in the early to mid-1950s, had watched their older brothers and sisters rebel and protest; for them, attacks against authority seemed second nature.

As Boomers grew older, they continued to have different experiences based on their time of birth. Thus, a Boomer born in 1964 had a different reaction to the disco scene in 1976 at age 12 than a Boomer born in 1946, who was then age 30—the first Boomer too young to get heavily involved, and the second Boomer too old, with adolescence, even youth, left behind for the world of work and raising a family. At the end of the cold war in 1990, the younger Boomer would have been 26, the older 44—and again likely to react to events differently.

This book, *Atlas of the Baby Boom Generation*, covers Boomer diversity extensively and recognizes that despite the differences among Baby Boomers, they carried a common cultural baggage packed with shared experiences from their formative years, a baggage they would continue to carry throughout their lives. Although they were not all children of prosperity, they were all children of a prosperous period,

Introduction

among the most dynamic in American history. They all grew up in a society increasingly geared to young people with a discernible (and for business, a profitable) adolescent subculture—teen movies, teen magazines, teen advertising, and the ubiquitous rock 'n' roll. They all felt the clout of suburban America, which shaped everything from political programs to television programs. They were enthralled by the Apollo missions but stirred by a series of violent tragedies that convinced many that something was seriously wrong with America: the assassinations of John Kennedy, Martin Luther King, Jr., and Robert Kennedy; the shootings at Kent State and Jackson State; the war in Vietnam.

They all shared a popular culture that separated them from earlier and later generations. For example, while the last Baby Boomers reached adolescence after the Beatles broke up, the rock group's continuing influence meant those Boomers could still identify with them, converse with older Boomers about them, and participate in the mental map that defined the entire generation. They shared a drug culture that separated them from older America as sharply as anything has ever separated generations. Not all Boomers took drugs, but most knew about them, knew what they did, knew the slang that referred to them . . . and felt their influence in art, music, and advertising.

Words spoken during events Boomer youths involved themselves in expressed their generation's belief in its distinctive nature and in its ability to redefine the world: "We are the delicate spores of the new fierceness that will change America," some political activists declared in 1968. But just a few years later, Boomers witnessed a tremendous change in the zeitgeist, or spirit of the times. After the idealism of the counterculture years, pessimism took hold in the mid-1970s, caused by the defeat in Vietnam, the Watergate scandal, inflation, and high unemployment.

A conservative reaction to the counterculture gained momentum in the 1980s. Symbolized by President Ronald Reagan, Americans in large numbers attacked liberal reforms, such as affirmative action. A cultural war erupted between those who wanted to return to "traditional values," often interpreted as a white, Christian, male-dominated society, and those who advocated minority rights and diverse thought. Society at large shifted from an "I'm more

▼ *School children duck and cover during an A-bomb drill in Brooklyn, New York, on February 1, 1951. (UPI/CORBIS-BETTMANN)*

▲ *A human footprint on lunar soil, on July 21, 1969, the date of the first moon landing. (Courtesy of NASA)*

concerned about the meaning of life than money" attitude—a prevailing mindset among Boomer youth in the 1960s—to "I'm more concerned about money." Material indulgence gave rise to the term "yuppies," applied to those Boomers who had forsaken their ideals. Although other Boomers rejected such materialism, the zeitgeist had clearly shifted away from 1960s liberal activism.

Another shift occurred in the 1990s as the cold war, which had for decades shaped the cultural climate, came to an end. At first the culture war raged on, made sharper by extremists who formed armed militias. But as some radicals became more strident, most Americans thought moderation best. Influenced by economic growth, they settled into a society exemplified by the Baby Boomer president, Bill Clinton: liberalism and conservatism avoided, a broad middle ground—critics called it a bland ground—championed. Many Boomers, in fact, as they aged and earned more money, turned their backs on the present and indulged in nostalgia. They listened to rock music from their younger days, reviving many musical careers in the process; they watched the "Nick at Nite" channel featuring old T.V. shows; and they attended movies based on those shows. Contemporary society, however, frequently jolted people from thoughts of earlier days with headline stories of violence against minorities, killings of abortion doctors, police brutality, and school shootings.

Introduction

As always in history, external developments shaped people. But the Boomers didn't simply react to the times; by force of numbers, economic clout, and their own determination, they continuously altered society. The *Atlas of the Baby Boom Generation* surveys the events that shaped Baby Boomer lives and the ways in which Boomers changed America from the 1940s onward. An intriguing final chapter envisions what might unfold for Boomers in the early decades of the 21st century.

After presenting an overview of American society during World War II, each chapter looks at the Boomer years decade by decade through topical sections. The first spreads in each chapter—Population and Family, Education, Economics, and Cultural Currents—describe key facets of American society through the lens of the Boomer generation. Recurring themes that helped define the Boomer experience—the cold war and nuclear threat (The Bomb), protest (The Protest), television (The Tube), and science (Technology)—follow the four introductory spreads. Other recurring material is included in each chapter: People, presenting short biographies of individuals who shaped the Boomer experience—people as varied as baseball great Joe DiMaggio, *Mad* magazine founder William Gaines, actress Mary Tyler Moore, black radical Angela Davis, and computer billionaire Bill Gates; and Trends detailing some of the fads and pop culture phenomena

▶ *Rock superstar Jimi Hendrix performs in 1967. (AP/Wide World Photos)*

ATLAS OF THE BABY BOOM GENERATION

▲ *Past and future sit side by side on a park bench in Atlanta, Georgia, circa 1995. (Imageworks)*

(from secret decoder rings to cellular phones) that characterized the Baby Boom generation.

To place events in relation to one another and make easy a sequential walk through Boomer history, each chapter contains an illustrated chronology. Meanwhile, placing American events in a larger context, chapters beginning with the late 1940s provide Big Picture maps that allow readers to visually pinpoint major world developments. A bibliography provides sources for additional investigation, and several appendixes round out the picture.

I n these pages readers discover the hula hoop, slinky, McDonald's—"It's ridiculous to call this an industry. . . . This is rat eat rat, dog eat dog . . ." said company leader Ray Kroc—Beat writers, Velcro, A-bomb tests, the Kitchen Debate between Nixon and Khrushchev. Television offers Howdy Doody and scenes of war; civil rights protesters seek justice, hippies seek love, social upheaval begets a sexual revolution; and blood flows in Vietnam while a man walks on the Moon. Women march for liberation, and people dance at discos as the economy melts—like Nero fiddling

while Rome burned, one critic said.

Pro-life and pro-choice crusaders engage in a moral fight while test-tube babies appear. Boomers contribute to a second boom in birthrates, see their kids enter high school and worry about violence and what's being taught, and find their lives changed by technology—by Walkmans, VCRs, computers, and the Internet. The future, a new century, portends problems with environmental crises, retirement, and old age, but offers hope with greater ethnic diversity and economic growth.

Kaleidoscopic would be one word to describe the Boomer decades, and with its diverse topics, illustrations, photos, maps, and colors, the *Atlas of the Baby Boom Generation* upholds that description. But it reflects as well the spirit of the Baby Boomers—a much-watched generation whose size, energy, and vitality reshaped America and left an imprint in history that future generations will study and talk about for years.

—Neil Hamilton
Spring Hill College
Mobile, Alabama

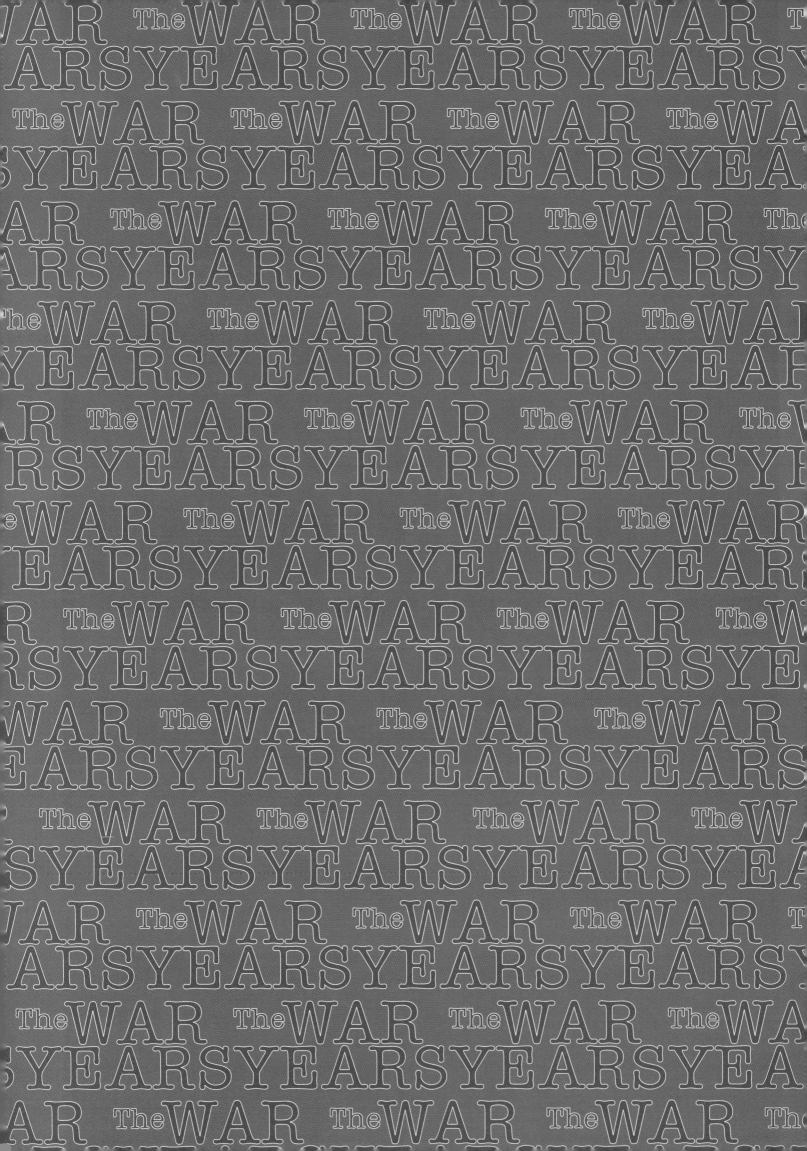

The WAR YEARS

The USO hosts a bicycle tour through New York City's Central Park, on June 4, 1942.
(CORBIS/BETTMANN-UPI)

The Home Front

▶ The proliferation of "Rosie the Riveter," like the woman pictured here who is making gas masks, blurred the line between men's and women's work. (CORBIS/BETTMANN)

W hen Norman Rockwell produced his drawing *Rosie the Riveter* for the *Saturday Evening Post*, he spotlighted one among several World War II economic developments that set the stage for change in the postwar period.

The American economy responded quickly to the Japanese attack on Pearl Harbor. In 1942, President Franklin Roosevelt established the War Production Board to mobilize industry, and the government removed nearly all risk for manufacturers by guaranteeing them profits. So rapidly did the economy switch from making consumer items to making war items that one government official recalled: "It was not so much industrial conversion as industrial revolution, with months and years condensed into days."

During the war, the manufacture of durable goods tripled. Among the most prominent developments—proving that if pressed, government and industry could move mountains or at least rubber trees—Roosevelt pursued a program to make synthetic rubber to substitute for the natural product made unavailable by Japan's military conquests in Asia. The government invested $700 million, built 51 factories, and then leased them to companies at nominal rates. By 1944, they made 87 percent of all rubber used in the nation. Since 1 armored tank required 1 ton of rubber, and a battleship 75 tons, synthetic rubber was sorely needed.

Between 1940 and 1945, the Gross National Product jumped from $100 billion to over $200 billion, and wages and salaries from $50 billion to $120 billion. The machinery was clearly in place for a postwar economic boom, due to begin as soon as factories could again produce consumer goods.

The war economy affected everyone, inciting profound social changes that Americans would grapple with for years to come. A *bracero* program, arranged with Mexico, brought thousands of Mexicans into the United States under short-term work contracts. In 1943, tension mounted between Mexicans and Anglos in Los Angeles that led to the Zoot-suit Riots. Anglos attacked young Mexicans who wore zoot suits—long coats with padded shoulders, pegged pants, wide-brimmed hats, and long watch chains—seeing in the people, their culture, and their clothes a threat to mainstream Anglo values.

> 66 *We Americans of today, together with our allies, are passing through a period of supreme test. It is a test of our courage—of our resolve—of our wisdom—our essential democracy.... I know that it is America's purpose that we shall not fail.* 99
>
> —**Franklin Delano Roosevelt**

▶▶ As male baseball players departed for the military, baseball owner Philip K. Wrigley decided to keep the sport (and the ballparks) alive by forming the All American Girls' Professional Baseball League in 1943. Lest the women players be perceived to resemble men, Wrigley established a charm school for them, instituted strict curfews, and required chaperons at all times. The league was limited to the Great Lakes region due to gasoline rationing and concerns about young women traveling alone.

More widespread conflict erupted between whites and African Americans. Thanks to the war economy, blacks were able to find jobs in industry. Moreover, they refused to accept discrimination at home while the United States was fighting against racism in Europe. In 1941, A. Philip Randolph, the leader of a black labor union, planned a huge march on Washington, geared to activating the black masses. Roosevelt feared that the march would disrupt the nation, and as a result, he and Randolph reached a deal whereby the president signed an executive order forbidding defense contractors from using racial discrimination in hiring and in return Randolph canceled the march.

Other blacks and their white supporters formed the Congress of Racial Equality to work for racial justice through nonviolent resistance. CORE activist James Farmer expressed the group's goals: "Not to make housing in ghettos more tolerable, but to destroy residential segregation; not to make Jim Crow facilities the equal of others, but to abolish Jim Crow; not to make racial discrimination more bearable, but to wipe it out."

Although CORE emerged from a pacifist group, it refused any permanent commitment to nonviolence while seeking radical change. "We dreamed of a mass movement," said Farmer, "and we did not think then that a revolution could be conducted by pacifists." CORE held its first successful sit-in in 1943 against a segregated restaurant in Chicago. Although CORE soon weakened, its tactics and ideals helped stimulate the postwar civil rights movement.

Despite gains for blacks, their migration into Detroit, Michigan, led to a riot in which police and black snipers exchanged gun fire, and whites invaded the black ghetto where they set fires and attacked African Americans. The riots ended only after 25 blacks and nine whites were killed, and 6,000 troops had entered the city to restore peace. In all, about 250 racial conflicts erupted in 47 cities that year. Americans faced unresolved racial problems they would have to confront in the postwar years.

The war economy changed the status of women, too. With posters proclaiming: "Longing won't bring him back sooner . . . . GET A WAR JOB!" more than six million women entered the workforce. Critics protested that women would abandon their children. To that complaint, Dr. Leslie Hohman wrote in the *Ladies' Home Journal* that "merely the presence of a mother in the house will not make children behave." Women received less pay than men, and government child-care programs helped only 10 percent of all working mothers. As the war continued more people accepted the idea of women as workers—but most considered the situation to be temporary, assuming the women would return to the kitchen when the men returned from the front.

While for many that indeed happened, others remained in the workforce, and many more entered it in the 1950s. The image of Rosie the Riveter, a woman doing "men's work," challenged society's ideas of what women could accomplish. As with industrial growth and race and ethnic relations, the war economy had permanently altered many women's lives, producing new opportunities and challenges for the postwar United States.

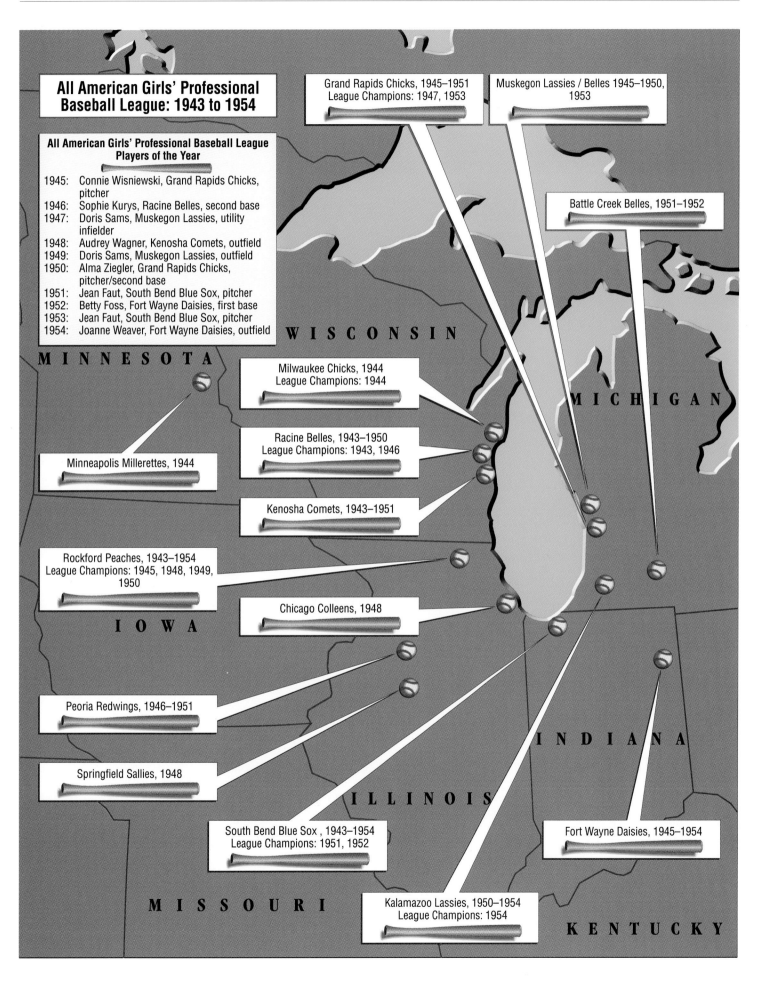

All American Girls' Professional Baseball League: 1943 to 1954

All American Girls' Professional Baseball League Players of the Year

1945: Connie Wisniewski, Grand Rapids Chicks, pitcher
1946: Sophie Kurys, Racine Belles, second base
1947: Doris Sams, Muskegon Lassies, utility infielder
1948: Audrey Wagner, Kenosha Comets, outfield
1949: Doris Sams, Muskegon Lassies, outfield
1950: Alma Ziegler, Grand Rapids Chicks, pitcher/second base
1951: Jean Faut, South Bend Blue Sox, pitcher
1952: Betty Foss, Fort Wayne Daisies, first base
1953: Jean Faut, South Bend Blue Sox, pitcher
1954: Joanne Weaver, Fort Wayne Daisies, outfield

Grand Rapids Chicks, 1945–1951
League Champions: 1947, 1953

Muskegon Lassies / Belles 1945–1950, 1953

Battle Creek Belles, 1951–1952

MINNESOTA

WISCONSIN

MICHIGAN

Milwaukee Chicks, 1944
League Champions: 1944

Minneapolis Millerettes, 1944

Racine Belles, 1943–1950
League Champions: 1943, 1946

Kenosha Comets, 1943–1951

Rockford Peaches, 1943–1954
League Champions: 1945, 1948, 1949, 1950

IOWA

Chicago Colleens, 1948

Peoria Redwings, 1946–1951

INDIANA

Springfield Sallies, 1948

ILLINOIS

South Bend Blue Sox , 1943–1954
League Champions: 1951, 1952

Fort Wayne Daisies, 1945–1954

MISSOURI

Kalamazoo Lassies, 1950–1954
League Champions: 1954

KENTUCKY

Chronology

Year	World	United States Politics	Arts
1939	World War II begins as Hitler and Stalin sign a nonaggression pact and Britain and France declare war on Germany.	The U.S. Supreme Court bans a new strategy used by workers called "sit-down strikes"; instead of leaving the factory the strikers sit at their machines and prevent their companies from employing strikebreakers.	Barred from performing at Constitution Hall, black contralto Marian Anderson sings at the Lincoln Memorial.
1940	Europe suffers as Germany conquers a host of nations and launches a bombing blitz against England.	▼ Franklin Delano Roosevelt wins an unprecedented third term as president.	The Disney film *Fantasia* pairs Mickey Mouse and conductor Leopold Stokowski.
1941	Nazi Germany sends millions to eventual death in concentration camps across Europe.	The Japanese attack on Pearl Harbor propels the United States into World War II.	Director and star Orson Welles releases *Citizen Kane*.
1942	American forces are captured by the Japanese in the Philippines, while Soviet forces battle the Germans at Stalingrad.	Japanese Americans on the Pacific coast are herded into internment camps.	▼ Humphrey Bogart reluctantly joins the war effort in *Casablanca*.
1943	Italy surrenders to the Allies, and Japan stumbles in the Pacific.	Congress authorizes employers to withhold income tax from employee paychecks.	*Oklahoma* opens on Broadway.
1944	The Allies invade Normandy under General Eisenhower on June 6 and liberate Paris on August 25.	Jettisoning running mate Henry Wallace in favor of Harry S. Truman, Roosevelt wins a fourth term as president.	In his play *No Exit*, which opens in Paris, author/philosopher Jean-Paul Sartre declares that "hell is other people."
1945	World War II comes to an end as Soviet forces take Berlin and the United States devastates Hiroshima and Nagasaki with atomic bombs.	President Roosevelt dies and is succeeded by his vice president, Harry S. Truman.	Richard Wright's *Black Boy* presents a searing account of poverty and prejudice.

UPI/CORBIS-BETTMANN

Science and Industry	Pastimes and Lifestyles	Sports	Year
The World's Fair, held in New York City, features "The World of Tomorrow," which displays modern innovations such as television and robots.	President Roosevelt announces that the Thanksgiving holiday will be moved from the fourth Thursday in November to the third, in order to increase the distance between Thanksgiving and Christmas.	The Baseball Hall of Fame opens in Cooperstown, New York.	1939
Women abandon silk for DuPont's new nylon stockings.	The 40-hour workweek becomes standard in the U.S.	The Chicago Bears upset the Washington Redskins in the NFL title game by a score of 73–0.	1940
German scientist Konrad Zuse develops the Z3 computer.	Bob Hope entertains U.S. troops with a United Service Organizations show at March Field in California.	New York Yankee Joe DiMaggio sets a baseball record by hitting safely in 56 consecutive games.	1941
Domestic automobile production is halted as industry moves to supply war matériel.	▼ Food rationing laws are in effect in the United States and across Europe.	Heavyweight boxing champion Joe Louis enlists as a private in the U.S. Army, serving with future baseball great Jackie Robinson in the then segregated army.	1942
Colossus, the first all-electronic calculating device, is built by British scientists to crack German codes during WWII.	Swiss scientist Albert Hoffmann hallucinates after experimenting with lysergic acid diethylamide (LSD).	The All American Girls' Professional Baseball League is founded by businessman Philip K. Wrigley.	1943
At Harvard University Howard Aiken develops the Mark I, the first full-scale programmable computer in the United States.	During a Ringling Brothers Circus performance in Hartford, Connecticut, a fire breaks out, collapsing the tent and killing 168 spectators.	The Olympic games are canceled because of WWII.	1944
On July 16, scientists detonate the first atomic bomb, at Alamogordo Air Base in New Mexico.	Earl Tupper founds the Tupperware Corp.	The Detroit Tigers beat the Chicago Cubs in a seven-game World Series.	1945

CORBIS

Between Alamogordo and Los Alamos, in a region Spaniards called *Jornada del Muerto*—the Journey of Death—an endless stretch of New Mexican desert gave way to a ranch house. From the house, under a blazing sun in 1945, workers put down a paved road that stretched 3,400 yards to the northwest, to a location labeled Ground Zero. From there, they put down three paved roads that led north, west, and south, to separate shelters 10,000 yards away. Thus emerged the Trinity test site, where that summer Americans exploded the world's first atomic bomb. The next year, the Baby Boom began. Bomb and Boom converged to create a generation defined by the specter of radioactive mushroom clouds.

> 66 *It has become appallingly clear that our technology has surpassed our humanity.* 99
>
> **—Albert Einstein**

Trinity was part of the World War II–era Manhattan Project, a top-secret program begun under President Franklin Roosevelt to beat Hitler in the race to develop an atomic bomb. The project cost $2 billion and employed 120,000 people at 37 installations in 19 states. Helped enormously by physicists who had fled Germany and Italy, it achieved a historic breakthrough when, underneath the football stadium at the University of Chicago, Enrico Fermi built a nuclear reactor and, with colleague Leo Szilard, produced a controlled chain reaction in December 1942.

▼ *Aerial view of the atomic test at the Trinity site in New Mexico. (Library of Congress)*

Secrecy so shrouded the Manhattan Project that Harry S. Truman, Roosevelt's vice president, had no idea what it was intended to accomplish. He learned more about it on April 13, 1945, one day after he assumed the presidency on Roosevelt's death. In his memoirs, Truman recalled that Secretary of War Henry Stimson "told me . . . about an immense project that was underway—a project looking to the development of a new explosive of almost unbelievable destructive power." Stimson withheld details, however, until several days later.

That summer, on June 27, scientists in the Manhattan Project finalized plans to ship an A-bomb nicknamed "Little Boy" to the Pacific for possible use against Japan. Three weeks later, on July 16, they gathered at the Trinity test site to watch the first explosion of an atomic bomb. Those present at the blast offered their accounts. "I saw first a yellow glow, which grew instantly to an overwhelming white flash, so intense that I was completely blinded," said Robert Serber. Emilio Segre said: "I was flabbergasted by the new spectacle . . . I believe that for a moment I thought the explosion might set fire to the atmosphere and thus finish the earth, even though I knew that this was not possible."

After the Japanese rejected Truman's continued demands for unconditional surrender, the president decided to use Little Boy. Most of the physicists in the Manhattan Project opposed the decision; they favored some kind of demonstration over an unpopulated area. Truman thought otherwise, however, and on the morning of August 6, 1945, the *Enola Gay,* an American B-29 aircraft, dropped the bomb on Hiroshima. The blast damaged or destroyed 70,000 of the city's 76,000 buildings, and killed 140,000 of the city's 350,000 population by the end of 1945, and 200,000 by the end of 1949 as radiation sickness took its toll. Truman followed the Hiroshima bombing with another one on August 9 of Nagasaki, after which Japan surrendered.

America's leaders offered strong arguments to support the nuclear attack. They pointed out that in August 1945 Japan still had an army of two million men in Manchuria, and over 5,000 kamikaze planes to use against any army invading the Japanese home islands. They insisted that Japan's militarists would fight to the end, and that an invasion would cost the United States more than 500,000 casualties, maybe more than one million.

But critics argued that instead of unconditional surrender Truman could have assured the Japanese that their emperor would retain his throne. Evidence indicates that under those terms Japan would have quit the war. As it turned out, after Hiroshima and Nagasaki Truman did permit Japan's emperor to remain in power (mainly as a means to maintain order in that devastated country and provide for a smoother transition to American occupation).

In *The Decision to Use the Atomic Bomb* (1995), Gar Alperovitz agrees with the critics and adds that by coupling retention of the emperor with having Russia declare war on Japan, the Japanese would most certainly have surrendered before Hiroshima. As it was, American actions delayed

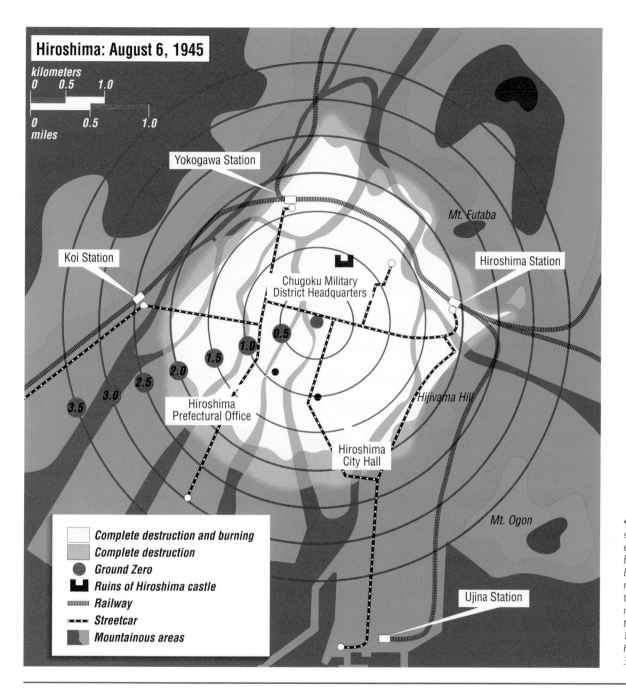

Hiroshima: August 6, 1945

kilometers
0   0.5   1.0

0   0.5   1.0
miles

Yokogawa Station

Koi Station

Mt. Futaba

Chugoku Military
District Headquarters

Hiroshima Station

0.5

1.0

1.5

2.0

2.5

3.0

3.5

Hiroshima
Prefectural Office

Hijiyama Hill

Hiroshima
City Hall

Mt. Ogon

Ujina Station

Complete destruction and burning
Complete destruction
Ground Zero
Ruins of Hiroshima castle
Railway
Streetcar
Mountainous areas

◄ *This map of Hiroshima and the surrounding areas shows the levels of destruction caused by the bomb called Little Boy. Everything within a 2-kilometer radius was decimated, including the military headquarters, government offices, and train lines. By the end of 1945, approximately 140,000 people had died, out of Hiroshima's population of 350,000.*

Russia's entry into the Asian war as Truman sought to limit Russian influence in that region. Why then did the United States drop the bomb? In large measure, Alperovitz argues, because Secretary of State James Byrnes convinced Truman that the United States needed to impress the Soviet Union with its strength and make the Russians more amenable to American demands in Europe and Asia.

Testimonials from those at Hiroshima offer a terrifying tale. Here is what three eyewitnesses had to say in interviews conducted at various times after the blast:

People came fleeing from the . . . streets. One after another they were almost unrecognizable. The skin was burned off some of them and was hanging from their hands and from their chins. . . .

Between the [heavily damaged] Red Cross

Hospital and the center of the city I saw nothing that wasn't burned to a crisp.

There were so many burned [at a first-aid station] that the odor was like drying squid. They looked like boiled octopuses. . . . I saw a man whose eye had been torn out by an injury, and there he stood with his eye resting in the palm of his hand. What made my blood run cold is that it looked like the eye was staring at me.

In retrospect, such reports fueled Baby Boomer anxiety about nuclear war. Journalist Edward R. Murrow recognized the predicament coming from the victory in World War II when he said: "Seldom, if ever, has a war ended leaving the victors with such a sense of uncertainty and fear, with such a realization that the future is obscure and that survival is not assured."

Things to Come

Some of the building blocks of Baby Boomer culture can be traced back to the war years and even earlier, long before the Boom had hit. Rhythm and blues groups, television experiments, and the first LSD trips—they were all harbingers of thing to come.

Rhythm and Blues

Sixties rock music had its roots in the music of '50s artists such as Elvis Presley and Bill Haley, but these men in turn owed their careers to the rhythm and blues artists of the '40s and early '50s. Rhythm and blues— black music marketed to the black population in the United States—evolved partly out of economic necessity. The costs of keeping big bands together proved prohibitive by the mid-'40s, and dozens of once-popular outfits began dissolving. African-American musicians found they could stay employed by forming bands of just five or six players. Some of these small groups were at the vanguard of the next evolution in jazz—bebop.

Some new bands developed a song-oriented approach with straight-ahead chord changes and a steady beat. Saxophone solos might be featured, but raucous, "honking" sax playing was more common than the fluid style heard in jazz. Similarly, piano playing in the new music was more clangorous and thumping. Lyrics ranged from hipster nonsense to thinly veiled sexual allusions. By the late '40s, songs such as "The Hucklebuck" and "All She Wants to Do Is Rock" were hits on black-oriented radio stations across the country. *Billboard* was the first publication to apply the label "rhythm and blues"—also known as R&B—to the new style and discard the unfashionable industry term, "race music."

White deejays of the '40s and early '50s were attracted to the work of R&B artists such as Wynonie Harris, Big Jay McNeely, and Louis Jordan, and featured their records during broadcasts. But white station executives discouraged the airplay of R&B. When Cleveland deejay Alan Freed succeeded in sidestepping the issue by introducing rhythm and blues singles to young white listeners as "rock and roll" music, the term stuck and a new market was created for white musicians and record companies.

Television

Although television did not become a national phenomenon until after World War II, TV experiments had been conducted decades before. As early as 1912, a primitive television system was developed in a Russian lab-

▶ *Louis Jordan (far right) and his group, in the 1947 movie Reet, Petite & Gone. (Archive Photos)*

oratory. Modest TV broadcasts were made in Germany, Britain, and the United States during the early '20s. In 1925, C. Francis Jenkins succeeded in transmitting motion pictures in halftone by radio, and dubbed the process "Radiovision." Commercial production of Radiovision sets—literally radios with small TV screens—began in 1927. Owners of the sets could watch Mickey Mouse and Felix the Cat during special broadcasts. But Radiovision sales, and most television research projects, ceased in the United States during the Depression.

Television development picked up again during the '30s. In Hitler's Germany, televised images of the 1936 Olympics were broadcast to hotel lounges in Berlin and Leipzig. In the United States, experimental telecasts were conducted by NBC and RCA; the 1939 World's Fair in New York City was a showcase for RCA's latest TV system. President Franklin Roosevelt appeared and spoke on television sets throughout the fairgrounds.

Further delays in TV innovation were caused by the war, but by 1945, the big three of TV—NBC, ABC, and CBS—geared up for commercial broadcasts. TV had Arthur Godfrey, Milton Berle, and Jackie Gleason in 1949. In 1951, after lengthy Federal Communications Commission (FCC) hearings over broadcast frequency standards, commercial television went into full swing.

LSD

▲ *A television receiving set, circa 1940s. (Library of Congress)*

Although artists and writers had described experiences with mind-altering substances for centuries, serious medical research on psychedelics began in the late 19th century. Peyote and mescal were cautiously used in patient treatment during the 1890s and the results were carefully documented. But it wasn't until 1943 that a synthesized psychedelic—lysergic acid diethylamide, or LSD—was developed and its effects recorded. The creation of LSD was an accident, and Dr. Albert Hoffmann's first "trip" came as a surprise—his original goal was a cure for migraine headaches. One week later, Hoffmann conducted a self-experiment with LSD and took notes. His research remained unpublished until 1947, after which experiments by other scientists followed throughout the '50s.

The medical professionals most curious about LSD were psychiatrists. LSD became the topic of medical conventions and published studies—98 documented experiments with the hallucinogen were conducted in 1955. While animals were the most frequent subjects in such projects, mental patients and epileptics also were treated with the new drug. From a 1956 medical conference came the term "psychedelic," derived from Greek and meaning either "mind-manifesting" or "mind-destroying," depending on the translation.

Artists picked up the thread and began experimenting with LSD during the '50s. Author and critic Aldous Huxley documented his experiences with the drug in *The Doors of Perception* (1954), and continued to write about the virtues of psychedelics for the rest of his career. Huxley became convinced that LSD could aid its users in achieving spiritual enlightenment. His thinking would have great impact on Timothy Leary and his followers only a few years later.

The late 1940s

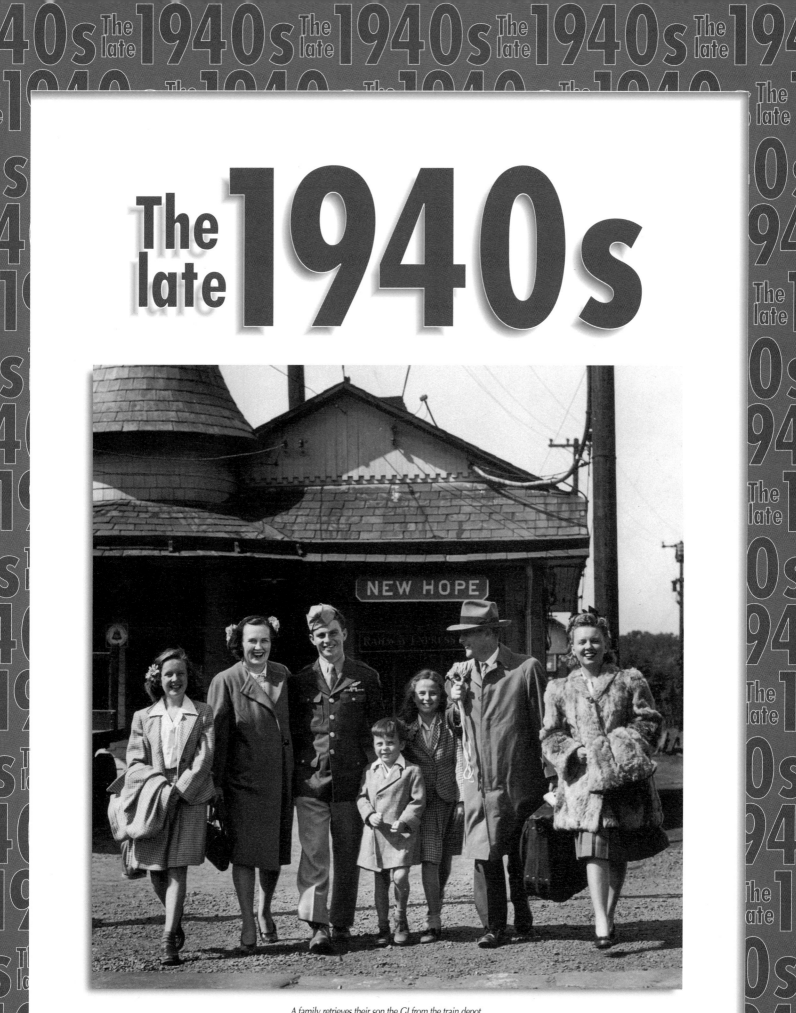

A family retrieves their son the GI from the train depot.
(ARCHIVE/LAMBERT)

The United States had never seen anything like it . . . an unprecedented, seemingly unceasing Baby Boom. Writing in the late 1940s, newspaper columnist Sylvia Porter proclaimed:

Boom. The biggest, boomiest boom ever known in history. Just imagine how much these extra people, these new markets, will absorb—in food, clothing, in gadgets, in housing, in services.

Births in America had actually increased earlier, nearing 3 million in 1942 and topping 3.1 million in 1943. But then birthrates dropped in 1944 and 1945. This encouraged demographic experts to insist that the birthrate would continue to decline, despite a temporary upsurge when men returned from the war. *Life* magazine said in 1945: "The U.S. will probably suffer an eight percent cut in its youth base between 1940 and 1970." And the Census Bureau claimed that the nation's population would peak at 163 million in 1965–1980, and then drop.

William F. Ogburn, a prominent sociologist at the University of Chicago, predicted there would be no population boom after the war. In fact, just the opposite would occur, "a cessation of population growth" that would mean "children of the next generation . . . should have room to move around and will not have to go hungry because of population pressure."

To reach their conclusions, the experts considered several factors. They pointed to the spread of urban, middle-class values that emphasized small families, as opposed to rural values that encouraged plenty of kids to work on farms. They noted the increased use of contraceptives, and the numerical decline of women in the fertile 20 to 29 age bracket. Finally, they said that working women, increasing in numbers and preoccupied with their jobs, would prefer to have few, if any, children.

They guessed wrong. One year alone, 1946, blew their theory apart: 206,387 births in February; 233,452 in May; 242,302 in June; and 349,499 in October. For the entire year, an all-time U. S. record 3.4 million babies were born . . . one every nine seconds!

The live birthrate per 1,000 women aged 15 to 44 jumped from 82.2 in 1945 to 110.1 in 1947, when total births reached 3,817,000. A drop occurred in 1948, and the number of births flattened for three years; as a result, the experts who had predicted at most a deviant rise in birthrates crowed. But

in 1951, births surged to over 3,823,000, greater than any other year prior to 1945, and a look at the entire picture from 1945 into 1950 revealed a startling increase in children.

No one knows for sure why births boomed. Obviously, marriages factored into the numbers. More women married in the late '40s than during the Depression or World War II, and they married younger: the median age at marriage for women decreased from 21.5 in 1940 to 20.3 in 1950. But that raises the question: Why marry in the first place? And then: Why choose to have children?

Other than personal and emotional reasons, economics exerted a strong influence. In the Western world, only the United States, Canada, Australia, and New Zealand experienced a Baby Boom. In each, substantial economic growth, along with optimistic attitudes about the future, encouraged women to have babies. In fact, in another miscalculation by experts, the Baby Boom defied those who claimed that economic prosperity would bring declining birth rates, a conclusion that assumed wealthier, more educated families produced fewer children than poorer, less literate ones.

Yet the experts had a point. Family size had dropped

▼ *This chart details the early years of the Boom by the women who began it: birthrates per 1,000 women, by age of mother, in the continental U.S.*

Birthrates Per 1,000 Women by Age of Mother

Year	10–14 years	15–19 years	20–24 years	25–29 years	30–34 years	35–39 years	40–44 years	45–49 years	total 15–44 years
1945	0.7	48.8	130.1	128.4	94.7	54.6	15.5	1.3	82.2
1946	0.7	56.9	171.7	157.3	103.6	56.7	15.6	1.2	98.3
1947	0.8	76.7	200.1	172.3	107.5	57.3	15.9	1.2	110.1

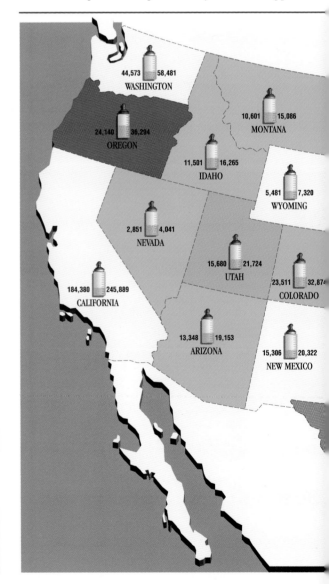

WASHINGTON 44,573 | 58,481
OREGON 24,140 | 36,294
MONTANA 10,601 | 15,086
IDAHO 11,501 | 16,265
WYOMING 5,481 | 7,320
NEVADA 2,851 | 4,041
UTAH 15,680 | 21,724
COLORADO 23,511 | 32,874
CALIFORNIA 184,380 | 245,889
ARIZONA 13,348 | 19,153
NEW MEXICO 15,306 | 20,322

since earlier in American history, and the Baby Boom, in a seeming contradiction, continued that trend. No longer did women give birth to seven or more children, as many once had. On the other hand, and this was an important source for the Baby Boom birthrates, families with no children, or with just one, declined. In short, Baby Boom couples saw medium-sized families as ideal, and they produced two to four children.

Interestingly, too, in the late '40s the Baby Boom involved not only women in their twenties, but also women over 35. They had delayed having children during the Great Depression and World War II, but had maintained their desire for them. Further, the Baby Boom crossed racial and ethnic lines, even though African Americans, for one, lived differently from whites—with more women working, fewer families living in suburbs, and lower incomes.

Thus, everywhere a boom. Historians have described the surging birthrate in exclamatory tones:

"The largest by far in the nation's history."

"The most amazing social trend of the postwar era."

"The most extraordinary population boom in history."

All these babies came at a time when a new youth culture waited to mold them. The word "teenager" appeared by the mid-'40s, and these youngsters used their voices, their energy, and their buying power to change families and society.

Seventeen, a groundbreaking magazine in its appeal to teenage girls, revealed the development early on, when it first hit newsstands in September 1944 and, over the next few months, presented articles such as "What You Wear," "Getting Along in the World," and "Your Mind." Alongside the articles, appeared ads for shoes, sweaters, Kotex, Dr. Pepper, and Odo-Ro-No (a deodorant).

Beyond *Seventeen*, with its appeal to the "clean teen," a more troubling development signified the youth culture: juvenile delinquency. Many newspapers offered stories about these rebels—trouble at home, trouble at school, trouble in the neighborhood.

In time, those born after World War II and through the '50s shaped this youth culture in their own ways. But the teens of the '40s laid the foundation for a distinct subculture and "the biggest, boomiest boom ever known in history" made society more youth-conscious than ever.

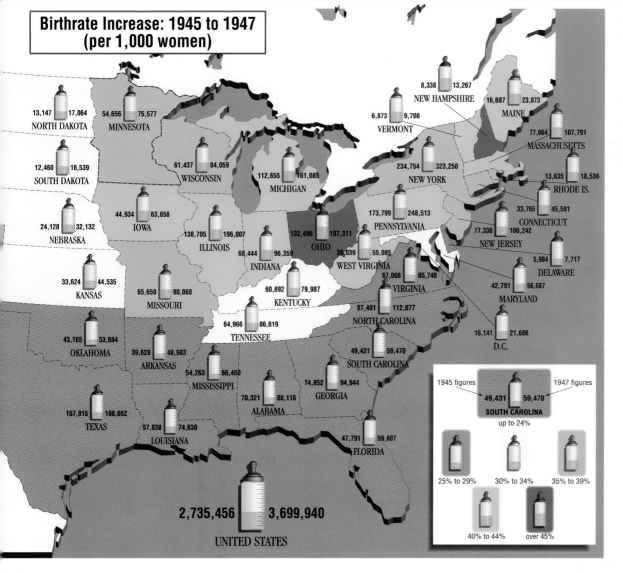

Birthrate Increase: 1945 to 1947 (per 1,000 women)

◀ This map shows the increase in births from 1945 to 1947, when the Baby Boom was in full swing. The percent change in birthrates is based on birthrates per 1,000 women in the continental U.S. population. South Carolina and Mississippi had the lowest growth, with 20 and 22 percent increases in births, respectively. New Hampshire had by far the largest growth—a 59 percent increase.

NORTH DAKOTA 13,147 17,064
MINNESOTA 54,656 75,577
NEW HAMPSHIRE 8,338 13,267
MAINE 16,687 23,873
VERMONT 6,873 9,708
SOUTH DAKOTA 12,460 16,539
WISCONSIN 61,437 84,059
MICHIGAN 112,655 161,085
MASSACHUSETTS 77,064 107,791
NEW YORK 234,754 323,250
RHODE IS. 13,635 18,536
IOWA 44,934 63,858
NEBRASKA 24,128 32,132
ILLINOIS 138,705 196,007
OHIO 132,496 197,311
PENNSYLVANIA 173,799 248,513
CONNECTICUT 33,765 45,581
NEW JERSEY 77,338 106,242
INDIANA 68,444 96,359
WEST VIRGINIA 39,039 55,085
DELAWARE 5,984 7,717
KANSAS 33,624 44,535
MISSOURI 65,659 90,060
KENTUCKY 60,892 79,987
VIRGINIA 67,068 85,740
MARYLAND 42,791 56,687
TENNESSEE 64,966 86,619
NORTH CAROLINA 87,401 112,877
D.C. 16,141 21,686
OKLAHOMA 43,165 53,684
ARKANSAS 39,628 48,983
SOUTH CAROLINA 49,431 59,470
MISSISSIPPI 54,263 66,450
GEORGIA 74,852 94,944
ALABAMA 70,321 88,116
TEXAS 157,915 198,662
LOUISIANA 57,838 74,630
FLORIDA 47,791 59,807

2,735,456   3,699,940

UNITED STATES

1945 figures   1947 figures
49,431   59,470
SOUTH CAROLINA
up to 24%

25% to 29%   30% to 34%   35% to 39%

40% to 44%   over 45%

As World War II ended, several observers testified about education in America. In a lengthy editorial, *Life* magazine declared: "Almost any experience of two years of full-time post-high-school study would be more humanizing than instantly to freeze, as so many young people must, into a rigid life pattern." A black teacher in Mississippi observed about her school's financial straits: "The money for the building was raised by the teachers, children, and patrons. . . . We have been able to put on one coat of paint, inside and out." An education writer insisted: "The political function of the schools is to teach Americanism, meaning not merely political and patriotic dogma, but the habits necessary to American life."

Each statement reflected a change sweeping through education from 1945 to 1949: colleges attracting students in ever larger numbers, public schools facing financial crises, and extremists restricting how and what children should be taught. Immersed in the euphoria of wartime victory, and beset by uncertainty as capitalism and communism battled for world domination, Americans projected society's concerns onto their schools.

In 1944, Congress passed the Servicemen's Readjustment Act, popularly called the GI Bill of Rights. "The bill came from the American Legion," claimed *Time* magazine, because the Legion, with the help of the American Council on Education, drafted it and lobbied hard for its passage. Among other benefits, the GI Bill provided money to veterans for education: $500 a year for tuition (then a substantial sum) in an elementary school, high school, business school, or college, depending on the needs of the veteran; $50 a month for subsistence; and an extra $25 for one or more dependents.

By the fall of 1946, over one million veterans had enrolled, far exceeding what had been expected. Many colleges, in fact, doubled their enrollments and handled the crunch by using more teaching assistants, setting up temporary buildings, and cramming students into large lecture halls.

Would the veterans be able to handle college courses? Professors often praised the GIs as more conscientious and harder working than traditional students. One newspaper columnist claimed: "The GIs are hogging the honor rolls and the Dean's lists; they are walking away with the top marks in all of their courses. . . . Far from being an educational problem, the veteran has become an asset to higher education."

The Veterans Administration later estimated that the bill resulted in degrees for 450,000 engineers; 180,000 doctors, dentists, and nurses; 360,000 schoolteachers; 150,000 scientists; 243,000 accountants; 170,000 lawyers; and 36,000 clergymen. The results showed that college degrees could be obtained by many in the middle class, and this changed the student population as well, making it racially and ethnically diverse, older, and married—no powder-puff races and other freshmen rites of initiation for this group.

Enrollment increases hit the public schools, too, amid widespread indications of a crisis. According to the *New York Times*, during the '40s, 150,000 teachers left the public schools for higher-paying jobs; the average weekly teacher salary stood at $37, a rate below the average for bartenders; 60,000 teachers had a high school education or less; and a great disparity existed between the best-funded school districts in the nation, where local governments spent $6,000 per classroom unit, and the worst, where they spent $100.

To make matters more difficult, racial segregation, especially Jim Crow laws in the South, crippled efforts to accelerate funding. When African Americans and white liberals criticized the racial caste system, and President Harry Truman appointed a Committee on Civil Rights in 1946 to investigate the status of civil rights and civil liberties, racial conservatives protested. They took a stand

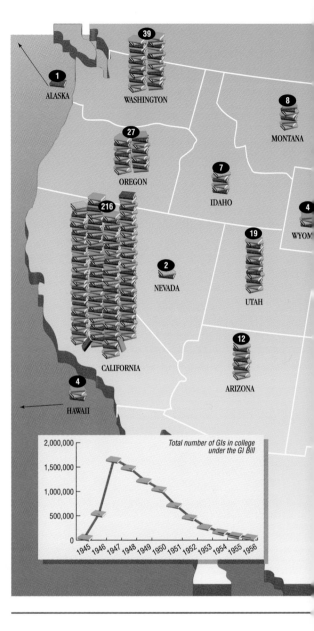

▼ *"GI Joe in College." Books and notebooks, as well as tuition, were furnished to veterans under the GI Bill of Rights. Here a new crop of solider-students purchases supplies for the term. (UPI/CORBIS-BETTMANN)*

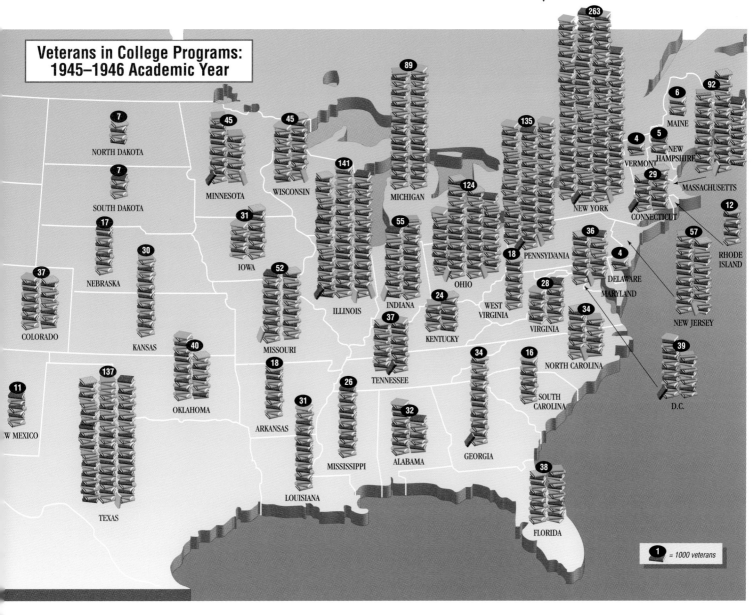

Veterans in College Programs: 1945–1946 Academic Year

263

89

92

6

7 NORTH DAKOTA

45 MINNESOTA

45 WISCONSIN

135

MAINE

4 VERMONT

5 NEW HAMPSHIRE

7 SOUTH DAKOTA

141

MICHIGAN

124

29 MASSACHUSETTS

NEW YORK

CONNECTICUT

12 RHODE ISLAND

17

31 IOWA

55

36

4

57

30 NEBRASKA

52

18 PENNSYLVANIA

DELAWARE MARYLAND

NEW JERSEY

37 COLORADO

KANSAS

ILLINOIS

INDIANA

24

OHIO

28

WEST VIRGINIA

34

11 W MEXICO

40 OKLAHOMA

18 MISSOURI

37 KENTUCKY

VIRGINIA

39 D.C.

137

31 ARKANSAS

26 TENNESSEE

34

16 NORTH CAROLINA

SOUTH CAROLINA

TEXAS

32 ALABAMA

GEORGIA

MISSISSIPPI

LOUISIANA

38 FLORIDA

1 = 1000 veterans

---

against federal funding for schools, fearing it would end segregation. They battled mightily against the funding— despite Copiah County, Mississippi, paying an abysmal average yearly salary for white teachers of $889.53, and for black teachers $332.58; and Alabama paying on average $976 and $600, respectively.

As more young people entered public schools, interest groups competed to shape classrooms. Some launched an assault on progressive education, which had dominated American curriculums since World War I. No one could precisely define it, and few progressives themselves agreed on specifics, but at its root the pedagogy stressed social utility over college preparation and a student-centered environment.

After World War II, progressive education unraveled, partly due to what some critics decried as laziness passing for creativity, but also due to a chilling hunt for communists. As early as 1934 Elizabeth Drilling named in her book *The Red Network* 460 organizations and 1,300 individuals she called communists. As the hunt intensified, the University of Washington fired three tenured professors in 1946 for

supposedly holding membership in the Communist Party. Three years later, the California Board of Regents required a loyalty oath of all its college professors. At the same time Red hunters lowered the ax on progressive curriculums, accusing educators who supported such practices of undermining American values by encouraging students to ask questions, rather than stick to mastering the 3Rs.

Schools, many Americans asserted, should be used to promote the corporate economy. Extremists attacked text- books that criticized business; a few burned them. Even the popular GI Bill fell under suspicion—much to the cha- grin of the American Legion. Senator John Rankin of Mississippi, at first lukewarm to the legislation, declared he didn't want a bunch of "overeducated" veterans studying under "red" professors.

"More humanizing . . . ," "One coat of paint . . . ," "Teach Americanism. . . ." These words echoed through U.S. colleges and public schools in the late '40s, reflecting changes, prob- lems, and fears in a society energized by victory in war and struggling to understand its many consequences.

▲ *The GI Bill of Rights opened up the doors of higher education to America's veterans. This map shows the number of GIs who took advantage of the opportunity in the 1945–1946 academic year.*

In 1945, as soldiers returned home from World War II, a hit song jumped from radios and climbed the record charts, "Let The Good Times Roll." Merry, upbeat, optimistic, it may have been more incantation than expectation. Although a writer for the *New York Times* predicted an economy similar to the prosperous Roaring Twenties, many Americans feared a return to the Great Depression, and many economists predicted such.

As the war neared its end, leaders in the federal government debated how to handle reconversion, returning factories to making consumer goods. In the first three months of 1945, military priorities ruled, but wartime economic controls soon came tumbling down as the government lifted prohibitions on the use of materials for civilian manufacturing. At the same time, the armed services canceled many war contracts, and by August more than three million workers left their jobs in defense factories.

The businessman, many Americans believed, should be left on his own to lead the postwar economy. Said economist Isador Lubin: "Businessmen are ingenious. They can be relied upon to find ways and means of reconverting their plants and going ahead with the production of the innumerable items required by the civilian economy."

Yet the war that protected free enterprise had produced an even bigger federal government, and a greater closeness between it and business. Thus the businessman would not be left to his own devices, nor did he want to be. Large corporations expected government help, especially corporations tied to the military. After all, the war had given birth to a military–industrial complex, whereby procurement officers for the armed services worked closely with manufacturers to assure a steady stream of weapons for the military and a steady stream of profits for industries. Although military spending in the late '40s dropped sharply from its World War II–level, a defense budget of $13.1 billion in 1947 maintained this cozy relationship.

As for the public at large, it had long been reliant on

Attack on Labor

In the late '40s, conservatives decided to assault the New Deal by taking aim at unions, a great source of voter support for that liberal program. Fred Hartley, a Republican congressman from New Jersey, and Robert Taft, a Republican senator from Ohio, drafted the Taft–Hartley Act. Perhaps the most important legislation passed by Congress in 1947, it allowed states to pass right-to-work laws that would prohibit union shops, meaning workplaces where all employees had to join the union that had organized the company. Union leaders called it a "slave labor act," and when President Truman vetoed it (only to have Congress override the veto), they rallied labor to support his reelection.

federal action during the Great Depression and the war, and thus welcomed the Employment Act of 1946 that committed Washington to move quickly at the first sign of recession. One senator said, "The federal government is the instrument through which we can all work to accomplish full employment and high annual income."

Government monies indeed helped create a robust economy. Although Congress decreased spending from $95.2 billion in 1945 to $36.5 billion in 1948, the amount was much higher than the $9.4 billion in 1939. Looked at another way, total federal government spending relative to gross national product climbed from 10.1 percent in 1940 to 15.6 percent in 1950. And state and local governments boosted their spending.

Beyond government expenditures, economic growth came from what Americans had saved during the war—some $140 billion. Freed from Depression-era, war-era constraints, they wanted to spend.

And spend they did. On cars, houses, hobbies; on such new inventions as electric clothes dryers, long-playing

▶ *The 1947 Studebaker, touted by the manufacturer as "the first genuine postwar automobile on the market." (Library of Congress)*

Percentage Change in Retail Sales: 1939 to 1948 and 1948 to 1954

1939–1948

PACIFIC
ALASKA & HAWAII
4,298,759
245%
14,838,410

WEST NORTH
CENTRAL
4,138,883
221%
13,268,206

MOUNTAIN
1,427,541
227%
4,665,554

UNITED
STATES
130,520,548
31%
170,568,377

WEST SOUTH
CENTRAL
3,101,358
252%
10,923,448

EAST NORTH
CENTRAL
9,251,114
212%
28,901,766

EAST SOUTH
CENTRAL
1,845,037
248%
6,417,719

SOUTH
ATLANTIC
4,368,947
238%
14,772,800

MIDDLE
ATLANTIC
10,291,937
174%
28,175,162

NEW
ENGLAND
3,318,214
158%
8,557,443

1948 figures → 14,772,800
percentage increase/decrease → **-43%**
1954 figures → 8,354,102

1948–1954

PACIFIC
ALASKA & HAWAII
14,838,410
0%
14,806,333

WEST NORTH
CENTRAL
13,268,206
22%
16,181,312

MOUNTAIN
4,665,554
342%
20,608,887

WEST SOUTH
CENTRAL
10,923,448
93%
21,039,501

EAST NORTH
CENTRAL
28,901,766
29%
37,256,221

EAST SOUTH
CENTRAL
6,417,719
-0.01%
6,356,734

SOUTH
ATLANTIC
14,772,800
-43%
8,354,102

MIDDLE
ATLANTIC
28,175,162
24%
35,053,819

NEW
ENGLAND
8,557,443
28%
10,911,468

UNITED
STATES
42,041,790
210%
130,520,548

1939 figures → 9,251,114
percentage increase → **212%**
1948 figures → 28,901,766

percentage change

- 300% increase and up
- 250%–299% increase
- 225%–249% increase
- 200%–224% increase
- 100%–199% increase
- 75%–99% increase
- 50%–74% increase
- 25%–49% increase
- 0%–24% increase
- decrease

records, Polaroid cameras, and automatic garbage disposals. New car sales jumped from 69,500 in 1945, to 2.1 million in 1946, to a record 5.1 million in 1949, a phenomenal rate that meant more road construction, filling stations, auto-repair shops, motels, and restaurants.

Demand so outstripped supply for consumer items that annual inflation jumped from 2 percent during the war years to 16 percent in the late '40s. Some home builders even held lotteries for customers. Buy a ticket and you might win a spot on the list to have a house built!

But problems existed. Labor unrest mounted as unions demanded pay hikes to compensate for price increases and reductions in overtime. Autoworkers went on strike in 1945, steelworkers and miners in 1946. That same year railroad workers held a brief walkout and threatened to shut down all the lines, so angering President Harry Truman that he, in response, threatened to seize the railroads and command the workers to run them.

A substantial disparity among classes existed as well. In 1947, the wealthiest 5 percent of families received 19 percent of the national income. At the same time, the richest 20 percent of families received 46 percent of the national income, while the lowest 20 percent received only 3.5 percent. Poverty rates remained high, too—in 1947 there were some 40 million poor people. In that same year, one-third of all homes lacked running water, three-fifths had no central heat, and four-fifths still heated by using coal or wood.

Another problem appeared when returning veterans forced women from their jobs. Although nearly three million women found jobs during the economic expansion, and by 1950 women made up 28 percent of the labor force compared to 24 percent a decade earlier, they held mainly entry-level or low-pay positions as secretaries, waitresses, and maids. In addition, they experienced heavy gender segregation, with 75 percent of them employed in female-only jobs in 1950, an increase from early in the century.

Yet as the wheels of industry sped up and consumer items abounded, more Americans than ever before entered the middle-class. They worked hard so they could buy those radios and hi-fi's and let the good times roll.

▲ As shown in the lower map, a postwar spending boom mirrored the childbirth boom. It's interesting to note, however, that spending in the late 1940s to early 1950s was actually settling down somewhat, after the sharp economic upturn that occurred during World War II. The upper map shows the remarkable increases in retail sales as the United States recovered from the Depression years.

Lights turned down, projector switched on, audiences in the late '40s watched as *D. O. A.* flickered on the screen. A dark movie in appearance and theme, it told about a man poisoned by a slow-working radioactive drug who hunts his murderer, finds him, kills him, and then surrenders to the police. Opposite such gloom, young people radiated joy as they hung around soda fountains and drank malts, and as bobby-soxers juked and jived at high school dances.

This contrasting scene reflects more than differences between young and old, for many teens saw *D. O. A.* Rather, it reveals a contradiction in American society between pessimism laced with fear and optimism infused with joy.

Fear emanated from the cold war, a showdown for global power between the United States and the Soviet Union. When President Harry Truman addressed Congress on March 12, 1947, he intended to scare the American people, and he did. "At the present moment in world history nearly every nation must choose between alternative ways of life," intoned Truman. He continued: "One way of life is based upon the will of the majority, and it is distinguished by free institutions. . . . The second way of life is based upon the will of a minority forcibly imposed on the majority. It relies upon terror and oppression."

As Truman saw it, the world had divided between good, represented by Americans, and evil, represented by Russians. To fight evil, he committed the United States to support "free peoples" everywhere in resisting "attempted subjugation by armed minorities."

That bold commitment, known as the Truman Doctrine, came as leftist rebels fought a rightist Greek monarchy. Truman believed that Soviet dictator Joseph Stalin intended to stir such rebellions in order to conquer all of Europe (although evidence failed to reveal any substantial Russian involvement in Greece).

Containment emerged as Truman's operative plan, advocated by State Department official George F. Kennan, who insisted that by using primarily economic and political measures to build a wall around the Soviet Union, its communist system would in time collapse. That a substantial number of Americans disagreed with this view was evident in the writing of a leading columnist, Walter Lippmann, who claimed containment would involve the United States in intervention around the globe, often to support oppressive regimes; and it was evident in a six-month-long debate in Congress over whether to approve the Marshall Plan, a program to rebuild Europe through American loans.

But many more Americans accepted containment as Soviet actions stoked additional fear. Stalin imposed a communist regime on Hungary, and overthrew the elected Czech government. In 1948, after provocative action by Truman, the Soviets blockaded land access to U.S.–dominated West Berlin. Americans applauded as Truman launched a massive airlift of goods into the embattled city and forced the Soviets to end their blockade.

Amid these actions and an ongoing communist revolution in China, a Red Scare captured America. The president issued an executive order requiring officials in the government to check loyalties and compile a list of subversive organizations, and the House Un-American Activities Committee (HUAC) began investigating Hollywood.

For some Americans, the Red Scare was actually a black one. They hated Truman's recent orders to end discrimination in federal employment and to desegregate the armed forces. They condemned a civil rights campaign to test a court order desegregating interstate buses. They watched in disgust as teenagers listened to rhythm and blues—"race music"—with its sexuality in beat and lyrics. They cringed when the Brooklyn Dodgers added Jackie Robinson to their roster and thus integrated major league baseball.

They blamed these developments on communist agitators who wanted to weaken U.S. society. That some Americans saw a connection between black civil rights and communism revealed itself when Attorney General Tom C.

> ❝The rights you have are the rights given you by this [House Un-American Activities] Committee. We will determine what rights you have and what rights you have not got. ❞
>
> —J. Parnell Thomas

▼ *After the lean years of the Depression and World War II, Americans enjoyed increased access to foodstuffs and energy resources as part of the postwar economic bonanza. More meat, more fruit, and most notably, more oil was consumed in the immediate postwar period: three times as many barrels of oil in 1947 as in 1942.*

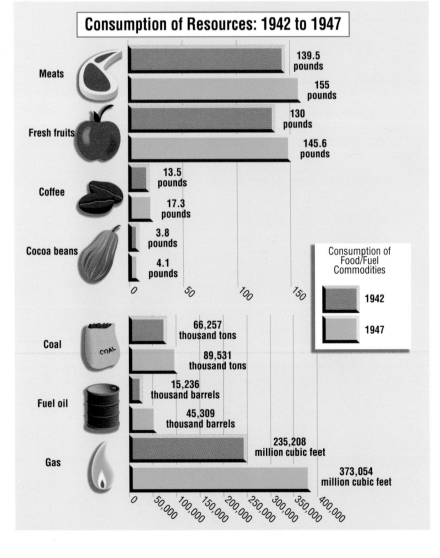

Consumption of Resources: 1942 to 1947

Meats — 139.5 pounds / 155 pounds
Fresh fruits — 130 pounds / 145.6 pounds
Coffee — 13.5 pounds / 17.3 pounds
Cocoa beans — 3.8 pounds / 4.1 pounds

Consumption of Food/Fuel Commodities: 1942 / 1947

Coal — 66,257 thousand tons / 89,531 thousand tons
Fuel oil — 15,236 thousand barrels / 45,309 thousand barrels
Gas — 235,208 million cubic feet / 373,054 million cubic feet

Clark listed among subversive groups several that advocated racial equality. But other Americans thought differently about civil rights and read with pride a *Time* magazine article that said Jackie Robinson acted with "intelligence, patience, and willingness."

As important to postwar culture as fear was the American dream, a belief in hard work leading to advancement, a faith in economic opportunity, and an unquenchable consumerism. Middle-class parents bought homes in the suburbs, setting the stage for residential patterns that would dominate the '50s. Teens found an economy in tune with their desires. One marketing firm discovered that in a typical week the nation's teenagers consumed 190 million candy bars, 130 million soft drinks, and 230 million sticks of gum.

Although some Americans worried about whether modern technology might destroy civilization—much as the protagonist in *D. O. A.* had been poisoned by radioactivity—many eagerly bought the new inventions. Television appeared for the first time as a widespread medium in 1946—like the suburbs, waiting to take center stage in the 1950s—and the *Washington Post* proclaimed it "good for a 1,000-year run."

So what was it to be: crusades against communism or ceaseless enjoyment? Film noir or soda fountains? For most Americans, the cold war, mixed with optimism, presented a bewildering jumble.

◄ *The Red Scare inspired numerous films with anticommunist themes—although in retrospect, the communists in Robert Stevenson's 1949 film noir look more like common thugs than wily Bolsheviks. But watch out for Janis Carter as Christine, the woman in red . . . in more ways than one. (Archive Photos)*

The Hollywood Ten

J. Parnell Thomas, HUAC chairman, had a mission: to purge Hollywood of communism. Thus when he and his committee descended on the movie capital in 1947, they intended to remove all obstacles to "truth." Although some celebrities, like actress Judy Garland, urged Americans to speak up about HUAC's assault on "free conscience," many in Hollywood cooperated with the committee when it started asking about their political beliefs.

Some refused, however. The most famous were a group of writers, including Alvah Bessie, Dalton Trumbo, and Ring Lardner, Jr., who came to be known as the Hollywood Ten. They argued that "freedom of speech" meant Americans could say whatever they wanted without being investigated. Liberals called them heroes, but HUAC cited them for contempt, and they went to prison for six months to a year, after which they found it impossible to get jobs when Hollywood blacklisted them.

Year	World	United States Politics	Arts
1946	▼ The Nuremberg Tribunal sentences 12 Nazi leaders to death.	The GI Bill sends millions of war veterans to college.	Parents rejoice at the down-to-earth advice offered in the new bestseller, *Common Sense Book of Baby and Child Care* by Dr. Benjamin Spock, and the first Cannes Film Festival is held on the French Riviera, presenting such films as Billy Wilder's *The Lost Weekend*, David Lean's *Brief Encounter*, and Roberto Rossellini's *Open City*.

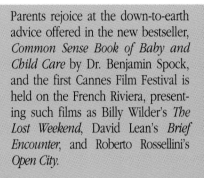

CORBIS/BETTMANN

Year	World	United States Politics	Arts
1947	India gains independence from Great Britain.	The Truman Doctrine declares American economic and military support for countries that resist communism.	The Hollywood Ten refuse to cooperate with the communist-hunting House Un-American Activities Committee.
1948	The Jewish state of Israel provides a new homeland to Europe's Jewish refugees while displacing thousands of Palestinian Arabs.	▼ Truman defeats Thomas Dewey in the presidential elections. The *Chicago Tribune* was premature in their pronouncement of Dewey's victory, in a famous journalistic blunder.	Abstract expressionism is born with Jackson Pollock's *Composition No.1*, a canvas of colorful paint splashes.

CORBIS/BETTMANN

Year	World	United States Politics	Arts
1949	Communist forces led by Mao Zedong take control of China, while Nationalists flee to the island of Taiwan.	The U.S. Senate ratifies and implements the North Atlantic Treaty, which aims to create a military counterbalance to the Soviet military presence in Eastern Europe after World War II.	*South Pacific* opens on Broadway; Katharine Hepburn and Spencer Tracy star in *Adam's Rib*.

Science and Industry	Pastimes and Lifestyles	Sports	Year
▼ Labor strikes paralyze U.S. industry, while government troops seize striking railways and coal mines.	Procter & Gamble introduces Tide, the first detergent for washing machines.	"Bullet Bill" Dudley of the Pittsburgh Steelers is awarded the "Triple Crown" for winning three individual statistical championships in one year—leading in rushing, punt returns, and interceptions. He also finishes first in lateral passing, becoming the first and only player in the NFL to lead in four categories.	1946

UPI/CORBIS-BETTMANN

Norwegian adventurer Thor Heyerdahl crosses the Pacific in the raft *Kon-Tiki*.	Christian Dior introduces his "New Look" to America, featuring long skirts, petticoats, and tiny waists.	After defending his heavyweight boxing title in a narrow victory over Jersey Joe Walcott, the "Brown Bomber" Joe Louis announces plans to retire.	1947
Ed Parson of Astoria, Oregon, develops the first Community Antenna Television (CATV) system, which consists of twin-lead transmission wire strung from housetop to housetop.	The McDonald brothers run a wildly popular self-service hamburger restaurant in California.	Negro Leagues legend Satchel Paige signs with the Cleveland Indians, becoming the first African American to pitch for a white major league team.	1948
Jean Paul Getty wins drilling rights to Middle Eastern oil lands that will make him the world's richest man.	RCA introduces a 45-rpm record, shortly after Columbia has introduced its 33 ⅓-rpm LP (long-playing) record. Much to the frustration of music lovers, they are not compatible with each other—nor are they compatible with the standard 78-rpm players.	The National Basketball League and the Basketball Association of America merge to found the National Basketball Association.	1949

The late 1940s   The Big Picture

As an iron curtain dropped across Europe, dividing the communist East from the capitalist West, the cold war entered American lives and took the shape it largely maintained for over 40 years. During the late 1940s, the Soviet Union and the United States engaged in tactics that would typify their confrontation for the rest of the century: military threats, economic pressure, propaganda, and involvement in the politics of other nations. For the generation that grew up after World War II, this brinkmanship would become a constant—frightening and seemingly immutable.

NORTH AMERICA AND EUROPE
NATO (1949)
The United States had not entered a peacetime military alliance in more than 150 years, but it did so in April 1949 when, along with Canada and 10 European governments, it established the North Atlantic Treaty Organization (NATO) to prevent Soviet expansion. Many in Congress complained that NATO would commit the United States to a ground war overseas, but after the Soviet Union exploded an atomic bomb in September 1949, the Senate approved military appropriations to aid the alliance. Two years later, President Truman sent the first American NATO troops to Europe.

ISRAEL
Israel Founded (1948)
A forceful push to found Israel began during World War II when the Holocaust convinced many Jews they needed a homeland. Zionists launched terrorist attacks in 1946 to evict the British from Palestine, and in 1947 the United Nations partitioned the land into two states—one Arab, one Jewish. Arab nations rejected the arrangement, however, and, after Israel declared itself independent in May 1948, war ensued. Israel prevailed in 1949 and forced the Arabs to sign an armistice. President Harry Truman backed Israel in the war, and thus brought the United States into the tinderbox of Mideast politics.

GERMANY
Berlin Airlift (1948-1949)

As youngsters, many Baby Boomers heard a heroic tale of how the United States and Britain airlifted supplies into West Berlin in the summer of 1948 after the Soviet Union blockaded that city. The Soviets thought they would cause enough hardship to prevent the Western powers from making West Germany autonomous. But the planes brought in up to 13,000 pounds of food, gas, and coal per day with flights landing every 90 seconds, and the publicity generated enormous praise for the West, and enormous criticism for the Soviets, who lifted their blockade in May 1949.

EASTERN EUROPE
The Iron Curtain Drops (1946)

"From Stettin in the Baltic to Trieste in the Adriatic," said Britain's former prime minister Winston Churchill in 1946, "an iron curtain has descended across the Continent." Although his speech drew an inaccurate line as to where the Soviet Union then dominated Europe, it provided an image that encapsulated the confrontation. To Americans, the Russians had dropped the curtain with their refusal to hold elections in Eastern Europe. The communist dictatorships in that region—what Churchill called "police governments"—and most especially the Soviet occupation of Poland, seemed to be the first step in a totalitarian march across all of Europe.

CHINA
China Falls to Communism (1949)

A communist revolution that began in 1927 achieved victory on October 1, 1949, when its leader Mao Zedong appeared in Peking's Tiananmen Square and proclaimed the People's Republic of China. This event stunned Americans, who assumed that the $2 billion in military aid they had given Mao's opponent, the nationalist Chiang Kai-shek, would defeat the communists. Chiang's army, however, was rife with corruption and the nationalists had alienated millions of peasants. After Mao's proclamation, Chiang fled to Taiwan, where the United States continued to back his claim of sovereignty over China, and thus added another tension point in the cold war.

VIETNAM
War in Vietnam (1945-1975)

When World War II ended, France decided to reconquer Vietnam, which the Viet Minh, a communist–nationalist group led by Ho Chi Minh, had declared an independent nation. In the fall of 1945, French troops drove the Viet Minh from Saigon, and in November 1946 French ships and airplanes bombarded Haiphong in North Vietnam, killing 6,000 civilians. The next month, Viet Minh troops attacked a French garrison in an act that signaled the start of the fight for independence. Under President Harry Truman, the United States backed France with arms, thus beginning a direct involvement in a war that would last nearly 30 years.

The end of World War II carried with it a development whose importance rivaled that of any other in the world's history: mushroom clouds that spread frightful radiation, first over Hiroshima and then over Nagasaki in Japan. The atomic bomb redefined America's standing in the world, while it redefined American society. Every Baby Boomer would grow up amid the promise of prosperity and the threat of death from the most destructive weapon ever known.

The dropping of the atomic bomb in August 1945 that led to Japan's surrender corresponded to a new crisis—the beginning of a cold war between the United States and the Soviet Union. Eastern Europe was the first battleground in which threats, propaganda, and intervention, short of actual combat between American and Russian forces, worked their influence. In Poland, both the United States and the Soviet Union wanted a government friendly to their respective interests. Soviet dictator Joseph Stalin declared that the question of Poland was crucial to Russia's survival. "Throughout history," he said, "Poland has been the corridor through which the enemy has passed into Russia."

When Allied leaders met at Yalta in 1945 to discuss postwar relations, President Franklin Roosevelt obtained from Stalin a promise to hold free elections in Eastern Europe. But with the Russian army occupying that region when World War II ended, Stalin broke his promise. In Poland, he ruthlessly crushed opposition to Soviet rule, as he did throughout Eastern Europe. Westerners felt betrayed and feared that Soviet communism, and with it a barbaric Russian horde, would sweep across Europe.

At that point, President Truman, who had succeeded Roosevelt, decided that the United States would defend Western civilization with two weapons: the A-bomb and the dollar. Truman thought that as the United States was the only nation with the atomic bomb, it would keep Russia in line. He thought also that the mighty American economy would make the Soviet Union flexible, for the Russians, devastated by war, badly needed economic help.

A meeting with Stalin at Potsdam, Germany, later in 1945 convinced Truman that Stalin understood only force. The following year, former British prime minister Winston Churchill gave a speech at Fulton, Missouri, in which he coined a term that expressed the hardening positions between East and West, and helped define more than 40 years of history. "From Stettin in the Baltic to Trieste in the Adriatic," Churchill declared, "an iron curtain has descended across the Continent." Truman concurred. He needed, however, to convince an American public—weary from World War II and disgusted with European affairs—that the Soviet Union posed a threat as great as any previously posed by Hitler.

Turmoil in Greece gave him his opportunity. As communist rebels tried to overthrow the corrupt Greek monarchy, Britain announced in February 1947 that it could no longer militarily support Greece. Truman listened to those in the State Department who argued that if Greece fell to communism so would Turkey, Italy, and France . . . like dominoes. Although Stalin had not incited the rebellion, Truman issued his statement, known as the Truman Doctrine, that equated anti-communism with freedom and said the United States would provide aid to any nation "resisting attempted subjugation by armed minorities." Thus at the very time the Baby Boom began, Truman laid out foreign policy that would shape relations with the Soviet Union—and mold Boomer mentalities—for decades to come.

Truman portrayed the world in stark terms: the United States stood for freedom, the Soviet Union for evil. In May 1947, Congress appropriated $400 million for aid to Greece and Turkey. Then as the war-torn European economy continued to suffer and a harsh winter gripped the continent— so bad even the gears of London's Big Ben froze and Churchill described society as "a rubble-heap, a charnel house, a breeding ground of pestilence and hate"—Truman convinced Congress to provide money to help rebuild the European economy ($13.33 billion between 1948 and 1952). Secretary of State George Marshall emphasized the humanitarian impulse behind what became known as the Marshall Plan, saying "Our policy is not directed against any country or doctrine, but against hunger, poverty, desperation and chaos." But ultimately the plan aimed at tying Western Europe to America's economy and averting the spread of communism. Under the plan, the United States shipped food and goods that ranged from aircraft parts to sulfur to oil—all intended to alleviate suffering and spark economic life. More extensively, the United States provided money to rebuild industries. Between 1947 and 1950, the plan expanded

---

Without the Marshall Plan
Your bread would be bare,
And so would your children...

Without the Marshall Plan
Your factory chimneys wouldn't smoke,
And neither would you.

But of course there is a Marshall Plan
And it costs every American 32 dollars a year
To help patch up old Europe.

It's easy to reach for help
We must reach for our tools!

—from **The Marshall Plan and You** by Jo Spiel,
distributed by the Dutch government,
November 1949

▼ A plane lands near the ruins of Berlin as part of the airlift. (UPI/CORBIS-BETTMANN)

industrial output 40 percent above that of 1938.

In 1947, George F. Kennan, an official in the U.S. State Department, laid out his "containment theory": the United States must use counterforce to meet changes in Soviet policy and action; by preventing Soviet expansion, the United States would force the communist system to collapse. Truman adopted the idea, adding military pressure to Kennan's call for political and economic pressure, and acted to form an alliance with Western Europe. This seemed particularly necessary to Truman after Stalin staged a communist coup against the government in Czechoslovakia. For his part, Stalin felt threatened: the Truman Doctrine, the Marshall Plan, the impending military alliance . . . all seemed intended to surround and ultimately destroy Russia.

Truman also worked with other Western nations in 1948 to make West Germany an independent nation. Stalin believed that such a move threatened Russian security, and he reacted by blockading West Berlin, a zone inside Soviet-occupied East Germany under the control of the Soviet Union, the United States, Britain, and France. Truman, in turn, responded with an airlift—tons of goods per day were

flown into West Berlin by American and British planes—and by stationing B-29 bombers, which could carry A-bombs, in Britain. This was a great, albeit symbolic, menace to the Soviet Union; the planes actually carried no bombs. At the same time, Truman reinstated the military draft and increased the size of the Army. Nuclear threat, military service, brinkmanship—the United States resorted to this formula time and again during the cold war, and it became the political backbeat of Baby Boomer lives.

Then, in April 1949, Truman formed the North Atlantic Treaty Organization (NATO) with Canada and several Western European nations. Members of NATO would consider an attack against one as an attack against all. The following month, Stalin lifted the Berlin blockade.

Despite Truman's efforts, communism advanced. In 1949, China fell to communist rebels, and the Soviet Union exploded its first A-bomb. Thus arose a world Baby Boomers considered frightening; a world where nations rattled nuclear weapons at each other; a world where the forces of "good" and "evil" battled for final control; a world always on the brink, always awaiting the next mushroom cloud.

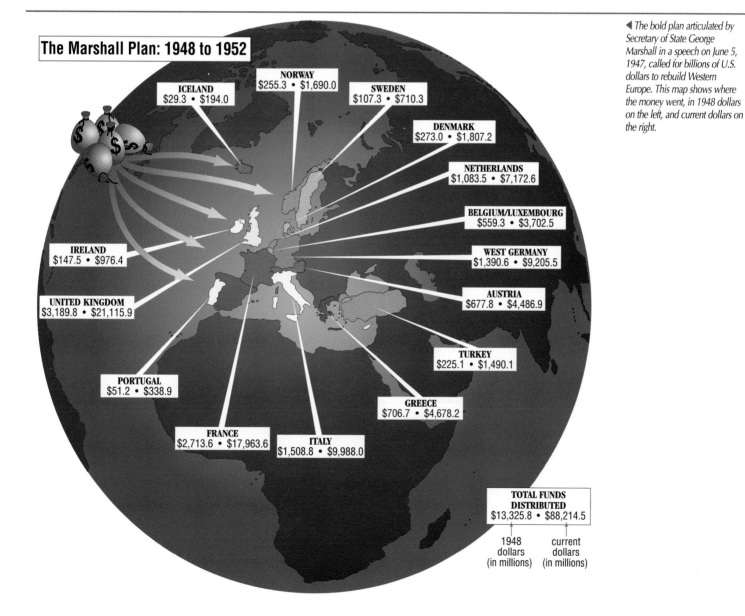

The Marshall Plan: 1948 to 1952

NORWAY
$255.3 • $1,690.0

ICELAND
$29.3 • $194.0

SWEDEN
$107.3 • $710.3

DENMARK
$273.0 • $1,807.2

NETHERLANDS
$1,083.5 • $7,172.6

BELGIUM/LUXEMBOURG
$559.3 • $3,702.5

WEST GERMANY
$1,390.6 • $9,205.5

AUSTRIA
$677.8 • $4,486.9

IRELAND
$147.5 • $976.4

UNITED KINGDOM
$3,189.8 • $21,115.9

TURKEY
$225.1 • $1,490.1

PORTUGAL
$51.2 • $338.9

GREECE
$706.7 • $4,678.2

FRANCE
$2,713.6 • $17,963.6

ITALY
$1,508.8 • $9,988.0

TOTAL FUNDS
DISTRIBUTED
$13,325.8 • $88,214.5

1948 dollars (in millions) | current dollars (in millions)

◄ The bold plan articulated by Secretary of State George Marshall in a speech on June 5, 1947, called for billions of U.S. dollars to rebuild Western Europe. This map shows where the money went, in 1948 dollars on the left, and current dollars on the right.

Political involvement—from canvassing to rallies to sit-ins to riots—shaped the Baby Boom generation. As children, Boomers heard about or witnessed civil rights protests in the 1940s and 1950s; as young adults, they joined them, or they threw their support behind antiwar, women's rights, environmental, and other causes.

The post–World War II civil rights movement set the tone, style, and strategy for Boomer protest. This movement gained momentum from a World War II catastrophe that galvanized black America. In July 1944, an explosion rocked the Port Chicago Naval Base in California, a blast so massive it sent fire and smoke 12,000 feet into the sky and shattered windows 20 miles away, and so devastating it killed 320 sailors—200 of them black. Because the Navy used only African Americans in the dangerous job of loading munitions at Port Chicago, their deaths raised questions about a policy that seemed racist. This perception was reinforced by a court of inquiry's written report, which stressed that "The consensus of the opinion of witnesses . . . is that the colored enlisted personnel are neither temperamentally nor intellectually capable of handling high explosives." After no exact cause could be found for the explosion, 258 blacks refused to work without guarantees for their safety.

In retaliation, the military court-martialed 50 of those it suspected of being either leaders or unwilling to obey all orders, and tried them for mutiny—the largest mass mutiny trial in American history. In October 1944, the Port Chicago Fifty were found guilty and given severe sentences. The verdict appalled blacks and many whites and led to protests, including mass meetings in several cities and a pro-clemency petition campaign organized by Eleanor Roosevelt and the National Urban League. Late in 1945, the 50 were released and granted clemency, but the incident had turned the spot-

> ❝ It is time for South Carolina to rejoin the union. ❞
>
> —Federal district judge **Waties Waring**, in 1947 ruling that blacks should be allowed to vote in Democratic primaries

light on racial segregation in the military and promoted alliances between African Americans and white liberals.

The National Association for the Advancement of Colored People (NAACP) benefited from such an alliance and heightened activism. Its membership surged from 50,000 in 1940 to 450,000 in 1946. In pursuing civil rights, the NAACP preferred court battles and political pressure to marches and boycotts. For example, in 1946 it represented Herman Sweatt, an African American who had applied to law school at the University of Texas and was told by the college he would be educated in a separate all-black institution. In another case, it represented 68-year-old G. W. McLaurin, who had enrolled in the doctoral program at the University of Oklahoma but was made to sit apart from white students, behind a railing marked "reserved for colored." The NAACP took both the Sweatt and McLaurin cases to the U.S. Supreme Court, claiming the plaintiffs had been denied equal education. In 1950, the court agreed, ruling that Sweatt and McLaurin must be admitted into the classrooms attended by whites.

In its pursuit of racial justice, the NAACP also sought to extend voting rights. Blacks and their white supporters believed that with the right to vote in southern states, many doors would open. The *Pittsburgh Courier* claimed: "Once Negroes start voting in large numbers . . . the Jim Crow laws will be endangered and . . . segregation . . . destroyed."

Oppressive Mississippi, where few African Americans voted, grabbed national headlines. In 1944, middle-class blacks in Jackson formed the Mississippi Progressive Voters League to register African Americans. The league ran up against Theodore "The Man" Bilbo, a powerful politician who used racist smears to keep blacks from voting. After Bilbo won a seat in the U.S. Senate, the NAACP challenged him, claiming his election had been rife with voter fraud. The NAACP had no hope of denying Bilbo his seat, but it used congressional hearings to expose the state's deep racism. Despite conservative white opposition, about 20,000 blacks registered to vote in Mississippi in the decade after World War II.

To supplement the NAACP, other leagues organized. In 1946 the Atlanta All Citizens Registration Committee helped 18,000 Georgia blacks register. In Winston-Salem, North Carolina, the local Congress of Industrial Organizations rallied black workers and, together with the NAACP, registered tens of thousands.

Voting drives often risked violence. In Fitzgerald, Georgia, notices appeared in 1946 on the doors of black churches: "THE FIRST NIGGER WHO VOTES IN GEORGIA WILL BE A DEAD NIGGER." A few days later, four whites accosted a black war veteran who had voted in Taylor County and killed him.

Despite these incidents, when blacks cast ballots they gained politically. Eager to court them, President Harry Truman formed a commission that issued *To Secure These Rights*, a report that called for federal protection of voting rights and desegregation of the armed forces, interstate transportation, and government employment. In 1948, Truman signed two executive orders, one establishing fair employment within the federal government, and another

▼ The charred hulls of two munitions ships protrude above the surface of the water in Port Chicago Harbor after the 1944 explosion that killed 320 people—nearly two-thirds of them black sailors—and injured many more. (UPI/COR-BIS-BETTMAN)

forming a committee to promote equal opportunity in the military.

In all, the voting rights drive bolstered black assertiveness, stirred the federal government into action, and provided lessons for the civil rights movement. Much work remained, however. A Gallup poll in 1948 showed that 56 percent of Americans thought even Truman's moderate approach to civil rights too extreme. Nevertheless, these early protests set strong examples for many Boomers about the strategies needed to fight injustice. Later Boomer activists would look back on the civil rights protests of the late 1940s as their moral seedbed.

A Plea to the United Nations

Based on the United Nations' aim of "universal respect for, and observance of, human rights and fundamental freedom for all without distinction to race, sex, language, or religion," prominent African Americans filed a petition in 1946 with its Economic and Social Council, seeking to get help in ending discrimination in the United States.

Several white Americans, taken aback by a move they said blemished the U.S. image in the world, criticized the petition; the NAACP defended it. One official, Charles Houston, said: "A national policy of the United States which permits disfranchisement in the South is just as much an international issue as . . . the denial of democratic rights in Franco Spain."

JIM CROW LAWS

In addition to laws designed to prevent African Americans from voting, a wide variety of other legislation existed across the United States, intended to separate blacks and whites from, quite literally, the cradle to the grave. These laws, nicknamed Jim Crow laws after a minstrel show character, extended far beyond the infamous segregated lunch counters—they also extended beyond the states in the "Deep South." Here is a small sample of legislation written after the Civil War that would not be torn down until the 1960s.

BARBERS: GEORGIA
No colored barber shall serve as a barber [to] white women or girls.

BURIAL: GEORGIA
The officer in charge shall not bury, or allow to be buried, any colored persons upon ground set apart or used for the burial of white persons.

CIRCUSES: LOUISIANA
All circuses, shows, and tent exhibitions, to which the attendance of . . . more than one race is invited or expected to attend shall provide for the convenience of its patrons not less than two ticket offices with individual ticket sellers, and not less than two entrances to the said performance.

EDUCATION: NEW MEXICO
Separate rooms [shall] be provided for the teaching of pupils of African descent, and [when] said rooms are so provided, such pupils may not be admitted to the school rooms occupied and used by pupils of Caucasian or other descent.

FISHING, BOATING, AND BATHING: OKLAHOMA
The [Conservation] Commission shall have the right to make segregation of the white and colored races as to the exercise of rights of fishing, boating and bathing.

INTERMARRIAGE: MARYLAND
All marriages between a white person and a negro, or between a white person and a person of negro descent, to the third generation, inclusive, or between a white person and a member of the Malay race; or between the negro and a member of the Malay race; or between a person of Negro descent, to the third generation, inclusive, and a member of the Malay race, are forever prohibited, and shall be void.

LIBRARIES: TEXAS
Any white person of such county may use the county free library under the rules and regulations, prescribed by the commissioners court and may be entitled to all the privileges thereof….Negroes of said county [shall] be served through a separate branch or branches of the county free library.

TELEPHONE BOOTHS: OKLAHOMA
The Corporation Commission is hereby vested with power and authority to require telephone companies . . . to maintain separate booths for white and colored patrons.

PRISONS: MISSISSIPPI
The warden shall see that the white convicts shall have separate apartments for both eating and sleeping from the negro convicts.

TEXTBOOKS: NORTH CAROLINA
Books shall not be interchangeable between the white and colored schools, but shall continue to be used by the race first using them.

POOL AND BILLIARD ROOMS: ALABAMA
It shall be unlawful for a negro and white person to play together or in company with each other at any game of pool or billiards.

MENTAL HOSPITALS: GEORGIA
The Board of Control shall see that proper and distinct apartments are arranged for said patients, so that in no case shall Negroes and white persons be together.

HOSPITAL ENTRANCES: MISSISSIPPI
There shall be maintained by the governing authorities of every hospital maintained by the state for treatment of white and colored patients separate entrances for white and colored patients and visitors, and such entrances shall be used by the race only for which they are prepared.

Nothing about the development of television from the mid-1920s to the 1940s gave the slightest clue that it would play such a critical role in shaping the ideas and attitudes of the Baby Boom generation. At the time, radio dominated communications, the movies provided mass entertainment, and television seemed little more than an intriguing novelty. Two New York City TV stations, which later became WNBC and WCBS, did provide programming during the 1930s, but it was largely experimental. Those telecasts, seen by very few people, centered on one-time events—baseball games, live theater, and selected speeches.

> 66 *Television is more interesting than people. If it were not, we should have people standing in the corners of our rooms.* 99
>
> **—Alan Coren**

Another station, in Schenectady, New York, near the General Electric labs where scientists were developing TV technology, also transmitted programs periodically. And occasionally in Washington or Philadelphia an event would be presented to demonstrate the new moving-image technology.

As late as 1941, TV sets were selling at the anemic rate of about 90 per month nationwide, but interest in television was growing and the technology behind it was improving. NBC had already made its first network broadcast—130 miles between stations in New York City and Schenectady—and the Federal Communications Commission (FCC) established uniform standards for TV transmission, approving a 525-line definition and 30 pictures per second for black-and-white television broadcasts. Many people who would later influence the growth of TV had become fans of the nascent medium, most notably David Sarnoff, a founder of NBC's parent company, RCA. Seeing the successful nationwide network of radio as a possible archetype, they began to envision TV's enormous potential to inform, entertain, and, above all, generate profits.

TV had barely begun to demonstrate its mainstream

appeal before World War II brought television programming to a standstill. Had the war not intervened, TV might have continued its slow-but-steady rise. Instead, the total absence of TV made its reemergence a development that caused a splash instead of a ripple. The postwar convergence of technological confidence and economic optimism created the climate to launch television and make it a cultural phenomenon. Thus TV became a force far greater than the sum of its vacuum tubes and circuitry.

The first bona fide TV hit made a superstar out of radio and vaudeville comic Milton Berle. *The Texaco Star Theater* premiered on June 8, 1948. It was a variety show that made optimum use of the new visual medium by relying heavily on sight gags and broad comedy to entertain its audience. As it was originally conceived, each week the show had a different host. "Uncle Miltie" emceed the first show. Morey Amsterdam, Jack Carter, and Henny Youngman were among those who took turns hosting throughout the summer.

In September Milton Berle was made the permanent host, and soon the show focused on him, with his wild costumes, corny jokes, and vaudeville-style clowning, as he perfected a TV genre that became known as "vaudeo." The original show, which spawned several copycats, including *Your Show of Shows* (1950–54) starring Sid Caesar, *Arthur Godfrey and His Friends* (1949–59), and *The Colgate Comedy Hour* (1950–55), lasted until 1956. It reappeared to a lukewarm reception in a slightly different format in 1958 for one year and then again in the mid-1960s for a season. But in those important first few years, Milton Berle was red-hot and made a lasting impression on a fledgling industry.

When *The Texaco Star Theater* premiered in 1948, only 172,000 households in the United States owned television sets, with the majority of viewers (about 35 percent) in New York. The small number of available TVs meant that most viewers gathered with others at the corner saloon or at the homes of friends to watch the show. Just one year later, nearly a million American households owned televisions, and by the end of Berle's reign in 1956, that number had increased to almost 35 million.

As there were more TV owners, so there was more TV to watch. From 1945 to 1950, the number of commercial television stations grew from nine to 103. This proliferation of local TV stations dealt a blow to many shows that had been developed from radio, especially the more ethnically oriented ones. Transplanted radio hits such as *The Goldbergs* (1949–54), *Life with Luigi* (1952–53), and *Amos 'n Andy* (1951–53) suffered, despite their popularity on radio. A number of factors appear to have contributed to their demise. Hollywood, not New York, was emerging as the TV capital. Racial and ethnic diversity seemed to be more easily tolerated when the characters were on the radio and therefore unseen. Advertisers, a generally conservative group, feared that shows depicting differences would inspire differences, threatening the herd mentality they depended on to sell their products. Furthermore, ethnic programming

▼ *The television invaded American homes with a speed that few other inventions can match. The remarkable growth of the industry is shown in this chart, detailing the number of homes with television sets in the late 1940s and 1950s.*

Year	# of households with TVs	Percentage increase
1946	8,000	
1947	14,000	43%
1948	172,000	92%
1949	940,000	82%
1950	3,875,000	76%
1951	10,320,000	62%
1952	15,300,000	33%
1953	20,400,000	25%
1954	26,000,000	22%
1955	30,700,000	15%
1956	34,900,000	12%
1957	38,900,000	10%
1958	41,924,000	7%
1959	43,950,000	5%

Note: 1959 is the first year to include Alaska and Hawaii.

◄ *Milton Berle hosts* The Texaco Star Theater. *(Photofest)*

that depended largely on negative stereotypes came under fire for being offensive and was driven from the airwaves.

Television had come a long way in a few short years. NBC, CBS, and ABC had risen from humble beginnings in New York to create nationwide TV networks. By using their radio network muscle to squeeze their only other competition, the Dumont network, out of business, the "Big Three" were establishing control over television. That control would last almost 40 years until cable and rival networks challenged them in the 1980s. By the dawn of the 1950s, it was clear that this "newfangled invention" was a force to be reckoned with.

Uncle Miltie

Milton Berle was instrumental in creating the excitement that fueled the TV-buying market in the late 1940s. But ironically, the subsequent decline of his *Texaco Star Theater* may have been a by-product of its huge success: as TV ownership rose, Berle's ratings slipped. Uncle Miltie, it turns out, "sold" a lot of TVs to people who didn't like him.

As it became more and more common to own a television, it became less and less necessary for people to gather in groups to watch. Berle's raucous comedic style played well in a crowded bar, but with just the family gathered in the living room, he was almost overpowering. His routines were steeped in vaudeville tradition, rooted in the urban experience, and flavored with Yiddish—they didn't have the same appeal to the demographically expanding audience. By the 1960s, Berle was largely considered a nostalgia act, a dinosaur from another time. But there is no reason to grieve for Uncle Miltie: he got the last laugh when in 1951 he signed a contract with NBC guaranteeing him a six-figure salary for 30 years . . . whether he worked or not.

DDT

Hailed as "the atomic bomb of pesticides," DDT promised to be the ultimate weapon in the war against bugs. A manmade chemical first synthesized by German chemist Othmar Zeidler in 1873, dichlorodiphenyl-trichlorethane received little attention until Swiss researcher Paul Muller discovered its insecticidal qualities in 1939.

DDT gained renown as a lifesaver in the hands of the U.S. Army during World War II. Used to wipe out malarial mosquitoes and disease-bearing lice, it dramatically halted a deadly typhus epidemic in Naples, Italy, during the winter of 1944. Released for civilian use after the war, DDT was widely adopted to control insect-borne diseases and agricultural pests around the world. Cheap, powerful, and unusually long lasting after its application, DDT quickly became the pesticide of choice for farmers and ordinary consumers as well as public health officials.

But DDT's success as a magic bullet was brief. Resistant houseflies were reported as early as 1946; by the end of the decade, resistant populations of mosquitoes and lice sent researchers scrambling to devise new and more deadly insecticides. In 1962, Rachel Carson's *Silent Spring* would spark a new movement with its warnings about the toxic effects of DDT in the environment. Soon the chemical that had once symbolized science's clearest triumph over pestilence and disease would become a symbol of environmental damage. Twenty-four years after its discoverer won the 1948 Nobel Prize for DDT's contributions to human health, DDT would be banned from use in the United States.

Atomic Testing

Less than a year after the bombings of Japan, the U.S. military launched Operation Crossroads in the Pacific's Marshall Islands. The first peacetime explosions of nuclear weapons, it was the beginning of a series of atmospheric, underwater, and underground nuclear tests that would continue in the Pacific and the Nevada desert until 1963.

▼ *Spectators at an atomic test in Las Vegas, Nevada. Those without protective goggles have wisely averted their eyes. (Archive Photos)*

Operation Crossroads played before a large crowd, including more than 42,000 military service personnel. Billed as an act of scientific research rather than a deterrent display of military might, atomic test "Able" exploded over Bikini Atoll on July 1, 1946. Doomsayers had predicted that the ocean floor would crack and vast catastrophes would ensue. When the actual explosion did not cause a cataclysm—and even left some targeted ships undamaged in the harbor—a nation was reassured that the mighty power of the atom could be harnessed by science.

The comforting news did not last long. The second atomic test on July 25 occurred under the waters of Bikini's lagoon, unleashing a plume of radioactive water and steam that quickly contaminated some 36 square miles of ocean. Bare-chested soldiers attempted to "scrub" the radiation off exposed ships, while some observers and members of the press began to question whether the effects of radiation, previously discounted, were more dangerous than military brass would admit. For many Americans, this was their first frightening glimpse of the long-term dangers of atomic weapons.

Public fears about radiation would inspire some memorable movie monsters of the 1950s—including *Godzilla* and the giant mutant ants of *Them!*—as well as repeated calls to end the tests. But in the panic that ensued following the first Soviet atomic test in 1949, the new Atomic Energy Commission would insist that aboveground nuclear testing was safe and vital to national security. For the people living downwind and the soldiers deliberately exposed to radioactive fallout, those assurances were of little comfort.

Velcro

Returning from a nature walk in 1948, Swiss inventor George de Mestral found himself picking off burrs stuck to the legs of his pants. Wondering how they adhered to fabric without tearing it, he inspected them under a microscope. Those burrs, covered with tiny hooks capable of grabbing fabric, became the inspiration for hook-and-loop fasteners—patented in 1951 under the name Velcro.

After much experimenting with fibers and manufacturing processes, de Mestral settled on a design that used opposing nylon strips: one covered with miniature nylon hooks and the other covered with fabric loops. Introduced into the United States in 1957, Velcro would find a use just about everywhere: clothing, footwear, astronauts' space suits, and on late-night TV, where David Letterman would make comic use of Velcro's adhesive powers by sticking himself to a fabric loop wall while wearing a Velcro suit.

ENIAC

Introduced to the public on February 16, 1946, the Electronic Numerical Integrator and Computer (ENIAC) contained more than 18,000 vacuum tubes, was more than 150 feet wide, and could perform 5,000 additions per second. A joint project of the University of Pennsylvania's Moore School of Electrical Engineering and the U.S. Army's Ballistic Research Laboratory, the creation of ENIAC was overseen by scientists John Presper Eckert and John Mauchly.

Work began on the ENIAC in 1943, and the first trials were run in November 1945. Built into a basement room at the Moore School, the superstructure covered 650 square feet and featured 300 neon lights. Running at full power, the ENIAC produced 150 kilowatts of heat, requiring the installation of two 20-horsepower fans to keep the unit cool. Everything about the ENIAC was large, except the amount of time it took to compute: capable of 5,000 operations per second, it was a thousand times faster than Harvard University's Mark I computer, which had been in the spotlight two years earlier. Eckert and Mauchly were known to boast that ENIAC could calculate the trajectory, or path, of a speeding object faster than the object could fly.

The ENIAC proved that an all-electronic calculating machine could provide industry with enormous power, leading to an explosion of new research. The excitement created by the unveiling brought numerous requests from the scientific community for more information about electronic computing. Eager to transmit technological knowledge, the university organized an invitation-only series of lectures at the Moore School. Taking place in the summer of 1946, the lectures explained ENIAC and, more importantly, revealed the design of EDVAC, a stored-program computer. Several dozen young scientists walked away with the framework of future computing scribbled in their notebooks.

The ENIAC would quickly be eclipsed by more advanced computers, including the EDVAC and the UNIVAC. But even before it made its public debut, ENIAC had already helped to shape the postwar world. In tests run in November 1945, ENIAC solved millions of calculations for Los Alamos scientists working on the hydrogen bomb.

Breaking the Sound Barrier

To fighter pilots in World War II, the so-called sound barrier was as tangible as a brick wall. As a plane approached the speed of sound—known as Mach I because the actual speed varies depending on altitude and weather conditions—it would be buffeted by wild shockwaves. Some planes disintegrated under the strain; others lost all navigational controls and crashed. Few pilots survived.

Throughout World War II, Germany, Britain, and the United States raced to create a supersonic fighter plane. But not until after the war did the Bell Aircraft Corporation find the right combination: thin wings, rocket fuel, reinforced construction, and a horizontal stabilizer on the tail. On October 14, 1947, over what is now Edwards Air Force Base, decorated combat pilot Captain Chuck Yeager flew the X-1 through the sound barrier, setting a new speed record and sending a sonic boom thundering across the California desert, ushering in a new era of supersonic flight. By the mid-1960s fighter planes such as the F-4 Phantom II and the MiG-21 would routinely exceed even Mach 2.

Jackie Robinson (1919-1972)

On April 18, 1946, in Jersey City, Jack Roosevelt Robinson stepped up to the plate for the minor league Montreal Royals. No African American had played professional baseball on a white team before, but Robinson, a four-sport varsity standout at UCLA, shone in his precedent-making appearance, batting .800 and scoring four times.

The next year, Robinson signed with the Brooklyn Dodgers, becoming the first black player to break the color barrier in major league baseball. For Robinson, who had faced court-martial rather than tolerate Jim Crow segregation in the U.S. Army, the terms of the deal would be tough. He pledged to Dodgers' president Branch Rickey that he would not respond to the taunts and humiliations that awaited him at the hands of the players and crowds. On the field with the Dodgers in 1947, he faced insults, physical attacks, even death threats. But, as Rickey had predicted, Robinson's courage and astonishing self-control in the face of provocation won the grudging respect of the nation. He helped spark the Dodgers to the 1947 National League pennant, and was named Rookie of the Year.

The psychic toll upon him was enormous. After two years of silence and passive resistance under his agreement with Rickey, Robinson reclaimed his right to speak out in 1949, and he did so with relish both on and off the field. A proud pioneer in the struggle against racial discrimination, Robinson retired from baseball in 1959 and was inducted into the Baseball Hall of Fame in 1962.

▼ *Jackie Robinson in 1947. (Archive Photos)*

The Good Doctors
Dr. Alfred C. Kinsey (1894–1956) and Dr. Benjamin Spock (1903–1998)

They were unlikely icons: a scientist previously distinguished for his exhaustive study of the gall wasp, and a mild-mannered pediatrician with an interest in psychoanalysis. Sex researcher Alfred Kinsey and child-rearing expert Benjamin Spock became household names as scientific authorities about the most personal details of the American family. Lightning rods for America's deep ambivalence about the role of science in effecting social and cultural change, Spock and Kinsey drew plaudits from progressives and the ire of cultural conservatives for the challenge their work posed to traditional moral standards.

Spock's *Common Sense Book of Baby and Child Care*, published in 1946, gave millions of young couples starting families advice that was both new and reassuring. Unlike previous guides, which called for draconian feeding schedules and harsh discipline, Spock counseled parents to trust their own instincts and make their own choices. He made Freudian theories of child development part of America's common parlance by translating them into simple, comforting homilies. Spock's book and its revised editions became enormously popular, eventually selling some 50 million copies around the world. When the first generation of Spock-raised babies reached young adulthood in the '60s—and Spock himself joined them in antiwar protests—the good doctor was blamed by conservative commentators for having fostered the breakdown of civil society with his permissive ways.

Kinsey, a professor at Indiana University, produced his own best-seller in 1948: *Sexual Behavior in the Human Male*. Based on interviews gathered over 10 years with some 12,000 men and women, Kinsey's data showed that while Americans might claim to practice monogamy and the missionary position, a high percentage of men had engaged in premarital sex, extramarital sex, and homosexual activity. His findings were shocking, but religious leaders were even more enraged by Kinsey's refusal to make moral judgments about sexual behaviors. He called this scientific objectivity; his opponents called it a subversive threat to American morals. After he published a follow-up work on female sexuality in 1953, his opponents prevailed—his research funding was slashed and his studies virtually halted.

Ingrid Bergman (1915-1982)

With her goddess-next-door looks and disarming disdain for Hollywood glamour, Ingrid Bergman was an audience favorite throughout the '40s. She played tramps, schemers, and even a nun, but moviegoers responded to her as the ideal feminine archetype created by David O. Selznick's studio publicity: the wholesome young wife and mother uncorrupted by fame.

Lurking behind the image was a determined woman growing bored with the limitations of acting in Hollywood—and stifled in her picture-perfect marriage to a stern Swedish neurosurgeon. In 1949 she fled them both for an experimental project with Italian director Roberto Rossellini. Her well-publicized affair with Rossellini ended her marriage, but the news of her out-of-wedlock pregnancy nearly ended her career. Once America's sweetheart, Bergman was assailed as immoral. Exiled to Italy, blacklisted in Hollywood, and denounced on the floor of the Senate as "a powerful influence for evil," she would not work in the United States again for nearly a decade.

R. Buckminster Fuller (1895-1983)

He was a transcendentalist for the 20th century, a prodigious intellect and inventor who believed that technology would remake human society, ending poverty, want, and war by allowing humanity to "do more with less"—a famous Fuller coinage, along with "Spaceship Earth."

In 1948 he introduced his best-known invention, the geodesic dome. Derived from a triangle-based geometry of his own devising, the geodesic dome enclosed the maximum amount of space within the minimum surface area. Between the dome and his "Witchita House" (1946), a circular home designed to be cheaply mass-produced, he claimed to have solved the problem of low-cost housing. Mainstream America wasn't buying, but many of his ideas would resurface in the nascent counterculture.

▲ Ingrid Bergman with Roberto Rossellini on the set of their film Stromboli, in 1949. (UPI/CORBIS-BETTMANN)

◄ R. Buckminster Fuller poses in front of his geodeisic dome. (Archive Photos)

THE 1950s

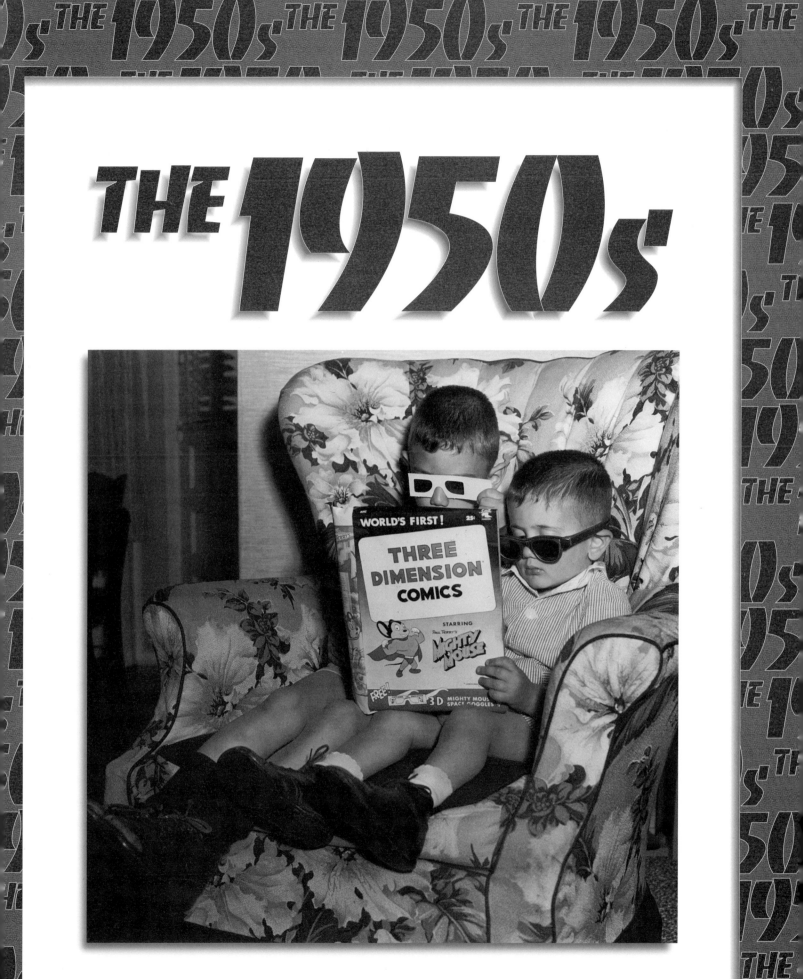

1953's latest novelty: 3-D comics!
(UPI/CORBIS-BETTMANN)

Population and Family

When the popular TV show *Father Knows Best* aired in the mid-'50s, it brought into millions of homes the ideal family . . . in size, in values, in actions. The show featured two parents with three children—what adults wanted and usually produced—with a father who worked and headed the household—what society expected. Television depicted the perfect, cohesive family unit—every week conflicts melted into happiness.

The Baby Boom that had begun so suddenly in the late '40s accelerated in the '50s, becoming, according to one observer, like a pig in a long, extended python of flat birthrates. Incredibly, more people were born between 1947 and 1953 than in the previous 30 years.

In 1954, the number of births topped four million for the first time in U.S. history. Despite this, families resembled less the old lady in the shoe than the comfortable suburbanites in *Father Knows Best*. Although by 1958 the number of families with two or more children had increased 46 percent from 10 years earlier, the number of families with more than five children had declined.

A procreation ethic propelled the mania for babies. Movies, magazines, industry, and television all promoted pregnancy. In a 1951 article for *Look*, movie star Rosalind Russell declared the end of Hollywood's "glamour era" and the debut of a child-centered, church-oriented community. The following year, General Electric offered five shares of common stock to any employee who had a baby on October 15, the company's 75th anniversary—and dozens did. With much fanfare, the hit TV show *I Love Lucy* promoted the happiness only a child could bring when Lucy, played by Lucille Ball, gave birth to Little Ricky. The event, splashed across the cover of *TV Guide*, coincided with Ball's real-life pregnancy, making fiction barely distinguishable from fact.

Society prescribed that women should stay home, have kids, and take care of them. Family counselor Paul Landis insisted "marriage is the natural state of adults." In the 1955 movie *The Tender Trap*, Debbie Reynolds preached: "A career is just fine. But it's no substitute for marriage. Don't you think a man is the most important thing in the world? A woman isn't a woman until she's been married and had children."

Societal norms dictated that women should feel creative and fulfill ambition through their roles as wives and mothers, supporting the husband as he builds his career, providing moral guidance to the children as they grow older. *McCall's* magazine implored: "For the sake of every member of the family, the family needs a head. This means Father, not Mother."

But contradictions abounded. While society as a whole emphasized the domestic role for women, glamorized by *Father Knows Best* and many other TV shows, more married women worked during the decade, increasing from 52 percent at the beginning of the decade to 60 percent by the end. At the same time, some women complained about their relegation to a secondary position in the economic and political world, and pursued a long-running campaign for an equal rights amendment to the Constitution (one that Congress finally approved in 1972, but that the states failed to ratify). Widespread rebellion, though, awaited another decade.

Fatherhood received devotional praise, too, both on TV shows such as *Leave it to Beaver* and *The Adventures of Ozzie and Harriet*, where the dads offered timely advice and received the respect and love of their sons, and in magazines, where writers advised fathers to be particularly careful in bringing up boys so as to ensure the youngsters did not become sissies. *American Home* magazine stated that a good dad should share in a son's hobbies and listen to his hopes and problems.

> 66 *I rarely get excited.*
> *I obey laws and rules.*
> *I respect authority.*
> *I conform to most customs.*
> *I am consistent with my actions.*
> *I am just an average person.* 99
>
> —from **"Stepping Stones to Happiness,"** Household *magazine. These were considered to be the most desirable personality traits.*

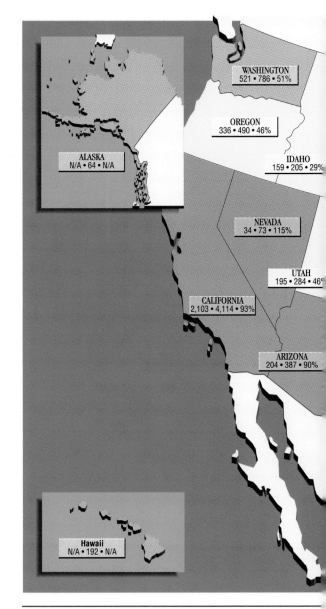

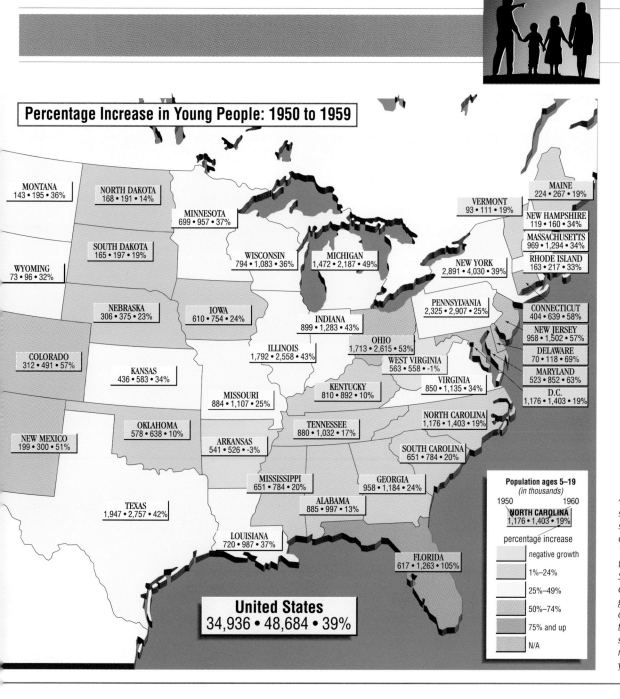

Percentage Increase in Young People: 1950 to 1959

MONTANA
143 • 195 • 36%

NORTH DAKOTA
168 • 191 • 14%

MINNESOTA
699 • 957 • 37%

VERMONT
93 • 111 • 19%

MAINE
224 • 267 • 19%

NEW HAMPSHIRE
119 • 160 • 34%

SOUTH DAKOTA
165 • 197 • 19%

WISCONSIN
794 • 1,083 • 36%

MICHIGAN
1,472 • 2,187 • 49%

MASSACHUSETTS
969 • 1,294 • 34%

WYOMING
73 • 96 • 32%

NEW YORK
2,891 • 4,030 • 39%

RHODE ISLAND
163 • 217 • 33%

NEBRASKA
306 • 375 • 23%

IOWA
610 • 754 • 24%

INDIANA
899 • 1,283 • 43%

PENNSYLVANIA
2,325 • 2,907 • 25%

CONNECTICUT
404 • 639 • 58%

NEW JERSEY
958 • 1,502 • 57%

COLORADO
312 • 491 • 57%

ILLINOIS
1,792 • 2,558 • 43%

OHIO
1,713 • 2,615 • 53%

WEST VIRGINIA
563 • 558 • -1%

DELAWARE
70 • 118 • 69%

KANSAS
436 • 583 • 34%

KENTUCKY
810 • 892 • 10%

VIRGINIA
850 • 1,135 • 34%

MARYLAND
523 • 852 • 63%

MISSOURI
884 • 1,107 • 25%

D.C.
1,176 • 1,403 • 19%

NEW MEXICO
199 • 300 • 51%

OKLAHOMA
578 • 638 • 10%

TENNESSEE
880 • 1,032 • 17%

NORTH CAROLINA
1,176 • 1,403 • 19%

ARKANSAS
541 • 526 • -3%

SOUTH CAROLINA
651 • 784 • 20%

MISSISSIPPI
651 • 784 • 20%

GEORGIA
958 • 1,184 • 24%

TEXAS
1,947 • 2,757 • 42%

ALABAMA
885 • 997 • 13%

LOUISIANA
720 • 987 • 37%

FLORIDA
617 • 1,263 • 105%

**United States
34,936 • 48,684 • 39%**

Population ages 5–19
(in thousands)

1950   1960
NORTH CAROLINA
1,176 • 1,403 • 19%

percentage increase

negative growth

1%–24%

25%–49%

50%–74%

75% and up

N/A

◀ *The Baby Boom went into full swing in the 1950s. This map shows the increase in the number of Americans aged 5 to 19; in the 10-year span from 1950 to 1959, the number of kids in the United States increased by nearly 40 percent. Note the divergent geographical trends in the upper part of the map; growth was slower in the Midwest and East, while some western states doubled or nearly doubled the number of young people.*

The conscientious father must also defeat the scourge of juvenile delinquency. As youths multiplied in numbers, teen culture seemed to expand exponentially, and with it a threat to the stable family. Publications broadcast a powerful message. Novels such as *Gutter Gang, Teen-Age Mafia,* and *The Young and the Violent* drew teen readers and adult worries. Writing in the *New York Times,* education editor Benjamin Fine stated that President Eisenhower's request for more money to fight juvenile delinquency showed that "the people of this country have awakened to the need for a concerted campaign to help our troubled boys and girls. Because in . . . 1955 we will have more than one million juvenile delinquents."

No one really knew if juvenile delinquency had grown appreciably from earlier decades; the press and politicians often exaggerated and sensationalized the matter. Teens themselves overwhelmingly rejected that part of their subculture; in fact, they rebelled little, donning cardigan sweaters and two-toned saddle shoes, and producing what many observers called a conformist "silent generation."

In all, the Baby Boom kids yet to enter their teen years had more to say in shaping society than did juvenile delinquents. Their sheer numbers alone jolted the economy, reshaping industries and producing entirely new ones dedicated to the needs, wants, and demands of a massive baby brigade.

POLIO

Population growth in the United States—to nearly 178 million in 1959—also owed something to the conquest of dangerous diseases, most notably polio. There were 40,000 new cases reported in 1954, the same year that Dr. Jonas Salk field-tested his vaccine in Philadelphia. Thousands of parents volunteered their children for the tests, and kids happily sported "Polio Pioneer" lapel buttons. When Salk announced in 1955 that his medicine was safe and effective, whole communities celebrated, honking car horns, ringing bells, and closing schools.

The U.S. Department of Health, Education, and Welfare helped bring the epidemic to an end by distributing the vaccine in the public schools. This, the largest ever mobilization of peacetime volunteers, involved 60,000 doctors and nurses and 50,000 teachers.

Elizabeth Eckford tried to keep her composure and dignity as young whites pushed menacingly close, taunting her, shouting "Nigger!" She kept walking toward the high school while inside she trembled—until she saw the National Guard lined up in front of the building. Surely they would help her enter on this, her first day of school. But when she reached the front steps, one guardsman refused to let her through. Confused, she walked down the helmeted line and tried again. This time, two soldiers blocked her, then others moved toward her with raised bayonets. Suddenly she realized the guard was there to stop her. Shaken, she turned and walked back through the mob, alone, fearful. "Lynch her! Lynch her!" someone shouted. When she made it to a bus bench, she sat down and started crying. A friendly white lady comforted her and admonished the taunters, saying, "She's just a little girl."

Eckford's ordeal outside Central High School in Little Rock, Arkansas, in 1957 displayed the challenge posed by racial integration, which together with enrollment growth and cold war fears, shaped education in the '50s.

Baby Boomers flooded the nation's schools. Public elementary school enrollments shot upward during the decade, from 18.4 million to 25.7 million, and public high school enrollments climbed from 5.7 million to 8.5 million. Although per pupil expenditures increased from $232 to $433, the nation suffered a serious shortage of teachers and classrooms. By 1959, 100,000 public school teachers had substandard credentials; and while some locations fought valiantly to expand facilities—California, for example, opened one new school per week throughout the decade—many instituted double and even triple shifts and portable classrooms. In Cape Canaveral, Florida, some classes met in school buses!

With such problems, many parents doubted their children would get the best education possible, and Americans debated what should be taught and whether schools had failed society. The Red Scare remained intense in the early '50s, and in several districts school boards fired supposedly subversive teachers, censored textbooks, and removed books about Russia from school libraries. Progressive education, defined haphazardly as any student-centered idea, or even anything different from traditional rote memorization, suffered attack from reactionaries who called it communistic, as they had in the '40s. To encourage students to question any authority, particularly that of the nation's leaders, was considered subversive.

By mid-decade the Red Scare had abated, but the Soviet menace remained. As Russia and the United States stockpiled nuclear weapons, many schools distributed maps to students showing American cities with bull's-eyes on them to indicate they had been targeted by the enemy. In elementary schools

▼ The Baby Boom generation staked out its first educational territory in the 1950s: the elementary school. Western states, in particular, underwent huge increases in enrollment. These disproportionate growth rates were due in large part to new employment opportunities arising from the war, especially in the electronics and aircraft industries, that drew workers to the region.

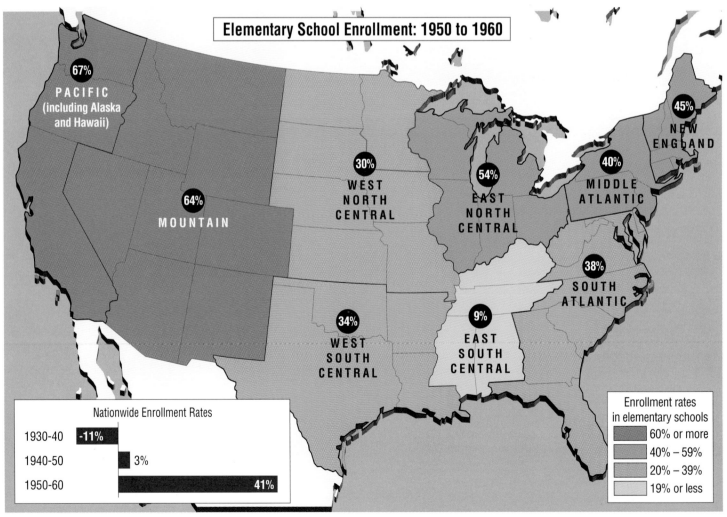

Elementary School Enrollment: 1950 to 1960

67% PACIFIC (including Alaska and Hawaii)

64% MOUNTAIN

30% WEST NORTH CENTRAL

54% EAST NORTH CENTRAL

40% MIDDLE ATLANTIC

45% NEW ENGLAND

38% SOUTH ATLANTIC

34% WEST SOUTH CENTRAL

9% EAST SOUTH CENTRAL

Nationwide Enrollment Rates

1930-40 -11%
1940-50 3%
1950-60 41%

Enrollment rates in elementary schools
- 60% or more
- 40% – 59%
- 20% – 39%
- 19% or less

◀ The nine African-American students attending Central High School in Little Rock, Arkansas, in 1957 are escorted off the school grounds under protection by the National Guard. (UPI/CORBIS-BETTMANN)

across the land, Baby Boomers went through frightening drills in which they scrunched under desks or stood in hallways, eyes closed, faces against the wall, to practice protecting themselves from a nuclear blast. Kids encountered the adult world at its most horrific, and often reacted with fatalism, fear, and nightmares. Historian Paul Boyer recounts a girl who, when asked what she wanted to be when she grew up, replied simply, "Alive."

After the Soviet Union launched the world's first space satellite, *Sputnik*, in 1957, America seemed more endangered than ever. "The schools are in terrible shape," said *Life* magazine in a feature series. "What had long been an ignored national problem, *Sputnik* has made a recognized crisis." *Life* juxtaposed two headlines that revealed the ominous development:

"IN U.S.S.R.: ROUGH HAUL ALL THE WAY"

"IN U.S.: RELAXED STUDIES"

The magazine contrasted the school life of Stephen Lapekas, a Chicagoan, and Alexi Kutzkov, a Muscovite. "Academically, Alexi is two years ahead of Stephen," said the writer, Sloan Wilson. One photograph showed that while Stephen recited a play, a fellow student ignored him and read *Modern Romances*; another showed Alexi's fellow students attentive while he stood and answered questions. According to *Life*, several ills had infected American education, including insufficient funds, lax grading, too many elective courses, and schools that "coddle and entertain the mediocre."

In focusing on a white student, *Life* failed to mention racial segregation as a problem. The National Association for the Advancement of Colored People obtained a momentous decision when, in 1954, the Supreme Court ruled in *Brown v. Board of Education* that public school segregation based on race violated the Constitution. The court declared:

"Separate educational facilities are inherently unequal."

The Deep South resisted *Brown* and defied the Court. Senator James Eastland of Mississippi linked the decision to communism. "The Negroes did not themselves instigate the agitation against segregation," he said. "They were put up to it by radical busybodies . . . intent on overthrowing American institutions." In March 1956, Southerners in Congress issued a manifesto calling *Brown* an abuse of judicial power, and saying they would resist integration by every lawful means. Nineteen of 22 Southern senators signed the manifesto, as did every congressman in Virginia, Arkansas, Alabama, Georgia, Louisiana, Mississippi, and South Carolina.

That defiance, along with the refusal of President Eisenhower to endorse *Brown*, precipitated the crisis at Little Rock and Elizabeth Eckford's traumatic ordeal. Although Eisenhower eventually sent in troops to control the mob and allow Eckford and eight other black students to attend Central High School, he considered his action "repugnant" because it violated states' rights and because he believed the courts were excessive, pushing black civil rights before whites were ready for them. Southern resistance continued, and as late as 1962 not a single African-American student attended school with whites in South Carolina, Mississippi, or Alabama.

Nevertheless, *Brown* had clearly moved the nation in a new direction. According to journalist David Halberstam, *Brown* "separated the old order from the new and helped create the tumultuous era just arriving"—the 1960s, the heart of the Baby Boomer upheaval.

❝ One of the great delusions of American educators has been that academic freedom is necessary for the achievement of material results. . . . Communists with their emphasis on science, foreign languages, and mathematics, are making tremendous progress. It is not a question of which system of education develops better-balanced personalities. The question is: Which system of education will win this universal war? ❞

—from **You Can Trust the Communists . . . To Be Communists** by Dr. Fred Schwartz

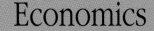

In 1959 the United States opened its National Exhibition in Moscow—a six-room California-style ranch house displaying appliances available to middle-class American consumers—and ignited an unexpected exchange between Soviet premier Nikita Khrushchev and U.S. vice president Richard Nixon. As the two men approached the kitchen, Nixon pulled Khrushchev aside and pointed to a built-in, panel-controlled washing machine. "We have such things," Khrushchev said defensively. "This is the newest model," Nixon retorted. "This is the kind which is built . . . for direct installation in the houses." Nixon insisted that the modern kitchen proved America's superiority.

Most Americans agreed with him. They measured their nation's standing in the '50s by that decade's pervasive materialism and unparalleled economic growth. Prosperity quickly choked off three recessions—the worst in 1957–58 when unemployment reached 7.5 percent—leaving the United States as the world's economic leader. Nixon bragged in Moscow: "The 67 million American wage earners are not the downtrodden masses depicted by the critics of capitalism. . . . They hold their heads high as they proudly enjoy the highest standard of living of any people in the world's history."

America's median family income rose 30 percent during the decade, and the Gross National Product climbed a whopping 37 percent. Americans had more autos, telephones, electric lights, bathtubs, and supermarkets per capita than any other nation.

Why the economic bonanza? Historians often pointed to long-term influences, such as abundant natural resources and individual initiative. But factors particular to the '50s worked their power, too. The Baby Boom supplied a ravenous appetite for consumer goods. Federal policies, especially low-interest home mortgages, encouraged spending. Research and development boosted productivity. Advertising, which jumped from $5.7 billion in 1950 to $11.9 billion in 1960,

turned luxuries into necessities, and made necessities urgent. And retailers offered more credit, with the first credit card, issued by Diners Club, appearing in 1950.

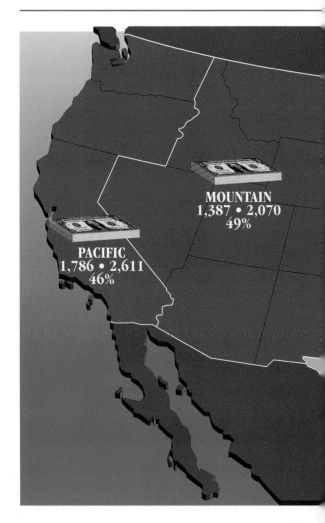

MOUNTAIN
1,387 • 2,070
49%

PACIFIC
1,786 • 2,611
46%

Further, no nation had the resources to challenge America. Western Europe, Russia, and Japan remained devastated by World War II. On top of that, the World Bank and International Monetary Fund, founded as the war ended to provide loans to European and Third World nations and to stabilize currencies, and dominated by American dollars, pursued policies that favored the United States in foreign trade.

The nation's economy grew hand-in-hand with its military. After previous wars, the United States had greatly reduced military spending. But after World War II, as cold war tension mounted, military expenditures that had been 1 percent of the GNP a few decades earlier, suddenly totaled 10 percent. Some companies, notably Boeing, General Dynamics, Raytheon, and Lockheed, obtained nearly all their income from defense contracts.

Ever larger corporations dominated the economy. They established oligopolies and conglomerates, owning firms engaged in diverse endeavors. Big even characterized agriculture, where corporate farms arose. By 1960, only 8.7 percent of the nation's population engaged in farming, yet America's dining tables displayed bounteous harvests.

Or generally so. A substantial minority of Americans lived in poverty. In his book *The Other America,* Michael Harrington claimed that some 40 to 50 million people were "denied the minimal levels of health, housing, food and education that our present age of scientific knowledge specifies as necessary for life as it is now lived in the United States."

Few Americans noticed the poor. Amid suburbs, shopping malls, and interstate highways, poor people had become invisible. They included many elderly, pockets of rural Americans, persons with skills made obsolete by new technology, and large numbers of blacks and other minorities.

Workers experienced many problems. Although African Americans found jobs in the expanding aircraft, electronics, auto, and chemical industries, they frequently endured menial work at low wages. Chicano tomato pickers in California were paid a meager 18 cents a bag, while the median annual earnings for all full-time women workers in 1960 reached only 60 percent of that earned by men. As mechanization continued apace, it often cost jobs. A drilling machine at one Ford plant lowered the number of workers from 117 to 41. At the same time, after a brief surge, nationwide union membership declined.

At the National Exhibition, Nixon told his Russian audience that "the caricature of capitalism as a predatory, monopolistic-dominated society is as hopelessly out of date, as far as the United States is concerned, as a wooden plow." That claim would soon be tested by the very Baby Boomers who grew up in the gadget-laden ranch-style houses.

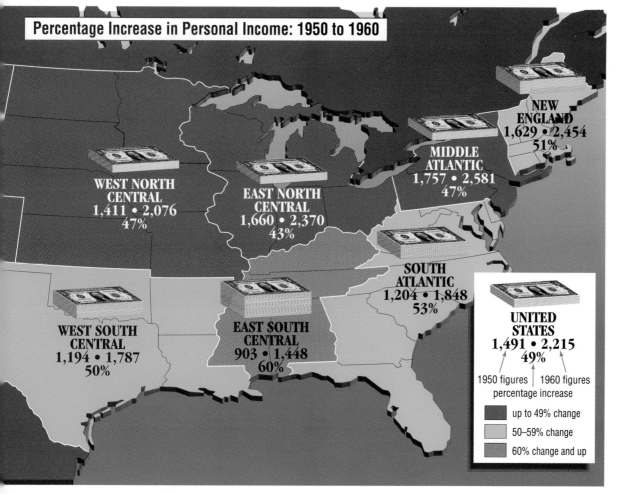

Percentage Increase in Personal Income: 1950 to 1960

NEW ENGLAND
1,629 • 2,454
51%

MIDDLE ATLANTIC
1,757 • 2,581
47%

WEST NORTH CENTRAL
1,411 • 2,076
47%

EAST NORTH CENTRAL
1,660 • 2,370
43%

SOUTH ATLANTIC
1,204 • 1,848
53%

WEST SOUTH CENTRAL
1,194 • 1,787
50%

EAST SOUTH CENTRAL
903 • 1,448
60%

UNITED STATES
1,491 • 2,215
49%

1950 figures | 1960 figures
percentage increase

up to 49% change
50–59% change
60% change and up

◀ *The 1950s lived up to its reputation as the decade of economic prosperity—for many Americans, at least. This map shows the increase in personal income from 1950 to 1960.*

It was drizzling and mysterious at the beginning of our journey. I could see that it was all going to be one big saga of the mist. "Whooee!" yelled Dean. "Here we go!" And he hunched over the wheel and gunned her; he was back in his element, everybody could see that.

A car speeding across highways meant rebelliousness and freedom for Jack Kerouac as described in his novel *On the Road* (1957). Millions more Americans took to their cars in the '50s, but unlike Kerouac, they engaged in one big saga of conformity that made all the world appear to be white middle-class.

The Red Scare that continued from the 1940s with investigations—some called them witch-hunts—led by Senator Joseph McCarthy from Wisconsin and by the House Un-American Activities Committee (HUAC) bred conformity. But so too did prosperity. As incomes rose, families fled cities for the suburbs, where homes could be bought cheaply and children raised securely.

In the 1940s, William Levitt and his brother acquired several thousand acres of potato farmland in Hempstead, 25 miles east of New York City, and began mass-producing houses. A two-bedroom Levittown Cape Cod sold for as low as $7,990 (with a free television included), well within reach of middle-class families helped by government mortgage policies. So much did Levittown attract Baby Boomer parents, some wags called it "Fertility Valley." Over the next decade other builders copied Levitt, and *Time* magazine gushed about another Levitt project in Pennsylvania, observ-

ing that "a new city for 60,000 people is rising dramatically from 5,000 acres that were wood lots and farmland less than a year ago." Every year during the '50s, one million acres of farmland disappeared under the concrete slabs that supported suburbia's dwellings.

Suburban developments often stretched mile after mile in monotonous sameness . . . all houses alike and all happiness invested within. By owning a home, a family had entered the front door of the American dream. Suburbia's rapture was reflected in spending patterns, as consumers bought more domestic items than they did clothes, or almost anything else. Up went the barbecues and the lawn and patio furniture that many Baby Boomer kids considered as natural as sod.

Television spread conformity, too. By 1960, TV sets could be found in 86 percent of all homes, and Baby Boomers by the millions watched *The Mickey Mouse Club* and *Howdy Doody*. That television could snare and influence even small children was clear in 1954 when Davy Crockett, played by Fess Parker, inspired kids to wear coonskin caps, Crockett T-shirts, and other items that, all told, cost their parents $100 million.

Reaching beyond suburban placidity, in the early '50s older youths tuned their radios to rhythm and blues. No blacks lived in the segregated suburbs—in the '60s Levitt publicly declared he would not sell to blacks, and in scores of suburban communities real estate agents refused to deal with them, arguing that sales to minorities would lower property values. But through R&B kids heard black artists with their distinctive musical beat. Disc jockey Alan Freed

▼ *The American love affair with the automobile intensified in the 1950s, as a healthy economy enabled Americans to buy more cars than ever before, and the Highway Revenue Act of 1956 gave them more places to go. This map shows the remarkable increase in the number of vehicles registered in the U.S. over the course of the 1950s.*

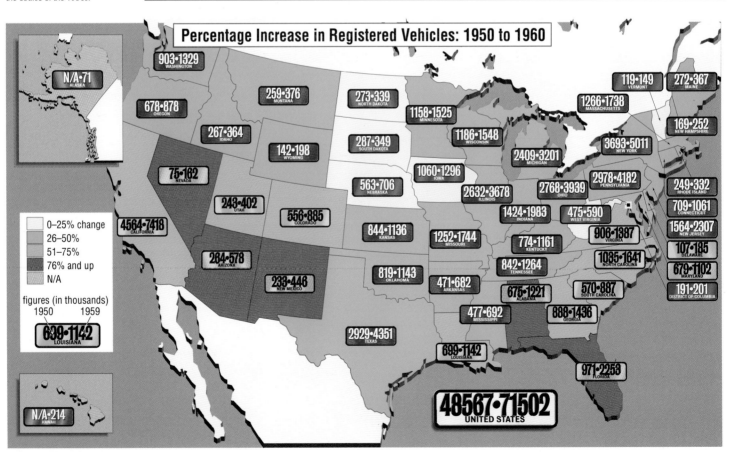

Percentage Increase in Registered Vehicles: 1950 to 1960

903•1329 WASHINGTON
N/A•71 ALASKA
678•878 OREGON
259•376 MONTANA
267•364 IDAHO
142•198 WYOMING
75•162 NEVADA
243•402 UTAH
4564•7418 CALIFORNIA
284•578 ARIZONA
233•446 NEW MEXICO
273•339 NORTH DAKOTA
287•349 SOUTH DAKOTA
556•885 COLORADO
563•706 NEBRASKA
844•1136 KANSAS
819•1143 OKLAHOMA
2929•4351 TEXAS
1158•1525 MINNESOTA
1186•1548 WISCONSIN
1060•1296 IOWA
2632•3678 ILLINOIS
1252•1744 MISSOURI
471•682 ARKANSAS
477•692 MISSISSIPPI
699•1142 LOUISIANA
2409•3201 MICHIGAN
1424•1983 INDIANA
2768•3939 OHIO
774•1161 KENTUCKY
842•1264 TENNESSEE
675•1221 ALABAMA
888•1436 GEORGIA
971•2253 FLORIDA
475•590 WEST VIRGINIA
906•1387 VIRGINIA
1035•1641 NORTH CAROLINA
570•887 SOUTH CAROLINA
3693•5011 NEW YORK
2978•4182 PENNSYLVANIA
119•149 VERMONT
272•367 MAINE
169•252 NEW HAMPSHIRE
1266•1738 MASSACHUSETTS
249•332 RHODE ISLAND
709•1061 CONNECTICUT
1564•2307 NEW JERSEY
107•185 DELAWARE
679•1102 MARYLAND
191•201 DISTRICT OF COLUMBIA
48567•71502 UNITED STATES

Legend:
0–25% change
26–50%
51–75%
76% and up
N/A

figures (in thousands)
1950 1959
639•1142 LOUISIANA

N/A•214 HAWAII

◄ Planned suburban communities were a nationwide phenomenon, but nowhere were they more popular than in the rapidly expanding western states. Pictured here is suburban sprawl in California, circa 1950s. (Archive/American Stock)

promoted R&B to a white audience, and the music evolved into rock 'n' roll around 1955, when "Rock Around the Clock" by Bill Haley and the Comets sold two million copies. Soon, rock music permeated teen lives.

About the same time, producer Sam Phillips at Sun Records listened to Elvis Presley sing and concluded: "Oh, man, that is distinctive. There is something there, something original and different." He signed Presley, who later recorded for RCA. In 1956, Elvis sold more than 10 million records. Many parents and publications, however, criticized him for his sensual motions on stage. The *Journal-American* said that Presley seemed to be performing "an aboriginal mating dance."

But as rock 'n' roll filled the airwaves and blasted from jukeboxes, commercial America diluted its rebelliousness. Dick Clark, for one, required the kids who danced on his TV show, *American Bandstand*, to dress conservatively (coats and ties for boys), and promoted performers whose saccharine style contrasted with the rockin' abandon of Chuck Berry.

For raw rebelliousness middle-class society had to look elsewhere. Beat writers such as Kerouac rejected excessive materialism, conformity, and consumerism. Although some suburbanites read *On the Road*, the Beats and beatniks remained a small minority, a few thousand at most. Much greater numbers in the African-American community challenged the social status quo by joining the fight for civil rights.

After 1955, the decade's pace quickened, partly owing to the launching of the space satellite *Sputnik* by the Soviet Union, an event that convinced many Americans that the communists had passed them in the technology race. Talk intensified that the Soviets even had an advantage in nuclear warheads. To experts, spy flights revealed otherwise, but the crisis atmosphere added an edge to society, as if someone had hunched over a wheel and gunned the nation into the next decade.

It's Howdy Doody Time!

TV brought conformist fun to kids across America when every weekday afternoon, beginning in 1947 (and lasting until 1960), they stopped whatever they were doing to watch the *Howdy Doody Show* with Buffalo Bob (played by Robert Schmidt). After a few revisions, Howdy Doody took shape as a 27-inch, big-eared boy puppet. Smith assembled a memorable cast to complement Howdy, including the human character Clarabelle the Clown, a mute who honked a horn to say yes or no and squirted Buffalo Bob with seltzer water.

Hardly any kid anywhere in America failed to identify the "Doodyville" residents. And they all knew the all-pervasive song that started the show:

It's Howdy Doody time
It's Howdy Doody time,
Bob Smith and Howdy, too,
Say "howdy do" to you.
Let's give a rousing cheer,
'Cause Howdy Doody's here.
It's time to start the show,
So kids, let's go!

Year	World	United States Politics	Arts
1950	The United States provides military and economic support to the Republic of Korea after communist forces from North Korea cross the 38th parallel and enter South Korea.	State Department official Alger Hiss is convicted of committing perjury before the House Un-American Activities Committee and sentenced to five years in prison.	Minnesota cartoonist Charles Schulz launches the syndicated comic strip "Peanuts."
1951	South Africa's white government classifies each resident by race as part of its apartheid policy.	General MacArthur returns from Korea to a hero's welcome but rejects calls that he run for president.	Reclusive author J. D. Salinger publishes the novel, *The Catcher in the Rye*.
1952	Britain's King George VI dies and is succeeded by his daughter, Queen Elizabeth II.	Dwight Eisenhower is elected president; his vice presidential nominee, Richard Nixon, must defend himself from corruption charges.	Ralph Ellison's award-winning novel, *Invisible Man*, paints a vivid portrait of postwar life in black America.
1953	The Korean War ends as North Korea and the United States sign the armistice agreement.	Convicted of stealing U.S. atomic secrets for the Soviet Union, Julius and Ethel Rosenberg are executed.	Arthur Miller's play, *The Crucible*, which serves as an allegory for the "Red Scare," has its premiere.
1954	Guatemalan rebels eject their communist ruler and install Colonel Carlos Castillo Armas as president.	The Supreme Court declares public school segregation unconstitutional in *Brown v. Board of Education.*	Audrey Hepburn wins a best actress Oscar® for her role as Princess Ann in *Roman Holiday.*
1955	Argentinean dictator Juan Peron is overthrown in a military coup.	Civil rights movement gains momentum with a bus boycott in Montgomery, Alabama, while in Mississippi 14-year-old Emmett Till is beaten to death for allegedly whistling at a white woman.	
1956	Soviet tanks crush Hungary's growing pro-democracy movement.	Dwight Eisenhower is reelected president in a landslide vote over Democrat Adlai Stevenson.	▲ Elvis Presley releases "Heartbreak Hotel," the first of many gold records.
1957	Millions of Chinese peasants are resettled in communes as part of Mao's Great Leap Forward.	President Eisenhower announces that the United States will intervene against communist aggression in the Middle East.	The Count Basie Band becomes the first African-American band to perform at the Waldorf-Astoria Hotel in New York City.
1958		President Eisenhower signs the Defense Reorganization Act, granting the defense secretary increased control over the military.	*The Ugly American*, by novelists Eugene Burdick and William Lederer, criticizes the insensitivity of American diplomats abroad.
1959	▲ Fidel Castro's rebels take control of Havana, forcing dictator Fulgencio Batista to flee Cuba.	Alaska and Hawaii become the 49th and 50th states.	The novel *Lady Chatterley's Lover* by D. H. Lawrence is banned from the mail by the U.S. Postmaster General, due to "obscene" content.

CORBIS/BETTMANN

Science and Industry	Pastimes and Lifestyles	Sports	Year
The FCC, in its Second Report on Color Television Issues, formally adopts the Field Sequential method proposed by CBS as the standard for color television in the United States.	Members of the Diners Club can charge restaurant meals using the first credit card.	The National Basketball Association holds its first championships.	1950
Edwin McMillan and Glenn Seaborg of the United States win the Nobel Prize in chemistry for their discovery of the chemical characteristics of transuranium.	Earl Tupper hires saleswoman Brownie Wise to help develop a direct selling system, known as the Tupperware party.	The Giants win the pennant over the Dodgers when Bobby Thomson hits a homer in the bottom of the ninth and scores three runs for a final score of 5–4.	1951
The CBS television network uses a UNIVAC computer to forecast the U.S. presidential election results.	The polio epidemic affects more than 47,000 people in the United States, especially children, triggering a widespread panic among parents.	Italian-American boxer Rocky Marciano wins the world heavyweight title.	1952
Geneticists James Watson and Francis Crick describe the structure of DNA as a double helix.	Hugh Hefner introduces the men's magazine *Playboy*.	Tennis player Maureen "Little Mo" Connolly, at 16, becomes the first woman to win the Grand Slam.	1953
Researchers at Bell Laboratories create the first solar batteries from silicon.	President Eisenhower signs a resolution that inserts the words "Under God" into the Pledge of Allegiance.	After surviving cancer, Mildred Didrikson returns to golf to win her third U.S. Women's Open championship.	1954
Physicist Albert Einstein dies in his sleep in Princeton, New Jersey.	The first nonstick cooking pans become available in Paris.	▼ The Brooklyn Dodgers defeat the New York Yankees to win their first World Series.	1955
Calder Hall, the first nuclear power plant to generate electricity for civilian use, begins operation in England.	The chess-playing computer program MANIAC I, designed by mathematician Stanislaw Ulam, becomes the first computer program to beat a human in a game.	*National Baseball Hall of Fame Library, Cooperstown, NY / Carl Kidwiler*	1956
Soviet launch of *Sputnik*, the first man-made satellite, initiates the space race.	Wham-O Manufacturing Company introduces the Frisbee.	The Brooklyn Dodgers and the New York Giants play their final games in New York. Both teams move to California the following year.	1957
Doctors first use ultrasound to monitor the development of a human fetus.	The first Pizza Hut opens in Wichita, Kansas.	The U.S. tennis team retakes the Davis Cup, an annual team competition played between nations, for the first time in three years.	1958
Xerox introduces its first fully automatic office copy machine.	The Barbie doll is unveiled at the Toy Fair in New York City; fashions introduced later that year include Commuter Set™, Plantation Belle™, and Wedding Day™.	Roger Ward wins the Indy 500, with an average speed of 135.857 mph.	1959

A mericans in the 1950s felt embattled: war in Korea, French withdrawal from Vietnam, Russia's crushing of the pro-democracy movement in Hungary, Castro's victory in Cuba ... all seemed losses to communism, the Red Menace. Amid a feeling of constant attack, many in the United States could not understand why some countries that wanted to exert their nationalism and independence, such as Egypt in the Suez Crisis, would declare neutrality in the cold war. Either you were for us, the capitalist good guys, or you were with them, the communist bad guys. The line had been drawn.

CUBA
Revolution (1953-1959)

A revolution in Cuba brought communism close to America's shores. It began in July 1953 when Fidel Castro led 165 men in attacking the Moncada army barracks in Santiago de Cuba, the first step in a plan to overthrow dictator Fulgencio Batista. Castro was captured, but after his release in 1955, he and Che Guevara resumed the fight. As Castro gained followers and Batista's regime suffered from corruption, the revolution's fortunes improved. On January 1, 1959, Castro and his small force of 1,000 guerrilla fighters marched into Havana triumphant; soon after, he declared himself a Marxist–Leninist.

GUATEMALA
CIA Coup (1954)

In 1954, the United States decided to use the Central Intelligence Agency (CIA) to contain communism in Latin America, where Jacob Arbenz had been elected president of Guatemala three years earlier. Allied with the Communist Party, Arbenz expropriated over 200,000 acres owned by the United Fruit Company, an American corporation, and received some arms from Russia. President Dwight Eisenhower subsequently approved covert action to topple Arbenz, and the CIA trained and supplied troops that pulled off a coup. That success set the stage for President John Kennedy to use the CIA in a disastrous attempt to overthrow Fidel Castro in Cuba in the early 1960s.

HUNGARY
Revolt (1956)

In October 1956, students and workers in Budapest took to the streets and demanded an end to their country's Stalinist regime. The Soviets agreed to allow Imre Nagy, a reformer, to rule, and they withdrew their troops from the country. But when Nagy renounced Hungary's membership in the Soviet-led Warsaw Pact, the Russians sent tanks into Budapest and elsewhere. The U.S. government called the Hungarians "freedom fighters," and through news stories many a young person in America remembered them for their bravery. Although desperate Hungarians sent a message to the West: "HELP—SOS!" President Dwight Eisenhower refused to send troops, and the Russians deposed Nagy and crushed the rebellion.

EGYPT
Suez Canal Crisis (1956)

Historian James T. Patterson has called the Suez Canal Crisis "one of the most frightening of the entire Cold War." In July 1956, Egyptian leader Gamal Abdel Nasser confiscated the Suez Canal from a British–French company. Together, Britain, France, and Israel then attacked Egypt. While President Dwight Eisenhower pressured the invaders to withdraw, the Soviet Union threatened to send in its own troops to help Nasser's beleaguered army. Eisenhower warned that if the Russians proceeded, the United States would respond in kind. With the world on the brink of a major war, the British, French, and Israelis ended their attack.

KOREA
War Between North and South (1950-1953)

The cold war turned hot on June 25, 1950, when the communist North Korean Army crossed the 38th parallel, which divided their land from South Korea, and tried to conquer the entire peninsula. Given the successful communist uprising in China, politics in the United States made it imperative for President Harry Truman to show that he would stand strong against the Red Menace. Thus, on June 30, the United States Army entered the war. At the insistence of General Douglas MacArthur, Truman ordered the Americans into North Korea, where they swept quickly toward China. But Chinese troops stormed into battle and pushed them back, and the two sides stalemated at the 38th parallel. In July 1953, President Dwight Eisenhower agreed to an armistice.

VIETNAM
Dien Bien Phu (1954)

In 1954, about 12,000 French troops garrisoned in the valley of Dien Bien Phu in North Vietnam suffered a withering assault from 40,000 communist-nationalist Viet Minh troops. On May 7, the French surrendered: their defeat lead to the decision to leave Vietnam. President Dwight Eisenhower had recently expressed his domino theory that if Vietnam fell to communism, so would the rest of Southeast Asia—"You knock over the first one, and what will happen to the last one is a certainty: it will go over quickly." As a result, he deepened the American involvement in Vietnam, furthering a conflict that would shape the Baby Boomer landscape.

SOUTH AFRICA
Apartheid (1950-1959)

At its inception in 1910, South Africa established a system whereby a minority white population ruled a large black one. After World War II, as an expanding economy required more black workers and, from the white perspective, more laws to control them, a segregationist system called apartheid emerged. In 1956, the government, which had previously restricted black voters, removed "coloured" voters—those of mixed race or Indian ancestry—from the common voter rolls. As the decade progressed, the government cracked down on black dissidents, among them Nelson Mandela, then the leader of the African National Congress. Apartheid in South Africa was a pointed reminder to many Americans that segregation existed in their country, too.

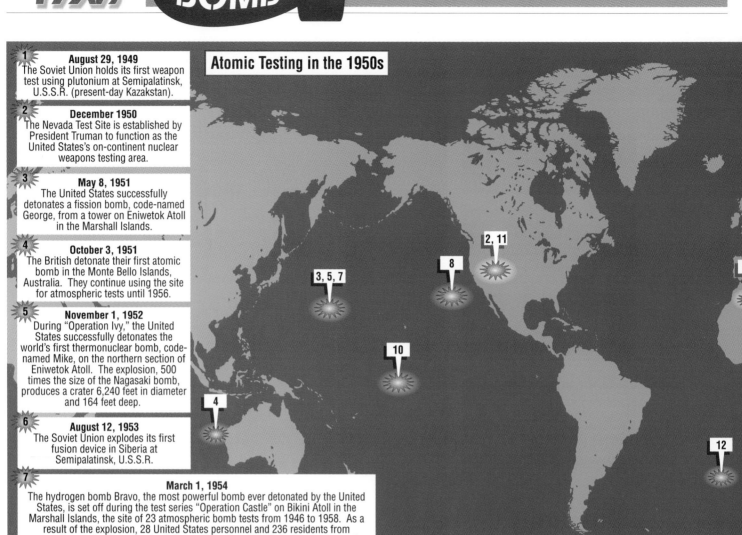

Atomic Testing in the 1950s

1
August 29, 1949
The Soviet Union holds its first weapon test using plutonium at Semipalatinsk, U.S.S.R. (present-day Kazakstan).

2
December 1950
The Nevada Test Site is established by President Truman to function as the United States's on-continent nuclear weapons testing area.

3
May 8, 1951
The United States successfully detonates a fission bomb, code-named George, from a tower on Eniwetok Atoll in the Marshall Islands.

4
October 3, 1951
The British detonate their first atomic bomb in the Monte Bello Islands, Australia. They continue using the site for atmospheric tests until 1956.

5
November 1, 1952
During "Operation Ivy," the United States successfully detonates the world's first thermonuclear bomb, code-named Mike, on the northern section of Eniwetok Atoll. The explosion, 500 times the size of the Nagasaki bomb, produces a crater 6,240 feet in diameter and 164 feet deep.

6
August 12, 1953
The Soviet Union explodes its first fusion device in Siberia at Semipalatinsk, U.S.S.R.

7
March 1, 1954
The hydrogen bomb Bravo, the most powerful bomb ever detonated by the United States, is set off during the test series "Operation Castle" on Bikini Atoll in the Marshall Islands, the site of 23 atmospheric bomb tests from 1946 to 1958. As a result of the explosion, 28 United States personnel and 236 residents from surrounding atolls (Rongelap Atoll, Rongerik Atoll, and Utirik Atoll) are relocated to Kwajelein Island as a precautionary measure against exposure to radiation.

▲ In the 1950s it sometimes seemed as though the entire planet was one enormous testing ground. This map shows the major nuclear weapons tests that were conducted in the 1950s, first by the United States and U.S.S.R., and later by the United Kingdom and France.

With the Korean War, and later talk of massive retaliation by the United States against any move by the Soviet Union to exert its influence, Baby Boomers inherited a world defined as much by nuclear fear and possible annihilation as by prosperous suburbs and a rosy future.

As the 1950s began, some American leaders saw the atomic bomb as a weapon that could defeat communism. Korea provided a possibility. On June 25, 1950, communist North Korea invaded South Korea, and President Harry Truman sent in troops. He did so without asking Congress to declare war, thus circumventing the Constitution and expanding presidential power. As it turned out, Congress applauded what it considered to be a strong stand against communism and provided him with money, authorized calling up the reserves, and extended the draft.

After General Douglas MacArthur launched a daring invasion at Inchon in September 1950, the Americans drove back the North Koreans. The United States relied heavily on air power, and through it—and a "scorched earth" policy—made devastating attacks on civilians. The Korean War had a higher ratio of civilian deaths to total deaths than in World War II, or later in Vietnam.

In the same month, Truman decided to liberate North Korea, but as American troops neared the Chinese border, China unleashed its army, and sent the Americans reeling. Truman wrote in his diary: "It looks like World War III is near." He almost made it much nearer by announcing his willingness to use the atomic bomb against China. At a press conference he said: "There has always been active consideration of its use. I don't want to see it used." A reporter asked: "Did we understand you clearly that the use of the bomb is under consideration?" Truman replied: "Always has been. It is one of our weapons."

Truman refrained from using the A-bomb, however, and he pulled back from trying to liberate North Korea. A ceasefire took effect in July 1953, after Dwight "Ike" Eisenhower became president. Despite the lessened tension in Korea, Eisenhower upped the nuclear ante. He and Secretary of State John Foster Dulles developed a policy called "massive retaliation," which envisioned using tactical nuclear weapons in the battlefield to counteract communist aggression. Said Eisenhower: "I see no reason why they shouldn't be used just exactly as you would use a bullet or anything else."

Eisenhower's tactical weapons were more powerful than the A-bomb dropped at Hiroshima—what the Japanese

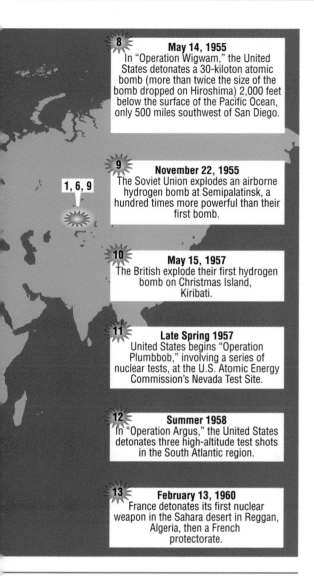

8
May 14, 1955
In "Operation Wigwam," the United States detonates a 30-kiloton atomic bomb (more than twice the size of the bomb dropped on Hiroshima) 2,000 feet below the surface of the Pacific Ocean, only 500 miles southwest of San Diego.

9
November 22, 1955
The Soviet Union explodes an airborne hydrogen bomb at Semipalatinsk, a hundred times more powerful than their first bomb.

10
May 15, 1957
The British explode their first hydrogen bomb on Christmas Island, Kiribati.

11
Late Spring 1957
United States begins "Operation Plumbbob," involving a series of nuclear tests, at the U.S. Atomic Energy Commission's Nevada Test Site.

12
Summer 1958
In "Operation Argus," the United States detonates three high-altitude test shots in the South Atlantic region.

13
February 13, 1960
France detonates its first nuclear weapon in the Sahara desert in Reggan, Algeria, then a French protectorate.

1, 6, 9

called *pika-don* for "thunder and flash"—and by this time the Soviet Union had its own nuclear weapons. In March 1954, the United States exploded the world's first hydrogen bomb, 750 times stronger than the A-bomb dropped on Hiroshima. Clearly nuclear weapons were unlike "a bullet or anything else." Their use threatened to destroy the world. Nevertheless, when, in 1955, the Chinese began shelling Quemoy and Matsu, two tiny islands between China and Taiwan, Eisenhower seriously considered dropping an A-bomb on China, and his advisors publicly said so. Although Ike decided otherwise after realizing the destruction the bomb would cause, his administration had frightened many with its loose talk.

In time, Eisenhower realized the danger and the financial burden a nuclear arsenal entailed, and so backed away from massive retaliation. But bomb tests continued. Between 1946 and 1961, the United States exploded at least 203 nuclear weapons in the Pacific and in Nevada, while the Soviet Union exploded its own, including an airborne H-bomb in November 1955. Neither nation cared much about protecting humans during these tests. The Russians exploded one A-bomb over an area with 45,000 of their army troops stationed near a village, in order to test the effects of radiation. In its

tests, the United States placed troops, who had little protective clothing, near ground zero.

The tests had health implications for private citizens, too. Fallout caused leukemia and birth defects. In 1958, *Consumer Reports* magazine sampled milk in 50 different locations and found it contained an increased amount of strontium-90. A radioactive isotope, strontium-90 could lodge in bones and cause cancer. A fearful public could only wonder "What next?" as both nations built intercontinental ballistic missiles (ICBMs) that could carry nuclear warheads long distances in a short time—much shorter than that required by aircraft.

The threat from Russian A-bombs helped stimulate a Red Scare in America that kept society on edge in the 1950s. Early in the decade, Senator Joseph McCarthy of Wisconsin pursued with a reckless disregard for facts those he deemed communists. McCarthy once listed as a communist sympathizer Howard Shipley, Harvard astrologer; no such person existed, although there was a Harlow Shapley, Harvard *astronomer*. Eisenhower detested McCarthy, but he refrained from publicly criticizing him, partly because he agreed with many of the senator's goals, partly because he believed a direct confrontation with McCarthy would only gain him more attention. Eisenhower hoped that McCarthy would ruin himself, and he did. His bellicose smearing of innocent people during the nationally televised Army–McCarthy hearings in 1954 brought about his downfall.

Cold war tension remained high, however, and the fear of communism intense, especially after the Soviet Union crushed a democratic uprising in Hungary in 1956. The nuclear arms buildup accelerated and left a deep fear, more so among Baby Boomers than anyone else. As Todd Gitlin has recalled in his book *The Sixties: Years of Hope, Days of Rage* (1989), whereas the older generation saw the A-bomb largely as a beneficial weapon that had ended World War II, the Baby Boomers saw it as a threat to their future: "Rather than feel grateful for the bomb, we felt menaced."

> 66 *Let us not assassinate this lad further, Senator. You've done enough. Have you no sense of decency, sir? At long last, have you left no sense of decency?* 99
> —Attorney **Joseph Welch** to Senator Joseph McCarthy, during the Army–McCarthy hearings, June 10, 1954

▼ *Brigadier General Courtney Whitney, General Douglas MacArthur (center), and Major General Edward Almond observe the shelling of Inchon, North Korea, from the U.S.S. Mt. McKinley, on September 15, 1950. (National Archives and Records Administration)*

In the 1950s, giant ants, the size of prehistoric dinosaurs, lumbered across southwestern deserts, terrorizing humankind. At least that's how the drama unfolded in *Them!* (1954), a movie that scored big in theaters. The creatures in *Them!* had mutated after atomic tests poisoned them with radiation—a horrible embodiment of American fears about the nuclear age.

The A-bomb saturated popular culture, taking center stage in print stories, movies, and TV shows. Baby Boomers and their parents wondered whether in developing nuclear weapons society had created a savior or a monster that might devour civilization. Some Americans expressed awe at the weapon; residents in Nevada awoke early during tests to see beautiful colors from the blasts. Others failed to comprehend it; one Arkansas farmer wrote to the government: "I have some stumps in my field that I should like to blow out. Have you got any atomic bombs the right size for the job? If you have . . . let me know how much they cost. I think I should like them better than dynamite."

But beyond the awe and misunderstanding stood the threat of annihilation that burned a deep imprint on Baby Boomer minds. The movie *The Day the Earth Stood Still* (1951) presented an alien visitor who warned earthlings they could destroy themselves with their nuclear weapons. *On the Beach* (1959) predicted the destruction of all human life after a nuclear war.

Fallout shelters appeared in suburbia. *Life* magazine told of an "H-bomb Hideaway" that could be bought for $3,000. The federal government suggested that shelters could be designed to double as playrooms or family dens . . . the family that stays together survives together—or, as critics said, dies together. Schools held regular A-bomb drills. In Los Angeles, teachers would, without warning, yell "Drop!" and kids would kneel down with their hands clasped behind their necks. In New York City, administrators issued 2.5 million ID tags to students, so they could be identified in the event of a nuclear attack.

In comic books and films Bert the Turtle advised kids

> " About the capitalist states, it doesn't depend on you whether or not [communists] exist. If you don't like us, don't accept our invitations and don't invite us to come and see you. Whether you like it or not, history is on our side. We will bury you. "
>
> —**Nikita Khrushchev**, *November 18, 1956. Some say the infamous last sentence was mistranslated and should actually read: "We shall outlive you."*

to find shelter: "Outdoors, duck behind walls and trees. Even a hollow in the ground . . . Do it instantly . . . Don't stand and look. Duck and cover!" The pervasive A-bomb seeped into the play lives of kids. One Boomer later recalled how he and his friends made imaginary fallout shelters from milk cartons; another how he converted his Ping-Pong table into a "shelter."

Years later, a Baby Boomer writing for the *Washington Post* stated: "Between the ages of 10 and 20, I had fairly regular nightmares about the destruction of the world with nuclear weapons." The Bronx High School of Science yearbook for 1959 captured the terrible threat: "In today's atomic age . . . the flames of war would write *finis* not only to our civilization, but to our very existence."

To many people, communism posed as big a menace to civilization as the A-bomb. Popular culture reflected the Red Scare, too. Politicians regularly engaged in Red-baiting—George Smathers, a Florida Democrat, said about Claude Pepper in a Democratic Senate primary: "Joe [Stalin] likes him, and he likes Joe." On the bookshelves, Mickey Spillane's Mike Hammer detective stories featured the title character chasing commies within the United States. "Real sons of b**** who should have died long ago," declared Hammer about the Reds. "They never thought there were people like me in this country."

Hollywood produced a wave of anti-communist movies, such as *I Was a Communist for the FBI* (1951). In *My Son John* (1952), patriotic parents suspected their son of being a Red. At the same time, Hollywood studio executives caved in to political pressure and compiled blacklists that banned from employment actors, directors, and writers suspected of being communists. The blacklists included people who had no attachment to communism, but who had supported left-wing causes. Among those blacklisted: Lee J. Cobb, Edward G. Robinson, and Orson Welles. In 1950, the book *Red Channels* listed 151 people in radio and television it said were subversives.

The Red Scare even ensnared the popular British-born comedian Charlie Chaplin, who on more than one occasion had criticized industrial capitalism as oppressive. Movie theaters rejected his films, and when he went abroad in 1952, the federal government denied him re-entry until he agreed to answer questions as to whether he was a communist or a communist sympathizer. Chaplin refused and stayed in Europe.

Between the bomb and the Red Scare, Baby Boomers grew up with their childhood happiness burdened by horrible possibilities. Behind every Howdy Doody puppet stood a mushroom cloud and a menacing Russian. A confused citizen in the '50s could well wonder who was the fearful "Them!"—the giant ants, the A-bomb, the communists, or maybe society itself.

Kix in the Nuclear Age

In *Life Under a Cloud* (1993), Allan M. Winkler relates how, shortly after World War II, Kix cereal urged kids to send in 15 cents and a box top for an "Atomic Bomb Ring." The ring had a chamber that showed "genuine atoms split to smithereens." Interestingly, the promotion corresponded with the arrival of the Baby Boom and was a curious welcome to life in the nuclear age.

Of course, A-bomb chic was not uncommon in the 1950s—for example, the word "Bikini" as a name for a woman's swimsuit was adopted by a French fashion designer from the name of the site of the first Pacific A-bomb test. And around 1950 a Boston restaurant served a new dessert—champagne-soaked sherbet spiced with liqueur—called the "Atomic Bomb."

INVASION: EARTH!

Date	Movie Title	Plot	Slogan
1951	The Day the Earth Stood Still	Alien comes to warn humankind of the perils of nuclear weapons.	*From out of space . . . a warning and an ultimatum!*
	The Thing (*a.k.a.* The Thing from Another World)	Scientists in the Arctic dethaw a violent alien and must fight to destroy it.	*It creeps...It crawls...It strikes without warning!*
1952	Captive Women (*a.k.a.* 3000 A.D.)	Survivors of a nuclear holocaust battle for dominance in what's left of New York City.	*(Not Available)*
	Invasion, U.S.A.	The home of the brave is invaded by communists.	*It will scare the pants off you!*
1953	War of the Worlds	Evil aliens land in a small town and begin terrorizing humans. From H.G. Wells's classic novel.	*Mighty panorama of Earth-shaking fury as an army from Mars invades!*
	It Came from Outer Space	Aliens crash on Earth and begin abducting humans.	*Amazing Sights Leap at You in 3-DIMENSION; In scientifically perfected, eye-resting, full sepia Monocolor!*
1954	Cannibal Attack	Enemy agents disguised as crocodiles try to steal cobalt from Johnny Weissmuller.	*(Not Available)*
1955	The Beast with a Million Eyes	Alien possesses the minds of animals and humans, compelling them to attack people.	*An unspeakable horror . . . Destroying. . . Terrifying!*
1956	Earth vs. the Flying Saucers	Earthlings must band together when aliens attack and begin destroying national monuments.	*Warning! Take Cover! Flying Saucers Invade Our Planet! Washington, London, Paris, Moscow Fight Back!*
	Godzilla, King of the Monsters	Awakened by nuclear tests, Godzilla rises from the deep and terrorizes Japan. (Released in Japan in 1954 as *Gojira!*; scenes with American actor Raymond Burr were added for 1956 version.)	*Incredible, unstoppable, titan of terror!*
	Invasion of the Body Snatchers	Alien impostors, disguised as their human victims, overrun a small town.	*Incredible! Invisible! Insatiable!*
1957	Attack of the Crab Monsters	Mutant crabs made gigantic, intelligent, and bloodthirsty by nuclear tests feast upon island-stranded scientists.	*From the depths of the sea . . . a tidal wave of terror!*
1958	IT! The Terror from Beyond Space (*a.k.a.* It! The Vampire from Beyond Space, The Terror from Beyond Space)	In the distant future (i.e., 1973) a blood-sucking alien stows away on an Earth spaceship and begins picking off astronauts one by one.	*IT! . . . Reaches through space! . . . Scoops up men and women! . . . Gorges on blood!*
	The Astonishing She-Monster (*a.k.a.* Mysterious Invader)	Sexy alien stripper with a deadly touch hunts human prey.	*A creature from beyond the stars. EVIL . . . BEAUTIFUL . . . DEADLY . . . !*
	The Space Children	Alien possesses the minds of children, forcing them to sabotage the nuclear test site where their parents work.	*Their Children Were The Slaves Of 'The Thing' From Outer Space!*
1959	The Hideous Sun Demon	A scientist exposed to radiation after a nuclear accident turns into a carnivorous reptile in the sun.	*The blaze of the sun made him a monster!*

◀ *The cold war played itself out in America's living rooms, on their televisions, and, perhaps most strikingly, in their cinemas. The twin demons of foreign invasion and out-of-control technology obsessed moviemakers throughout the dark years of the Red Scare and on into the 1960s. The classic giant ant movie* Them! *was just one of many films exploring the invasion theme; this chart recalls some others. Aliens and monsters may have been standing in for Bolsheviks, but the message was clear. . . . Watch the skies.*

On May 18, 1954, the headline in the *New York Times* read: "HIGH COURT BANS SCHOOL SEGREGATION: 'SEPARATE BUT EQUAL' DOCTRINE HELD OUT OF PLACE IN EDUCATION." No other court decision in the 1950s proved so important in stimulating civil rights protests as *Brown v. Board of Education*. No other moment seemed more laden with legal principles that could reform a major institution—public schools—and with it society at large. Coupled with a highly publicized bus boycott at Montgomery, Alabama, black protest punctured the conformist '50s and signaled greater changes ahead.

Although the civil rights movement gained most notice during this period, there were other influential protests. For example, a small political left advocated radical social and economic change. In 1954, Irving Howe began publishing *Dissent*, a democratic socialist quarterly. Another socialist, I. F. Stone, issued *Weekly*, a newsletter in which he exposed government deceit. At the same time, a vigorous peace movement appeared, stirred into action by the world's mounting arsenal of nuclear weapons. In 1957, Norman Cousins, an essayist and editor of the *Saturday Review*, joined with chemist Linus Pauling and others to found the National Committee for a Sane Nuclear Policy. SANE demanded an end to nuclear weapons buildups and to the cold war, and by 1958 it had 25,000 members in 130 chapters.

As for the *Brown* case, it was touched off by a seven-year-old girl. Segregation laws in Topeka, Kansas, prevented Linda Brown from attending a white school only blocks from her house, and forced her to walk across dangerous railroad tracks each morning so she could catch a bus to an all-black school several miles away. In 1951, Linda Brown's father, Oliver Brown, sued the Topeka school board. The National Association for the Advancement of Colored People (NAACP) had already resolved to attack public school segre-

gation and was looking for cases that would provide an opportunity to challenge racist laws. Thurgood Marshall, who headed the NAACP's Legal Defense Fund, argued for Brown as the case made its way to the Supreme Court.

Marshall hoped for a broad ruling that would strike down school segregation everywhere. He and his legal team insisted that such segregation violated the Constitution: "No state," they declared, "has any authority under the equal protection clause of the Fourteenth Amendment to use race as a factor in affording educational opportunities among its citizens."

But Marshall went beyond legal argument and introduced a study by Harvard psychologist Kenneth Clark, which would become a landmark work in showing that racially segregated facilities harmed blacks, that "separate but equal" could never be equal. Using two dolls, one brown the other white, Clark had interviewed African-American children in segregated elementary schools and found that when they identified with the brown doll, they often expressed regret and saw themselves as inferior. His findings implied that segregation debased African Americans and was by its nature prejudicial and damaging.

When the Supreme Court voided school segregation in *Brown*, it echoed Clark's study by declaring: "Separate educational facilities are inherently unequal." Reaction to *Brown* among African Americans ranged from a newspaper that called it America's "second emancipation proclamation," to conservative writer Zora Neale Hurston, who complained that it denigrated black schools. Naturally, positive reactions were most prevalent.

Many southern states defied *Brown*, and several attacked the NAACP with investigations and restrictive laws. Although 723 school districts desegregated by 1957 (most of them in the Upper South), the Supreme Court had failed to establish a strict time frame, and this only encouraged delinquent states to delay.

Brown emboldened blacks to fight harder for their rights. On December 1, 1955, in Montgomery, Alabama, an African-American woman named Rosa Parks refused to move to the back of a bus despite being ordered to do so. Inspired by the incident, E. D. Nixon, who had founded the local NACCP chapter, promoted a boycott to desegregate the city's buses. Nixon recruited black church leaders to direct the effort, among them the new pastor of the Dexter Avenue Baptist Church, Martin Luther King, Jr. They formed the Montgomery Improvement Association (MIA) and elected King its president.

When the boycott began on December 5, King expected only modest support, but the buses ran practically empty. He later said: "A miracle had taken place. The once dormant and quiescent Negro community was now fully awake."

With his strong leadership—"King excelled in the pulpit and enjoyed it, both its high theatrics and warm spontaneity," reported one chronicler—King gained national attention. He preached Gandhian nonviolence, asking protesters to reject hate and practice *agape*—love and goodwill toward all.

As the boycott rolled on, week after week, those participating in it did so with great sacrifice, many of them maids

> " *Our mistreatment was just not right, and I was tired of it.* "
>
> —**Rosa Parks**,
> *reflecting on December 1, 1955*

▼ *On February 23, 1956, a crowd of some 5,000 gives a standing ovation to the leaders of the Montgomery bus boycott, during a rally at Montgomery's First Baptist Church. (UPI/COR-BIS-BETTMANN)*

and day laborers forced to get rides from those who had cars. In January 1956, the *Montgomery Advertiser* reported that blacks had given up, but the story, a false one, was planted to cause confusion among the protesters. Meanwhile, the Montgomery police harassed carpool drivers, stopping them to check registration, or for other minor reasons such as failing to signal properly.

Harassment bordered on the deadly that January 30 when someone bombed King's home, and, the following night, that of E. D. Nixon. In February, a Montgomery County grand jury indicted King and more than 100 MIA activists for violating an anti-boycott law. Tried and found guilty, King remained free on appeal. In June, the state attorney general,

John Patterson, obtained an unusual court order banning most activities by the NAACP on the grounds that it had organized and financed an illegal boycott through the MIA.

Finally on November 13, 1956, the U.S. Supreme Court ordered Montgomery to desegregate its buses. King subsequently joined E. D. Nixon, fellow black minister Ralph Abernathy, and Glenn Smiley, a white minister and civil rights activist, on a bus ride. Over the ensuing days whites shot at the buses, an act attesting to continued resistance and hate. That American society remained unjust, and that some still fought change every step of the way, led to intensifying protests in the 1960s, spreading beyond civil rights to question the very foundations of American society.

▼ A.   An excerpt from the laws of Montgomery, Alabama. On December 1, 1955, Rosa Parks was charged with violating Section 11.
B.   African-American residents of Montgomery presented the following (excerpted) list to the Montgomery City Council in 1955. Although the list predated the boycott, segregated buses were already a concern.
C.   After the Supreme Court ruled in favor of the protesters, Reverends King and Powell circulated the following letter of advice to black bus riders.

THE MONTGOMERY BUS BOYCOTT

Ⓐ

c. 6, § 10   MONTGOMERY CITY CODE   C. 6, § 13

Sec. 10. Separation of races—Required

Every person operating a bus line in the city shall provide equal but separate accommodations for white people and negroes on his buses, by requiring the employees in charge thereof to assign passengers seats on the vehicles under their charge in such manner as to separate the white people from the negroes, where there are both white and negroes on the same car; provided, however, that negro nurses having in charge white children or sick or infirm white persons, may be assigned seats among white people.

Nothing in this section shall be construed as prohibiting the operators of such bus lines from separating the races by means of separate vehicles if they see fit. (Code 1988, §§ 603, 606.)

Sec. 11. Same—Powers of persons in charge of vehicle; passengers to obey directions.

Any employee in charge of a bus operated in the city shall have the powers of a police officer of the city while in actual charge of any bus, for the purpose of carrying out the provisions of the preceding section, and it shall be unlawful for any passenger to refuse or fail to take a seat among those assigned to the race to which he belongs, at the request of any such employee in charge, if there is such a seat vacant. (Code 1938, § 604.)

Ⓑ

NEGROES' MOST URGENT NEEDS

FOLLOWING ARE A FEW OF THE MOST URGENT NEEDS OF OUR PEOPLE. IMMEDIATE ATTENTION SHOULD BE GIVEN TO EACH OF THESE. WHAT IS YOUR STAND TOWARD THEM?

The present bus situation. Negroes have to stand over empty seats of city buses, because the first ten seats are reserved for whites who sometimes never ride. We wish to fill the bus from the back toward the front until all the seats are taken. This is done in Atlanta, Georgia, Mobile, Alabama and in most of our larger southern cities...

Sub-division for housing. Just recently a project for subdivision for Negroes was presented before the City Commission for approval. Protests from whites and other objections prevented the development. There is no section wherein Negroes can expand to build decent homes....

Negro representation on all boards affecting Negroes. Negroes are taxpayers; they are property owners or renters. They constitute about forty percent of the city's population. Many boards determine their destinies without any kind of representation whatsoever. Only Negroes are qualified to represent themselves adequately and properly....

Gentlemen, what is your stand on these issues? What will you do to improve these undemocratic practices? Your stand on these issues will enable us to better decide on whom we shall cast our ballot in the March election.

Very truly yours,
Montgomery Negroes

Ⓒ

December 19, 1956

INTEGRATED BUS SUGGESTIONS

This is a historic week because segregation on buses has now been declared unconstitutional. Within a few days the Supreme Court Mandate will reach Montgomery and you will be re-boarding integrated buses. This places upon us all a tremendous responsibility of maintaining, in the face of what could be some unpleasantness, a calm and loving dignity befitting good citizens and members of our Race. If there is violence in word or deed it must not be our people who commit it.

For your help and convenience the following suggestions are made. Will you read, study and memorize them so that our non-violent determination may not be endangered. First, some general suggestions:

1. Not all white people are opposed to integrated buses. Accept goodwill on the part of many.
2. The whole bus is now for the use of all people.
3. Pray for guidance and commit yourself to complete non-violence in word and action as you enter the bus.
4. Demonstrate the calm dignity of our Montgomery people in your actions.
5. In all things observe ordinary rules of courtesy and good behavior.
6. Remember that this is not a victory for Negroes alone, but for all Montgomery and the South. Do not boast! Do not brag!
7. Be quiet but friendly; proud, but not arrogant; joyous, but not boistrous [sic].
8. Be loving enough to absorb evil and understanding enough to turn an enemy into a friend.

Now for some specific suggestions:

1. The bus driver is in charge of the bus and has been instructed to obey the law. Assume that he will cooperate in helping you occupy any vacant seat.
2. Do not deliberately sit by a white person, unless there is no other seat.
3. In sitting down by a person, white or colored, say "May I" or "Pardon me" as you sit. This is a common courtesy.
4. If cursed, do not curse back. If pushed, do not push back.
5. In case of an incident, talk as little as possible, and always in a quiet tone. Do not get up from your seat! Report all serious incidents to the bus driver.
6. For the first few days try to get on the bus with a friend in whose non-violence you have confidence. You can uphold one another by a glance or a prayer.
7. If another person is being molested, do not arise to go to his defense, but pray for the oppressor and use moral and spiritual force to carry on the struggle for justice.
8. According to your own ability and personality, do not be afraid to experiment with new and creative techniques for achieving reconciliation and social change.
9. If you feel you cannot take it, walk for another week or two. We have confidence in our people. GOD BLESS YOU ALL.

THE MONTGOMERY IMPROVEMENT ASSOCIATON
THE REV. M. L. KING, JR., PRESIDENT
THE REV. W. J. POWELL, SECRETARY

In the 1950s, TV established itself as a focus of daily living. It molded the American consciousness—influencing fashion, furnishings, behavior, and buying habits. It was an advertiser's dream. Commercials created the desire, the need, the uncontrollable yearning for, well, nearly everything. In one convenient location advertisers could tell you exactly how to be the envy of friends and neighbors. They had the solution for everything from dirty ovens to painful bunions.

Housewives weren't the only target. Programming geared to children promoted toys, snacks, and breakfast cereals that Boomers begged their mothers to buy. *Howdy Doody* (1947–60) was the first show to capture the children's audience; as early as 1949, *Howdy Doody* merchandise topped $11 million in sales. This fact was not lost on advertisers, who quickly made children the focus of their relentless product pitches. The rampant consumerism that came to characterize the Baby Boom generation had officially begun.

Merchandising was big business and it wasn't limited to Davy Crockett coonskin caps and Mickey Mouse ears. The omnipresent TV created a completely new market for items designed specifically to enhance the TV-watching experience. Designers made couches that were slung low to make eye-level viewing easier and chairs with wider arms to accommodate a glass and ashtray, essential viewing accessories. Lightweight, foldable TV tables also made their debut, enabling meals to be served in front of the television. As TVs became the focal point of many living rooms, television makers stopped trying to disguise TVs as more conventional furniture.

The viewing audience grew exponentially and soon living rooms and playrooms gave way to the TV room. In April 1950, television was in 5,343,000 American homes. That number increased to more than 7,500,000 by September. Americans couldn't get enough TV.

The variety shows that had first captured the TV audience still retained a prominent spot in the nightly lineup of programs. In the end, Ed Sullivan, a sportswriter turned gossip columnist, hosted the show that survived the longest. Sullivan became a legend and his show, *The Toast of the Town,* later renamed *The Ed Sullivan Show* (1948–71), was a Sunday night institution for more than two decades. Over the years, Sullivan cultivated a reputation for discovering new talent, a distinction that helped ensure his longevity. He also had something for everyone. On the same night Sullivan might show-

case the Bolshoi Ballet to appease his critics, Richard Pryor to appeal to a sophisticated audience, Topo Gigio the mechanical Italian mouse for the kids, and fire juggling, plate-spinning acrobats . . . for no good reason. Oddly enough, this unlikely emcee knew how to plug into pop culture to deliver just what the country wanted. He proved that when he booked Elvis and the Beatles. In all, Sullivan used his programming instincts to create 1,087 memorable "rilly big shews."

In the early '50s another staple of TV, the situation comedy, began its rise to prominence. The venerable sit-com, a format borrowed from radio, was well suited for the confines of the average living room. Many of the familiar characters that audiences had come to know on radio moved comfortably into TV shows. The characters seemed like old friends and viewers adapted easily to the change. But it wasn't until the tremendous success of *I Love Lucy* (1951–57) that the sit-com would be guaranteed a permanent place on the prime-time TV schedule.

Lucille Ball had achieved some favorable notices in movies and starred on a radio program entitled *My Favorite Husband* (1948) before she made her way to TV. She was a recognizable Hollywood actress but by no means a star. But when she and real-life husband Desi Arnaz revamped her radio program for TV, cast Desi as her television husband, and renamed the show *I Love Lucy* everything changed. Lucille Ball instantly became a household name and the undisputed queen of television comedy.

Despite network interest in their show, Desi and Lucy had difficulty securing sponsors. As a result, they founded their own Hollywood production company, Desilu Productions, and assumed most of the financial risk for making the show. Together, they introduced several innovations. The most important change was not broadcasting their show live as most shows originating in New York had done. Broadcasting live meant that shows aired once for the TV audience tuned in at that time, but were not preserved on film. It wasn't until *I Love Lucy* that programs were regularly produced with the idea of rebroadcast in mind.

By preserving their programs on film, Ball and Arnaz pioneered the concept of reruns and syndication, a development that revolutionized the TV industry. Filming in front of a live audience and using three cameras so that shows could be edited for broadcast were two other innovations that distinguished the show. *I Love Lucy* premiered in 1951 and was an overnight success that made Hollywood, not New York, the TV mecca.

Other family comedies such as *The Adventures of Ozzie and Harriet* (1952–66), *Leave It to Beaver* (1957–63), and *Father Knows Best* (1954–63) all followed, but none could compare to the popularity of *I Love Lucy.* Those shows relied heavily on depicting an idealized version of harmony and domestic tranquillity. They whitewashed the family to remove any offensive blemishes and, consequently, any semblance of reality. During their original broadcast runs, none of them was a consistent ratings winner. In its final two seasons, *Father Knows Best*

▼ *One of television's first superstars, comedienne Lucille Ball, pictured here in the episode "Sales Resistance," from* I Love Lucy. *(CORBIS/BETTMANN)*

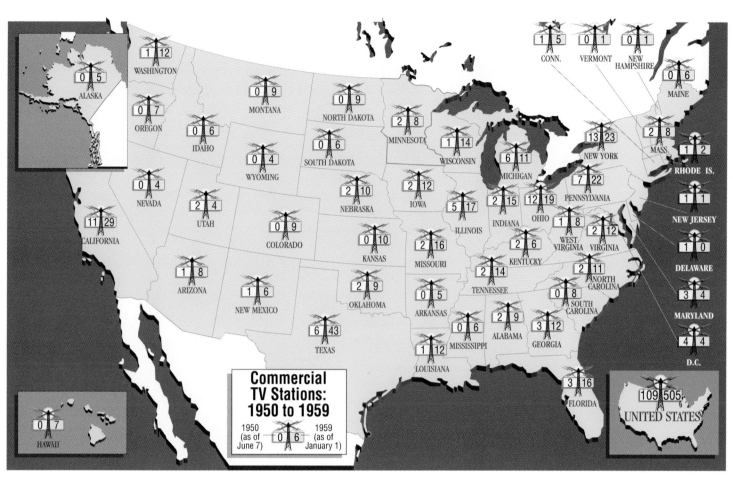

Commercial TV Stations: 1950 to 1959

1950 (as of June 7) — 1959 (as of January 1)

---

finally managed to make its way into the top 15 shows. The mythology of these "perfect" families has grown with time and their perceived popularity reflects a nostalgia for an imagined simpler time, when Boomers were still babies.

Late in the decade, the TV cowboys ambushed the airwaves, introducing some of TV's most enduring characters—Matt Dillon, Wyatt Earp, Brett Maverick, Hoss and Little Joe Cartwright. *Gunsmoke* (1955–75), TV's longest running Western, kicked off a trend that produced a steady stream of adult Westerns right into the next decade. These shows appealed especially to men and introduced more mature themes to regular TV programming. All the Westerns were filmed and most were produced by Hollywood studios that had, just a decade earlier, refused to be associated with TV. At their peak, in the 1958–59 season, 31 adult Westerns played in prime time.

By the end of the decade, live production had all but disappeared and it was generally accepted that TV shows, in order to generate real money, needed to be captured on film for later distribution and sale. Advertisers exerted more influence over programming content in order to appeal to broader markets. Movie studios entered the TV business and movie celebrities who had once shunned the small screen began to warm up to the idea. These developments changed the "texture" of TV. TV production moved decidedly away from innovation and embraced homogeneity.

As the 1950s drew to a close, television's detractors had already begun their drumbeat of criticism. They wondered if television was good for children and whether it encouraged violence. They attacked shows they had previously liked and bemoaned TV's banality and commercialism. But their warnings came too late. The genie was out of the bottle and America had fallen deeply and irreversibly in love with TV.

▲ *Although the 1940s saw remarkable growth in the number of households with TV sets, it wasn't until the 1950s that there was expansion in the number of TV stations.*

The Quiz Show Scandal

During 1959 hearings before a U.S. House of Representatives investigative committee, it came to light that television was fake. A nation that had made TV quiz shows some of the most popular programs of the 1950s found out from contestant Charles Van Doren that he had not won and retained his title as champion of *Twenty-One* because he was brilliant. Mr. Van Doren, smart as he was, had become a national celebrity because he was coached—given the questions and answers ahead of time. And he was only one of the contestants who had agreed to be pre-rehearsed.

Columnists, commentators, and politicians feared for America's collective soul. Networks responded by removing many TV quiz shows from the air. Fearing that advertisers had negatively influenced the content of shows, networks eliminated the last vestiges of advertiser-controlled programming. From the late 1950s on, corporate interests could buy commercial spots only during network shows, rather than buying blocks of time to air programs they produced themselves.

Giving contestants the answers wasn't illegal at the time, but the revelation that such a fraud could be perpetrated on an unwitting public shook the era's prevailing innocence. Baby Boomers grew up in the shadow of that skepticism. The scandals of the sixties and seventies—lies about Vietnam, political blacklists, Watergate—served to institutionalize cynicism among Americans such that in the 1990s, the uproar caused by the quiz show scandal seems positively quaint.

L ike a mutant creature from outer space, television swiftly conquered the American media. Wartime staples like *Life* magazine and the *Saturday Evening Post* ran into financial problems when advertisers began abandoning print for TV. Annual sales of radios plummeted from 8,175,000 in 1950 to 2,998,000 in 1955, and ratings dropped. But this is nothing compared to the impact of television on the film industry.

Hollywood had its own problems before TV came along. The studio system came under attack by the Justice Department, which charged that studio ownership of movie theaters constituted an unfair monopoly. The 1948 decision in *United States v. Paramount et al.* dealt a severe economic blow to Hollywood: finding in favor of the Justice Department, the Supreme Court defended the separation of production and exhibition. Meanwhile, the House Un-American Activities Committee (HUAC) dealt another blow with the Hollywood blacklist. The Red Scare shook the foundations of the industry and tarnished its image in the country at large.

> 66 *It is a certainty that people will be unwilling to pay to see poor pictures when they can stay at home and see something which is, at least, no worse.* 99
> —**Samuel Goldwyn**

An even more alarming trend was afoot. Movies had enjoyed unprecedented popularity after the war; in the years 1946-48, 90 million Americans went to the movies every week. In the early '50s attendance dropped steadily, and in 1958 attendance hit 40 million, its lowest point since 1922. The reasons for the pre-television drop are unclear, though some blamed the Baby Boom itself. Was it as difficult to find a baby-sitter then as it is now? But by 1952 Hollywood had seen the enemy, and it wasn't the Boomers, HUAC, or the Justice Department. "Don't be a Living Room Captive!" pleaded an ad, "Step out and see a great movie!"

If television was the craze keeping the masses at home, studios reasoned, Hollywood needed a better craze. First came 3-D. The concept goes all the way back to 19th-century stereoscopic viewers, but when an otherwise forgettable jungle adventure named *Bwana Devil* began packing theaters in 1952, movie producers hoped they had found their savior. Briefly, it seemed every film could be improved by viewing it through red-

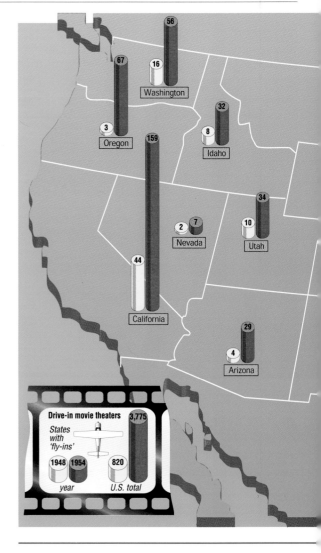

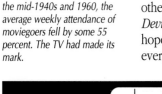
▼ *Between the boom years of the mid-1940s and 1960, the average weekly attendance of moviegoers fell by some 55 percent. The TV had made its mark.*

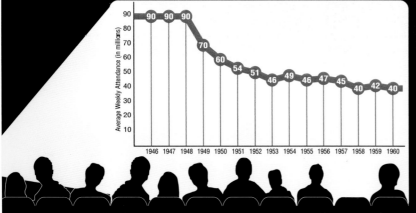

and-blue colored lenses, from the horror classic *House of Wax* to the splashy musical *Kiss Me Kate.* But it didn't take audiences long to grow weary of the migraine-inducing 3-D specs, and the craze faded fast. Alfred Hitchcock shot *Dial M for Murder* in 3-D, but by the time of the film's release the fad was already over. 3-D was "a nine-day wonder," Hitchcock observed, "and I came in on the ninth day."

Quick on the heels of 3-D came Cinerama and Cinemascope, both promising to replicate the 3-D experience without the glasses. Requiring several screens and projectors to work its magic, Cinerama never really caught on. But the Cinemascope process, which uses a special lens to create an image more than twice as wide as it is tall, took off. The acclaim was not universal: "Cinemascope is fine," remarked director George Stevens, "if you want a system that shows a boa constrictor to better advantage than a man." But spectacle-hungry audiences loved it, and like any successful enterprise, it spawned imitators—Superscope, Super Totalscope, and Super Technorama to name a few. Comedies (*Desk Set*, 1957), musicals (*Carousel*, 1956), and even dramas (*Picnic*, 1955) received the wide-screen treatment. Some felt the studios went too far. In 1953 the directors of *Julius Caesar* and *Shane* were horrified that their non-wide-screen films were altered in

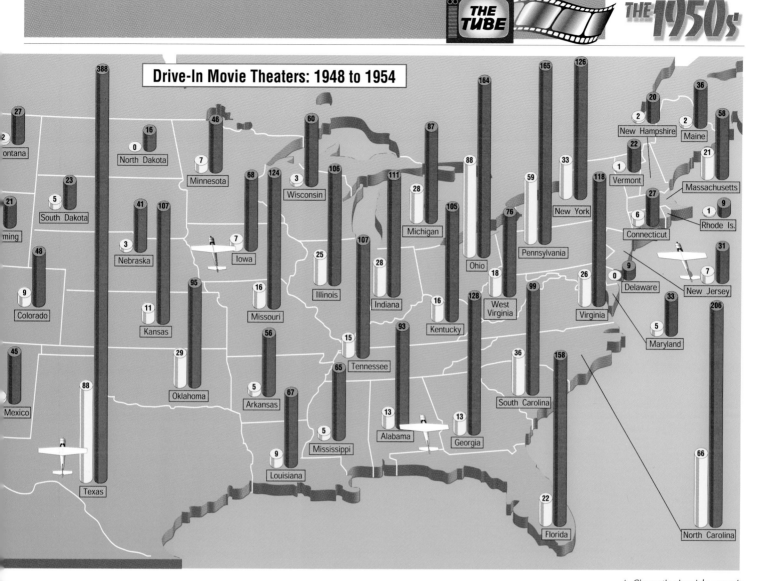

Drive-In Movie Theaters: 1948 to 1954

State	Count
Montana	27
2	
ontana	
Wyoming	21
South Dakota	23
5	
North Dakota	0
16	
Minnesota	46
7	
Wisconsin	60
68	
124	
3	
Michigan	87
28	
164	
165	
126	
New Hampshire	2
20	
Maine	36
2	
58	
Vermont	22
1	
Massachusetts	21
Nebraska	41
3	
Iowa	7
106	
111	
Ohio	88
105	
New York	33
Pennsylvania	59
76	
Connecticut	27
6	
Rhode Is.	1
9	
Colorado	48
9	
Kansas	107
11	
Missouri	95
16	
Illinois	25
Indiana	107
28	
West Virginia	128
18	
Virginia	118
26	
0	
Delaware	9
New Jersey	31
7	
Kentucky	16
99	
Maryland	33
5	
Oklahoma	29
Arkansas	56
Tennessee	15
65	
93	
South Carolina	36
158	
Mexico	45
Texas	88
388	
5	
Mississippi	67
Louisiana	9
Alabama	13
Georgia	13
Florida	22
North Carolina	206
66	

the name of giving the people what they wanted.

Audiences didn't want just spectacle, however. Boasting neither color nor Cinemascope, *From Here to Eternity* (1953) was nonetheless a moneymaker for Columbia Pictures. Of course, it did have that steamy beach scene—the world's oldest gimmick, one might say—and something television couldn't offer. As TV became more ubiquitous, it became increasingly antiseptic. Sponsors held editorial control in an iron fist: in addition to bans on sexual and political content, even the "downbeat" story was discouraged. Movies, on the other hand, received First Amendment protection in 1952.

Encouraged by the popularity of more risqué foreign films, Hollywood stepped in to fill the titillation gap. The Production Code, Hollywood's censorship organ, lost its influence and eventually collapsed. Thanks in no small part to its battle with the tube, Hollywood explored more mature themes, bringing sex (*Peyton Place*, 1957), drugs (*The Man With the Golden Arm*, 1955), and rebellion (*Blackboard Jungle*, 1954; *Rebel Without a Cause*, 1955) to the screen with unprecedented candor.

The competition with television led to further innovation and loosening of standards in the 1960s. But as the fifties closed, Hollywood was still in search of a new identity.

▲ Cinematic gimmicks weren't the only way to seduce audiences away from their TVs. In the early 1930s, Richard Hollingshead mounted a projector to the hood of his car, and the first drive-in was born. No baby-sitter was necessary, and parking was guaranteed—by the early 1950s it was an idea whose time had come. While more than 20 percent of indoor theaters went out of business by mid-decade, the number of drive-ins more than quadrupled.

Shock Titan: William Castle (1914-1977)

In the quest to out-gimmick television, nobody did it better—or, at least, tried harder—than B-movie director William Castle. Castle promoted his 1958 film *Macabre*, about a murderous rampage in a small town, by taking out a policy with Lloyd's of London to insure audiences in case of "death by fright." He positioned nurses in the lobby, hearses on the street outside—it was a hit.

Castle's *Citizen Kane* was *The Tingler* (1959), filmed in Percepto and starring Vincent Price as (what else?) a mad scientist. According to the trailer, "When the Tingler's victims scream in fright—YOU TOO will feel every shocking sensation!" Castle wasn't kidding: the secret of Percepto was the electric buzzers attached to the theater seats. Other thrills followed in the 1960s, including *13 Ghosts* (1960) filmed in Illusion-O, as well as *Strait-Jacket* (1964) and *I Saw What You Did* (1965), vehicles for the ever-shocking Joan Crawford.

Attack of the Suburb!

A young postwar couple might have believed they were realizing the American dream: the chance to raise children in a roomy, inexpensive new house of their own. Just such an opportunity was offered by the suburban communities blossoming around American cities during the '50s. Building techniques perfected in the Army enabled designer William Levitt to construct low-cost housing with remarkable speed. Levittown, Long Island—begun in 1947—became the model for suburbs across the United States, towns with row upon row of single-family homes built with assembly-line exactness and sameness. Mortgages, already inexpensive, were made more attractive by government subsidies for war veterans. The houses were occupied virtually overnight.

> 66 *Little boxes on the hillside,*
> *Little boxes made of ticky-tacky,*
> *Little boxes, little boxes,*
> *Little boxes all the same . . .* 99
> — **"Little Boxes,"** *folk song by Malvina Reynolds*

By the mid-'50s, the now-classic suburban family model dominated America. When in 1956 Washington convened the First Women's Congress on Housing to discover "what American families needed and wanted," the focus was almost entirely on the single-family home, presumably inhabited by a wage-earning man and a housewife raising young children. Culturally, the model was reinforced by suburban-set TV sitcoms such as *Ozzie and Harriet, Leave It to Beaver,* and *The Donna Reed Show.* Legally, the suburban cookie-cutter pattern was overseen by the Federal Housing Authority (FHA). The FHA's technical bulletin, *Planning Profitable Neighborhoods,* encouraged builders to aim at markets based on similarities of economic level, age, and race. Indeed, it was no accident that the early suburban communities were invariably populated by whites—the original Levittown deeds restricted the sale of houses to Caucasians.

Suburban expansion also contributed to another crucial event of the Baby Boom—the explosive growth of American highways. In 1948, anticipating military remobilization, Congress ordered a study of improvements for the interstate highway system. The Defense Department, the National Security Resources Board, and State Highway departments contributed to the project. A series of congressional acts allotting funds to highway development followed, culminating in the Federal-Aid Highway Act of 1956. The passage of this bill raised funding authorizations to $2.2 billion per year. So the toll roads and interstates rolled out across the nation, each of them scientifically designed to accommodate passenger cars, trucks, and military vehicles traveling at high speeds.

As the highways expanded, so did the suburbs and industry. Use of the new roads by commuters and truckers increased dramatically—demand and construction spiraled upward. By 1958, highway development was an industry in itself, and Congress increased its funding yet again in an attempt to pull the nation out of recession.

The highway was becoming a mythic creature for Americans, and once more Hollywood was ready to tell the tales. The highway was a lifeline—if your car left the big road's protective confine, you might tumble into the lair of a knife-wielding killer (*Psycho,* 1960). The highway could be fickle—it might offer to carry you to freedom in a high-speed getaway from police, but suddenly end in midair just as escape was within reach (*The Lineup,* 1958). TV police adventures, previously confined to cities, took to the roads in '50s programs such as *Highway Patrol* and *M Squad.* And more than a few citizens found themselves involved in real-life highway dramas, as freeway planners targeted their property to make way for expansion—legal protection to persons displaced by highway projects would not become federal law until 1970.

Looking at the histories of the suburbs and the highways, and the commerce they spawned, one easily could conclude that Henry Ford's system of mass production had worked its way deeply into American culture by the '50s. The material legacy of the '50s lives today, in planned communities, fast-food chains, and shopping malls tied together by the federal roadways threading their way across the nation.

▶▶ *Suburban developments like Levittown were an American dream come true for many young families. As the map on the right shows, homeownership rates increased dramatically during the course of the postwar period, particularly in the South.*

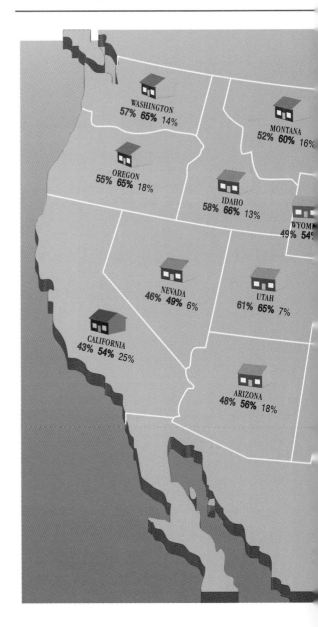

WASHINGTON
57% 65% 14%

MONTANA
52% 60% 16%

OREGON
55% 65% 18%

IDAHO
58% 66% 13%

WYOM
49% 54%

NEVADA
46% 49% 6%

UTAH
61% 65% 7%

CALIFORNIA
43% 54% 25%

ARIZONA
48% 56% 18%

McDonald's

For some, the sprawl of suburbia and the network of roadways presented great entrepreneurial opportunities. In 1954 Ray Kroc, the proud distributor of an electric mixer that made six milkshakes at once, visited San Bernardino to investigate a restaurant busy enough to need eight of his machines. He found a food stand owned by the McDonald brothers, who were applying fast-service factory-line techniques to the preparation of hamburgers. Kroc talked the McDonalds into letting him franchise the store, and eventually gained the rights to the restaurant's name and the golden arch design.

Kroc opened his first McDonald's in 1955, and in 10 years he had hundreds of shops dotting cities and roadways in dozens of states, with sales totaling in the millions. He shaped a model that would inspire similar restaurant chains and shopping-mall enterprises to come: low price for product, high customer turnover, cheap labor (often high school students), rental income from franchisers, and massive advertising campaigns. Kroc's philosophy was as blunt as a bulldozer leveling ground for the next suburban development: "It is ridiculous to call this an industry. It is not. This is rat eat rat, dog eat dog. I'll kill 'em, and I'm going to kill 'em before they kill me."

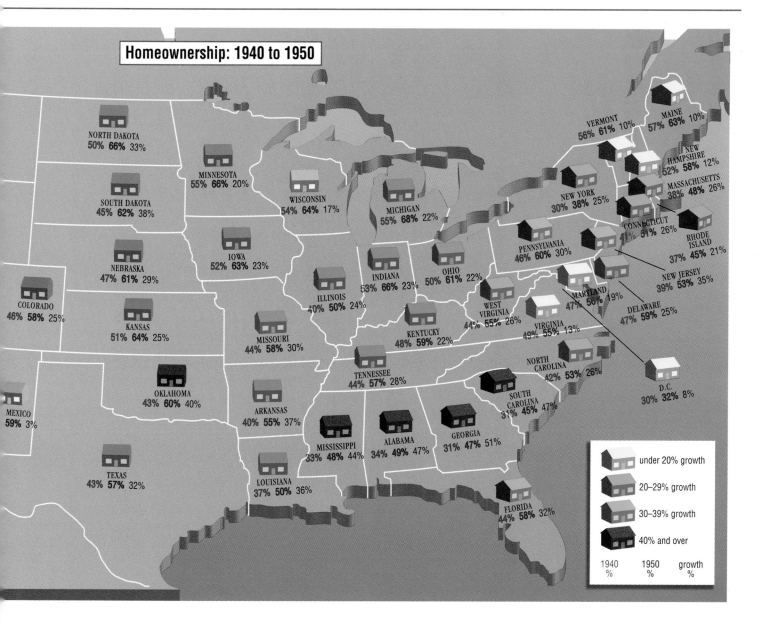

Homeownership: 1940 to 1950

NORTH DAKOTA
50% **66%** 33%

MINNESOTA
55% **66%** 20%

SOUTH DAKOTA
45% **62%** 38%

WISCONSIN
54% **64%** 17%

MICHIGAN
55% **68%** 22%

VERMONT
56% **61%** 10%

MAINE
57% **63%** 10%

NEW HAMPSHIRE
52% **58%** 12%

NEW YORK
30% **38%** 25%

MASSACHUSETTS
38% **48%** 26%

NEBRASKA
47% **61%** 29%

IOWA
52% **63%** 23%

INDIANA
53% **66%** 23%

OHIO
50% **61%** 22%

PENNSYLVANIA
46% **60%** 30%

CONNECTICUT
41% **51%** 26%

RHODE ISLAND
37% **45%** 21%

COLORADO
46% **58%** 25%

KANSAS
51% **64%** 25%

ILLINOIS
40% **50%** 24%

KENTUCKY
48% **59%** 22%

WEST VIRGINIA
44% **55%** 26%

VIRGINIA
49% **55%** 13%

MARYLAND
47% **56%** 19%

NEW JERSEY
39% **53%** 35%

DELAWARE
47% **59%** 25%

MISSOURI
44% **58%** 30%

MEXICO
59% 3%

OKLAHOMA
43% **60%** 40%

ARKANSAS
40% **55%** 37%

TENNESSEE
44% **57%** 28%

NORTH CAROLINA
42% **53%** 26%

D.C.
30% **32%** 8%

SOUTH CAROLINA
31% **45%** 47%

TEXAS
43% **57%** 32%

LOUISIANA
37% **50%** 36%

MISSISSIPPI
33% **48%** 44%

ALABAMA
34% **49%** 47%

GEORGIA
31% **47%** 51%

FLORIDA
44% **58%** 32%

under 20% growth

20–29% growth

30–39% growth

40% and over

1940 %	1950 %	growth %

The Birth of Cool

Americans understandably made the adjustment to postwar life more quickly than Europeans. While we went "back to work," those overseas were faced with the job of rebuilding their lives from the surrounding rubble. European Existentialism grew from these ruins. Taking their cue from Kierkegaard and Nietzsche, French writers Jean-Paul Sartre, Simone de Beauvoir, and Albert Camus published literature centered on the ideas of an absurd and godless universe, individual action, and solitary responsibility. This philosophy caught on with artists and authors the world over.

Existentialist tenets gradually made their way to America; doubt and disquiet crept into American minds as consumerism saturated everyday life. The cold war took hold, and big existential-flavored questions began to be posed by screenwriters and popular novelists. Suspense author Jim Thompson created a parade of murderous male losers who imparted their insights into life's terrifying absurdity before dying in spectacularly unpleasant ways (*The Killer Inside Me*, 1952; *After Dark, My Sweet*, 1955).

▼ *Miles Davis in the studio, circa 1950s. (Florence and Carol Reiff/ CORBIS-BETTMANN)*

Existential dread would become a pop horror theme in TV's *The Twilight Zone*, with its many tales of people who suddenly find themselves in deserted towns or exitless rooms, desperate to discover who and where they are. The nightmarish existential fiction of Czech author Franz Kafka grew in reputation. Soon the adjective "Kafkaesque" was used by people who had never touched a copy of *The Trial* or *The Metamorphosis*. The word has kept a place in our language for more than 40 years ("Sex with you is truly a Kafkaesque experience."—Shelley Duvall to Woody Allen, *Annie Hall*).

The New York–based artists and writers of the Beat movement picked up the other half of the Existentialist equation: that of the man or woman of action. Confronting what they saw as mindless consumption and blind conformity in America, the Beats celebrated and created poetry, music, painting, sculpture. Self-discovery was key; psychoanalytic theory, Eastern philosophy, abstract art, and mind-altering drugs were a few of the tools. Groundbreaking works such as Jackson Pollock's painting *Lavender Mist* (1950), Allen Ginsberg's poem *Howl* (1955), and Jack Kerouac's novel *On the Road* (1957) were hailed by the Beats as feats of feverish self-exploration and rebuffs to conservative mass culture. Each of the men eventually was recognized as a key artist of the century.

The "beatniks," as they were known in the mass media, quickly become objects of ridicule and stereotyping. An exaggerated mythology of the Beats evolved during the '50s, suggesting that all male beatniks spent their days playing bongos and reciting poetry, and that all the women were subject to fits of uncontrolled interpretive dance. By the end of the decade, beatnik costume kits with prepackaged berets, cigarette holders, and paste-on goatees were marketed to children during Halloween. The image of the smoke-and-jazz-filled coffeehouse became a convenient symbol of loose morals and youthful self-indulgence, turning up again and again in movies and television. An embarrassing attempt to bring Kerouac's *The Subterraneans* to the big screen featured the songs "Coffee Time," "Analyst," and "Look Ma, No Clothes."

The movies at least had one thing right: the importance of jazz to the Beat aesthetic. Bebop, with its wild improvisations and defiant attitude, embodied the exploration and confrontation that appealed to the Beat community. Bop king Charlie Parker's trumpeter, young Miles Davis, turned things around in 1949 and 1950 with experimental recordings that toned down bop's aggressiveness but increased its melodic complexity. These records inspired a style that became known as "cool."

Cool jazz had catchy tunes, was easily commodified, and was largely white. Fronted by white West Coast players such as Gerry Mulligan and Chet Baker, cool caught on with the college crowd and "sophisticated" middle-class listeners. The dominance of the style already was clear when Dave Brubeck's infectious and easily digested cool tune "Take Five" began appearing on radio stations everywhere. "It was the same old story, black s*** was being ripped off all over again," said Miles. Davis's earlier recordings were reissued in 1954 as a 10-inch LP titled *The Birth of the Cool*, and Davis

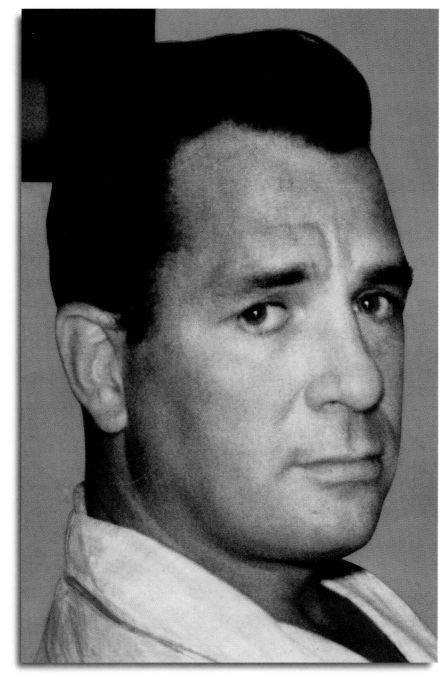

▲ *Jack Kerouac. (Archive Photos)*

would be forever identified as the father of a style he had come to scorn. In 1955 he formed a hard-driving bop quintet that included tenor sax god John Coltrane and didn't look back.

Davis went on to become one of the most successful musicians of the '50s. His records were hits, and he became rich. The image of the uncompromising black artist solidified —a tough guy capable of astonishing lyricism. Davis even gained the dubious distinction of making *Playboy*'s list of America's best-dressed men.

When *Playboy* hit the scene in 1953, its glossy pages touted the notion that the average guy consumer could acquire a hip cachet if he dressed sharp, bought the right record albums, and learned to pronounce "Sartre" correctly. For many young white men with disposable cash during the '50s, it was an alluring package. It was cool.

Transistors

William Shockley, John Bardeen, and Walter Brattain, all researchers at Bell Laboratories in Murray Hill, New Jersey, had something interesting to show their colleagues on December 23, 1947. Using the semiconductor material germanium, gold wires, and insulators, they were able to amplify an electronic signal—a voice transmitted over a loudspeaker.

Their invention, which would be dubbed a "point-contact transistor," was presented to the public with little fanfare the following year. The *New York Times* reported on the invention on July 1, 1948, noting that the device "has several applications in radio where a vacuum tube is ordinarily employed." In fact, the transistor would go on to replace the vacuum tube, at a fraction of the vacuum tube's size and cost.

Almost impossibly complicated to produce, the transistor had to wait until 1951 and the development of a simpler, more reliable junction transistor before finding a manufacturer willing to tackle the complex fabrication process. First used in telephone systems and hearing aids, the transistor attracted the attention of companies including IBM, General Electric, and Texas Instruments. In 1954 the first transistor radio delighted consumers, particularly teenagers.

Further research led to the development of silicon transistors, the building blocks for both the silicon chip and integrated circuits. In 1956, Shockley, Brattain, and Bardeen won the Nobel Prize in Physics for their work on the transistor. The future barons of Silicon Valley were still in diapers, but the Silicon Age had begun.

Contraceptive Pills

She launched the birth control movement in 1914 and fought for decades to make contraception legal. But in 1950, at the age of 71, activist Margaret Sanger determined that her crusade was not yet over. Recruiting the pathbreaking biologist Gregory Pincus to develop a drug that could prevent conception, Sanger persuaded heiress Katharine Dexter McCormick to underwrite the cost of the research, setting in motion a mighty social revolution.

Pincus and his associate M.C. Chang focused their attention on the contraceptive possibilities of the steroid hormone progesterone. Meanwhile, researcher Carl Djerassi, working independently in Mexico City, synthesized an oral form of progesterone for the first time in 1951. Although Djerassi had not intended to create a method of birth control, his discovery—along with the news of Pincus's successes—sparked a race among drug companies to test and market the first oral contraceptive.

Introduced in 1960, the earliest version of what would come to be known as "the pill" contained large amounts of progesterone and estrogen, leading to a significant number of side effects. Although the risk of side effects—including potential risks from long-term use—led to the development of a lower-dosage pill, the pill's popularity

was little affected by the potential risks. Given credit for everything from the sexual revolution and the women's movement to being the cure for world overpopulation, the pill allowed millions of women to exercise greater control over their bodies.

Stretch Yarn

First introduced in 1947 by a Swiss company, the earliest stretch yarn was produced by putting nylon thread through a heat-set process that added crimp and curl to its texture. Unlike traditionally produced stretch fabrics, the crimped nylon fiber had an astonishing ability to stretch up to five times its own length—and then return to its original shape.

An instant hit in European ski clothes, stretch yarn slowly infiltrated the American market in the '50s, becoming commonplace in socks and foundation garments before Italian designer Emilio Pucci would make stretch yarn a fashion statement in its own right. In 1959, the addition of DuPont's Spandex, whose elasticity results from its chemical structure, opened the way for a whole new era in athletic wear.

Photocopiers

As an employee of the electronics firm P.R. Mallory Company in the 1930s, Chester Carlson was called upon to make copies of patents or design specifications by hand. Nearsighted and arthritic, Carlson had strong motivation for seeking a better way to make reproductions. Several companies were already testing photographic methods for copying documents, such as thermography, which involved the use of infrared rays.

Working out of his apartment in New York, Carlson took a different path, experimenting with electrostatic charges and heat. By 1937, he had invented xerography (in Greek, "dry writing"). He patented his idea in 1940, but it would be years before Carlson's work caught the eye of the Haloid Company. Finally, in 1958, Haloid introduced the first commercial copier using the xerographic method. Three years later the company changed its name to Xerox Corporation, and soon thereafter it changed the business environment forever.

In addition to improving the lives of white-collar workers around the globe and making Carlson a millionaire, Xerox would later take the lead in the digital revolution; Xerox PARC (Palo Alto Research Center) was founded in 1970 and incubated numerous wizards of the personal computer and the Internet.

Credit Cards

Charge it! Before 1950, gas stations and stores issued their own charge plates—metal tags with raised letters—for use only in their own establishments. But in 1949, over lunch in New York City, Alfred Bloomingdale, Francis McNamara, and Ralph

Snyder came up with a plan that would eventually launch the multibillion-dollar consumer credit industry. They would form an independent company to act as a middle-man between consumers and businesses, charging fees to offer credit to consumers while shielding businesses from the financial risk if the consumer defaulted.

Within a month, Diners Club was born. Beginning in New York City and Los Angeles, the partners recruited restaurants to accept the Diners Club charge card. Their first customers were traveling salesmen who often needed to entertain on the road. By the late 1950s, Diners Club had gone nationwide and branched into travel and retail. It also had competition: on October 1, 1958, American Express offered its first charge card. These two companies vied with a sudden proliferation of bank-issued credit cards, including cards from banking powerhouses Chase Manhattan and Bank of America. In 1958, these bank cards, which did not charge consumers an annual fee for their use, hit upon the idea of charging interest on unpaid balances. Consumer culture would never be the same.

It would be another 20 years before the credit card industry would assume its now-familiar shape—plastic charge cards with a magnetic strip, the Visa and MasterCard networks, and interest fees on unpaid balanes. But in the interim, the enormous expansion of consumer credit fueled a buying binge. By the mid-1990s, credit cards would be an ubiquitous feature of everyday life, with the average American owning 3.9 credit cards.

TV Dinners

An entire meal portioned into compartments on an aluminum tray, the frozen TV dinner was the brainchild of Clarke and Gilbert Swanson. Introduced in supermarkets at the end of 1953, the original Swanson's TV Dinner contained turkey with gravy and dressing, mashed sweet potatoes, and buttered peas. By simply popping the whole tray into the oven, a harried housewife could make dinners for the whole family in 30 minutes. Best of all, the tray was easy to carry into the living room—allowing the family dinner to take place around the television set instead of the kitchen table. By 1955, Swanson was selling 25 million TV dinners a year.

▼ *A scene to warm the hearts of credit card companies. Women inspect the merchandise at Alexander's Department Store, New York City, in the 1950s. (CORBIS/BETTMANN)*

Chuck Berry (1926-)

He played the guitar for girls he dated and sang in a reform-school quartet, but Chuck Berry didn't start performing professionally until 1952. At the Cosmopolitan Club in East St. Louis, Missouri, Berry jumped the musical color line, covering both the blues standards beloved by black audiences and the country-western songs popular with whites. With pungent guitar riffs influenced by jazz guitar masters like Charlie Christian, Berry's new sound drew integrated crowds in a segregated town.

His big break came in 1955 after blues legend Muddy Waters connected him with Chess Records in Chicago. One of rock's first singer-songwriters, Berry scored a crossover hit on the white popular music charts with his first release, the country-flavored "Maybellene." Then came the songs that defined the sound and spirit of the new rock and roll: "Roll Over Beethoven," "Johnny B. Goode," "Rock & Roll Music," "Sweet Little Sixteen," and "Reelin' and Rockin'." Lyrically capturing the longings of love-struck, car-crazy teens, his music became an anthem for American adolescence.

But while a rising generation of rock musicians on both sides of the Atlantic took inspiration from his signature guitar riffs, Berry's own career was paralyzed by racially loaded

▼ *Chuck Berry. (Archive Photos)*

legal battles over his indiscretions with young white women. Arrested in 1959 under the rarely enforced Mann Act, forbidding the transport of women across state lines for "immoral purposes," Berry would spend the early '60s in prison.

William M. Gaines (1922-1992)

William Gaines inherited the family business, publishing comic-book versions of Bible stories and syrupy animal fables. But saccharine wasn't selling, so in 1950 he introduced a new line of horror comics illustrated by a talented group of offbeat artists. Cult favorites with children and teens, comic books like *Tales from the Crypt* jumped off the shelves, turning a major profit for Gaines in less than a year.

In 1953, the Senate launched an inquiry into the morals of comic books, prodded by outraged newspaper editorials deploring an increase in juvenile delinquency. Wholesalers saw the writing on the wall and refused to carry horror comics, forcing Gaines to discontinue the horror titles. He had only one moneymaker left: *Mad*, a loony, sophomoric, and sometimes subversive parody. To save his business and escape new industry rules governing the content of comic books, Gaines changed its format in 1954 from 10-cent comic to 25-cent magazine.

Mad allowed Gaines to go on corrupting the morals of generations of delighted teenagers with its wacky spoofs on just about every part of American culture. An outpost of rebellion in a conformist age, *Mad* encouraged its fans with the responsibility-shucking slogan of poster boy Alfred E. Neuman: "What — me worry?"

Adlai Stevenson (1900-1965)

He was the great liberal hope of the '50s, an intellectual with an easy patrician charm, a quick wit, and a passion for issues. His success as the reform-minded governor of Illinois brought him to the attention of a Democratic Party desperate for leadership as the Truman presidency limped to its unpopular end. He coveted a national office but initially refused offers to run in the 1952 presidential elections, believing that no candidate could beat Army hero Dwight D. Eisenhower. As the reluctantly drafted Democratic nominee, he proved himself right, losing to Eisenhower by tremendous margins both in 1952 and in 1956. But he made the most of his position as sacrificial lamb, engineering a campaign that would be remembered for its unusual intelligence and integrity.

His platform was ahead of its time, promoting a nuclear test ban during McCarthy-era saber-rattling and proposing government-sponsored health insurance for the elderly years before the creation of Medicare. But his campaign was strictly old-fashioned. He turned a blind eye to television's growing political power, refusing to consult the new breed of media-savvy imagemakers. Instead he wrote speeches, shunning audience-pleasing rhetoric to talk seriously about sophisticated issues in the most unlikely forums. To a group of coal miners, he spoke on foreign policy; to McCarthy-lean-

Joe DiMaggio (1914-1999)

A 56-game hitting streak that has never been equaled. Nine world championships as the star of the outfield for the New York Yankees. He was Joltin' Joe, the Yankee Clipper: tall, dark, handsome, and the idol of base-ball-loving Americans everywhere.

His romantic involvement with screen goddess Marilyn Monroe seemed like a celebrity merger made in heaven. The media breathlessly covered every step of their two-year courtship, and fans mobbed the San Francisco courthouse where they tied the knot early in 1954.

But DiMaggio was an intensely private man. The crowd of gawkers cheering Monroe as she filmed the famous skirt-lifting scene over a New York subway grating for *The Seven-Year Itch* was more than his dignity could take. He left her that night, and they divorced by the end of 1954.

Later Monroe would say that he had been the one great love of her life. And DiMaggio, who never married again, sent roses to her grave three times a week for 20 years.

◀◀ *Ayn Rand testifies before the House Un-American Activities Committee, left. (UPI/CORBIS/BETTMANN)*

▼ *Joe DiMaggio and Marilyn Monroe at their wedding in 1954. (CORBIS/BETTMANN)*

ing businessmen, on the need to protect civil liberties.

In a famous exchange on the campaign trail, a woman shouted out to Stevenson that he was the candidate of "every thinking person." He thanked her, but replied that it wouldn't be enough: "We need a majority," he said. Stevenson never could find that majority, even in his own party. Called one of the most influential losers in American politics, his ideas helped reinvigorate the Democratic Party, laying the groundwork for its comeback in the '60s.

Ayn Rand (1905-1982)

B orn Alice Rosenbaum, she fled the turmoil of Soviet Russia to reinvent herself in Hollywood, where she worked as a scriptwriter while devising the philosophy she called Objectivism. Molded by her deep revulsion for Soviet collectivism, it postulated that self-interest is the highest form of ethical behavior. Celebrating heroic individualism, laissez-faire capitalism, and a thoroughly un-postmodern belief in the omnipotence of reason, Objectivism attracted a small legion of devoted followers, particularly after the 1957 publication of her novel, *Atlas Shrugged*.

Hailed less for its literary qualities than for its function as parable, *Atlas Shrugged* used a turgid romance about the mysterious disappearance of American industrialists as a vehicle to exemplify the principles of Objectivism. Reviewers found little to recommend in either her novel or her philosophy, and mainstream conservatives denounced her strident antireligious stance. But Rand struck a chord in a segment of the American public, especially on college campuses, where she was a sought-after speaker. Like her previous novel, *The Fountainhead* (1943), *Atlas Shrugged* was a perpetual best-seller and a harbinger of the Reagan era.

Fashion

In 1950s America, fashion drew from the era's fascination with modernism and futuristic design, rock and roll culture, and Parisian haute couture. Some highlights:

● A dark suit with a white shirt was the standard work uniform for the American middle-class company man. But the collegiate look gradually came into its own, and jacket, slacks, and thin tie combos were seen more often on young adult men.

● Women were offered a variety of stylistic choices. Depending on her age or social status, a '50s woman could pick from fashions that included collegiate looks, "sweater girl" outfits, the glamorous and expensive Dior "New Look," or from styles influenced by movie stars such as Jane Russell and Marilyn Monroe ("Le véritable busty-look Americain," the French called it).

● Rock and roll culture made its contribution to '50s fashion—there were poodle skirts and circle skirts for the girls, gabardine pants and patterned "rock and roll" shirts for the guys.

● The '50s styles at large were reflected in casual wear, and clothes with "atomic" prints and abstract patterns echoed the designs of formica kitchen tabletops. "Hawaiian" themes took off in a big way in short-sleeved men's shirts, swim trunks, and underwear—you even could own the "Duke Champion Kahanomoku" swim trunks modeled after those worn by Montgomery Clift in *From Here to Eternity*.

● Synthetics made their mark. The word "nylon" became synonymous with women's stockings, and the press-free wonders of rayon and dacron were trumpeted far and wide. Brightly colored vinyl or lucite accessories became common. Synthetics made molding easy—the adventurous shopper could choose from handbags shaped like guitars, pagodas, or birdcages!

Toys!

When they weren't worrying about nuclear war, flying saucers, or the communist affiliations of the local scoutmaster, Americans found time for play in the '50s. A number of toy innovations became absolute crazes during the decade:

● **Silly Putty.** "The real solid liquid" debuted in 1950. It bounced, it stretched, it copied newspaper comics, and it melted into the carpet if you left it lying around.

● **Slinky.** The sinuous steel spring that compelled

users to obsessively bounce it from hand to hand reached its peak popularity in 1953. Remembered for its won't-leave-your-head commercial jingle as much as its ability to walk down stairs, alone or in pairs.

● **_The Hula Hoop._** Wham-O eclipsed its 1957 invention, the Frisbee, with this 1958 release. The lightweight plastic hoop truly caught on like wildfire. Children and adults alike desperately shimmied and twisted to keep the hoop twirling around their waists. Endurance competitions sprang up nationwide. Multi-hoop novelty acts went on the road. Older hoopsters were hospitalized when they threw out their backs. The craze even spread overseas, but the Japanese weren't having any of it and banned the hoop from city streets. The Hula Hoop fad, perhaps thankfully, died as suddenly as it began.

The Cult of the Teen

"What are you rebelling against?"
"What've ya got?"
—_The Wild One_ (1954)

A distinct teen culture developed in America during the '50s, and the entertainment industry was quick to exploit it. Movies and popular music dwelt on the themes of youthful love, youthful pain, and youthful rebellion. Rock and roll was the teen music of choice, and rock stations sprang up all over the United States as Hollywood cranked out dozens of movies with rock and roll scenarios.

Lurid tales of teen violence and leather-jacketed gangs became the grist for paperback novels and films. Evan Hunter's _The Blackboard Jungle_, the story of a dedicated high school teacher attempting to weed out the punks from the angry-but-basically-good students, was a best-seller. The movie treatment (1955) became famous as the first film with a rock and roll theme song, Bill Haley's "Rock Around the Clock."

The movies also delivered full-blown teen melodramas playing on alienation felt by young adults who were treated as children by society. None of these films could match the high-octane Freudian juice of _Rebel Without a Cause_ (1955). Natalie Wood's dad eyes her lustfully! James Dean's dad wears an apron! Car wrecks! Knife fights! The movie was an instant classic.

By the end of the decade, the teen romance formula was so well-established that it lent itself easily to a musical theater update of Shakespeare, _West Side Story. Romeo and Juliet_ had the makings of an ideal teen tale: misunderstood youth, domineering parents, exalted love, disruptive violence. _West Side Story_ became a hit both on Broadway (1957) and later in movie houses (1961). The music wasn't Chuck Berry or Elvis Presley, but the drama was all '50s.

THE 1960s

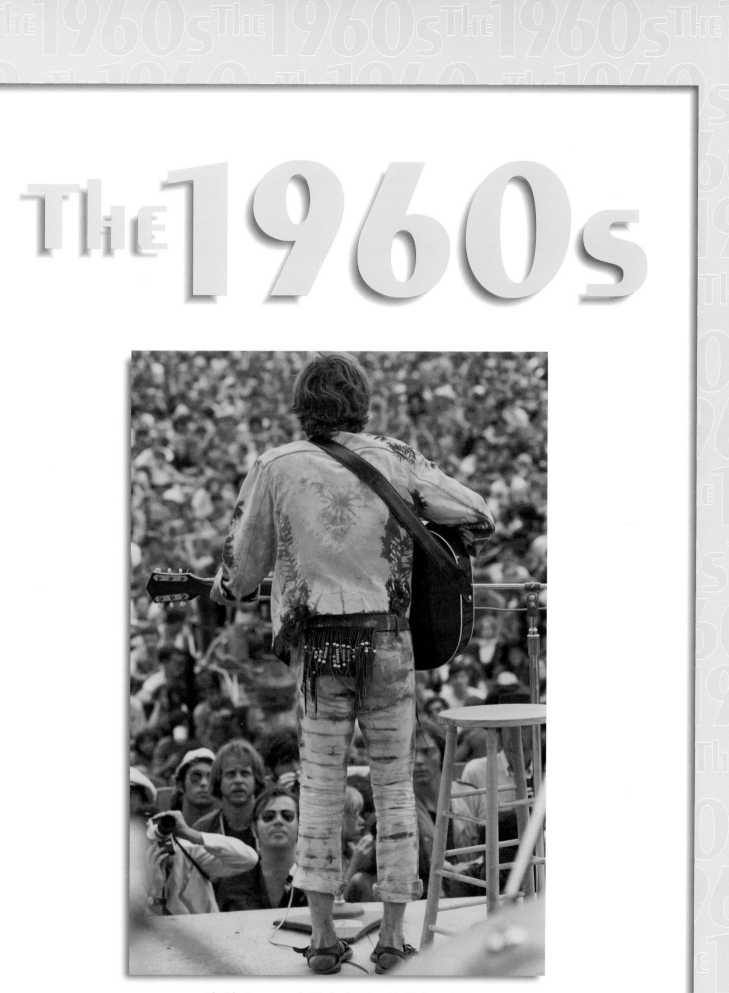

John Sebastian onstage at the Woodstock Music and Art Fair, August 1969.
(Henry Ditz/CORBIS/BETTMANN)

Suburban contentment surrounded many Baby Boomers as the 1960s began: ranch houses amid new plantings, bicycles in driveways, TVs in living rooms, dad at the office, mom in the kitchen. But the confines of middle-class life caused a reaction that soon challenged the domestic equilibrium suburbia had promised.

The Baby Boom of the 1950s continued, adding four million children each year until 1964, when the birthrate finally began to drop. Total live births per 1,000 women aged 15 to 44 went from 23.7 in 1960, to 21.0 in 1964, to 17.8 in 1969. At the same time, Boomers born in the late 1940s and early 1950s reached their teens in numbers modern America had never known.

The first challenge to traditional family values emerged not from the Baby Boomers, but from older women. Throughout the 1950s society had insisted that both personal security and feelings of self-worth came from marriage and family. That prescription did indeed appear to produce contentment: one survey in 1955 found that about 80 percent of husbands and wives rated their marriages "above average," and about two-thirds called them "extraordinarily happy" or "decidedly happier than average."

Beneath the veneer, however, trouble loomed. When questioned further in the same survey, women sometimes

> 66 I have an I.Q. in the 145-150 range. I "caught" a husband at 19, married him on my twentieth birthday, quit school pregnant, and now have six children! I am the typical stay-at-home, domineering mother and wife. I love my children yet I hate them, have actually wished them dead. 99
>
> —**South Carolina housewife**, in a letter to Betty Friedan, 1964

expressed regret about their marriages, more so than their husbands, and criticized their subordination to men. Suburban homes, filled with kids, toys, and TVs, also held within them discontent.

Women remained largely quiet, however, until Betty Friedan's *The Feminine Mystique* appeared in 1963. A wealthy homemaker, Friedan felt unhappy about being relegated to suburbia. She surveyed friends who had graduated with her from college and discovered they felt the same way. "The problem that has no name," she wrote, was gnawing at women. "We can no longer ignore that voice within women that says, 'I want something more than my husband and my children and my home.' "

While Friedan's book questioned the family status quo, President John Kennedy established the Commission on the Status of Women, and in 1963 Congress passed the Equal Pay Act, followed the next year by Title VII of the Civil Rights Act that prohibited discrimination in employment based on race or sex. These actions said that women would no longer quietly accept a second-class social status. In 1966, Friedan formed the National Organization for Women (NOW), devoted to obtaining equal rights.

The concept that women could fulfill themselves outside

▶ Births were already in decline at the beginning of the 1960s, but it was the sharp and sustained decrease in newborns between 1964 and 1969 that led demographers to declare 1964 to be the final year of the Boom.

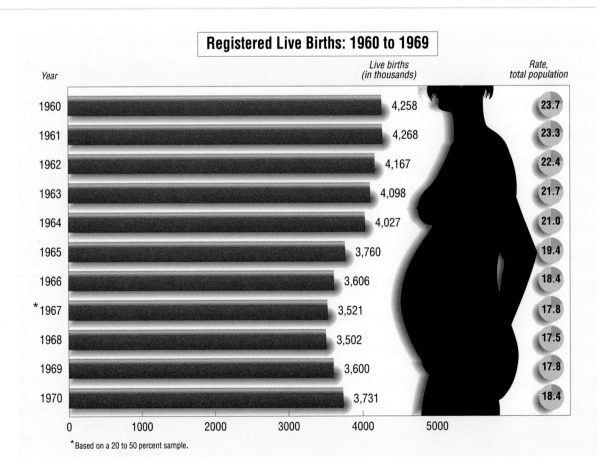

Registered Live Births: 1960 to 1969

Year	Live births (in thousands)	Rate, total population
1960	4,258	23.7
1961	4,268	23.3
1962	4,167	22.4
1963	4,098	21.7
1964	4,027	21.0
1965	3,760	19.4
1966	3,606	18.4
*1967	3,521	17.8
1968	3,502	17.5
1969	3,600	17.8
1970	3,731	18.4

*Based on a 20 to 50 percent sample.

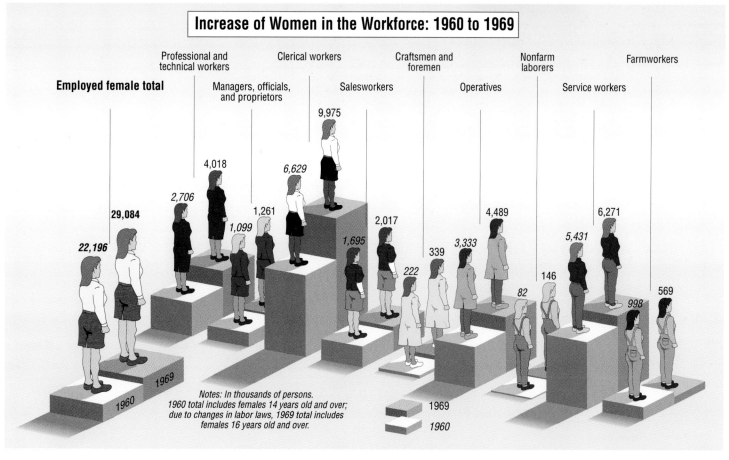

Increase of Women in the Workforce: 1960 to 1969

Employed female total

Professional and technical workers

Managers, officials, and proprietors

Clerical workers

Salesworkers

Craftsmen and foremen

Operatives

Nonfarm laborers

Service workers

Farmworkers

22,196
29,084
2,706
4,018
1,099
1,261
6,629
9,975
1,695
2,017
222
339
3,333
4,489
82
146
998
5,431
6,271
569

1960
1969

Notes: In thousands of persons.
1960 total includes females 14 years old and over;
due to changes in labor laws, 1969 total includes
females 16 years old and over.

1969
1960

the home, either through political activism or by obtaining jobs traditionally held by men, produced tension in marriages. Yet as radical as Friedan seemed to traditionalists, other, often younger, women advocated more extreme measures. As discontent spread throughout the 1960s and engendered ever-greater protest, they condemned the family unit as dysfunctional and oppressive, attacked pervasive sexism, and wanted nothing to do with marriage or social cooperation with men. The group Redstockings issued a manifesto in 1969 that declared:

Women are an oppressed class. Our oppression is total, affecting every facet of our lives. We are exploited as sex objects, breeders, domestic servants, and cheap labor. . . . We identify the agents of our oppression as men. . . . All other forms of exploitation and oppression (racism, capitalism, imperialism, etc.) are extensions of male supremacy. . . . All men have oppressed women.

Feminist attitudes affected even moderates: in 1957, 35 percent of women surveyed considered the ideal family size to be four or more children; in 1971 only 23 percent said this. Meanwhile the divorce rate shot up, and many younger women delayed marriage or vowed they would never marry at all.

Another challenge to traditional family values came from teen culture. Advertisers and television producers aimed a strong appeal at the seemingly endless procession of Baby Boomer kids and encouraged teenagers to feel independent of their parents. At the same time, peer pressure favored rebelliousness and added gray hairs to elders who fought to maintain their authority. Teens developed a powerful subculture—in time labeled a counterculture, or a revolt against middle-class values—often expressed through alienation. One 18-year-old told *Look* magazine in 1966 that kids were "very discontented" with their lives. Baby Boomers who attended college established enclaves where they exerted power denied them in adult society, living amid cultural influences their parents neither approved of nor understood.

When in 1966 John Lennon announced that the Beatles were more popular than Jesus, his words shook adults who saw in them a declaration that young people would reject traditional values. Their worries proved legitimate when Baby Boomers expressed a greater acceptance of premarital sex. Many wanted intimacy, but considered edicts about sex outside of marriage, and indeed the institution of marriage itself, to be hypocritical.

A curious contradiction flowed through the youth subculture. On the one hand, young people looked back with longing on their childhood and regretted their loss of innocence. "You can't be twenty on Sugar Mountain," sang Neil Young, "though you're thinking that you're leaving there too soon." On the other hand, Boomers had seen in the suburbs, in their own family ranch houses, a confinement they disliked and wanted desperately to avoid.

▲ *Perhaps for financial reasons, or perhaps in hopes that greater personal fulfillment could be found outside the home, the number of women in the workforce increased slowly but steadily throughout the 1960s. This chart shows the total numbers of women working in various professional categories.*

The college students seethed with anger as they crowded around the police cruiser and prevented it from moving. Mario Savio, a philosophy major, climbed atop the car and spoke out. He railed against authority saying: "There is a time when the operation of the machine becomes so odious . . . you've got to put your bodies . . . upon all the apparatus and you've got to make it stop."

The confrontation that unfolded in 1964 at the University of California-Berkeley stunned older Americans who thought their children had entered college at a time when higher education could provide unparalleled opportunities. By 1969, such optimism lay tattered as student upheaval, surges in enrollment, and racial controversy shook academia.

Enrollment in secondary schools and colleges reached new heights. For all high schools, the number jumped from about 9.6 million in 1960 to over 14 million in 1970; for colleges, degree-credit enrollment jumped from 3.6 million to nearly 8 million. In the high schools, educators in the early 1960s reacted to the Soviet Union's continued lead in space by scrambling to reform teaching methods. After Harvard psychologist Jerome Bruner claimed in his book *The Process of Education* that "any subject can be taught effectively . . . to any child at any stage of development," some schools had students engage in hands-on activities to learn how scientists and social scientists did their work. In this context, schools emphasized new technology, such as multimedia classrooms, to encourage student initiative. In all, however, these reforms paled in comparison to the upheaval that swept colleges.

> **❝** *I am a student. Please do not fold, spindle, or mutilate me.* **❞**
> —*slogan of the* **Free Speech Movement**, *1964*

On many campuses, student population doubled. Schools such as the University of California at Berkeley developed complex bureaucracies, placing students in classes that numbered in the hundreds. Bountiful higher education had suddenly turned impersonal, and students felt like cogs in a thought factory.

Mario Savio made his heated declaration after college administrators had prohibited students from distributing political pamphlets. To students, this restriction proved that the university, and society as a whole, supported free speech

only when it agreed with mainstream views. The Free Speech Movement, led by activists who had learned from their participation in civil rights protests, demanded freedom of political expression. Before long, other campuses erupted in similar fashion.

Some of the upheaval was stirred by Students for a Democratic Society (SDS). Founded in 1960, SDS set up programs to help ghetto residents and staged marches to protest the Vietnam War. At its height, its membership topped 100,000—a minority of students, but an outspoken and highly active one. SDS gained widespread attention in 1968 when it helped lead a student uprising at Columbia University to protest the building of a gym in Harlem and the close relationship between Columbia and government weapons research. More than 1,000 students occupied several buildings before police moved in with billy clubs flailing and evicted the protesters.

Three other campus upheavals convinced mainstream America that college students had gone too far. A few months after Columbia, the Black Student Union at San Francisco State College advised African Americans on campus to defend themselves against racist administrators by carrying guns. Student strikes, police arrests, and fire bombings rocked the campus. On May 4, 1970, National Guard troops at Kent State University in Ohio fired into a crowd of protesters, resulting in four deaths. Two of the dead had been passersby, walking to class. The shootings polarized the nation, as did comments

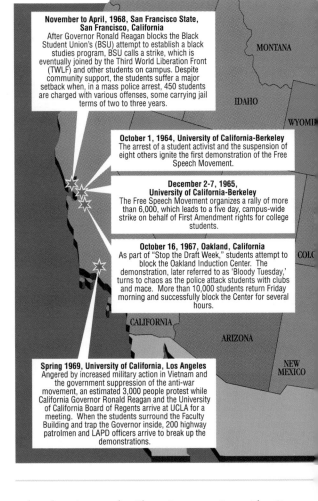

November to April, 1968, San Francisco State, San Francisco, California
After Governor Ronald Reagan blocks the Black Student Union's (BSU) attempt to establish a black studies program, BSU calls a strike, which is eventually joined by the Third World Liberation Front (TWLF) and other students on campus. Despite community support, the students suffer a major setback when, in a mass police arrest, 450 students are charged with various offenses, some carrying jail terms of two to three years.

October 1, 1964, University of California-Berkeley
The arrest of a student activist and the suspension of eight others ignite the first demonstration of the Free Speech Movement.

December 2-7, 1965, University of California-Berkeley
The Free Speech Movement organizes a rally of more than 6,000, which leads to a five day, campus-wide strike on behalf of First Amendment rights for college students.

October 16, 1967, Oakland, California
As part of "Stop the Draft Week," students attempt to block the Oakland Induction Center. The demonstration, later referred to as 'Bloody Tuesday,' turns to chaos as the police attack students with clubs and mace. More than 10,000 students return Friday morning and successfully block the Center for several hours.

Spring 1969, University of California, Los Angeles
Angered by increased military action in Vietnam and the government suppression of the anti-war movement, an estimated 3,000 people protest while California Governor Ronald Reagan and the University of California Board of Regents arrive at UCLA for a meeting. When the students surround the Faculty Building and trap the Governor inside, 200 highway patrolmen and LAPD officers arrive to break up the demonstrations.

▼ *On December 4, 1964, Free Speech Movement leader Mario Savio addresses a rally at the University of California-Berkeley for political freedom on campus. (UPI/CORBIS-BETTMANN)*

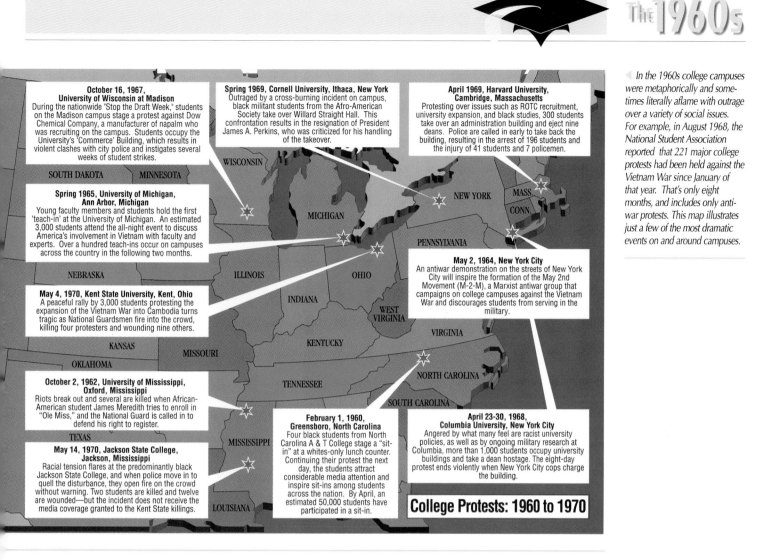

October 16, 1967, University of Wisconsin at Madison
During the nationwide "Stop the Draft Week," students on the Madison campus stage a protest against Dow Chemical Company, a manufacturer of napalm who was recruiting on the campus. Students occupy the University's 'Commerce' Building, which results in violent clashes with city police and instigates several weeks of student strikes.

Spring 1965, University of Michigan, Ann Arbor, Michigan
Young faculty members and students hold the first 'teach-in' at the University of Michigan. An estimated 3,000 students attend the all-night event to discuss America's involvement in Vietnam with faculty and experts. Over a hundred teach-ins occur on campuses across the country in the following two months.

May 4, 1970, Kent State University, Kent, Ohio
A peaceful rally by 3,000 students protesting the expansion of the Vietnam War into Cambodia turns tragic as National Guardsmen fire into the crowd, killing four protesters and wounding nine others.

October 2, 1962, University of Mississippi, Oxford, Mississippi
Riots break out and several are killed when African-American student James Meredith tries to enroll in "Ole Miss," and the National Guard is called in to defend his right to register.

May 14, 1970, Jackson State College, Jackson, Mississippi
Racial tension flares at the predominantly black Jackson State College, and when police move in to quell the disturbance, they open fire on the crowd without warning. Two students are killed and twelve are wounded—but the incident does not receive the media coverage granted to the Kent State killings.

Spring 1969, Cornell University, Ithaca, New York
Outraged by a cross-burning incident on campus, black militant students from the Afro-American Society take over Willard Straight Hall. This confrontation results in the resignation of President James A. Perkins, who was criticized for his handling of the takeover.

April 1969, Harvard University, Cambridge, Massachusetts
Protesting over issues such as ROTC recruitment, university expansion, and black studies, 300 students take over an administration building and eject nine deans. Police are called in early to take back the building, resulting in the arrest of 196 students and the injury of 41 students and 7 policemen.

May 2, 1964, New York City
An antiwar demonstration on the streets of New York City will inspire the formation of the May 2nd Movement (M-2-M), a Marxist antiwar group that campaigns on college campuses against the Vietnam War and discourages students from serving in the military.

February 1, 1960, Greensboro, North Carolina
Four black students from North Carolina A & T College stage a "sit-in" at a whites-only lunch counter. Continuing their protest the next day, the students attract considerable media attention and inspire sit-ins among students across the nation. By April, an estimated 50,000 students have participated in a sit-in.

April 23-30, 1968, Columbia University, New York City
Angered by what many feel are racist university policies, as well as by ongoing military research at Columbia, more than 1,000 students occupy university buildings and take a dean hostage. The eight-day protest ends violently when New York City cops charge the building.

College Protests: 1960 to 1970

In the 1960s college campuses were metaphorically and sometimes literally aflame with outrage over a variety of social issues. For example, in August 1968, the National Student Association reported that 221 major college protests had been held against the Vietnam War since January of that year. That's only eight months, and includes only anti-war protests. This map illustrates just a few of the most dramatic events on and around campuses.

by Vice President Spiro Agnew, who called the event "predictable" given the "traitors and thieves and perverts in our midst." A few days after Kent State, police reacted to a disturbance at all-black Jackson State College in Mississippi by strafing a dorm and killing two students.

Upheaval penetrated public schools, too. High school students emulated their older brothers and sisters and staged antiwar protests. They rebelled against authority and demanded rights. In an interview with a newspaper reporter investigating youth protest in 1968, one student in New York City complained "The main thing that's taught us in school is how to obey the rules. . . . Don't mention the curriculum. They'll tell us what to learn."

Some educators considered U.S. schools to be too authoritarian. They studied news of a highly successful reform in Britain called open education, which made the teacher a facilitator of knowledge, a person who provided ways for children to develop their own questions and find the answers. Many school districts in America experimented with open education, but it faltered in the early 1970s as parents complained that it ignored the basics.

Race relations were also a volatile issue. Many southern schools had failed to desegregate; as a result, beginning in 1965, the federal government withheld aid to those that practiced de jure discrimination. Although many districts then integrated, problems remained with northern schools that, as a result of housing patterns, practiced de facto segregation.

The federal courts sought to remedy this by ordering student busing, and in doing so sparked yet another controversy. Perhaps unsurprisingly, given the kaleidoscope of ideas in the 1960s, some blacks began arguing against integration, saying competition from middle-class white kids discouraged black children and that white schools ignored black culture.

At decade's end, schools and colleges exhibited the same questioning and doubt found in society at large. Yet resiliency existed too. Young people kept enrolling in college, keeping the faith that education would improve their lives.

Free Universities

Responding to the countercultural call for liberated education, in 1965 James Mellen and other political activists founded Free University in New York's Greenwich Village. The two-room college, nicknamed FUNY, offered courses such as Marxist Geography, Life in Mainland China, and Imperialism in Latin America.

While the school engaged in serious intellectual pursuits, unusual events happened too, such as peace demonstrations and hippies playing rock music in class. Before internal bickering caused FUNY's collapse in 1966, it had by example encouraged free universities in other locations, including Chicago, Illinois; Detroit, Michigan; and Gainesville, Florida.

In 1965, a bright young lawyer, Ralph Nader, recounted disturbing findings from his investigation of the automobile industry in his book *Unsafe at Any Speed*. He found that manufacturers compromised safety for style, and in particular he criticized General Motors for making the Chevrolet Corvair. Nader asserted that GM knew the car had a faulty suspension system but continued to produce it anyway.

GM reacted by investigating Nader and harassing him, a tactic that, when uncovered, raised a controversy as great as the one caused by Nader's book. As sales of the Corvair plummeted, GM ceased production, while Congress passed legislation in 1966 that set safety standards for cars. The episode raised the entire issue of corporate responsibility to consumers, and it expanded government regulation of business while revealing that the public, accustomed to prosperity, considered abundance and safe products an entitlement.

As prosperous as the 1950s had been, Americans had seen only bounty's leading edge. During the 1960s the nation experienced its longest period of uninterrupted economic growth. In terms of constant 1958 dollars, per-capita income jumped from $2,157 in 1960 to $3,050 in 1970—a massive 41 percent increase. Over the same period, the per-capita Gross National Product went from $2,699 to $3,555.

This growth had several causes. The Trade Expansion Act of 1962 reduced some tariffs, thus boosting exports. Then in 1964, President Lyndon Johnson pushed through Congress a tax cut, and unemployment quickly dropped from 5 percent that year to 4.4 percent in 1965, to 3.7 percent in 1966. (Throughout the decade, economic growth created 10 million new jobs.) Government spending on social welfare programs stimulated the economy, as did spending on internal improvements, such as interstate highways and, even more so, on the Vietnam War.

In addition, the Baby Boomers entered the economic equation in a big way. Teen money flowed as readily as hormones jumped. Adolescents spent $12 billion a year. They bought 55 percent of all soft drinks, 53 percent of all movie tickets, 43 percent of all records. Teenage girls spent $3.5 billion a year on clothes. More than one out of every five high school seniors drove their own cars, taking them to fast-food hangouts where teen dollars helped propel an entirely new industry.

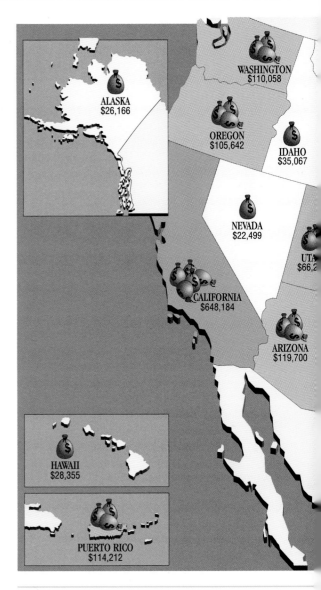

▼ President Johnson greets teacher Marie Perry and some students in the Rose Garden, at the press conference for "Project Head Start," a War on Poverty Program aimed at preparing underprivileged kids for school. (UPI/CORBIS-BETTMANN)

Advertisers and corporations quickly recognized and encouraged the youth market. Pepsi-Cola heralded the era with its slogan, "For those who think young," and tied itself to the Boomers with, "Come Alive! You're in the Pepsi Generation!" Auto manufacturers plied the youth market with cool designs, such as the Ford Mustang. Teen dollars appeared in the money spent on Beatles records, movies, magazines, calendars, even wigs. The Beatles set an entertainment industry record when they earned $150,000 for a one-night performance in Kansas City.

The nation still struggled with poverty (and a great disparity between white and black incomes), but amid the economic boom it decided to do something about it. In his 1964 State of the Union address, President Johnson declared "Unconditional War on Poverty." As part of what he called the Great Society, he convinced Congress to establish an array of programs. Some, such as Medicare, benefited the middle class more than any other group; others helped the poor. The Office of Economic Opportunity coordinated Head Start, which established free nursery schools to prepare poor children for kindergarten; the Job Corps provided jobs for young people; and the Community

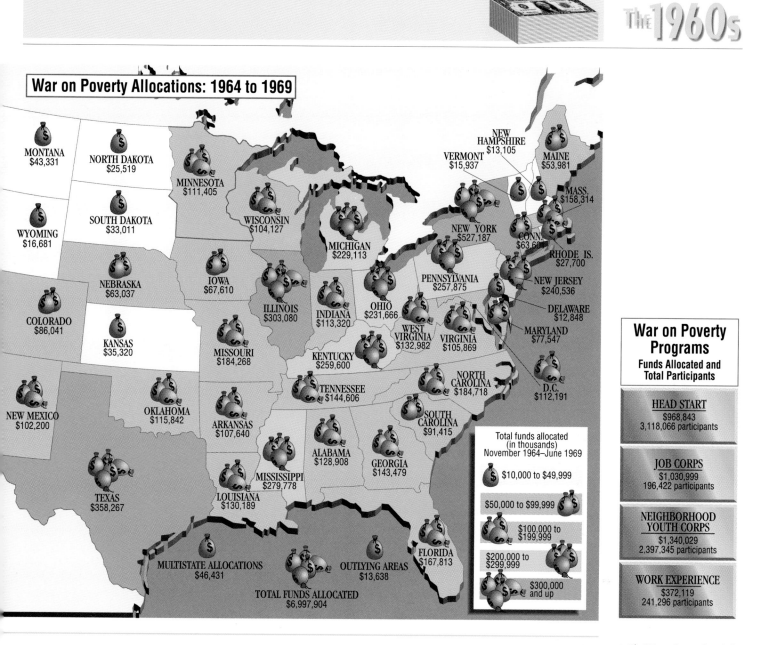

War on Poverty Allocations: 1964 to 1969

MONTANA $43,331
NORTH DAKOTA $25,519
MINNESOTA $111,405
NEW HAMPSHIRE $13,105
VERMONT $15,937
MAINE $53,981
WYOMING $16,681
SOUTH DAKOTA $33,011
WISCONSIN $104,127
MASS. $158,314
NEW YORK $527,187
CONN. $63,601
RHODE IS. $27,700
NEBRASKA $63,037
IOWA $67,610
MICHIGAN $229,113
PENNSYLVANIA $257,875
NEW JERSEY $240,536
COLORADO $86,041
KANSAS $35,320
ILLINOIS $303,080
INDIANA $113,320
OHIO $231,666
DELAWARE $12,848
MARYLAND $77,547
MISSOURI $184,268
WEST VIRGINIA $132,982
VIRGINIA $105,869
NEW MEXICO $102,200
KENTUCKY $259,600
NORTH CAROLINA $184,718
D.C. $112,191
OKLAHOMA $115,842
ARKANSAS $107,640
TENNESSEE $144,606
SOUTH CAROLINA $91,415
TEXAS $358,267
MISSISSIPPI $279,778
LOUISIANA $130,189
ALABAMA $128,908
GEORGIA $143,479
MULTISTATE ALLOCATIONS $46,431
OUTLYING AREAS $13,638
FLORIDA $167,813
TOTAL FUNDS ALLOCATED $6,997,904

Total funds allocated
(in thousands)
November 1964–June 1969

$10,000 to $49,999

$50,000 to $99,999

$100,000 to $199,999

$200,000 to $299,999

$300,000 and up

War on Poverty Programs
Funds Allocated and Total Participants

HEAD START
$968,843
3,118,066 participants

JOB CORPS
$1,030,999
196,422 participants

NEIGHBORHOOD YOUTH CORPS
$1,340,029
2,397,345 participants

WORK EXPERIENCE
$372,119
241,296 participants

The War on Poverty funneled millions of dollars to the needy in the mid- and late-1960s, creating jobs and educational opportunities for young and old.

Action Program encouraged the poor to demand greater participation in political decision making.

Critics attacked the last program when, through its efforts, some poor people began demanding public services from local governments and began forming tenants' right groups. Chicago's Woodlawn Organization, an African-American group, declared: "It is a war against the poor when we are told by the President and Congress that we can plan for ourselves, but then find we can only stand in the waiting rooms of . . . city hall, while plans are made for us." Critics saw in such complaints and demands turmoil; the program's supporters saw in them long-overdue empowerment.

Poverty declined in the 1960s, from 20 percent in 1963 to 13 percent in 1968. The War on Poverty, though, may have contributed less to that improvement than the economic boom. After all, government spending on social programs, $1.2 billion in 1966, seemed substantial but paled in comparison with spending on the Vietnam War, $22 billion that same year. Further, Johnson's programs assumed poor people were responsible for their poverty, thus the government ignored structural changes causing unemployment, such as coal mines closing in Appalachia.

Late in the decade businesses faced more federal regulation as society grappled with what to do about hazardous working conditions. Congress formed the Occupational Safety and Hazards Administration (OSHA) in 1970 to issue regulations for factories and other workplaces. At the same time, deteriorating air and water quality spurred environmental reform, as did Rachel Carson's *Silent Spring* (1962). "The most alarming of all man's assaults upon the environment is the contamination of air, earth, rivers, and sea with dangerous and lethal materials," she wrote in discussing chemical pollution. In 1970, Congress established the Environmental Protection Agency and soon required it to oversee thousands of factories and other potential polluters.

Nevertheless, America remained a throwaway society, immersed in plastic cigarette lighters, plastic cups, and plastic pens. Detroit produced 367 car models in 1967—obsolescence planned, disposal encouraged. The environmental and social implications behind waste raised the consciousness of many Baby Boomers and caused some to question their society in ways that went beyond Ralph Nader, to the essence of whether a person's life should be defined by what he or she bought.

In the book *It's Happening* (1966) by J. L. Simmons, a youthful character addresses a member of the older generation:

Look at you, brainwashing a whole generation of kids into . . . buying your junk. . . . Look at you, screwing up the land and the water and the air for a profit, and calling this nowhere scene the Great Society! And you're gonna' tell us how to live? C'mon, man, you've got to be kidding.

Listening to such talk in the 1960s, adults often reacted with incredulity—"What were youths complaining about?" After all, they had education, prosperity, security. But many Baby Boomers felt otherwise, and their discontent led to a youth-dominated counterculture, a revolt both political and cultural against middle-class values and practices.

An event on February 1, 1960, stimulated the counterculture: four black students began a sit-in at the segregated Woolworth's lunch counter in Greensboro, North Carolina. By week's end 1,000 other protesters had joined them to demand integration. Several hundred young protesters subsequently formed the Student Nonviolent Coordinating Committee (SNCC) and committed themselves to bold activism. Said one: "Instead of sitting idly by, taking the leavings of a sick and decadent society, we have seized the initiative."

> 66 *I went over to the sergeant and I said 'Sergeant, you got a lot a d*** gall to ask me if I've rehabilitated myself! I mean, I mean... I'm sittin' here on the bench, I'm just sittin' here on the Group W bench, cause you want to know if I'm moral enough to join the army and burn women, kids, houses, and villages after bein' a litterbug.'*
>
> *He looked at me and he said, 'Kid, we don't like your kind.'* 99
>
> —**Arlo Guthrie**, *"Alice's Restaurant"*

Greensboro and SNCC breached suburbia, stirring white youths, who now realized something was seriously wrong with American society. Other factors also stirred them: the idealistic image projected by President John Kennedy and, in 1963, his assassination, which shattered hopes; fears of nuclear annihilation made worse by the 1962 Cuban Missile Crisis; the Vietnam War, just then gaining significant attention; and their sheer numbers, a Jonah inside the societal whale, seeking deliverance.

In the first half of the 1960s, it was SNCC that sounded the loudest alarm. When the group launched its Mississippi Freedom Summer Project in 1964 to register black voters, hundreds of white northern college students joined the effort. They quickly learned how racist American society truly was; when the FBI refused to protect them, they learned just how cruel and calculated the federal government could be.

At the same time, discontented white youths organized Students for a Democratic Society (SDS), committed to making America a participatory democracy. SDS was part of an emerging political side to a counterculture that soon became even more radicalized. SNCC, for example, declared Black Power in 1966—meaning African Americans should define their own goals and lead their own organizations to fight racism—and the following year ousted its white members. The Black Panthers, organized in California in 1966, combined a drive for African-American self-determination with socialism and paramilitary training.

Mainstream society trembled at these developments, made all the more ominous by urban riots, such as the one in Watts, a black ghetto in Los Angeles, that exploded in August 1965 and resulted in 34 deaths. That protest seemed everywhere—antiwar, women's rights, gay rights, ad infinitum—that assassins killed Martin Luther King, Jr., and Robert Kennedy in 1968, and that America's crime rate shot upward in the 1960s—violent crimes jumped an astonishing 10 percent a year—seemed all the more indicative of social collapse.

Amid political revolt, a pervasive cultural protest emerged. Beginning in San Francisco's Haight-Ashbury district around 1965, hippies professed a communal society based on love and peace . . . and fostered by LSD.

Although Haight-Ashbury disintegrated after the disastrous, drug-saturated 1967 Summer of Love, the idealistic message and psychedelic images wafted through suburbia as pungently as the marijuana smoked by ever-larger numbers of youths. According to *Life* magazine in 1967: "Every city worthy of the name has at least one psychedelic store that sells everything a 'head' could want, short of the grass itself."

Drugs acted as an initiation, for getting high meant getting hip to society's hypocrisies and cruelties. In that sense, they represented a merging of the political and cultural

▶ Burning of the U.S. flag during a 1969 antiwar protest called "March Against Death," in Washington, D.C. (Archive Photos)

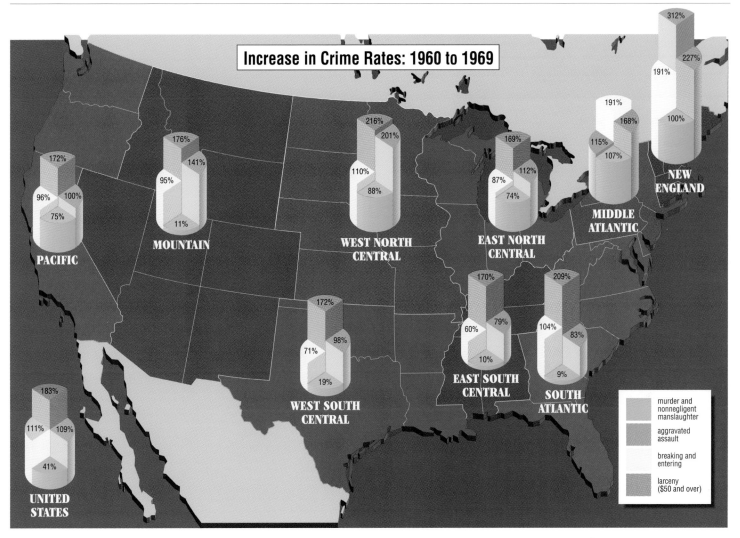

Increase in Crime Rates: 1960 to 1969

PACIFIC — 172%, 96%, 100%, 75%
MOUNTAIN — 176%, 141%, 95%, 11%
WEST NORTH CENTRAL — 216%, 201%, 110%, 88%
EAST NORTH CENTRAL — 169%, 112%, 87%, 74%
MIDDLE ATLANTIC — 191%, 168%, 115%, 107%
NEW ENGLAND — 312%, 227%, 191%, 100%
WEST SOUTH CENTRAL — 172%, 98%, 71%, 19%
EAST SOUTH CENTRAL — 170%, 79%, 60%, 10%
SOUTH ATLANTIC — 209%, 104%, 83%, 9%
UNITED STATES — 183%, 111%, 109%, 41%

Legend: murder and nonnegligent manslaughter; aggravated assault; breaking and entering; larceny ($50 and over)

counterculture, evident throughout the youth uprising. Cultural and political protesters both smoked pot and became alienated, wore long hair, listened to folk and rock music, and watched anti-establishment movies, such as *Easy Rider*. In 1969 both bathed in Woodstock's glow and absorbed the shocking violence of the riot at Altamont Raceway.

Rock music defined the counterculture. "For our generation, music is the most vital force in most of our lives," said one prominent activist. Heavily influenced by Bob Dylan and by the Beatles, rock evolved into a new form dealing with social issues and mystical experiences. The Beatles' 1967 album *Sgt. Pepper's Lonely Hearts Club Band* presented a pathbreaking format, uniting its songs to a common theme, and displaying the band's immersion in drugs and psychedelia. As America polarized in the late 1960s, rock music likewise went in two directions, with some

musicians—such as Crosby, Stills, Nash, and Young—employing a mellow, escapist country sound, and others—such as Steppenwolf and MC5—a harsh, anticapitalist message.

The counterculture sharply divided Baby Boomers from their parents. In declaring the generation its 1966 "Man of the Year," *Time* magazine said: "The young have . . . staked out their own minisociety, a congruent culture that has . . . alarmed their elders."

Time claimed the Boomer generation would "land on the moon, cure Cancer [*sic*]. . . lay out blight-proof, smog-free cities . . . and, no doubt, write finis to poverty and war." Even youths who believed that in 1966 felt differently as the decade ended. They felt violated by a nation whose war against them and against Vietnam had produced oppression. From young idealism they shifted to hardened cynicism. America limped into the 1970s doubting its future.

▲ *Reinforcing the mainstream view that the United States was headed for complete social breakdown was an alarming rise in crime rates throughout the 1960s. Pictured here are the percentage increases in four categories of crime, based on incidents reported to police.*

Boohoo Faith

The counterculture held little sacred, and that included religion. In 1966, Arthur Kleps founded the Neo-American Boohoo Church, which declared LSD a sacrament. Kleps infused his church with self-deprecating humor and satire. He issued a psychedelic coloring book, and his *Boohoo Bible* contained cartoons and true-or-false tests. The Boohoos used *Row, Row, Row Your Boat* as their hymn and tried to get the legal system to recognize their use of LSD as protected by religious freedom. Inexplicably, the courts refused to consider the Boohoos' request!

Year	World	United States Politics	Arts
1960	In Africa, 11 former European colonies form independent governments, including Nigeria, Chad, Gabon, Somalia, and Madagascar.	▼ Democrat John F. Kennedy narrowly edges out Richard M. Nixon for the presidency.	Pop art guru Andy Warhol exhibits the painting *Campbell's Soup Can (Tomato and Rice)*.
1961	East Germany constructs the Berlin Wall to halt the flow of refugees to West Berlin.		The film *Breakfast at Tiffany's* opens, starring Audrey Hepburn as the free-spirited Holly Golightly.
1962	The Cuban Missile Crisis brings the United States and the Soviet Union to the brink of nuclear war.		Marilyn Monroe, 36, dies of an apparent overdose of sleeping pills.
1963	The United States, the U.S.S.R., and Great Britain sign the Nuclear Test Ban Treaty, allowing only underground atomic weapons tests.	President Kennedy is assassinated in Dallas, Texas. He is succeeded by Lyndon Johnson.	The record album *The Freewheelin' Bob Dylan* is released, featuring the songs "Blowin' in the Wind" and "A Hard Rain's Gonna Fall."
1964	The Gulf of Tonkin Resolution grants the United States the right to use "all necessary measures" to "prevent further aggression" in Southeast Asia.	President Johnson, elected to his first full term in office, announces a war on poverty.	Lenny Bruce, the controversial comedian known for his satirical routines, is arrested for swearing in public at the Cafe A Go-Go in New York City.
1965	The United States begins heavy bombing of North Vietnam and sends in combat troops as the war escalates.	Civil rights demonstrators face brutal police violence in Selma, Alabama.	Bob Dylan is booed by folk purists at the Newport Folk Festival when he "plugs-in" and plays an electric guitar with a rock band.
1966	The Cultural Revolution begins in China, with protesters demanding that the people conform to the communist principles of ruler Mao Zedong.	Women's rights activist Betty Friedan founds the National Organization for Women.	Mia Farrow, age 21, weds Frank Sinatra, age 50, in a Las Vegas ceremony.
1967	Israel captures the Golan Heights, the West Bank, and Arab Jerusalem during the Six-Day War.	Thurgood Marshall becomes the nation's first African-American Supreme Court justice.	Dustin Hoffman is seduced by Anne Bancroft in Mike Nichols's film *The Graduate*.
1968	In France, college students take over 23 universities and workers seize factories and strike.	Richard Nixon wins a presidential race marred by the assassination of Democratic candidate Robert F. Kennedy and civil rights leader Rev. Martin Luther King, Jr.	Tom Wolfe releases *Electric Kool-Aid Acid Test*, an account of his journey across America with author Ken Kesey and the Merry Pranksters on a psychedelic bus.
1969	The United States secretly bombs communist bases in Cambodia.	The drowning death of Mary Jo Kopechne ends Senator Edward Kennedy's hopes of pursuing the 1972 presidential nomination.	500,000 young people converge on Max Yasgur's farm for "Three Days of Peace and Music" at the Woodstock music festival.

Archive Photos

Science and Industry	Pastimes and Lifestyles	Sports	Year
Research scientists perfect the laser, an acronym for **l**ight **a**mplification by **s**timulated **e**mission of **r**adiation.	Chubby Checker's "The Twist" creates an international dance craze.	The Winter Olympics are held in Squaw Valley, California.	1960
Astronaut Alan Shepard becomes the first American in outer space.		Roger Maris hits his 61st home run, breaking Babe Ruth's single-season record.	1961
Biologist Rachel Carson's *Silent Spring* warns that pesticides endanger the environment.		Wilt Chamberlain of the Philadelphia Warriors sets the NBA single-game scoring record in a 169-147 win over the New York Knicks, completing the game with a total of 100 points.	1962
Aboard *Vostok 6*, cosmonaut Valentina Tereshkova becomes the first woman in space.		Arthur Ashe is the first black man to play on the U.S. Davis Cup tennis team.	1963
Surgeon General Luther Terry links cigarette smoking to lung cancer.	▲ Beatlemania grips the U.S. as the Fab Four arrive for their first extended American tour and a historic appearance on *The Ed Sullivan Show*.	In an upset over Australian Ron Clarke, Billy Mills becomes the first American to win the 10,000-meter race in the Summer Olympics, held in Tokyo.	1964
Cosmonaut Aleksei Leonov completes the first spacewalk, while Americans Virgil Grissom and John Young orbit the Earth three times in a *Gemini* spacecraft, and the unmanned *Mariner IV* comes within 12,000 km (7,500 mi.) of Mars.	London designer Mary Quant introduces the miniskirt.	In hockey, the first Conn Smythe Trophy is awarded to Jean Beliveau of the Montreal Canadiens, as the most valuable player to his team in the play-offs against the St. Louis Blues.	1965
William H. Masters and Virginia E. Johnson publish the results of their controversial research in *Human Sexual Response*.	California outlaws LSD, a mainstay of the counterculture.	The American Football League and National Football League merge, as the AFL becomes the first league to successfully challenge the NFL in pro football.	1966
Dr. Christiaan Barnard of South Africa performs the first human heart transplant on Louis Washkansky, who lives 18 days.	50,000 convene at the Monterey International Pop Festival in California, which features the greatest number of rock performances ever assembled.	The Green Bay Packers win the first Super Bowl under legendary coach Vince Lombardi.	1967
Oil is discovered on Alaska's North Slope.	Dr. Spock is tried and convicted for illegally counseling young people to resist the draft; the conviction will later be overturned on appeal.	U.S. medalists Tommie Smith and John Carlos are ejected from the Olympics in Mexico City for giving the Black Power salute.	1968
Apollo 11 astronauts Neil Armstrong and Buzz Aldrin walk on the surface of the moon.	Fueled by "clues" in Beatles' songs, a rumor spreads that Paul McCartney died in 1966. McCartney declares the "Paul is Dead" story to be a hoax.	The New York Mets beat the Baltimore Orioles in the fifth series game by 5–3, clinching their first World Series title.	1969

Archive Photos/Popperfoto

THE BIG PICTURE

A s Americans experienced domestic turmoil in the 1960s, disruptions overseas added to the sense that the world was a ball of confusion. The decade began with Africans declaring their independence from European rule, thus dismantling a powerful colonialist system. India and China waged war, while within China a Cultural Revolution shook society. The world neared nuclear destruction when Russia and the United States had a nerve-rattling showdown over Cuba. Russia saw its domination of Eastern Europe threatened by an uprising in Czechoslovakia, which it brutally suppressed, while riots in France nearly toppled the Fifth Republic.

CUBA
Missile Crisis (1962)

On October 14, 1962, American spy planes photographed launch pads in Cuba that could handle Russian missiles armed with nuclear warheads. President John Kennedy publicly accused the Soviet Union of an unprovoked act that threatened American security. He blockaded Cuba and ordered the Soviets to remove the missiles. The crisis ended when Premier Nikita Khrushchev acquiesced, in return for Kennedy's pledge not to invade Cuba and to dismantle American missiles in Turkey aimed at the Soviet Union. Baby Boomers would long remember the frightening time when Kennedy and Khrushchev stood "eyeball to eyeball," and nuclear war seemed near.

CHINA
Cultural Revolution (1966-1976)

A great upheaval shook China in 1966 when protesters took to the streets and demanded that those who had deviated from ruler Mao Zedong's communist principles be purged. This began the Cultural Revolution, during which Red Guards zealously enforced Mao's drive for ideological conformity. Many political leaders were removed from office, intellectuals were attacked for their "bourgeois" ideas, and Mao was worshiped as a savior. The upheaval caused clashes between armed factions and brought economic turmoil. Before the Cultural Revolution ended with Mao's death in 1976, it influenced young radicals in the United States, who adopted Maoism in their struggle to overthrow capitalism.

FRANCE
Student Protests (1968)

While protests shook the United States in 1968, in France college students took over 23 universities, and workers seized factories and went on strike. Militants clashed with police in Paris, and plastic bombs exploded in Marseilles, but the protesters failed to present a united front as their demands ranged from reforming college curriculums to replacing capitalism with communism. In general, they detested France's leader, Charles de Gaulle, and wanted him removed. De Gaulle, however, rallied his supporters, and the violence ended when he won parliamentary elections. His victory proved short-lived, though: in 1969 he lost a vote of confidence and quit.

CZECHOSLOVAKIA
Prague Spring (1968)

In 1968, Russia faced a great challenge to its hold on Eastern Europe. That January, Alexander Dubcek won election as first secretary of Czechoslovakia's Communist Party and quickly declared freedom of speech and other reforms. Czechoslovaks dubbed that period "Prague Spring," meaning the winter of oppression had ended, but when some called for their nation to quit the Soviet-dominated Warsaw Pact, winter returned. The month of August saw an invasion of 200,000 troops from five Warsaw Pact countries. Young people in Prague surged atop Soviet tanks and in a futile act chanted "U.S.S.R. go home!" Many American youths saw in that scene similarities to their own protests.

CHINA AND INDIA
Sino-Indian War (1962)

Many Americans saw the cold war in simplistic terms, but a conflict between India and China revealed complexity. Ever since gaining independence in the late 1940s, India had been involved in a border dispute with China in the Himalayas. In 1962, war erupted when Chinese troops overran India's northern outposts and advanced through the plains of Assam. A simplistic assessment would have concluded that communist China acted with the blessing of communist Russia. Yet both Russia and the United States aided India, the former to contain China, the latter to contain communism. The aid resulted in China withdrawing its troops.

VIETNAM
War (1965-1975)

Despite warnings from advisors that America could never win a war in Southeast Asia, in 1965 President Lyndon Johnson landed the first American combat troops in South Vietnam while launching massive air attacks against the communists in North Vietnam. American involvement in Vietnam deepened dramatically. By 1968, America had about 500,000 troops in South Vietnam, but the communist-led Tet Offensive early that year proved more would be needed to win. Dispirited, Johnson decided to open peace talks with North Vietnam. His successor, Richard Nixon, began bringing American troops home.

AFRICA
End of Colonialism (1960-1970)

During the 1960s, the African continent underwent enormous changes as colony after colony declared independence from European rule. In 1960 alone, Congo, Cameroon, Madagascar, Nigeria, Senegal, and Somalia, among others, "decolonized." By 1970, only Portugal retained its colonies. Many young Americans, especially young blacks, took pride in African nationalism. As with most international developments, the cold war played an important role. While the new nations struggled to choose between capitalist and socialist economies, the United States, the Soviet Union, and China worked to exert their influence and gain strategic advantage.

> President John Kennedy pauses while addressing the nation via television about the Cuban Missile Crisis, right. (Archive Photos)

Eyeball to eyeball. Nuclear warhead to nuclear warhead. So the United States and the Soviet Union stood in 1962 during a crisis over Cuba, a crisis that threatened to unleash a nuclear holocaust.

John Kennedy entered the presidency in 1961 believing he could bring peace and prosperity to the world, and that if the United States failed, freedom failed. With such vision, and with his vigor, he appealed to Baby Boomers, then still in their teens and by and large still in their innocence. Said one teenager as he reflected on Kennedy's administration: "The whole idea was that you can make a difference. . . . I really believed that I was going to be able to change the world."

Despite the powerful optimism of the early 1960s, many feared the world might not last long, that at any minute a nuclear war could wipe out everyone and everything. Ironically, Kennedy, the president who brought optimism, fed such pessimism with an arms buildup. Even though the Russians had only a small number of intercontinental ballistic missiles (ICBMs) and showed no desire to greatly increase them, between 1961 and 1963 Kennedy added several hundred to America's arsenal. Soviet Premier Nikita Khrushchev responded by ordering a 58-megaton nuclear bomb exploded on August 30, 1961—the largest such detonation in history. The bomb, said one observer, seemed to "suck the whole earth into it." Krushchev's act broke a moratorium on nuclear tests and caused Kennedy to respond with a series of his own—30 explosions in all. Baby Boomers faced a more contaminated atmosphere and a more harrowing existence.

Early in 1961, Kennedy approved a daring assault on Cuba. He wanted to overthrow that nation's Marxist dictator, Fidel Castro; to do so, he set in motion a CIA plan to equip Cuban exiles for an invasion. In April, the exile force landed at the Bay of Pigs. Kennedy had promised the soldiers air cover, but at the last minute withdrew it. Exposed to Castro's army, and lacking any support from the Cuban people, who either supported Castro or considered the American invasion an affront to their sovereignty, the invaders failed.

General "Buck" Turgidson: *Mr. President, we are rapidly approaching a moment of truth both for ourselves as human beings and for the life of our nation. Now, truth is not always a pleasant thing. But it is necessary now to make a choice, to choose between two admittedly regrettable, but nevertheless distinguishable, postwar environments: one where you got twenty million people killed, and the other where you got a hundred and fifty million people killed.*

President Muffley: *You're talking about mass murder, General, not war!*

Turgidson: *Mr. President, I'm not saying we wouldn't get our hair mussed.*

—*from* **Dr. Strangelove or: How I Learned to Stop Worrying and Love the Bomb**, *screenplay by Peter George, Stanley Kubrick, and Terry Southern*

Close to the Edge

How near had the world come to a nuclear war during the Cuban Missile Crisis? On Saturday, October 27, 1962, as tension between the Soviet Union and the United States remained high, an American U-2 spy plane flew off course into Siberia. Had the Russians shot it down, war might have resulted. To make matters worse, that same day, Soviet antiaircraft guns did down a U-2 over Cuba, but President Kennedy decided to let the incident pass. Near the same time, a technological breakdown caused the advance warning station in Moorestown, New Jersey, to send a message that a nuclear missile had been fired from Cuba, headed to Tampa. Only discovery of the error by radar tracking stations prevented disaster.

The fiasco fed Kennedy's obsession with Cuba and encouraged a brinkmanship that nearly caused a world war during the Cuban Missile Crisis, which erupted in 1962 when Khrushchev began building missile sites in Cuba. To this day, the reasons for his action remain unclear; however, he said after the event: "We had to establish a tangible and effective deterrent to American interference in the Caribbean." On October 14, 1962, United States spy planes photographed the launchpads under construction. Although nuclear missiles had not yet been put in place, Khrushchev had sent several to the island. The launchpads would be able to fire medium-range missiles a distance of 1,000 miles, and longer-range ones that could reach as far as Seattle to the north and Lima, Peru, to the south.

Kennedy met for several days with his advisors. They had to act quickly, because the Soviet missiles would soon be operational and could thus be used to retaliate for any decision Kennedy might make. Kennedy opted for a blockade, or what he called a "quarantine," of Cuba.

On October 22, 1962, the president presented his case to the American people on national television in a broadcast that helped define the Baby Boom generation. He warned that an attack on any nation in the Western Hemisphere by nuclear missiles from Cuba would be considered an attack by the Soviet Union on the United States and would be met with a nuclear response. The U.S. Air Force stood at DEFCON 2, an alert just short of war, and ICBMs were prepared for firing.

The world stood on edge. Kennedy called his wife and children back to Washington so they could go to a fallout shelter if necessary. Some students at New England colleges hurriedly packed their cars and fled to Canada. The *Los Angeles Times* reported that high school students were breaking down in class and crying, "I don't want to die!"

Fortunately, Khrushchev ordered Soviet ships carrying nuclear missiles to turn away from Cuba and return to Russia.

He and Kennedy reached an agreement that publicly stated the Soviet Union would dismantle the launchpads in return for the United States promising never to invade Cuba. In secret, Kennedy agreed to something else: he would dismantle American missiles stationed in Turkey and aimed at the Soviet Union.

Stepping back from the brink, Kennedy and Khrushchev plunged into building more missiles. Both the United States and the Soviet Union pursued MAD—mutual assured destruction. This strategy asserted that nuclear war could be avoided by each nation building more weapons to guarantee that neither side would win a world war, thus making it improbable they would use their nuclear arsenals.

With so many nuclear weapons, Baby Boomers felt increasingly nervous about the prospects of an aggressive leader unleashing a world war or even of an accident that would kill many people. In 1966, for example, a B-52 bomber and a jet tanker collided over Spain, and four hydrogen bombs dropped from the B-52. Only safety devices kept them from exploding; as it was, three of them spread plutonium over a wide area.

In the late 1960s, the United States deployed MIRVs, multiple independently targetable reentry vehicles, meaning that each ICBM could carry up to 10 separately targeted warheads. MAD thus reached a level more mad.

Baby Boomers flocked to movies related to nuclear fears. *Fail-Safe* (1962) presented a failure in technology that sent American bombers toward Russia, with no way to call them back. After the bombers nuked Moscow, the Russians were allowed to nuke New York City. A pitch-black comedy called *Dr. Strangelove or: How I Learned to Stop Worrying and Love the Bomb* (1964) told the story of an insane American general and a Soviet Doomsday Machine that led to nuclear annihilation.

The United States and the Soviet Union made some progress in controlling nuclear weapons with the 1963 Limited Test Ban Treaty. In 1964 China exploded its own A-bomb; the nuclear powers had enough weapons to destroy the world several times over. Little comfort existed, then, for Baby Boomers brought to the edge during the Cuban Missile Crisis and left staring into a looming holocaust.

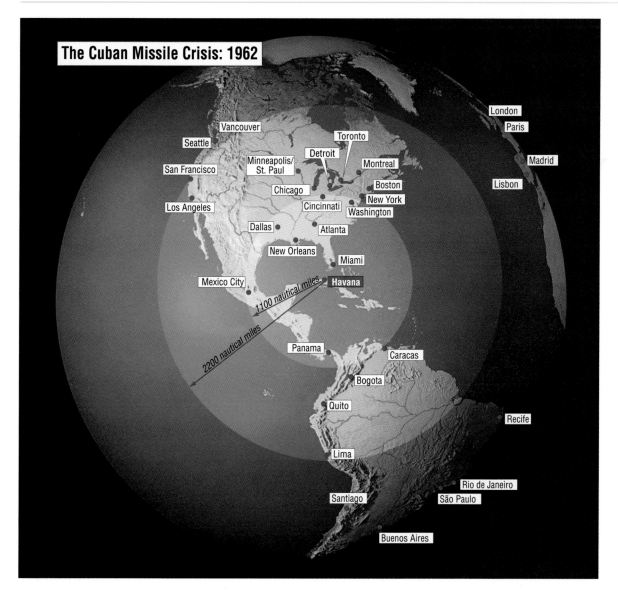

The Cuban Missile Crisis: 1962

London
Paris
Madrid
Lisbon
Vancouver
Seattle
Toronto
Detroit
Minneapolis/St. Paul
Montreal
San Francisco
Boston
Chicago
New York
Los Angeles
Cincinnati
Washington
Dallas
Atlanta
New Orleans
Miami
Mexico City
Havana
1100 nautical miles
2200 nautical miles
Panama
Caracas
Bogota
Quito
Recife
Lima
Rio de Janeiro
Santiago
São Paulo
Buenos Aires

◀ A nuclear conflict on the island of Cuba would risk plunging most of the Western Hemisphere into chaos, as this map shows. From Cuba ICBMs could reach as far north as Seattle, Washington, and as far south as Lima, Peru.

PROTEST PROTEST PROTEST PROTEST

FROM CIVIL RIGHTS TO BLACK POWER

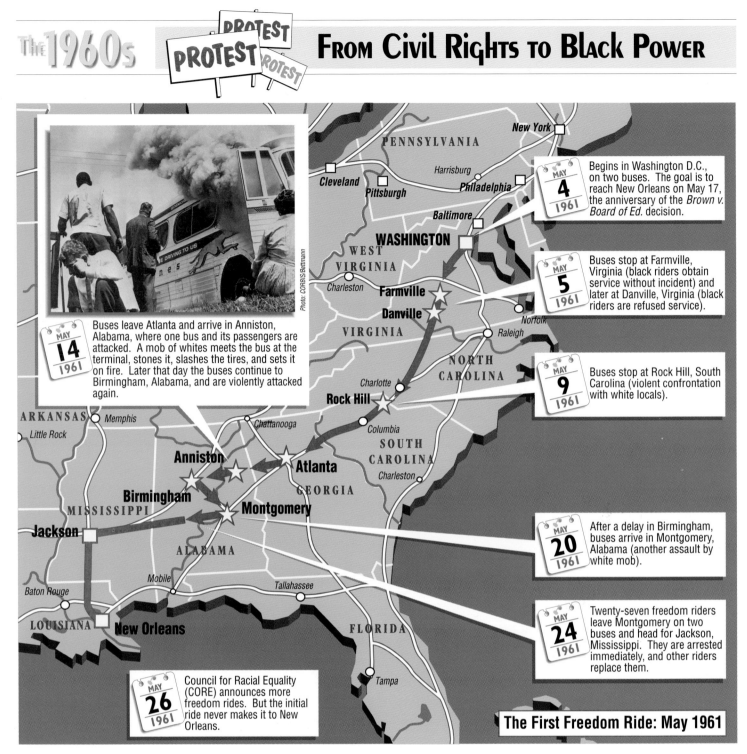

Photo: CORBIS/Bettmann

MAY 14 1961 Buses leave Atlanta and arrive in Anniston, Alabama, where one bus and its passengers are attacked. A mob of whites meets the bus at the terminal, stones it, slashes the tires, and sets it on fire. Later that day the buses continue to Birmingham, Alabama, and are violently attacked again.

MAY 4 1961 Begins in Washington D.C., on two buses. The goal is to reach New Orleans on May 17, the anniversary of the *Brown v. Board of Ed.* decision.

MAY 5 1961 Buses stop at Farmville, Virginia (black riders obtain service without incident) and later at Danville, Virginia (black riders are refused service).

MAY 9 1961 Buses stop at Rock Hill, South Carolina (violent confrontation with white locals).

MAY 20 1961 After a delay in Birmingham, buses arrive in Montgomery, Alabama (another assault by white mob).

MAY 24 1961 Twenty-seven freedom riders leave Montgomery on two buses and head for Jackson, Mississippi. They are arrested immediately, and other riders replace them.

MAY 26 1961 Council for Racial Equality (CORE) announces more freedom rides. But the initial ride never makes it to New Orleans.

The First Freedom Ride: May 1961

▲ This map shows the points of major conflict along the route of the first Freedom Ride buses, in May 1961.

The black waitress looked at the four young African-American college students, and said: "Fellows like you make our race look bad." By sitting at the F. W. Woolworth lunch counter in Greensboro, North Carolina, on February 1, 1960, the students challenged segregation law that forbade blacks from eating with whites. The effect of their action went well beyond Greensboro and ignited a new era in the civil rights movement, one that dominated the '60s: public protest that turned radical.

The four students intended to occupy seats at the Woolworth lunch counter every day until they were served. Other protesters had earlier used such a tactic, called a sit-in, but perhaps because of the nation's exploding youth population and its impatience with the status quo, this one had a greater effect. Within days, the number of protesters at Woolworths and a nearby S. S. Kresge store reached into the

hundreds. Over the following weeks, sit-ins erupted in 31 southern cities in eight states. Despite some gains, most of the South rejected desegregation.

Angered by resistance to change, and worried that President John Kennedy would fail to pursue civil rights reform, James Farmer, national director of the Congress of Racial Equality (CORE), decided to have his organization's white and black members stage a Freedom Ride that would challenge the South's segregated interstate bus system. On May 4, 1961, 13 protesters left Washington, D.C., some on a Trailways bus, others on a Greyhound, to travel through the Deep South and, along the way, use "white only" facilities at bus terminals.

The Freedom Riders encountered their first large-scale violence on May 14 in Anniston, Alabama, where whites attacked them with fists, chains, and iron bars . . . while the

police watched. Then, as the Greyhound sped out of town, the attackers pursued it in 50 cars, pulled it over, and fire-bombed it. With smoke billowing from the bus windows, the Freedom Riders fled the vehicle, only to be beaten again. More assaults occurred later that day at Birmingham, Alabama, where chief of police Bull Connor told the Ku Klux Klan it could have time with the protesters.

When, after the violence, it appeared that the Freedom Ride would end, the Student Nonviolent Coordinating Committee (SNCC), formed by college students who participated in or supported the Greensboro protest, sent volunteers to board the buses. On May 20, the protesters continued their ride to Montgomery after Alabama's Governor John Patterson assured Attorney General Robert Kennedy that "the state of Alabama had the will, the force, the men, and the equipment to give full protection to everyone in Alabama." But Patterson, a committed segregationist who hated the Freedom Riders, failed to keep his promises, and thugs attacked the Freedom Riders in Montgomery.

Robert Kennedy sent federal marshals to accompany the buses, but when the Freedom Riders reached Jackson, Mississippi, the police threw them in jail. Kennedy subsequently convinced the Interstate Commerce Commission to quickly enforce an earlier Supreme Court ruling making segregated inter-state bus systems illegal.

> 66 *We can not be satisfied as long as a Negro in Mississippi can not vote, and a Negro in New York believes he has nothing for which to vote.* 99
> —**Martin Luther King, Jr.**, *at the 1963 March on Washington*

The Freedom Rides were only one tactic in the escalating fight for civil rights. In April 1963, Martin Luther King, Jr., led marches in Birmingham to protest segregation there. Bull Connor arrested King, and on April 16 the civil rights leader wrote his "Letter from a Birmingham Jail," in which he argued breaking the law was justified when the law itself degraded human dignity. The Birmingham protest led businessmen in that city to begin desegregating and hiring blacks for clerical and sales jobs.

Later in 1963, at a massive March on Washington to pressure President Kennedy and Congress into enacting a civil rights bill, more than 250,000 people participated and heard King tell of his dream to one day be able to proclaim: "Free at last! Free at last! Thank God almighty we are free at last!" But Kennedy demonstrated the limits to his liberalism when he assigned an aide to pull the plug on the public address system should any speechmaker turn too radical. And although the march generated extensive press coverage, a civil rights bill remained stalled in Congress. Perhaps most telling, and certainly most horrifying, just 18 days after the march four African-American girls were killed when a church in Birmingham, Alabama, was dynamited.

In 1964, SNCC took the lead in launching Freedom Summer, a drive to register black voters in Mississippi, where laws and fear had kept them from casting ballots. Whites retaliated with violence and, near the town of Philadelphia, killed three student volunteers. The horrible murders, abetted by local law enforcement, revealed the length to which the white establishment would go to protect its power.

An Unequal Burden

One troubling aspect of the school desegregation story is often overlooked: when school boards carried out integration, they usually did so by transferring blacks to white schools and shutting down the black schools. With that, African Americans lost part of their tradition and heritage. In Gainesville, Florida, blacks complained in 1969 about phasing out all-black Lincoln High School. Black leader Charles Chestnut III asked: "Why not zone some whites [to] Lincoln and leave it as it is?" Historian David Ashwell has found that blacks considered the closing of Lincoln as the end of their central cultural institution.

To many young urban blacks, voting campaigns moved too slowly and too condescendingly. As a result, in October 1966, Huey Newton and Bobby Seale formed the Black Panther Party for Self-Defense in Oakland, California. Newton insisted that the Panthers would create a "democratic socialist society free of racism." Their 10-point program demanded an end to police brutality and the release of all blacks in jail . . . victims, they said, of racist persecution. By 1970, the Panthers had 30 chapters and several thousand members. Among whites they gained notoriety for parading militia-style, shouting "Power to the people!" and riding in cars on armed patrol to confront any police who engaged in brutality. Black Panther action merged with Black Power, a term that meant African Americans should define their goals, lead their own organizations, and reject white racism.

To most whites, the Black Panthers and Black Power spelled trouble. Blacks with guns, guts, and revolutionary spirit equaled blacks who would no longer accept the granting of rights at the pace whites and black moderates wanted them granted. The line between the races hardened while many African Americans agreed with what novelist James Baldwin had written early in the decade: "To be a Negro in this country and to be relatively conscious is to be in a rage all the time."

▽ Protesters arrive at the Lincoln Memorial in Washington, D.C., as part of the historic March on Washington on August 28, 1963. (UPI/CORBIS-BETTMANN)

Helmeted Chicago police raised their billy clubs into the night air, smashing them across skulls and pushing them deep into abdomens. Protesters cried out in anguish and pain, as did bystanders, while the blue phalanx snarled, surged, and struck indiscriminately. Television cameras caught the chaos outside the 1968 Democratic National Convention, and middle-class America watched in shock and disgust, condemning not the police, but the protesters—the hippie activists who represented yet another disruption, another assault planting odious ideas inside young skulls, ideas that proclaimed American society sick, cruel, or unjust. More protests erupted in the 1960s than in any other decade in the 20th century, and the New Left and the antiwar movement epitomized this turmoil.

> 66 *The confrontation was not created by the police. The confrontation was created by the people who charged the police. Gentlemen, get the thing straight, once and for all: the policeman isn't there to create* disorder, *the policeman is there to preserve* disorder. 99
>
> —**Mayor Richard Daley**, *on the 1968 Democratic National Convention*

"We have spoken at last with vigor, idealism, and urgency, supporting our words with picket lines, demonstrations, money, and even our own bodies. . . . Pessimism and cynicism have given way to direct action," proclaimed radical leader Al Haber in 1960 as the New Left emerged. At first no one could precisely define New Left. Generally speaking, it was an effort born on college campuses to restore community and uplift individuals. Unlike the Old Left, which had matured during the Great Depression of the 1930s, the New Left at first rejected ideological debates about capitalism and communism—in fact, rejected all ideology and operated on gut feeling. However, the New Left changed over the course of the 1960s, as increasingly radicalized and highly ideological groups such as Weatherman rejected all middle-class values, and embraced Marxism and Maoism.

The rise of the New Left can be explained in part by the sheer number of young people expressing youthful discontent. More important, it grew from the glaring contradictions between prevailing democratic ideals on the one hand, and existing racial segregation and corporate power on the other; from discontent with a technocracy that said only "experts" knew what was best for America, and from a cold war that, rather than making the world safe for democracy, instead raised fears of nuclear annihilation.

When Students for a Democratic Society (SDS) emerged as the leading New Left organization, it did so around the slogan "One man, one soul," which proclaimed individuals to be more important than any doctrine. Al Haber formed SDS at the University of Michigan in 1960, and it attracted young activists, among them Tom Hayden, editor of the campus newspaper. In 1962, Hayden drafted a manifesto, and 43 SDSers (along with several other leftists) debated it at the Port Huron Conference in June of that year. The document they approved, titled "the Port Huron Statement," opened by announcing: "We are people of this generation, bred in at least modest comfort, housed now in universities, looking uncomfortably to the world we inherit." Few outside the SDS leadership read the cumbersome document, but the SDS itself activated dissidents on college campuses, those disgusted with racism, poverty, undemocratic rule, and the Vietnam War.

In 1964, the SDS launched its Economic Research and Action Project, through which its members worked in ghettos to help the poor, particularly to politicize them and show them how to lobby local governments and landlords. SDS membership lagged, however, until the group associated itself with antiwar protests. In 1965, the SDS sponsored a march on Washington that attracted 25,000 protesters. In its wake, the SDS grew to over 100 chapters with about 4,000 members. John Stennis, a conservative senator from Mississippi, warned that the government had better "jerk this movement up by the roots and grind it to bits before it had the opportunity to spread further."

But spread it did, rising to 30,000 members after sponsoring a massive draft card burning in New York City on April 15, 1967. The following year, an SDS chapter led a protest at Columbia University in which 1,000 students occupied five buildings to condemn racist, militaristic, and oppressive college policies. The protest ended in bloodshed when police forcibly cleared the buildings.

While the SDS grew, leaders within the organization worried that its emphasis on the war might make it a one-issue group. At the same time, the autonomy given its chapters produced factional fights. In 1968, Bernardine Dohrn won election as SDS interorganizational national secretary and proclaimed herself a "revolutionary communist." Many within the SDS considered her too radical, and with the organization's membership at a peak—well over 100,000—infighting caused the SDS to quickly unravel. In 1969, one faction formed Weatherman (later called Weather Underground) and, under Dohrn's leadership, dedicated itself to advancing communism through violent revolution. By 1970, the SDS had disintegrated into little more than a skeletal group.

The greater antiwar movement and the SDS often worked together. No one ever controlled the movement, however, and along with SDS and even-more-radical groups such as Third World Marxists, who advocated street fighting to topple the U.S. government, it included such liberal groups as Women's Strike for Peace, Americans for Democratic Action, and Catholic Worker. While liberals in the movement called for a cease-fire in Vietnam and a negotiated settlement, radicals demanded "Out Now!"

▼ A protester vents his anger at the advancing National Guard troops, who have come to clear out Grant Park, outside the 1968 Democratic National Convention in Chicago. (UPI/CORBIS-BETTMANN)

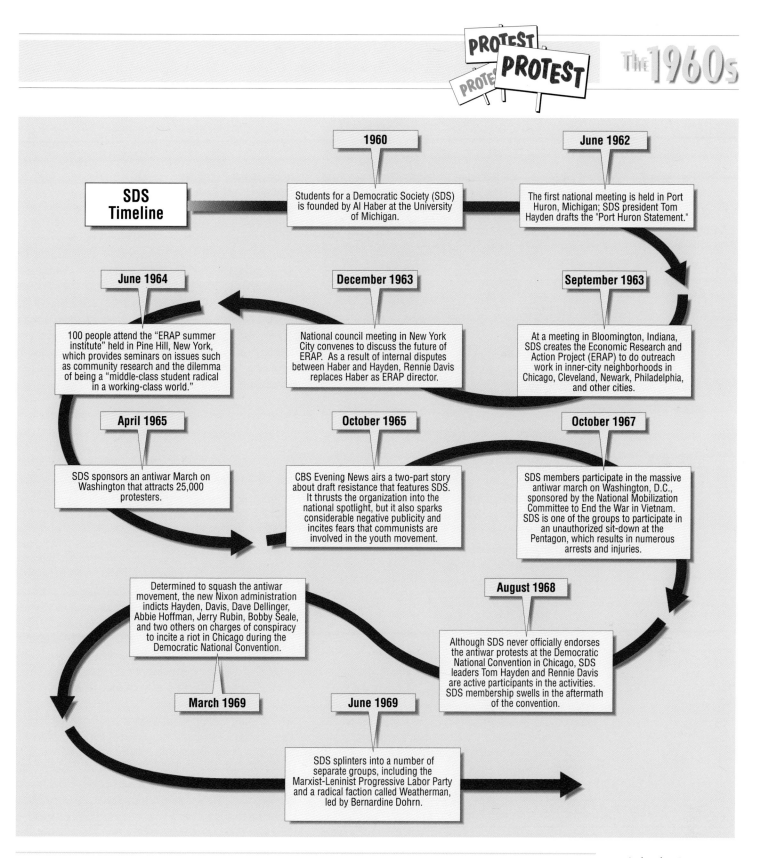

SDS Timeline

1960
Students for a Democratic Society (SDS) is founded by Al Haber at the University of Michigan.

June 1962
The first national meeting is held in Port Huron, Michigan; SDS president Tom Hayden drafts the "Port Huron Statement."

June 1964
100 people attend the "ERAP summer institute" held in Pine Hill, New York, which provides seminars on issues such as community research and the dilemma of being a "middle-class student radical in a working-class world."

December 1963
National council meeting in New York City convenes to discuss the future of ERAP. As a result of internal disputes between Haber and Hayden, Rennie Davis replaces Haber as ERAP director.

September 1963
At a meeting in Bloomington, Indiana, SDS creates the Economic Research and Action Project (ERAP) to do outreach work in inner-city neighborhoods in Chicago, Cleveland, Newark, Philadelphia, and other cities.

April 1965
SDS sponsors an antiwar March on Washington that attracts 25,000 protesters.

October 1965
CBS Evening News airs a two-part story about draft resistance that features SDS. It thrusts the organization into the national spotlight, but it also sparks considerable negative publicity and incites fears that communists are involved in the youth movement.

October 1967
SDS members participate in the massive antiwar march on Washington, D.C., sponsored by the National Mobilization Committee to End the War in Vietnam. SDS is one of the groups to participate in an unauthorized sit-down at the Pentagon, which results in numerous arrests and injuries.

Determined to squash the antiwar movement, the new Nixon administration indicts Hayden, Davis, Dave Dellinger, Abbie Hoffman, Jerry Rubin, Bobby Seale, and two others on charges of conspiracy to incite a riot in Chicago during the Democratic National Convention.

August 1968
Although SDS never officially endorses the antiwar protests at the Democratic National Convention in Chicago, SDS leaders Tom Hayden and Rennie Davis are active participants in the activities. SDS membership swells in the aftermath of the convention.

March 1969

June 1969
SDS splinters into a number of separate groups, including the Marxist-Leninist Progressive Labor Party and a radical faction called Weatherman, led by Bernardine Dohrn.

A march on the Pentagon in October 1967 attracted more than 100,000 largely peaceful protesters. Organized by the National Mobilization Committee to End the War in Vietnam, nicknamed MOBE, the protest included writers and political ideologues, as well as people dressed as witches and others wearing black-magic garb, who surrounded the Pentagon and attempted to levitate the building and expel its evil spirits. The next summer, protest erupted at the Democratic National Convention in Chicago and again included a diverse collection of people, from antiwar hardliners to Yippies, who mixed opposition to the war with cultural revolution, demanding (among other things) the legalization of psychedelics and the abolishment of money.

The antiwar movement received its greatest support on October 16, 1969, when millions of people from all walks of life wore black armbands, held vigils, and marched through streets as part of "Moratorium." One public opinion survey found people agreeing in overwhelming numbers with the statement "I am fed up and tired of the war." President Richard Nixon had already begun withdrawing American troops from Vietnam . . . now the pressure to quicken the pace and steady the resolve intensified.

▲ Students for a Democratic Society (SDS) was not originally an antiwar organization, but as the conflict in Vietnam expanded, resistance expanded as well, and SDS was right in the middle of the storm. This time line highlights a few of the major events in the life of SDS, a seminal group that characterized many of the best and worst aspects of 1960s activism.

▲ Members of the National Organization for Women picket the White House on May 7, 1969, demanding equal rights for women. (UPI/CORBIS-BETTMANN)

These conditions stimulated the women's movement. So, too, did a book written by Betty Friedan in 1963, *The Feminine Mystique*, in which she criticized society's conformist demand that women stay at home and tend to domestic chores. Such a restriction, she argued, was frustrating and oppressive. Through example, civil rights and anti-war protesters also encouraged women to act.

Like so many other protests in the 1960s, the women's movement displayed a split between moderates and radicals. The moderates, often called feminists and represented most prominently by the National Organization for Women (NOW), sought equal rights and wanted to integrate women into mainstream society. The radicals, often called liberationists and represented most prominently by the group Redstockings, condemned men and wanted a revolutionary movement, peaceful or otherwise. Liberationist Robin Morgan said: "We women must seize control over our own lives and try . . . to salvage the planet from the ecological disaster and nuclear threat by male-oriented power nations."

A circular issued by a protest group in August 1968 and titled "No More Miss America" proclaimed:

There will be Picket Lines; Guerrilla Theater; Leafleting; Lobbying Visits to the contestants urging our sisters to reject the Pageant Farce and join us; a huge Freedom Trash Can (into which we will throw bras, girdles, curlers, false eyelashes, wigs . . .); we will announce a Boycott of all those commercial products related to the Pageant, and the day will end with a Women's Liberation rally at midnight when Miss America is crowned on live television.

Liberationists considered the family structure to be oppressive, chaining women to men. They wanted to destroy patriarchy and capitalism, which they argued exploited women as part of a male supremacist system. "Sexism has no chance of being eliminated under capitalism," claimed Marilyn Salzman Webb in 1970. "Should some of us think that we have 'made it,' whatever that means, the rest of us will still be used to supply cheap, free, and reserve labor, to consume, to scab on each other."

> ❝ If assertiveness . . . is a virtue in a man, it is a virtue in a woman; if forbearance is a virtue in a woman, it is likewise a virtue in a man. ❞
> —*Lilith's Manifesto*, 1970

Liberationists insisted women must gain control over their own bodies, such as in determining whether to have children. Ironically, many saw the sexual revolution as anything but liberating; to them, free love was another form of oppression. Robin Morgan insisted: "The invention of the Pill made millions for the drug companies, made guinea pigs of us, and made us all the more 'available' as sexual objects." Believing that the mainstream feminist movement was limited by its white, upper-middle-class roots, and that the fight against oppression required unity, the radicals sought to bring together women different in racial, class, and ethnic background. They even organized in secondary schools—the New York High School Students' Union formed a women's collective, and one young female said: "Now, with awakened eyes, I could see all the brainwashing of my sisters that goes on at school."

More than 100 women gathered along the famed boardwalk at Atlantic City, New Jersey, to demonstrate against the Miss America pageant for treating women as sex objects. They shouted "Liberation Now!" and thus provided a phrase that soon entered the popular mind: "women's liberation."

The women's movement emerged at a time of massive gender discrimination. In the 1950s few women held professional jobs, such as lawyers, doctors, and college professors; few earned anywhere near what men earned; and many suffered from state laws that treated them as second-class citizens, prohibiting them, for example, from starting a business, or from obtaining a loan without a man's cosignature.

Black women experienced double oppression, based on their race and sex. Radical Frances M. Beal, writing in 1969, said black women had been "sexually assaulted by the white colonizer," and forced into economic subservience as the white woman's maid. Such radicals claimed that black women had been ignored by mainstream feminism—and even liberationists—and had little in common with moderates such as NOW. They claimed their exploitation came not just from male chauvinism—which the moderates protested—but also from racism embedded in capitalism. Beal

Birth Control

Q: In some places in the United States it is not legal to supply birth control information. How do you feel about this—do you think birth control information should be available to anyone who wants it, or not?

Interview date: December 3 through 8, 1959		Interview date: May 2 through 7, 1963		Interview date: November 20 through 25, 1964	
Should be available:	72%	Should be available:	74%	Should be available:	81%
Should not be available:	14%	Should not be available:	17%	Should not be available:	11%
No opinion:	14%	No opinion:	9%	No opinion:	8%

insisted: "If the white groups do not realize they are in fact fighting capitalism and racism, we do not have common bonds." It was felt that liberation for black women would require a revolutionary overthrow of the economic system.

As the 1960s came to an end, women, radical and otherwise, confronted men in several high profile actions. They staged a sit-in at the offices of the *Ladies' Home Journal* to demand a free day-care center and an end to sexist

---

Abortion

Q: As you may have heard or read, an Arizona woman recently had a legal abortion in Sweden after having taken the drug thalidomide, which has been linked to birth defects. Do you think this woman did the right thing or the wrong thing in having this abortion operation?

Interview date: August 23 through 28, 1962

Right:	52%
Wrong:	32%
No opinion:	16%

Q: Do you think abortion operations should or should not be legal in the following cases:

Interview date: December 11 through 16, 1965

A. Where the health of the mother is in danger?

Should be legal:	77%
Should not be legal:	16%
Don't know:	7%

B. Where the child may be born deformed?

Should be legal:	54%
Should not:	32%
Don't know:	14%

C. Where the family does not have enough money to support another child?

Should be legal:	18%
Should not:	72%
Don't know:	10%

Q: Would you favor or oppose a law that would permit a woman to go to a doctor to end pregnancy at any time during the first three months?

Interview Date: November 12 through 17, 1969

Favor:	40%
Oppose:	50%
No opinion:	10%

By Sex

Women		Men	
Favor:	40%	Favor:	40%
Oppose:	53%	Oppose:	46%
No opinion:	7%	No opinion:	14%

By Religion

Protestants		Catholics	
Favor:	40%	Favor:	30%
Oppose:	50%	Oppose:	58%
No opinion:	10%	No opinion:	11%

By Education:

College		High School		Grade School	
Favor:	58%	Favor	37%	Favor	31%
Oppose:	34%	Oppose:	53%	Oppose:	57%
No opinion:	8%	No opinion:	10%	No opinion:	12%

By Age

21-29 Years		30-49 Years		50 Years and Over	
Favor:	46%	Favor:	39%	Favor:	38%
Oppose:	50%	Oppose:	50%	Oppose:	50%
No opinion:	4%	No opinion:	11%	No opinion:	12%

Appearance

Q: Do you approve or disapprove of women wearing slacks in public?

Interview date: October 19 through 24, 1961

Approve:	
Disapprove:	67%
No opinion:	26%
	7%

Q: Do you approve or disapprove of women wearing shorts in public?

Interview date: February 10 through 15, 1966

Approve:	
Disapprove:	27%
No opinion:	66%
	7%

Q: Which do you consider to be in "bad taste"?

Interview date: February 10 through 15, 1966

	Men	Women
Wearing stretch pants in public	40%	48%
Women smoking while driving or walking	45%	57%
Women wearing shorts in public	53%	67%

Although the women's liberation movement was associated with "radicals" in its early years, in reality many women's issues were very much on the minds of the general public. The Gallup poll results shown here offer a window into mainstream opinions on some typical "women's issues."

---

advertisements. They demonstrated against radio station WBCN in Boston for running a help wanted ad that carried the statement, "If you're a chick, we need typists." On August 26, 1970, NOW sponsored a nationwide Women's Strike for Equality that aimed to build support in Congress for an equal rights amendment (ERA) to the Constitution, spotlight discriminatory practices against women in the workplace, and promote equal educational opportunities, day-care centers, and abortion rights. Thousands marched in Boston, San Francisco, Los Angeles, Washington, and Chicago. The largest demonstration occurred in New York City—40,000 marchers. The protest prompted Congress to begin considering the ERA, and it caused businesses and governments to start reforming their discriminatory policies. NOW and other groups representing women felt energized, and they carried their protests onward, through the 1970s. Said women's leader Kate Millett of August 26: "Today is the beginning of a new movement."

Stonewall

At the close of the '60s, the trend toward protests against sexual discrimination expanded to include gays and lesbians. On June 27, 1969, during a routine raid on the Stonewall Inn, a gay bar in New York City's Greenwich Village, police encountered unexpected defiance. After a woman dressed in men's clothes struggled to resist arrest, other patrons assailed the police with bottles, and a melee resulted in injuries to four officers.

The police returned to the neighborhood the following night and made additional raids, but a crowd of 400 young men and women hurled bottles at them and chanted "Gay Power!" The newspaper *The Village Voice* called the event "a kind of liberation, as the gay brigade emerged from the bars, back rooms, and bedrooms of the Village."

After Stonewall, gays formed the Gay Liberation Front, and in 1970 organized the first Gay Pride Week. Reflecting on the early days of the Gay Rights movement, author Edmund White says, "'Gay is good' sounded preposterous, even to our own ears. But the more we said it, the more we began to believe it."

As the 1960s dawned, television had settled into a comfortable groove. Viewers were tuning in regularly, networks were making money, and sponsors were churning out products to meet consumer demands. Why fix something that wasn't broken? In the spring of 1961, however, the status quo got a jolt when, in a speech to the National Association of Broadcasters, Chairman Newton Minow of the Federal Communications Commission (FCC) described TV as a "vast wasteland." That remark launched a crusade for TV reform and has been the rallying cry of critics ever since.

Improving educational programming, especially children's TV, became a subject of debate. Advancing public television was also on the activist agenda. The U.S. Senate convened a Senate Subcommittee to Investigate Juvenile Delinquency that examined whether TV violence had been a factor in the recent rise in youth crime. Educators, politicians, parents, and even some TV executives moved to "improve" TV, insisting that, with adjustments, it could be a positive force for education. *Sesame Street* (1969–present) was born from this movement and after 30 years it continues to set the standard for educational TV.

Joan Ganz Cooney, a New York public-TV producer, developed the show based on in-depth research about the ways kids learn. Combining that knowledge with information about why TV appeals to kids, she created a fast-moving, funny show with inner-city sensibilities. Memorable characters—Big Bird, Kermit the Frog, Cookie Monster, and their diverse group of human friends—used advertising techniques (*"Today's show is brought to you by the letter 'T'"*) to sell education. Catchy tunes, repetition, short segments, and visually appealing colors drew the audience in. What kept them coming to *Sesame Street* is not entirely clear. Despite few changes in format and what some critics have called its excessive political correctness, *Sesame Street* has remained a perennial favorite, and, while it may or may not have proved its educational value, its staying power—even in the competitive children's TV market of the '90s—showed that if viewers are given a choice, quality can prevail.

Quality TV might have been the rallying cry when it came to America's youth, but generally Americans have rejected the idea that TV should be edifying. Advertisers were satisfied to sponsor shows that raised no serious issues, offended no one, and nurtured mindless acceptance of the world according to TV. Nothing confirmed that more than the "hayseed comedies" that flooded the prime-time schedule in the early '60s. Leading the pack was the *Beverly Hillbillies* (1962–71), a comedy for the common man about uneducated, unsophisticated bumpkins that poked fun at highfalutin city folk. Not surprisingly, the *Beverly Hillbillies* was vilified by the educated elite, many of them city folk

> **"** When television is good—not the theater, not the magazines, or newspapers—nothing is better. But when television is bad, nothing is worse. I invite you to sit down in front of your television set when your station goes on the air and stay there without a book, magazine, or newspaper, profit-and-loss sheet or rating book to distract you, and keep your eyes glued to that set, until the station signs off. I can assure you that you will observe a vast wasteland. **"**
>
> —**Newton Minow**, *FCC Chairman, May 9, 1961*

themselves, and quickly became synonymous with bad TV. But the program with its catchy theme song, "The Ballad of Jed Clampett," hit number one within three weeks of its first broadcast and lasted 10 seasons. Along with *Gomer Pyle, U.S.M.C.* (1964–70), *Petticoat Junction* (1963–70), and *Green Acres* (1965–71), the *Beverly Hillbillies* presented an image of simple folk leading silly but uncomplicated lives that stood in stark contrast to the uncomfortable realities of the 1960s.

As a cultural phenomenon, these shows have been the subject of much analysis. Many have dismissed the genre as "idiot TV" produced to appeal to the lowest levels of American intelligence. Others have argued that by promoting traditional values, these programs were an antidote to the acute insecurity induced by the Kennedy assassination, the war in Vietnam, and the rising unrest at home. But when Paul Henning, creator of the *Beverly Hillbillies* and *Green Acres*, was asked why he thought his shows were so popular he answered, "My shows are pure fun, just escape."

TV in the 1960s certainly was fun. Besides the backwoods comedies depicting rural America, cold war politics inspired TV spy shows. *The Man from U.N.C.L.E.* (1964–68) was a small screen version of the ever-suave James Bond, while *Get Smart* (1965–70), a satire developed by Mel Brooks and Buck Henry, became a TV classic spoofing the espionage genre. Reflecting real-world interest in outer space, the western frontier was replaced by "the final frontier." For three seasons in the late 1960s, *Star Trek* (1966–69) followed the adventures of Captain Kirk, Mr. Spock, and the crew of the starship U.S.S. *Enterprise*. In their exploration of worlds unknown, *Star Trek's* crew reflected contemporary social issues. In its original run, *Star Trek* was consistently on the low end of the ratings scale. It was only the persistence of "trekkies" that built the cult following that revived the show and made it one of the most successful TV franchises ever.

Silly shows like *Gilligan's Island* (1964–67) and *My Favorite Martian* (1963–1966) moved television comedy away from the suburban family programs like *The Donna Reed Show* (1958–66). In *My Favorite Martian*, reporter Tim O'Hara befriends a Martian after discovering his downed spacecraft. Uncle Martin, as the Martian becomes known, will reveal his identity and otherworldly powers only to Tim, leading to all sorts of complications. Like the *Beverly Hillbillies*, this show popularized a "fish out of water" sitcom ploy, taking characters from their usual settings and plopping them down in a whole new environment. *Gilligan's Island*, despite its total implausibility, also stretched the limits of conventional sit-coms by putting unrelated people of different backgrounds in a situation where they were forced to interact. Where else in America but on TV would the wealthy Mr. and Mrs. Thurston Howell III rub elbows with the likes of

Gilligan? Hardly biting social criticism, but the program did show that *Ozzie and Harriet* (1952–66) weren't the only people in the world. Overall, '60s TV introduced a string of odd and often memorable characters in shows like *F-Troop* (1965–67), *The Flying Nun* (1967–70), *The Munsters* (1964–66), and *The Addams Family* (1964–66).

As the decade progressed, this escapist fare seemed increasingly out of sync with the times. Eventually, even the behemoth that was television programming was touched by countercultural ideas, airing programs that would have been unthinkable just a few years earlier. For example, *I Spy* (1965–68), not a typical espionage show, starred black comedian Bill Cosby in a dramatic role—until then, blacks had been seen only in subservient roles or not at all. In 1968, Diahann Carroll was cast in the title role of *Julia* (1968–71), making her the first black woman to star in a TV show. Also in 1968, the comedy variety show, *Rowan and Martin's Laugh-in* (1968–73) brought the fast pace of the restless youth culture into American living rooms. And the politically inspired humor of *The Smothers Brothers Comedy Hour* (1967-69) caused numerous much-publicized run-ins with network TV censors.

TV also made its presence felt on the political scene, beginning with the Nixon–Kennedy presidential debates, and earned a central role in every subsequent major election. It is widely accepted that Kennedy's victory in the 1960 presidential election was influenced by public reaction to the debates. The factor that seemed to tip the scales in Kennedy's favor was not what he said but how he looked on TV. Richard Nixon, with his stilted delivery and five-o'clock shadow, appeared awkward, almost sinister in comparison to the handsome and genial senator from Massachusetts. The rise of TV as a political tool meant that building political careers would no longer rely as heavily on ideas and achievements.

The rise of TV news and live coverage of news stories brought TV audiences face-to-face with disturbing realities: assassinations, dramatic reports from Vietnam, and late-decade war protests and urban riots. The interaction of television and current events lent a newfound seriousness to TV journalism. We were no longer isolated by geography. The experience of sharing key events—the Kennedy assassination, the riots at the 1968 Democratic National Convention, and the moon landing—transformed our national self-image. The powerful TV images seen in the '60s both unified and divided us.

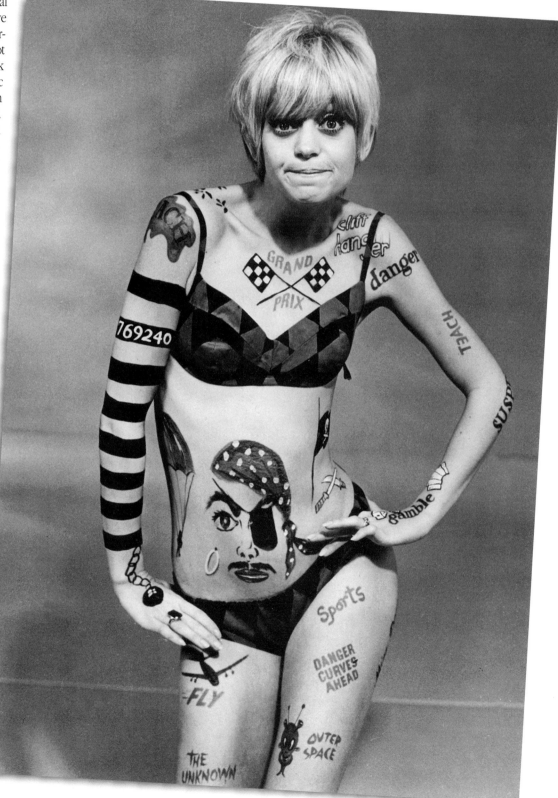

▼ A perky Goldie Hawn exhorted viewers to "sock it to me" along with the rest of the cast of Rowan and Martin's Laugh-in. You bet your bippy. (UPI/CORBIS-BETTMANN)

President Lyndon Johnson once described the country of Vietnam as insignificant. In fact the Vietnam War turned out to be anything but: nearly 60,000 Americans and more than one million Vietnamese were killed; the land of Vietnam was ravaged by defoliants, napalm, and carpet bombing; the entirety of Southeast Asia was destabilized; and American society was torn asunder. But early in the war, few in the United States felt anything less than confidence; few suspected the war—at first portrayed by politicians as a limited "police action"—would drag on with such devastating effect. Even Baby Boomers believed in their country's infallibility—believed, at first, that America should be in Vietnam to contain communism.

> ❝ No event in American history is more misunderstood than the Vietnam War. It was misreported then, and it is misremembered now. Rarely have so many people been so wrong about so much. Never have the consequences of their misunderstanding been so tragic. ❞
>
> —Richard Nixon

America's involvement in Vietnam began in the late 1940s, when President Harry Truman supported the French, who were then fighting the Viet Minh led by Ho Chi Minh. Ho, a communist and a nationalist, wanted to prevent the French from reclaiming his country, which they had ruled for decades prior to World War II. Truman sent arms and ammunition to the French, but, in 1954, the Viet Minh defeated the French army at Dien Bien Phu.

France then decided to withdraw. Under terms of the Geneva Accords, Ho controlled North Vietnam as an administrative unit, while another government ruled in the south. Elections were to be held in 1956 to determine the ruler for all of Vietnam. With the ink on the Accords still wet, President Dwight Eisenhower sent weapons to South Vietnam—in direct violation of the provision prohibiting such assistance. He later sent military advisors to the south and encouraged the ruler there, Ngo Dinh Diem, to sabotage plans for the 1956 election, thus preventing a likely victory by Ho Chi Minh. Diem, who claimed he had no use for democracy, faced a severe threat when South Vietnamese rebels, the Viet Cong, rose up against his dictatorship.

In 1961, President John Kennedy insisted that the United States must use its power to stop communism in Vietnam. Many Baby Boomers, enamored with the charismatic Kennedy and immersed in an upbringing that told them America could do little wrong, supported him. Kennedy increased the number of American troops in Vietnam from 1,364 in 1961 to 16,000 in November 1963. That same month, the South Vietnamese army, ARVN, overthrew and killed Diem (with CIA approval).

After Kennedy's assassination later in November, Lyndon Johnson continued the slain president's foreign policy. A major turning point in the war occurred in 1964 with the Gulf of Tonkin Resolution. In August of 1964, Johnson claimed that American ships had been attacked in the Gulf of Tonkin, adjacent to North Vietnam, by the North Vietnamese navy. The assault, he said, occurred on two different nights. He asked Congress to provide him with a blank check to fight the war. With little debate, Congress agreed. Johnson failed to tell the American people, however, that doubt existed as to whether enemy ships had attacked on the second night; and that, in any event, the American ships had provoked North Vietnam by helping commandos infiltrate that region from the south.

Military commanders assured Johnson that air power could bring the communists to their knees. In February 1965, after Viet Cong troops killed several Americans at the U.S. air base at Pleiku, Johnson implemented a full-scale air campaign by launching regular raids, called Rolling Thunder, against the north. He was convinced that within three months the raids would stop the now substantial flow of arms and soldiers from North to South Vietnam and that he could avoid sending in large numbers of American troops.

But the communists kept their supply lines open, ARVN fought poorly, and by late summer of 1965 Johnson had deployed 125,000 American soldiers in South Vietnam. They soon took over the ground fighting, and a mournful procession of body bags into the United States began. As Johnson reached deeper into the draft pool and boosted American troop strength to about 500,000, many Baby Boomers marched off to war, while many others marched against it.

In 1968, Ho's army launched its Tet Offensive (at the time of the Tet religious holiday), in which it captured several South Vietnamese cities. The Americans beat back Ho's forces, but Tet showed that many more bombings and many more soldiers would be needed to even approach a victory in the war. As more Boomers joined antiwar protests and Democrats challenged Johnson in 1968 for his party's nomination, the president announced a peace initiative with North Vietnam and his decision not to seek reelection.

Johnson's successor, Richard Nixon, pursued "Vietnamization," which meant gradually withdrawing American troops and turning the fighting over to ARVN, while intensifying bombing raids over North Vietnam to force a favorable peace settlement. Peace talks between the Americans and North Vietnamese dragged on until January 1973, when an agreement enacted a cease-fire and allowed Nixon to withdraw the last American troops. Both the United States and North Vietnam subsequently violated the cease-fire. Finally, on

▼ *U.S. rescue helicopters land in Vietnam. (Archive Photos/London Daily Express)*

May 1, 1975, Saigon fell to the North Vietnamese army.

Nixon's policy from 1969 to 1973 prolonged Vietnam's, and America's, agony. In South Vietnam, all involved committed atrocities. In North Vietnam, Nixon launched bomb attacks that appalled people worldwide. During the 1972 Christmas bombing of Hanoi, American B-52 planes dropped 36,000 tons of explosives, more than the total dropped in the war from 1969 to 1971. (For the entire war, the United States dropped far more bombs on North Vietnam than it had dropped on Germany during World War II.) Nixon had told his Joint Chiefs of Staff: "I don't want any more of this crap about the fact that we can't hit this target or that one." The Americans targeted hospitals and civilian settlements in an attempt to shatter North Vietnam's morale.

Under Nixon, American troops limped home, demoralized. Before leaving Vietnam, fraggings—where enlisted men tried to kill their officers—had reached alarming levels; desertions had climbed; and by one estimate 40,000 of the 250,000 personnel still in Vietnam in 1971 had become heroin addicts. Nixon, however, claimed he had continued the fight to protect America's honor—its ability to stand by its commitment to contain communism.

▼ *This map gives an overview of some significant events of the Vietnam War.*

August 2, 1964 — North Vietnamese PT boats fire upon the U.S.S. *Maddox* in the **Gulf of Tonkin**. When a second attack allegedly occurs on August 4, President Johnson gains enough support to launch retaliatory attacks against North Vietnam. On August 7 U.S. Congress passes Gulf of Tonkin Resolution, allowing President Johnson to defend Southeast Asian by "all necessary measures." [1]

March 2, 1965 — U.S. begins Operation Rolling Thunder, a bombing offensive that lasts until November 1, 1968. By its conclusion, Operation Rolling Thunder has claimed 818 U.S. pilots, an estimated 182,000 North Vietnamese civilians, and some 20,000 Chinese support personnel.

January 8, 1966 — U.S. launches Operation Crimp, an enormous offensive that includes more than 8,000 troops; despite a massive search effort, U.S. troops fail to find Viet Cong headquarters.

March 9-11, 1966 — U.S. Special forces camp at **A Shau** decimated. [2]

September 14, 1966 — North of **Tay Ninh**, U.S. 196th Light Infantry Brigade spearheads Operation Attleboro, a search and destroy mission that lasts until November 26—resulting in the deaths of more than 150 Americans and 1,000 Viet Cong. [3]

June 8, 1969 — President Nixon orders the withdrawal of 25,000 troops at a meeting with South Vietnamese President Nguyen Van Thieu on **Midway Island**. [13]

May 10, 1969 — Battle for **Ap Bia Mountain**, later known as "Hamburger Hill," begins. By the time U.S. troops declare victory on May 20, the United States has suffered 460 casualties and 597 Vietnamese have been killed. [12]

March 18, 1969 — The secret bombings of Cambodia, also known as Operation Menu, begin under President Nixon's command.

February 22, 1969 — Communist forces launch full-scale assault on **South Vietnam**, striking many southern Vietnamese towns and killing 1,140 US soldiers. U.S. troops repel communists by March 15, 1969. [11]

April 24-May 5, 1967 — 160 U.S. troops are killed and 764 are wounded at the battle near North Vietnam's airfield, **Khe Sanh**; North Vietnam loses more than 940 troops. [4]

July 16-October 31, 1967 — An ambush near **Dac To**, in the Kontum Province, devastates company of 173rd U.S. Airborne Brigade, killing 80 and wounding 34, out of 130 troops. [5]

September 4-7, 1967 — Battle in **Que Son Valley** results in the deaths of 114 U.S. Marines. [6]

November 3-22, 1967 — 4,500 U.S. troops hold off 6,000 North Vietnamese troops in a battle near **Dac To**; 285 U.S. troops are killed and 985 are wounded, and 1,455 North Vietnamese troops are killed. [7]

January 21, 1968 — North Vietnamese begin shelling U.S. base at **Khe Sanh**. The battle continues until April 8, 1968, when U.S. forces recapture Route 9. [8]

March 16, 1968 — A platoon of U.S. troops led by Lieutenant William Calley kills more than 200 unarmed civilians in what comes to be known as the **My Lai Massacre**. [10]

January 30, 1968 — Viet Cong launch Tet Offensive, invading **Saigon** and over 100 other cities and towns. Although U.S. troops successfully defend Saigon, the temporary Viet Cong capture of the U.S. Embassy marks a turning point in U.S. morale. [9]

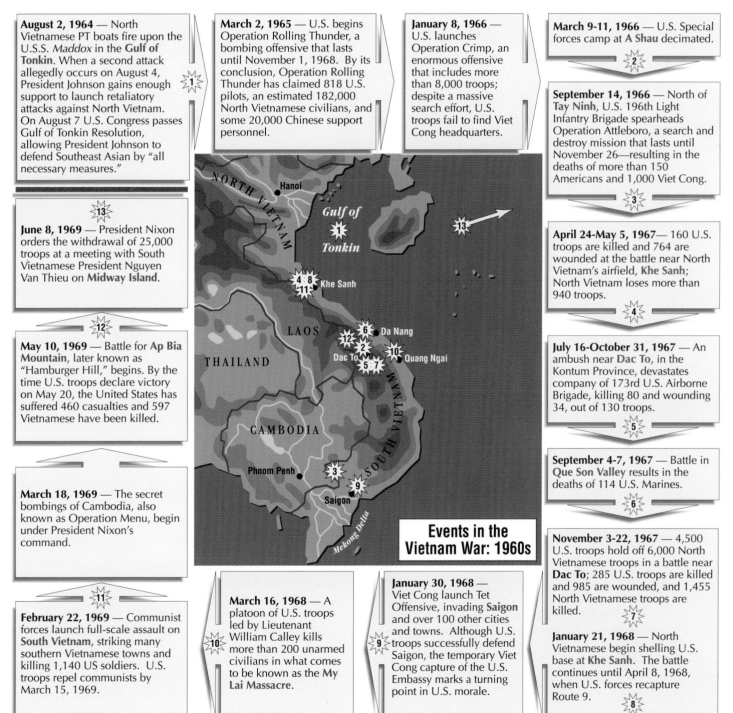

Events in the Vietnam War: 1960s

L ush greenery spread like a ribbon along the curving white beach. When the first American combat troops sent to Vietnam landed at Da Nang in March 1965 they brought with them tanks, bulldozers, and radar equipment. They dug foxholes. They feared the worst. They expected to be bombed. But young Vietnamese girls brought them garlands of flowers. If an attack occurs, said a general, "We'll just have to move out to the next ridge." For eight years American troops moved across the ridges. But Vietnam swallowed many of them whole.

On a strategic level, no one knew what to expect in Vietnam. The war offered few clear battlefields, little of what had been seen in World War II or in Korea. Villages would be cleared of enemy in the day, only to be surrendered at night. Guerrilla warfare—a part of the communist strategy— meant a civilian could never be viewed as simply a civilian— the next grenade could come from a child's hand, the next rifle buried in potted plants carried to markets on bicycles.

Youth defined the soldiers, at least before war made them old. Most came from the Baby Boom generation. Unlike in World War II and Korea where the average age was 27, in Vietnam it was 19—high school a recent memory. Most stayed in Vietnam for a year-long tour of duty. And for most, the year became a lifetime.

As to why they served, the reasons varied. Large numbers of combat soldiers were draftees, so they had no choice. Early in the war, many expressed optimism and idealism. "Some people wonder why Americans are in Vietnam," said Jack Swender in a letter home to Kansas. "I would rather fight to stop communism in South Vietnam than in . . . Kansas City."

Nurses in the military or in civilian groups often expressed humanitarian motives. "I couldn't get away from the feeling that there were guys over there like my brother," said Cherie Rankin, "guys who grew up with apple pie and country, guys who did what they were told . . . I didn't want to support the war, but I wanted to support those guys."

Nurses faced an increasing flow of soldiers wounded by weapons built to inflict multiple injuries. Among the injured were victims of friendly fire, for 15 to 20 percent of all casualties among the American troops came from accidental attacks by their own military. Commanders often relied too heavily on air and artillery strikes when American soldiers were entangled in combat and sometimes misdirected the fire.

In the early years, American forces fought well; they showed bravery in battle and usually inflicted more devastation on the enemy

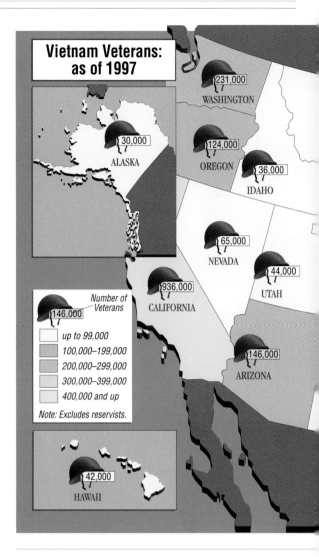

Vietnam Veterans: as of 1997

231,000 WASHINGTON
30,000 ALASKA
124,000 OREGON
36,000 IDAHO
65,000 NEVADA
44,000 UTAH
936,000 146,000 CALIFORNIA
146,000 ARIZONA
42,000 HAWAII

Number of Veterans
146,000

up to 99,000
100,000–199,000
200,000–299,000
300,000–399,000
400,000 and up

Note: Excludes reservists.

▼ The strain of battle shows on the faces of a commander and radio operator from the 101st Airborne Division, stationed in Vietnam. (Archive Photos)

than the enemy did on them. Even late in the war, one combatant proclaimed: "As far as being soldiers, we're proud of our outfit and its history." But camaraderie often proved hard to come by. After the war, a North Vietnamese soldier, Nguyen Hung, revealed a difference between the two sides: "For us, the army was like a family, because unlike American soldiers who came to Vietnam for one year and then got out, . . . we had to go on fighting . . . The only way we could live together for that long was to treat each other like brothers, so we became very close."

Racism reared its head, too. Until the late 1960s, African-American soldiers suffered fatalities out of proportion to their presence in the military. In 1965, blacks made up only 12.6 percent of the troops, but suffered 24 percent of American combat deaths. Back in the States, racism further robbed the dead. For example, residents of Wetumpka, Alabama, forbade PFC Jimmy Williams, a 19-year-old African American, from being buried in the white cemetery. His mother protested: "He was not fighting a second-class war, and did not die a second-class death."

American forces faced fierce combat, as in 1968 at Khe Sanh, where 6,000 Marines stubbornly held their base and outposts against 20,000 enemy. "I never thought incoming artillery sounded so terrible—it just screams out of the sky," said one soldier.

When the men and women who served in Vietnam returned home, many did so to a cool—sometimes even chilling—welcome. It would be years before the national scars left by the conflict would heal sufficiently for the vets to get their due. By the end of the 20th century, the sacrifices of these soldiers had finally come to be broadly recognized. This map shows a state-by-state population count of Vietnam veterans as of 1997.

Letters from the war expressed the agony: "For the last week we have been waiting for an attack, and last night it came in full force," wrote Allen Paul to his wife. "Honey, I was never so scared in my life . . . The noise from shooting is enough to drive a person crazy." "When I think about the hell I've been through the last few days, I can't help but cry and wonder how I am still alive," said Kenneth Peeples.

Some comments showed the dehumanizing side of combat. "I get all excited when I see VC, just like when I see a deer," said one soldier. "I go ape firing at him." Such attitudes contributed to the My Lai Massacre in 1968, when American troops set houses in the hamlet afire and shot civilians as they fled them. They gathered other civilians in a ditch—many women and children—and fired at them point blank.

Frustration took its toll in a war where territorial gains often meant little and strategy seemed senseless. Along a ridgeline bordering the A Shau Valley in May 1969 American troops battled for 11 days through jungle, taking intense fire from the enemy and suffering so many casualties—460—before capturing it, they named it "Hamburger Hill." They soon gave up the hill after commanders changed their minds and decided it had no military value.

By the late 1960s, disillusionment among soldiers resembled an Asian monsoon, dreary and unremitting: "This country is no gain that I can see, Dad," said Phillip Woodall in a

letter home. "We're fighting, dying, for a people who resent our being here." After the war Larry Gwin commented that "Any American soldier who went to Vietnam, didn't have to stay there long before he knew there was something wrong with our presence there."

Vietnam veterans had to wait a long time for national recognition of their sacrifices. Using private donations, the Vietnam Veterans Memorial was built on the mall in Washington, D.C., a stark double wall made from black granite; it was dedicated in 1983. Visitors placed flowers near it, on the lush green lawn. When they stared at the names of 58,132 war dead engraved in the wall, its shiny surface caught their reflection. They saw the names, and they saw themselves.

The Class-Bias Theory

In the years since the Vietnam War, sociologists have debated a class-bias thesis that says men from working-class and poor families were more likely to serve in Vietnam than those from professional class and wealthy families. In 1995, Thomas C. Wilson used new evidence to show that class bias did play a role in the war, although not nearly as much as some earlier analysts thought. He found that men of lower social class were more likely to serve than other men: "The Vietnam war was almost certainly not an equal opportunity war," he wrote. He went on to say, however, that "class-bias seems to have benefited only a relative few near the top of the American social hierarchy."

What a Long, Strange Trip

The rapid evolution of rock music could be observed in 1967, just by visiting your local record shop. That year, debut albums by The Doors and the Grateful Dead, *Are You Experienced?* by Jimi Hendrix, and *Sgt. Pepper's Lonely Hearts Club Band* by the Beatles all hit the shelves. Rock and roll had undergone serious changes since Carl Perkins' "Blue Suede Shoes."

A corner was turned in American music with the unexpected popularity of the Beatles in 1963. By '64 and '65, American pop charts were loaded with tunes by British bands, most notably the shaggy-but-clean-cut Beatles and the more bluesy, danger-tinged Rolling Stones. The "British Rock Invasion" of the early '60s irritated many Americans who weren't in high school, not least of all the musicians who had been riding the crest of America's folk music craze. Rock and roll was simply ugly and frivolous to many folkies, who made a point of distancing themselves from rock musicians.

The picture changed in 1965 when folk music's shining star, Bob Dylan, performed at the Newport Folk Festival with an electric band. Scuffles broke out, and folk legend Pete Seeger attempted to cut Dylan's power line with an ax. But subsequent albums demonstrated Dylan's firm commitment to electric music. And rock musicians were listening—the influence of Dylan's social criticism and surreal imagery began to be heard in new recordings.

The Beatles also showed increasing sophistication. By

▼ *The Grateful Dead had an eventful 1969, including involvement in two watershed events in '60s rock history: Woodstock and Altamont. They performed at Woodstock, but they canceled their scheduled Altamont performance due to "bad vibes." This map tracks their travels between the two festivals.*

"Tell Me, Who Are You?"

They came and went. A few even had hit singles. Diligent collectors continue to unearth their records, and occasionally their songs are covered by contemporary bands.

Ultimate Spinach	H.P. Lovecraft
The Chocolate Watchband	Free Design
The Godz	Rhinoceros
The Status Quo	Elephant's Memory
Insect Trust	Bubble Puppy
The Grass Roots	The Electric Prunes

1966, they sounded very different from the band who had rattled off "I Wanna Hold Your Hand" two and a half years before. *Revolver* distinguished itself with ingenious arrangements and stylistic diversity, and their next album, *Sgt. Pepper's Lonely Hearts Club Band* (1967), was an instant popular and critical success. Sgt. Pepper's "concept album" approach—weaving together separate songs with a unifying theme or story line—broke new ground, and other bands followed the example. The trend peaked with the Who's ambitious rock opera, *Tommy* (1969).

Instrumental virtuosity was showcased more insistently in rock performances by the late '60s, and the soloist's weapon of choice was usually the electric guitar played at high volume. At the 1967 Monterey Pop Festival, the brilliant guitarist

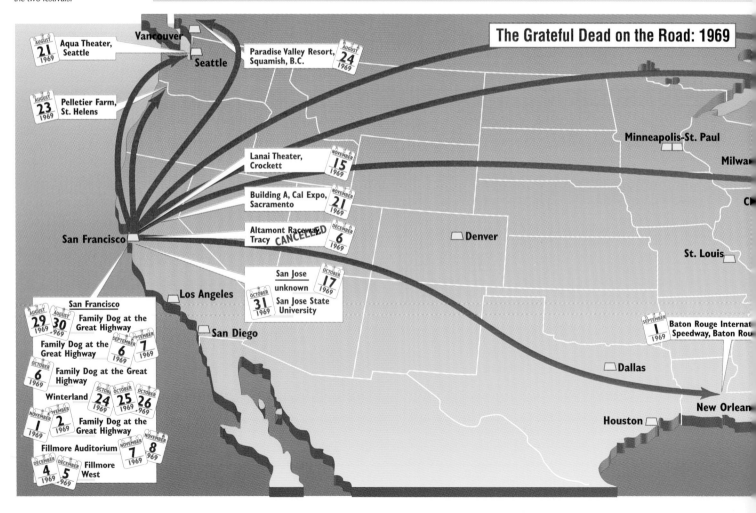

The Grateful Dead on the Road: 1969

Aqua Theater, Seattle — AUGUST 21 1969
Paradise Valley Resort, Squamish, B.C. — AUGUST 24 1969
Pelletier Farm, St. Helens — AUGUST 23 1969
Lanai Theater, Crockett — NOVEMBER 15 1969
Building A, Cal Expo, Sacramento — NOVEMBER 21 1969
Altamont Raceway Tracy CANCELLED — DECEMBER 6 1969
San Jose unknown / San Jose State University — OCTOBER 17 1969 / OCTOBER 31 1969
San Francisco — Family Dog at the Great Highway — AUGUST 29 1969 / AUGUST 30 1969
Family Dog at the Great Highway — SEPTEMBER 6 1969 / SEPTEMBER 7 1969
Family Dog at the Great Highway — OCTOBER 6 1969
Winterland — OCTOBER 24 1969 / OCTOBER 25 1969 / OCTOBER 26 1969
Family Dog at the Great Highway — NOVEMBER 1 1969 / NOVEMBER 2 1969
Fillmore Auditorium — NOVEMBER 7 1969 / NOVEMBER 8 1969
Fillmore West — DECEMBER 4 1969 / DECEMBER 5 1969
Baton Rouge International Speedway, Baton Rouge — SEPTEMBER 1 1969

Vancouver
Seattle
Minneapolis-St. Paul
Milwa[ukee]
Denver
St. Louis
Los Angeles
San Diego
Dallas
New Orleans
Houston

Jimi Hendrix cemented his reputation not only by out-performing and out-playing everyone else, but also by setting his instrument on fire. "Blue Suede Shoes" seemed far away.

Rock music culture reached both its high and low points during 1969. The Woodstock Art and Music Fair, in Bethel, New York, in August was attended by hundreds of thousands and featured many of the most popular acts. Woodstock became a national symbol for "peace, love, and music," and a defining moment of the Baby Boom generation. The festival was followed by a best-selling live recording and an Oscar-winning documentary film.

Woodstock's evil twin was California's Altamont Music Festival, held the following December. The audience was nervous and aggressive, spurred on by the Hell's Angels, who were hired as security. Several clashes between audience members and the Angels climaxed with the stabbing death of a concertgoer by a gang member. For some, Altamont was an indicator of the counterculture's imminent collapse. Certainly it ended the decade on a downbeat note.

By 1970 several important rock musicians had died and many prominent groups had dissolved. Musical values of the '60s would be largely eclipsed by disco and other pop trends. However, a somewhat overlooked album from 1967 would have lasting impact on the music of the '70s and '80s. *The Velvet Underground and Nico*, featuring Lou Reed, would be a key inspiration to musicians for the next 25 years.

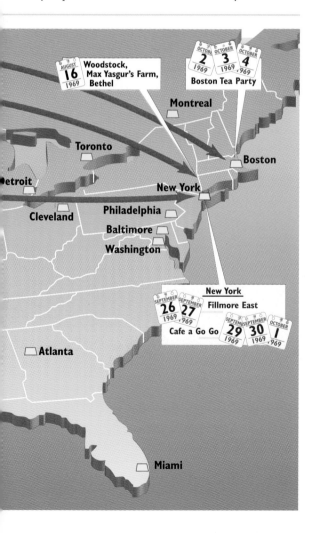

Fans of rock music had an abundance of records and concerts from which to choose, and many styles to explore. Here are a few highlights:

Psychedelic and Funky Flavors

Jefferson Airplane — epitomized the "San Francisco sound" of electric guitars backing trippy lyrics. The songs "White Rabbit" and "Somebody to Love," from the album *Surrealistic Pillow* (1967), put the Airplane on the map.

Big Brother and the Holding Company — known to some as one of the worst groups ever to back a great blues singer: Janis Joplin, who went on to a successful solo career and an early death in 1970.

Sly and the Family Stone — African-American artists who created a unique pop-funk sound, hugely popular with white audiences. Their performance at Woodstock was one of the festival's highlights.

Quicksilver Messenger Service — one of the better guitar-centric bands specializing in long jams and psychedelic noise. Their rendition of Bo Diddley's "Who Do You Love" took up an entire album side.

Artists and Poets

The Doors — rock's bad boys of dark poetry, the '60s group who spun chart-topping music from bits of verse by Blake and Rimbaud. Bandleader Jim Morrison's death in 1971 only added to his cult status.

The Byrds — sometimes known as the "American Beatles." Among the carefully wrought Byrds hit tunes was "Eight Miles High" (1966), which featured an adventurous backward-tracked guitar solo.

The Mothers of Invention — Frank Zappa and the Mothers spun satirical fare such as "Who Are the Brain Police?" and "America Drinks and Goes Home," tangled in dense improvisations and non sequitur edits.

Virtuosos, or Just Really Loud?

Cream — the premier "jamming" band of the '60s, with drums, bass, and guitar often improvising all at once. Guitarist Eric Clapton survived the '60s and moved on to a successful solo career.

Iron Butterfly — the popularity of this group's "In-A-Gadda-Da-Vida" (1968) with its meandering solos and senseless lyrics, appalled serious musicians. But high schoolers around the country tapped out the drum solo on their desktops with #2 pencils.

Blue Cheer — proud to be loud, perhaps the loudest of '60s rock bands. Reputedly, Blue Cheer could be heard for miles during an open-air concert. Their thick, screaming guitar 'n' drums style prefigured '80s "metal" rock.

> **The Man can't bust our music!**
> —**Columbia Records** *ad slogan*

If You're Going to San Francisco . . .

A flower child—literally—enjoys a "be-in" in New York's Central Park, March 26, 1967. (UPI/CORBIS-BETTMANN)

Communes. Pot. Free love. Acid. Hippies. By 1967, these terms were known to most Americans, even those in the smallest rural towns. The revolution in youth lifestyle had become a major media event, and it was impossible to escape images of long-haired social dropouts on television and in the newspapers.

The hippies, as they were popularly known, were in part the progeny of the Beats. In fact, the epicenter of the hippie movement was San Francisco, home to much Beat activity during the '50s and the early '60s. The new counterculture, however, did not follow the Beat model, that of artistic creation and social criticism in willful isolation. The hippies were a mass movement infused with a utopian vision. Central to this movement were tenets of peace, physical pleasure, and spiritual exploration through communal solidarity, rock music, and mind-altering drugs.

Drugs were central to hippie society. Marijuana was the day-to-day favorite, but synthetic psychedelics were seen as key to spiritual awakening. Timothy Leary, famous for being fired from Harvard University in

1963 for experiments with LSD, morphed from academic to guru and media star when he founded the League for Spiritual Discovery. From his Millbrook, New York, mansion Leary made the call to "Turn on, tune in, and drop out." By 1966, LSD, or "acid," was an integral part of hippie culture.

LSD also loomed large in the average American's imagination. Tales began to circulate about the horrors of "bum acid trips." LSD, the stories went, compelled the users to jump from windows, set themselves on fire, or stare at the sun until blind. Instructional films were made to inform teens of the dangers of marijuana and LSD, becoming, with driving-safety and dating-tips movies, part of the high school health class repertoire.

In part, mainstream Americans saw the hippie movement for what it was—a rejection of their core values. It wasn't surprising, then, that movies and TV programs took opportunities to ridicule and vilify the movement. Hippies made colorful additions to sit-coms, detective films, and ham-fisted TV shows like *Dragnet*. Of course, admonitions from the older generation only made the social phenomenon more attractive to young people. Continual media coverage reinforced

> " *May the Good Lord Shut Your Mouth and Open Your Mind.* "
> —*motto of the* **Avalon Ballroom**

the fascination. Youths began sporting long hair and hippie attire in cities all over the country, as the San Francisco scene continued to grow.

By 1967, the San Francisco hippie community was feeling the combined pressures of media exposure and a steady influx of young people, some of them teenage runaways, into the Haight-Ashbury district. The resultant population explosion could not have been handled gracefully without the Diggers.

San Francisco's Diggers took their name from a 17th-century English community that provided for the poor and took a philosophic stance against private property. In 1966, the Diggers began scouring San Francisco for cheap or discarded furniture, clothing, and food, and holding events at which these items were given away to anyone who wanted them. As the Diggers became more organized, they opened Free Stores in which everything displayed could be had, literally, for free, and to which anyone could materially contribute what they wished. The hippie community learned to expect regularly held Free Food gatherings from the Diggers. Along with the food and the material goods, the Diggers posted scores of printed broadsides outlining the Free philosophy and giving their spin on community news. One of the earliest of these summed up Digger thinking concisely: "Give up jobs. Be with people. Defend against property."

The Diggers became the organizational heart of San Francisco hippie culture, where men and women were able to realize, in part, the utopian vision of the community. "Create the condition you describe" was one of their mottoes—act and build in the here and now. A number of the Diggers had worked with the San Francisco Mime Troupe, whose blend of activism and theater inspired the Digger conception of "life-actors," people who worked on a grassroots level to radically reshape social realities.

When the "Summer of Love" arrived in 1967, the Diggers attempted to provide for the flood of out-of-state youths. Unfortunately, the San Francisco scene was changing, and not for the better. Police harassment was more frequent. Casual use of LSD had been made illegal in California, and stronger and more dangerous drugs were circulating, including heroin. Organized crime was attempting to control drug sales. Already the Diggers had circulated a broadside decrying the commercial exploitation of the scene, which included the seduction of naive teenage girls into prostitution. "Rape is as common as bull**** on Haight Street," said the Digger paper. "Minds & bodies are being maimed as we watch, a scale model of Vietnam . . ."

Hippies began moving out of the city, hoping that communal living in outlying areas would be more conducive to their ideals. The San Francisco scene continued for years, but many felt that its spirit had dissipated. Appropriately, one of the Diggers' last works of street theater in San Francisco was a mock funeral celebrating the "Death of Hippie, Son of Media."

▼ The epicenter of the 1960s countercultural earthquake was the corner of Ashbury and Haight Streets in San Francisco. The top map shows "the Haight," as it was commonly known, in relation to the rest of San Francisco. The bottom map offers a small sampling of the places where hippies passed the time during the "Summer of Love."

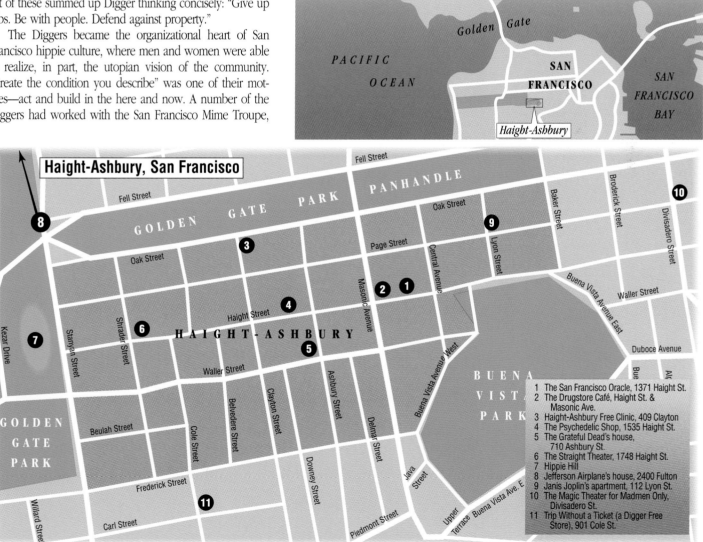

Golden Gate

PACIFIC OCEAN

SAN FRANCISCO

SAN FRANCISCO BAY

Haight-Ashbury

Haight-Ashbury, San Francisco

Fell Street
PANHANDLE
GOLDEN GATE PARK
Oak Street
Page Street
Baker Street
Broderick Street
Divisadero Street
Central Avenue
Lyon Street
Masonic Avenue
Buena Vista Avenue East
Waller Street
Haight Street
HAIGHT-ASHBURY
Stanyan Street
Shrader Street
Kezar Drive
Duboce Avenue
Waller Street
Ashbury Street
Clayton Street
Belvedere Street
Cole Street
Delmar Street
Downey Street
Buena Vista Avenue West
BUENA VISTA PARK
GOLDEN GATE PARK
Beulah Street
Frederick Street
Carl Street
Willard Street
Piedmont Street
Java Street
Upper Terrace Buena Vista Ave. E.

1 The San Francisco Oracle, 1371 Haight St.
2 The Drugstore Café, Haight St. & Masonic Ave.
3 Haight-Ashbury Free Clinic, 409 Clayton
4 The Psychedelic Shop, 1535 Haight St.
5 The Grateful Dead's house, 710 Ashbury St.
6 The Straight Theater, 1748 Haight St.
7 Hippie Hill
8 Jefferson Airplane's house, 2400 Fulton
9 Janis Joplin's apartment, 112 Lyon St.
10 The Magic Theater for Madmen Only, Divisadero St.
11 Trip Without a Ticket (a Digger Free Store), 901 Cole St.

Agent Orange

Frustrated by the enemy's ability to hide in lush jungles, the U.S. military recognized the enormous tactical advantage to be gained by massive defoliation of the South Vietnamese countryside. Launched by President John Kennedy in 1962 and halted by President Richard Nixon in 1970, Operation Ranch Hand sprayed some 19 million gallons of herbicide on the forests and croplands of South Vietnam. Fifteen different herbicides were shipped to Vietnam, all referred to by their color-coded containers, but none would attain the notoriety of Agent Orange.

Agent Orange was chemically similar to herbicides in wide agricultural use in the United States. But as early as 1964, prominent scientists wondered about the long-term health effects of widespread spraying in Vietnam. In a 1967 petition to the president's scientific advisor, more than 5,000 scientists asked that the herbicide program be halted. Sparked by those scientists' protests, the first study to address the issue concluded in late 1967 that herbicidal spraying would cause no long-term health effects in exposed soldiers.

Only later would it be revealed that Agent Orange was contaminated with dangerous concentrations of dioxin, a by-product of the herbicide manufacturing process. After

▶ In September 1966, Air Force planes spray the Cambodian countryside to defoliate the area and expose Viet Cong troops. (CORBIS/BETTMANN)

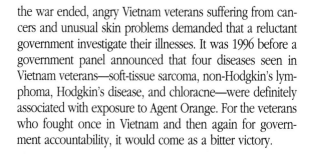

the war ended, angry Vietnam veterans suffering from cancers and unusual skin problems demanded that a reluctant government investigate their illnesses. It was 1996 before a government panel announced that four diseases seen in Vietnam veterans—soft-tissue sarcoma, non-Hodgkin's lymphoma, Hodgkin's disease, and chloracne—were definitely associated with exposure to Agent Orange. For the veterans who fought once in Vietnam and then again for government accountability, it would come as a bitter victory.

Athletic Shoes

A century after its invention, a sneaker was still just a sneaker: rubber bottoms attached to canvas uppers. In 1966, Converse, the American company that dominated the market with its distinctive high-topped sneakers, introduced its most radical innovation in years by offering the consumer a choice of colors instead of the usual black and white.

But far more radical changes were in the air. In 1962, a young Stanford business school student submitted a school paper about marketing specialized running shoes. Two years later, that student founded Blue Ribbon Sports to market running shoes designed by his college track coach. Selling his first 1,300 pairs out of his car trunk at local track meets, Phil Knight introduced a series of innovations to the design of the running shoe. By 1980, Knight and his company, renamed Nike, would overtake Adidas as the dominant force in sneakers, becoming the powerhouse of a multibillion-dollar athletic shoe industry—just in time to catch the wave of Boomer aerobics and jogging fads.

Teflon

Invented accidentally in 1938 by DuPont researcher Roy Plunkett, polytetrafluoroethylene—better known by the trade name Teflon—found widespread use in military, scientific, and industrial applications. A chemically inert, heat-tolerant polymer with a uniquely slippery texture, Teflon was hailed as a milestone in plastics research. But not until 1960 was Teflon introduced to American consumers in what is now its most familiar form: nonstick cookware.

Teflon-coated pans were the brainchild of French engineer Marc Gregoire and his wife Colette. Watching her husband try to bond Teflon to aluminum in order to make a nonstick mold for a new fishing rod, Mme. Gregoire suggested that her husband use the same technique on her aluminum fry pan. The result, imported from France by Macy's department store for the 1960 Christmas season, was an instant sales success. Though the early nonstick pans scratched easily, American cooks loved how easy they were to use and clean. By the summer of 1961, Americans were buying over a million nonstick pans a month. Our taste for Teflon still hasn't changed: 40 years and a low-fat cooking revolution later, over a billion Teflon-coated pans have been sold. An instantly recognizable cultural icon, Teflon even entered the American political lexicon in the 1980s, when Congresswoman Pat Schroeder dubbed scandal-proof Ronald Reagan "the Teflon president—nothing sticks to him."

Thalidomide

It was mother's little helper: a nontoxic sedative that also relieved morning sickness and nausea in pregnant women. Considered so safe that it was available over the counter in many countries, thalidomide was widely adopted for use around the world after its introduction in Germany in 1958.

The application to market thalidomide in the United States arrived at the federal Food and Drug Administration in early September 1960. But FDA officer Dr. Frances Kelsey found troubling inconsistencies and incomplete data in the thalidomide application, and delayed the approval pending further review.

It was a decision that would save thousands of American children. In November 1961, German physician Dr. W. Lenz linked the use of thalidomide to a huge upswing in several rare birth defects, including facial deformities and the absence of arms and legs. Although thalidomide was removed from most markets by the fall of 1962, some 10,000 children would be born with birth defects caused by thalidomide. In the United States, thanks to Dr. Kelsey's refusal to rubber-stamp the application, only 17 such children were born.

Provoked by the close call that averted an American thalidomide disaster, in the early 1960s Congress passed the Kefauver-Harris Bill, which lengthened the FDA's approval process for new drugs. Then hailed as a model of concern for consumer safety, the FDA would later come under fire from AIDS and cancer activists for delaying or preventing patients from obtaining experimental drugs whose safety was not yet proven. In an ironic twist, one of the experimental drugs in demand by activists would be thalidomide. Bowing to activist pressure, in 1998 the FDA approved thalidomide for use in AIDS, cancer, and leprosy patients.

Laser

An acronym standing for "light amplification by stimulated emission of radiation," lasers were the work of two physicists at Bell Labs in Murray Hill, New Jersey. Charles Townes and Arthur Schawlow, both of whom would go on to win Nobel Prizes for their work, discovered in 1958 that atoms and molecules could be forced to emit a burst of extremely intense, focused light.

The first working laser was constructed in 1960, and the technology was quickly applied to several different fields. In 1964 Bell Labs scientist Kumar Patel devised a carbon dioxide laser used for medical surgery. Industry found lasers useful for boring and cutting metals. But not until the 1970s, and the invention of hair-thin glass strands called fiber-optic wave guides, would lasers become a driving force in telecommunications.

Technology: To the Moon

No Camelot would be complete without a quest, and on May 25, 1961, President John Kennedy revealed his holy grail to a joint session of Congress:

I believe that this nation should commit itself to achieving the goal, before this decade is out, of landing a man on the moon and returning him safely to the Earth. No single space project in this period will be more impressive to mankind, or more important in the long-range exploration of space; and none will be so difficult or expensive to accomplish.

With those words, Kennedy launched the Apollo space program. Perhaps the most massive scientific mobilization in world history, the quest for the moon demanded an effort involving more than $20 billion and some 400,000 people.

But nothing easier would have accomplished the same political goal. Apollo was as much a competition as a quest, an implicit challenge to the Soviets, transforming the cold war into a game of wits fought by brilliant scientists and brave heroes in the new frontier of outer space.

For the United States, the moon race was a calculated gamble. The technology to bring a man to the moon and back did not exist in 1961. To create it, American scientists and engineers burst into a frenzy, developing advanced rockets, powerful computers, sophisticated navigational aids, life-support systems, and portable energy systems. During a period of war abroad and massive social upheaval at home, critics decried the incredible resources poured into the space race. But once the goal had been declared, any diminution of support for it would have handed the Soviets an enormous symbolic victory.

▶ *In pursuit of their ultimate goal, putting a man on the moon, NASA undertook a series of unmanned lunar explorations throughout the mid-1960s—the Ranger, Surveyor, and Lunar Orbiter missions. This map shows the landing sites of those missions, plus the late Apollo missions.*

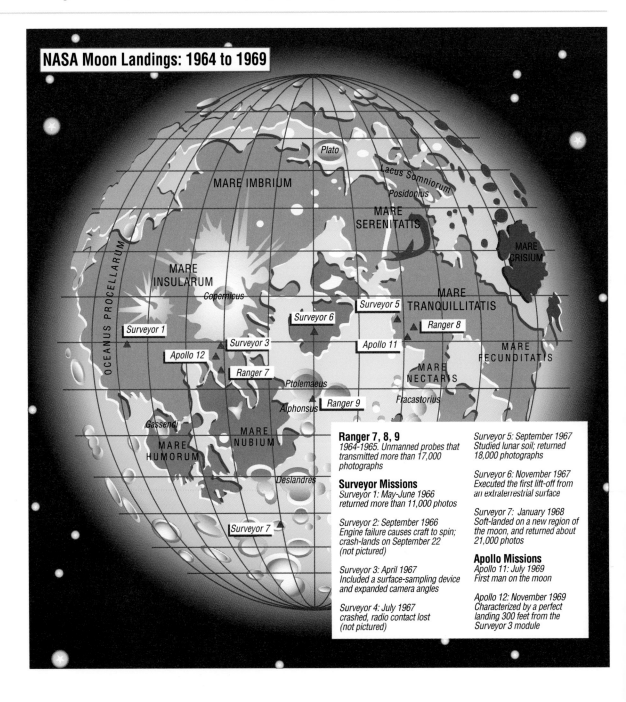

NASA Moon Landings: 1964 to 1969

Ranger 7, 8, 9
1964-1965. Unmanned probes that transmitted more than 17,000 photographs

Surveyor Missions
Surveyor 1: May-June 1966 returned more than 11,000 photos

Surveyor 2: September 1966 Engine failure causes craft to spin; crash-lands on September 22 (not pictured)

Surveyor 3: April 1967 Included a surface-sampling device and expanded camera angles

Surveyor 4: July 1967 crashed, radio contact lost (not pictured)

Surveyor 5: September 1967 Studied lunar soil; returned 18,000 photographs

Surveyor 6: November 1967 Executed the first lift-off from an extraterrestrial surface

Surveyor 7: January 1968 Soft-landed on a new region of the moon, and returned about 21,000 photos

Apollo Missions
Apollo 11: July 1969 First man on the moon

Apollo 12: November 1969 Characterized by a perfect landing 300 feet from the Surveyor 3 module

From 1957, when the radio signals of the Soviet satellite *Sputnik* were first detected over the skies of an anxious nation, the Soviets had a commanding lead in the space race. With limited funds and support shaken from a reluctant Eisenhower administration after the humiliation of *Sputnik*, NASA began its first manned space program in 1958. Despite numerous mishaps, including the very public failure of the first Mercury-Redstone rocket test in 1960, Mercury succeeded in sending the first American astronaut, Alan B. Shepard, into space for 15 minutes of suborbital flight on May 5, 1961. But the jubilation over Shepard's flight was dimmed by a Soviet triumph: just three weeks earlier, Soviet cosmonaut Yuri Gagarin had not only become the first man in outer space, but had also completed a full orbit of the Earth. NASA would not equal that effort until John Glenn's historic flight aboard the Mercury-Atlas *Friendship 7* on February 20, 1962.

Kennedy's tight deadline left little time to catch up. NASA and a host of industrial contractors had to work on several fronts simultaneously to build the knowledge base required for Apollo. The moon itself was an unknown. Throughout the 1960s a barrage of unmanned NASA probes visited the moon to collect precious information about the conditions of the lunar surface. Thousands of photographs were beamed from the Ranger and Lunar Orbiter probes back to Earth, and a map of the rocky and desolate moonscape began to take shape.

The Apollo program needed a cadre of rigorously trained astronauts. Seven astronauts served in the Mercury program from 1961 to 1963, flying six missions that established that humans suffered no ill effects in weightlessness. While the Soviets continued to dazzle the world with the records set by their cosmonauts, caution was NASA's watchword. The length of the Mercury flights was slowly increased, from Alan Shepard's 15 minutes to a day and a half for Gordon Cooper in the last Mercury mission. The nine astronauts added to the roster for the Gemini program (1965-1966) spent two years in training before the first mission. *Gemini 4*, the second manned mission of the program, made history when astronaut Ed White, in a pressurized space suit tethered to the ship, took America's first spacewalk on June 3, 1965—a feat the Russians had accomplished two and a half months earlier.

NASA hoped that the rapid successes of Gemini would continue with the Apollo program. The Johnson administration, hounded by turmoil at home and abroad and hoping to win back the approval of the nation, urged NASA to work faster. But the first launch of *Apollo 1* was dogged with technical problems, and then tragedy. On January 27, 1967, during the first manned test of Apollo on the launch pad, a fire swept through the cockpit of the ship, killing astronauts Gus Grissom, Ed White, and Roger Chaffee trapped inside.

The deaths of the three astronauts shocked the nation. But after the disaster, NASA and its contractors instituted stringent new quality-control measures that brought the program back on track. Meanwhile, the Soviet space program ground to a halt after the death of a cosmonaut and the explosive failure of the massive N-1 rocket built to go to the moon.

After nearly two more years of furious work, the Apollo program had its first major triumph: *Apollo 8*, propelled by the behemoth three-stage Saturn V rocket, arrived in orbit around the moon. On Christmas Eve, 1968, the three-person crew of *Apollo 8* took turns reading from the book of Genesis on a live television broadcast beamed from lunar orbit to millions of awestruck people on Earth.

Seven months later, astronauts Neil Armstrong, Edwin "Buzz" Aldrin, and Michael Collins would again command the attention of the world as *Apollo 11* blasted off from Cape Canaveral, Florida. Hundreds of thousands of people gathered around the launching site; millions more watched on TVs around the world. Four days after launch, Neil Armstrong and Buzz Aldrin detached from the main ship in a lunar module named *Eagle*. At 4:17 P.M. U.S. eastern daylight time on July 20, 1969, the world heard the historic words: "Houston, Tranquility Base here. The *Eagle* has landed."

It was America's shining hour, when a nation wracked by assassinations, protests, and war stood united for a moment, watching the grainy television images of Neil Armstrong's giant leap for mankind. NASA, shorn of its quest, would stumble in the years that followed. But though the public's enthusiasm for grandiose space programs would cool, the profound impact of the Apollo program would remain. Beyond its technical advances and scientific discoveries, the moon quest bequeathed to us a strange new vision of our world seen from the desolation of outer space. It will remain one of the most beautiful images of the twentieth century: the blue Earth rising over the cold gray surface of the moon.

▲ *Neil Armstrong takes one small step for man. (NASA)*

▶ *Cesar Chavez ends a 23-day hunger strike and breaks bread with Robert Kennedy at a protest in 1968. (UPI/CORBIS-BETTMANN)*

Cesar Chavez (1927-1993)

Cesar Chavez defied poverty, racism, and the limits of an eighth-grade education to become one of the most successful union organizers in United States history. A former migrant field-worker, Chavez went to the heart of California farm country to launch the National Farm Workers Association (NFWA) in 1962. It marked the first attempt to organize Mexican-American farmworkers, who labored long days under grueling conditions for the lowest wages of any occupation in the country.

In 1965, the NFWA joined Filipino workers in a strike against local grape growers. Chavez led striking Chicano workers on a march to the state capital in the first major Latino political protest, a watershed event that solidified his standing as a preeminent voice in the civil rights movement.

As the grape strike spread across California, Chavez joined forces with the Filipino union to form the United Farm Workers of the AFL-CIO. As UFW leader, Chavez continued to rely on nonviolent protest in response to intimidation by growers and local police. Though his tactics won the support of civil rights groups, it took five long years of strikes and an unprecedented nationwide grape boycott before growers agreed to higher wages and improved working conditions. A compelling example of the brief convergence between the labor and civil rights movements, Chavez led the UFW until his death.

Helen Gurley Brown (1922-)

"Nice girls *do*," announced Helen Gurley Brown in her controversial 1962 best-seller *Sex and the Single Girl*. Brown encouraged her female readers to seize all the freedoms traditionally accorded single men—including recreational sex.

Though she shocked older Americans, her message resonated with young women, leading to Brown's 1965 appointment as editor-in-chief of *Cosmopolitan*. She radically refashioned the long-established women's magazine, finding a new target audience in young professional women who "love men and children but don't want to be solely identified as wife, girlfriend or mother." Mixing a proto-feminist for-

▶▶ *Helen Gurley Brown, right. (Archive Photos)*

mula with an inspired combination of careerism, sex, and beauty tips, Brown told women that they could go out and achieve fulfillment for themselves—and look beautiful doing it. That message made *Cosmo* the best-selling women's magazine of the next 30 years.

Marshall McLuhan (1911-1980)

"Marshall McLuhan, what are you doin'?" The famous one-liner from *Rowan and Martin's Laugh-in* paid satiric homage to the academic pop-culture hero of the decade. A once-obscure Canadian literary critic, he captured fevered media attention with *The Gutenberg Galaxy* (1962) and *Understanding Media* (1964). In these and later books, McLuhan argued that technological developments in communication changed the balance between the five senses. He claimed that the invention of typography led to an overemphasis on the visual, creating individualization and alienation; while the new electronic media, like radio, television, and computers, would realign human sensory responses, paving the way for a global "retribalization."

Intriguing, eccentric, and downright cryptic, McLuhan became famous for aphorisms—like "the medium is the message"—that revolutionized the way people thought about media. But his puzzling prose and his fantastically broad generalizations eventually undermined his standing with the pundits of pop culture. Not until the rise of a new wired generation would the man and his theories take on a new cultural resonance.

I'm With the Band
Linda Eastman McCartney (1941–1998) and Yoko Ono (1933–)

Sixties rock bands drew legions of groupies and hippie chicks eager for their idols' attention, but few young fans had the success of Linda Eastman, a sunny blonde photographer. Using her camera to gain access to the icons of youth culture, she captured classic photographs of the Rolling Stones, Janis Joplin, Jimi Hendrix, Jim Morrison, and Eric Clapton. On a 1967 photo shoot with the Beatles, she captured the interest of Paul McCartney.

Two years later, Eastman and McCartney married, much to the dismay of heartbroken fans, who angrily denounced her as a gold digger. When the Beatles broke up the following year, popular wisdom blamed Linda—whose entertainment lawyer father had waged an unsuccessful campaign to represent the Beatles—along with John Lennon's new wife, Yoko Ono.

Ono, a Japanese performance artist, drew the most vehement public hatred. A member of the loosely organized avant-garde Fluxus Group and an associate of composer John Cage, she staged experimental art "happenings" that demanded audience participation. Ono had no previous experience in rock music, and Lennon no experience in performance art, but the two clicked at a showing of Ono's work in 1966. They moved in together in 1968 and married in March 1969.

Public reaction was profoundly negative. Fans disapproved of Ono's incursions into John's music and blamed her when their extraordinarily public marriage turned itself into performance art through the infamous "bed-ins for peace." Openly disliked by the other members of the Beatles, Ono was accused of diverting Lennon's talent to leverage her own career through his fame and fortune. While Linda McCartney would be largely redeemed in the public mind, Ono's demonization would continue long after Lennon's death.

Muhammad Ali (1942-   )

"I am the greatest," he said, and who could argue? Born Cassius Clay in Louisville, Kentucky, Ali won a gold medal as a light heavyweight at the 1960 Olympics before turning professional. Brash and playful, with a face that the camera adored, his exuberant egotism made him a media darling, while his speed in the ring made him almost unbeatable. In 1964 he defeated heavily favored champion Sonny Liston for the world heavyweight title, then stunned the nation by announcing that he had joined the Nation of Islam and changed his name to Muhammad Ali.

It was the beginning of a controversy that suspended his career just as he reached his physical peak. In 1967 he refused to comply with a draft notice from the Army, declaring himself a conscientious objector because of his religious beliefs. In response, the World Boxing Association stripped him of his heavyweight title and suspended him from boxing. Sentenced to five years in prison for evading the draft, he spent years appealing his conviction before being acquitted by the Supreme Court in June 1970. "The Greatest of All Time" returned to the ring a different, slower fighter, shadowed by the loss of what were probably his prime competitive years.

▼ *Cassius Clay (later Muhammad Ali) before the famous Sonny Liston fight, February 1964. (UPI/CORBIS-BETTMANN)*

Secret Agents

"Do you expect me to talk, Goldfinger?"
"No, Mr. Bond. I expect you to die."

The secret agent craze was at full steam when *Goldfinger* reached American movie theaters in 1964. James Bond knockoffs were filmed world- wide, and secret agent TV shows crowded the airwaves. Trading cards with images of the Bond films' Sean Connery and TV's *The Man From U.N.C.L.E.*, Robert Vaughn, were packaged with bubble gum and sold to schoolchildren. *Playboy* proudly published new Bond adventures by the arch-spy's creator, Ian Fleming—and of course the magazine featured photo spreads of the movies' latest Bond Girls. The media were saturated with fantasies of ruthless-but-suave superagents outwitting power-crazed criminal masterminds, studly heroes who never seemed to tire from their enormous intake of liquor, cigarettes, and women. The concoction was "crude but effective," as a Bond villain would put it.

Serious secret agent dramas were filmed—*The Spy Who Came in from the Cold* (1965) and *The Quiller Memorandum* (1966) were two attempts at realistic espionage tales—but such movies didn't catch on with filmgoers. Spies who led lonely, slow-paced lives and packed no technogadgets just weren't credible to the public. Where were the babes?

James Bond the film character is still with us. But the cultural phenomenon he inspired, a bizarre celebration of the cold war as an arena of machismo, glamour, and beautiful women with pornographic names, is entirely a creature of the '60s.

Your Friendly Local Head Shop

During the late '60s, American cities were dotted with small retail stores known as head shops. If you were a hippie, these were the places to get certain vital household supplies. If you wanted to be a hippie, you could browse a head shop to get an idea of the stuff you should own. Convenient! The inventory of such a shop might include the following:

- **Comics.** Graphic depictions of sex, violence, and drug use abounded in "underground" cartoon publications such as *Zap Comix*. They also contained some remarkable art. These magazines were the first to showcase Robert Crumb, the creator of Mr. Natural and the famous "Keep On Trucking" cartoon.

- **Newspapers.** Counterculture papers such as New York's *The East Village Other* and *The L.A. Free Press* dished the latest about drug laws, political action, music, and local scenes. Always stacked beside them were *The Village Voice* and *Rolling Stone*, both of which still exist, albeit in more mainstream incarnations.

● **Posters.** Countless posters with political slogans, old movie stills, or images of rock stars filled the walls of these little shops. This was the easiest way to obtain a psychedelic art reproduction. Ads for music events at the Fillmore concert halls often featured first-class poster art by psychedelic stylists, and a good head shop always stocked a few of these best-sellers.

● **Buttons.** There always were bucketsful of pin-on buttons with slogans serious, ridiculous, or suggestive. "Frodo Lives" (for the Tolkien fans), "I am a human being: do not fold, spindle, or mutilate," and "War is not healthy for children and other living things" were popular favorites. There also was "LXIX" for those who wanted to get kicked out of Latin class.

● **Drug paraphernalia.** Hash pipes. Hookahs. Bongs. Designer roach clips. Rolling papers. It *was* called a head shop, after all.

Fashion

"Mod" fashion rode into the States on the heels of the early '60s "British Rock Invasion." Longer hair for men and shorter skirts for women were the trends. Suits with ties had become associated with conservative values, and young men took to wearing "effeminate" colors and textures. Women were encouraged to squeeze into formfitting outfits, perhaps accompanied by tall shiny vinyl boots. Pop art, with its comic-book colors and broad-stroke patterns, began to influence women's fashion—a white plastic handbag adorned with black zebra stripes might complement the latest Carnaby Street fashion special.

Clothing styles became more relaxed as they were influenced, in the later '60s, by the hippie movement and the popular fascination with Eastern culture. Of course, if you were a genuine dropout from society, you couldn't afford —and wouldn't be interested in—East Indian blouses, flower-patterned bell-bottom pants, or tinted eyeglasses with rectangular frames. But it cost nothing to grow your hair.

Indeed, long hair had become a political issue by 1967. Many men felt as strongly about their right to shoulder-length hair as they did about the Vietnam War

and civil liberties. For others, it was simply a matter of style, and in some ways they were right. Young men's hair length would remain long—by today's standards, anyway— throughout the '70s, years after the hippie counterculture had waned.

The 1970s

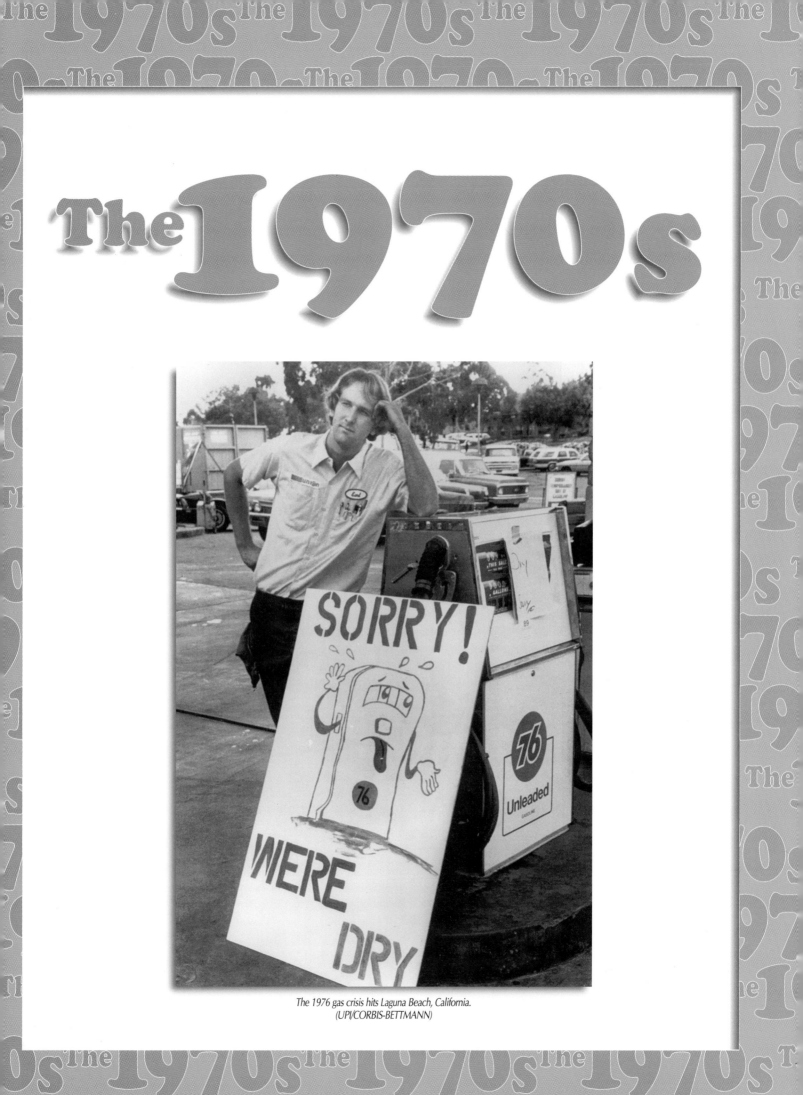

The 1976 gas crisis hits Laguna Beach, California.
(UPI/CORBIS-BETTMANN)

According to Arlie Hochschild, author of *The Second Shift* (1989), when more women obtained jobs in the 1970s, they labored not only at the office or factory, but also at home—a "second shift" that meant they worked longer each week than did men. This caused tension in many marriages as wives demanded their husbands assume more of the household chores. Along with a declining birthrate and a new immigration, the movement of women into the workforce presented society with serious changes and challenges.

Much as the Census Bureau had been proved wrong in the late 1940s when it failed to predict the Baby Boom, it stood corrected again in the early 1970s—this time for failing to predict the sharp decline in fertility among Baby Boomer women. As some women sported buttons proclaiming "Stop at Two" and "None is Fun," lifetime births expected per 1,000 wives aged 18–24 dropped from 2,375 in 1971 to 2,134 in 1980. Whereas the President's Commission on Population Growth and the American Future had insisted in 1970 that births for the next 20 years would remain above that year's level, births actually dropped below it in 1971.

What prevented the Baby Boomers from booming? Concern with overpopulation played a role. In 1969, Paul Ehrlich had founded Zero Population Growth, which advocated increased birth control, and dire predictions sounded in newspapers and magazines warning that if Baby Boomers reproduced at the rate their parents had, the nation would suffer from overcrowding. "Our view," said the President's Commission, "is that population growth of the magnitude we have had since World War II has aggravated many of the nation's problems and makes their solution more difficult."

That women delayed marriage also worked against a high birthrate. Further, unlike their parents who averaged three-child families, Baby Boomers stopped at two. Use of the contraceptive pill, first marketed in 1960, allowed couples to more reliably plan the size of families. And a soaring divorce rate added its influence: divorce often occurred during a woman's most fertile years, disrupting reproduction.

Despite the drop in birthrates, America's population continued to expand, helped along by a new immigration. Almost 4.5 million legal immigrants entered the nation during the 1970s, surpassing the rate of the preceding two decades. Unlike previous voluntary immigrants, most were people of color.

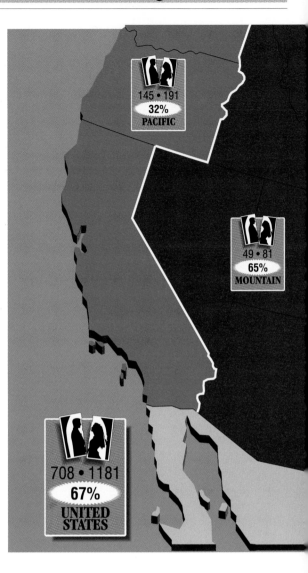

Women for Tradition

Although Phyllis Schlafly had gone against the restrictions that society traditionally imposed on women and earned a law degree, she emerged in the 1970s as the most visible female opponent of both gay rights and of feminist reforms such as the Equal Rights Amendment. A mother of five, Schlafly extolled families in which men worked and women stayed at home. In her "Stop ERA" campaign, she believed the amendment would ruin families by permitting women to be drafted and, by creating a "unisex society," legalizing homosexual marriages.

As immigration reshaped society, so too did women entering the workforce in large numbers—what Hochschild called "the basic social revolution of our time." That both parents frequently worked in the 1970s probably affected families more than any other change from previous decades. Where wives worked, they often felt more independent and exerted more power within the family—a development that caused discord within many marriages. Husbands considered their authority under attack, and wives disliked the expectation, one prevalent before the late 1970s, that in addition to their jobs, they should also wash clothes, clean house, and cook dinner.

Divorce rates doubled during the decade and, in 1975, exceeded one million for the first time. This increase was caused by more than conflict over who would clean house. Some Baby Boomers may have been trapped in oppressive, even abusive, relationships, while others—and many observers claim this was the most important reason—desired instant gratification and exhibited less willingness to compromise than their forebears; thus when turbulence appeared, they bailed out. *Mad* magazine satirically offered kids a Divorce Survival Badge for doing such things as agreeing with father that the "silly young lady he is dating is 'real swell

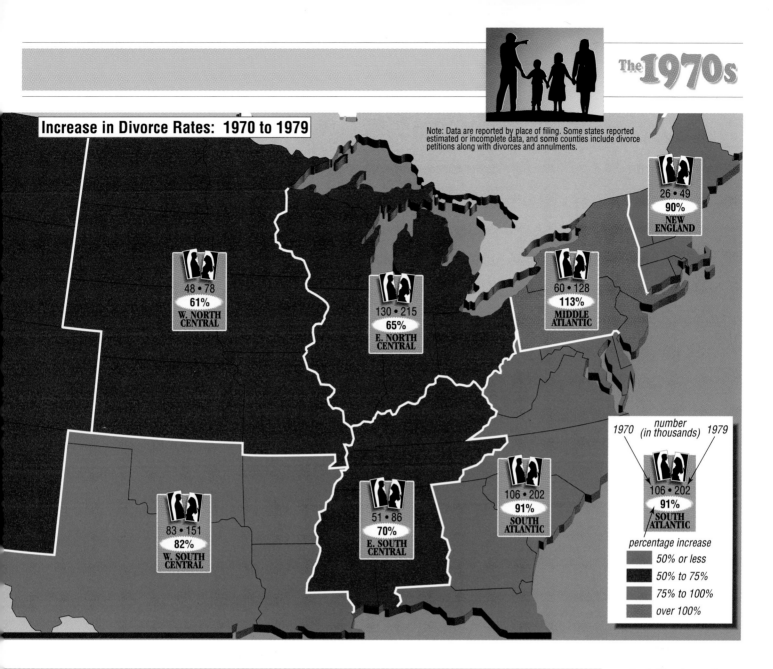

Increase in Divorce Rates: 1970 to 1979

Note: Data are reported by place of filing. Some states reported estimated or incomplete data, and some counties include divorce petitions along with divorces and annulments.

26 • 49
90%
NEW ENGLAND

48 • 78
61%
W. NORTH CENTRAL

130 • 215
65%
E. NORTH CENTRAL

60 • 128
113%
MIDDLE ATLANTIC

83 • 151
82%
W. SOUTH CENTRAL

51 • 86
70%
E. SOUTH CENTRAL

106 • 202
91%
SOUTH ATLANTIC

1970 — number (in thousands) — 1979

106 • 202
91%
SOUTH ATLANTIC

percentage increase
- 50% or less
- 50% to 75%
- 75% to 100%
- over 100%

and a lot of fun.'" On the serious side, divorces traumatized many children. In addition, divorce often resulted in dire economic consequences as more than half of all female-headed households lived in poverty.

Not even children kept marriages together. Many Boomers rejected the idea, a strong one among their parents, that a bad marriage should be endured for the children's sake. In fact, when it came to kids, they showed a sharp divergence from earlier generations. Half of all Boomer parents in one survey agreed with the statement they "should not sacrifice" to give their children "the best."

But then Boomers saw neither family nor children as sure routes to happiness. Of 50,000 parents who responded to a questionnaire issued by newspaper columnist Ann Landers, 70 percent said if they had it to do over again, they would *not* have kids. From the Boomer perspective, personal fulfillment overshadowed family responsibility—thus the desire to marry late or stay single. Although most Boomers still opted for marriage and parenthood, they stayed single longer than any generation this century; and although the large number of Baby Boomers produced a record number of marriages in 1979, the *percentage* of people getting married had dropped.

Conservatives attacked these developments. They decried the American family's collapse, supposedly crafted by wild hippies and other irresponsible counterculture youths. Traditionalists such as Phyllis Schlafly riled feminists by beginning her speeches with, "I'd like to thank my husband for letting me be here tonight." Despite conservative efforts, Boomers would not revert to the 1950s or any other era traditionalists considered better.

▲ *Family life underwent sharp breaks with tradition in the 1970s, as more marriages were terminated than ever before.*

▼ *Many women decided to put childrearing on hold in the 1970s.*

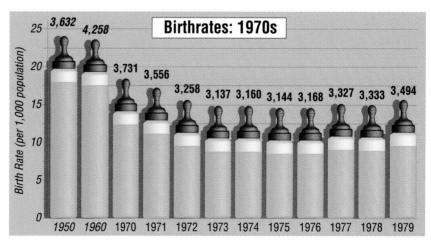

Birthrates: 1970s

Birth Rate (per 1,000 population)

1950	1960	1970	1971	1972	1973	1974	1975	1976	1977	1978	1979
3,632	4,258	3,731	3,556	3,258	3,137	3,160	3,144	3,168	3,327	3,333	3,494

SAT Score Averages for College-Bound Seniors: 1970-1979

Year	Verbal	Math
1970	460	488
1971	455	488
1972	453	484
1973	445	481
1974	444	480
1975	434	472
1976	431	472
1977	429	470
1978	429	468
1979	427	467

▲ *Parents and educators alike were distressed by plummeting Scholastic Aptitude Test (SAT) scores in the 1970s.*

As society struggled with aftershocks from the 1960s, so too did education. Schools in the 1970s bore the brunt of reform campaigns meant to correct failures from the previous decade or to build on challenges to tradition. These efforts generated additional controversy.

Convinced that earlier reforms sponsored by the federal government had faltered because they had been haphazard and limited, President Richard Nixon proposed an ambitious Experimental Schools Program (ESP). Under legislation passed by Congress, school districts could receive federal funds to support innovative "comprehensive plans," an amorphous phrase that implied reform of all 12 grade levels, along with staff development, community outreach, and curriculum changes. Eighteen districts received such funding; for example, Berkeley, California, won a $7 million grant to establish 24 alternative schools dedicated to decreasing institutional racism. But in short order, ESP failed . . . only one of Berkeley's alternative schools survived, and no one in the 18 districts could point to concrete gains. The inability to precisely define "comprehensive plans," disputes among local interests, and misunderstanding by federal officials as to what schools needed all contributed to ESP's end.

At the same time, disturbing news led the public to question what was going on in the schools. As Baby Boomers born in the late 1950s prepared to graduate from high school, Scholastic Aptitude Test scores, in decline since the 1960s, accelerated their plunge. Between 1970 and 1974, the average SAT verbal score fell 16 points; in just one year, from 1974 to 1975, it dropped another 10. In that same one-year period, the average math score, which had dropped eight points from 1970 to 1974, nose-dived another eight.

Although part of the decline could be attributed to the increased number of students taking the test—thus bringing into the calculations low-scorers who, in previous times, would not have considered going to college—the trouble went deeper. Experts blamed the results on family instability from increased divorce, youthful alienation produced by the

1960s upheaval, declining attention spans caused by television, and poor teaching as evident in the use of "dumbed-down" textbooks and the reluctance to assign homework. As a result, parents demanded that schools shift from reform to teaching in the way *they* had been taught. In response to the question "Do you favor or oppose a back-to-basics movement?" 83 percent of those sampled in a 1977 Gallup poll said "favor."

Despite such growing enthusiasm for tradition, court rulings and congressional action regarding civil rights pointed schools in a progressive direction. In 1970, the federal government's Office for Civil Rights (OCR) declared that discrimination against children deficient in English violated the 1964 Civil Rights Act and that school districts had to provide special programs for them. The Supreme Court upheld the OCR in 1974, and Congress passed the Bilingual Education Act that made English-deficient children eligible for bilingual programs. Many parents and politicians attacked the legislation, though, for promoting a splintered society over one united by a common language. More controversy emerged when researchers found that English-deficient children in bilingual programs learned no better than those outside them.

Advocates for handicapped children saw success in 1970 when Congress redefined handicapped to include the learning-disabled and, in 1973, when Congress declared that schools must provide full access for handicapped students or risk losing federal funds. Critics worried that the requirement would cost schools enormous amounts of money, taking resources away from mainstream students, but Congress moved ahead and in 1975 passed the Education for All Handicapped Children Act that detailed how districts had to provide an "individualized program."

Of all the federal mandates on education, busing raised the greatest fury, one that threatened to harm race relations irreparably. In 1971, the Supreme Court issued its landmark decision in *Swann v. Charlotte–Mecklenburg Board of Education.* About 24,000 black students were enrolled in that North Carolina district, 14,000 of whom attended schools with few, if any, whites. The justices ruled unanimously that federal courts could require busing to desegregate schools. "Today's objective is to eliminate . . . all vestiges of state-imposed segregation," said the court. Few people supported the decision—a 1971 Gallup poll showed that 76 percent of the nation's eligible voters opposed busing; only 18 percent favored it. That same year, in Pontiac, Michigan, opponents to a busing order dynamited 10 school buses.

In Boston, white parents, mainly Irish-American, organized ROAR—Restore Our Alienated Rights—to protest federal judge W. Arthur Garrity's order, issued in 1974, that the city desegregate its public schools through busing. The school board claimed that segregation grew from housing patterns beyond its control. But Garrity claimed that the board had sustained and even expanded segregation through such tactics as busing black children past white schools. Interestingly, ROAR and its conservative supporters demonstrated by using the same tactics, marches and sit-ins, for example, used in the 1960s by civil rights workers and antiwar Boomer youths, even down to the chant: "Hell, no! We

▼ *On September 13, 1974, police escort black students to the primarily white South Boston High School. (UPI/CORBIS-BETTMANN)*

October 1970, The Massachusetts Commission Against Discrimination files a suit when black student Christine Underwood is denied entry to *Roslindale High School* ❶.

May 1971, In order to create racial balance in the schools, the state board begins the redistricting of four elementary schools in Dorchester: the *Joseph Lee* ❷ and *John Marshall* ❸ schools in mixed neighborhoods and the nearby *Fitfield* ❹ and *O'Hearn* ❺ schools attended by mostly white students. Both white and black parents disregard this ruling by refusing to send their children to the reassigned schools.

March 15, 1972, Civil rights lawyers file a suit in U.S. district court on behalf of black Dorchester parents against the Boston School Committee, which becomes known as the *Morgan v. Hennigan* case.

April 3, 1974, Approximately 15,000–25,000 antibusing demonstrators gather on *Boston Common* ❻ while hundreds fill the auditorium at the *State House* ❼, where the Joint Subcommittee on Education listens to eight hours of testimony on desegregation issues.

January 7, 1975, The Boston School Committee submits a plan to the court with no forced busing. Backing down from his initial threats, Judge Garrity rules that the committee's "plan" complies with the court's order and removes Kerrigan, Ellison, and McDonough from contempt of court, signaling a small victory for antibusing groups in Boston.

December 19, 1974, Three of the five members of the Boston School Committee, John Kerrigan, Paul Ellison, and John McDonough, remain defiant and refuse to comply with Judge Garrity's order to establish a new desegregation plan for year two, despite being held in contempt of court until they submit a new busing plan.

December 11, 1974, A 17-year-old white student, Michael D. Faith, is stabbed at *South Boston High School* ⓫, resulting in angry white protests and a walkout at *Hyde Park High School* ❿ of 200 white students.

May 10, 1974, Governor Sargent announces his decision to replace the Racial Imbalance Act with a proposition that would rely heavily on the voluntary busing of minority students into white neighborhoods, the expansion of voluntary busing to the suburbs, and magnet schools.

June 21, 1974, Disregarding the governor's decision, Judge W. Arthur Garrity, Jr., gives his ruling in the federal court suit *Morgan v. Hennigan*, finding the school committee guilty of maintaining a segregated school system and ordering the state busing plan to be put into effect in September at the start of the school year.

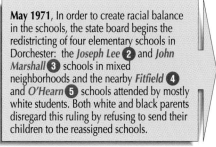
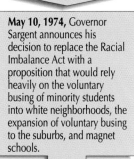

North End ❼❻
East Boston
Brighton (Allston)
South End **South Boston** ⓫
Roxbury
Jamaica Plain ❾ ❸ ❽
Boston Harbor
Roslindale ❷ **Dorchester** ❺
❶ ❹
West Roxbury
Mattapan
❿

Busing Crisis in Boston: 1970 to 1975

October 15, 1974, A black student stabs a white student at *Hyde Park High School* ❿. In reaction to white protest, Governor Sargent calls in 500 National Guardsmen.

December 6, 1974, Adults from the South Boston Information Center (SBIC) enter *South Boston High School* ⓫ and provoke the white students into a frenzied rally in the auditorium and then throughout the school. The police remove approximately 300 whites.

October 8, 1974, When 1,500 students pour out of *English High School* ❾ following a false alarm, a mob of black students moves into the Mission Hill projects and begins throwing rocks and starting skirmishes. By evening, MBTA cancels all buses traveling into Roxbury-Dorchester and Mission Hill.

September 1974, As the court-ordered buses begin to run, rifle shots are fired at the *Boston Globe building* ❽. The newspaper has consistently supported the Racial Imbalance Act and the court-ordered busing.

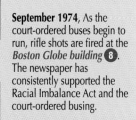
▲ *One of the most divisive struggles over de facto segregation in the 1970s occurred in the Boston area as white and black parents battled authorities over forced busing of high school students.*

won't go!" Nationally, as busing and other desegregation measures took hold, middle-class whites fled public schools for private ones, or they fled to the suburbs, creating a racial imbalance much like the one that existed before the court decisions.

Racial controversy enveloped colleges, too, as the federal government pursued affirmative action programs to boost black student enrollment. In 1974, Alan Bakke, a white student, claimed he had been discriminated against by the University of California–Davis Medical School when it denied him admission while accepting minority applicants with lower test scores. Bakke sued, and a divided Supreme Court

ruled he had to be admitted by UC–Davis, but that the school could consider race in future admissions. Irrespective of the ruling, black enrollment at American colleges increased with affirmative action in place, as did that of women.

Federal programs and regulations raised the specter of communities losing control over their public schools. Between 1965 and 1977, such regulations increased from 92 to nearly 1,000. A Gallup poll found that by a two-to-one margin adults believed the national government should allow school districts to spend federal moneys as local officials saw fit. But total abandonment of federal requirements seemed about as distant as a return to the one-room schoolhouse.

Total Unemployed: 1970 to 1979

Year	Total
1970	4,088,000
1971	4,994,000
1972	4,840,000
1973	4,304,000
1974	5,076,000
1975	7,830,000
1976	7,288,000
1977	6,855,000
1978	6,047,000
1979	5,963,000

▼ Cars lined up at a gas station in Los Angeles, California, during gas rationing. (UPI/CORBIS-BETTMANN)

An editorial cartoon drawn in 1976 showed the over-sized face of an Arab sheikh with the acronym OPEC (for Organization of Petroleum Exporting Countries) affixed to his forehead and his cavernous mouth swallowing whole a huge automobile emblazoned with the caption, "American Lifestyle." To many Americans, it appeared as if the Arab oil nations had combined with bewildering, threatening forces to devour a once-prosperous economy.

Perhaps there was some irony in a Baby Boomer generation conditioned to consume suddenly encountering limitations as its older members reached adulthood. Boomers had been raised on TV commercials that preached instant gratification, and, despite the soured economy, they pursued it. They preferred spending to saving—economists attributed 20 percent of the decline in America's savings rate to the appearance of the Boomer consumer.

To survive and prosper, many corporations changed focus as the Boomers moved into their twenties. For example, McDonald's shifted its appeal from teenagers to adults by replacing its red building color with subdued brown, and by introducing a breakfast menu that appealed to young workers who rushed to their jobs in the morning. Beer companies promoted light beer with fewer calories. Adidas sold 13 million pairs of running shoes in one year as these young people indulged in a jogging craze. However strong youthful anti-materialism may have been in the 1960s, it beat a hasty retreat. *Playboy* called the behavior a "new materialism." The author Tom Wolfe, although not specifically talking about Boomers, referred to the 1970s as the "Me Generation."

The economy, already shaken by Vietnam-era spending that helped create government deficits, showed signs of turmoil as the Baby Boomers flooded the job market. It took a shattering blow when, in 1973, OPEC suspended oil shipments to the United States in hopes of influencing U.S. policy in the Middle East. The yearlong embargo and subsequent price hikes by OPEC stunned Americans. They had relied increasingly on foreign oil—in 1960, 19 percent of the oil they consumed came from abroad; in 1972, 30 percent did so—and they consumed wasteful amounts in homes, in industries, and in large, gas-guzzling cars. Few Americans knew the phrase "energy efficiency," and fewer cared about applying it.

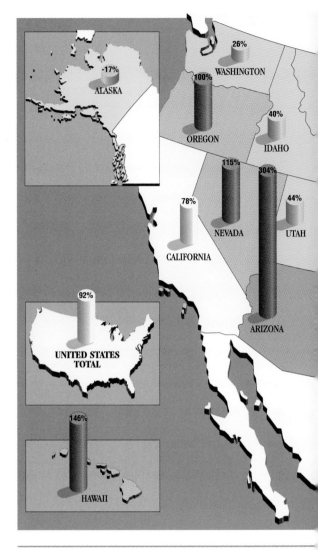

By the middle of 1974, prices for heating oil and gasoline had risen as much as 33 percent. By 1980, the price of crude oil was nearly seven times higher than 10 years earlier. The multinational oil companies realized a 70 percent increase in profits in 1973, and 40 percent the following year. Although Americans still paid less for oil than did people in most industrialized nations, the crisis worsened already intense feelings of despair and decline flowing from the debacle in Vietnam and the Watergate scandal. After the federal government mandated rationing, motorists found themselves stuck in long lines at service stations, their lives fueled as much by frustration and anger as by gasoline. When oil prices went up, so did inflation, from 3 percent in 1972 to a staggering 11 percent in 1974. Industrial output fell 10 percent in that year alone, and unemployment nearly doubled.

Caused in part by the oil crisis, but more by longer-term problems, factories reduced their workforces or shuttered their doors. Chrysler closed 13 plants, costing 31,000 jobs; and newspapers recited a tiring, depressing refrain: "Weyerhauser Co. may trim about 1,000 employees from its 11,000-member workforce over the next year"; "500 workers are scheduled to be laid off from Westinghouse's 85-year-old fortress-like factory"; "Food Fair, Inc. plans to close 89 supermarkets in New York and Connecticut."

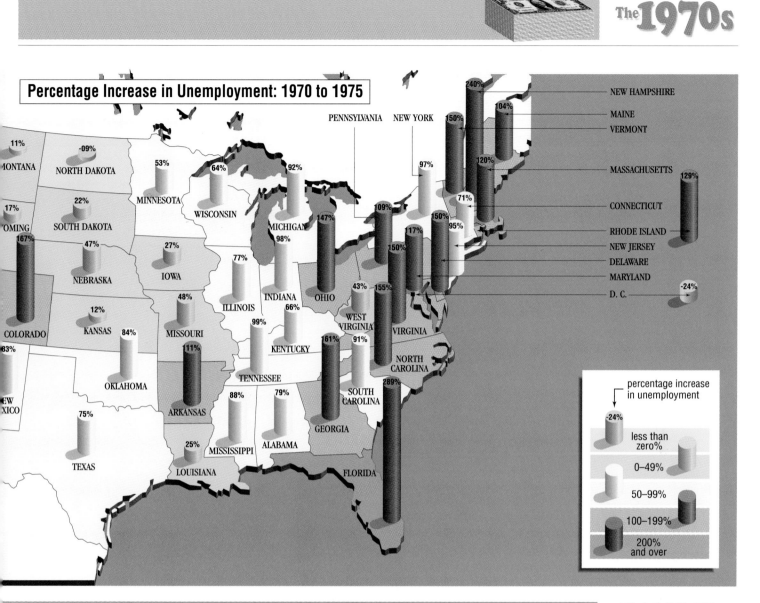

Percentage Increase in Unemployment: 1970 to 1975

percentage increase in unemployment

-24% less than zero%

0–49%

50–99%

100–199%

200% and over

While the Northeast "Rust Belt" suffered the most, every sector experienced losses. A few economists called the closings painful but necessary—a way for the economy to rebuild, like an old tree falling in the forest and replenishing the Earth. The metaphorical tree, however, fell on real people. Although 27 million new jobs were created in the 1970s, laid-off factory workers watched in despair as America's shift to a service economy often forced them to trade in their wrenches for spatulas and flip burgers in low-pay, fast-food eateries.

Some conservative commentators blamed America's economic ills on laziness, a decline in the work ethic, as evident in the rise of leisure. George Gilder asserted in *Wealth and Poverty:* "The problem of contemporary capitalism lies . . . in a persistent subversion of the psychological means of production—the morale and inspiration of economic man."

But few factory managers agreed. Productivity certainly slipped, with output per hour in the business sector falling 0.3 percent in 1980, but this was largely due to a younger, more inexperienced workforce and the hike in oil prices that caused industries to spend more money on energy-efficient rather than labor-efficient equipment. Everywhere Americans looked, economic decline slapped them in the face. The nation's share of manufacturing exports dropped from 25 to

17 percent; unemployment reached 8.5 percent in 1975; and inflation soared to 13 percent in 1979.

In 1980, the consumer price index climbed 10.3 percent, and in a short while America tumbled from its position as world leader in standard of living and was surpassed by nine other nations as measured by per-capita GNP. The typical family faced the 1980s with only 7 percent more real purchasing power than a decade earlier—and all of that increase came in 1970–73, before OPEC's oil embargo and the cavernous mouth that swallowed the economy whole.

▲ *The first half of the 1970s witnessed a desperate surge in unemployment rates, with the number of jobless increasing more than 100 percent in many states. A gradual improvement began in the late 1970s, but real recovery would await the Reagan Revolution of the early 1980s.*

Steel and Decline

Steel exemplified America's manufacturing decline in the 1970s. Once the largest exporter of steel, the United States produced only 16 percent of the world's output by 1979. U.S. Steel closed 14 plants and mills in eight states, costing 13,000 jobs.

Notably, the United States fell behind Japan. American steel manufacturers had failed to invest in efficient equipment, and when the world demand for steel dropped, they suffered. Meanwhile the fittest plants, those in Japan, flourished. Rather than invest in new plants, many American companies sought profits by putting their money in various businesses, such as chemical plants and shopping malls. For every new dollar U.S. Steel invested, 46 cents went into non-steel activities.

By the 1970s, older Baby Boomers looked back at their suburban past and wrapped it in nostalgia. What else could be done as the government and economy unraveled around them? What else could be done as pessimism and self-indulgence engulfed their generation?

With its ad slogan, "Where Were You in '62?," the movie *American Graffiti* (1973) exemplified Boomer immersion in nostalgia. Set in 1962, it followed a group of small-town California teenagers the night after they graduated from high school, an adolescent world untouched either by John Kennedy's assassination or other events that later shattered innocence. Young people watching *American Graffiti* on its release, or

its rerelease in 1978, could escape the dispiriting violence and corruption of the 1960s, and the depressed economy of the 1970s . . . as they could, too, by watching *Happy Days* on TV (1974–1984) or collecting old comic books. A widespread infatuation with the conformist 1950s was a staple of '70s pop culture.

Boomers embraced nostalgia for other reasons. Having

grown up in a fast-paced society characterized by fleeting relationships, many had little attachment to person or place; they yearned for something to hold on to. Having questioned tradition and rejected long-standing values, they lacked an identity; remembrances provided them with one. Having reached the age of 30, older Boomers felt limitations; nostalgia reminded them of when opportunity seemed boundless.

Stripped from this affair with the past, Boomers exhibited rampant pessimism. According to a survey conducted by the University of Michigan, the "level of worry" among young people 21 to 39 years old climbed from 30 percent in 1967 to 50 percent in 1976. Suicide rates for Boomers exceeded those of all other generations in American history. While the nation's overall rate remained stable, that for 20- to 24-year-olds in the mid-1970s rose, as it did a few years later for 25- to 29-year-olds, when many Baby Boomers reached that age bracket.

Influential books reinforced feelings of despair. Barry Commoner's *The Closing Circle: Nature, Man and Technology* (1971) portrayed a country and world facing collapse from environmental degradation. Although Commoner

> ❝ *Avoid all needle drugs. The only dope worth shooting is Richard Nixon.* ❞
> —**Abbie Hoffman**

▼ *The 1970s witnessed the dimming of American expectations, as shown by these opinion polls, taken in even-numbered years in the 1960s and 1970s. Respondents felt they were worse off, they had made less progress, and they expected less from the future. The same is true of their feelings about the nation; less well off, less progress, less expected. Note the upswing in hopes for the future shown in the 1980 surveys.*

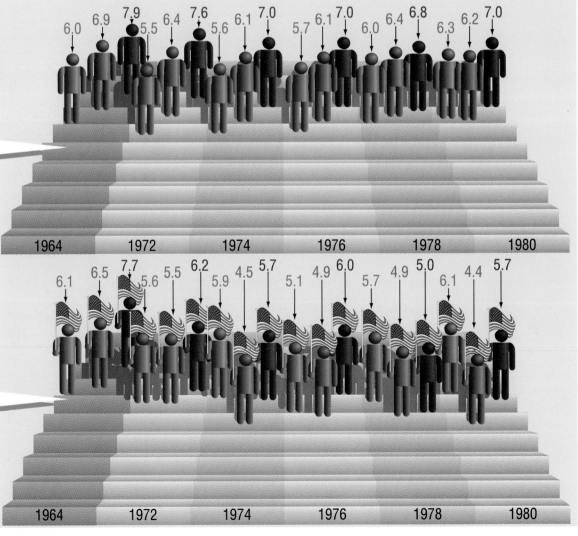

Opinion Ratings on Quality of "Your Life" and "The Situation of the Country"

Question: "Here is a ladder representing the 'ladder of life.' Let's suppose the top of the ladder represents the *best* possible life for you [at 10], and the bottom, the *worst* possible life for you [at 0]. On which step of the ladder do you feel you personally stand at the present time? Five years ago? Five years from now?"

Question on "the Situation of the Country": "Looking at the ladder again, suppose the top represents the *best* possible situation for our country; the bottom the *worst* possible situation. Please show me on which step of the ladder you think the United States is at the present time...five years ago...five years from now."

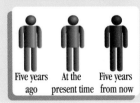

Five years ago | At the present time | Five years from now

said "there is reason to find in the very depths of the environmental crisis itself a source of optimism," the crisis portended disaster. There will have to be a rational use and distribution of the Earth's resources, warned Commoner, or humankind will sink into barbarism.

In *An Inquiry Into the Human Prospect* (1974), Robert L. Heilbroner squelched any hope Commoner may have offered. Damage to the environment, high birthrates, excessive armaments, and an unbalanced distribution of wealth among nations all threatened human survival. He insisted: "If, then, by the question 'Is there hope for man?' we ask whether it is possible to meet the challenges of the future without the payment of a fearful price, the answer must be: No, there is no such hope." The worst, he said, awaits.

But too much can be made of society's pessimism being generational. Class and occupational differences also played a role. Another survey by the University of Michigan, this one in 1970, found that while 40 percent of professionals placed little trust in government, 66 percent of unskilled blue-collar workers distrusted Uncle Sam. Such distrust, in fact, permeated the whole society in the wake of deceit surrounding the Vietnam War and Watergate. In 1972, 53 percent of the respondents to a poll agreed with the statement that a few big interests ran the federal government. Three years later, another poll found public confidence in the military had plunged from 62 percent in 1966 to 30 percent, confidence in Congress from 42 percent to 12 percent.

Either as antidote or as complement to pessimism, self-indulgence engulfed the Boomer generation. In 1978, a writer for the *Washington Post* described how young men spent more time than ever primping and no longer worried that others knew about it. They were motivated, said the author, not by love of beauty, but by self-love.

As advertisers intensified their drive to have people satisfy their wants now and be judged by money spent, Boomers immersed themselves in self-actualization programs, jogging, mountain climbing, and the great escapist fad, discos. Unlike 1960s rock, disco songs contained no strong political message, no hippie love ideals—just losing mind to body and a pulsating sexual beat.

Yet here, too, a theme can be overplayed, for social reform efforts remained vibrant. The women's movement accelerated as feminists pushed for an equal rights amendment to the Constitution. The American Indian Movement (AIM) staged its "Trail of Broken Treaties" in 1972, when 2,000 Native Americans traveled in a caravan to Washington, D.C., and protested violations of treaty rights. AIM activism included, in 1973, the much-publicized violent showdown with federal troops at Wounded Knee. Taking a different tack, the once-militant Black Panthers turned to working within the system to promote welfare programs, increase housing opportunities, and provide legal representation in the ghettos. Other 1960s' radicals emerged as environmental activists. The spectacular revelation in 1978 that houses had been built over a chemical dump at Love Canal in New York boosted the environmentalist ranks, as did the ominous near-meltdown in 1979 at Pennsylvania's Three Mile Island nuclear power plant.

Boogie Fever

Discos found life during the late 1960s in New York City's black and Latin neighborhoods, and among gays who wanted places where they could dance. Unlike most rock, disco made the audience important, and discos displayed this with their gaudy trappings. At the famous Studio 54 in New York City, 450 special effects included plastic snowfalls.

Nothing emblazoned disco in the popular imagination more than the hit movie *Saturday Night Fever* (1977), starring John Travolta. After the movie appeared, a disco craze swept America, from New York City, where more than 1,000 discos opened, to Fennimore, Wisconsin, a small town that opened a $100,000 club.

"Discos," says historian David Szatmary, "embodied the narcissistic extravagance of the mid- and late-seventies," with their sex and drugs—especially cocaine. But they also provided real opportunity for the gay men who owned many of the clubs and helped bring gay culture out of the closet.

As for why people flocked to discos, one culture analyst commented: "They are depressed by taxes and inflation. They want to party. . . . I call it, 'The music that fiddles while Rome burns.'"

But in most ways America seemed exhausted in the 1970s, economically prostrate, politically bankrupt, and socially spent. For many, life had been reduced from pursuing ideals to, as the Bee Gees sang, "staying alive."

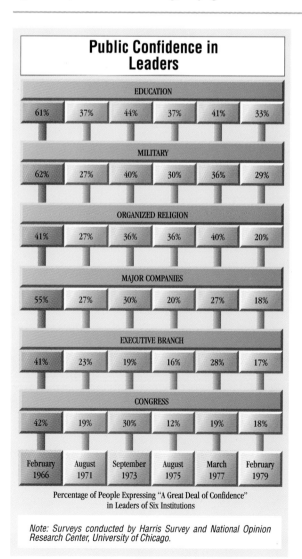

Public Confidence in Leaders

	February 1966	August 1971	September 1973	August 1975	March 1977	February 1979
EDUCATION	61%	37%	44%	37%	41%	33%
MILITARY	62%	27%	40%	30%	36%	29%
ORGANIZED RELIGION	41%	27%	36%	36%	40%	20%
MAJOR COMPANIES	55%	27%	30%	20%	27%	18%
EXECUTIVE BRANCH	41%	23%	19%	16%	28%	17%
CONGRESS	42%	19%	30%	12%	19%	18%

Percentage of People Expressing "A Great Deal of Confidence" in Leaders of Six Institutions

Note: Surveys conducted by Harris Survey and National Opinion Research Center, University of Chicago.

◀ In addition to the lessening of personal expectations, opinion polls in the 1970s also revealed a declining faith in the institutions that were once considered to be the bedrock of American society. It's hardly surprising that public confidence in the Executive Branch nose-dived during the Watergate years—more revealing, perhaps, is the dwindling confidence in leaders of other institutions, especially when compared to the more optimistic 1960s.

Year	World	United States Politics	Arts
1970	The new social-liberal cabinet in West Germany begins direct negotiations with East Germany in order to normalize relations between the two German states.	Four students at Ohio's Kent State University are killed by National Guardsmen firing on an antiwar rally.	Drug overdoses kill Woodstock veterans Jimi Hendrix and Janis Joplin; the Beatles break up.
1971	Protests by Bengali nationalists lead to war in East Pakistan (Bangladesh) and inspire ex-Beatle George Harrison to host the Concert for Bangladesh.	Defense Department official Daniel Ellsberg leaks the "Pentagon Papers" to the *New York Times*, revealing the extent of U.S. involvement in Southeast Asia.	Dee Brown publishes *Bury My Heart at Wounded Knee: An Indian History of the American West*.
1972	The "Bloody Sunday" deaths of 13 Catholics precipitate violence in Northern Ireland.	Nixon is reelected, but a break-in at Democratic national headquarters in the Watergate building casts a shadow over his presidency.	Claes Oldenburg, a Swedish-American sculptor who is a leader in the creation of the pop art era, receives the Skowhegan Medal for Sculpture.
1973	Arab nations, incensed by Western support for Israel in the Yom Kippur War, reduce their oil production, causing an energy shortage.	The Supreme Court overturns state bans on abortion in *Roe v. Wade*.	*The Godfather* and *Cabaret* split the major Academy Awards, but Marlon Brando refuses to accept his best actor prize as a protest against discrimination toward Native Americans.
1974	In Portugal, the Armed Forces Movement overthrows the civilian dictator and installs a military leader.	▼ Facing impeachment for his role in the Watergate scandal, President Nixon resigns from office.	Russian ballet dancer Mikhail Baryshnikov joins the American Ballet Theatre (ABT) in New York City.
1975	The war in Vietnam ends with the fall of Saigon, but neighboring Cambodia begins a reign of terror under Pol Pot.		Young movie director Steven Spielberg scores his first hit with *Jaws*.
1976	In Soweto, an African township in South Africa, children demonstrate against a government order calling for all classes to be taught in Afrikaans rather than English. Police attempt to restore order and open fire, killing at least 100 people.	*UPI/BETTMANN*	Alex Haley's historical epic *Roots* is a best-seller; the award-winning TV adaptation will air the following year.
1977	The Spanish Communist Party (Partido Comunista De España or PCE) is legalized in Spain.	President Jimmy Carter is criticized for the Panama Canal Treaty, which arranges for control of the canal to be turned over to Panama.	Critics love Woody Allen's film *Annie Hall*, while kids flock to George Lucas's *Star Wars*.
1978	President Jimmy Carter brings Egypt's President Anwar Sadat and Israel's Prime Minister Menachem Begin to Camp David to begin negotiations that lead to the 1979 treaty.	President Carter postpones production of the controversial neutron bomb.	*Dallas*, a television drama about Texas oil barons, begins a 10-year run.
1979	An Islamic revolution deposes the Shah of Iran, who flees to the United States, while angry Iranians seize U.S. hostages.	President Carter signs the SALT II agreement with Soviet leader Leonid Brezhnev, which aims to limit the U.S. and Soviet Union's strategic arms.	The Sugar Hill Gang releases "Rapper's Delight," the first commercial rap hit.

Science and Industry	Pastimes and Lifestyles	Sports	Year
The Clean Air Act forces automobile manufacturers to limit tailpipe emissions.	Elvis Presley and President Richard Nixon meet at the White House to discuss possible solutions to America's drug problem.	Diane Crump becomes the first female jockey in the Kentucky Derby, finishing 12th in the race.	1970
Amtrak, the National Railroad Passenger Corporation, begins operation and takes over the nation's inter-city passenger rail services.	The Disney World theme park opens in Lake Buena Vista, Florida.	The Supreme Court clears ex-boxer Muhammad Ali of draft-dodging charges.	1971
TWA and American Airlines announce that they will begin inspecting passengers' luggage before they board planes in order to reduce incidents of terrorism.	American Bobby Fischer beats Russian Boris Spassky at the World Chess Championships in Reykjavik, Iceland.	Eleven Israeli athletes are killed by Palestine Liberation Organization terrorists at the Munich Olympics.	1972
Scientists Stanley Cohen and Herbert Boyer accomplish the first gene-splicing.	Pong, the digital version of Ping-Pong, becomes an arcade hit.	Billie Jean King beats Bobby Riggs in a "Battle of the Sexes" tennis match.	1973
Intel introduces the 8080 micro-processor with 64K memory.	Streaking becomes headline news when Robert Opal runs naked across the stage of the Academy Awards.	Hank Aaron breaks Babe Ruth's lifetime record with his 715th home run.	1974
The parents of coma-stricken Karen Anne Quinlan file suit to force a New Jersey hospital to allow their daughter to die naturally.	Phillip Morris introduces low-calorie Miller Lite beer, rekindling the brewery's popularity.	Fred Lynn of the Boston Red Sox is the first and only baseball player to win both the Rookie of the Year and the MVP awards.	1975
Fear of the "swine flu" leads millions of Americans to receive flu shots that cause paralysis in 535 people.	The International Telegraph and Telephone Consultative Committee (CCITT) issues the Group 2 fax standard, which is able to transmit a one-page document in approximately three minutes.	The Summer Olympics in Montreal, Canada, features dramatic victories by Bruce Jenner in the decathlon, Nadia Comaneci in gymnastics, and brothers Leon and Michael Spinks in boxing events.	1976
	◄ *The Complete Book of Running* by James Fixx inspires a jogging fad, while the record-breaking *Saturday Night Fever* sound track fuels the disco fever.	Unprecedented bidding wars for top baseball players are sparked by the new practice of free agency.	1977
Contamination from an old chemical dump forces the evacuation of Love Canal in New York State.	In the first transatlantic balloon crossing, three Americans set an endurance record of 138 hours and 6 minutes in the air.	The U.S. Open switches to hardcourt, becoming the only Grand Slam competition to have been played on three surfaces; the previous court surfaces included grass and clay.	1978
A reactor overheats at the Three Mile Island nuclear power plant in Harrisburg, Pennsylvania.	The new Sony Walkman allows listeners to take their music anywhere.	Star fullback O. J. Simpson retires from the San Francisco 49ers.	1979

CORBIS/James L. Ames

The Big Picture

Although the defeat of the United States in Vietnam—signaled by the fall of Saigon in 1975—made Americans both weary and wary of overseas involvement, they remained inextricably bound to the greater world. Whether attending rock concerts to benefit the poor in Bangladesh, encouraging agreements to bring peace to the Middle East, or watching in horror as Iranian revolutionaries ransacked a U.S. embassy and grabbed hostages, Americans realized that the world was both small and unstable, neither beyond their concern nor pliant to their desires.

NORTHERN IRELAND
Constitution Suspended (1972)

Stirred by what the civil rights movement in the United States had accomplished for African Americans, Catholics in Northern Ireland organized shortly before 1970 to protest oppression by Protestants. The movement took a violent turn, however, when radical Catholics acting through the Provisional wing of the Irish Republican Army (IRA), and Protestants acting through their own paramilitary units, attacked each other. The IRA wanted to end Protestant domination and British rule and used bombings, assassinations, and other terrorist tactics to achieve its ends. As violence spread, Britain sent troops into Northern Ireland and suspended Northern Ireland's constitution and its Parliament. Between 1972 and 1976, the conflict caused an average of 275 deaths per year.

GREECE AND SPAIN
Democracy Takes Hold (1974-1975)

Politics in Greece and Spain took a surprise turn when both countries replaced dictatorships with democracies. The Greek military regime was destroyed by an invasion of Cyprus by Turkish forces in 1974; the following year a new constitution established a Greek republic. In Spain, fascist ruler Francisco Franco died in 1975, and King Juan Carlos took power. Few expected Carlos to make anything more than minor changes, but working with Prime Minister Adolfo Suarez Gonzalez, he formed a legislature based on universal suffrage. Amid the cold war, Americans hailed the Greek and Spanish reforms as victories for democracy.

PANAMA
The Panama Canal Treaty (1977-1978)

Ever since the 1960s, American presidents had negotiated with Panama to change how the Panama Canal was governed. In 1977, President Jimmy Carter signed a treaty that returned the Canal Zone to Panamanian rule but stipulated that the United States would operate the canal itself until the year 2000. Many in and outside Congress claimed the treaty placed a critical facility under foreign control and weakened American power. One senator remarked: "We stole it [Panama] fair and square," and thus should keep the canal. Carter, however, pushed the treaty hard, and in 1978 the Senate ratified it.

CHILE
Pinochet Obliterates Allende's Socialist Program (1970-1973)

The postwar years saw escalating political upheaval in nearly all regions of Latin America. Perhaps nowhere was this turmoil more vivid to the Boomer experience than in Chile when, after Salvador Allende's election to power in 1970, his rule was cut down in 1973 by a military coup under the direction of General Augusto Pinochet. In the short two years of Allende's rule, he nationalized U.S.-owned mines and launched economic support programs, pushing inflation upwards, which, in itself, added to civil strife. In 1973, Pinochet's coup—supported by the U.S. government—marked the beginning of a 16-year dictatorship notorious for its brutal suppression of human rights.

EGYPT AND ISRAEL
War and Peace (1973-1979)

America's Secretary of State Henry Kissinger scoffed at any suggestion that Egypt might go to war against Israel. "I regarded it as empty talk," he said. But on October 6, 1973, Egypt and Syria attacked during the Jewish religious holiday, Yom Kippur. The Arabs wanted to regain land they had lost in 1967 and drove their enemy from the Sinai Peninsula and the Golan Heights, until a few days later when American arms shipments allowed Israel to recover. A cease-fire followed and, in 1979, with the help and encouragement of the United States, Egypt and Israel established diplomatic relations: in so doing, they kindled hope that peace might come to a region Americans had long thought incurably explosive.

MIDDLE EAST
Civil War (1975-1976)

The Middle East erupted in violence again in 1975 when religious factions went to war in Lebanon. Palestinian and leftist Muslim militias fought Maronite (Syrian Catholic), Phalange, and other Christian militias. Several Arab countries aided the Palestinians, and Israel aided the Christians, thus extending long-standing enmities into Lebanon. The conflict grew more complex in 1976 when Syrian troops entered the country and fought against the Palestinians to restore order. A cease-fire was declared, but more than 60,000 people had been killed and the atmosphere within Lebanon remained tense, with continued battles, an ineffective central government, and, in 1978, an incursion by Israeli troops against Palestinian militia bases.

IRAN
Revolution Overthrows the Shah (1979-1981)

To the surprise of President Jimmy Carter, in 1979 Islamic revolutionaries led by Ayatollah Khomeini overthrew Iran's shah. That November, an angry mob attacked the U.S. embassy in Tehran and held Americans hostage. The crisis perplexed Carter, conditioned like most Americans to see the world in cold war terms, but now confronted by an event that defied that definition. In April 1980, Carter used military commandos in a failed attempt to rescue the hostages. He did not reach a deal with the Iranians until his last day as president, after the crisis had humiliated him and contributed to his defeat in the 1980 election.

BANGLADESH
Independence and Turmoil (1971-1979)

When in 1971 ex-Beatle George Harrison sponsored a "Concert for Bangladesh," he called attention to a country ravaged by war and famine. In the spring of 1971, Pakistani troops swept through Dacca, the major city in Bangladesh, or what was then East Pakistan. The troops slaughtered civilians in an attempt to crush a surging independence movement, but Bangladeshis still declared their nationhood. In an ensuing war, more than one million Bangladeshis died. In December, India deployed its army, igniting war between itself and Pakistan. A few days later, Pakistan surrendered and recognized Bangladesh's independence. Turmoil, however, continued; in 1975 alone a flood killed 500,000 people and two bloody military coups shook the nation.

CAMBODIA
Khmer Rouge Atrocities (1975-1979)

As the 1970s began, the United States, as part of the Vietnam War, launched massive attacks against enemy encampments in Cambodia. These attacks destabilized the Cambodian government and unintentionally helped the Khmer Rouge, a communist guerrilla group within Cambodia. Led by Pol Pot, the communists gained power in 1975 and suppressed Buddhism, placed the economy under state control, and forcibly relocated urban residents to rural districts. The Khmer Rouge built terror centers and killed their enemies—at least one million and perhaps as many as three million Cambodians had been killed by 1979. That year, Vietnamese troops drove the Khmer Rouge from power.

VIETNAM
Fall of Saigon (1973-1975)

In January 1973, delegates from the United States and North Vietnam met in Paris where they signed a peace agreement. Although America still provided massive military supplies to South Vietnam in its continuing war with the communists, on April 30, 1975, the South Vietnamese government surrendered. Just two days earlier, viewers in the United States watched as television broadcast scenes of Americans and a few Vietnamese boarding emergency helicopters to flee the communist forces, while U.S. Marines kept many more panic-stricken Vietnamese away from the choppers—a horrible end to a horrible war.

With the massive buildup of nuclear weapons by the United States and the Soviet Union in the 1950s and 1960s, "the bomb" had become for Baby Boomers a sword of Damocles over their heads. Few expected the technology to be contained, let alone eliminated. With a few notable exceptions, events in the 1970s fulfilled that expectation.

Perhaps no other politician had entered the American presidency provoking more intensity of feeling than Richard Nixon in 1969. Many admired him for his firm opposition to communism; many despised him for his history of duplicitous behavior. He began his term with the nation deeply divided over Vietnam. The war, in fact, influenced almost every important foreign policy decision during Nixon's presidency. Nixon appointed Henry Kissinger, a Harvard professor, as his national security advisor. The two men could hardly stand each other—Nixon thought Kissinger had psychological problems, and Kissinger said Nixon had a "meatball mind"—but together they embraced the philosophies of "realpolitik" and "linkage." Realpolitik meant they believed foreign policy should be purged of moral crusades. They insisted the United States should pursue its strategic interests, first and foremost.

According to the theory of linkage, world developments could be directed by the United States, the Soviet Union, and China. The Soviets and the Chinese supported the communists in Vietnam, thus agreements with those two nations at one level would lead to arrangements at another to end the Vietnam War.

Nixon pursued his strategy through secret deals and through grand theater, carefully staged for television. In a surprise move, in February 1972, he journeyed to Peking (now Beijing), China. His trip astonished many Baby Boomers, for they knew his reputation as the unrelenting congressman who had hunted communists on the domestic scene and who had vilified those he held responsible for "losing China" to communism back in 1949. In China, Nixon met with Mao Zedong, the mastermind of that nation's communist revolution. From the visit—during which in a toast before TV cameras Nixon proclaimed, "This was the week that changed the world"—the United States and China promised to normalize relations.

Whether Nixon's trip to China lessened the threat of nuclear war, however, was debatable. After all, by 1972, the Soviet Union had 1,200 ICBMs, 200 long-range bombers equipped with nuclear weapons, and 200 nuclear missiles aboard submarines. The United States had 1,054 ICBMs, 540 long-range bombers equipped with nuclear weapons, and 656 nuclear missiles aboard submarines—enough firepower to kill each Russian 50 times over.

By making the Russians worry about a possible U.S.–China alliance, Nixon may have propelled the signing of SALT I, the Strategic Arms Limitation Treaty, with the Soviet Union, at the time of his visit to Moscow in 1972. SALT I set a ceiling on ICBMs, and a related agreement limited both nations in employing antiballistic missile systems. The two nations also signed The Basic Principles of Relations,

U.S. Nuclear Warheads: 1970 to 1979

Year	Strategic Warheads				Non-Strategic Warheads	Stockpiled Warheads
	ICBM	SLBM	Bombers	Total Strategic Warheads		
1970	1,306	1,630	6,465	9,401	16,341	25,742
1971	1,516	2,587	6,252	10,355	15,632	25,988
1972	1,726	3,276	7,360	12,363	14,556	26,919
1973	1,936	4,318	6,991	13,244	14,714	27,958
1974	2,041	4,654	6,788	13,483	14,310	27,793
1975	2,251	4,771	6,911	13,933	12,742	26,675
1976	2,251	5,359	6,647	14,257	11,321	25,579
1977	2,251	5,477	6,592	14,320	10,402	24,722
1978	2,251	5,712	6,264	14,227	9,639	23,866
1979	2,251	5,645	6,252	14,148	9,582	23,730

UNITED STATES

which stressed peaceful coexistence. *Time* magazine said about Nixon's trip to Russia: "It had all been stage-managed carefully, and the accords had been worked on for months or even years. . . . They could have been revealed to the world without the Kremlin spectacular, yet the way in which they were signed gave them special import."

SALT I stood at the center of détente, a policy intended to reduce tension between the United States and the Soviet Union. Accordingly, the nuclear threat diminished. In application, however, SALT I did little; it said nothing about multiple independently targetable reentry vehicles (MIRVs)—where one missile carried several nuclear warheads, each programmed to hit a different target—and both nations added greater numbers of them to their arsenals. While Soviet leader Leonid Brezhnev met with Nixon in 1973 and signed a statement called the Prevention of Nuclear War, Henry Kissinger spoke realpolitik when he said privately that "the way for us to use [SALT] is for us to catch up." Soon, the United States had 10,000 nuclear warheads, the Soviet Union 4,000. Laurence Martin, director of war studies at the University of London, observed that SALT I accelerated rather than restrained strategic arms procurement.

In spite of all the symbolism surrounding the American–Soviet agreements, détente proved illusory. In 1975, the Russians voided an earlier trade agreement with the United States; they argued that congressional legislation had changed it. *Time* pondered: "Three years of delicate and arduous negotiations were . . . aborted. Was something else aborted as well—namely the whole carefully crafted structure of détente between Washington and Moscow?"

In the end, Nixon's linkage theory failed. Neither the Soviet Union nor China backed away from supporting the communists in Vietnam. Although Russian pressure contributed to North Vietnam reaching a cease-fire agreement with the United States that took effect in 1973, so too did the American bombing raids on Hanoi. "The bastards have never been bombed like they're going to be bombed this time," declared Nixon before a particularly brutal assault. After U.S. troops left Vietnam with the cease-fire, the war continued. American and Russian weapons, and some Chinese ones, flowed into Vietnam, and the casualties continued to mount until, in 1975, the American-backed South Vietnamese government collapsed.

The 1970s ended on an ominous note, suggesting that the bomb still ruled, that détente had suffered, and that for all their might, the superpowers were limited in their ability to dictate world events. In 1979, President Jimmy Carter signed SALT II with the Soviet Union; that treaty restricted the number of MIRVs and froze the number of delivery systems. But then the Russians invaded Afghanistan, and the U.S. Senate rejected the treaty. That same year, fundamentalist Muslims in Iran ransacked the U.S. embassy and took Americans hostage. Try as Carter did, he failed to get them released during his presidency. Persons overseas, who felt oppressed by the United States and suffocated by its power, pursued terrorism and would pursue it on a yet grander scale.

▼ *In the 1970s the United States and the U.S.S.R. pursued an aggressive policy of stockpiling nuclear weapons. Competition between the two superpowers became more fierce with every passing year, despite attempts, like the SALT treaties, to slow things down.*

U.S.S.R. Nuclear Warheads: 1970 to 1979

Year	Strategic Warheads				Non-Strategic Warheads	Stockpiled Warheads
	ICBM	SLBM	Bombers	Total Strategic Warheads		
1970	1,546	301	596	2,443	9,200	11,643
1971	1,616	380	596	2,592	10,500	13,092
1972	1,600	481	596	2,678	11,800	14,478
1973	1,635	584	596	2,815	13,100	15,915
1974	1,666	722	596	2,985	14,400	17,385
1975	2,277	869	596	3,743	15,700	19,443
1976	2,607	1,002	596	4,205	17,000	21,205
1977	2,838	1,309	596	4,744	18,300	23,044
1978	3,666	1,531	596	5,793	19,600	25,393
1979	4,833	1,605	596	7,035	20,900	27,935

U.
S.
S.
R.

In February 1973 about 300 Native Americans barricaded themselves at Wounded Knee on the Pine Ridge Reservation in South Dakota, guns pointed at federal marshals, who pointed guns at the Indians. The scene resembled warfare from a hundred years earlier when whites had swept across the Great Plains, forcing Native Americans into retreat and destroying their culture. This time Indian leader Russell Means declared: "We've got the whole Wounded Knee Valley, and we definitely are going to hold it until death do us part."

As the tumultuous 1960s ended, two groups kept alive their countercultural protests into the next decade: Native Americans and women. Both determined they would fight for the rights long denied them.

Native American protest had erupted four years before Wounded Knee, when, in 1969, dissidents occupied Alcatraz, an island off San Francisco where a fortresslike prison had recently been abandoned by the federal government. They reclaimed the land as Native American property and demanded that the United States fund the building of a cultural center. The government refused and evicted the protesters in 1971. But the occupation had generated enormous publicity and exposed the horrendous conditions Indians faced on their reservations: an average of only 5.5 years of schooling; 90 percent of housing substandard; unemployment reaching 80 percent; alcoholism epidemic.

The Alcatraz protest also encouraged Native Americans to build the nascent American Indian Movement (AIM) into a national organization. Founded in 1968, AIM established "survival schools" in cities and formed neighborhood patrols to prevent police brutality. Folk singer Buffy Sainte-Marie captured the discontent among Native Americans when she sang: "When a war between nations is lost/The loser, we know, pays the cost/But even when Germany fell to your hands/You left them their pride and you left them their land."

In 1972, Russell Means led AIM into Gordon, Nebraska, where it protested the refusal of the local authorities to file charges against two white men implicated in the murder of

> **"** We weren't meant to be tourist attractions for the master race. **"**
> —**Lehman Brightman**, *South Dakota Sioux, 1970*

▼ *Members of the American Indian Movement stand guard outside the Sacred Heart Church in Wounded Knee, South Dakota, during the 1973 standoff. (UPI/CORBIS-BETTMANN)*

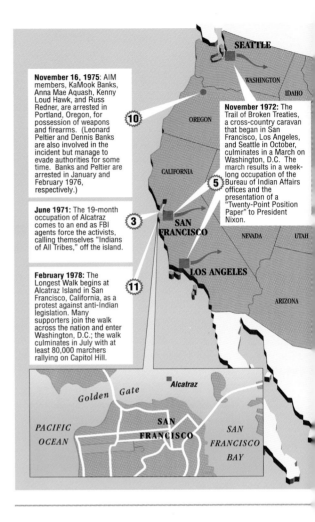

November 16, 1975: AIM members, KaMook Banks, Anna Mae Aquash, Kenny Loud Hawk, and Russ Redner, are arrested in Portland, Oregon, for possession of weapons and firearms. (Leonard Peltier and Dennis Banks are also involved in the incident but manage to evade authorities for some time. Banks and Peltier are arrested in January and February 1976, respectively.) **10**

November 1972: The Trail of Broken Treaties, a cross-country caravan that began in San Francisco, Los Angeles, and Seattle in October, culminates in a March on Washington, D.C. The march results in a week-long occupation of the Bureau of Indian Affairs offices and the presentation of a "Twenty-Point Position Paper" to President Nixon. **5**

June 1971: The 19-month occupation of Alcatraz comes to an end as FBI agents force the activists, calling themselves "Indians of All Tribes," off the island. **3**

February 1978: The Longest Walk begins at Alcatraz Island in San Francisco, California, as a protest against anti-Indian legislation. Many supporters join the walk across the nation and enter Washington, D.C.; the walk culminates in July with at least 80,000 marchers rallying on Capitol Hill. **11**

an Oglala Lakota man. The arrest of the two men, their trial, and their subsequent conviction boosted AIM's prestige among Native Americans.

The showdown at Wounded Knee—site of an 1890 massacre when the U.S. Army killed hundreds of Sioux, mainly old men, women, and children—occurred after some of the Oglala Sioux on the Pine Ridge Reservation asked AIM to help them oppose Richard Wilson, a tribal leader whom they considered corrupt. The federal government supported Wilson because he was willing to allow the development of uranium mines, although the mines would encroach on the reservation and likely contaminate the land.

When the AIM protesters arrived at Wounded Knee, Wilson's Indian police surrounded them. The protesters then ransacked a trading post, confiscated its guns, and erected barricades. The federal government responded with a massive show of force: 17 armored personnel carriers, 130,000 rounds of M-16 ammunition, 12 M-79 grenade launchers, several helicopters, and Phantom jets. Sporadic gunfire and a long siege ensued. Finally, on May 7, AIM gave up after the government made promises, which were never fulfilled.

The government then prosecuted Means, but failed to get a conviction for Wounded Knee. At the same time, the FBI compiled 316,000 files on Sioux connected with AIM, made 562 arrests, and obtained 185 indictments—which led to only 15 convictions, all on minor charges. Another violent confrontation erupted at Pine Ridge in 1975, when several Native

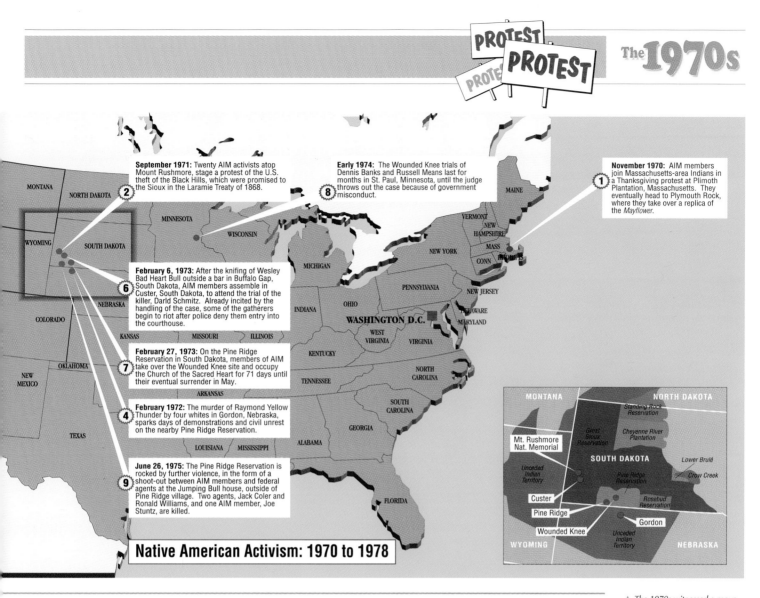

September 1971: Twenty AIM activists atop Mount Rushmore, stage a protest of the U.S. theft of the Black Hills, which were promised to the Sioux in the Laramie Treaty of 1868.

Early 1974: The Wounded Knee trials of Dennis Banks and Russell Means last for months in St. Paul, Minnesota, until the judge throws out the case because of government misconduct.

November 1970: AIM members join Massachusetts-area Indians in a Thanksgiving protest at Plimoth Plantation, Massachusetts. They eventually head to Plymouth Rock, where they take over a replica of the *Mayflower*.

February 6, 1973: After the knifing of Wesley Bad Heart Bull outside a bar in Buffalo Gap, South Dakota, AIM members assemble in Custer, South Dakota, to attend the trial of the killer, Darld Schmitz. Already incited by the handling of the case, some of the gatherers begin to riot after police deny them entry into the courthouse.

February 27, 1973: On the Pine Ridge Reservation in South Dakota, members of AIM take over the Wounded Knee site and occupy the Church of the Sacred Heart for 71 days until their eventual surrender in May.

February 1972: The murder of Raymond Yellow Thunder by four whites in Gordon, Nebraska, sparks days of demonstrations and civil unrest on the nearby Pine Ridge Reservation.

June 26, 1975: The Pine Ridge Reservation is rocked by further violence, in the form of a shoot-out between AIM members and federal agents at the Jumping Bull house, outside of Pine Ridge village. Two agents, Jack Coler and Ronald Williams, and one AIM member, Joe Stuntz, are killed.

Native American Activism: 1970 to 1978

Americans and FBI agents exchanged gunfire. The FBI arrested the Indians, among them Leonard Peltier, for killing two agents. In a controversial trial, one many outside observers called inconclusive, even prejudiced against the defendant, Peltier was found guilty and sentenced to two consecutive life terms. AIM collapsed as a national organization in the late 1970s, although local chapters continued to operate.

Amid Native American activism, women expanded their protest, fighting for numerous changes in what historian Terry Anderson has called "a Feminist Renaissance." In the early 1970s, Congress passed the Equal Rights Amendment (it was never ratified by the states) and Title IX of the Educational Amendments Act, which prohibited colleges that received federal funds from engaging in sex discrimination. About the same time, San Diego State University began the first women's studies program, and by 1980 such classes existed on 500 campuses.

In what many women considered a major victory for their rights, in 1973 the Supreme Court decided in *Roe v. Wade* that states could no longer ban abortions conducted during the first three months of pregnancy. The following year, Congress passed the Equal Credit Opportunity Act that stipulated a woman could get credit without her husband's co-signature and based on her income, without reference to his.

In the early 1970s complaints were filed against 1,300 corporations that received federal funds, demanding equal employment. Protests even involved nuns who organized to denounce the Catholic Church as a male church that relegated women to a secondary status.

As the 1970s ended, dissension within the women's movement slowed its progress. Radicals and moderates disagreed as to whether men should be included or excluded from the movement—should they be treated as equals, as misguided souls, or as oppressive beasts. Feminists divided along lines of age, class, and race, with criticism by some that the movement had generally helped white middle-class women but had abandoned the poor and ignored minorities. For their part, conservatives, both male and female, questioned whether change had come too fast and threatened the traditional family. Yet from Native Americans to Catholic nuns, society felt the effects of protest and change.

▲ The 1970s witnessed a movement among Native Americans akin to the civil rights movement of the 1960s. This map details some key moments of resistance, particularly those involving the American Indian Movement (AIM). While AIM protests—often dramatic and sometimes violent—tended to dominate the headlines, other advocacy groups also existed, including the National Congress of American Indians, the National Indian Youth Council, and the Native American Rights Fund.

Big Brother

Throughout the 1960s and into the 1970s the federal government operated a secret counterintelligence program, called COINTELPRO, to crush protest groups. The FBI employed 2,000 agents in COINTELPRO. They infiltrated organizations and used many dirty tricks, illegally wiretapping phones and breaking into homes and offices.

COINTELPRO even encouraged or helped arrange political assassinations, such as when it provided the Chicago police with information that helped the cops murder Black Panther leader Freddie Hampton. At the same time, through another secret program, Army agents compiled dossiers on 25 million Americans. When these efforts came to light, critics warned that an oppressive, omnipresent government had arrived—Big Brother dressed to lie, destroy, and kill.

Environmentalism

Two events served as bookends for the environmental movement in the 1970s: one signaled hope, and the other danger. On April 22, 1970, Americans by the millions celebrated the first Earth Day, showing their support for environmental reform. Nine years later, on March 28, 1979, a nuclear accident at the Three Mile Island power plant in Pennsylvania sent thousands of residents scurrying in panic and caused millions more to live in dread that a similar accident could occur near their own neighborhood.

The environmental movement gained momentum in 1969 after a massive oil spill ruined beaches and killed wildlife at Santa Barbara, California. National attention was also drawn to the environment that year when scientists discovered salmon laced with DDT (a pesticide damaging to the entire food chain) in Wisconsin and Minnesota, and the Cuyahoga River near Cleveland, Ohio, filled with oil sludge, caught fire. Many 1960s activists joined the environmental movement and used tactics, such as sit-ins and building mass support, they had learned and developed in the fight for civil rights and against the Vietnam War.

Americans first engaged in large-scale activities to promote environmental reform with Earth Day. The recognition of Earth Day took many shapes, from Girl Scouts in canoes removing garbage along the Potomac River, to blacks in St. Louis using street theater to dramatize health problems caused by lead paint, to 5,000 protesters gathering at the Washington Monument and singing along with folk musicians before marching on the Interior Department.

More than 20 million people participated in Earth Day activities, and as politicians counted heads and saw potential votes riding on environmental issues, Congress passed several clean air and water acts, and many states passed favorable legislation. Some historians have gone so far as to call the 1970s the "golden age of environmentalism."

In December 1970, President Richard Nixon established the Environmental Protection Agency (EPA), which consolidated several government agencies to handle problems facing the nation's environment. "As concern with the condition of our physical environment has intensified . . ." said Nixon, "it . . . has become increasingly clear that only by reorganizing our Federal efforts can we develop the knowledge, and effectively ensure the protection, development, and enhancement of the total environment itself." That same year, he signed the Clean Air Act, which toughened standards for auto emissions in order to reduce air pollution. In 1972, he signed into law the Clean Water Act, which set as a goal the total elimination of pollutant discharges by 1985 (which was never met), and the Pesticide Control Act, which banned the use of DDT.

Other accomplishments followed. The Endangered Species Act of 1973 pledged the federal government to protecting those species and their habitats threatened with extinction. Among the first was the northern spotted owl and its home among the ancient forests of the Pacific Northwest. Between 1974 and 1977, clean-air laws reduced the number

> 66 *The conservation movement is a breeding ground of Communists and other subversives. We intend to clean them out, even if it means rounding up every bird watcher in the country.* 99
>
> — **John Mitchell**
> U.S. Attorney General, 1969-1972

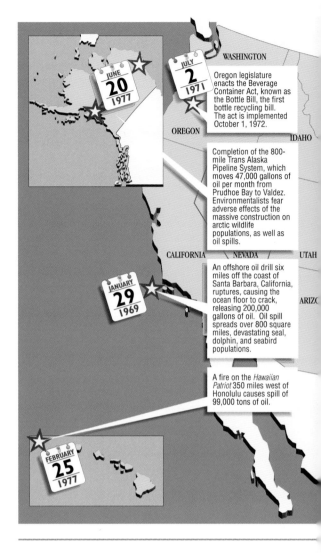

WASHINGTON

JULY 2 1971 — Oregon legislature enacts the Beverage Container Act, known as the Bottle Bill, the first bottle recycling bill. The act is implemented October 1, 1972.

OREGON   IDAHO

JUNE 20 1977 — Completion of the 800-mile Trans Alaska Pipeline System, which moves 47,000 gallons of oil per month from Prudhoe Bay to Valdez. Environmentalists fear adverse effects of the massive construction on arctic wildlife populations, as well as oil spills.

CALIFORNIA   NEVADA   UTAH

JANUARY 29 1969 — An offshore oil drill six miles off the coast of Santa Barbara, California, ruptures, causing the ocean floor to crack, releasing 200,000 gallons of oil. Oil spill spreads over 800 square miles, devastating seal, dolphin, and seabird populations.

ARIZONA

A fire on the *Hawaiian Patriot* 350 miles west of Honolulu causes spill of 99,000 tons of oil.

FEBRUARY 25 1977

---

of unhealthy days in 25 major cities by 15 percent—largely by reducing auto exhaust emissions—and the number of *very* unhealthy days by 35 percent. Not to be outdone by Congress, Colorado, Wyoming, New Mexico, Nevada, and Utah each enacted tougher clean-air standards on utilities than did the federal government.

In the late 1970s, President Jimmy Carter established a $1.6 billion superfund to clean up abandoned chemical-waste sites. By executive order, he protected about 100 million acres of land in Alaska as national parks, forests, or wildlife refuges. He appointed 18 environmentalists to important government posts, and signed legislation setting stiffer controls for strip mining.

But for all its success, the environmental movement underwent changes that caused some to claim that, as the decade ended, it had fallen on hard times. For one, the movement—highly decentralized like protest movements had been in the 1960s—splintered, and arguments arose among those who wanted to cooperate with business and those who wanted confrontation. For another, economic upheaval tested the nation's commitment to environmental reform. An Arab oil embargo boosted oil prices, inflation reached debilitating heights, and recession cost many people their jobs. As a result, business leaders and many others

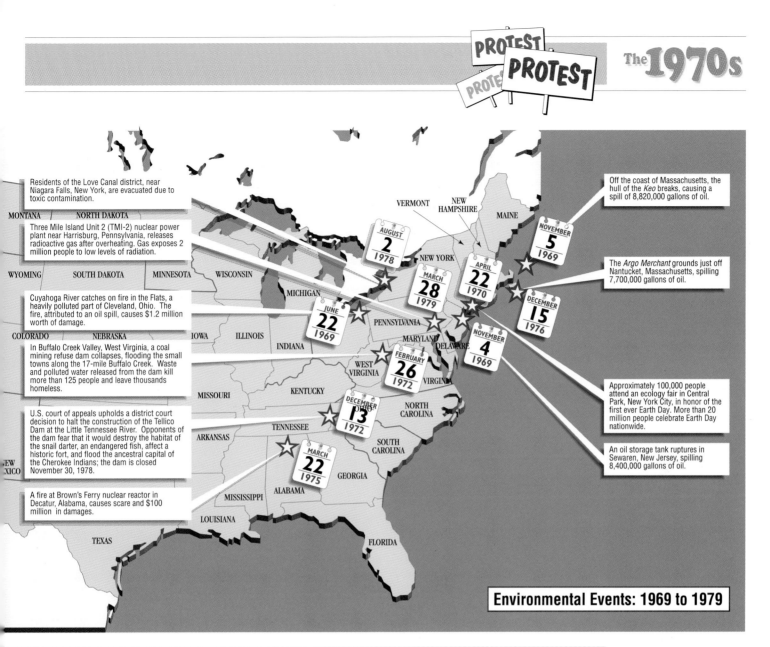

Residents of the Love Canal district, near Niagara Falls, New York, are evacuated due to toxic contamination.

Three Mile Island Unit 2 (TMI-2) nuclear power plant near Harrisburg, Pennsylvania, releases radioactive gas after overheating. Gas exposes 2 million people to low levels of radiation.

Cuyahoga River catches on fire in the Flats, a heavily polluted part of Cleveland, Ohio. The fire, attributed to an oil spill, causes $1.2 million worth of damage.

In Buffalo Creek Valley, West Virginia, a coal mining refuse dam collapses, flooding the small towns along the 17-mile Buffalo Creek. Waste and polluted water released from the dam kill more than 125 people and leave thousands homeless.

U.S. court of appeals upholds a district court decision to halt the construction of the Tellico Dam at the Little Tennessee River. Opponents of the dam fear that it would destroy the habitat of the snail darter, an endangered fish, affect a historic fort, and flood the ancestral capital of the Cherokee Indians; the dam is closed November 30, 1978.

A fire at Brown's Ferry nuclear reactor in Decatur, Alabama, causes scare and $100 million in damages.

Off the coast of Massachusetts, the hull of the *Keo* breaks, causing a spill of 8,820,000 gallons of oil.

The *Argo Merchant* grounds just off Nantucket, Massachusetts, spilling 7,700,000 gallons of oil.

Approximately 100,000 people attend an ecology fair in Central Park, New York City, in honor of the first ever Earth Day. More than 20 million people celebrate Earth Day nationwide.

An oil storage tank ruptures in Sewaren, New Jersey, spilling 8,400,000 gallons of oil.

Environmental Events: 1969 to 1979

---

insisted that the cost of environmental regulation, which they said held back economic growth, was a luxury that could no longer be afforded.

Employment and energy development seemed more important than ever. Congress granted auto manufacturers more time to meet emission standards, and it dropped legislation that would have imposed strong environmental controls on new offshore oil leases. Even President Carter, a strong environmentalist, relaxed the enforcement of federal antipollution standards.

Much opposition came from rural communities where people needed work, such as the residents of Eastport, Maine, who, over environmentalist objections, supported in the mid-1970s a proposed oil refinery that would create 1,400 jobs near their town. Others criticized environmentalists for being too zealous in choosing animal welfare over human welfare. One shopping mall developer in Rensselaer County, New York, dropped his project entirely after a court ordered him to regulate the temperature of water discharged into a nearby stream so as to protect 3,000 trout—at a cost of $100 per fish to install the needed equipment, and $10 per fish to operate it.

Yet the catastrophe at Three Mile Island near Harrisburg, Pennsylvania, in 1979 brought home the threat posed by

modern technology and reinforced long-held environmentalist views that the danger from nuclear power far outweighed any benefits. According to some, radioactivity released into the air by the accident resulted in retardation of children and an unusually high number of cancer cases in people living near the plant. Whatever problems beset the environmental movement at decade's end, Three Mile Island and earlier work by environmental protesters to alert the public left a deep impression; thus even though the 1980 election brought to power a president unfriendly to environmental reform, only one in five voters believed environmental standards should be relaxed for economic development.

▲ As the 1970s dawned, it became clear to many Americans that the needs of Mother Nature could no longer be ignored. This map shows some of the major environmental disasters and victories in the 1970s.

◄ On March 30, 1979, a cow is treated to radiation exposure as it grazes in front of the Three Mile Island nuclear power plant in Harrisburg, Pennsylvania—just two days after the accident. (CORBIS/BETTMANN-UPI)

At the start of the 1970s, American families could sit in front of their TV sets over TV dinners and see the world on the nightly news. With each bite of salisbury steak, Walter Cronkite, by then America's most trusted newsman, would report the day's events. The fighting in Vietnam was still fierce and reports of both Viet Cong and American casualties scrolled across the bottom of the screen like baseball scores.

With the war, racial conflict, antiwar protests, the sexual revolution, drug use, and the women's liberation movement as the uneasy subtext of American life, it is no wonder that TV looked the way it did for the first half of the 1970s. The extraordinary character comedy *All in the Family* (1971–79) held the top spot in the TV ratings for five years from the 1971–72 season until the 1975–76 season. Created by Norman Lear, *All in the Family* brought to life Archie Bunker, an equal opportunity bigot who believed every stereotype imaginable. Archie and those surrounding him—his wife Edith, daughter Gloria, son-in-law Michael "Meathead" Stivic, and neighbors the Jeffersons—gave Americans a way to laugh with one another and often talk to each other in a disturbed time in a divided country. From the on-air toilet flush that opened the first episode to an interracial smooch between Archie and guest-star Sammy Davis, Jr., *All in the Family* broke TV convention in ways no other show had ever done.

All in the Family and its spin-offs, *Maude* (1972–78), *The Jeffersons* (1975–85), and *Good Times* (1974–79), tackled difficult issues: the Vietnam War, abortion, women's rights, integration, mixed marriages, class differences, rape, impotence, menopause, racism, premarital sex, religion, electoral politics, and child abuse. The frank portrayal of these subjects opened television to a kind of realism it had never shown before. The lasting influence is seen not only in fictional television but in talk TV and news entertainment.

▼ *John Belushi, as Jack Ruby, assassinates Lee Harvey Oswald, played by Bill Murray, with a pie in a Saturday Night Live skit. (CORBIS/Owen Frankl)*

x

In a polite, Mary Richards kind of way, *The Mary Tyler Moore Show* (1970–77) also brought innovations to TV. As the first workplace comedy, it showed a new type of "family" that could offer support and love. The lead character, Mary Richards, became the model for many single women who were entering the workplace in growing numbers. She expressed both the courage and the uncertainty women felt as they began to assume positions of authority on the job. Like the characters in *All in the Family*, the audience saw these characters, Mary, Rhoda, Ted, Mr. Grant, and the others, struggle and evolve over the years (well, not Ted).

In addition to comedies that made real-life a legitimate TV topic, the '70s introduced the miniseries. Faltering in the ratings, ABC took a chance on *Roots* in early 1977. The network's executives originally shied away from the project, uncertain of how a predominantly white audience would receive the epic story of four generations of American slavery. In the end they were convinced to present this 12-hour television event because, being third in the ratings, they had nothing to lose.

The unprecedented decision to air this sensitive and powerful story of the African-American experience over eight consecutive nights had a tremendous, if unexpected, impact. The compressed time frame built a momentum that put *Roots*, our nation's divided history, and racial discrimination at the center of conversations all across America—not just the week it was shown but for months afterward.

More than 100 million viewers—nearly half the population of the United States—were tuned in to the last installment. Some analysts attributed its success to a new American consciousness. Many even predicted a new era in race relations. Others thought it was just Hollywood cashing in with a black soap opera that trivialized slavery. Twenty years later *Roots* is remembered as a remarkable TV event because so many Americans shared the experience. But the national reconciliation around race never materialized. That the miniseries has lasted as a TV genre is perhaps the most enduring legacy of *Roots*.

Saturday Night Live (1975–present) is another television landmark that began in the mid-seventies. The late night Saturday comedy show, featuring the "Not Ready for Prime Time Players," and with its mix of outrageous sketches and wild characters, revived live comedy. Chevy Chase, Dan Aykroyd, Gilda Radner, Jane Curtin, Garrett Morris, John Belushi, and Laraine Newman were the first crop of comics in a long line of performers who made names for themselves on this show. Tuned into the post-hippie Baby Boomers, the show was cool but not too controversial. *Saturday Night Live* stretched comedic boundaries with racy language and pointed social commentary that made everything, even TV, a target. With sketches featuring the Killer Bees, the Coneheads, Emily Litella and the Samurai Warrior, the show capitalized less on outrage and more on outrageous.

As the decade drew to a close, audiences were beginning to tire of the in-your-face realism that ushered in the decade. The political climate had changed and the first wave of Baby Boomers had begun their own families. By 1975, complaints about TV's candid handling of controversial topics had begun and the backlash began to be felt. Complaints about questionable subject matter and TV violence led government to push for programming geared for the whole family. Networks were forced to sanitize their early evening lineup and provide programs suitable for "family viewing." Abortion, drug use, sex, and other sensitive subjects were exiled from the 8:00 P.M. to 9:00 P.M. time slot.

Reaching again for those values that had once offered security, *Happy Days* and *Laverne and Shirley* topped the ratings from 1977 to 1979. For the first time in television history, ABC, not CBS, won first place in the year-end ratings. The Reagan–Bush era in politics was about to dawn and America was trying to put the controversy and unrest of the early '70s behind. Gripped with nostalgia, TV underwent a transformation and turned back to a kinder, gentler time, or so it imagined.

M*A*S*H

"I don't think this place is turning out to be that great an experience for me. I mean I work under terrible pressure and everything and there's a lot of death and destruction and stuff, but outside of that I don't think I'm really getting much out of it."

—Radar O'Reilly

It was 1972, the United States was still mired in its most unpopular war. Based on a satirical Robert Altman film of the same name, *M*A*S*H* was the story of a medical unit stationed in Korea in the early 1950s, but its ambivalent, sometimes absurdist portrayal of war could easily have applied to American feelings about Vietnam. The doctors and staff were, for the most part, reluctant soldiers drafted to provide medical care to wounded servicemen. For 11 years, Hawkeye Pierce, Klinger, Radar, and the others pushed the limits of television by taking a realistic look at war with sardonic humor and bittersweet drama. One of the most popular shows of all time, it drew one of the largest TV audiences ever for its final episode in 1983.

When Richard Nixon ran for the presidency in 1968 he said: "Let us begin by committing ourselves to the truth—to see it like it is, and tell it like it is—to find the truth, to speak the truth, and to live the truth."

He said this in part because many people already distrusted him, thanks to his controversial political past, but more so because faith in the presidency had been undermined by his predecessor, Lyndon Johnson, who had misled the public about U.S. involvement in Vietnam. For many a Baby Boomer brought up on patriotic principles, the experience with Johnson was shattering, and much as they doubted Nixon, they hoped he would abide by his statement. Unfortunately for them and the nation, he lied, broke laws, violated the Constitution—making Johnson's transgressions seem Lilliputian.

On June 17, 1972, operatives for the Nixon reelection campaign broke into Democratic Party headquarters in Washington, D.C., at an apartment and office complex called Watergate. The word "Watergate" soon acquired a meaning beyond the burglary and attempts to cover it up; it came to mean a whole parcel of covert, and usually illegal, domestic activities under Nixon.

66 *Whether ours shall continue to be a government of laws and not of men is now for Congress and ultimately the American people.* 99

—*Special Prosecutor* **Archibald Cox**, *after being fired by President Nixon in the "Saturday Night Massacre"*

In his book *Time of Illusion* (1975), Jonathan Schell likens Nixon's administration to the performance of an evil magician: the president appeared to be open, compassionate, and truthful (thus winning considerable popular support), while in actuality he was secretive, hateful, and deceitful. In short, he spun his illusions and made his audience see something that wasn't there. On one occasion Nixon stayed up at night, listing the images he wanted projected of himself so as to appear a "viable" leader: "humane, fatherly, warmth . . . trustworthy, boldness, fairness to opponents . . . "

Nixon's crimes began well before the break-in at Watergate. His illegal acts are evident in conversations recorded in the Oval Office and elsewhere by a tape system that, ironically enough, Nixon himself had ordered installed. He sold ambassadorships for $250,000 and extracted money from business executives and labor leaders so he could amass a slush fund. He ordered illegal wiretaps on political opponents and antiwar activists, and, in June 1971, urged his chief of staff, Bob Haldeman, to have someone burglarize the Brookings Institute, a Washington think tank. "I want the break-in . . . ," said the president. "You're to break into the place, rifle the files, and bring them in. . . . You go in to inspect the safe. I mean, *clean it up.*"

In September 1971, the secret White House Special Investigative Unit, known as the Plumbers, broke into the offices of Daniel Ellsberg's psychiatrist. Ellsberg, a former official in the Defense Department, had leaked a classified government document, the "Pentagon Papers," to the *New York Times.* That same month, Nixon agreed with John D. Ehrlichman, his legal counsel, that secret papers about Vietnam should be purloined. "Now, I'm going to steal those documents out of the National Archives," said Ehrlichman. "You can do that, you know," Nixon replied.

Also in 1971, the president discussed using the Internal Revenue Service to go after his political opponents. To Ehrlichman he said: "And on the IRS, you could—are we looking into [Edmund] Muskie's return? . . . Teddy [Kennedy]? Who knows about the Kennedys? Shouldn't they be investigated?" Nixon's anti-Semitism flared as he urged Haldeman, "Bob, *please* get me the names of the Jews, you know, the big Jewish contributors of the Democrats."

In June 1972, Nixon and Haldeman tried to quash an FBI investigation of the Watergate break-in by telling the bureau's acting director, Patrick Gray, that the burglary was a CIA job, and the FBI should stay away. Nixon said that Gray should be told the investigation "will open the whole, the whole Bay of Pigs thing. . . ." Nixon desperately wanted to cover up the Watergate break-in—he realized that if details about it surfaced, so too would details about his administration's other illegal acts. Thus in August he expressed pleasure at the payment of hush money to the Watergate defendants. "It's worth it . . . ," he told Haldeman. "They have to be paid. That's all there is to that."

In September, Nixon agreed that Senator Edward Kennedy should get Secret Service protection during his bid for the Democratic presidential nomination. Nixon, however, wanted the agents to spy on Kennedy. "Plant one, plant two guys on him," Nixon said. "This will be very useful."

On March 21, 1973, Nixon, Haldeman, and John Dean, another presidential legal counsel, discussed paying additional money to the Watergate defendants. When Dean said that another million dollars might be required, Nixon insisted: "And you could get it in cash. I, I know where it could be gotten."

By that time, Congress had begun investigating the Watergate break-in, in part because two reporters for the *Washington Post,* Bob Woodward and Carl Bernstein, suspected a cover-up and doggedly pursued the story. When, in July 1974, Congress finally obtained the Oval Office tapes—after the Supreme Court ordered Nixon to turn them over—it heard in the president's own words how he had directed break-ins, installed illegal wiretaps, approved the payment of bribe money, and obstructed justice.

In July, a committee of the House recommended that Nixon be impeached. The tape that recorded the president's effort to end the FBI's Watergate investigation by invoking the CIA became public in August, and Nixon's remaining support in Congress collapsed. The president realized he could no longer avoid impeachment, and that he would likely be convicted and removed by the Senate. On August 9, 1974, he resigned.

For many Baby Boomers, Nixon's acts came as no surprise. They had long distrusted him. Said one at a later date: "I think Watergate showed the rest of the country exactly what kind of 'Law and Order' Nixon and his cronies were after!" If Lyndon Johnson and Vietnam had eroded the Boomer faith in America's democratic institutions, Watergate practically destroyed it.

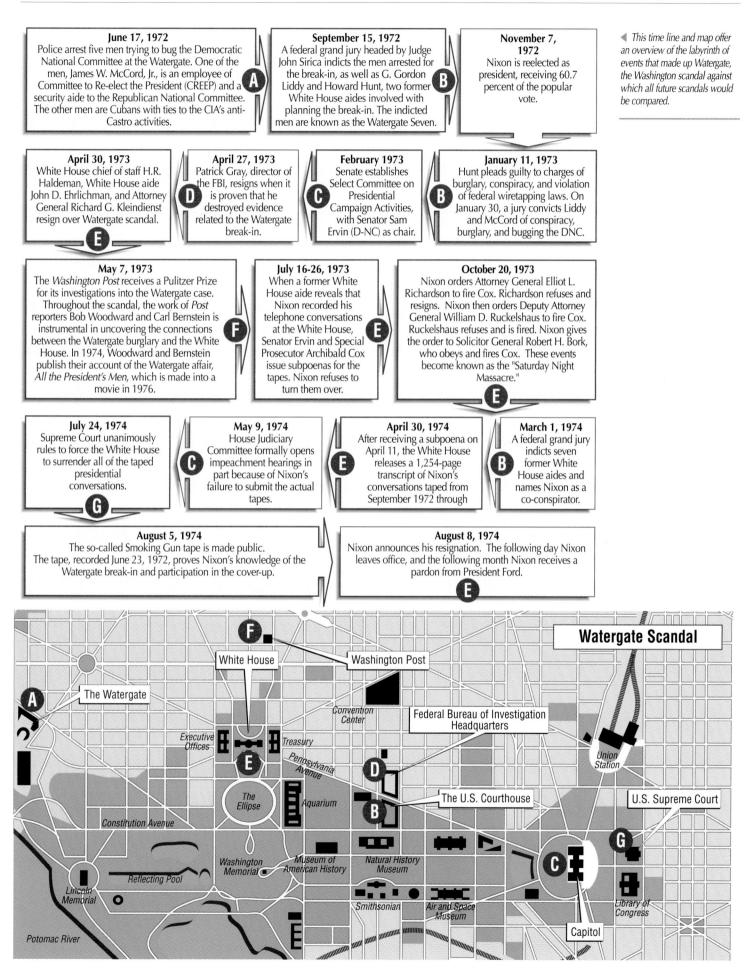

June 17, 1972
Police arrest five men trying to bug the Democratic National Committee at the Watergate. One of the men, James W. McCord, Jr., is an employee of Committee to Re-elect the President (CREEP) and a security aide to the Republican National Committee. The other men are Cubans with ties to the CIA's anti-Castro activities.

September 15, 1972
A federal grand jury headed by Judge John Sirica indicts the men arrested for the break-in, as well as G. Gordon Liddy and Howard Hunt, two former White House aides involved with planning the break-in. The indicted men are known as the Watergate Seven.

November 7, 1972
Nixon is reelected as president, receiving 60.7 percent of the popular vote.

◄ *This time line and map offer an overview of the labyrinth of events that made up Watergate, the Washington scandal against which all future scandals would be compared.*

April 30, 1973
White House chief of staff H.R. Haldeman, White House aide John D. Ehrlichman, and Attorney General Richard G. Kleindienst resign over Watergate scandal.

April 27, 1973
Patrick Gray, director of the FBI, resigns when it is proven that he destroyed evidence related to the Watergate break-in.

February 1973
Senate establishes Select Committee on Presidential Campaign Activities, with Senator Sam Ervin (D-NC) as chair.

January 11, 1973
Hunt pleads guilty to charges of burglary, conspiracy, and violation of federal wiretapping laws. On January 30, a jury convicts Liddy and McCord of conspiracy, burglary, and bugging the DNC.

May 7, 1973
The *Washington Post* receives a Pulitzer Prize for its investigations into the Watergate case. Throughout the scandal, the work of *Post* reporters Bob Woodward and Carl Bernstein is instrumental in uncovering the connections between the Watergate burglary and the White House. In 1974, Woodward and Bernstein publish their account of the Watergate affair, *All the President's Men*, which is made into a movie in 1976.

July 16-26, 1973
When a former White House aide reveals that Nixon recorded his telephone conversations at the White House, Senator Ervin and Special Prosecutor Archibald Cox issue subpoenas for the tapes. Nixon refuses to turn them over.

October 20, 1973
Nixon orders Attorney General Elliot L. Richardson to fire Cox. Richardson refuses and resigns. Nixon then orders Deputy Attorney General William D. Ruckelshaus to fire Cox. Ruckelshaus refuses and is fired. Nixon gives the order to Solicitor General Robert H. Bork, who obeys and fires Cox. These events become known as the "Saturday Night Massacre."

July 24, 1974
Supreme Court unanimously rules to force the White House to surrender all of the taped presidential conversations.

May 9, 1974
House Judiciary Committee formally opens impeachment hearings in part because of Nixon's failure to submit the actual tapes.

April 30, 1974
After receiving a subpoena on April 11, the White House releases a 1,254-page transcript of Nixon's conversations taped from September 1972 through

March 1, 1974
A federal grand jury indicts seven former White House aides and names Nixon as a co-conspirator.

August 5, 1974
The so-called Smoking Gun tape is made public. The tape, recorded June 23, 1972, proves Nixon's knowledge of the Watergate break-in and participation in the cover-up.

August 8, 1974
Nixon announces his resignation. The following day Nixon leaves office, and the following month Nixon receives a pardon from President Ford.

Watergate Scandal

White House · Washington Post · The Watergate · Convention Center · Executive Offices · Treasury · Pennsylvania Avenue · Federal Bureau of Investigation Headquarters · Union Station · The Ellipse · Aquarium · The U.S. Courthouse · U.S. Supreme Court · Constitution Avenue · Washington Memorial · Museum of American History · Natural History Museum · Lincoln Memorial · Reflecting Pool · Smithsonian · Air and Space Museum · Capitol · Library of Congress · Potomac River

Alternative Energy

In the early '70s, as U.S. oil production began to decline and American demand for oil continued to rise, the U.S. turned increasingly to the oil-producing nations of the volatile Middle East. It was a strategy that would ultimately send shock waves through the U.S. economy. An OPEC oil embargo in the fall of 1973 launched a decade of high oil prices and uncertain supply levels, creating skyrocketing inflation and repeated economic recessions. While the government experimented with gasoline rationing and price controls, researchers raced to develop alternative sources of energy.

Funding for the research came in large part from the Department of Energy (DOE), created in 1977 as a response to the oil crisis. Charged with developing more efficient and practical alternatives to oil, the DOE poured billions of dollars into the creation of cheaper and more effective solar cells, quieter windmills, hydroelectric projects, and plant-based substitutes for gasoline. It also supported research on improving fuel efficiency and minimizing pollutants in existing fuels.

The infusion of funding made the U.S. a world leader in innovative alternative energies, but American leadership would prove short-lived. Cheaper oil prices in the 1980s discouraged interest in renewable energy sources, and the Department of Energy would see its research budget shrink dramatically. A decade after the oil crisis, the DOE's mission would be reduced to cleaning up after the problems caused by an energy source once hoped to be the solution to America's energy needs: nuclear power.

Test-tube babies

Even before she was born, she made headlines around the world. Commentators furiously debated the ethical implications of her existence, many called for a complete ban on the revolutionary technique that created her, and the *New York Times* called her an example of the Frankenstein myth made real.

The cause of all the commotion was little Louise Joy Brown, born to delighted parents on July 25, 1978, at Oldham District General Hospital in England. Her birth was unremarkable, but her conception was extraordinary: unable to conceive naturally due to a blockage in her Fallopian tubes, Lesley Brown had an egg extracted from her ovaries using laparoscopy and placed in a test tube, where it was fertilized by sperm from her husband Gilbert. After fertilization, the minute embryo was placed in Lesley Brown's uterus. Nine months later, the "baby of the century," the first human being to be conceived outside the human body, was born.

British gynecologist Patrick Steptoe and biologist Robert Edwards pioneered the experimental technique, known as in vitro fertilization. Then so controversial that Edwards lost his research funding soon after Louise's birth, in vitro fertilization would quickly become a popular treatment for infertility; by the end of the 1980s, there would be thousands of "test-tube babies."

Coin-operated video games

For more than a decade after physicist Willy Higginbotham created the first computer game for visitors to Brookhaven National Laboratory, computer games remained the province of geeky college pranksters with access to university-owned mainframe computers. All that changed in 1971, when California engineer Nolan Bushnell introduced Computer Space, a coin-operated video version of a game first invented at MIT in 1961. The game was a commercial failure, but, convinced that the concept was worth pursuing, Bushnell took his few hundred dollars in profits and formed a new company named Atari.

Atari's first video arcade game was installed in a bar in Sunnyvale, California, in September 1972. A simulated version of Ping-Pong, Pong proved wildly popular with customers, who in a few weeks time stuffed the machine with so many quarters that it needed repairs. By 1974, more than 100,000 Pong games and Pong clones were scattered in arcades and bars across America.

But the video game frenzy was only just beginning. *Star Wars* fans flocked to Space Invaders, which blasted out of arcades in 1978 to pop up in restaurants, ice cream shops, and pizza parlors around the country. Atari countered in 1979 with its biggest-selling game, Asteroids.

Critics called the games violent and a waste of time. But as players shot, jumped, and mazed their way through the video game revolution, for the first time computer technology became part of daily life. And the stage was set for personal computers to make the leap from the garages of dedicated computer nerds to the homes and offices of ordinary people.

Supermarket scanners

Forced to keep track of thousands of small items in stock, grocers needed a technological solution to their inventory dilemmas that would save time and expense at the checkout counter. Based on an idea patented in 1952 by Norman Woodland and Bernard Silver, the solution would involve the use of coded information that could be read automatically by machine—the ubiquitous bar code that appears on the back of almost every product sold in the United States. But it would not be until the invention of the laser in the 1960s that their idea would become possible.

RCA tested the first laser-read supermarket scanner in a Kroger's Supermarket in 1972. Their bull's-eye design proved unworkable because of printing difficulties. But in 1973, George J. Laurer of IBM, working with a team including Woodland, introduced the Universal Product Code: a standardized system of straight black and white lines that encoded 12 numerical digits. On June 16, 1974, the first UPC scanner went into operation at Marsh Supermarket in Troy, Ohio, and a package of chewing gum became the first item to usher in a new, bar-coded era.

Louise Joy Brown, the first test-tube baby, shortly after she was born on July 25, 1978. (AP Photo/Pool)

CAT scans and MRIs

Together they inaugurated a new era in medical diagnosis and cancer detection. Computerized axial tomography was the brainchild of two researchers, American physicist Allan MacLeod Cormack and British industrial engineer Geoffrey Newbold Hounsfield, working separately an ocean apart. Where doctors had been limited to a two-dimensional X-ray image, CAT scans combined multiple X rays taken from various angles to produce a three-dimensional image of the inside of the body. First introduced by Hounsfield's employer in 1972, CAT scans offered physicians a detailed accuracy previously unknown.

Magnetic resonance imaging opened a window into the human body without the use of X rays. Relying on a phenomenon long known to physicists, it read tiny signals emitted by human cells—signals that differed substantially between normal cells and cancerous tumor cells. First tested in 1977 by inventor Raymond V. Damadian, the MRI offered a powerful new tool for cancer detection without exposing patients to dangerous radiation.

Their diagnostic advantages encouraged hospitals across the country to purchase the new machines. But the high cost of the technology and equipment, and burgeoning numbers of patient tests, helped launch two decades of skyrocketing health care costs.

Public Enemies?
Angela Davis (1944–) and Leonard Peltier (1944–)

The government called them murderous anti-American fanatics, but activists charged that Leonard Peltier and Angela Davis were victims of J. Edgar Hoover's legacy—COINTELPRO, a brutal FBI campaign to crush militant leftist organizations.

A Marxist and a member of the Black Panther party, philosophy professor Angela Davis was a vocal supporter of George Jackson, a Black Panther accused of killing a white guard in California's Soledad Prison. Her articulate, effective defense of Jackson, who was believed to be the victim of a setup, made her a prime target of the FBI. In August 1970, following the deaths of four people during a shoot-out between law enforcement officers and a small group led by George Jackson's younger brother, Davis was charged with murder. These charges were based only on her known association with the younger Jackson, who sometimes worked as her bodyguard and possessed handguns registered to her. After two months in hiding as the FBI's most wanted fugitive, Davis was captured in New York City and spent more than a year in prison. After a jury acquitted her of all charges, she returned to activism and academia.

Leonard Peltier was not so lucky. The Ojibwa–Lakota activist was accused of the 1975 murders of two federal agents during a shoot-out between the FBI and members of the radical American Indian Movement (AIM) on the Pine Ridge Reservation in South Dakota. Although three of Peltier's codefendants had been acquitted in earlier trials amid allegations of federal misconduct, the judge refused to let attorneys argue Peltier's case along similar grounds. A

cause célèbre among international human rights groups, who questioned whether he received a fair trial, Peltier was convicted in 1977 on two counts of first-degree murder and has been in prison ever since.

Henry Kissinger (1923-)

He was the lone cowboy of Washington bureaucracy—an overweight intellectual with a heavy Bavarian accent, a legacy of the birthplace he fled as a teenage refugee from Nazi Germany. As first the national security advisor and then secretary of state in the Nixon Administration, he ran United States foreign policy with a combination of personal charisma, ingenious shuttle diplomacy, and hardheaded realpolitik.

Widely celebrated for successful peace initiatives in the Middle East and China, he came under fire from both sides of the political spectrum for promoting policies that divorced the strategic interests of the United States from moral concerns. While outraged doves condemned his role in the 1970 United States invasion of Cambodia and the CIA campaign against Chile's Salvador Allende, conservative hawks accused him of knuckling under to the Soviet Union's "evil empire" in a one-man quest for détente.

The sole survivor of the tarnished Nixon administration, he became a political liability during the Ford–Carter presidential election, and returned in 1977 to a well-publicized private life as a high-profile consultant.

Mary Tyler Moore (1936-)

A heroine for a decade of narrowing horizons and shaky optimism, she tossed her hat into the cold Minneapolis air every week on *The Mary Tyler Moore Show*. The Brooklyn-born dancer and actress became famous as Dick Van Dyke's better half in the '60s classic, *The Dick Van Dyke Show*. In 1970 she began a seven-year run as the perennially single thirty-something career woman Mary Richards. She survived bad dates, good friends, and a mediocre job—all with her trademark niceness and unsinkable smile. While the show gave working women a slice of sit-com life more in tune with the times, Moore herself was not content to be only an actress. She and her husband, producer Grant Tinker, formed MTM Enterprises, a production company that launched several acclaimed sit-coms and groundbreaking dramas, including *Hill Street Blues* (1981–1987).

Two Guys in a Garage
Steve Jobs (1955–) and Steve Wozniak (1950–)

They were nerds united by the California counterculture and a love of electronics. Graduates of the same Silicon Valley high school, their first short-lived business venture manufactured and sold illegal "blue boxes." Using these devices, merry nerd pranksters exploited a weakness in Ma Bell's technology to make free long-distance calls,

▶ *Angela Davis awaiting trial, 1972. (UPI/CORBIS-BETTMANN)*

as did Wozniak, who posed as Henry Kissinger to place a late-night phone call to the Pope from a Berkeley dormitory.

While Jobs left college to experiment with drugs and Eastern religions, Wozniak took a job designing calculators for Hewlett-Packard. Their paths crossed again at the Homebrew Computer Club, a Palo Alto–based group of computer enthusiasts. Wozniak wowed Homebrewers in 1976 by building his own rudimentary personal computer, the Apple I. Struck by the amount of interest in Apple I, Jobs persuaded Wozniak to go into business with him. Financed with capital from the sale of their most prized possessions, Jobs's VW bus and Wozniak's programmable calculator, the little start-up company run out of Jobs's garage quickly turned a profit and attracted the attention of adult investors.

Wozniak's next invention, the user-friendly Apple II, was showcased at the 1978 West Coast Computer Faire as a consumer-ready product. Sales soared, launching the personal computer revolution and making the young entrepreneurs a fortune. When Apple Computers, Inc., went public two years later, Jobs and Wozniak would become the first multimillionaires of the fledgling personal computer industry.

Jim Henson (1936–1990)

The first person to design puppets specifically for use in front of the television camera, Jim Henson threw his peculiar genius into the creation of a Muppet menagerie that would redefine the landscape of childhood in America. Joining forces with the Children's Television Workshop, Henson and his collaborators brought a host of furry, fuzzy, and friendly monsters to *Sesame Street* (1969–present); they soon became as familiar to parents as the words of Dr. Spock.

The antics of Kermit the Frog, Cookie Monster, and Big Bird delighted preschool children, but Henson's sly parodies of popular culture—like oily Muppet game show host Guy Smiley—entertained parents as well. The combination was irresistible, and Henson soon entered prime time with *The Muppet Show* (1976–1980), an all-ages musical variety show, drawing on Boomer luminaries such as Arlo Guthrie and Joan Baez for guest hosts. It firmly established Henson as one of the most beloved giants of the entertainment field.

Disco

"Ummm. Love to love you, baby."
"Ohhhhh. Love to love you, baby."
"Ahhhhhhh. Love to love you, baby . . ."

—Donna Summer,
"Love to Love You, Baby," 1975

The insistent pulse of disco music filled the radio airwaves from 1975 through the early '80s. The songs' lyrics usually urged listeners to dance and have sex and go to discos, those busy nightclubs where men and women went to find people who wanted to dance and have sex and spend time in discos.

Discos housed loud bacchanals, with participants doing their best to impress each other with sharp clothes, good grooming, and flashy dance steps. Alcohol and recreational drugs were part of the mating ritual—cocaine use among young adults increased during the disco years. Discos' late-night schedules gave their guests lots of time to snag bed partners for the evening, or at least to obtain phone numbers from promising prospects. And the music's steady dance beat thrummed through the night.

With disco music edging out rock from radio air play, backlash was inevitable. "Disco Sucks!" rallies appeared around the country. Such events usually were organized by local rock deejays and almost always concluded with a bonfire fed by hundreds of disco record albums.

But the popularity of disco and its culture wouldn't lose steam for years. The phenomenon was boosted nationwide with the release of the movie *Saturday Night Fever* (1977), starring teen heartthrob John Travolta as a young Brooklynite obsessed with disco nightlife. The film was a hit and songs from its sound track topped the charts. More clubs opened, more disco-themed movies were churned out, and disco-centric dance shows and advertising began filling more TV airtime. ("I taught John Travolta to dance, and I can teach you," went one particularly insistent commercial.)

The public had their fill of disco by 1982, and the clubs began closing because of low attendance. But disco and its trappings live on, celebrated as retro kitsch in MTV programming and, more modestly, novelty gift shops.

Fashion

Seventies disco culture swept fashion along with it. A few highlights:

- Open-necked synthetic shirts and tight pants for men. Gold jewelry optional.

- Dresses for women who were out on the town. The blouse-and-skirt combo for an evening of dancing was a thing of the past.

● Hair: highly styled, men and women alike. Men put lots of work into their hair, wearing it fuller and longer than in today's fashion. "Unisex" hair salons came into prominence during the '70s.

Satan Wore a Leisure Suit

A peculiar creature known as a leisure suit became popular with men in the early '70s. This matching jacket-and-slacks outfit, intended to be worn with open-necked print shirts, was cheaply made and looked it. Designed for the average Joe who wanted a low-cost "dressy" outfit, synthetic leisure suits flooded the racks of men's bargain clothing shops. It didn't take long for them to become a sign of bad taste and poor judgment. A then-popular TV comedy show took the fashion crisis head-on. Featured was a sketch in which a scientist detailed the effects on laboratory rats of tiny custom-made leisure suits. The results? "Leisure suits cause cancer," proclaimed the doctor.

Mime

Young Woman: "Mom, Dad, I . . . I have something to tell you."
Mother: "What is it, darling?"
Father: "It's okay, honey, we're here for you."
Young Woman: "I want to be a mime."
Mother: [shrieks]
Father: "You ungrateful little b****!"

—Chicago Second City Theater sketch, 1980

If pantomime were a human being, one would feel sorry for it. The once-esteemed French art enjoyed a burst of popularity during the mid-'70s, but by 1979 it had been overexposed by television. Mime artists suddenly were the butt of cruel jokes and scorn that would continue for decades.

It's uncertain why mime street performers began appearing more frequently in urban centers, especially San Francisco, around 1974. But it's a matter of history that a man-and-wife mime team, Shields & Yarnell, were given a crack at network television during the summer of 1977 and early in 1978. Their program's popularity was brief, but the media exposure was enough to boost the enrollment in mime classes around the country. The number of young mimes performing in public parks increased exponentially. What once seemed a unique art became ubiquitous, and the public began expressing impatience. Audiences today are more likely to be entertained by parodies of pantomime rather than the real thing.

Pantomime did, however, produce a notable success story. In 1978, a young street mime and comedian was cast as the lead in the TV sitcom *Mork & Mindy*. Robin Williams has since become one of America's leading movie stars. He has not felt compelled to simulate an invisible wall for years.

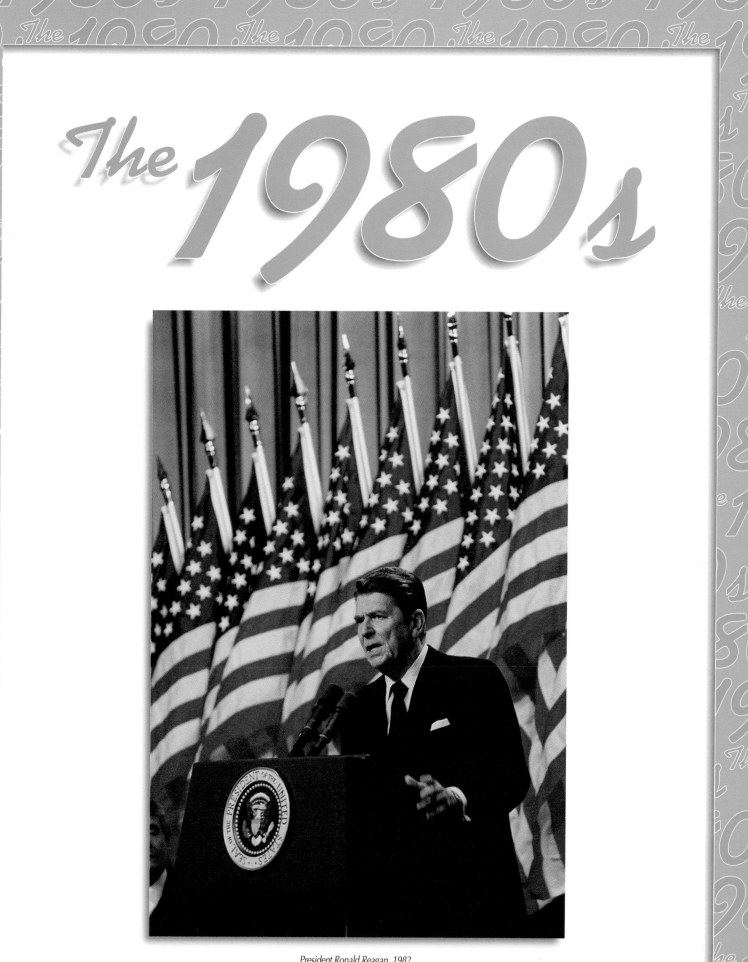

President Ronald Reagan, 1982.
(Courtesy of Ronald Reagan Presidential Library)

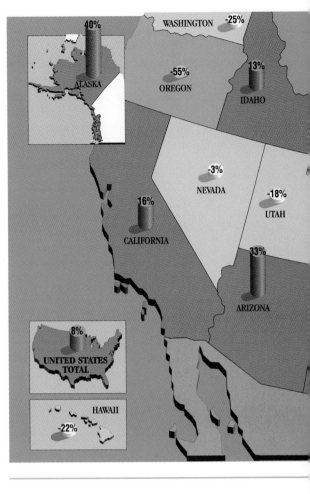

In December 1986, the *Miami Herald* reported a chilling story: "Joseph Savino [confessed] that after drinking and taking drugs last Christmas Eve at his Southwest Broward trailer, he 'smacked' [his six-year-old son] in the face and punched him in the stomach because the boy splashed water on the bathroom floor. He knocked the boy against the toilet bowl, he said. The child died two days later." Similar stories appeared in newspapers across the country and raised dark questions: Had American families given themselves over to violence and abuse? Had they collapsed? Or did such stories distort the overall picture? The responses produced heated debate—but everyone agreed that families and population had changed in ways that caused great anxiety.

In 1980, total births per 1,000 women age 15 to 44 stood at 71.1, a sharp drop from 1970, and the decline continued, reaching 67.0 in 1990. In contrast, the birthrate per 1,000 women age 30 to 44 increased from 35.4 in 1980 to 44.7 in 1990. This meant that women born largely in the 1950s gave birth at a higher rate than those born largely in the late 1930s and 1940s, the pre–Baby Boom. Women who had delayed marriage or delayed having children had decided to have families.

The new immigration that began in the 1970s accelerated in the 1980s: it boosted population, while changing America ethnically and causing tension. Six million legal immigrants entered the United States in the 1980s, more than any other decade except 1900–1910, and another three to five million entered illegally.

Immigrants from Asia outnumbered those from any other region; at 44 percent. Immigrants from Latin America came in a close second, with 40 percent of all immigrants hailing from that area. Many Asian-American immigrants quickly earned household incomes higher than other immigrant groups, even higher than many natives. The median household income of Asian Americans topped $31,000 in 1988, exceeding the nearly $29,000 for non-Hispanic whites. Success bred antagonism. Blacks criticized Asian Americans who owned businesses in Harlem, while white fishermen in Texas actually attacked Vietnamese fishermen who competed with them. One Asian-American leader was quoted as saying: "We are seeing a trend of racially motivated violence directed against Asians which we believe is a national phe-

▼ *Boomer women continued to make their mark on the nation's birthrates, as the number of new mothers over 30 increased significantly in the 1980s. Many of these women will become the influential "soccer moms" of the 1990s.*

nomenon." Yet for all the influx of people, America had a lower percentage of its population as immigrants than did other Western nations.

As Baby Boomers raised their kids in the 1980s, they faced changes, several so tumultuous they raised questions as to whether families could survive. As in the 1970s, some marriages collapsed under the weight of women working outside the home when couples failed to allocate housework—largely because men refused to do their share. "The last several years of my marriage we had lists of household chores to be done," said one divorced husband. "I hated that . . . list." According to Arlie Hochschild in *The Second Shift* (1989), a survey in 1983 found that "the more housework a wife saw her husband do, the less likely she was to think of divorce." Between outside employment and housework, wives typically worked 71 hours a week; their husbands, 55. Of course more than disputes about housework brought divorce; other influences included a weak sense of commitment, abusive relationships, and the belief by women who worked that, since they were earning their own income, they no longer had to put up with bad marriages.

With both parents working, and with single parenthood increasing, the latchkey child phenomenon appeared. While 12 percent of children in 1970 lived with one parent, 25 percent did so by 1990. According to one study, such kids were more likely to abuse tobacco, marijuana, and alcohol. They perhaps had more opportunity for sexual relations, too. Latchkey kids and other youngsters contributed to a notable

Mothers over Thirty: 1980 to 1989
(in thousands)

Age	1980	1985	1989
10–14	1.1	1.2	1.4
15–19	53.0	51.0	57.3
20–24	115.1	108.3	113.8
25–29	112.9	111.0	117.6
30–34	61.9	69.1	77.4
35–39	19.8	24.0	29.9
40–44	3.9	4.0	5.2
45–49	0.2	0.2	0.2

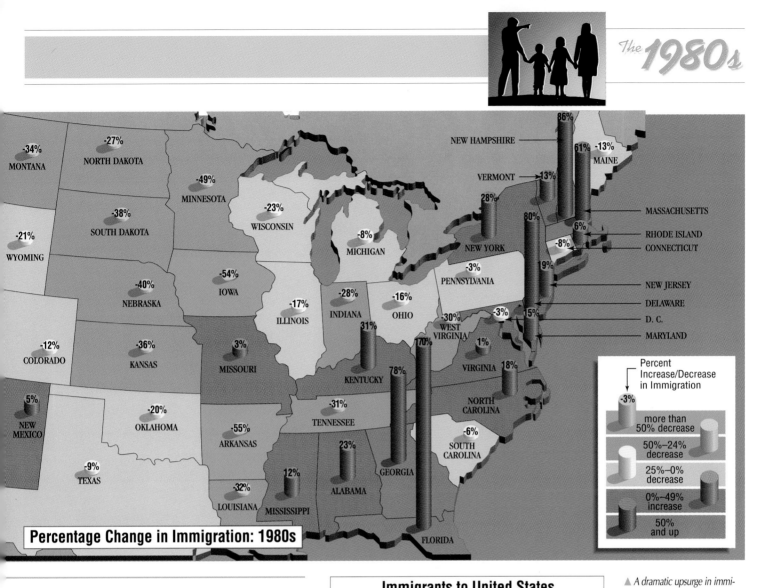

Percentage Change in Immigration: 1980s

MONTANA -34%
NORTH DAKOTA -27%
MINNESOTA -49%
SOUTH DAKOTA -38%
WISCONSIN -23%
WYOMING -21%
NEBRASKA -40%
IOWA -54%
MICHIGAN -8%
COLORADO -12%
KANSAS -36%
MISSOURI 3%
ILLINOIS -17%
INDIANA -28%
OHIO -16%
NEW MEXICO 5%
OKLAHOMA -20%
ARKANSAS -55%
KENTUCKY 78%
TENNESSEE -31%
WEST VIRGINIA -30%
VIRGINIA 1%
NORTH CAROLINA 18%
TEXAS -9%
LOUISIANA -32%
MISSISSIPPI 12%
ALABAMA 23%
GEORGIA 70%
SOUTH CAROLINA -6%
PENNSYLVANIA -3%
NEW HAMPSHIRE 86%
MAINE 61% -13%
VERMONT 13%
NEW YORK 28% 80%
MASSACHUSETTS
RHODE ISLAND 6%
CONNECTICUT -8%
NEW JERSEY 19%
DELAWARE -3%
D. C. 15%
MARYLAND
FLORIDA 31%

Percent Increase/Decrease in Immigration
-3%
more than 50% decrease
50%–24% decrease
25%–0% decrease
0%–49% increase
50% and up

rise in births to unmarried teens, from 11 percent in 1970 to 22 percent in 1985.

Problems with children figured prominently in news reports, and research often supported the sensational stories. "A rise in brutal crimes by the young shakes the soul of society," proclaimed *Time* magazine. *Time* went on to concede that adolescent violence existed earlier, but, it insisted, "juvenile crime appears to be more widespread and vicious than ever." The FBI reported that between 1983 and 1987 arrests of those under 18 for murder increased 22.2 percent, for aggravated assault 18.6 percent, and for rape 14.6 percent. *Time* recounted how a 16-year-old boy shot to death a woman he had never met before, and then after the crime told police he "just wanted to get away and kill somebody." Violence was blamed on biological impulses, or "raging hormones"; children growing up in single-parent families, where the mother or father paid them little attention; movies and TV shows soaked in blood—by age 16 the typical child had witnessed about 200,000 violent acts—and drug use.

Yet for all the problems, families showed remarkable resiliency. According to the Institute for Social Research at the University of Michigan, most Americans still considered a happy marriage and family life important to them. Writing in *The State of Families, 1984–85*, R. Morton Darrow asserted that richness, diversity, and vitality characterized the modern family, and that "for those who succeed, the quality of family life . . . is immeasurably superior to the more constrained family models of an earlier age when less was expected and

Immigrants to United States by Country of Origin

Country of origin	total 1982	total 1988	% change
Laos	36,528	10,667	-71%
Vietnam	72,553	25,789	-64%
Taiwan	9,884	6,888	-30%
United Kingdom	14,539	13,228	-9%
China	27,100	28,717	6%
Jamaica	18,711	20,996	12%
Philippines	45,102	50,697	12%
India	21,738	26,268	21%
Thailand	5,568	6,888	24%
Poland	5,874	9,507	62%
Mexico	56,106	95,039	69%
El Salvador	7,107	12,045	69%
Cuba	8,606	17,558	104%
Haiti	8,779	34,806	296%

less was achieved."

Many parents who started families in the 1980s reported that children gave them love and companionship, and caused them to reach beyond themselves. Families in which both parents worked often handled their responsibilities well. The *Ladies' Home Journal* (1985) stated: "Although the potential problems of the latchkey child cannot be ignored," by and large these children were "doing just fine." The magazine continued: "The family . . . whether it is a single-parent family, stepfamily, extended family, or traditional family, is strengthening bonds in new ways . . . that we can all celebrate."

▲ A dramatic upsurge in immigration occurred during the 1980s, with immigrants unevenly distributed to a few key states, as seen in the map. There was also a shift in the immigrants' countries of origin, shown in the chart; emigration from nations in Southeast Asia began to drop, while emigration from Latin and Central American nations increased sharply.

NOTE: Selected countries only; not a complete list.

▲ *Education Secretary William Bennett observes kindergartners in 1987. (UPI/CORBIS-BETTMANN)*

▼ *This chart shows mean salaries for entry-level teachers, as compared to the salaries corporations offered to recent college graduates.*

In his own remarks, Bell warned that if Americans failed to correct education, their economy would fall behind the Japanese and West German economies. He blamed the mess on families where both parents worked and had little time to meet with teachers, on increased drug use among teens, and on lowered academic standards in high schools. Teachers, he said, gave too many A's.

Many a Baby Boomer parent gave public schools low marks for achievement and thus agreed with *A Nation at Risk*, with Bell, and with other critical reports and books issued during the decade—so numerous that some accused their authors of "school bashing." *The Mathematics Report Card—Are We Measuring Up?* claimed that more than 25 percent of all 13-year-olds could not handle elementary school math, and that only 16 percent of 17-year-olds could handle algebra.

In his book, *Cultural Literacy: What Every American Needs to Know*, E. D. Hirsch, Jr., claimed that public schools had failed to transmit a shared cultural knowledge important to critical thinking. "It will not do to blame television for the state of our literacy," he said. "Schools have, or should have, children for six or seven hours a day, five days a week, nine months a year, for thirteen years or more. To assert they are powerless to make a significant impact on what students learn would be to make a claim about American education that few . . . would find it easy to accept."

Teachers felt assaulted, and they fumed when few parents, Baby Boomer and otherwise, recognized the difficulties they faced and the low pay they received. Into urban classrooms, and many rural ones, came students of diverse economic, ethnic, and racial backgrounds, many part of a new immigration, many unable to speak English. Into these same classrooms came kids experienced in drugs, crime, and violence; kids from broken homes; pregnant girls or girls with

In 1983 the National Commission on Excellence in Education, established by Secretary of Education Terrell Bell, issued *A Nation at Risk*, a report whose horror stories grabbed the nation's attention: 13 percent of all 17-year-olds were functionally illiterate; in 19 academic achievement tests given in 21 countries, students in the United States never finished first or second, while they finished last seven times; and between 1975 and 1980, the number of remedial math courses rose 72 percent at four-year public colleges. "A rising tide of mediocrity in elementary and secondary education," said the report, threatened to ruin America.

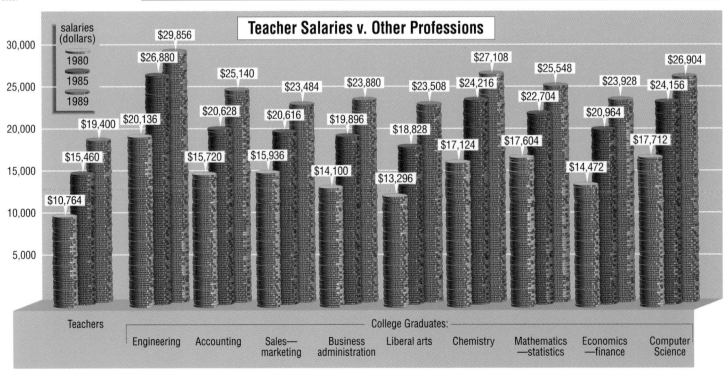

Teacher Salaries v. Other Professions

salaries (dollars)

1980 / 1985 / 1989

Teachers: $10,764 / $15,460 / $19,400

College Graduates:

Engineering: $20,136 / $26,880 / $29,856
Accounting: $15,720 / $20,628 / $25,140
Sales—marketing: $15,936 / $20,616 / $23,484
Business administration: $14,100 / $19,896 / $23,880
Liberal arts: $13,296 / $18,828 / $23,508
Chemistry: $17,124 / $24,216 / $27,108
Mathematics—statistics: $17,604 / $22,704 / $25,548
Economics—finance: $14,472 / $20,964 / $23,928
Computer Science: $17,712 / $24,156 / $26,904

young children. Teachers often had to spend as much time dealing with social problems as they did with furthering knowledge.

Teacher salaries had improved since the 1970s, but only minimally, and in general pay lagged behind comparable professional jobs. In addition to inadequate salaries, teachers suffered from burdensome bureaucracies that limited their authority and made them feel like, well, children—always being told what to do rather than being asked for their professional advice. Said one education leader: "Unless the country deals with the issue of declining pay and status of teachers, the talk about reform . . . is pure rhetoric."

As it turned out, many school districts tried reforms—everything from experimental programs to stricter discipline. In Philadelphia, educators responded to complaints about too little homework with a study plan that mandated three nights of homework per week for high school students. To get parents more involved in its schools, El Paso, Texas, sent teachers out to visit the homes of elementary students. To ensure qualified teachers, 46 states required them to pass competency exams. To encourage teachers and use their expertise, Miami set up a school-based management plan.

Did the efforts work? From 1980 to 1985—a transitional period from Boomer to post-Boomer college students—average SAT scores climbed 16 points. At about the same time, high school graduates who completed English, math, science, and social studies courses as opposed to less stringent electives increased from 13.4 percent to 30 percent. But after 1985, national SAT scores flattened, and students still packed remedial courses at colleges.

In that situation, President George Bush and numerous educational leaders proposed allowing parents to choose whichever schools they wanted to send their children to,

The Failure of Higher Education?

With his best-selling book *The Closing of the American Mind* (1987), professor Allan Bloom offered a searing condemnation of higher education. But he didn't stop with educational theory: he called rock music a "gutter phenomenon" and asserted that "it ruins the imagination of young people." About the 1960s he claimed: "So far as universities are concerned, I know of nothing positive coming from that period; it was an unmitigated disaster for them." About relativism he said: "History and the study of cultures do not teach or prove that values or cultures are relative."

Bloom's belligerent stand against popular culture, diversity, and cultural relativism, combined with his arguments for a return to a Great Books curriculum, made him a controversial figure—a champion of those disgusted with changes that began in the 1960s, a monster to those who thought such changes liberating.

even if it meant crossing district lines. Some saw choice as the only way to foster competition and excellence by breaking the routine of providing even the worst schools a guaranteed enrollment. Critics claimed, however, that choice would encourage white parents to remove their kids from schools with black students, and thus promote segregation. Others feared that proposals to give tax breaks to parents who sent their kids to private schools, or to provide parents with vouchers that would allow them to use public tax moneys to pay for private school education, would destroy public schools.

In the early 1980s, Ernest Boyer, president of the Carnegie Foundation for the Advancement of Teaching, complained that during the previous decade "schools [had become] more and more adrift until they didn't know what they were supposed to do." Had they now found their rudders and steered a better course? Or did the crisis warrant bolder action?

▼ *Americans were no closer to understanding "why Johnny can't read" in the 1980s than they had ever been—but polls showed a wide variety of opinions on what ailed schools. This chart tracks public opinion on educational problems throughout the 1980s. Note that some concerns of the early 1980s, such as discipline and integration, fade into the background late in the decade, while drug use jumps to the foreground. School violence, a constant concern in the 1990s, is not even on the radar here.*

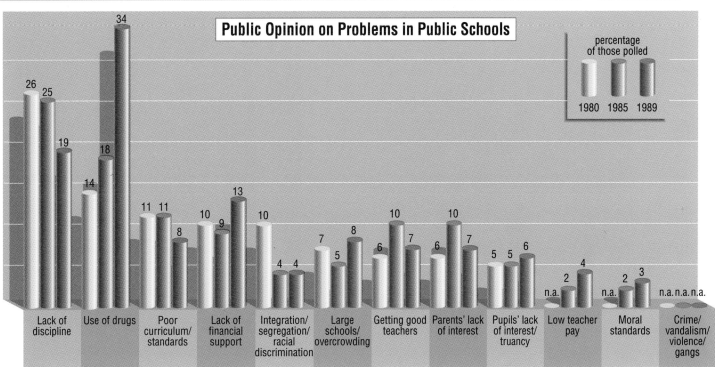

Public Opinion on Problems in Public Schools

percentage of those polled
1980 1985 1989

Lack of discipline	Use of drugs	Poor curriculum/ standards	Lack of financial support	Integration/ segregation/ racial discrimination	Large schools/ overcrowding	Getting good teachers	Parents' lack of interest	Pupils' lack of interest/ truancy	Low teacher pay	Moral standards	Crime/ vandalism/ violence/ gangs
26 25 19	14 18 34	11 11 8	10 9 13	10 4 4	7 5 8	6 10 7	6 10 7	5 5 6	n.a. 2 4	n.a. 2 3	n.a. n.a. n.a.

They were the best of times and they were the worst of times. A split personality ran through the 1980s economy: prosperity and progress on the one hand, poverty and limits on the other. Baby Boomers exhibited the split; like the characters in the popular movie *The Big Chill* (1983), they pursued materialism; unlike those characters, many experienced setbacks that kept them financially strapped.

More than any other individual, Ronald Reagan characterized the decade and shaped its economy. When he campaigned as the Republican candidate for president in 1980, he promised "morning in America"—a break with the inflation and recession (and negative attitudes) of the previous decade. Reagan promoted supply-side economics, meaning he wanted the federal government to create investment incentives for the economic elite, which would, in theory, increase production, employment, and the supply of goods, and end inflationary pressure.

As president, Reagan cut income taxes and other taxes 23 percent over a three-year period. As a result, by 1984 disposable income for the top 0.2 percent of all tax filers increased about 25 percent. At the same time, the gain in disposable income for those at the median point rose a scant 3.5 percent, and due to changes in tax laws, families who earned under $10,000 saw their net income drop more than 15 percent.

Reagan reduced spending for Medicare, Medicaid, food stamps, and school meals. To ease business regulations, he weakened enforcement of laws meant to protect the environment. He also attacked unions. When federal air traffic controllers went on strike, he fired them and destroyed their union. And he made decidedly anti-union appointments to the National Labor Relations Board and to federal courts. His actions and, even more so, a decline in blue-collar manufacturing jobs, gutted union membership, dropping it from 19.6 percent of the civilian labor force in 1980 to 13.4 percent at decade's end.

Critics called Reagan's economic measures largess for the rich, and the president's own economic advisor, David Stockman, admitted in retrospect: "Do you realize the greed that came to the forefront? The hogs were really feeding." Reagan's critics howled in derision when the economy displayed the ugly side of its split personality, and in 1982–83 plunged downward. Unemployment climbed to around 10 percent, with black unemployment hitting 20 percent. In the Midwest, many farmers, beset by heavy debts and falling crop prices, lost their farms.

But 1984 told a different story. A 7 percent rise in the GNP surpassed every year since 1951. Then in 1987, the Dow Jones Industrial Average topped 2,700, a record. Although later that year the Dow dropped 508 points in a single day, by 1989, as the Reagan recovery continued, it had again reached its 1987 record.

Mergers and leveraged buyouts made a few opportunists wealthy. Financiers Ivan Boesky and Michael Milken pursued

▼ *The "trickle-down" economic policies of the Reagan administration seem in retrospect to have created a "trickle up" as far as income was concerned. This chart shows how the distribution of aggregate income—the total amount of income in a particular year—gradually shifted in favor of those in the highest income brackets.*

Percentage Distribution of Aggregate Income: 1980 to 1989

percent of population / year	bottom 20%	20% to 40%	40% to 60%	60% to 80%	top 20% — 80% to 95%	top 5%
1980	5.3%	11.6%	17.6%	24.4%	26.5%	14.6%
1981	5.3%	11.4%	17.5%	24.6%	26.8%	14.4%
1982	5%	11.3%	17.2%	24.2%	26.9%	15.3%
1983	4.9%	11.2%	17.2%	24.5%	27.1%	15.3%
1984	4.8%	11.1%	17.1%	24.5%	27.1%	15.4%
1985	4.8%	11%	16.9%	24.3%	27%	16.1%
1986	4.7%	10.9%	16.9%	24.1%	26.9%	16.5%
1987	4.6%	10.7%	16.8%	24%	26.6%	17.2%
1988	4.6%	10.7%	16.7%	24%	26.8%	17.2%
1989	4.6%	10.6%	16.5%	23.7%	26.7%	17.9%

◄ A view of the floor of the New York Stock Exchange, in October 1989. (UPI/CORBIS-BETTMANN)

undervalued firms and took them over by offering junk bonds, so named for their high risk, to stockholders. Boesky—"Ivan the Terrible," fellow investors called him—amassed millions through insider trading, an illegal activity whereby he received information about corporate mergers and buyouts from investment houses. As part of a plea bargain with federal prosecutors, he turned in Milken, who had violated securities laws. Milken was convicted on six felony counts, paid $1 billion in fines, and served a jail term. Boesky paid $100 million in civil penalties and also served time in jail.

Scandal embroiled savings and loan institutions, too. Bad investments, along with top managers draining funds in order to finance luxuries for themselves, caused a rash of S&L failures. Government bailouts cost taxpayers dearly—they were still paying the bill in the 1990s.

High living led to *Newsweek* magazine labeling 1984 the "Year of the Yuppies." The word stood for young, upwardly mobile, urban professionals—supposedly former Baby-Boomer hippies who had lost their ideals and gone ballistic with the materialistic. *The Big Chill* captured this with its portrayal of a group of friends, all former college radicals, who pursued success in mainstream society. For yuppies, imported beer ruled over domestic beer; ice cream with foreign names over ice cream with plain English ones; products from Bloomingdale's over most anything from Sears. To many observers, it seemed that yuppies pursued the material with little remorse and great intensity. "Their lives are so busy," said one critic, "that merely to give someone the time of day seems to be an act of charity."

Popular images aside, more than half of all Baby Boomers earned under $20,000 a year. Only a minority of Boomers could afford to own homes—ownership rates for householders under 35 declined from 41 percent in 1982 to 39 percent in 1989, with younger Baby Boomers hit the hardest.

With its split personality, the expanding 1980s economy reduced the size of America's middle class by kicking many people down the income ladder. Between the mid-1970s and late 1980s, the middle class declined a whopping 20 percent. Adding to the bad news, poverty increased, reaching 13 percent overall, but 26 percent among Hispanics and 33 percent among blacks. As many families lived in poverty by 1990 as had in 1964.

As homeless people crowded America's city streets in ever-increasing numbers, it became impossible to ignore the fact that a massive inequality of wealth prevailed. During the decade, income for the bottom fifth of families decreased, while income increased for the top fifth. Said one analyst: "The tax cut of 1981, the high interest rates of 1981–82, and the growing federal deficit went far to generate new sources of wealth for those who already had more money than virtually everyone else in America."

At the same time, Reagan's deficit spending exceeded all previous presidents combined, with the accumulated national debt topping $1 trillion in mid-decade and $3 trillion by 1990. His tax cuts, combined with massive military spending, guaranteed the expansion of the deficit.

Supply-side economics thus stimulated both growth and inequality, selective prosperity and deeper poverty—a split personality in the U.S. economy that carried into the 1990s.

President Ronald Reagan's revolution hardly looked like one, what with the sight and smell of money saturating his inauguration in 1981. But this was a conservative revolution that, according to some critics, was intended to dismantle the 1960s Great Society, keep the underclass contained, beat back countercultural ideas, and promote religion and nationalism.

Reagan won the presidency by reaching beyond his own Republican Party to appeal to Democrats, often called "Reagan Democrats," with a message that stressed traditional values, economic rebirth, and an optimistic faith in America's future. Many Americans reacted enthusiastically to his message, especially his optimism, after the 1970s—when everything from Watergate to the economy was depressing. A former movie actor, Reagan could touch his audiences and earned a reputation as "the Great Communicator." *Time* magazine said that "Reagan is a sort of masterpiece of American magic—apparently one of the simplest, most uncomplicated creatures alive, and yet a character of rich meanings, of complexities that connect him with the myths and powers of his country in an unprecedented way."

Along with an appeal that won over many moderates, Reagan and a vibrant New Right joined forces and tried to reshape American society by emphasizing moral issues. Showing its expanding reach, the New Right allied with the New Religious Right, evangelicals who believed that the constitutional ban on official prayers in public schools, the Supreme Court support of abortion, and the spread of gay rights and feminist ideas had corrupted society and threatened its survival.

▼ *Reverend Jerry Falwell at a press conference for his group, Family Forum 88, organized in time for the 1988 presidential race. (UPI/CORBIS-BETTMANN)*

MTV Cops?

Miami Vice (1984-1989) was a TV police drama—but no ordinary one. Set in tropical surroundings with stories focused on "glamorous" drug deals, it displayed an excess that both contradicted and complemented '80s conservatism. Its rock music score—often featuring contemporary hits—along with its cinematic style, reflected the heavy influence of MTV. In fact, Brandon Tartikoff, head of programming at NBC, first conceived the idea when, at a lunch with producer Anthony Yerkovich, he scribbled on a napkin "MTV cops."

In 1979, Reverend Jerry Falwell founded the Moral Majority. He declared it would battle "the obscenity, vulgarity, profanity that under the guise of sex education and 'values clarification'" dominated public schools. Each Sunday, Falwell taped the *Old Time Gospel Hour* in his imposing red brick church in Lynchburg, Virginia. Nearly 400 TV stations carried the show, and through it Falwell raised millions of dollars to fight "heathen" influences. In 1980, the Moral Majority supported Ronald Reagan for the presidency after he won them over by declaring the theory of evolution "a scientific theory only" whose validity even some scientists doubted.

With battle lines clearly drawn, acrimony characterized debates—especially those over abortion. New Rightists organized Operation Rescue, which demonstrated outside abortion clinics. In 1987, pro-choice groups joined civil libertarians to defeat the nomination of Robert H. Bork, a conservative who had criticized liberal judicial activism, to the Supreme Court. Nevertheless, two years later the court upheld a Missouri statute that greatly limited women's access to abortions.

Many Boomers joined the conservative tide; others, seeking spiritual fulfillment, but turned off by traditional religion, plunged into the New Age movement. A curious, nebulous combination of spirituality and superstition, New Age had its roots in faith healing and the belief that souls migrated into different realms. New Agers channeled voices from outer space and the supernatural world. J. Z. Knight, for one, said she spoke with Ramtha, a 35,000-year-old warrior who once lived on Atlantis.

Actress Shirley MacLaine, an unofficial spokeswoman for the New Age movement, claimed to have been reincarnated. She led past-life regressions—at $300 per person. According to *Time* magazine, her advice to others typified New Age talk: "There is so much you need to know," she said. "See the outer bubble of white light watching for you. It is part of you. It is showing itself, that part of God that you have not recognized."

Business attested to the New Age appeal. Bantam Books increased its New Age titles tenfold, while New Age radio stations featured intergalactic, lost-in-space type music, and MacLaine sold eight million copies of five books dealing with self-exploration and past-life regression therapy.

New Agers earned notoriety when they proclaimed August 16, 1987, the day of harmonic convergence—cartoonist Gary Trudeau ridiculed it by calling it "moronic convergence"—when the heavens would be in a rare alignment. There would occur from this, they predicted, visits by UFOs and the raising of the dead. Objective reports failed to confirm that these events occurred.

If average Americans were confused by the New Age movement, they were alarmed by rap music, which became popular with young people of all races in the mid-1980s. Many teenagers were introduced to rap by MTV, the music channel that went on the air in 1981 and began presenting music videos 24 hours a day. Some condemned the videos as nothing more than poorly packaged commercials; others praised them as innovative and experimental. Whatever the case, by the late 1980s, even aging Baby Boomer rockers—Eric Clapton, the Rolling Stones—were making videos.

As the decade ended, political conservatism had begun to lose its vitality. The Iran-Contra scandal—in which Reagan sold weapons to Iran in exchange for the release of American hostages, and then used the money from the arms sales to fund the Contras in Nicaragua—rocked his presidency. At the same time, the New Religious Right suffered when televangelist Jim Bakker was convicted in federal court of having bilked contributors to his ministry and diverted funds to support his luxuries, including an air-conditioned dog house. Soon after, another televangelist, Jimmy Swaggert, who had loudly condemned Bakker for his sins, was forced to confess his own, begging forgiveness for having had sex with prostitutes. As if signaling conservatism's retreat, in 1989 Falwell dismantled the Moral Majority.

Voting Patterns: 1980, 1984, 1988

Year	Voting Age Population (in millions)			Percent of Voting Age Population Reporting They Voted		
	1980	1984	1988	1980	1984	1988
18-20 years old	12.3	11.2	10.7	35.7	36.7	33.2
21-24 years old	15.9	16.7	14.8	43.1	43.5	38.3
25-34 years old	35.7	40.3	42.7	54.6	54.5	48.0
35-44 years old	25.6	30.7	35.2	64.4	63.5	61.3
45-64 years old	43.6	44.3	45.9	69.3	69.8	67.9
65 years old and over	24.1	26.7	28.8	65.1	67.7	68.8
Male	74.1	80.3	84.5	59.1	59.0	56.4
Female	83.0	89.6	93.6	59.4	60.8	58.3
Black	137.7	146.8	152.9	60.9	61.4	59.1
White	16.4	18.4	19.7	50.5	55.8	51.8
Hispanic**	8.2	9.5	12.9	29.9	32.6	28.8
Total*	157.1	170.0	178.1	59.2	59.9	57.4
School years completed:						
8 years or less	22.7	20.6	19.1	42.6	42.9	36.7
High School: 1-3 years	22.5	22.1	21.1	45.6	44.4	41.3
4 years	61.2	67.8	70.0	58.9	58.7	54.7
College: 1-3 years	26.7	30.9	34.3	67.2	67.5	64.5
4 years or more	24.0	28.6	33.6	79.9	79.1	77.6

* Total includes other races not shown separately.
** Hispanic persons may be of any race.

◀ An ironic aspect of the Reagan revolution was that comparatively few Americans actually participated—voter disaffection, which had been on the rise for decades, meant that fewer than half of eligible voters bothered to go to the polls on election day. Although Reagan's reelection campaign in 1984 was able to galvanize a small amount of extra participation in some quarters, overall the chart and map show a gradual erosion of interest in electoral politics, across demographic categories of age, gender, race, education, and, in the map below, region.

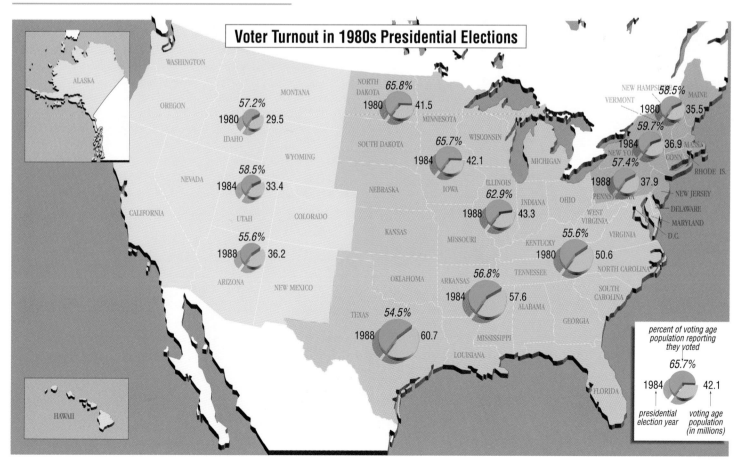

Voter Turnout in 1980s Presidential Elections

percent of voting age population reporting they voted

65.7%
1984 — 42.1
presidential election year — voting age population (in millions)

Year	World	United States Politics	Arts
1980	In Quebec, residents vote overwhelmingly against a measure initiated by the Parti Québécois government that would allow the French-speaking province to negotiate sovereignty-association with the rest of Canada.	Ronald Reagan captures the presidency as Republicans take control of the Senate.	John Lennon is murdered in New York City by a crazed fan.
1981	Polish leaders impose martial law and outlaw the independent labor union Solidarity.	Sandra Day O'Connor is sworn as the U.S. Supreme Court's first female justice.	Cable subscribers can watch rock music videos on MTV (Music Television).
1982	Britain delivers a humiliating defeat to Argentina in a battle over the Falkland Islands.	The proposed Equal Rights Amendment to the Constitution fails to meet the ratification deadline.	Steven Spielberg's *E.T.* warms America's heart and breaks box-office records.
1983	President Ronald Reagan orders an invasion of Grenada after a bloody coup brings a leftist regime to power.	Calling the Soviet Union an "evil empire," President Reagan proposes the Strategic Defense Initiative, a space-based missile defense program.	Hit film *The Big Chill* packs Baby Boomers into the theaters, and the sound track puts "oldies" back on the charts.
1984	A toxic leak at a Union Carbide pesticide plant in Bhopal, India, kills 3,500 people.	President Reagan easily wins re-election over Democrats Walter Mondale and Geraldine Ferraro, the first woman to run for vice president on a national ticket.	Madonna tops the charts with her album, *Like a Virgin.*
1985	New Soviet leader Mikhail Gorbachev institutes economic and cultural reforms that bring *glasnost,* or "openness," to the U.S.S.R.	Bernhard Goetz, who had confessed to shooting four blacks, is acquitted on attempted murder charges and convicted on an illegal weapons charge.	Bob Geldof organizes British pop stars to record the song "Do They Know It's Christmas?" to raise money for famine relief in Ethiopia.
1986	In the Filipino elections Corazon Aquino defeats corrupt President Ferdinand Marcos.	Justice William Rehnquist's nomination to be the next chief justice of the United States is confirmed by the Senate.	Paul Simon's *Graceland,* a collaboration with South African artists, wins a Grammy for "Album of the Year."
1987	During the annual pilgrimage to Mecca, Iranian Shiite Muslims protest against Sunni Muslims, leading to riots and the death of over 400 pilgrims.	A Senate investigation into Iranian arms sales turns up links to the Nicaraguan Contras and the Reagan cabinet.	University professor Allan Bloom attacks moral relativism in *The Closing of the American Mind.*
1988	Benazir Bhutto becomes president of Pakistan and the first female to lead a Muslim nation in modern history.	George Bush wins the presidency with the campaign promise "Read my lips: no new taxes."	Novelist Salman Rushdie infuriates fundamentalist Muslims with *The Satanic Verses.*
1989	▶ Populist movements overthrow communist rule across Eastern Europe, but the Tiananmen Square massacre ends pro-democracy protests in China.		Conservatives threaten to withdraw funding for the National Endowment for the Arts.

CORBIS/Kevin R. Morris

Science and Industry	Pastimes and Lifestyles	Sports	Year
Mount St. Helens in Washington erupts with an explosion killing eight people and producing tremors felt over 100 miles away.		◁ The U.S. Olympic hockey team beats the Soviets for the gold medal at Lake Placid, New York.	1980
The AIDS epidemic emerges in New York and San Francisco, baffling doctors.		Martina Navratilova, who dominates women's tennis, becomes an American citizen.	1981
Telephone giant AT&T is broken up as part of an antitrust settlement.		American swimmer Steve Lundquist sets the world record in the 100m breaststroke at the Pan American games in Venezuela with a time of 1:02.28.	1982
Launched into space 11 years earlier, *Pioneer 10* passes the outermost planet of our solar system and becomes the first man-made craft to enter deep space.	Nancy Reagan asks kids to "Just Say No" to drugs, but highly addictive crack cocaine begins to wreak havoc on American cities.	The United States loses the America's Cup yacht race for the first time in 132 years.	1983
For the first time, the American Heart Association classifies smoking as a risk factor leading to strokes.	Board game Trivial Pursuit sells some 20 million copies.	At the Olympics, Mary Lou Retton wins a gold medal in the all-around individual competition, becoming the first American woman to win an individual gold medal in any gymnastics event.	1984
Researchers detect a hole in the protective ozone layer over Antarctica.	Oceanographers in the North Atlantic locate the wreckage of the *Titanic*.	Mike Tyson becomes world heavyweight champion.	1985
A nuclear accident at Chernobyl in the Ukraine exposes much of Europe to radioactive fallout.	Nintendo video games enchant millions of American children.	American Greg LeMond wins the Tour de France for the first time; he will also win in 1989 and 1990.	1986
The stock market falls 508 points on Black Monday.	Prozac, manufactured by American pharmaceutical firm Eli Lilly, is approved in the United States to treat depression.	NFL players go on strike for free agency rights; a month later they agree to restricted player movement in exchange for a salary cap.	1987
NASA climatologist James Hansen sounds a dire warning about global warming.	Northwest Airlines announces that it plans to ban smoking on most domestic flights.	The Baltimore Orioles set a new major league baseball record after they lose their first 21 games of the season.	1988
Sony produces its 50-millionth Walkman.	The U.S. Supreme Court rules in *Texas v. Johnson* that the First Amendment upholds the right to burn the American flag as symbolic political speech.	A San Francisco earthquake jolts the World Series at Candlestick Park.	1989

CORBIS/BETTMANN

Before the Berlin Wall fell in 1989, Americans were caught in global crises that sent U.S. troops overseas to fight and die. The downing of a Korean passenger jet by the Soviet air force and the invasion of Afghanistan by the Soviet army worsened relations between the Soviet Union and the United States, and a disaster at a nuclear reactor soured relations between the Soviets and several European nations. In addition, world terrorist activity increased, and Americans felt fearful and even helpless after a bomb on Pan Am Flight 103 destroyed an airliner over Lockerbie, Scotland, killing 270 people. The decade ended on a remarkable note, as the Berlin Wall fell, Germany unified, and prodemocracy movements swept across Europe.

EAST GERMANY
Berlin Wall Torn Down (1989-1990)
To Americans growing up during the cold war, the Berlin Wall symbolized communist repression. The wall, actually a series of walls topped with barbed wire and fortified with watchtowers, gun emplacements, and mines, had, since 1961, prevented East Berliners from traveling to West Berlin. Nearly 200 people had been killed trying to breach it. But on November 9, 1989, the East German government, beset by protesters, opened the wall. Over the next several months, German crowds—including punk rockers clad in leather jackets—took hammers and chisels to the concrete barrier and smashed it; entrepreneurs tried to sell the rubble.

LEBANON
Civil War Intensified (1982-1990)
While civil war wracked Lebanon in 1982, Israel invaded that country to crush the Palestine Liberation Organization. The invasion only intensified the turmoil. After Christian militias, working with the Israelis, slaughtered 1,000 Palestinians in refugee camps, President Ronald Reagan sent U.S. Marines into Beirut and ordered warships to bombard the Lebanese countryside. That, however, led to terrorists detonating a TNT-loaded truck at Marine headquarters, killing 230 soldiers. With no way to control the civil war, Reagan withdrew American troops in 1984. Israel followed suit in 1985 (except for some troops in the south), but fighting among various groups and the Syrian army continued, leaving Beirut a devastated shell.

GRENADA AND PANAMA
Two U.S. Invasions (1983 and 1989)
With Cubans building an airfield on Grenada while a bloody coup brought to power a stridently leftist regime, President Ronald Reagan ordered an invasion of that country in October 1983. About 10,000 paratroopers battled several hundred Cuban workers, along with 100 or so Cuban soldiers. The Americans quickly won, and a new Granadan government reversed the leftist policies. A few years later, grand juries in Tampa and Miami indicted Panamanian dictator Manuel Antonio Noriega on charges of drug trafficking and money laundering. After fraudulent elections kept Noriega in power, President George Bush launched Operation Just Cause in 1989 and sent in American troops. They captured Noriega, and the ex-strongman was placed on trial in Florida and convicted.

UKRAINE, U.S.S.R.
Nuclear Disaster (1986)

On April 26, 1986, an explosion blew apart the heavy steel and concrete lid of the Chernobyl nuclear power station, 65 miles north of Kiev, in the worst accident in the history of nuclear energy. Thirty-five people died almost immediately, several hundred others were hospitalized, and over 100,000 were relocated. Radioactive emissions—exceeding the A-bomb blasts at Hiroshima and Nagasaki—spread across Europe, contaminating farmland, livestock, and people. The catastrophe shook Baby Boomers in the United States, who remembered the less severe accident at Three Mile Island in Pennsylvania, and it gave strength to an anti-nuclear power movement.

IRAN-IRAQ
War (1980-1990)

For several years after war erupted between Iran and Iraq in 1980, Iran held the advantage. But after Iran fired missiles at oil tankers in the Persian Gulf flying the U.S. flag, the American Navy responded by attacking Iranian oil facilities and vessels. In July 1988, the U.S.S. *Vincennes* mistakenly shot down an Iranian airliner, killing 290 passengers and crew. After the tragedy, Iran and Iraq agreed to a cease-fire, and in 1990 signed an agreement ending hostilities. The war had cost hundreds of thousands of lives—including those of rebellious Kurds killed by Iraqi chemical weapons—while the American intervention had helped Iraq and its dictator, Saddam Hussein.

KOREA
Korean Airliner Downed by Soviets (1983)

On the night of August 3, 1983, a Soviet jet fighter shot down Korean Air Lines flight 007 inside Soviet airspace, near Sakhalin Island. The attack, which killed all 269 on board, enraged Americans. President Ronald Reagan called it "an act of barbarism." We now know that the airliner had been warned by the Soviet fighter, but for some reason failed to respond. To this day it is unclear why KAL 007 was far off course. Had the triple-check navigation equipment failed? Had the United States involved the airliner in a spy mission? A Russian investigation later said its air defense commanders had operated incompetently and from panic.

AFGHANISTAN
Russia's Quagmire (1980-1989)

When Islamic fundamentalists, the Mujahedeen, began fighting a Marxist regime in Afghanistan, Soviet leaders faced a predicament. Should the Mujahedeen win, their religious crusade might spread to the Soviet Union and threaten its stability. But should the Soviets invade Afghanistan to help the Marxists, they might get bogged down in what the Soviet military called "Russia's Vietnam." In December 1979 Russia sent in troops. The United States considered this a threat to its nearby oil interests and by 1987 was spending $630 million to support the Mujahedeen rebels. Russia had its Vietnam—a quagmire that consumed men and money. In 1989 its last demoralized troops left Afghanistan.

CHINA
Tiananmen Square (1989)

In the spring of 1989, students in Beijing, China's capital, began hunger strikes and mass demonstrations at Tiananmen Square to demand democratic reforms. The number of protesters soon swelled as workers and bureaucrats joined the ranks. On May 19 the government declared martial law and the following day sent troops and tanks into Tiananmen Square, while a crowd numbering one million tried to block them. Then in early June, Premier Deng Xiaoping ordered the army to shoot the unarmed protesters, and hundreds died. President George Bush stated he "deplored" the massacre, but within weeks he pursued expanded economic relations with China.

If Baby Boomers thought they lived in one big nuclear arsenal from the 1950s through the 1970s, they hadn't seen anything yet: in the early 1980s nuclear armaments expanded at an unprecedented rate, producing an equally unprecedented danger. Yet as the decade ended, President Ronald Reagan and Soviet leader Mikhail Gorbachev reached a momentous arms reduction agreement.

Reagan entered the presidency in 1981 as a fierce cold warrior committed to defeating communism. "The Soviet Union is the focus of evil," he proclaimed in 1983. In his first administration, he promoted a 41 percent increase in defense spending while pledging to build 17,000 nuclear weapons.

Reagan cared little for detail, and little for facts that contradicted his war against communism. In one unabashed error, he once claimed that ICBMs could be called back after they were launched. That he made irresponsible comments, that the Soviet Union reacted to American defense spending by accelerating its own, and that annual worldwide military spending in the early 1980s reached $550 billion, all caused a dormant anti-nuclear weapons movement to awaken and place pressure on the bomb builders.

> **❝** To this day, America is still the abiding alternative to tyranny. This is our purpose in the world—nothing more and nothing less. **❞**
>
> —**Ronald Reagan**

One group, Physicians for Social Responsibility (PSR) organized a high-profile meeting in 1980. Prominent scientist George Kistiakowsky declared: "I personally think that the likelihood for an initial use of nuclear warheads is really quite great between now and the end of the century." PSR called for dismantling nuclear arsenals. Partly because Baby Boomers supported the group's activities, its membership climbed from 3,000 in 1981 to 16,000 in 1982.

The Fate of the Earth (1982) by Jonathan Schell captured Baby Boomer attention. Schell lamented American complacency. "At present, most of us do nothing," he said. "We take refuge in the hope that the holocaust won't happen, and turn back to our individual concerns." He graphically showed what would result if a one-megaton A-bomb were dropped over New York City. A fireball, he said, would grow "until it was more than a mile wide, and rocketing upward, to a height of over six miles. For ten seconds, it would broil the city below. Anyone caught in the open within nine miles of ground zero would receive third-degree burns and would probably be killed." His litany of charred bodies, flattened buildings, and irradiated landscapes—"the city and its people would be mingled in a smoldering heap"—chilled most everyone who read it.

Schell informed Americans that in a first attack, the Russians would use the equivalent of 800,000 Hiroshima bombs. Television reinforced the possible horror with the movie *The Day After*, which aired in 1983. An estimated 100 million viewers watched as a fictional nuclear attack leveled Kansas City.

In reality, nuclear missiles remained on their launchpads, but in ever greater, ever more frightening numbers. The Soviet Union had placed 345 SS-20 missiles, each with three nuclear warheads, in Eastern Europe; through NATO the United States had placed 500 cruise missiles in Western

Europe. Alongside the arsenals, several regional conflicts threatened world peace. Reagan saw them linked to the larger nuclear issue, for he believed the Soviet Union was behind most world upheaval; thus if the Russians were beaten at bomb building, they would quit making trouble in the world. In the meantime, their adventures in other countries must be stopped, their evil deeds frustrated.

Consequently, Reagan intervened in several hot spots. In October 1983 he invaded Grenada with 2,000 Marines. The Caribbean island had undergone a communist revolution, and several hundred Cubans had been sent there by Fidel Castro to build an airport. Reagan sent troops to evict the Cubans and overthrow the communist government, which they did. Most Americans hailed this victory, and many believed their nation had overcome its post-Vietnam malaise and could again exert its military power.

Reagan considered Marxist-influenced rebels in El Salvador and the Sandinistas in Nicaragua a great threat to American security. He believed the Soviet Union backed both and planned to make Central America another Cuba. Thus in 1983 Contras (counterrevolutionaries) trained by the CIA invaded Nicaragua and attacked the Sandinista government. The action raised a storm of controversy in the United States. Reagan called the Contras "freedom fighters," but many Baby Boomers, raised on the Vietnam War, argued that

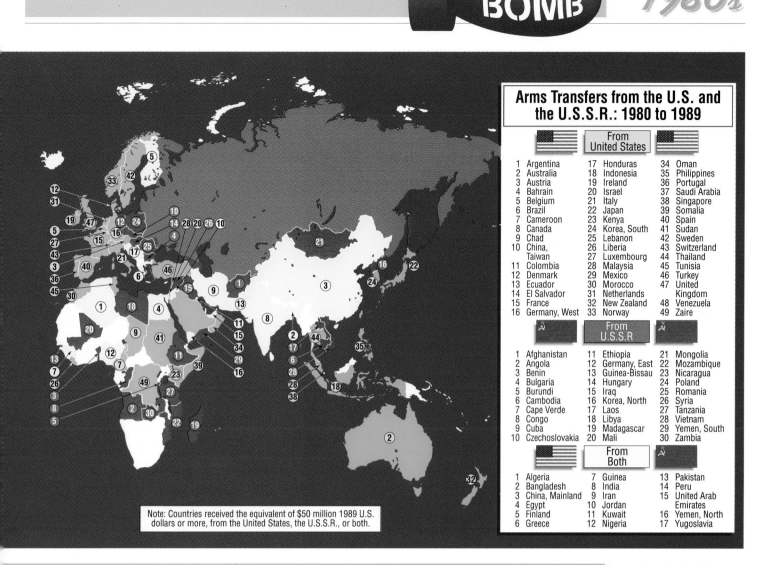

Arms Transfers from the U.S. and the U.S.S.R.: 1980 to 1989

From United States

1 Argentina	17 Honduras	34 Oman
2 Australia	18 Indonesia	35 Philippines
3 Austria	19 Ireland	36 Portugal
4 Bahrain	20 Israel	37 Saudi Arabia
5 Belgium	21 Italy	38 Singapore
6 Brazil	22 Japan	39 Somalia
7 Cameroon	23 Kenya	40 Spain
8 Canada	24 Korea, South	41 Sudan
9 Chad	25 Lebanon	42 Sweden
10 China,	26 Liberia	43 Switzerland
Taiwan	27 Luxembourg	44 Thailand
11 Colombia	28 Malaysia	45 Tunisia
12 Denmark	29 Mexico	46 Turkey
13 Ecuador	30 Morocco	47 United
14 El Salvador	31 Netherlands	Kingdom
15 France	32 New Zealand	48 Venezuela
16 Germany, West	33 Norway	49 Zaire

From U.S.S.R

1 Afghanistan	11 Ethiopia	21 Mongolia
2 Angola	12 Germany, East	22 Mozambique
3 Benin	13 Guinea-Bissau	23 Nicaragua
4 Bulgaria	14 Hungary	24 Poland
5 Burundi	15 Iraq	25 Romania
6 Cambodia	16 Korea, North	26 Syria
7 Cape Verde	17 Laos	27 Tanzania
8 Congo	18 Libya	28 Vietnam
9 Cuba	19 Madagascar	29 Yemen, South
10 Czechoslovakia	20 Mali	30 Zambia

From Both

1 Algeria	7 Guinea	13 Pakistan
2 Bangladesh	8 India	14 Peru
3 China, Mainland	9 Iran	15 United Arab
4 Egypt	10 Jordan	Emirates
5 Finland	11 Kuwait	16 Yemen, North
6 Greece	12 Nigeria	17 Yugoslavia

Note: Countries received the equivalent of $50 million 1989 U.S. dollars or more, from the United States, the U.S.S.R., or both.

Central America would become a quagmire as deep as had been the one in Southeast Asia.

Many other Boomers, however, supported Reagan in everything from his nuclear arms buildup to the military action in Grenada and Central America. The reinvigorated military boosted national pride, erased bad memories from Vietnam, and restored confidence in the fight against communism.

In the mid-1980s, Reagan advanced his program called the Strategic Defense Initiative (SDI), or Star Wars. With SDI, he wanted to build a defensive shield using lasers to knock down nuclear missiles entering the United States. Critics in America ridiculed the idea as fantasy; Russian leaders called it "irresponsible" and "insane."

The cold war took another turn when Soviet premier Mikhail Gorbachev, under enormous pressure in his country to cut defense spending and reform a crumbling economy, proclaimed his desire to end the arms race. In December 1987, Reagan and Gorbachev signed the Intermediate Nuclear Force Treaty (INF) that provided for the dismantling and destruction of short- and medium-range missiles in Europe. The treaty, Gorbachev later claimed, "represented the first well prepared step on our way out of the cold war, the first harbinger of the new times." The following year,

Gorbachev stunned the world by announcing a unilateral withdrawal of Soviet troops from Eastern Europe, along with tanks, artillery pieces, and combat aircraft.

A scandal rocked the Reagan administration in the late 1980s, when it was disclosed that the president had illegally funded the Contras. The scandal showed that in some ways little had changed since Richard Nixon's duplicity. But in other ways a new world beckoned, for cold war tension had declined considerably. On a summit trip to Moscow in 1988, a newspaper reporter asked Reagan: "Do you still think you're in an 'evil empire,' Mr. President?" He replied: "I was talking about another time and another era."

▲ *In the 1980s the cold war was no longer confined to two super-powers; virtually every nation, no matter how small or seemingly insignificant, chose one "side" or the other. This map shows the competition for global influence in the form of arms transfers. Most intruiging, perhaps, are nations shown here in yellow, receiving arms shipments from both the United States and the U.S.S.R., playing both sides against the proverbial middle.*

A Buttery Crisis

As Allan M. Winkler points out in *Life Under a Cloud* (1993), much like writers in the 1950s, several novelists in the 1980s explored the theme of nuclear holocaust. For example, Pulitzer Prize winner Bernard Malamud portrayed life after a nuclear war in *God's Grace* (1982).

But the nuclear weapons buildup entered children's literature, too, when the famed writer Dr. Seuss wrote his satirical *The Butter Battle Book* (1984), intended for Baby Boomer parents and their kids. In it, he tells of an arms race between the Yooks, who eat bread with the butter side up, and the Zooks, who eat it butter side down. As they developed powerful weapons, they developed the desire to use them in order to settle their differences.

"We must do everything we can under our constitutional system to stop the killing of unborn children. We're talking about life and death," said Carl Anderson, an aide to a conservative Republican senator, about abortion. "Nothing like [abortion] has separated our society since the days of slavery," said Surgeon General Dr. C. Everett Koop. Given the divisive protests fueled by Baby Boomer discontent in the 1960s, Koop may have overstated his case, but many Boomers, older now, would have agreed as they either joined or witnessed the conflict over abortion.

Although as an issue abortion generated the most heated protest of the 1980s, other protests also appeared. Mitch Snyder, a former prison inmate, raised a furor in 1984 when, as an activist for the homeless, he went on a 51-day hunger strike to convince the federal government to improve shelters in Washington, D.C. He eventually obtained funding for a 1,400-bed shelter. One supporter said that Snyder symbolized for him "that meaningful change doesn't happen for poor people in our country unless you fight."

Through the National Organization for Women (NOW), liberal feminists, many of them Baby Boomers, continued their push for women's rights. But progress was hampered by conservative opposition—as evident in the failure to obtain ratifi-

cation of the Equal Rights Amendment—and internal conflict. Betty Friedan, who in the early 1960s had ignited the women's movement, declared a newfound caution. In *The Second Stage* (1981), she argued that equality for women should never mean destruction of the family or sexual war against men. More controversy arose in 1989 when NOW proposed forming a political party dedicated to feminist issues, especially women's right to abortion. Even many pro-choice activists criticized NOW for the proposal, claiming it would hurt the Democratic Party, which they saw as the best hope for achieving their goals.

In opposition to the pro-choice stance, the political New Right opposed abortions except to save the life of the mother, and, as the number of abortions nationally climbed from 744,600 in the 1970s to 1.5 million in the early 1980s, a pro-life movement emerged, heavily populated by Baby Boomers. Most in the movement protested peacefully; but a violent minority engaged in bombings of abortion clinics—30 attacks occurred between 1982 and 1985.

The pro-life movement gained its strength from those who considered abortion murder and who perceived it as a threat to family values. They believed abortion promoted sexual promiscuity, and they complained that teenagers could get abortions without their parents knowing, thus undermining

AIDS Activism

With its slogan "Silence = Death," the organization ACT UP used public protests to pressure for the release of experimental AIDS drugs and to get pharmaceutical companies to cut the prices for such drugs. ACT UP was founded in 1987 by playwright and author Larry Kramer, and held its first demonstration that March on Wall Street in New York City, picketing and blocking traffic.

Other noteworthy demonstrations included a sit-in at the offices of *Cosmopolitan* magazine in 1988 to challenge an article that claimed few women were in danger of contracting AIDS, as well as protests at the Food and

Drug Administration and the White House. ACT UP was a reflection of its Baby Boomer roots: its protest strategy owed much to the civil rights movement; and its loose, almost chaotic, structure resembled the 1960s group Students for a Democratic Society.

Pictured here, Kansas City, Missouri, police officers hold ACT UP protesters while waiting for handcuffs to arrive. The AIDS activists were protesting a medical convention, claiming the group of doctors were trying to prevent the use of alternative treatments for their disease. (AP/WIDEWORLD PHOTOS) ▲

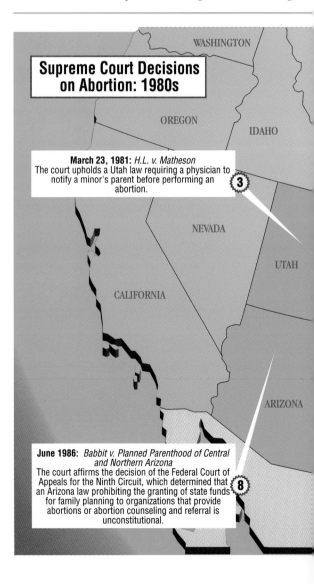

Supreme Court Decisions on Abortion: 1980s

WASHINGTON

OREGON

IDAHO

March 23, 1981: *H.L. v. Matheson*
The court upholds a Utah law requiring a physician to notify a minor's parent before performing an abortion. ③

NEVADA

UTAH

CALIFORNIA

ARIZONA

June 1986: *Babbit v. Planned Parenthood of Central and Northern Arizona*
The court affirms the decision of the Federal Court of Appeals for the Ninth Circuit, which determined that an Arizona law prohibiting the granting of state funds for family planning to organizations that provide abortions or abortion counseling and referral is unconstitutional. ⑧

relations within families. Some observers argued, however, that pro-life men sometimes acted out of frustration with feminists who promoted issues that threatened male authority.

Pro-life groups incited controversy in the early 1980s when they released *Silent Scream*, a movie that purported to show what happened to a 12-week-old fetus in a woman's womb when it was subjected to surgical instruments used in an abortion. The fetus squirmed to avoid the instruments, and its mouth opened, emitting a silent scream. But doctors criticized the movie for its inaccuracies, claiming that the mouth was really a space between the fetal chin and chest, and that trick photography had been used to show the fetus "thrashing about in alarm."

A political war erupted between pro-life and pro-choice groups. President Ronald Reagan issued an executive order withholding federal money for clinics that discussed abortion when counseling women. In 1987, he nominated pro-life Robert H. Bork to the Supreme Court; in response, pro-choice groups teamed with civil libertarians to defeat Bork's nomination. In 1989, the court upheld a Missouri statute that greatly limited women's access to abortions. Yet pro-lifers had a difficult time getting other state legislatures to emulate Missouri.

While these disputes unfolded, Randall Terry, a Baby Boomer, formed Operation Rescue (OR), a militant pro-life group that demonstrated in front of abortion clinics and blocked access to them. In *Wrath of Angels* (1998), James Risen and Judy L. Thomas called OR "the organization that completed the sudden transformation of anti-abortion activism from a movement of scattered and easily ignored pockets of local protest into a national phenomenon." OR gained widespread media attention in May 1988 with its protests at clinics in New York City and on Long Island. The group followed those with protests in July at Atlanta—so extensive some called it a siege—and in October at clinics in 32 cities that resulted in 2,600 arrests. The latter effort included "rescues," where protesters convinced women entering the clinics to reject abortion and keep their babies.

Terry likened OR to the civil rights movement with its use of civil disobedience. Terry himself was arrested in 1989 after he blocked an Atlanta clinic, and was sentenced to a 24-month prison term. (His time in jail and internal disputes led to the breakup of OR in 1990.) He defended his actions by asserting: "You would do whatever you could to physically intervene and save the life of [a] child. That is the appropriate response to murder."

▼ *Like the rest of the United States, Supreme Court justices in the 1980s spent a great deal of time thinking about abortion. This map shows the decisions handed down by the court on abortion issues.*

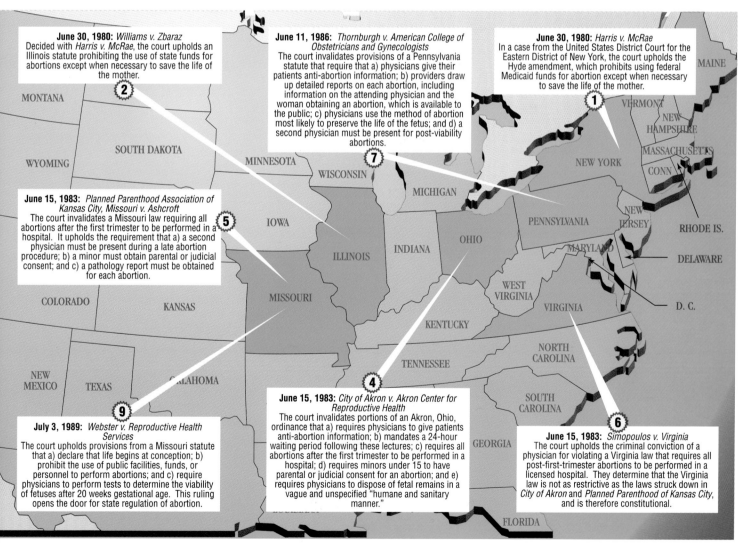

June 30, 1980: *Williams v. Zbaraz*
Decided with *Harris v. McRae*, the court upholds an Illinois statute prohibiting the use of state funds for abortions except when necessary to save the life of the mother.
2

June 11, 1986: *Thornburgh v. American College of Obstetricians and Gynecologists*
The court invalidates provisions of a Pennsylvania statute that require that a) physicians give their patients anti-abortion information; b) providers draw up detailed reports on each abortion, including information on the attending physician and the woman obtaining an abortion, which is available to the public; c) physicians use the method of abortion most likely to preserve the life of the fetus; and d) a second physician must be present for post-viability abortions.
7

June 30, 1980: *Harris v. McRae*
In a case from the United States District Court for the Eastern District of New York, the court upholds the Hyde amendment, which prohibits using federal Medicaid funds for abortion except when necessary to save the life of the mother.
1

June 15, 1983: *Planned Parenthood Association of Kansas City, Missouri v. Ashcroft*
The court invalidates a Missouri law requiring all abortions after the first trimester to be performed in a hospital. It upholds the requirement that a) a second physician must be present during a late abortion procedure; b) a minor must obtain parental or judicial consent; and c) a pathology report must be obtained for each abortion.
5

July 3, 1989: *Webster v. Reproductive Health Services*
The court upholds provisions from a Missouri statute that a) declare that life begins at conception; b) prohibit the use of public facilities, funds, or personnel to perform abortions; and c) require physicians to perform tests to determine the viability of fetuses after 20 weeks gestational age. This ruling opens the door for state regulation of abortion.
9

June 15, 1983: *City of Akron v. Akron Center for Reproductive Health*
The court invalidates portions of an Akron, Ohio, ordinance that a) requires physicians to give patients anti-abortion information; b) mandates a 24-hour waiting period following these lectures; c) requires all abortions after the first trimester to be performed in a hospital; d) requires minors under 15 to have parental or judicial consent for an abortion; and e) requires physicians to dispose of fetal remains in a vague and unspecified "humane and sanitary manner."
4

June 15, 1983: *Simopoulos v. Virginia*
The court upholds the criminal conviction of a physician for violating a Virginia law that requires all post-first-trimester abortions to be performed in a licensed hospital. They determine that the Virginia law is not as restrictive as the laws struck down in *City of Akron* and *Planned Parenthood of Kansas City*, and is therefore constitutional.
6

Before television threw open its doors to all manner of taboo topics, talk shows like *The Phil Donahue Show* (1970–96) had begun to introduce them as a matter of education. The television talk-show format, which originated in the wake of the women's movement as a way to expose educated homemakers to a wider world, pioneered the trend toward providing expert advice, bringing topics like sexual dysfunction, domestic violence, and alcoholism "out of the closet." By the 1980s, talk TV had moved beyond experts. It was no longer enough to hear about rape from the medical professional who treated victims; we needed to hear from the victims themselves. The age of confessional television had dawned.

By the mid-1980s, TV characters were making the same kinds of admissions. Gone was the unapologetic, unenlightened character of Archie Bunker; in his place was the complicated, neurotic self-examination of Frasier Crane of *Cheers* (1982–93). But flaws and self-doubt were not just for comic characters. *Hill Street Blues* (1981–87), one of the finest TV dramas of any era, presented cops as they had never been seen before. Instead of invincible crime fighters, *Hill Street* cops were troubled and flawed. The conflicts often centered on how relationships were affected when police work seeped into everyday life.

Hill Street Blues, with its large cast, open-ended plots, and complex storytelling engaged a new, upscale audience. This wealthy Boomer viewing audience appealed to advertisers and ensured the success of *Hill Street Blues*, despite ratings that were mediocre by usual standards. *Hill Street Blues* blended good TV and good demographics and opened the door for other yuppie-oriented entertainment. Advertisers were willing to shell out for airtime on shows that, while not necessarily ratings blockbusters, consistently put grown-up Boomers in front of their TV sets: *St.*

Elsewhere (1982–88), *Moonlighting* (1985–89), and *thirtysomething* (1987–91) are just a few examples.

A depiction of self-absorbed yuppies struggling with "having it all," *thirtysomething* was a perfect reflection of the audience advertisers hoped to reach. The characters seldom deprived themselves or their children of anything, yet they were troubled by a nagging emptiness. These well-off but brooding, overachieving but dissatisfied Baby Boomers lived the 1980s ideal—striving and acquiring—while wondering openly about the meaning of it all. Every personal obstacle in the lives of Michael, Hope, Elliot, Nancy, Gary, Melissa, and Ellyn—disintegrating relationships, serious illness, births, deaths, and career changes—were opportunities for self-examination that touched a nerve with audiences.

Educated urbanites appreciated *thirtysomething* with all its nuances. Much of the rest of the country preferred the pure entertainment value of *Dallas*—a brash, unapologetic indulgence in everything despicable.

The other breakaway hit of the '80s was *The Cosby Show* (1984–92). In an era where sit-coms had fallen on hard times, this show introduced a new kind of family comedy in the tradition of *Father Knows Best*, but different. This show about an upper-middle-class black family featured several children but was presented through the eyes of adults. Baby Boomers related to the working parents, who were doing their best to raise a family in demanding times. *The Cosby Show* was the forerunner of the second generation of family comedies, such as *Roseanne* (1988–97), *Married With Children* (1987–97), *Home Improvement* (1990–99), and even *The Simpsons* (1989–present), that depicted family life as less than entirely harmonious.

In the 1980s, TV ratings and demographics became more important to the networks than ever before. Fox TV, the first new network to emerge since the late 1940s, began regular programming in 1986 with the premiere of the *Late Show with Joan Rivers*. Cable TV, with its niche programming, had begun chipping away at network TV supremacy. Favorable changes in government regulations sparked an explosion of growth in the cable industry so that by 1987, 50 percent of American homes were wired for cable. For the first time since the 1950s, the "Big Three Networks"—NBC, CBS, and ABC—were facing possible competition. HBO, which began testing the market for pay-TV in 1972 with 365 subscribers, had topped a million subscribers by the late 1970s and was continuing to grow rapidly.

WTBS, the first superstation and the brainchild of Ted Turner, began beaming old shows, via satellite, to independent cable TV providers around the country. Soon Turner's all-news TV station, CNN, would forever change TV news on international, national, and local levels. CNN could not then, and could not even in the late 1990s, compete head-to-head with network news. But because it was dedicated only to news and had made immediacy its priority, CNN found itself in the center of breaking news long before the networks had dispatched their teams to cover events. For instance, CNN was the only station carrying the *Challenger* space shuttle disaster live in January 1986.

Who Shot J.R.?

One of the biggest '80s successes was the antithesis of *thirtysomething*. While *thirtysomething* focused on real people with problems, *Dallas* (1978–91) was about people with *real problems*. The characters lived at least a few lives every episode—plotting corporate takeovers, arranging murders, committing adultery, and bribing government officials. From the time that TV viewers turned their backs on Milton Berle for being "too New York," there have always been shows that played well on the coasts and those that were popular with the nation in between. *Dallas* appealed to the "heartland" audience—the very audience that critics liked to blame for television's mediocrity.

The first successful prime time "soap opera," *Dallas* had an enormous cast of regulars and elaborate plot lines that carried over from show to show. The program centered on two wealthy, rival Texas oil families, the Barneses and the Ewings. J.R. Ewing, the man *Time* once called "that human oil slick," was the embodiment of self-centered greed in a decade characterized by hostile takeovers and unbridled corporate power. The second season ended with the much hyped cliffhanger that had the whole country wondering, "Who shot J.R.?" The next season's opening episode, which revealed the identity of the gunman, attracted the second largest audience in TV history. *Dallas* stayed on top into the 1990s and was one of the few TV dramas to ever rank number one in TV ratings. It also has the distinction of being the first network show that became a monster hit overseas. That success opened the networks' eyes to moneymaking TV syndication possibilities outside the United States.

It is true that CNN-style continuous news coverage has brought events in the United States and around the world closer to viewers. But it has also led the way in sensationalizing news—blurring the line between entertainment, commentary, and news—in order to generate ratings. The legitimate historic events of the 1980s, the Tiananmen Square protests, the Gulf War, and the fall of the Berlin Wall produced large audiences. Baby Boomers, weaned on TV, witnesses to assassinations and civil unrest, expect to be at the scene of every news story. And news programming has evolved to meet that expectation for firsthand reports. In the process, especially as local news has replaced national news as the primary source for information, all news programming has veered toward tabloid sensationalism.

The other major cable breakthrough in the '80s was MTV. Television had never really succeeded in capturing the youth market with musical programming. Under pressure to appease sponsors, censors, and parents, commercial television hadn't found a format that really worked—producing instead middle-of-the-road fare like *American Bandstand* (1957–89), *Shindig* (1964–66), and *Hullabaloo* (1965–66), which appealed more to young teenyboppers than to their rebellious older siblings. MTV debuted on August 1, 1981, and changed that for good.

In 1981, Baby Boomers were ages 17–34, a valuable target age for advertisers. The older Boomers who had come of age in the '60s still clung to music as their symbol of rebellion. And the younger Boomers were setting the new rock and roll trends. MTV was the first real attempt to reach music fans with *their* music, rather than a sanitized version of music intended to appeal to a vast TV audience. By deciding to "narrowcast," MTV created an edgy cable-TV product that won over viewers, especially teenagers who generally tuned into music and stayed away from TV (on average teenagers constituted only 10 percent of the TV audience). Putting aside the network TV formula that produced shows with something for everyone or shows so innocuous that no one was offended, MTV went right to the heart of the new generation gap and made something that young people would like and parents would not.

MTV was launched with an advertising blitz that featured rock stars like Mick Jagger demanding, "I want my MTV." By the decade's end, MTV had come to influence nearly all aspects of American culture. It isn't surprising

that as MTV skewed more toward the younger end of the Boomer age bracket, a new music TV network, VH-1, would emerge to satisfy the rock and roll interests of aging Boomers.

Several trends that surfaced in the 1980s would strongly influence television in the next decade. Public disclosure of previously private matters fueled the taste for even more juicy personal stories. The line between news and entertainment got fuzzier. Cable TV grew exponentially. VCRs drove the video movie market. And as this happened, TV network hegemony was disintegrating.

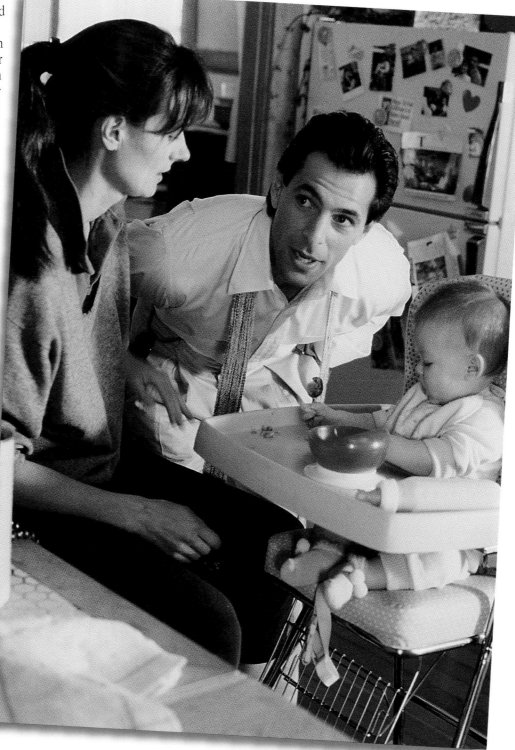

▼ *Mel Harris and Ken Olin play Hope and Michael on the Boomer hit,* thirtysomething. *(Photofest)*

The '80s are often cast as years of conservatism, overspending, selfishness, and greed. This was the Reagan era, and federal deregulation of business went hand-in-hand with what appeared to be tacit government support for laissez-faire capitalism. The money-and-power culture embraced by some Boomers during the '80s certainly was not the only way of life in America, but it was a noisy and distinctive one. It was a time in which books with such titles as *Looking Out for Number One* and *Winning Through Intimidation* were popular, and in which a 2,500-year-old essay by an Asian military tactician, Sun Tzu's *The Art of War*, was a best-seller. The new folk heroes were not those who stole from the rich, but those who became rich.

Consumer culture had become something of a science by the '80s. Baby Boomers learned to shop at an early age; malls and shopping centers grew up alongside the Boomer generation. During the 25 years since architect Victor Gruen had designed the first fully-enclosed two-story structure devoted to retail commerce, shopping malls had mushroomed in American suburbs and cities. The malls literally contained almost anything a shopper might want—clothes, food, music, electronics, toys, restaurants, movie the-

> 66 *I was actually less concerned about the market than the potential for collapse of the world financial system.* 99
>
> **—Mary Farrell**,
> *investment strategist, on Black Monday*

aters. Business owners liked the shelter provided by the malls; stores housed in a mall did not need to be built to resist the elements. They also liked that customers stayed longer at the retail coliseums than they would at a single street-level shop—teenagers and adults alike socialized at shopping malls for hours, increasing the chances there would be further sales as the day went by.

The '80s introduced plenty of products to stock the malls' shelves. Many now-standard home electronics made their premieres during the '80s—video players, compact discs, desktop computers, cable television. The new corporate culture inspired lines of "executive toys," which might include exercise equipment, computer chess games, or elaborately designed clocks, all with high price tags. New merchandise appeared faster than it could be coveted. Acquisition was celebrated in the popular TV program *Lifestyles of the Rich and Famous*, in which a nationwide audience was permitted to visit the expensively outfitted homes of celebrities.

In the second half of the decade, the stock market, something of a playground for ambitious '80s speculators, began to show signs of overextension and abuse. In 1986, Ivan Boesky, the high-rolling investor who inspired the slo-

▼ *Boomers "felt the burn" as the aerobics craze swept the United States. (The Image Works)*

▲ Many investors could not believe their eyes when they saw the results of Black Monday, October 19, 1987. (James Marshall/The Image Works)

gan "Greed is good!" in Oliver Stone's film *Wall Street*, was prosecuted for insider trading—making investments based on privileged information. His case was seen as representative of widespread excesses in the financial arena.

Less than a year later, during October 1987, the stock market crashed. Analysts had warned for months that stocks were overvalued and that something had to give. But no one had anticipated the major role that computer technology would play in what became known as Black Monday. Computers had become critical to the market during the '80s. Not only did the machines allow traders to communicate buys and sells immediately to the exchange floor, but they also enabled complex orders involving huge blocks of different stocks to exchange hands within seconds; in many cases, these computer trades were programmed to be made automatically, without human intervention. When a selling panic kicked in on Monday, October 19, an unprecedented flood of computer-transmitted sales led to a 508-point loss. At the close of the day, the Associated Press announced that it would take until 9:30 P.M. to sort through the rubble and send closing prices to the world's news agencies.

High-stakes financial gamesmanship wasn't a feature of just the stock market. In 1988, the leveraged buyout came into its own. "Corporate raiders" borrowed money by issuing low-credit, high-yield junk bonds, and used the funds to buy controlling interests in targeted companies. By the end of the decade, RJR Nabisco, Kraft, Pillsbury, and Montgomery Ward were just a few of the corporations that had fallen to buyouts, takeovers, and mergers.

If the '80s were years of conspicuous consumption, they also were the era during which Americans were handed the bill for the party. Waste management was a mounting problem, and neighborhood-level recycling programs were instituted as a partial solution. Unfortunately, the handling of industrial toxic waste couldn't be dealt with as readily. New facilities intended to recycle or contain hazardous waste were designed, and most citizens were glad of it. No one, however, wanted such a plant to be built in his or her neighborhood. The federal government stuck to its deregulation stance as battles over siting of waste treatment facilities were fought state by state. Public hearings over the issue sometimes crumbled into brawls between citizens and local officials. The term "NIMBY Syndrome" entered the language—Not In My Back Yard. NIMBYism is alive today, any time someone demands that a problem be solved . . . by someone else, somewhere else.

AIDS Research

It was the disease that crept out of nowhere. In 1979, puzzled physicians began noticing a rash of unusual illnesses plaguing young gay men in New York, San Francisco, and Los Angeles. Helpless doctors watched men die from a constellation of maladies that included a skin cancer called Karposi's sarcoma; a rare form of pneumonia; swollen lymph nodes; and widespread yeast infections.

The first research article on the phenomenon appeared in June 1981, from the national Centers for Disease Control. As the death toll rose, an avalanche of articles on the epidemic followed. The most notorious, a 1983 editorial in the *Journal of the American Medical Association,* suggested that this new disease, dubbed Acquired Immunodeficiency Syndrome (AIDS), could be transmitted by casual contact. Although doctors now know this to be untrue, at the time fear gripped the general public, leading to an upsurge of harassment against so-called high risk groups, gay men and Haitians, and a fevered reevaluation of the Sexual Revolution of the 1960s.

In reality scientists still had no idea what caused AIDS or how it was spread. Heavily funded research powerhouses expressed no interest in the disease, while doctors and researchers on the front lines struggled for enough funding to obtain basic laboratory equipment. Two feuding labs on different continents—a French team from the Pasteur Institute, and the National Cancer Institute's Dr. Robert Gallo—began to investigate the possibility that a new type of disease agent called a retrovirus might be the cause of AIDS. From 1983 until their dispute was settled by an international committee in 1986, internecine warfare between the labs held up study on the newly discovered human immunodeficiency virus (HIV).

By the end of the 1980s research had led to AZT (Retrovir®), the first drug that appeared to lengthen the lives of HIV-positive patients. But, with the barriers facing the development of an AIDS vaccine or cure continuing to prove formidable, new drugs and treatments have not halted the epidemic. At the end of 1998, more than 33 million people around the world were infected with HIV.

Walkmans

On July 1, 1979, the first Walkman rolled off Sony production lines. One decade later, on June 27, 1989, Sony produced its 50 millionth Walkman. During that decade, the portable cassette players swept across America like an irresistible force.

The concept of the Walkman was beautifully simple: Sony engineers adapted a portable dictation machine to play stereo formats and added a headset instead of speakers. Unlike the boom boxes that proliferated during the 1970s, Walkmans were easy to carry and didn't bother the neighbors. Their popularity grew hand-in-hand with the Boomer jogging craze.

Critics fretted that a nation of "Walkpeople" would be alienated, isolated, and hard-of-hearing. But for legions of commuters and teenagers, the Walkman provided a sound track for the mundane moments of daily life. Its ability to create a sense of personal space even in the middle of a crowd gave people a feeling of control over their surroundings. Best of all, it let children listen to music that their parents hated at full volume without provoking an argument.

VCRs

The year was 1980. A recession weighed down the economy, and gloomy retailers forecast a poor sales season for nonessentials, particularly home-entertainment items. With a sale price ranging from more than $600 to $1,500, the home videocassette recorder (VCR)—first introduced in Betamax format by Sony in 1975—seemed a likely candidate for failure.

Instead, analysts were astonished to note a VCR sales boom. Despite high prices and the confusion created by the incompatible VHS and Betamax formats, VCR sales rose 60 percent from 1979 to 1980. Asian electronics manufacturers flooded the market, driving down prices, and the sales curve continued to rise. By 1985 nearly a quarter of all U.S. homes with a television set also owned a VCR, which made Hollywood and the television networks very nervous.

Despite the doomsayers, the rapid market conquest by the VCR did not put an end to big-screen movies, or destroy television's profitability by allowing viewers to fast forward through the commercials in previously taped programs. But, with sales continuing at a rate of a million units a month, the VCR spawned what would quickly become a multibillion-dollar business in prerecorded videocassettes: movies, children's programming, workout tapes, and more. Consumer demand would not be limited to the United States—by 1990, more than a third of the world's TV-owning households also contained a VCR.

The WELL

An offshoot of the *Whole Earth Catalog,* the influential counterculture catalog and magazine, the Whole Earth 'Lectronic Link (WELL) yanked the communal ethos of the 1960s into a new, wired era. Born out of a conversation between *Whole Earth* publisher Stewart Brand and entrepreneur Larry Brilliant, whose Network Technologies International sold computer conferencing systems to businesses, the WELL would become legendary in the history of the Internet as one of the first virtual communities—a fractious collection of people linked together by nothing but a computer and a modem.

The WELL opened shop in Sausalito, California, in March 1985. With one employee—Matthew McClure, recently returned from a 12-year stint on a Tennessee commune—and six modems, the WELL drew its first few hundred subscribers largely from the *Whole Earth* readership. Highly educated and computer-savvy, they filtered

in and out of various "conferences," virtual locations modeled on French literary salons, where online conversations were organized by topic. Whether they logged on for friendly chatter, or for information on anything from parenting to UNIX hacking, within the space of a year the members of the WELL had bonded together in a unique and very real community. When three members opened up a new conference on the Grateful Dead in April 1986, hundreds of Deadheads from around the country rushed to join the WELL, providing the group with a much-needed financial boost.

Although the growth of the World Wide Web and its mammoth entities, like America Online, would soon overshadow the few thousand hippies and intellectuals on the WELL, its influence would go far beyond numbers. The earliest online haunt of some of today's most influential cyber-thinkers, the WELL provided our first glimpse of the way computer technology would transform our definition of society and self.

Polartec

A polyester fabric engineered to have the warmth and texture of fleece, Polartec rejuvenated the slipping reputation of polyester and reinvigorated the sagging fortunes of its inventors at Malden Mills, a 100-year-old Massachusetts textile company. Lightweight, breathable, and easy to care for, Polartec offered all the benefits of wool with none of wool's scratchy drawbacks. An instant success for cold-weather outerwear and sports gear, Polartec was widely imitated by other manufacturers.

Cheaper types of synthetic fleece made market inroads, but Polartec continued to develop new and more sophisticated fabrics, including water-repellent fleece and windproof fleece. But Polartec's finest moment would come in 1996, when a public weary of corporate downsizing made a hero of Malden Mills's owner Aaron Feuerstein for keeping all of his employees on at full salary while rebuilding the mills after a devastating 1995 fire.

▼ *Dr. Robert Gallo and Health and Human Services Secretary Margaret Heckler at a press conference on the cause of AIDS, April 23, 1984. (CORBIS/BETTMANN)*

Bruce Springsteen (1949-)

A blue-collar troubadour from industrial New Jersey, Bruce Springsteen won critical acclaim and the devotion of fans for his poignant, hard-driving ballads of working-class desperation. But Springsteen went from star to cultural icon with the 1984 release of his seventh album, *Born in the U.S.A.*

Though the title song was actually an angry anti-anthem about a Vietnam veteran's sense of betrayal, Springsteen's regular-guy image and heavy visual reliance on American flags made him a sudden symbol of resurgent American optimism and patriotism. Springsteen tolerated the irony of his new popularity as the poster boy for American jingoism. But his tolerance had its limits: he soundly rejected Ronald Reagan's attempts to appropriate "Born in the U.S.A." as a campaign theme song for the 1984 elections. Springsteen aged gracefully in the '90s as he transformed again, this time from fist-pumping rock god to reflective, socially conscious solo artist.

▼ *The Boss performs "Born in the U.S.A." in 1985. (UPI/CORBIS-BETTMANN)*

No Limits
Sandra Day O'Connor (1930–) and Sally Ride (1951–)

Equal opportunity for women got a boost in the '80s from Supreme Court Justice Sandra Day O'Connor and astronaut Sally Ride, who shattered the glass ceiling of two extremely male-dominated fields. Twenty years apart in age, their different paths to success also illustrated just how expectations for women would change over the course of a generation.

Graduating third in her class at Stanford Law in 1952, O'Connor never forgot that private law firms refused to consider her for any job but legal secretary. Following her husband to Arizona, she began to build a private law practice while raising three children. But it was her volunteer work with Arizona's Republican Party that gave her career a boost, leading to an appointment as the state's assistant attorney general. O'Connor was serving as a judge on Arizona's Court of Appeals when Ronald Reagan, making good on a campaign promise to appoint the first woman to the Supreme Court, chose her to fill a 1981 vacancy. A conservative centrist and advocate for women's rights, O'Connor helped swing the ideological balance of the Supreme Court to the right after years of liberal domination.

For Baby Boomer Sally Ride, there would be no suggestions that she pursue secretarial work. Ride was working on a doctorate in astrophysics at Stanford when she responded to a NASA advertisement recruiting women for the space program. Selected in 1978 as one of 35 female candidates for spaceflight training, she made history in 1983 when, as part of the crew of the space shuttle *Challenger STS-7*, she became the first American woman in outer space. A member of the committee that investigated the 1986 explosion of the *Challenger 51-L*, she left NASA in 1987 for academia, where she has made it a priority to attract more women to the sciences.

What Happened?
Jerry Rubin (1938–1994) and Jane Fonda (1937–)

Stalwarts of the fading counterculture reinvented themselves for the '80s by getting down to business. Most startling was the transformation of former Yippie leader Jerry Rubin, whose memorable media antics helped define the '60s protest movements. Rubin once demonstrated the absurdities of capitalism by tossing dollar bills to a throng of frantic stockbrokers on the New York Stock

Dismissed by white political pundits as too radical, too inexperienced, and too narrow in his appeal, Jackson galvanized African-American voters, who turned out to support him in record numbers.

His 1984 campaign suffered a sudden meltdown after Jackson was quoted calling Jews "Hymies" and New York City "Hymietown." But he still won enough support in the primaries to be a keynote speaker at that year's Democratic National Convention, helping to establish him as the first serious African-American presidential candidate in American history.

Back on the campaign trail in 1988, he electrified audiences with a populist platform for people left behind by the decade's economic boom: African Americans, family farmers, struggling Rust Belt laborers. A fiery orator, Jackson led his "Rainbow Coalition" to primary victories in several states. He captured 29 percent of the popular vote—second only to Michael Dukakis—but could not overcome the suspicion of Democratic leaders, who considered him to be a rogue outsider. While Democrats continued their march to the right in an attempt to woo back voters lost to Reagan and George Bush, Jackson would emerge from his presidential campaigns as a powerful voice for progressive issues and a source of hope and pride for African Americans.

Jerry Rubin at the office, left. (UPI/CORBIS-BETTMANN)

Exchange. But in August 1980, Rubin joined the ranks of his former enemies, taking a job on Wall Street as a securities analyst.

While Rubin clashed with his old friend Abbie Hoffman in a series of well-publicized "Yippie vs. Yuppie" debates, another radical threw herself into venture capitalism. Known in the '70s for her antiwar activism and the infamous "Hanoi Jane" radio broadcasts, Jane Fonda became best known in the '80s as the hard-nosed businesswoman directing a multi-million dollar fitness empire. Like Rubin, who eventually left Wall Street to become a distributor for a Colorado health-drink company, Fonda insisted that her new career was consistent with the revolutionary ideals she once loudly espoused. But for Americans still smarting from the excesses of the Vietnam era—or leery of the consumer nirvana promised by the Reagan revolution—the corporate conversions of Rubin and Fonda looked like the ultimate sell-out.

Jesse Jackson (1941-)

A civil rights activist who worked under Dr. Martin Luther King, Jr., the Reverend Jesse Jackson astonished the leadership of the Democratic Party with two quixotic campaigns for the presidential nomination.

Jesse Jackson at a press conference. (UPI/CORBIS-BETTMANN)

Cocaine

It might be difficult to believe that an ode to an addictive, debilitating drug could become a top-40 radio hit. Nevertheless, Eric Clapton's "Cocaine" was a chart-topper in the late '70s and remained in the pop star's repertoire through the '80s.

The song only reflected reality. Powdered cocaine, inhaled, was the recreational drug of choice among the affluent in the early '80s. Unconcerned about its addictive effects, some partygoers thought little of offering cocaine to people they had met just minutes before. When sealing a business deal or negotiating sex, cocaine was a hip substitute for an alcoholic drink.

Powdered cocaine fell out of fashion with Boomer partyers when its very real dangers were made known by the media and, in many cases, experienced firsthand. Tragically, the more powerful and more addictive version of cocaine, crack, appeared in the mid-'80s and was marketed by drug dealers to the urban poor. Crack use remains a critical social problem.

Way Back Yonder in Vietnam

After the fall of Saigon in 1975, Americans lost no time in using movies and TV to process their pain and doubt about the Vietnam War. Several war-themed Hollywood dramas of the late '70s—*The Deer Hunter, Coming Home, Apocalypse Now*—were followed in the '80s by a virtual flood of 'Nam-centric movies and TV programs. Sometimes the war itself was the focus, as in the Academy Award-winning *Platoon* (1986) and Stanley Kubrick's *Full Metal Jacket* (1987).

Also popular were ridiculous, "This time we win!" actioners, in which war veterans returned to Vietnam or Cambodia to free P.O.W. buddies held prisoner by sadistic Asians—Chuck Norris's *Missing in Action* series and Sylvester Stallone's *Rambo* are prime examples. Even when the stories weren't set in Southeast Asia, '80s movies and TV programs often featured American men who had matured during, been traumatized by, or learned their craft in the Vietnam War. Vietnam became the word that spoke volumes about a character's psychological makeup. ("He's a little crazy—worked with the CIA's Phoenix operation in 'Nam," they whisper about Mel Gibson in *Lethal Weapon.*)

Little thought was given to the tragic experience of the Vietnamese people as America looked to Hollywood for exorcism of wartime demons. The lone exception didn't come until 1993 with the release of *Heaven & Earth*, based on the memoirs of Vietnamese author Le Ly Hayslip. Significantly, the movie was made through the efforts of Oliver Stone, creator of the our-boys-in-'Nam epic, *Platoon*.

The Vietnam movie cycle slowed by the end of the '80s, but along the way Hollywood learned how to keep selling Vietnam to the American public. James Cameron's film *Aliens* (1986) gave viewers a science-fiction 'Nam, with U.S. Marines on a distant planet battling hordes of monsters in close combat.

Fashion

With most traces of '60s youth counterculture gone by 1980, Boomers were faced with the prospect of making a living in a conservative era. In great part, fashion trends for a generation now in their thirties and forties were dictated by the down-to-business attitude of Reaganite America. Former radicals donned suits on behalf of "working within the system."

Suits were standard work wear for the Boomer middle class, men and women alike. The game became one of dressing at once conservatively and stylishly, so your intelligence, taste, and seriousness were announced before you uttered a word. Businessmen adopted the practice of wearing "power ties," neckties with elaborate patterns and bright colors meant to indicate aggressiveness. Businesswomen wore jacket, blouse, and skirt combinations that bespoke a careful blend of "femininity" and professionalism. "Dress for success" was the popular maxim.

Casual wear, on the other hand, offered the fashion-conscious a wider range of choice. A few highlights:

- Denim jeans, especially pricey name brands, were very popular—and late in the decade it became fashionable to deliberately rip holes in the new jeans for which you paid $30.

- Izods—short-sleeved pullover shirts with collars— were seen on men everywhere.

- Hollywood had its moments of influence, in particular the ripped sweatshirts of *Flashdance* and the T-shirt-and-jacket combos of *Miami Vice*.

- Inexpensive, garish plastic wristwatches, especially those by Swatch, became the rage.

The 1990s

A fan in a pinstriped suit mourns Grateful Dead singer Jerry Garcia, who died on August 9, 1995.
(REUTERS/MARK CARDWELL/ARCHIVE PHOTOS)

"No American is typical anymore," said a writer for *American Demographics* in 1995. "There is no average family. . . . the body politic has become a motley crowd." To critics, motley brought chaos; but others insisted that by decade's end the American family, although new in form, had largely stabilized.

As they had done several times before, Baby Boomers surprised demographic experts, this time by setting off a "baby boomlet" that lasted from 1977 to 1994. The boomlet produced 72 million children, compared to 77 million during the boom (1946–64), and owed its strength to women who began childbearing late. Of course, by far the greatest number of babies born were to women in their 20s; but Boomer women in their 30s and older contributed more than one-third of all births. Although the birthrate jumped up for all age groups, it did so fastest for 30- to 39-year-old women.

Similar to the Baby Boom, the boomlet stimulated everything from toy sales to college enrollments, as youths born in the late 1970s squeezed into overcrowded dormitories on campuses across the nation. Yet because there were so many aging Baby Boomers, young people made up a smaller percentage of the population than they did in the 1960s.

With Baby Boomers moving out of their childbearing years, and with their much smaller successor generation, the baby busters, or Generation X, entering, the number of births and the birthrate began declining in the mid-1990s. But this overall trend belies growth in certain subgroups, such as Hispanics.

With Baby Boomer women more likely than those in previous generations to remain childless, and with Boomers getting older, only one-third of all households had kids under 18 living in them. Further, although married couples still dominated, almost 25 percent of all households consisted of people living alone.

That more women worked meant fewer households had a traditional working dad and a stay-at-home mom—in 1995 only 25 percent fit that profile. Although popular magazines carried stories about mothers opting to stay home with their kids, women in the workplace actually climbed slightly from 57.9 percent in 1993 to 58.8 percent in 1994.

▼ A demographic portrait of the Baby Boom generation in 1990.

Baby Boomers as of 1990

URBAN V. RURAL RESIDENCE

Total population	76,968,012
Urban population	58,584,681
% of total	76.1
Rural population	18,383,331
% of total	23.9
Farm population	1,086,627

NATIVITY & PLACE OF BIRTH

Native population	69,138,123
% born in state of residence	62.0
Foreign-born population	7,829,889
Entered the U.S. 1980 to 1990	3,729,686

DISABILITY OF CIVILIAN NONINSTITUTIONAL PERSONS

With a mobility or self-care limitation	2,832,844
With a mobility limitation	1,201,451
With a self-care limitation	2,208,184
With a work disability	4,705,755
In the labor force	2,414,084
Prevented from working	1,919,528

CHILDREN EVER BORN PER 1,000 WOMEN

26 to 34 years old	1,381
35 to 44 years old	1,960

VETERAN STATUS

Civilian veterans 26 to 44 years old	7,865,225

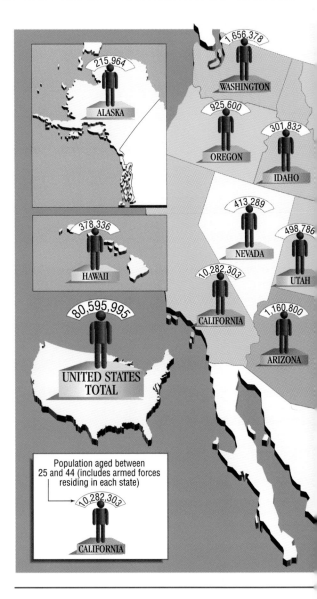

Population aged between 25 and 44 (includes armed forces residing in each state)
→ 10,282,303
CALIFORNIA

The resurgence of "traditional family values" may have had some effect, however, in women deciding against abortions. The abortion rate declined from 29.3 per 1,000 women in the early 1980s to 25.9 in 1992. As an issue, though, abor-

Baby Boomers as of 1990

ANCESTRY

Arab	302,798	German	18,239,038	Scotch-Irish	1,502,739
Austrian	267,295	Greek	351,004	Scottish	1,724,346
Belgian	126,901	Hungarian	505,612	Slovak	599,658
Canadian	166,236	Irish	12,197,666	Subsaharan African	212,087
Czech	530,364	Italian	4,634,338	Swedish	1,512,125
Danish	491,312	Lithuanian	256,634	Swiss	300,907
Dutch	1,850,705	Norwegian	1,238,351	Ukrainian	245,686
English	9,308,016	Polish	3,001,006	United States or American	3,527,739
Finnish	206,696	Portuguese	373,104	Welsh	661,199
French (except Basque)	3,199,771	Romanian	120,511	West Indian (excluding Hispanic origin groups)	416,474
French Canadian	970,303	Russian	973,491	Yugoslavian	162,022

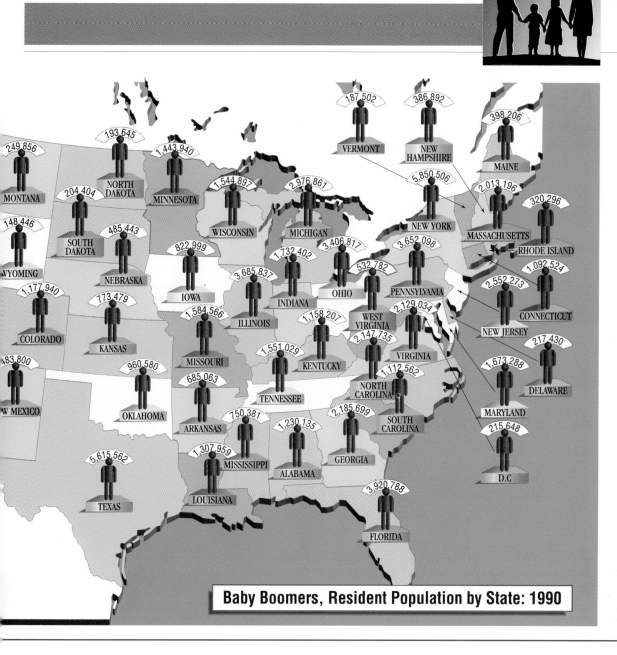

Baby Boomers, Resident Population by State: 1990

◀ *In 1996 the U.S. Census Bureau released a report on the Baby Boom generation, "Selected Social Characteristics of Baby Boomers 26 to 44 Years Old." Among the subjects covered by the report were where Boomers were as of 1990 (shown here in the map) and who they were (shown in the charts at left).*

tion produced a firestorm. Most Americans were pro-choice and believed women should decide about pregnancy, but Christian fundamentalists saw abortion as murder and claimed it destroyed families. Randall Terry, who founded Operation Rescue in the 1980s, declared: "We must strive to build a Christian democratic republic. . . . The only alternative is a pagan nation with rampant murder, rape, drug abuse, gang warfare."

In the 1990s, pro-life activists picketed abortion clinics and distributed "wanted" posters displaying the names and photos of abortion doctors labeled as murderers. Anti-abortion fanatics shot and killed three doctors and bombed several abortion clinics. Protest tactics both peaceful and violent led to federal laws protecting access to the clinics, but also to state laws that made abortions more difficult to obtain. Many of the clinics closed, and about 80 percent of counties in the United States had no doctors who performed abortions.

If fundamentalists thought abortion shattering to families, numerous instances in which students shot and killed teachers and fellow students led many Americans to conclude that society was sick. While a majority of parents no longer considered schools safe, debates raged as to what

caused the violence: was it the "jock" culture found in the schools, the availability of guns, the example set by violent movies and TV shows? Personal problems confronting the assailants? A materialistic society that treated human beings callously? "This is not about the weapons used or how many there were," said the principal of the Jonesboro, Arkansas, middle school where two boys ambushed and killed four students and a teacher in 1998. "It is about our society, what is happening to our children."

Children in the United States seemed to be growing up faster and faster in the 1990s. The teen birthrate reached 61 per 1,000 women in 1992, with a sharp increase among unmarried teens. Yet for all these problems, some developments indicated greater stability. Between 1992 and 1995 teen pregnancy rates decreased significantly, juvenile crime dropped during the decade, and in 1998 the U.S. government reported a decline in sexual intercourse among adolescents. The Centers for Disease Control and Prevention attributed the last to sex education in schools, intervention by churches, and "more family discussions around the dinner table between parents and their children." The "motley crowd" and its families may have started coming together.

Nathan Glazer, professor at the Harvard University Graduate School of Education, stated in the early 1990s: "America's population is changing in its racial and ethnic composition. Its values are changing. Its notions of the proper relation of groups and individuals to the national society are changing." Such changes stirred renewed controversy about schools and colleges: Were academic standards improving? Should multiculturalism be promoted? Had affirmative action enriched society? Should high schools as we know them be ended?

In 1993, the U.S. Department of Education issued several reports to commemorate the tenth anniversary of *A Nation at Risk*, the analysis that had ripped public schools with such statements as: "If an unfriendly power had attempted to impose on America the mediocre educational performance that exists today, we might well have viewed it as an act of war." The reports cited numerous advances, such as an increase in high school students taking academic rather than vocational courses.

Terrell Bell, the former secretary of education who had put together the commission that authored *A Nation at Risk*, claimed it had made educational reform a priority, and that few could deny improvement had occurred with on-site decision-making, smaller bureaucracies, and other changes. Yet some analysts thought the impact much less. College admission standards remained the same, school systems remained underfinanced and teachers underpaid, and homework assignments remained too shallow or few.

Deciding to pursue further improvements, in 1994 Congress passed the Goals 2000: Educate America Act. It called for all students leaving grades four, eight, and twelve to demonstrate "competency" in core courses with challenging academic content. The act encouraged states to undertake strategic planning for reform by the year 2000, and its sponsors claimed that it helped 36 states establish content standards in core academic subjects and 17 states develop performance standards.

After Goals 2000 passed Congress, the National History Standards Project issued its proposal for public school history courses and stirred a multicultural dispute that had been brewing for some time. Ever since the 1960s, African Americans, and to a lesser extent Mexican Americans, Puerto Ricans, and other ethnic groups, had advocated that liberal arts courses include study of minorities and their role in America's development. In short, they wanted a multicultural curriculum.

Opponents believed multiculturalism would cause America to lose its attachment to a common culture. Said one critic of the proposed curriculum: "Omitted . . . in the name of respect for diversity were, among other touchstones of traditional American history, the First Continental Congress, Robert E. Lee, Alexander Graham Bell, Thomas Edison, Albert Einstein, Jonas Salk, and the Wright Brothers." They also feared multiculturalism would encourage hatred of the dominant Anglo-Saxon culture by portraying it as oppressive.

While battles raged over that issue, conservatives attacked affirmative action. The program had been started in the 1960s to correct past discrimination against minorities by giving them preferential treatment in hiring, in awarding of government contracts, and in college admissions. In the 1990s, critics said that affirmative action caused colleges to accept inferior students. One report claimed that blacks graduating from high school scored lower on achievement tests than whites still in the eighth grade. As a result, affirmative action encouraged poorly prepared blacks to enter college and led to their dropping out. Better to improve earlier education, said the critics, and bring blacks into college at the same academic standing as whites. That proposal, however, ignored abysmal conditions found in central city schools.

After a federal court struck down affirmative action in Texas, the number of blacks admitted into the University of Texas law school dropped from 75 in 1996 to 11 in 1997. Through Proposition 209, California banned race as a consideration in public college admissions. Consequently, African Americans and other minorities in the freshman class admitted to the University of California–Berkeley decreased from 23.1 percent in 1997 to 10.4 percent in 1998.

A pathbreaking study that year, *The Shape of the River* by William Bowen and Derek Bok, showed that although blacks had higher dropout rates than whites, and lower grade point averages, when they graduated from college they were as likely as other students to pursue advanced degrees; as a result, they formed the backbone of a black professional class. Further, by socializing in college, blacks and whites learned about each other.

▼ A boy looks through the fence at the Columbine High School tennis courts in Littleton, Colorado, April 24, 1999. Thirteen roses were placed on the fence in remembrance of the 13 people killed by two gun-wielding students on April 20, 1999. (AP Photo/Eric Gay)

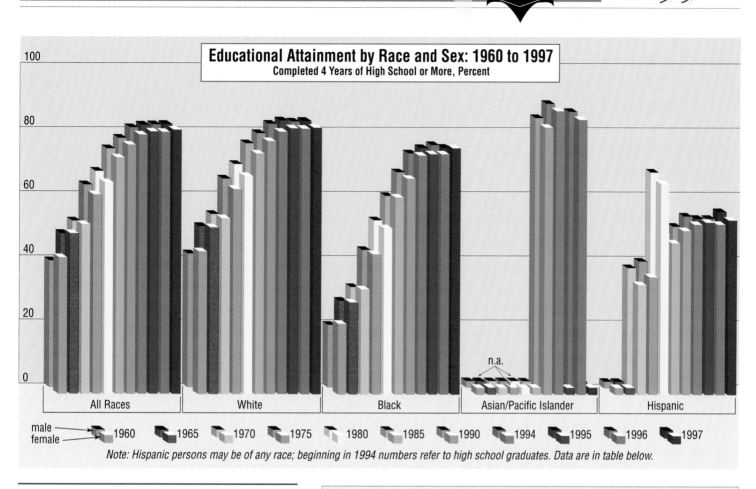

Educational Attainment by Race and Sex: 1960 to 1997
Completed 4 Years of High School or More, Percent

male
female
1960 1965 1970 1975 1980 1985 1990 1994 1995 1996 1997

All Races   White   Black   Asian/Pacific Islander   Hispanic

n.a.

Note: Hispanic persons may be of any race; beginning in 1994 numbers refer to high school graduates. Data are in table below.

The authors said affirmative action should be supported as a way to provide a better future for both races.

Parents watching the evening news in the late 1990s can be forgiven for wondering if their children would have any future at all: in February 1996, a 14-year-old boy in Moses Lake, Washington, used an assault rifle to kill two classmates and a teacher at his junior high school; in October 1997, a 16-year-old boy killed his mother and then shot nine students, killing two of them, at his high school in Pearl, Mississippi; December of that year saw a 14-year-old boy open fire on a student prayer circle at his high school in West Paducah, Kentucky, killing three students.

Outdoing these crimes, both in the age of the perpetrators and in premeditated coldness, two boys, 11 and 13 years old, donned camouflage outfits and, in March 1998, fired on students and teachers who were leaving their Jonesboro, Arkansas, middle school in response to a fire alarm the boys had set off. They fired 26 shots in 15 seconds, wounding 11 classmates and killing four, along with a teacher.

Tragedy struck again, in April 1999, when two students entered Columbine High School in Littleton, Colorado, and opened fire. They killed a teacher and 12 fellow students and wounded several more, before killing themselves with their own guns. Later, police found several bombs planted by the shooters at the school.

Even though Department of Education statistics showed that nationwide only 10 percent of public schools reported any major violent crimes, one survey soon after the Columbine attack revealed that a majority of parents feared

	Completed 4 Years of High School or More, Percent									
	All Races		White		Black		Asian/Pacific Islander		Hispanic	
year	male	female	male	female	male	female	male	female	male	female
1960	39.5	42.5	41.6	44.7	18.2	21.8	n.a.	n.a.	n.a.	n.a.
1965	48.0	49.9	50.2	52.2	25.8	28.4	n.a.	n.a.	n.a.	n.a.
1970	51.9	52.8	54.0	55.0	30.1	32.5	n.a.	n.a.	37.9	34.2
1975	63.1	62.1	65.0	64.1	41.6	43.3	n.a.	n.a.	39.5	36.7
1980	67.3	65.8	69.6	68.1	50.8	51.5	n.a.	n.a.	67.3	65.8
1985	74.4	73.5	76.0	75.1	58.4	60.8	n.a.	n.a.	48.5	47.4
1990	77.7	77.5	79.1	79.0	65.8	66.5	84.0	84.0	50.3	51.3
1994	81.0	80.7	82.1	81.9	71.7	73.8	88.6	88.6	53.4	53.2
1995	81.7	81.6	83.0	83.0	73.4	74.1	n.a.	n.a.	52.9	53.8
1996	81.9	81.6	82.7	82.8	74.3	74.2	86.0	86.0	53.0	53.3
1997	82.0	82.2	82.9	83.2	73.5	76.0	n.a.	n.a.	54.9	54.6

for the safety of their children at school. That they had reason to fear was reinforced that May when a student at Heritage High School in Conyers, Georgia, shot six students. None of the victims died, but it was yet another reminder that such brutal attacks could happen at any school.

Critics pointed to the cliques that alienated some students, and to the domination of schools by athletes, or what was called a "jock culture." One prominent educator even argued that high schools be done away with as more harmful than beneficial to young people. Violence, performance standards, race relations—all put public schools under great pressure in the 1990s.

▲ Despite the many challenges confronting the U.S. educational system, in the 1990s more students successfully completed high school than ever before. The increasingly multicultural makeup of graduating classes is proof positive of gains made since the 1960s.

As the United States entered the 1990s, its trade with Asia topped that with Europe; of all the domestically manufactured computers 62 percent were sold to overseas customers; one of the country's most prestigious newspapers, the *New York Times*, published a national edition by bouncing information from satellites to printing plants. New trade and new technology indicated that a global economy had arrived, an era filled with bigger businesses, faster-paced communication, and seemingly unlimited growth.

The decade began with a recession dogging the economy and ever-mounting budget deficits threatening to send it into a tailspin. As a result, President George Bush agreed to a $146 billion tax hike in return for Congress promising to lower the deficit by $500 billion over five years. In doing so, however, Bush broke his "no new taxes" pledge and convinced many voters that he had betrayed them. Despite his efforts, unemployment topped 7 percent in 1992, and the budget deficit for the year neared $300 billion.

By 1993 low interest rates had stimulated a recovery, just as Bill Clinton won the presidency by never forgetting that "It's the economy, stupid." America's commitment to a global economy went into full swing. Clinton had highlighted that shift in 1993 when he convinced Congress to ratify the North

▼ *A portrait of the Boomer labor force, as reported by the U.S. Census Bureau.*

American Free Trade Agreement (NAFTA), which Bush had negotiated. NAFTA lowered trade barriers between the United States, Mexico, and Canada. Clinton followed that by negotiating the replacement of the General Agreement on Tariffs and Trade (GATT) with the new World Trade Organization (WTO), which involved 92 countries. The change in 1994 lowered tariffs and banned import quotas.

These agreements corresponded with the Soviet Union's collapse, and many American economic leaders lauded what they called a global economy, one in which capitalism prevailed and money flowed from wealthy nations to poor ones as corporations maximized profits. Many American businesses relocated their plants overseas in order to take advantage of low wages.

Globalism could be seen, too, in the prominent organizations that brought countries together. The Group of Seven, or G-7, the world's largest economic powers, met yearly to discuss problems, and added Russia to their group, making it the G-8. The Organization of Economic Cooperation and Development, with 29 members, the United States, Britain, Germany, Canada, and France among them, promoted economic growth, while the World Trade Organization oversaw trade agreements and enforced trade rules.

The United States dominated the global economy. By 1995, it claimed 41 of the world's largest corporations, including the top two in sales, General Motors and Ford, and was by far the world's largest importer and exporter. Trade in 1996 made up 23 percent of the U.S. Gross Domestic Product, a jump from 11 percent in 1990.

While the International Monetary Fund reported that world output grew more than 4 percent in 1996, the greatest in a decade, the American economy prospered. Late that year, the United States entered its 26th consecutive quarter of growth, the second-longest stretch in peacetime. Some economists, doubting that the pace could be sustained, predicted a recession in another year. Economic indicators sagged early in 1998, but by July they had rebounded, and in August the economy grew for the 88th month in a row. Low interest rates, stable financial markets, and low inflation—under 2 percent—all encouraged the boom.

So, too, did increased productivity. George David, CEO of United Technologies, reported that his company reduced its U.S. workforce from 108,000 in 1991 to 72,000 in 1998, but upped its production by 25 percent. Federal Reserve Board Chairman Alan Greenspan declared: "The current economic performance, with its combination of strong growth and low inflation, is as impressive as any I have witnessed in my near half-century of daily observation of the American economy."

Another massive wave of corporate mergers, akin to those of the 1980s, swept America. But whereas leveraged buyouts dominated the previous decade, buyouts by businesses seeking to obtain similar companies and expand markets, or reduce costs, dominated the 1990s. In 1994 alone, American Home Products acquired American Cyanamid for $9.27 billion, Bell Atlantic merged with Nynex in a $13 billion deal, and Martin Marietta bought out Lockheed for $5.2 billion.

In all, mergers valued at over $328 billion prompted *Business Week* to proclaim: "A stampede of deals, unmatched

Selected Labor Characteristics of Baby Boomers (26 to 44 years old, 1990)

Labor Force Status	
In labor force	64,272,064
Percent in labor force	83.5
Civilian labor force	63,407,323
Employed	59,975,248
Unemployed	3,432,075
Percent unemployed	5.4
Armed forces	864,741
Not in labor force	12,695,948
Males	**38,244,126**
In labor force	35,170,696
Percent in labor force	92.0
Civilian labor force	34,397,616
Employed	32,556,567
Unemployed	1,841,049
Percent unemployed	5.4
Armed forces	773,080
Not in labor force	3,073,430
Females	**38,723,886**
In labor force	29,101,368
Percent in labor force	75.2
Civilian labor force	29,009,707
Employed	27,418,681
Unemployed	1,591,026
Percent unemployed	5.5
Armed forces	91,661
Not in labor force	9,622,518

Industry	
Employed	59,975,248
Agriculture, forestry, and fisheries	1,415,546
Mining	448,685
Construction	4,071,070
Manufacturing, nondurable goods	4,347,051
Manufacturing, durable goods	6,853,545
Transportation	2,840,098
Communications and other public utilities	1,880,876
Wholesale trade	2,779,801
Retail trade	8,091,539
Finance, insurance, and real estate	4,281,087
Business and repair services	2,995,097
Personal services	1,673,580
Entertainment and recreation services	747,945
Health services	6,298,001
Educational services	4,801,707
Other professional and related services	3,327,107
Public administration	3,122,513

Class of Worker	
Employed	59,975,248
Private wage and salary workers	44,806,106
Government workers	9,438,788
Local government workers	4,349,927
State government workers	2,897,559
Federal government workers	2,191,302
Self-employed workers	5,543,738
Unpaid family workers	186,616

Commuting to Work			
Workers	59,739,675	% using other means	1.2
% drove alone	75.1	% walked or worked at home	5.3
% in carpools	13.2		
% using public transportation	5.2	Mean travel time (minutes)	22

Wealth and Poverty Characteristics of Baby Boomers (26 to 40 years old, 1990)

Poverty Status	
Persons for whom poverty status is determined	75,923,302
Below poverty level	7,580,476
Unrelated individuals	13,283,951
Below poverty level	2,087,359
Families	29,947,561
Below poverty level	3,437,999
With related children under 18 years	23,900,540
Below poverty level	3,233,246
With related children under 5 years	10,840,552
Below poverty level	1,581,270
Female householder families	5,104,898
Below poverty level	1,898,601
With related children under 18 years	4,508,275
Below poverty level	1,841,853
With related children under 5 years	1,423,245
Below poverty level	794,975
Families	11.5
With related children under 18 years	13.5
With related children under 5 years	14.6
Female householder families	37.2
With related children under 18 years	40.9
With related children under 5 years	55.9

Baby Boom Income in 1989	
Households	38,764,962
Less than $5,000	1,725,997
$5,000 to $9,999	1,971,433
$10,000 to $14,999	2,454,118
$15,000 to $24,999	6,403,905
$25,000 to $34,999	7,064,248
$35,000 to $49,999	8,615,079
$50,000 to $74,999	6,937,464
$75,000 to $99,999	2,044,584
$100,000 to $149,999	1,018,864
$150,000 or more	529,270
Median household income (dollars)	34,601
Families	29,947,561
Less than $5,000	1,309,748
$5,000 to $9,999	1,506,518
$10,000 to $14,999	1,759,817
$15,000 to $24,999	4,432,824
$25,000 to $34,999	5,160,995
$35,000 to $49,999	6,893,378
$50,000 to $74,999	5,858,040
$75,000 to $99,999	1,722,607
$100,000 to $149,999	850,639
$150,000 or more	452,995
Median family income (dollars)	36,434
Nonfamily households	8,817,401
Less than $5,000	416,249
$5,000 to $9,999	464,915
$10,000 to $14,999	694,301
$15,000 to $24,999	1,971,081
$25,000 to $34,999	1,903,253
$35,000 to $49,999	1,721,701
$50,000 to $74,999	1,079,424
$75,000 to $99,999	321,977
$100,000 to $149,999	168,225
$150,000 or more	76,275
Median nonfamily household income (dollars)	29,225

in number and scale since the heyday of junk-bond financed takeovers in the late 1980s, is sweeping through corporate America." Rising stock values, more available cash, and favorable government policies drove the mergers, but critics condemned them for creating bloated bureaucracies and corporations powerful enough to pressure Congress and state legislatures into tariff protection and tax policies that hurt consumers.

By the late 1990s, clouds loomed. For one, median family income remained lower than in 1989, and the average job growth rate lagged behind that of the mid- and late 1980s. The *New York Times* reported that wages for workers in the "statistical middle," those earning $23,000–$32,000 a year for a 40-hour week, increased less than for those at the lower and upper ends.

More disturbingly, the 1998 economic collapse in Asia threatened to wreck the American economy—and, in fact, the nation's exports began declining and its trade deficit began deepening, with experts saying it might reach a record $150 billion. As the Asian economies set out on the road to recovery in 1999, an important lesson had been learned: As far as the global economy is concerned, it is indeed a small world after all.

◀◀ *Baby Boomers come in all economic brackets, as shown by the U.S. Census report, "Selected Social Characteristics of the Baby Boom Generation."*

▼ *Housing data on Boomers, from the U.S. Census Bureau's report.*

Selected Housing Characteristics of Baby Boomers (26 to 44 years old, 1990)

Occupied housing units	38,337,994

Year Structure Built	
1989 to March 1990	955,065
1985 to 1988	4,578,751
1980 to 1984	4,626,715
1970 to 1979	8,748,514
1960 to 1969	5,374,005
1950 to 1959	4,783,284
1940 to 1949	2,940,056
1939 or earlier	6,331,604

Bedrooms	
No bedrooms	845,227
1 bedroom	4,866,594
2 bedrooms	10,885,532
3 bedrooms	15,675,941
4 bedrooms	5,089,125
5 or more bedrooms	975,575

Selected Characteristics	
Lacking complete plumbing facilities	260,858
Lacking complete kitchen facilities	262,151
Condominium housing units	1,683,153

House Heating Fuel	
Utility gas	19,339,490
Bottled, tank, or LP gas	2,024,533
Electricity	10,720,562
Fuel oil, kerosene, etc.	4,100,964
Coal or coke	131,347
Wood	1,600,817
Solar energy	25,175
Other fuel	142,844
No fuel used	252,262

Mortgage Status and Selected Monthly Owner Cost	
Specified owner-occupied housing units	
	17,278,219
With a mortgage	15,863,031
Less than $300	373,637
$300 to $499	2,341,092
$500 to $699	3,524,687
$700 to $999	4,469,902
$1,000 to $1,499	3,253,878
$1,500 to $1,999	1,127,353
$2,000 or more	772,482
Median (dollars)	757
Not mortgaged	1,415,188
Less than $100	108,078
$100 to $199	549,716
$200 to $299	448,286
$300 to $399	173,421
$400 or more	135,554
Median (dollars)	209

Gross Rent	
Specified renter-occupied housing units	
	16,120,532
Less than $200	772,960
$200 to $299	1,544,076
$300 to $499	6,015,868
$500 to $749	4,860,763
$750 to $999	1,578,038
$1,000 or more	716,559
No cash rent	632,268
Median (dollars)	481

Year Householder moved into Unit			
1989 to March 1990	10,651,856	1970 to 1979	4,968,607
1985 to 1988	15,535,912	1960 to 1969	401,733
1980 to 1984	6,511,331	1959 or earlier	268,555

▲ A December 16,1996, White House photo shows President Clinton and White House intern Monica Lewinsky at a Christmas party. The photo was part of the 3,183 pages of evidence collected by the office of Independent Counsel Kenneth Starr. (AP Photo/OIC)

Driven by the racial and social tumult Baby Boomers had stirred in the 1960s, and by a changed world order, Americans in the 1990s engaged in a culture war intended to define society.

As the decade began, the United States defeated Iraq in the Persian Gulf War—a victory so quick that President George Bush declared: "By God, we've licked the Vietnam syndrome once and for all." Just one year later, however, riots wrecked the national euphoria. They erupted in south central Los Angeles after a predominantly white jury acquitted four white police officers of having beaten black motorist Rodney King. The jury reached its verdict even though the assault had been captured on videotape. Blacks concluded that the police and courts stood for white oppression. A great divide between southern California's largely prosperous white suburbs and its largely poor black or ethnic inner cities added to their anger.

The riots spread quickly to Long Beach and Hollywood, and at least 1,000 businesses blazed. Black rapper Ice-T said: "This is not right . . . but it's like, if you put somebody in a jail cell and they can't get out, they're going to set fire to their own cell." By the time the riots ended, 44 people were dead, 2,000 injured, and more than $1 billion in property damaged. Most whites condemned the King verdict, but neither did they condone the riots. The opinions on race of many people—on both sides—were hardened by the events in L.A.

Many conservatives thought the riots came from a widespread disrespect for order and a pandering to minorities that dated from the 1960s. According to this perspective, it was not only the empowerment of racial minorities, but also a '60s-style liberal worldview that had weakened America's traditional values. To many conservatives, affirmative action had rewarded people for their skin color while oppressing whites, feminists had ruined the all-American family, and cultural malcontents—everyone from Hollywood filmmakers to novelists to rock stars—had promoted immorality.

Conservatives went to war against these influences, and in one prominent battle they tried to end federal funding for the arts. Led by Senator Jesse Helms and egged on by right-wing radio hosts such as Rush Limbaugh, conservatives protested "immoral works" supported with tax dollars. The dispute sharpened political discourse and brought into focus the concept of the "culture war," a vaguely defined but highly influential struggle between left- and right-wing ideologies that would dominate the political scene throughout the nineties.

Government support of radical and even inflammatory artwork also stirred extremists who believed that an intrusive, powerful government threatened morality and liberty. Some right-wingers formed militias and a handful went further; in April 1995 Timothy McVeigh bombed a federal building in Oklahoma City, Oklahoma, killing 168 people. It seemed as if America's metaphorical culture war might become a literal one.

The nation's racial divide widened in 1995 when a largely African-American jury in Los Angeles acquitted black football and entertainment star O. J. Simpson of having murdered his ex-wife Nicole Brown Simpson and her friend, Ron Goldman. Whites reacted in disgust and anger—the evidence against O. J. appeared to be irrefutable. Many African Americans, however, cheered and celebrated— right or wrong, O. J. had beaten a racist police force and judicial system.

As the 1990s ended, several sensational events kept the culture war alive, even as the economy grew and the FBI reported sharp drops in violent crime. In August 1997, several white police officers in New York City brutalized Abner Louima, a 32-year-old Haitian immigrant whom they had arrested during a brawl. In addition to its racist overtones, the attack may have also signified law and order at almost any cost, a tactic favored by many conservatives angered by societal decay.

In June 1998, three white supremacists in Jasper, Texas, tied an African American, James Byrd, Jr., to the back of their pickup truck and dragged him for three miles, tearing Byrd's body to shreds. "It looked like an animal drug down the road," said a man who testified at the trial of John William King, one of those convicted of the murder. For Baby Boomers raised on the optimism of the civil rights movement, the many clashes between blacks and whites during the 1990s raised the sad question of whether or not Americans would, ultimately, overcome their differences someday.

Another event reflected the cultural divide on the issue of sexual preference. Early in 1999, Russell Henderson pleaded guilty to beating and killing a 22-year-old homosexual, Matthew Shepard, the previous fall in Laramie, Wyoming. Outside the courthouse where Henderson appeared, a demonstration took place. One fundamentalist preacher declared: "God hates fags!" Retorted another demonstrator: "I would like to see if Christ were standing here today. Christ would have judged you!"

FBI agents continued their hunt in the mountains of North

Carolina for Eric Rudolph, charged with bombing abortion clinics, a gay nightclub, and the 1996 Summer Olympics in Atlanta. Some extremists considered Rudolph a hero in the fight for traditional moral values. Meanwhile, the April 1999 shooting at Columbine High School in Littleton, Colorado, excited the cultural debate: what social development should be blamed? Conservatives complained about a decline in moral values; liberals about the proliferation of guns.

No single event revealed the widening cultural divide more profoundly than the Clinton/Lewinsky scandal. Special prosecutor Kenneth Starr charged that, in trying to hide an adulterous relationship with a White House intern, the pres-ident had perjured himself and obstructed justice. Congress impeached Clinton on those charges, while Clinton support-ers protested that the president was the victim of a conserv-ative witchhunt. Although early in 1999 the Senate failed to convict him, the episode greatly sullied his presidency and stoked discussions about America's moral decline. The great promise of the Camelot-inspired Clinton administration seemed, by its end, to have been destroyed by self-interest. In the eyes of many conservatives, Clinton, our first Baby Boomer president, was a living symbol of the loose morals and muddled thinking born of the 1960s counterculture, now tearing apart the social fabric of the United States.

Race Relations

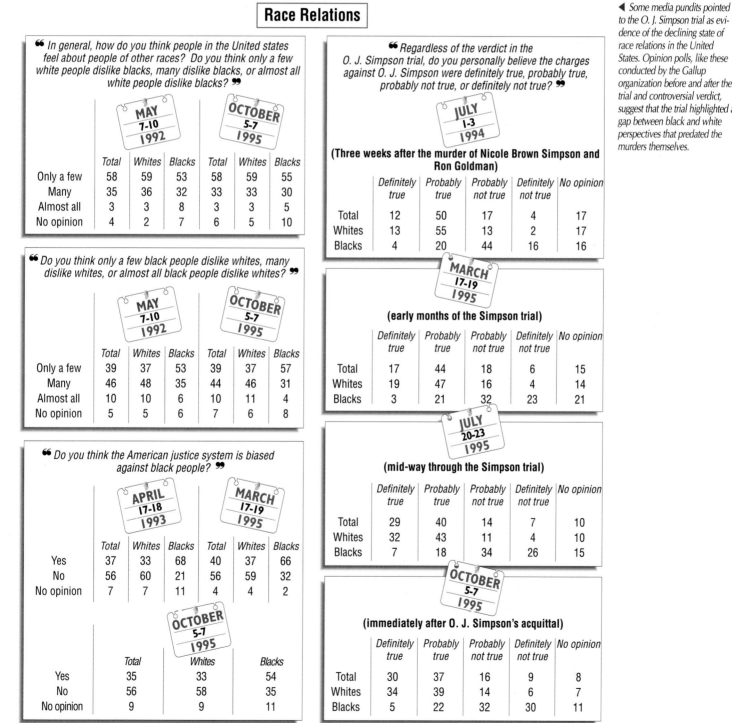

◄ Some media pundits pointed to the O. J. Simpson trial as evi-dence of the declining state of race relations in the United States. Opinion polls, like these conducted by the Gallup organization before and after the trial and controversial verdict, suggest that the trial highlighted a gap between black and white perspectives that predated the murders themselves.

" In general, how do you think people in the United states feel about people of other races? Do you think only a few white people dislike blacks, many dislike blacks, or almost all white people dislike blacks? "

	MAY 7-10 1992			OCTOBER 5-7 1995		
	Total	Whites	Blacks	Total	Whites	Blacks
Only a few	58	59	53	58	59	55
Many	35	36	32	33	33	30
Almost all	3	3	8	3	3	5
No opinion	4	2	7	6	5	10

" Do you think only a few black people dislike whites, many dislike whites, or almost all black people dislike whites? "

	MAY 7-10 1992			OCTOBER 5-7 1995		
	Total	Whites	Blacks	Total	Whites	Blacks
Only a few	39	37	53	39	37	57
Many	46	48	35	44	46	31
Almost all	10	10	6	10	11	4
No opinion	5	5	6	7	6	8

" Do you think the American justice system is biased against black people? "

	APRIL 17-18 1993			MARCH 17-19 1995		
	Total	Whites	Blacks	Total	Whites	Blacks
Yes	37	33	68	40	37	66
No	56	60	21	56	59	32
No opinion	7	7	11	4	4	2

	OCTOBER 5-7 1995		
	Total	Whites	Blacks
Yes	35	33	54
No	56	58	35
No opinion	9	9	11

" Regardless of the verdict in the O. J. Simpson trial, do you personally believe the charges against O. J. Simpson were definitely true, probably true, probably not true, or definitely not true? "

JULY 1-3 1994
(Three weeks after the murder of Nicole Brown Simpson and Ron Goldman)

	Definitely true	Probably true	Probably not true	Definitely not true	No opinion
Total	12	50	17	4	17
Whites	13	55	13	2	17
Blacks	4	20	44	16	16

MARCH 17-19 1995
(early months of the Simpson trial)

	Definitely true	Probably true	Probably not true	Definitely not true	No opinion
Total	17	44	18	6	15
Whites	19	47	16	4	14
Blacks	3	21	32	23	21

JULY 20-23 1995
(mid-way through the Simpson trial)

	Definitely true	Probably true	Probably not true	Definitely not true	No opinion
Total	29	40	14	7	10
Whites	32	43	11	4	10
Blacks	7	18	34	26	15

OCTOBER 5-7 1995
(immediately after O. J. Simpson's acquittal)

	Definitely true	Probably true	Probably not true	Definitely not true	No opinion
Total	30	37	16	9	8
Whites	34	39	14	6	7
Blacks	5	22	32	30	11

Year	World	United States Politics	Arts
1990	Iraq's Saddam Hussein orders an invasion of neighboring oil-rich Kuwait.	President George Bush violates his 1988 "no new taxes" campaign promise.	The warning "Parental advisory—explicit lyrics" is added to music albums containing lyrics about sex, drugs, or violence.
1991	The Soviet Union dissolves amid political and economic chaos as its republics demand autonomy from Moscow.	Despite sporadic antiwar protests, public sentiment supports President Bush's Operation Desert Storm in defense of Kuwait against Iraq.	*Thelma and Louise* gives the buddy picture a feminist twist.
1992	The breakup of Yugoslavia ignites genocide in Bosnia–Herzegovina.	President Bush, hobbled by an economic recession, loses his re-election bid to Arkansas Democrat Bill Clinton.	Johnny Carson retires from *The Tonight Show* after 30 years; controversially, NBC replaces him with Jay Leno, rather than David Letterman.
1993	Nelson Mandela and President Willem de Klerk of South Africa are jointly awarded the Nobel Peace Prize for working to terminate the apartheid regime.	President Bill Clinton appoints Janet Reno as attorney general, the first woman to head the Department of Justice.	African-American novelist Toni Morrison wins the Nobel Prize for literature.
1994	Two million refugees from Rwanda's civil war inundate neighboring Zaire.	Republicans gain majorities in the House and Senate in what House Speaker Newt Gingrich calls a "Republican revolution."	Woodstock II is held in Saugerties, New York. Returning acts include Crosby, Stills, and Nash, Joe Cocker, and Santana, mixing with newer acts, such as Sheryl Crow and Nine Inch Nails.
1995	A Jewish extremist assassinates the Israeli prime minister, Yitzhak Rabin, halting the peace process.	A bomb outside of the Alfred P. Murrah Federal Building in Oklahoma City, Oklahoma, kills 168 people.	Deadheads mourn the death of Grateful Dead leader Jerry Garcia, age 53.
1996	A pipe bomb explodes at the Olympic games in Atlanta, killing 1 person and injuring more than 100 others.	President Clinton signs a sweeping welfare reform bill that ends federal cash payments to individuals.	*Rent*, a musical that updates *La Bohème* to modern New York, moves to Broadway to rave reviews.
1997	A Thai currency collapse destabilizes the Asian economy.	President Clinton decides to cut federally funded research into human cloning.	Director James Cameron's *Titanic* grosses more than $600 million, the highest total ever for a motion picture.
1998		◀ Independent Counsel Kenneth Starr's investigation into allegations of corruption and sexual indiscretions imperils the Clinton presidency.	The Chairman of the Board, Frank Sinatra, dies at 82.
1999	After NATO intervenes in Kosovo in order to halt Serbian leader Slobodan Milosevic's plan of ethnic cleansing, three American soldiers are taken as prisoners of war; with the help of Jesse Jackson they are released after 32 days of captivity.	The New Jersey Supreme Court unanimously rules that the Boy Scouts of America's dismissal of openly gay Scout leader James Dale solely because of his sexual orientation is illegal based on a state anti-discrimination law.	Stanley Kubrick's last film, *Eyes Wide Shut*, opens in theaters just a few months after his death, starring real-life husband and wife Tom Cruise and Nicole Kidman.

CORBIS ONLINE

Science and Industry	Pastimes and Lifestyles	Sports	Year
The death of young AIDS activist Ryan White spurs Congress to allocate millions of dollars for health services to AIDS victims.	The Classification and Ratings Administration (CARA) replaces the X rating for movies with NC-17 (no children under 17).		1990
Tim Berners-Lee and his team of programmers create the programs that run the World Wide Web.	On Independence Day, President Bush celebrates the fiftieth anniversary of Mount Rushmore with a rededication ceremony.		1991
The FDA calls for a suspension on silicone gel-filled breast implants; three months later, they are allowed on the market under controlled clinical studies.	The Internet becomes easier to use as the World Wide Web expands.		1992
The North American Free Trade Agreement eases tariffs and barriers to trade between Mexico, the United States, and Canada.	Reports that prolonged exposure to the flickering lights of video games can lead to epileptic fits prompt Nintendo and Sega to place warnings on game cartridges.	▲ Chicago Bulls star Michael Jordan announces his retirement from basketball, but he soon returns.	1993
Congress passes legislation to compensate approximately 3,000 Gulf War veterans suffering from ailments known as Gulf War syndrome.	The famous photo of the Loch Ness monster is proved to be a fake, created by Marmaduke Wetherell.	An attack on U.S. figure skater Nancy Kerrigan is traced to rival skater Tonya Harding.	1994
Microsoft introduces the new Windows® '95 operating system.	Martha Stewart parodies her domestic goddess image in a popular TV commercial in which she tiles a swimming pool with credit cards.	After a 234-day strike by major league baseball players, team owners agree to the reinstatement of free-agent bidding and salary arbitration.	1995
A "mad cow" scare links tainted British beef to a fatal brain disease in humans.	California voters approve measure allowing critically ill patients to use marijuana when prescribed by a doctor.	Three-time amateur golf champion Tiger Woods, 20, turns professional.	1996
Scots scientists, led by Ian Wilmut, create Dolly, a genetic clone of an adult sheep.	Heaven's Gate, a San Diego-based cult that supports itself by designing Web pages, commits mass suicide, believing that a UFO concealed behind the Hale-Bopp comet will take them to the stars.	The AFC Denver Broncos finally break the NFC dominance in the Super Bowl by defeating the Green Bay Packers with a final score of 31 to 24.	1997
Seventy-seven-year-old John Glenn becomes the world's oldest astronaut when he returns to space aboard the shuttle *Discovery*.	Viagra, an "anti-impotence pill," flies off drugstore shelves.	Roger Maris's 1961 single-season home run record is shattered by Mark McGwire and Sammy Sosa.	1998
Astronomers announce that they have detected the first multi-planet solar system similar to our own, observed around Upsilon Andromedae, a solar-type star located 44 light-years away.	Visions of apocalyptic Y2K scenarios—ranging from stock market collapses and airplane disasters to ATM malfunctions and power outages—bestir a nervous public and also allow many opportunists to cash in on the hype.	U.S. women's soccer team wins the World Cup, defeating China by a score of 5–4.	1999

CORBIS/Scott Wachter

As the cold war came to an end, President George Bush talked about a New World Order. But crises in the 1990s led many to think the more accurate phrase was New World Disorder. The end of the Soviet Union left many questions about whether Russia and Eastern Europe could be integrated into the global economy. Although changes in South Africa marked progress, genocide in Rwanda horrified the world. The United States went to war in both the Persian Gulf and the Balkans, while Asia presented problems with oppression in Indonesia and in China—the latter nation apparently trying to build its nuclear weapons with secrets stolen from American government laboratories.

YUGOSLAVIA
War in the Balkans (1991-1999)

The Balkans knew little peace in the 1990s. First, war erupted among Serbia (Yugoslavia), Croatia, and Bosnia, marked by Serbian atrocities. After the warring sides reached a peace agreement at Dayton, Ohio, American and other NATO troops enforced it. Then in 1999, Serbian president Slobodan Milosevic rejected NATO demands that Serbia's province of Kosovo with its 90 percent ethnic Albanian population—and a guerrilla group called the Kosovo Liberation Army that engaged in terrorism—be given autonomy. With Milosevic beginning ethnic cleansing in Kosovo, NATO went to war, launching the heaviest air attacks in Europe since World War II. Kosovar refugees flooded neighboring nations while bombs devastated Serbia.

RWANDA
Genocide (1994-1998)

In the early 1990s, it looked as though a civil war in Rwanda between Hutus and Tutsi would be settled peacefully. Then in April 1994 a rocket downed a plane carrying Rwanda's Hutu president, killing him. The civil war raged anew, and over a 100-day period Hutu extremists slaughtered 800,000 Tutsi and Hutu moderates. The Tutsi army drove the Hutu militias into neighboring countries, while the turmoil produced two million refugees. Firing squads in 1998 executed 22 people accused of genocide. A former prime minister, Jean Kambanda, pleaded guilty before a U.N. tribunal and received a life sentence.

EAST TIMOR
Timorese Demands and Suharto's Fall (1999)

After Indonesia invaded the Portuguese colony of East Timor in 1975, it brutally suppressed Timorese demands for independence. More than 100,000 Timorese were killed from 1975 into the 1990s. Seeking to end the upheaval, in October 1999 the Indonesian government formally ended 24 years of occupation, and the Timorese began the slow process of constructing an independent state. Unrelated to East Timor, an economic collapse forced from power in 1998 President Suharto, Indonesia's dictator for more than 30 years.

SOUTH AFRICA
Apartheid Ends (1990-1996)

As seemingly impregnable institutions—East European communism, the Soviet Union—collapsed, so too did apartheid in South Africa. In February 1990, President Willem de Klerk lifted the ban on the African National Congress and released its leader, Nelson Mandela, from prison. Later in the year, de Klerk announced that he would support electoral reforms that would give blacks and other non-whites much more political power. The government repealed all apartheid laws in 1992, and in 1994 Mandela won election as president. He promised reconciliation with whites, rather than revenge. A bill of rights approved in 1996 provided one of the broadest guarantees of liberty found in any country.

IRAQ
Persian Gulf War and Its Aftermath (1991-1999)

As the cold war ended, Americans hoped they had found peace, but in August 1990, Iraqi troops invaded Kuwait. President George Bush considered Kuwait's oil vital to the United States and Europe, and feared that Iraqi dictator Saddam Hussein would grab another oil-rich nation, Saudi Arabia. Aided by a multinational force, the American military struck at Iraq. Massive air raids began on January 17, 1991, followed by a ground assault on February 23. The Iraqi army was destroyed within 100 hours. Trouble with Iraq continued, however, as Hussein frustrated weapons inspections. American warplanes bombed Iraq several times, most notably late in 1998, and an embargo devastated the Iraqi economy.

THE U.S.S.R.
A Communist Collapse (1991)

From Stettin in the Baltic to Trieste in the Adriatic, an iron curtain dissolved as the 1990s began, taking with it the Soviet Union in 1991, which collapsed under the weight of its own political system. With startling speed the Soviet "republics" declared their independence. On December 25, 1991, the gold hammer-and-sickle flag of the Soviet Union was lowered over the Kremlin for the last time. Americans brought up in a world divided between two superpowers, one capitalist, the other communist, could hardly believe that the cold war was over. Yet Russia lived constantly on the edge—an attempted coup later in 1991, war with Chechnya, and economic chaos were just some of the challenges it faced.

CHINA
Repression and Espionage (1990-1999)

Although China celebrated the peaceful transfer of Hong Kong from Britain in 1997, America's relations with the most populous Asian nation remained troubled. Actions by the Chinese government in the 1990s to repress dissidents and its continued oppression of Tibet produced tension. President Bill Clinton tried to liberalize China's policies by encouraging more economic contact between China and the United States, what he called "engagement," but the policy had little effect. Then in 1999 it was revealed that Chinese spies—at work since the 1980s but most heavily since the mid-1990s—had stolen American atomic secrets. Reports claimed that the entire U.S. nuclear arsenal had been compromised.

KENYA AND TANZANIA
Terrorists Strike U.S. Embassies (1998)

Terrorists bombed two U.S. embassies in August 1998. An explosion at Nairobi, Kenya, killed more than 200 people, including 12 Americans; another at Dar es Salaam, Tanzania, killed 11 people. The United States blamed Osama bin Laden, a Saudi Arabian, for the attacks, and later in August the American navy fired missiles at his base in Afghanistan and a factory in Sudan that supposedly made chemical weapons. In November, a federal court indicted bin Laden and five others, but the men remained at large. The embassy bombings contributed to a record high worldwide death and injury toll in 1998 from terrorist attacks.

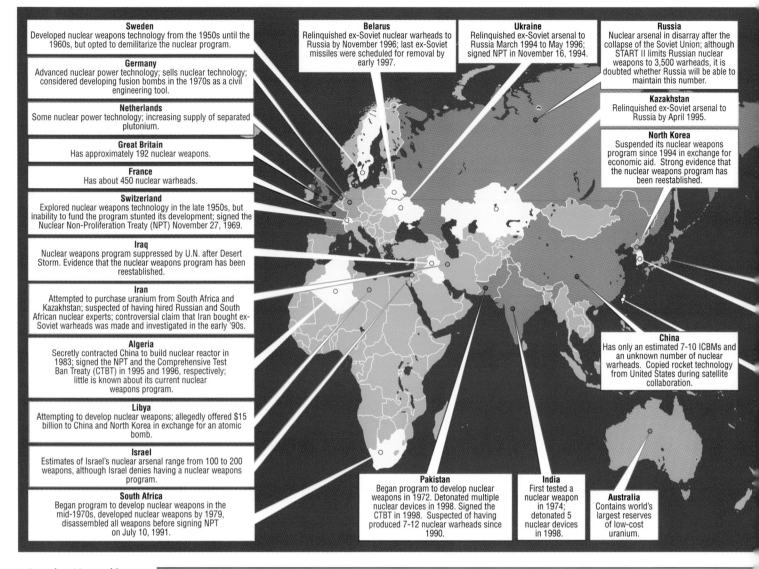

Sweden
Developed nuclear weapons technology from the 1950s until the 1960s, but opted to demilitarize the nuclear program.

Germany
Advanced nuclear power technology; sells nuclear technology; considered developing fusion bombs in the 1970s as a civil engineering tool.

Netherlands
Some nuclear power technology; increasing supply of separated plutonium.

Great Britain
Has approximately 192 nuclear weapons.

France
Has about 450 nuclear warheads.

Switzerland
Explored nuclear weapons technology in the late 1950s, but inability to fund the program stunted its development; signed the Nuclear Non-Proliferation Treaty (NPT) November 27, 1969.

Iraq
Nuclear weapons program suppressed by U.N. after Desert Storm. Evidence that the nuclear weapons program has been reestablished.

Iran
Attempted to purchase uranium from South Africa and Kazakhstan; suspected of having hired Russian and South African nuclear experts; controversial claim that Iran bought ex-Soviet warheads was made and investigated in the early '90s.

Algeria
Secretly contracted China to build nuclear reactor in 1983; signed the NPT and the Comprehensive Test Ban Treaty (CTBT) in 1995 and 1996, respectively; little is known about its current nuclear weapons program.

Libya
Attempting to develop nuclear weapons; allegedly offered $15 billion to China and North Korea in exchange for an atomic bomb.

Israel
Estimates of Israel's nuclear arsenal range from 100 to 200 weapons, although Israel denies having a nuclear weapons program.

South Africa
Began program to develop nuclear weapons in the mid-1970s, developed nuclear weapons by 1979, disassembled all weapons before signing NPT on July 10, 1991.

Belarus
Relinquished ex-Soviet nuclear warheads to Russia by November 1996; last ex-Soviet missiles were scheduled for removal by early 1997.

Ukraine
Relinquished ex-Soviet arsenal to Russia March 1994 to May 1996; signed NPT in November 16, 1994.

Russia
Nuclear arsenal in disarray after the collapse of the Soviet Union; although START II limits Russian nuclear weapons to 3,500 warheads, it is doubted whether Russia will be able to maintain this number.

Kazakhstan
Relinquished ex-Soviet arsenal to Russia by April 1995.

North Korea
Suspended its nuclear weapons program since 1994 in exchange for economic aid. Strong evidence that the nuclear weapons program has been reestablished.

China
Has only an estimated 7-10 ICBMs and an unknown number of nuclear warheads. Copied rocket technology from United States during satellite collaboration.

Pakistan
Began program to develop nuclear weapons in 1972. Detonated multiple nuclear devices in 1998. Signed the CTBT in 1998. Suspected of having produced 7-12 nuclear warheads since 1990.

India
First tested a nuclear weapon in 1974; detonated 5 nuclear devices in 1998.

Australia
Contains world's largest reserves of low-cost uranium.

▲ *Just as the originators of the first A-bomb had feared, the nuclear genie would not be kept in the bottle. This map shows the status of nuclear powers all around the world, as of the late 1990s.*

As America entered the 1990s, the cold war world that Baby Boomers had known all their lives came tumbling down. The Berlin Wall that divided East Berlin from West Berlin—representing a seemingly permanent confrontation between the United States and the Soviet Union—toppled in 1989. Communist governments in Eastern Europe collapsed in 1989–90, and the Soviet Union itself collapsed in 1991.

So swift was the change, and in some quarters so little understood, there actually were Americans who believed the end of the cold war meant nuclear weapons had been eliminated. The bomb, however, remained a threat, although in a different guise—hemmed in by treaties and challenged by other weapons of mass destruction in its ability to incite fear. With so many nations in possession of these weapons, and with them readily available to small groups of people, Baby Boomers lived in a world different from the "one" big enemy portrayed in the cold war—now there were many smaller ones.

The nuclear threat eased in July 1991 when President George Bush and Soviet leader Mikhail Gorbachev signed the Strategic Arms Reduction Treaty, START I. The treaty pledged each nation to reduce its strategic offensive nuclear arms by 30 percent over seven years. After the Soviet Union broke up, the four former Soviet republics with these weapons—Russia, Ukraine, Kazakhstan, and Belarus—agreed to abide by the treaty. (The last three eventually gave up all their nuclear weapons.) In 1993, the United States and Russia signed START II, in which they promised to reduce their long-range nuclear arsenals to about one-third of their existing levels. Two years later, they agreed to an indefinite extension of the Non-Proliferation Treaty, originally signed in 1968.

The United States and Russia reached yet another agreement in 1996, the Comprehensive Test Ban Treaty (CTBT). Soon 168 nations signed the CTBT, all pledging to refrain from testing nuclear weapons. In the United States, "New Abolitionists" now argued that America should destroy all its nuclear weapons. They said the fear of nuclear war had to be totally eliminated, and they claimed that nuclear weapons drained money from projects more suitable to a new world order where regional conflicts prevailed. In contrast with earlier anti-nuclear movements, the New Abolitionists consisted substantially of hard-nosed government specialists rather

Nuclear Proliferation: 1990s

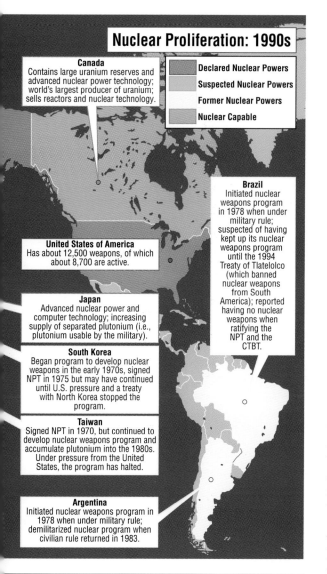

Canada
Contains large uranium reserves and advanced nuclear power technology; world's largest producer of uranium; sells reactors and nuclear technology.

Declared Nuclear Powers
Suspected Nuclear Powers
Former Nuclear Powers
Nuclear Capable

United States of America
Has about 12,500 weapons, of which about 8,700 are active.

Japan
Advanced nuclear power and computer technology; increasing supply of separated plutonium (i.e., plutonium usable by the military).

South Korea
Began program to develop nuclear weapons in the early 1970s, signed NPT in 1975 but may have continued until U.S. pressure and a treaty with North Korea stopped the program.

Taiwan
Signed NPT in 1970, but continued to develop nuclear weapons program and accumulate plutonium into the 1980s. Under pressure from the United States, the program has halted.

Argentina
Initiated nuclear weapons program in 1978 when under military rule; demilitarized nuclear program when civilian rule returned in 1983.

Brazil
Initiated nuclear weapons program in 1978 when under military rule; suspected of having kept up its nuclear weapons program until the 1994 Treaty of Tlatelolco (which banned nuclear weapons from South America); reported having no nuclear weapons when ratifying the NPT and the CTBT.

of highly enriched uranium to make a Hiroshima-size bomb, and that instructions for making a nuclear weapon could be found on the Internet.

Terrorists had access to weapons other than nuclear ones, however, and those they used. In 1993, radical Muslims bombed the World Trade Center in New York City—the first attack within the United States by international terrorists. Shortly after, Lt. Gen. Robert Schweitzer, a former National Security Council official, warned about such groups: "We'll see them again, armed probably with biological or nuclear weapons." In 1995, terrorists did strike using chemical weapons, but in Tokyo. The group Aum Shinrikyo released the nerve gas sarin that killed 12 people and injured 5,000. The attack rattled Americans. Then, in April, terrorists struck at home and bombed the Alfred P. Murrah Federal Building in Oklahoma City. To the surprise of most Americans, these were domestic terrorists—no one could be sure who the enemy was, or where he might strike. In May, Congress appropriated $100 million to fund a national counterterrorism center.

Weapons of Mass Destruction (WMD), a catchall phrase referring to nuclear, biological, and chemical weapons, seized center stage. The Department of Defense called them an urgent threat, and President Bill Clinton pledged his administration to counterproliferation, meaning developing the military capability to knock out or limit WMD within any nation. At a meeting in France in 1998, the heads of the world's leading industrial nations declared: "Special attention should be paid to the threat of utilization of nuclear, biological, and chemical materials, as well as toxic substances, for terrorist purposes."

Critics, however, accused Clinton of being a paper tiger when it came to fighting proliferation. They said that through leaks of high technology, especially the export of super-computers, his administration had contributed to the spread of weapons. China appeared to be a major culprit by obtaining information from the United States that improved its missile systems and by exporting WMD. Russia also played a role. "We know that Russia has either actively been involved or permitted others in its country to sell ballistic missile components and design and production equipment to Iran," claimed Senator Thad Cochran in January 1998. "These are very troubling matters." Fortunately, the United States avoided any new terrorist attacks within its borders. But the nation's vulnerability overseas appeared evident when in August 1998 a terrorist group blew up the U.S. embassies in Kenya and Tanzania, killing 263 people, including 12 Americans.

Baby Boomers received a jolt of déjà vu in 1999 when President Clinton pledged $7 billion to pursue research on a missile defense system. His decision seemed like Ronald Reagan's Star Wars all over again. Unlike Reagan, however, Clinton envisioned a modest system able to intercept only a few incoming missiles. North Korea had developed improved missiles, and other nations might do the same. Thus the Clinton administration believed the threat from ICBMs had increased—in other words, a nemesis from the cold war had returned.

than dreamy-eyed idealists. General Lee Butler, former head of the U.S. Strategic Air Command, said: "Accepting nuclear weapons as the ultimate arbiter of conflict condemns the world to live under a dark cloud of perpetual anxiety."

Yet with the dismantling of nuclear missiles came a problem: how to keep fissile, or fissionable, materials from falling into the hands of dangerous countries or groups. Some analysts argued, too, that as America disarmed, nations such as Germany and Japan that relied on U.S. nuclear weapons for protection might develop their own.

In 1998, India and Pakistan shattered the optimism surrounding disarmament when they tested nuclear bombs. Some analysts worried that these two enemies might use them in a war against each other. One claimed: "The . . . explosions have destroyed the facade of nonproliferation."

For Baby Boomers, in some ways the end of the cold war brought less security. Terrorists stood ready to tap into an atomic lode. Russia still had a large nuclear complex in the mid-1990s, with enough fissile material in storage to make 100,000 nuclear bombs. Some of the material was confiscated in European countries as smugglers attempted to transport it. More than one expert warned that it took only 25 pounds

Few could imagine as the 1990s began that a confrontation at a remote cabin in Idaho would energize a protest movement where thousands of people, many of them Baby Boomers, joined militias. But it did.

Large numbers of Americans grew scared and angry in the early 1990s as the economy turned sour and the nation faced an uncertain post–cold war future riddled with terrorist threats from foreign enemies and cultural battles between liberals and conservatives. At Ruby Ridge, a lonely promontory deep in the forests of Idaho, 40-something Randy Weaver lived in a crude cabin with his family. In 1992, federal agents tracked him down for having failed to appear in court on charges related to selling illegal firearms. As members of a surveillance team approached the cabin, they stumbled across Weaver's 14-year-old son, Samuel; the family dog; and a family friend, Kevin Harris. An agent fired at the dog, and Samuel and Harris fired back. The exchange left Samuel and agent William Degan dead.

The agents then surrounded Weaver's cabin. A siege ensued, during which an agent fired at an open door and killed Weaver's wife, Vicki, while she stood unarmed, holding her baby. After capturing Randy Weaver and Kevin Harris, the government tried them for murder in the death of Degan. A jury acquitted them of the charge, and a subsequent government investigation revealed that the agents at Ruby Ridge had violated rules of engagement that stipulated shots be fired only at armed adults and had violated Vicki Weaver's civil rights. In 1995, the government settled a civil damage suit filed by Randy Weaver and awarded his family more than $3 million. Ruby Ridge served as a tocsin within the far right and convinced many in mainstream America that federal power had gone too far.

Soon after Ruby Ridge, in 1993, federal agents claimed that the Branch Davidians, an armed religious group, and their leader David Koresh—like Weaver, a Baby Boomer—had stockpiled illegal guns at their compound, Mount Carmel, near Waco, Texas. The agents raided Mount Carmel, only to be met by gunfire that killed several of them. They then laid siege to the compound, while accusing Koresh of dealing in drugs and abusing children.

Koresh preached an apocalyptic future and isolated his group from a society he thought evil; but he neither sold drugs nor abused children—those charges the government contrived. After several weeks, government tanks punched holes in the walls of the compound and pumped tear gas inside. A fire erupted that quickly killed Koresh and 74 other Davidians, including more than 20 children.

Although 11 Davidians were tried for killing four agents in the original raid, a jury acquitted them (while finding seven guilty of a lesser charge). The *New York Times* called the verdict a "stunning defeat" for the government. Waco reinforced the extreme right's view that America had become a police state.

Militias organized, and even some middle-class Americans, suffering from economic hardship and frightened by government power, joined them. The militias, whose membership never exceeded 100,000, varied their actions from staging paramilitary training to handing out leaflets, giving lectures, and setting up Web sites. For many the militias struck a responsive chord, while for others they indicated dangerous times, filled with intrigue and hate.

Among the militias, MOM, or the Militia of Montana, gained the most attention. Founded by John Trochmann in 1994, MOM claimed that the federal government had fallen under the control of ungodly humanists and that the nation's leaders were moving the United States toward a One World government, a socialist state with no national boundaries. MOM distributed a training manual that advised: "The placement of a bomb . . . of great destructive power, which is capable of effecting irreparable loss against the enemy . . . is an action the urban guerrilla must execute with the greatest cold-bloodedness." Overall, the militia movement embraced common themes: gun control threatened the Second Amendment; powerful leaders were plotting to create a One World government; a conspiracy existed to destroy liberty.

Some observers noted that even though, between the 1960s and 1990s, protest movements and the Baby Boomers who populated them had gone from left-wing to right-wing, they converged ideologically in their distrust of the federal government. The charge that a conspiracy existed to destroy liberty rang true for both New Leftists and New Rightists, but they disagreed over solutions, with New Left extremists (a few of whom eventually joined the right wing) having proposed socialism, and New Right extremists proposing libertarianism.

In April 1995 came a powerful explosion at a federal building in Oklahoma City, Oklahoma. The blast killed 168

> 66 *We want a bloodless revolution. But if the bureaucrats won't listen we'll give them a civil war to think about.* 99
>
> —**Samuel Sherwood,**
> *founder of the United States Militia Association*

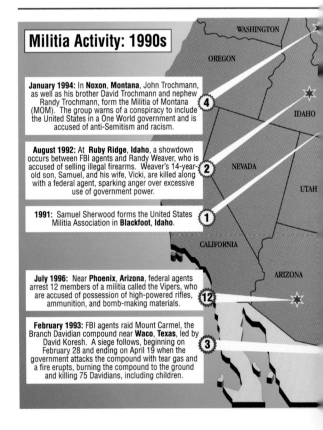

Militia Activity: 1990s

January 1994: In **Noxon**, **Montana**, John Trochmann, as well as his brother David Trochmann and nephew Randy Trochmann, form the Militia of Montana (MOM). The group warns of a conspiracy to include the United States in a One World government and is accused of anti-Semitism and racism. ④

August 1992: At **Ruby Ridge, Idaho**, a showdown occurs between FBI agents and Randy Weaver, who is accused of selling illegal firearms. Weaver's 14-year-old son, Samuel, and his wife, Vicki, are killed along with a federal agent, sparking anger over excessive use of government power. ②

1991: Samuel Sherwood forms the United States Militia Association in **Blackfoot, Idaho**. ①

July 1996: Near **Phoenix, Arizona**, federal agents arrest 12 members of a militia called the Vipers, who are accused of possession of high-powered rifles, ammunition, and bomb-making materials. ⑫

February 1993: FBI agents raid Mount Carmel, the Branch Davidian compound near **Waco, Texas**, led by David Koresh. A siege follows, beginning on February 28 and ending on April 19 when the government attacks the compound with tear gas and a fire erupts, burning the compound to the ground and killing 75 Davidians, including children. ③

people, including many children. Some militia supporters blamed the government. "I definitely believe [the government] did the bombing," said Linda Thompson. "I mean, who's got a track record of killing children?"

The government arrested Timothy McVeigh, a veteran of the Persian Gulf War who had associated with militia figures, for planting the bomb, and in 1997 a jury found him guilty of murder. Another jury found an accomplice, Terry L. Nichols, guilty of involuntary manslaughter. Although never directly tied to any militia, the bombing put militias under scrutiny. Many Americans condemned them for their anti-Semitism, racism, and hate. Some militias, however, had legitimate political complaints.

While militias formed, in 1997 the debate over abortion remained intense. Pro-life groups rallied support for legislation in Congress that would ban what they called "partial-birth abortion," a late-term procedure that involved partially delivering a fetus, collapsing its skull, and then delivering it. Congress passed the ban, but President Bill Clinton vetoed it.

That setback and others emboldened a minority among pro-lifers to mix with militias that embraced the abortion issue. Extremists bombed abortion clinics and killed abortion doctors. A mysterious group that called itself Army of God issued an underground manual telling how to attack clinics with homemade explosives.

While economic prosperity weakened the militia movement in the late 1990s, memories of the besieged cabin at Ruby Ridge remained strong enough, and the abortion issue heated enough, to guarantee continued protests from those, extremists and otherwise, who saw the federal government as responsible for killing babies and liberty.

Million Man March

Reminiscent of the mass rally for civil rights at the Washington Mall in 1963, on October 16, 1995, at least 400,000 demonstrators turned out at the same location for the Million Man March, a "Holy Day of Atonement and Reconciliation." Nation of Islam leader Louis Farrakhan organized the march to promote self-help and self-esteem among black men. Afterwards, participants spoke of feeling more committed to the black community, to supporting its businesses, and to supporting their families. The march was also cited as the reason for a jump in 1996 in voter turnout among black men. Farrakhan, a controversial leader who has often been criticized for his anti-Semitism, spoke out against white supremacy. He also said: "We are not here to tear down America. America is tearing itself down. We are here to rebuild the wasted cities." (AP/WIDE WORLD PHOTOS) ▼

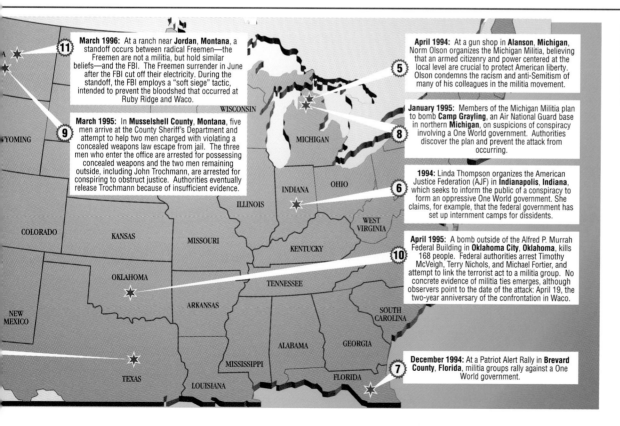

◀ Contrary to the stereotype, militia activity was not the sole province of rugged loners in the Pacific Northwest. This map details some of the most noteworthy militia-related events in the 1990s.

March 1996: At a ranch near **Jordan, Montana,** a standoff occurs between radical Freemen—the Freemen are not a militia, but hold similar beliefs—and the FBI. The Freemen surrender in June after the FBI cut off their electricity. During the standoff, the FBI employs a "soft siege" tactic, intended to prevent the bloodshed that occurred at Ruby Ridge and Waco.

March 1995: In **Musselshell County, Montana,** five men arrive at the County Sheriff's Department and attempt to help two men charged with violating a concealed weapons law escape from jail. The three men who enter the office are arrested for possessing concealed weapons and the two men remaining outside, including John Trochmann, are arrested for conspiring to obstruct justice. Authorities eventually release Trochmann because of insufficient evidence.

April 1994: At a gun shop in **Alanson, Michigan,** Norm Olson organizes the Michigan Militia, believing that an armed citizenry and power centered at the local level are crucial to protect American liberty. Olson condemns the racism and anti-Semitism of many of his colleagues in the militia movement.

January 1995: Members of the Michigan Militia plan to bomb **Camp Grayling,** an Air National Guard base in northern **Michigan,** on suspicions of conspiracy involving a One World government. Authorities discover the plan and prevent the attack from occurring.

1994: Linda Thompson organizes the American Justice Federation (AJF) in **Indianapolis, Indiana,** which seeks to inform the public of a conspiracy to form an oppressive One World government. She claims, for example, that the federal government has set up internment camps for dissidents.

April 1995: A bomb outside of the Alfred P. Murrah Federal Building in **Oklahoma City, Oklahoma,** kills 168 people. Federal authorities arrest Timothy McVeigh, Terry Nichols, and Michael Fortier, and attempt to link the terrorist act to a militia group. No concrete evidence of militia ties emerges, although observers point to the date of the attack: April 19, the two-year anniversary of the confrontation in Waco.

December 1994: At a Patriot Alert Rally in **Brevard County, Florida,** militia groups rally against a One World government.

The 1990s ushered in an era of competition in the television business. Cable networks and syndication flourished by producing inexpensive shows with low production values or by repackaging old movies and network reruns. Meanwhile, the 1990s saw a steady erosion in "Big Three" network viewership.

In an effort to retain their dominance, CBS, NBC, and ABC became increasingly influenced by the bottom line, making profit the primary arbiter of programming. Entertainment magazines, celebrity biographies, game shows, and "real video" compilations of natural disasters and stunts gone wrong were a regular TV staple. Nick at Nite and TV Land became popular networks simply by airing old television shows as "TV classics." And *Mystery Science Theater 3000* (1988–99), hosted by one human and two puppets, all acting like class clowns, made cheesy sci-fi movies seem cool by making sarcastic running comments about the on-screen action.

Evidently all this rummaging in the past inspired only a greater hunger for "used" TV and movies. Old movies were the mainstay of cable networks AMC, TNT, and TBS. The Cartoon Network presented round-the-clock cartoons—some

> **❝** *Television! Teacher, mother, secret lover.* **❞**
>
> **—Homer Simpson**

new and some old. And in the mid-'90s, the channel TV Land was launched, dedicated entirely to vintage TV shows.

Cable also settled in to create original programming that rivaled the quality of the best network presentations, original movies and series, such as *The Larry Sanders Show* (1992–98) and *The Sopranos* (1999–present). With so many new outlets for programming, non-network series filled the airwaves on weekends and early evenings. S*tar Trek: Deep Space Nine* (1993–99), *Baywatch* (1989–present), and *Hercules: The Legendary Journeys* (1995–present) were among the most popular syndicated series.

All the viewer options made the '90s the era of choice. In addition to the many cable stations, two networks emerged. The WB network debuted with *The Wayans Brothers* and UPN took off with *Star Trek: Voyager* in 1995. By the end of the decade, the WB had made inroads in the lucrative teen market with shows such as *Dawson's Creek* (1998–present). The Fox Network, formed 15 years earlier, had two breakthrough shows, *The X-Files* (1993–present) and *Ally McBeal* (1997–present), which drew critical acclaim and generated a "buzz" that propelled them from cult favorites to bona fide hits. At award time, when *The X-Files* and *Ally McBeal* garnered the trophies, the "Big Three" networks were left scrambling to develop programming that could compete.

Television news magazines and celebrity gossip programs like *Hard Copy* (1989–present), *Inside Edition* (1989–present), and *Entertainment Tonight* (1981–present) made use of audiences' taste for lurid stories and entertainment hype to build huge markets for tabloid-style news. Audiences tuned in with rapt attention to the unprecedented media coverage given the O. J. Simpson saga, from the slow-speed chase in the white Bronco to the DNA evidence to the final verdict. The ratings success of the murder trial helped to ensure that such stories would have a central place in our daily viewing.

In 1999, *The Simpsons* (1989–present), TV's most popular prime-time animated show since *The Flintstones*, was the longest running half-hour comedy on television. Bart Simpson, his long-suffering mother Marge, sisters Lisa and Maggie, and his lazy, intellectually challenged, doughnut-loving father Homer were a far cry from *The Brady Bunch*. The cartoon took a jaundiced view of small-town America and delivered some of the most pointed commentary on our times, launching barbs at religious fundamentalism, corporate greed, political opportunism, public education, and gratuitous violence. Perhaps audiences were more able to accept the exaggerated stupidity of Homer, the machinations of his boss Mr. Burns, and the antics of Bart, the perpetual fourth-grader, because they were cartoons. Cartoons were able to push the boundaries of typical comedies by creating characters who never had to be "softened" by humanity. The success of *The Simpsons* inspired other adult cartoons, including *Beavis and Butt-head* (1993–97), *Dr. Katz, Professional Therapist* (1995–present), and *South Park* (1997–present).

Even the more conventional styles of TV entertainment were different in the 1990s. The most popular sit-com, *Seinfeld* (1990–98), revolved around a circle of self-centered thirtysomethings—Jerry, Elaine, George, and Kramer—who made the self-involved yuppies of the 1980s look like saints by

The X Files (1993–present)

At a time when the saying "Question Authority" first became fashionable, J. Edgar Hoover, the head of the Federal Bureau of Investigation, gave his blessing to a TV show about his agency that depicted agents as the patriotic protectors of American ideals (*The FBI* [1965-1972]). All the while, Hoover compiled blacklists, plotted against presidents, and made feminine fashions a private hobby. Those secrets—along with unanswered questions about assassinations, U.S. covert operations and the lies of the Nixon administration—planted conspiratorial seeds that blossomed as Baby Boomers reached adulthood.

Fox Mulder, television's FBI guy for the '90s, is the product of that pervasive distrust. As guardian of the X Files, the final resting place of the FBI's weird, logic-defying cases, he became a sort of conscience for a generation convinced that there was more to everything than met the eye. Mulder's specialty was the unexplained, and his life was guided by just one belief, that "the truth is out there."

While conspiracy theories were his obsession, his partner was the unflappable Agent Dana Scully, a medical doctor and born skeptic, who applied science to the X Files. Despite alien abductions, confrontations with duplicitous agents, run-ins with clones, and discoveries of semi-human life forms lurking in sewers, Scully never let go of her trademark logic. Sci-fi's very own Woodward and Bernstein, Mulder and Scully were the cynical 1990s protectors of the truth, standing united against the shadow government conspiracy. (Photofest) ▶

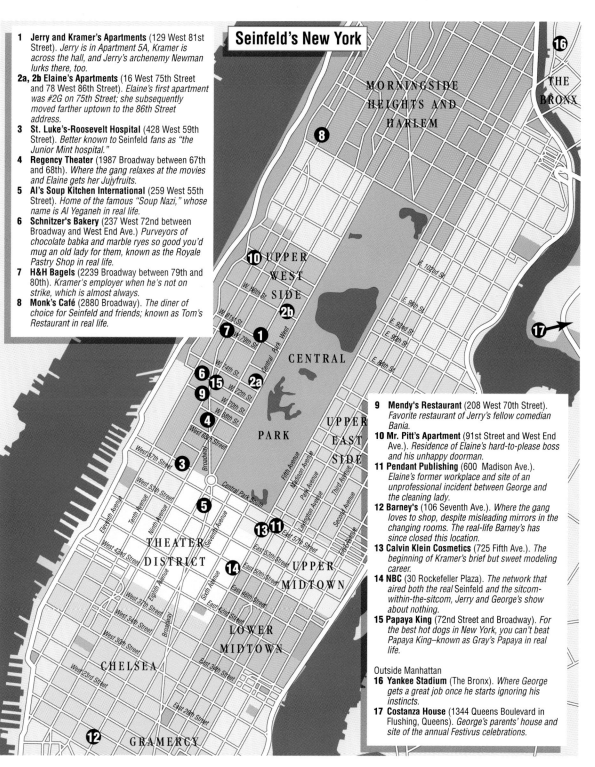

Seinfeld's New York

1 **Jerry and Kramer's Apartments** (129 West 81st Street). *Jerry is in Apartment 5A, Kramer is across the hall, and Jerry's archenemy Newman lurks there, too.*

2a, 2b **Elaine's Apartments** (16 West 75th Street and 78 West 86th Street). *Elaine's first apartment was #2G on 75th Street; she subsequently moved farther uptown to the 86th Street address.*

3 **St. Luke's-Roosevelt Hospital** (428 West 59th Street). *Better known to* Seinfeld *fans as "the Junior Mint hospital."*

4 **Regency Theater** (1987 Broadway between 67th and 68th). *Where the gang relaxes at the movies and Elaine gets her Jujyfruits.*

5 **Al's Soup Kitchen International** (259 West 55th Street). *Home of the famous "Soup Nazi," whose name is Al Yeganeh in real life.*

6 **Schnitzer's Bakery** (237 West 72nd between Broadway and West End Ave.) *Purveyors of chocolate babka and marble ryes so good you'd mug an old lady for them, known as the Royale Pastry Shop in real life.*

7 **H&H Bagels** (2239 Broadway between 79th and 80th). *Kramer's employer when he's not on strike, which is almost always.*

8 **Monk's Café** (2880 Broadway). *The diner of choice for Seinfeld and friends; known as Tom's Restaurant in real life.*

9 **Mendy's Restaurant** (208 West 70th Street). *Favorite restaurant of Jerry's fellow comedian Bania.*

10 **Mr. Pitt's Apartment** (91st Street and West End Ave.). *Residence of Elaine's hard-to-please boss and his unhappy doorman.*

11 **Pendant Publishing** (600 Madison Ave.). *Elaine's former workplace and site of an unprofessional incident between George and the cleaning lady.*

12 **Barney's** (106 Seventh Ave.). *Where the gang loves to shop, despite misleading mirrors in the changing rooms. The real-life Barney's has since closed this location.*

13 **Calvin Klein Cosmetics** (725 Fifth Ave.). *The beginning of Kramer's brief but sweet modeling career.*

14 **NBC** (30 Rockefeller Plaza). *The network that aired both the real* Seinfeld *and the sitcom-within-the-sitcom, Jerry and George's show about nothing.*

15 **Papaya King** (72nd Street and Broadway). *For the best hot dogs in New York, you can't beat Papaya King–known as Gray's Papaya in real life.*

Outside Manhattan

16 **Yankee Stadium** (The Bronx). *Where George gets a great job once he starts ignoring his instincts.*

17 **Costanza House** (1344 Queens Boulevard in Flushing, Queens). *George's parents' house and site of the annual Festivus celebrations.*

◀ *Seinfeld brought television audiences full circle from the late '40s when programs like* The Texaco Star Theater *and* The Goldbergs *were denounced as "too New York." Nothing was too New York for* Seinfeld *writers, who utilized real sites for the fictional characters' exploits. This map offers a small sampling of the* Seinfeld *gang's favorite spots.*

comparison. There were no heartwarming scenes on *Seinfeld*; if the show had a motto it was, according to cocreator Larry David, "No learning, no hugging." For the first time in TV's 55-year history, there was a show that did not expect more from TV than it could deliver. *Seinfeld* didn't aspire to change lives or provide great insights. By accepting TV for what it was, this "show about nothing" made audiences laugh.

Seinfeld was a monster, decade-defining hit, but ironically it did not compare to past hits such as *All in the Family, The Cosby Show,* and *M*A*S*H* in terms of audience share. The rise

of cable and the introduction of new broadcast networks spread the audience thin. But by the end of the decade, there were indications that network TV had accepted the realities of a more competitive marketplace. There seemed to be a slight trend back toward allowing low-rated shows to build audience loyalty before yanking them from the lineup. Networks were beginning to see the value of diverse segments of viewers—such as the 50-plus viewer, who had long been ignored in order to appeal to younger people. Or maybe they were doing what TV has always done . . . aim for the Baby Boomers.

▲ *Customers inspect a new Volkswagen Beetle convertible, circa 1950s. (CORBIS)*

In the decade following World War II, the American landscape was swept by Levittown-style suburbs linked by the highways of the new Eisenhower interstate system. The resulting boom in automobile use and sales dwarfed anything that had come before it, but the American love affair with the automobile was only warming up.

Commuters drove to workplaces increasingly distant from outlying bedroom communities. While their husbands took the car to work, stay-at-home moms found they needed a second car to reach "miracle miles," sprawling new shopping centers along major road arteries. Businesses catered to young families in automobiles, building drive-thru windows, drive-in movies, fast-food restaurants, and motels. Whether traveling down the road to the supermarket or across the country for a family vacation, Americans found unprecedented freedom and convenience in their cars.

To kids growing up in the backseat of chrome-fitted convertibles and lumbering tail-finned Eldorados, the importance of owning a car would be as obvious as the color of the sky. Even before they were old enough for bicycles, Baby Boom children raced up and down the driveway in pedal cars—a toy-store staple, often lovingly detailed to replicate the popular cars of the day. Though their fathers coveted Detroit's new sporty cars—like the iconic Chevy Corvette, introduced in June 1953, or the legendary Ford Thunderbird, introduced as a two-seater in 1954—Baby Boomers took their first rides in more prosaic family vehicles, like the Ford Country Sedan, the Chevy Bel Air, and the Nash Rambler.

Throughout the 1950s and 1960s, Detroit churned out larger and heavier cars. Increased horsepower helped power these behemoths, which continued to sell well to families and older adults. But the notorious "land barges" were too expensive for young people buying their first car. When the first wave of Baby Boomers reached driving age, they flocked to the Volkswagen Beetle. With its easily maintained rear engine and bare-bones interior, the famously cheap Beetle was the perfect starter car. Better yet, the German

Beetle had no ties to American car companies tarred by the counterculture as part of the military-industrial complex. Volkswagen bugs and busses became the vehicle of the protester, and imported cars began making their first noticeable dent in Detroit's sales figures.

The Big Three American automakers tried to fight back, aiming at the young Boomer market with a new series of "compact" cars like the Chevy Corvair and the Ford Falcon. Smaller and lighter than standard American cars, they also had a smaller price tag. But Volkswagens were still cheaper, and though the American compacts sold well, they could not end the gathering onslaught of imports. Detroit was dealt a major blow when Washington activist Ralph Nader accused the Chevy Corvair of being an irresponsibly designed deathtrap in his landmark 1965 exposé *Unsafe at Any Speed*. Though General Motors fought back with a lawsuit against Nader, the damage was already done. In 1966 Corvair production dropped by more than half, and three years later the model was terminated. Nader would return to haunt the auto industry, becoming the catalyst for a new era of government regulation that began in 1966 with the U.S. Motor Vehicle Safety Act, mandating seatbelts and other safety features.

Burned in the budget-car market, Detroit had more success catering to drivers looking for speed and performance. The first muscle car, the 1964 Pontiac GTO created by engineer John DeLorean, was a full-sized car with a need for speed. Young Boomers also flocked to the 1964 Ford Mustang, a low-priced, compact sporty car that could do 0-60 m.p.h. in 6.1 seconds and topped off at a speed of 110-127 m.p.h. In its first four years, nearly 2.1 million Mustangs were sold. Rivals GM and Chrysler scrambled to enter the market with their own "pony cars," the Chevy Camaro and the Pontiac Firebird. But while these classic American sports cars beguiled enthusiasts, their future was threatened by Detroit's unwillingness to explore engineering alternatives that would bring their cars into line with 1970 Clean Air Act emissions requirements without threatening performance.

In 1972, the 15-millionth Volkswagen Beetle rolled off German production lines, topping the Ford Model T as the top-selling car in world history. More ominously for Detroit, in 1970 Japanese automaker Honda entered the American automobile market for the first time. Japanese companies like Toyota and Datsun had made little mark on American consumers since they began selling cars in the late 1950s.

▶▶ *Reconceptualized as a status symbol, the revamped Volkswagen Beetle hits the road in 1998. (AP/WIDEWORLD PHOTOS)*

But the demographics of the American car market were changing. Inexpensive, fuel-efficient subcompacts like Toyota's Corona and Corolla and Honda's Civic endeared themselves to a second wave of young Boomers making their first car purchase in the early 1970s. When Arab oil embargoes sent the price of gasoline sky-high, Americans of all ages forsook their U.S.-built gas-guzzlers for Japanese cars. In 1977, Japanese automakers stunned the industry by capturing more than 10 percent of the American passenger car market for the first time in history.

It was the beginning of a new era of reduced expectations for GM, Ford, and Chrysler. Roundly criticized for their failure to adapt to the changing realities of the American road, the Big Three struggled to regain the loyalties of consumers even after the gas crunch had passed. The Baby Boom market proved particularly tough to crack. First-time buyers impressed with the reliability and overall quality of their Japanese economy cars became repeat customers, maturing into mid-level sedans like the Honda Accord, first introduced in 1976, and the Toyota Camry, introduced in 1983. The Accord and the Camry have dominated the passenger car market ever since. The only American car joining them on the best-seller lists has been the Ford Taurus, introduced in 1986. But Detroit's talent for big vehicles has given it an edge in the market as Boomers started having children of their own. In 1984, Chrysler's Dodge Caravan and Plymouth Voyager became the vehicles of choice for harried parents. High off the ground, with cargo space and seating for an entire family, the innovative minivan threatened to replace the venerable station wagon altogether.

The minivan's success cleared the way for the trend of the 1990s: sport utility vehicles. Built on truck platforms and boasting off-road capability, SUVs like the Jeep Cherokee and the Ford Explorer appealed to soccer moms tired of the minivan's stodgy image and to Boomers addicted to outdoor recreation. Automakers rushed to bring more luxurious versions to market, hoping to cash in on a trend fueled by economic prosperity and the lowest gas prices in recent history. Meanwhile, Volkswagen reassessed the generation that had made it successful decades earlier, and revamped its iconic Beetle—reconceptualizing its anti-establishment vehicle as a status symbol. A clever marketing campaign capitalized on Boomer nostalgia for their misspent youth, combined with the desire for a chic vehicle.

In 1995, American households spent almost 20 percent of their annual income on buying or maintaining their cars, spending more only on housing. But with the advent of cellular phones, personal entertainment systems, and other diversions for the car, people have less and less need to go home.

If the past 50 years have witnessed the triumph of the automobile, it is still unclear what the future will bring. In 1995 alone, Americans drove some 2.2 trillion miles in more than 200 million vehicles—quadruple the number of autos on the roads in 1950. Though the ugly realities of incurable gridlock, shrinking oil supplies, and environmental damage loom on the horizon, any number of strategies for luring us out of our cars have failed. For now it remains our most cherished liberty, the very essence of being an American: the freedom to get in the car and drive away.

▼ The latest in family-oriented vehicles: Mazda's 1999 minivan. (AP/WIDE WORLD)

Don't Trust Anyone UNDER Thirty

"Do you ever just want to get the hell out of this country?"

"And go where?"

"I don't know. Anywhere. Doesn't matter. Just some other place."

"I dunno. I've traveled. And all it is, is bad water, bad food, you get sick, you gotta deal with strange people — then when you get back, you can't tell whether it really happened to you, or you just saw it on TV."

— **Slacker** *(1991)*

They were dubbed "Generation X" by author Douglas Coupland, and the name has stuck. The young people of today—roughly, those born between 1965 and 1976—have no single cultural identity. They are liberals and conservatives, gay and straight, cyberculture gearheads, technophobe artists, critical theorists, sex radicals on book tours, corporate climbers intent on retiring by age 40, aspiring actors obsessed with fame. But, cultural differences aside, most Gen Xers would agree that their parents' "revolution" was bungled, and that they each must create their own futures rather than looking to sweeping social movements.

Possibly the only thing all Gen Xers have in common is the way in which movies and television dominate their lives. Ben Stiller's movie *Reality Bites* (1994) portrays young people so saturated by electronic media that they rattle off movie references and commercial catchphrases as readily as the Bloomsbury writers made literary allusions. One of the characters in Stiller's film even attempts to "authenticate" her life, and those of her friends, by constantly videotaping them. Authors Neil Howe and Bill Strauss also stress young Americans' close relationship to electronic sound and image—in their book, *13th Gen* (1993), they contrast the elder "Atari Wave" of the generation with the junior "Nintendo Wave."

Critics have condemned electronic media for ruining the minds of Gen Xers, blaming it for shortened attention spans and learning disabilities. Others counter that "progressive" changes made in America's education system during the '70s are the cause of today's failures in education. But it does appear irrefutable that the way information and images are processed today—quickly, repetitiously, briskly edited—affects how people think about narrative, time, and work. This is an era in which live theater is filled with movie-like special effects, in which digital graphics make movies look like video games, and in which personal achievement is validated by television coverage. The Gen

▶ *Technology? You're soaking in it. In the late 1990s, patrons of the "@ cafe" in New York City could surf the Net during dinner. (Kevin Flemming/CORBIS)*

Xers flourish in this environment.

If image dominates Generation X, the image often is soaked in nostalgia. Nineties youth have shown great attraction to artifacts and styles of earlier postwar decades—it's as if the young people of today focus on the past as intently as those in the '60s looked to the future. Gen Xers might attend a '70s blaxploitation film festival, or a coffeehouse program of '50s high school "dating tips" movies. Disco kitsch is in vogue, and VH1 reinforces the trend by rerunning old dance shows such as *Solid Gold.* Sixties psychedelia has reemerged in the late-night dance marathons called "raves," with their throbbing lightshows and recreational drugs. Even those archaic icons of '50s cool, the Frank Sinatra/Dean Martin "Rat Pack," are hip again. Hollywood is cashing in on the refreshed popularity of the old Vegas bad boys with new movie-bio treatments, and classic Rat Pack film vehicles, such as *Ocean's Eleven* and *Robin and the Seven Hoods,* are resurfacing on TV. Television also is increasingly devoted to resuscitated programs such as *I Dream of Jeannie* and *Bewitched,* repackaged for nostalgic allure as "vintage" or "classic" TV. The target market, of course, is the aging Boomer population, but programmers have been pleasantly surprised to find they've acquired a big audience of Gen Xers.

Nineties nostalgia fads have surfaced most clearly in music. Twentysomethings jump, jive, and wail to the tune of contemporary swing bands like the Squirrel Nut Zippers and the Cherry Poppin' Daddies, as well as reissues of the greats, like Louis Prima. CD reissues of '50s and '60s kitsch and exotica are also brisk sellers and have earned their own "Lounge" and "Easy Listening" bins at music shops. Juan Garcia Esquivel was one of the first of the 1950s orchestral novelty artists to be revived, closely followed by Les Baxter and Martin Denny. The recycling gates opened wide as the revival grew to embrace stripshow music, Italian exploitation sound tracks, jazz and string orchestra fusions, pre-Moog electronics, even Robert Mitchum's calypso recordings. With the '90s came retro theme nights at bars and nightclubs, for which customers are encouraged to dress-to-match the moods of *The Exotic Moods of Les Baxter* or Esquivel's *Space-Age Bachelor Pad Music* thrumming in the background.

An odd circularity has evolved, in which forward-looking advances in technology, media, and culture are employed to evoke the past, a past consumed eagerly by the Boomers' children. The circle comes into sharp focus at Gen X social events—Boomers attending such get-togethers watch young people consuming martinis, smoking cigars, and playing swing albums, and wonder how their children became their parents.

▼ *In a mind-boggling convergence of generational overtones, guitarist Brian Setzer, who became an MTV icon in the 1980s with his 1950s-derived band the Stray Cats, is pictured on-stage at the 1960s-inspired "Woodstock '99" festival with the Brian Setzer Orchestra, a 1940s-style swing band. (AP/WIDE WORLD PHOTOS)*

Family and Faith Revisited

In her book, *The Master Trend: How the Baby Boom Generation Is Remaking America* (1993), demographer Cheryl Russell argues that Boomers in the '90s were marked by a broad-based generational midlife crisis. According to Russell, many Boomers feel that, somewhere along the line, they have lost their way. The generation that rejected the traditional values of its parents appears increasingly drawn to "old-fashioned" commitments of family and faith. In turn, the old values are reshaped to fit '90s concerns.

Working Mothers

Political activism of the '70s and '80s succeeded in increasing the presence of women in the national labor force, including in executive positions previously held only by men. Women did not, however, give up their options to be mothers when they became employed. With the fading of the '50s housewife role—by 1989, fewer than 7 percent of U.S. families followed the man-as-breadwinner, woman-as-homemaker model—came that of the working mother. By 1991 60 percent of married women with children under the age of 6 were employed.

Besides economic necessity, one of the most common motivations for women who desire work is personal fulfillment, and surveys have indicated that most women would not leave their jobs even if financial pressures were reduced. But the double commitment to parenting and

career has produced a particularly '90s stress, common enough to inspire a television advertising campaign, in which a working mother is asked by her daughter, "Mommy, when do I get to be the client?" To the tune of Cyndi Lauper's "Girls Just Wanna Have Fun," Mom tosses a cellular phone into her attaché kit, confident that AT&T conference calling will allow her to conduct her meeting while surrounded by sand-flinging children.

Most working mothers probably wish that similar crises of their own could be handled as simply. But women are undeterred, and hold fast to their right to both employment and parenthood. They show every indication of continuing to accept the challenge of their position well into the next century.

Religion

Despite the agnostic tone of the '60s and '70s, religious practice never faded completely from the American scene—although it did appear to sit on the sidelines during the tumult of those years. Religion is back in the '90s. Radio stations featuring the music of forthrightly Christian singers, such as Amy Grant, are enjoying new listeners. Publishers of religious books say that sales are up. And of course, there's the Religious Right—vociferous, organized, and growing. Spokespeople for these groups acknowledge that their constituents vary in age, class, race, and gender, but all of them

▼ *Women attempted the delicate balancing act between career and children in ever-increasing numbers throughout the late 1980s and 1990s.*

Mothers in the Workforce
(numbers in thousands)

	Total Married Couples With Children Under 18	Percentage with Wife in Labor Force	Total Married Couples With Children Under 6	Percentage with Wife in Labor Force
1986	24,630	61.4%	11,924	53.9%
1987	24,645	64.0%	11,966	57.0%
1988	24,600	65.2%	11,915	57.3%
1989	24,735	65.7%	12,011	57.6%
1990	24,537	66.5%	12,051	59.1%
1991	24,397	67.1%	12,100	60.2%
1992	24,420	68.1%	11,925	60.3%
1993	24,707	67.8%	11,942	60.0%
1994	25,058	69.4%	12,118	62.2%
1995	25,241	70.4%	11,951	63.9%
1996	24,920	70.3%	11,782	63.0%
1997	25,083	71.3%	11,584	63.9%
1998	25,269	70.9%	11,773	64.0%

are quick to point to the aging Boomers in their ranks.

Some elements of Boom Generation faith have a familiar '60s ring. Writers on the subject point to a postmodern religious sensibility among Americans in their 40s and 50s, a quest for growth and self-fulfillment that contrasts with older religious tenets of self-denial. In this scenario, aging Boomers draw on their sense of personal autonomy to choose from religious options in an exploratory, experimental manner.

The current popularity of "self-improvement" texts lends support to theories of renewed Boomer religiosity. A visit to any large book store will turn up titles such as *Spiritual Crisis: What's Really Behind Loss, Disease, and Life's Major Hurts, Inner Simplicity: 100 Ways to Regain Peace and Nourish Your Soul,* and *Spiritual Literacy: Reading the Sacred in Everyday Life.* One of the grandfathers of self-improvement, M. Scott Peck, is still going strong—Peck's *The Road Less Traveled: A New Psychology of Love, Traditional Values and Spiritual Growth* (1978) remains a best-seller after 20 years.

It may be a trend rather than a movement. But if a new spirituality does become fully manifest among the Baby Boomers—the Older Generation of the '90s—then perhaps their "long strange trip" will continue for decades to come.

Aging Parents

Studies indicate that the fastest growing segment of the population today are those 85 and older. The implication for Baby Boomers is clear—the possibility that they might soon be caring for their elderly parents is very real.

Today, it's estimated that more than 22 million American families are involved in providing long-term care for parents or other relatives. In the face of the growing expense of long-term care and the time it consumes, Boomers have striven for the best compromise in dividing their attention between their own lives and those of their parents. Often the solution has been a long-distance arrangement, with the out-of-town caregiver paying his or her parents' bills as well as hiring and managing an on-site caretaker. Still, the process can be difficult. It has been determined that a full half of employed caretakers have taken time off work to care for their elders during the '90s.

The picture is further complicated by the spectre of Alzheimer's disease. People who already are caring for their parents find that they must make important determinations if the disease is diagnosed—their elders' wishes for care and housing, as well as their important papers, their insurance information, even their house keys, immediately become critical issues.

In '90s America, with federal funding stripped from the public health system and an insurance industry that views long-term care as a growth market, the prospects for the elderly and their caregivers look dire. As of this writing, congressional hearings are being held regarding substandard treatment and widespread patient abuse in nursing homes for the elderly. One only can hope that the hearings will result in legislation that will improve the lot of older citizens who need care, and of their children who attend to them.

Caring for the Elderly
(numbers in thousands)

Home Health and Hospice Care Patients

	Home	Health Hospice
Total, 1991	1,237.1	47.2
Total, 1993	1,451.2	50.1
Total, 1996	2,427.5	59.4

Characteristics of Home Health Care Patients 65 Years or Older, 1996

Total	1,763,000

Percentage Received Help With
Bathing, showering	53.2
Dressing	45.8
Eating	9.2
Moving in/out of bed or chair	29.6
Using the toilet	22.6
Light housework	38.9
Managing money	2.8
Shopping	14.1
Using the telephone	2.7
Preparing meals	23
Taking medications	23.4

Primary Source of Payment
Private insurance	3.7
Own income	2
Medicare	79.6
Medicaid	7
Other	7.7

Nursing Home Residents 65 Years or Older, 1995

Total	1,385,000

Percentage Distribution
Male	24.7
Female	75.3
65 to 74 years	17.5
75 to 84 years	42.3
85 years and over	40.2
White	89.5
Black	8.5
Other	2

Type of Nursing Care
Skilled care	46.1
Intermediate care	50.4
Residential Care	3.5

Primary source of payment
Private sources	28.9
Medicare	12.7
Medicaid	55.7
Other	2.7
Vision impaired	28.4
Hearing impaired	22.4
Using wheelchair	64.5
Using walker	24.9

Percentage Receiving Assistance With
Bathing, showering	86.3
Dressing	66.6
Eating	45.1
Moving out of bed or chair	23.8
Using toilet	57.8
Using telephone	68.2

◀ *In the 1990s many Baby Boomers were called upon to parent their parents, especially their mothers. As the nation continues to age, reliance on services such as home health care, nursing homes, and hospice services will continue to increase.*

Cloning

With mild eyes in a white face, Dolly looked like a surefire favorite at the petting zoo. But in the February 27, 1997, edition of *Nature*, Scots scientist Ian Wilmut revealed the Finn Dorset lamb to be a creature from the pages of science fiction. Dolly is a clone—a genetically identical duplicate—of another adult sheep. Her birth in July 1996 made her the first animal ever to be cloned from the cells of an adult mammal.

Wilmut and his colleagues at the Roslin Institute outside Edinburgh had found a way to overcome what many scientists believed was an absolute barrier. In the early embryonic stage of development, cells are generalized—every cell resembles every other cell. But, as the animal's organs develop, cells quickly take on specific functions.

Scientists believed that the specialized cells, though they still contain their original DNA, had permanently lost the ability to copy that DNA to recreate an entire animal.

Wilmut's team overcame this barrier by taking udder cells from an adult ewe, starving them of nutrients, and then removing their nuclei. Each nucleus was electronically fused to an egg cell from another sheep, replacing the egg's own DNA. The eggs were then implanted in the womb of yet another sheep. The revolutionary process had an astonishing failure rate—of 277 embryos created from the udder cells, only Dolly survived gestation to be born without massive birth defects.

A study of animal clones created since Dolly suggests that clones may suffer from severe medical problems and brief life spans. Still, scientists agree that the technology to create human clones will be tested—if not perfected—

▼ *Pictured in 1997, Dolly, below right, is the first cloned sheep, produced from adult sheep cells at the Roslin Institute in Edinburgh. Polly, below left, is the world's first transgenic lamb. (AP/ WIDE WORLD PHOTOS)*

in the foreseeable future. In response, many governments have outlawed or restricted further research on cloning. Most cloning experiments, however, seek to create transgenic clones—clones that combine DNA from different species. For example, in addition to Dolly, the Roslin Institute also created transgenic sheep named Molly and Polly; they were cloned partially from human genes, in the hope that their milk will produce a human blood-clotting protein for use in treating hemophiliacs.

Lifestyle Drugs

Amidst spiraling health care costs, drug companies targeting the massive Baby Boomer markets have introduced new products aimed at treating aging consumers' self-esteem. Whether they treat hair loss or sexual problems, some of the most popular new drugs, dubbed "lifestyle drugs," offer Baby Boomers the chance to turn back the hands of time.

Intended to treat men with serious erectile dysfunction caused by physical debilities, Viagra has rapidly become the drug of choice for older men looking to regain the sexual stamina they had as teenagers. While insurers debate whether Viagra should be covered under health plans, men have turned to the Internet to obtain the drug with little or no input from a physician. The price is not cheap: beyond the $9 or $10 cost per pill, Viagra can cause serious side effects, and has been associated with more than 100 deaths since its introduction in March 1998. Propecia, also available over the Internet, may halt hair loss, but also can cause impotence and, if pregnant women handle broken tablets, birth defects. But sales of both drugs continue to rise, leaving analysts to wonder if pharmaceutical companies won't soon find it more profitable to minister to Americans' obsession with youth and beauty instead of their health.

Virtual Pets

They dangle from key chains, clamoring for food and attention. If ignored or mistreated, they become foul-tempered or sick, and may even die. Virtual pets, a craze imported from Japan with the 1996 release of Tamagotchi, gave children and adults alike a chance to try their hand at parenting. The "parents" of virtual pets have to care for their small plastic wards by pressing buttons under an LCD screen. With their incessant demands, the pets have proved to be a tough responsibility, particularly for young children, who frequently leave the pets for parents to babysit. Responding to complaints from stressed-out parents, manufacturers have added a suspend feature to many models, allowing the toy to shut down without "killing" the pet. Toys have come a long way from the Davy Crockett caps and secret decoder rings of the early Baby Boom generation: in 1999 the Sony Corporation introduced Aibo, a robot dog that barks, wags its tail, and responds to commands.

High-tech Pregnancy

Since the introduction of in vitro fertilization (IVF) into the United States from England in 1981, at least 300 fertility clinics have sprung up around the country. Privately owned, these for-profit clinics have become the unregulated center of research into assisted fertility technology. The market they serve is a large one: according to recent estimates, some 15 percent of women of childbearing age have sought treatment to help them have children.

Success is by no means guaranteed. Each cycle of IVF can cost up to $10,000; but women have less than a 30 percent chance of becoming pregnant from any one cycle—and for women over 40, the rate is less than 10 percent. For those women who do become pregnant, slightly more than half give birth to one child, 25 percent have twins, nearly 6 percent have triplets or more, and the rest end in miscarriages. For Boomer women looking to beat the odds, some clinics offer services ranging from donated eggs to donated embryos.

Despite the drawbacks, and a number of troubling ethical questions raised by such sophisticated techniques as the freezing of embryos, increasing numbers of couples have turned to the clinics. In 1996 alone, assisted reproductive technology helped to conceive more than 20,000 babies.

World Wide Web

At the beginning of the decade, it didn't exist. By the end of the decade, it has become a central part of daily life for millions of Americans. Whether we use it to show off family pictures to relatives thousands of miles away, to trade on the stock market, to buy books and records, to play online games with people all over the world, or to just read the news in the morning, the World Wide Web has rapidly insinuated itself into our lives.

Born from a 1989 proposal by British physicist Tim Berners-Lee, the Web created a global network of information accessible through hypertext links. Berners-Lee and his colleagues created a hypertext browser and editor in 1990, calling the program "WorldWideWeb." Placed on a server at the Center for Nuclear Research (Centre Européen pour la Recherche Nucléaire, or CERN) in Switzerland in 1991, it grew exponentially: in 1993, the year that the Mosaic browser debuted for the PC and Macintosh, the number of Web servers grew from 50 to 500. By the end of 1994, there were 10,000 servers; by 1997, more than 650,000.

The rapid advance of the Web has still left behind millions of Americans unable to afford a computer. Poverty and restrictive governments have also prevented its spread in other countries. Nevertheless, by allowing information to flow freely around the globe as text, graphics, sounds, and video, the World Wide Web has already begun to change the way we look at the world.

Robert Bly (1926-)

He was an obscure poet from rural Minnesota until he tapped into the New Age with *Iron John: A Book About Men* (1992). Constructed from Jungian theories and eclectic fragments of mythology and folklore from around the world, Iron John argued that the masculine psyche was grievously wounded when the factories of the Industrial Revolution removed fathers from homes and farms, leaving them with little time to spend with young sons. In Bly's analysis, boys left to the care of women are unable to find models for adulthood, instead spending a prolonged adolescence perpetually grieving over their abandonment. To solve this crisis of manhood, he urged male readers to separate themselves from the "feminine" legacy of their mothers by coming together in all-male initiation ceremonies where they could collectively mourn and make a formal transition to a truly "masculine" adulthood.

Critics howled. Feminists accused Bly of launching a backlash against women's rights, while conservatives and cultural critics laughed at his eager pastiche of various native, folk, and tribal traditions. But others acknowledged that Bly articulated a very real despair and anger felt by men trying to make sense of changing gender roles. His message found a large and enthusiastic audience: *Iron John* spent a full year on best-seller lists and was called the seminal work of the men's movement.

Oprah Winfrey (1954-)

▼ *Oprah has a ball, below (CORBIS/Mitchell Gerber).*
▶▶ *Bill Gates does some charity work, far right. (AP/WIDE WORLD PHOTOS)*

Critics used her name as shorthand to deplore a decade fascinated with tell-all sensationalism, but the popularity of Oprah Winfrey sprung from more than the titillating topics of her enormously popular day-time talk show. Though she joined the ranks of the most highly paid entertainers in the United States, devoted fans loved her for the obstacles she overcame, most notably a childhood spent in rural poverty and an adolescence marked by sexual abuse.

Her success and incredible wealth only heightened audience appreciation for her ability to empathize with her troubled talk-show guests with tears, hugs, and startling personal revelations of her own. Her well-publicized struggles to control

her weight helped fans identify with her even further. Sympathizing with her failures, inspired by her successes, they embraced Oprah as a combination of big sister and best friend, an intimate confidante and trusted authority figure wrapped into one.

The emotional bond she forged with her audiences made her a cultural force to be reckoned with. In 1996, driven by a desire to become a more uplifting influence on her immense audience, she introduced a book club segment to her television show. She promptly turned the publishing industry on its head as each of her monthly choices—many of them difficult novels by self-consciously literary authors—flew out of bookstores and dominated best-seller lists.

Bill Gates (1955-)

When the personal computer revolution swept across America in the '90s, a run on high technology stocks made computer-industry pioneers multimillionaires. First among geeks to inherit the earth was Microsoft founder Bill Gates. A mercurial visionary whose dead-on instincts and sometimes

ruthless business practices made Microsoft the titan of the software industry, Gates rolled over his competitors with an intensity that invited comparisons with the robber barons of a previous century. As his personal fortune mushroomed by tens of billions of dollars, Gates leaped to the top of the list of wealthiest Americans.

But money couldn't buy him popularity. Long known for his brusque manner and inattention to social graces, Gates seemed to make enemies at the same speed with which he made money. The complaints of bested competitors and prominent consumer advocates persuaded the

◀ The Clintons and Gores on the campaign trail in 1992. (COR-BIS/Joseph Sohm; ChromoSohm Inc.)

Justice Department to launch an antitrust investigation into the Microsoft empire in 1997, while average citizens used their personal computers to make Gates-bashing an Internet cottage industry.

Though Gates typically met public criticism with a less-than-endearing mix of defensiveness and disdain, the Justice Department investigation and the bad press surrounding it encouraged him to pay more attention to public relations. Looking to soften his image, he began a series of talk-show appearances and high-profile charitable donations to schools and libraries. Critics argued that his philanthropy hardly matched the grandeur of his fortune, but others suggested that Gates might slowly be awakening to the social expectations that come with being America's richest person.

Bill Clinton (1946-) and Hillary Rodham Clinton (1947-); Al Gore, Jr., (1948-) and Tipper Gore (1948-)

They conquered the White House amid fanfare about the transfer of political power from one generation to the next, ending decades of political domination by the men who had served in the armed forces during World War II. The new leadership took to the national stage possessing radically different cultural landmarks than their predecessors. Children of prosperity and the cold war, raised on television and nuclear air-raid drills, they experienced John F. Kennedy's assassination as teenagers and faced the moral quagmire of Vietnam as college students. Products of the tumultuous era that bore them, the Clintons and the Gores would inherit the strengths—and the weaknesses—of their clamorous generation.

Clinton's tremendous personal warmth appealed to Boomers who preferred the easy garrulousness of a talk-show host to the distant statesmanship of older leaders. But, as he repeatedly staked out positions on issues only to abandon them in the face of criticism, Clinton fell prey to the same charges of expediency that haunted a generation perpetually reinventing itself to suit changing times.

Clinton easily won reelection in 1996, but his second term was marred by a scandal concerning his sexual involvement with a White House intern. While attacks on Clinton became more rabid with every salacious revelation and even his supporters began to lose faith, the president withstood the attacks, escaped impeachment, and emerged with his approval ratings virtually unscathed.

Meanwhile, first Lady Hillary Rodham Clinton's hopes to exert her own influence on public policy were dashed by fierce public opposition, evidence that the feminist gains of the Boomer era still elicited profound hostility from a nation troubled by the resulting permutations of the American family. The more traditional Gores—he a second-generation senator, she the stay-at-home mother of four—avoided most of the First Family's controversy, but largely failed to capture the imagination of voters.

Buffeted by the media they courted, these Baby Boomers in the White House seemed to personify the idealism, contradictions, and squandered promise of their generation.

Fashion

From the '80s onward, corporate fashion became less strict for "creatives." Those laboring as copywriters or design artists often have not been held to suit-and-tie rules. In the '90s, this looser standard became the everyday norm in the new media and software start-up companies that mushroomed throughout the marketplace.

This corporate-casual style spawned "dress-down Fridays," adopted by many major corporations in the early '90s. The policy allowed employees to shift readily into weekend mode by permitting casual wear in the workplace on Fridays. Slacks, sweaters, and expensive sneakers became commonplace at the end of the workweek. Guidebooks dictating dress-down do's and don'ts were distributed to employees, stressing the importance of dressing "tastefully" and avoiding shorts and tank tops.

Clothing chains responded to the trend with Dress-Down Friday promotions. Their marketing instincts were correct—researchers found that sales in casual business attire, especially men's, grew 12 percent between 1993 and 1995. As the decade comes to a close, the "once-a-week-casual" policy is a corporate standard.

Selling the Past

Nostalgia became a big-dollar marketing tool during the '90s, targeting Baby Boomers with numerous campaigns associating products with music and images of the '50s, '60s, and '70s. Often the product is an artifact of Boom Generation youth in '90s format—a digitally enhanced reissue of vintage music or a big-budget movie remake of an old TV show. With few exceptions, such marketing campaigns and their products score millions of dollars.

● One of Hollywood's earliest attempts to recycle Boomer television, 1987's *Dragnet*, was followed in the '90s by a string of movies based on "classic" television shows. Among these were *The Addams Family* (1991), *The Brady Bunch Movie* (1995), *Mission Impossible* (1996), *Lost in Space* (1998), and *The Mod Squad* (1999). Hollywood promises to deliver further treatments of old TV shows in shiny new cinematic packages.

● With the advent of compact discs during the '80s, record shops suddenly were awash with digital reissues of classic LP recordings in all genres. In recent years, these re-releases have taken aim at a vulnerable spot in buyer psychology: nostalgia for the increasingly rare vinyl record. CDs of old music often are packaged in the manner of the vinyl original, with cardboard sleeves instead of clear plastic cases. The compact disc itself sometimes is designed to look like a small vinyl LP, with a reproduction of the recording's original label in the center.

● It's an everyday, every-hour occurrence: a TV commercial promoting a car, a bank, or a computer is accompanied by the music of Marvin Gaye, John Lennon, or David Bowie. The songs are selected for maximum nostalgic rush as well as for lyrics that complement the advertiser's message. The spots can elicit groans from viewers, but the product is remembered. Early successes in exploiting Boomer nostalgia have made advertisers more brazen—characters in a recent ad are shown "evolving" from hippies to middle-aged consumers. Then there's the Volkswagen commercial with the already infamous slogan, "If you sold your soul during the '80s, here's your chance to buy it back."

The World at My Ear

When cordless telephone technology became widely available in the '80s, a future was envisioned in which one could make a phone call immediately, wherever the location. It took only a few years for pocket-sized cellular phones to become widely used. Today drivers, pedestrians, and restaurant customers often are seen keeping in touch with their offices or families through a cell phone.

If cellular phones were just the beginning, the pager business also took off in the 1990s, creating another way to stay in constant contact with the world. Not only do on-the-go adults want pagers, phone-happy teens need them too. Manufacturers have responded to youth demand with pagers in shocking pink and bright yellow.

Now pocket-sized computers that handle e-mail, as well as keep track of memos and addresses, are becoming popular. Comic strip detective Dick Tracy comes to mind—he kept touch with headquarters through his trusty two-way wrist radio. The demand in today's culture for personal electronic accessibility has made the cartoon less of a fantasy, and possibly made today's culture more of a cartoon.

THE FUTURE

Anna Walter, age nine, teaches a class about the Internet.
(AP/WIDE WORLD PHOTOS)

B aby Boomers, most of whom will *not* die before they get old, will be unlike any aging generation that has come before. Said one Boomer confronting the future, "I just go day to day. . . . I have a tendency to spend. Unfortunately, I have converted my wife to *my* way!" Most experts claim that the consumption-saturated Boomers, conditioned to buy, will continue to do so into the 21st century, and that they will, in many forms, display characteristics peculiar to their experience.

The dawning 21st century promises to alter the status of Boomers. For one, demographic changes will remove that generation from its place as the largest segment of the population. Between 2005 and 2025, Boomers will see their share of the overall population drop from 27 to 19 percent. Taking their place will be their children, or the Baby Boomlet, born between 1977 and 1995, which by 2015 will outnumber the Boomers. America's youthfulness will be reinforced by what the Census Bureau expects to be an increase in births after the year 2000 that will continue at least until 2050.

When Boomers look around in the 21st century, they will notice a more diverse population, one in which non-Hispanic whites will decline from 75 percent of the population in 1990 to 68 percent in 2010, and even more later. Almost all the population growth for non-Hispanic whites will come from births, but 57 percent of the growth for Asian Americans, 36 percent for Hispanics, and 20 percent for blacks will result from immigration. As the Boomers grow older, more and more service workers will come from these groups, a trend social analyst Peter G. Peterson considers dangerous. Writing in the *Atlantic Monthly*, he calls it "a potentially explosive situation in which largely white senior Boomers will be increasingly reliant on overtaxed minority workers."

One historian believes that the aging Baby Boomer cohort will bring as much social change as did the Industrial Revolution, with its urban development and immigrant labor. By the year 2040 the number of Americans 65 or older will reach 55 million, compared to 25 million in 1980 . . . more than doubling, then, in just 60 years. With people living longer, there will be a higher proportion of Boomers entering old age than did people in previous generations. Peterson insists that all of America will one day resemble Florida: "By 2022 at the latest, the proportion of Americans who are elderly will be the same as the proportion in Florida today. America, in effect, will become a nation of Floridas." The Census Bureau claims that while America's elderly population will increase 26 percent by 2010, it will increase 50 percent in Florida and Arizona.

With the high divorce rate among Boomers, and with women having longer lifespans than men, many women will live alone in old age. That situation raises the question of who will take care of the Boomers when they get old. Their children could, of course, and in a recent interview one Boomer expressed the hope that in retirement she would

> **❝** *Sooner or later I'm going to die, but I'm not going to retire.* **❞**
>
> **—Margaret Mead**

travel the country with her daughter. But many of them expect their children to go their own way. Without a doubt, the large number of Boomers will strain those social institutions and government agencies involved in providing care for the elderly.

As the generally thrifty parents of Baby Boomers pass away, they will leave substantial inheritances to their generally not-so-thrifty Boomer heirs. In what the *New York Times* described as "the largest intra-generational transfer of wealth in history," approximately $12 trillion in funds, property, and heirlooms will have to be split among the surviving generation. The fallout from this transfer is likely to touch Boomers in deeply personal ways. According to psychoanalyst Dr. Henry F. Smith, "Money is a way to quantify love. And both anticipating and receiving the inheritance intensifies both the loving and hating aspects of relationships

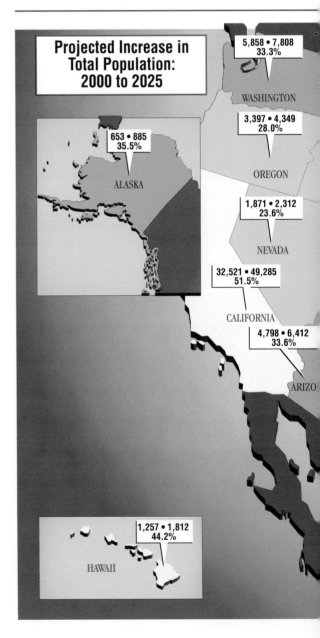

Projected Increase in Total Population: 2000 to 2025

5,858 • 7,808
33.3%

WASHINGTON

3,397 • 4,349
28.0%

653 • 885
35.5%

ALASKA

OREGON

1,871 • 2,312
23.6%

NEVADA

32,521 • 49,285
51.5%

CALIFORNIA

4,798 • 6,412
33.6%

ARIZO.

1,257 • 1,812
44.2%

HAWAII

THE FUTURE

between child and parent, and sibling and sibling." When Baby Boomer Richard Nelson's father died, his relationship with his brother nearly dissolved over the issue of who would receive their father's glockenspiel: "We fought like Cain and Abel over that glockenspiel," Nelson told the *New York Times*, "because it represented the hours we spent [with him]."

As Boomers themselves reach old age, they will not suddenly start listening to Lawrence Welk. They will listen to the Beatles, the Rolling Stones, the rock music they grew up with. They will continue to consume fast food and pizza—their traditional nutritional mainstays. In general, they will be more tolerant than the previous generation toward sex, for they themselves grew up in a permissive era.

Yet Boomers have never made up a homogeneous group. Differences in gender, race, ethnicity, and class exist and will complicate the general picture. Spending, traveling, and entertaining will be more thoroughly indulged in by a favored minority, particularly those born in the late 1940s and

early 1950s whose opportunities for career advancement were greater than those for later Boomers.

Boomers will work longer, perhaps into their seventies. One study predicts that in Wisconsin between 2005 and 2010 those 65 and older in the labor force will climb from 10.8 to 13.3 percent. Computers will make working at home more possible. Psychologist Ken Dychtwald, author of *Age Wave*, predicts: "It will become 'normal' for 50-year-olds to go back to school and for 70-year-olds to start new careers. In addition, the average 'first' retirement age will rise from 62 in 1995 to 70 in 2020 in reflection of greater vitality and longevity."

Boomers will, in the end, be as shaped by their cohort experiences, a shared desire for education, self-fulfillment, and comfortable lives, as they had been from the very beginning. Boomerdom has come a long way from the 1960s, when the Who sang "Hope I die before I get old." As the 21st century approached, one Boomer said: "If you have all your ducks in order, retirement is something to look forward to."

▼ *As the U.S. population grows in the first quarter of the 21st century, the proportion of Boomers in that population will be considerable.*

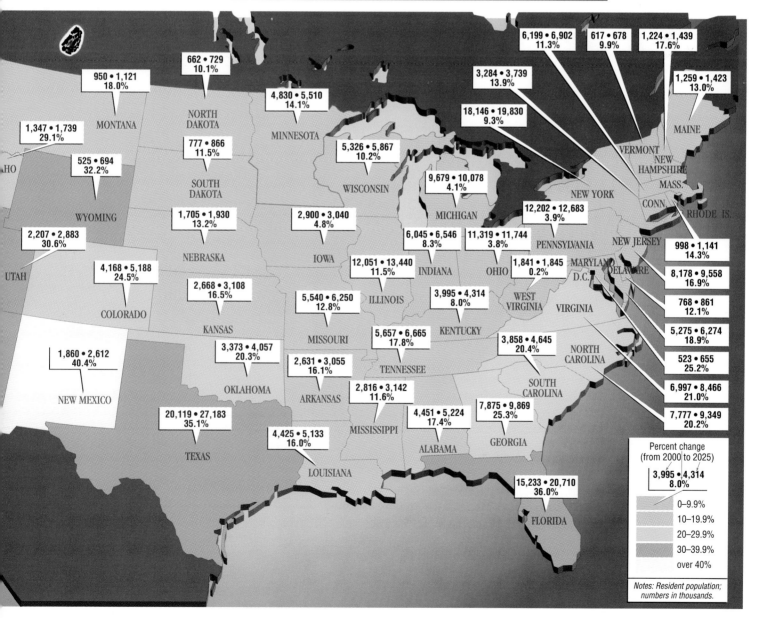

Percent change (from 2000 to 2025)

3,995 • 4,314
8.0%

0–9.9%
10–19.9%
20–29.9%
30–39.9%
over 40%

Notes: Resident population; numbers in thousands.

Map data labels (state • 2000 • 2025 • percent):

- MONTANA: 950 • 1,121 — 18.0%
- NORTH DAKOTA: 662 • 729 — 10.1%
- MINNESOTA: 4,830 • 5,510 — 14.1%
- IDAHO: 1,347 • 1,739 — 29.1%
- 525 • 694 — 32.2% (WYOMING area)
- SOUTH DAKOTA: 777 • 866 — 11.5%
- WISCONSIN: 5,326 • 5,867 — 10.2%
- MICHIGAN: 9,679 • 10,078 — 4.1%
- WYOMING: 2,207 • 2,883 — 30.6%
- NEBRASKA: 1,705 • 1,930 — 13.2%
- IOWA: 2,900 • 3,040 — 4.8%
- UTAH: 4,168 • 5,188 — 24.5%
- COLORADO: 2,668 • 3,108 — 16.5%
- KANSAS: 5,540 • 6,250 — 12.8% (ILLINOIS area)
- ILLINOIS: 12,051 • 13,440 — 11.5% (INDIANA area)
- INDIANA: 6,045 • 6,546 — 8.3%
- OHIO: 11,319 • 11,744 — 3.8%
- PENNSYLVANIA: 12,202 • 12,683 — 3.9%
- NEW YORK: 18,146 • 19,830 — 9.3%
- 3,284 • 3,739 — 13.9%
- 6,199 • 6,902 — 11.3%
- 617 • 678 — 9.9%
- 1,224 • 1,439 — 17.6%
- MAINE: 1,259 • 1,423 — 13.0%
- NEW MEXICO: 1,860 • 2,612 — 40.4%
- OKLAHOMA: 3,373 • 4,057 — 20.3%
- MISSOURI: 5,657 • 6,665 — 17.8%
- ARKANSAS: 2,631 • 3,055 — 16.1%
- TENNESSEE: 2,816 • 3,142 — 11.6%
- TEXAS: 20,119 • 27,183 — 35.1%
- LOUISIANA: 4,425 • 5,133 — 16.0%
- MISSISSIPPI: 4,451 • 5,224 — 17.4%
- ALABAMA: 7,875 • 9,869 — 25.3% (GEORGIA area)
- GEORGIA: 7,875 • 9,869 — 25.3%
- KENTUCKY: 3,995 • 4,314 — 8.0%
- WEST VIRGINIA: 1,841 • 1,845 — 0.2%
- VIRGINIA: 3,858 • 4,645 — 20.4%
- NORTH CAROLINA: 6,997 • 8,466 — 21.0%
- SOUTH CAROLINA: 7,777 • 9,349 — 20.2% / 523 • 655 — 25.2% / 768 • 861 — 12.1%
- MARYLAND: 5,275 • 6,274 — 18.9%
- NEW JERSEY: 8,178 • 9,558 — 16.9%
- 998 • 1,141 — 14.3%
- FLORIDA: 15,233 • 20,710 — 36.0%

In 1999, many educators looked toward the Internet and computers in general as their best opportunity to advance learning and help young people address glob-al challenges. The children of the later Baby Boomers, and the grandchildren of the early ones, will in ever-larger num-bers attend schools and colleges equipped with new com-puter technology. One teaching technique gaining in popu-larity in the late 1990s was called inquiry-learning, in which students are directed to find answers to questions via the World Wide Web, rather than by relying on teachers to pro-vide the solutions. Students could go online and use satellite data to plot whale and seal movements; or they could study Monarch butterflies through a university project. More teach-ers will likely use this pedagogy and its technology in the 21st century.

Colleges turned increasingly to distance learning in the 1990s, employing interactive television systems that broadcast via satellite, and creating Internet courses. About 750,000 stu-dents enrolled in distance education during the 1994-95 aca-demic year, mainly through community colleges. Nationwide, about 10,000 college-level courses could be found in 1997 on the Internet. The coming decades promise more. Said one educator: "Web-based courses are going to be mainstream in the future. Many . . . colleges do not understand that their ability to survive in the 21st century depends on the new technologies."

But critics worry that schools might use computers as a panacea that will hurt the quality of the overall educational programs. In the 1990s, a high school in Massachusetts spent $330,000 on computers with money acquired from cutting proposed teacher positions in art, music, and physical edu-cation. Another school in Virginia converted its art room into a computer lab. As the 21st century nears, debate rages as to whether computers encourage students to see factual link-ages—the "hypertext mind"—or whether they promote one-dimensional thinking and numb any ability to investigate more than a single problem at one time. A prominent engi-neer has claimed that computers foster linear thought detri-mental to innovation.

Many questions have also been raised about the so-called "digital divide." Research by groups such as the National Telecommunications and Information Administration (NTIA) suggest that, while computers and the Internet certainly hold out the promise to improve education, gen-erally speaking the students who have access to high technology are already successful both in terms of education and economics. For example, in July 1999 NTIA reported that 61.6 percent of people with col-lege degrees now use the Internet, while only 6.6 percent of those with an elementary school education or less use it. In the period between 1997 and 1998, the gap in Internet use between the most and the least educated increased by 25 percent. Observers worry that rather than creating new opportunities and narrowing the gap between upper and

lower classes, high technology might be making it worse, with poorer students being poorly trained in using comput-ers and the Internet. As U.S. employers will require more and more technology skills in the future, this situation sug-gests an unsettling self-fulfilling prophecy. The challenge for the future will be to extend the ben-efits of high technology from the "haves" to the "have nots."

Some critics have disparaged the trend toward viewing computers as a panacea for what ails America's schools. Steve Jobs, founder of Apple computers, insists: "No amount of technology will make a dent. . . . We can put a Web site in every school—none of this is bad. It's bad only if it lulls us into thinking we're doing something to solve the problem with education." With the federal gov-ernment and computer companies fervently pushing schools to buy computers, and with experts insisting computers are essential in a technology-driven world, their pervasive pres-ence in schools seems all but assured for the 21st century.

> 66 *There won't be schools in the future.... I think the computer will blow up the school. That is, the school defined as something where there are classes, teach-ers running exams, people structured in groups by age, following a curriculum, all of that.* 99
>
> —**Seymour Papert**

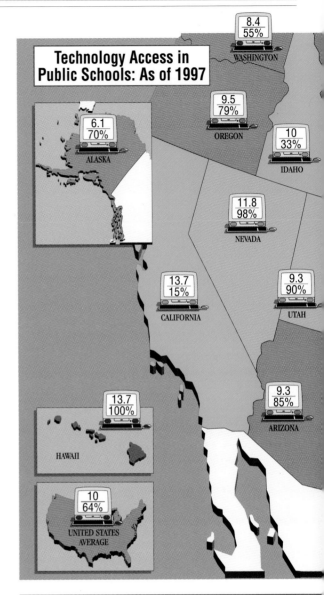

Technology Access in Public Schools: As of 1997

8.4 / 55% — WASHINGTON
9.5 / 79% — OREGON
10 / 33% — IDAHO
6.1 / 70% — ALASKA
11.8 / 98% — NEVADA
13.7 / 15% — CALIFORNIA
9.3 / 90% — UTAH
13.7 / 100% — HAWAII
9.3 / 85% — ARIZONA
10 / 64% — UNITED STATES AVERAGE

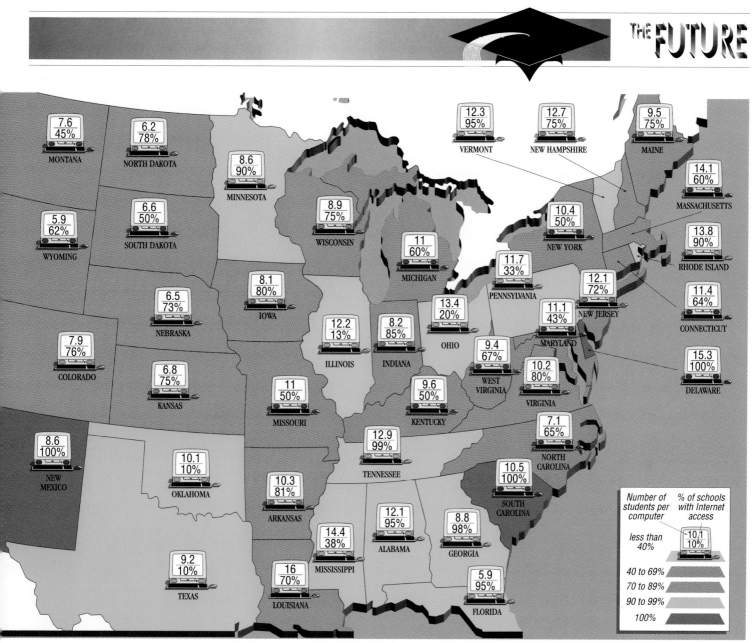

VERMONT	12.3 / 95%									
NEW HAMPSHIRE	12.7 / 75%									
MAINE	9.5 / 75%									

Map of United States showing number of students per computer and % of schools with Internet access:

- MONTANA: 7.6 / 45%
- NORTH DAKOTA: 6.2 / 78%
- MINNESOTA: 8.6 / 90%
- WYOMING: 5.9 / 62%
- SOUTH DAKOTA: 6.6 / 50%
- WISCONSIN: 8.9 / 75%
- MICHIGAN: 11 / 60%
- VERMONT: 12.3 / 95%
- NEW HAMPSHIRE: 12.7 / 75%
- MAINE: 9.5 / 75%
- MASSACHUSETTS: 14.1 / 60%
- RHODE ISLAND: 13.8 / 90%
- NEW YORK: 10.4 / 50%
- PENNSYLVANIA: 11.7 / 33%
- NEW JERSEY: 12.1 / 72%
- CONNECTICUT: 11.4 / 64%
- NEBRASKA: 6.5 / 73%
- IOWA: 8.1 / 80%
- ILLINOIS: 12.2 / 13%
- INDIANA: 8.2 / 85%
- OHIO: 13.4 / 20%
- MARYLAND: 11.1 / 43%
- COLORADO: 7.9 / 76%
- KANSAS: 6.8 / 75%
- MISSOURI: 11 / 50%
- KENTUCKY: 9.6 / 50%
- WEST VIRGINIA: 9.4 / 67%
- VIRGINIA: 10.2 / 80%
- DELAWARE: 15.3 / 100%
- NORTH CAROLINA: 7.1 / 65%
- NEW MEXICO: 8.6 / 100%
- OKLAHOMA: 10.1 / 10%
- ARKANSAS: 10.3 / 81%
- TENNESSEE: 12.9 / 99%
- SOUTH CAROLINA: 10.5 / 100%
- TEXAS: 9.2 / 10%
- LOUISIANA: 16 / 70%
- MISSISSIPPI: 14.4 / 38%
- ALABAMA: 12.1 / 95%
- GEORGIA: 8.8 / 98%
- FLORIDA: 5.9 / 95%

Legend:
Number of students per computer — % of schools with Internet access
10.1 / 10%
- less than 40%
- 40 to 69%
- 70 to 89%
- 90 to 99%
- 100%

But bad teaching and bad programs . . . those no computer can cure.

In search of better education, a small but growing number of parents have decided to take their children out of schools and teach them at home. Home schooling attracts Christian fundamentalists who distrust secular education, back-to-earth people who distrust all institutions, parents whose kids have emotional problems or learning disabilities, and, increasingly, middle-class parents who simply think schools have failed their children. As with computers in education, debate continues over the effectiveness of home schooling, but many believe the trend will expand.

Americans face a great challenge entering the 21st century: how to maintain or restore community, prevent machine contact from overwhelming human contact, and prevent selfish economic agendas from condemning large numbers of people to an isolated second-class life. Like the plot in the 1968 movie *2001: A Space Odyssey*, a favorite among Baby Boomers, the question begs for an answer: Will all achievement come through machines and make human beings insignificant, or will human beings regenerate into a higher consciousness and build a more enlightened future?

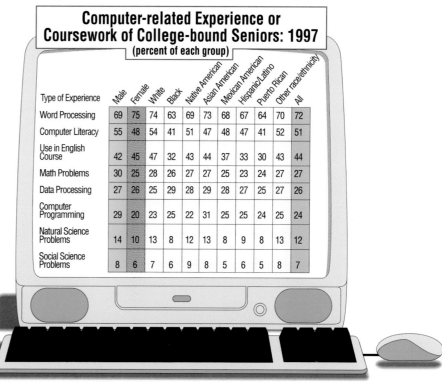

Computer-related Experience or Coursework of College-bound Seniors: 1997
(percent of each group)

Type of Experience	Male	Female	White	Black	Native American	Asian American	Mexican American	Hispanic/Latino	Puerto Rican	Other race/ethnicity	All
Word Processing	69	75	74	63	69	73	68	67	64	70	72
Computer Literacy	55	48	54	41	51	47	48	47	41	52	51
Use in English Course	42	45	47	32	43	44	37	33	30	43	44
Math Problems	30	25	28	26	27	27	25	23	24	27	27
Data Processing	27	26	25	29	28	29	28	27	25	27	26
Computer Programming	29	20	23	25	22	31	25	25	24	25	24
Natural Science Problems	14	10	13	8	12	13	8	9	8	13	12
Social Science Problems	8	6	7	6	9	8	5	6	5	8	7

" As almost every factor of production . . . moves effortlessly across borders," wrote Robert Reich in *The Work of Nations* (1991), "the very idea of an American economy is becoming meaningless, as are the notions of an American corporation, American capital, American products, and American technology." A global economy has overtaken the United States and the world—but will it mean boom or bust for the 21st century?

By almost every measurement, the United States experienced an economic surge in the mid-1990s; and by almost every measurement that surge intensified an already high concentration of income and wealth—the highest among all industrialized nations. Around the globe three billion people lived on the equivalent of less than two dollars a day; the world's 356 billionaires possessed more wealth than that of countries with 45 percent of the world's population.

Several economists predict that this domestic and international concentration of wealth will worsen as the global economy enters the 21st century. Robert Reich insists that a decline in worldwide transportation and communication costs, coupled with an emphasis on high technology, will result in more opportunity and wealth for an educated one-fifth of the American people, while the other four-fifths will fall rapidly behind, their plight worsened by labor-saving machines that will take their jobs. By 2020, he predicts, the top one-fifth will have 60 percent of all income, the bottom one-fifth only 2 percent. In effect, the upper ranks will secede from the union as they surround themselves with plush houses, good schools, and walled communities protected by security guards. The nation needs policies to expand ownership in companies, he insists, and increase the financial return to individuals, or the middle class will disappear.

Surveying the world scene, some political scientists forecast that the increasing concentration of wealth will threaten democracy. North America, Western Europe, and East Asia possessed three-quarters of the gross world product in the early 1990s, and 80 percent of the value of world trade. Unless policies change, the economic gaps within countries, as well as between have and have-not countries, will continue to widen . . . and most believe policies will not change. Sudden economic downturns such as that which sent Asia into an economic depression in the late 1990s may well mean the new century could see a rise in politics geared to class difference.

Profound social change will also be exerted by the exponential increase in elderly Americans as the graying of the Baby Boom continues. Already the federal government has realized what this might mean for its leading retirement program, Social Security. The ratio of workers to beneficiaries will decline from 4.8 to 1 in 1990, to 3.6 to 1 in 2020; and to

▼ *Baby Boomers will continue to be a part of the workforce well into the 21st century.*

Estimated Labor Activity of Mature and Older Workers: 1990 to 2020

Status and Age Group	1990	1995	2000	2005	2010	2020	% change 1995 to 2005
Employed							
45 to 49 years old	11.1 million	14.1 million	15.9 million	17.7 million	17.7 million	15.1 million	25.5%
50 to 54 years old	16.1 million	10.2 million	12.8 million	14.5 million	16.1 million	14.6 million	42.2%
55 to 59 years old	11.8 million	7.1 million	8.4 million	10.4 million	11.8 million	13.1 million	46.5%
60 to 64 years old	6.8 million	4.2 million	4.5 million	5.4 million	6.8 million	8.5 million	28.6%
65 to 69 years old	2.3 million	2 million	2.2 million	2.1 million	2.3 million	3.2 million	5%
70 and older	2.4 million	2 million	2.2 million	2.6 million	2.4 million	2.8 million	30%
Unemployed							
45 to 49 years old	487,200	617,400	697,200	777,000	770,000	663,600	25.9%
50 to 54 years old	373,800	445,200	558,600	634,000	706,000	638,400	42.4%
55 to 59 years old	298,200	310,800	369,600	458,000	516,000	575,400	47.4%
60 to 64 years old	196,800	180,400	192,700	229,000	291,000	364,900	26.9%
65 to 69 years old	92,400	92,400	101,200	97,000	105,000	149,600	5%
70 and older	90,000	110,000	120,000	135,000	125,000	150,000	22.7%

2.8 to 1 in 2030. According to the Congressional Budget Office, with no changes in benefits or revenues Social Security will be exhausted in the year 2044. Making the problem worse, Congress has over the years drawn money from Social Security to help finance the mammoth $5 trillion national debt, and Medicare, beset by higher health costs and by retirees living longer, could go broke.

In January 1998, President Bill Clinton began pushing for Social Security reform and advocated using a budget surplus to strengthen the system's finances. Congress, however, pushed to use the money for a tax cut. Whatever the final decision, it will take several hundred billion dollars to begin making Social Security solvent for Boomer retirees. Perhaps realizing this, Boomers have expressed pessimism, with nine out of ten agreeing that "the government has made financial promises to [their] generation that it will not be able to keep."

Boomers were often criticized by their elders for failing to save adequately for the future. Yet pre-Boomers had not done much better and instead had benefited from government programs such as Medicare, from Social Security being indexed to inflation, and from large increases in house values during the 1970s and 1980s. These benefits have so far largely escaped Boomers, and in any event many of them face the 21st century with inadequate funds for retirement. They know it, too—67 percent worry about their financial future, and 68 percent said they have not done enough to plan for retirement. But much as some Boomers started raising families late, they may start saving late. The proportion of those 30 to 44 years old who say they will likely put money into a retirement plan jumped from 14 percent in 1992 to 32 percent in 1995. Of course, saying you will save and actually saving are two different things, and the savings rate remained weak as the next century approached.

As Baby Boomers grow older, they will change their behavior to reflect their aging bodies; infirmities will slow them down. But despite that, they will reflect their cohort experience; their propensity to spend will continue. "We don't plan to give a child who's 35 or 40 a whole lot of money," said one. "If we live that long, we will enjoy what's left." Companies are already reshaping their advertising to attract older Boomers, reshaping automobile ads for the fifty-plus crowd, for example.

Some economic analysts forecast a rosy future, led as usual by the Boomer generation. In *The Roaring 2000s*, Harry S. Dent., Jr., predicts unprecedented prosperity, at least until 2015, based on the demographics of the Baby Boomers. They will, he said, be the most comfortable retirement generation, and their spending, combined with more widespread use of modern technology such as the Internet, will make for the greatest economic growth in history.

▼ *Unfortunately, not all Boomers will benefit from turn-of-the-century economic growth—for some, old age will mean hard times.*

Projected Number of Mature and Aged Adults in Poverty: 1990 to 2020							
Status and Age Group	1990	1995	2000	2005	2010	2020	% change 1995 to 2005
Low Earnings Workers							
45 to 49 years old	3 million	3.8 million	4.3 million	4.8 million	4.8 million	4.1 million	26.3%
50 to 54 years old	2.3 million	2.8 million	3.5 million	3.9 million	4.3 million	3.9 million	39.3%
55 to 59 years old	1.8 million	1.9 million	2.3 million	2.8 million	3.2 million	3.6 million	47.4%
60 to 64 years old	1.3 million	1.1 million	1.2 million	1.5 million	1.8 million	2.3 million	36.4%
65 to 69 years old	0.6 million	0.6 million	0.6 million	0.6 million	0.6 million	0.9 million	0%
70 and older	0.5 million	0.5 million	0.6 million	0.6 million	0.6 million	0.8 million	20%
Below Poverty Level							
45 to 49 years old	1.1 million	1.4 million	1.6 million	1.8 million	1.8 million	1.6 million	28.6%
50 to 54 years old	0.9 million	1.1 million	1.3 million	1.5 million	1.7 million	1.6 million	36.4%
55 to 59 years old	0.9 million	0.9 million	1 million	1.3 million	1.5 million	1.7 million	44.4%
60 to 64 years old	0.8 million	0.7 million	0.8 million	1.1 million	1.4 million	1.5 million	57.1%
65 to 69 years old	1 million	0.9 million	0.9 million	1 million	1.2 million	1.6 million	11.1%
70 and older	2.5 million	2.8 million	3 million	3.3 million	3.4 million	4.3 million	17.9%

The he map of potential world hot spots in the 21st century will look familiar to Baby Boomers, for it features many of the same locations that grabbed headlines and produced crises during the second half of the 20th century. Of course no one can foresee what new hot spots will emerge, and thus break the pattern, but that the map repeats the past reveals how much must still be resolved where diplomacy, money, and lives have already been committed.

YUGOSLAVIA
Balkan Hot Spot

A threat to world order in much of the 20th century, the Balkans promise to hold the same distinction in the 21st. Conflict among ethnic and religious factions contributed to the outbreak of World War I; in the 1990s such conflict led to war among Serbia, Bosnia and Croatia, and to war between Serbia and NATO, the outcome of which could produce a settlement leading to the deployment of a multinational peace force in Kosovo. But will that bring long-lasting stability? Many observers doubt it, and fear more atrocities and turmoil that could cause a large-scale war.

CUBA
After Castro . . . What?

Americans gave the Cuban National Baseball Team a friendly reception when it appeared in Baltimore in May 1999 for a game with the Orioles, but such warmth belied political tension. A few years earlier, in an attempt to topple dictator Fidel Castro, the United States hit Cuba with tighter economic sanctions. Although Castro claims the action has made his country stronger, Cuba's economy faces declining sugarcane harvests, massive interest payments on foreign loans, and a crumbling infrastructure. Many believe that Castro's death will bring his brother Raul to power, a development fraught with implications for stability in the Caribbean and for potential American economic investments in Cuba.

IRAQ
The Hussein Factor

With U.N. weapons observers booted from Iraq in 1998, the possibility exists that dictator Saddam Hussein will make weapons of mass destruction. He might, in fact, be close to nuclear capability. Will he use such weapons to grab Middle Eastern oil fields and disrupt supplies to Europe and the United States? Will he attack Israel? Or is he acting more defensively than offensively? And what about a post-Hussein Iraq? There seems to be opportunity for an open society, but also the potential for continued dictatorship under Hussein's successors—alternatives loaded with consequences for American influence and world stability.

CHINA
Trade, Human Rights, and Nuclear Weapons

Post–cold war China has befuddled and frustrated American leaders. Presidents George Bush and Bill Clinton believed that expanded economic ties with China would lessen human rights abuses there. That hasn't happened, thus the question remains: When will China stop oppressing its dissidents? And will it pursue democratic reform? Americans worry, too, about China's nuclear arsenal. The theft of atomic secrets from the United States reveals China's sense of nuclear inferiority and its ambition to improve its weapons. Some observers warn that China's export of nuclear technology to the Middle East and its own nuclear buildup pose a tremendous danger to world peace.

NORTH KOREA
Another Nuclear Threat

A missile fired across Japan, chemical weapons, what may be a nuclear site beneath a mountain—American and Asian leaders worried that North Korea had committed itself in the 1990s to programs that in the years ahead could threaten its neighbors and even the United States, which it had warned of "annihilating strikes" should any provocation occur. North Korea, devastated by famine, could attack wealthier South Korea out of desperation. The *Christian Science Monitor* says North Korea has been keeping "the outside world on edge"—evidenced by the United States testing its radar system to prepare for a possible North Korean nuclear missile strike on the West Coast.

ISRAEL
Arabs and Jews

Relations between Israelis and Palestinians remain tense despite peace agreements. In 1999 Yasir Arafat, leader of the Palestine Liberation Organization, threatened to establish an independent Palestinian state in the West Bank and Gaza Strip with or without Israel's cooperation, and Israel rejected any large withdrawal from the West Bank without assurances of safety from Palestinian terrorist attacks. Thus there continues the long-standing question of whether Arabs and Jews can live together peacefully in the Middle East, or whether the two sides, engaged in battle so many times, will again resort to war.

ASIA
Needed: Another Economic Miracle

Economists applied the label "economic miracle" to the boom in much of Asia from the late 1980s into the mid-1990s. But a crash that began in 1997 ruined national economies and toppled governments. Unemployment soared and malnutrition spread. In East Timor, some residents took to eating bark to survive. With 60 percent of the world's population, Asia is important, even vital, for economies elsewhere. Pessimists foresee a prolonged depression that could drag down the thriving U.S. economy; they see little hope of another miracle. Optimists stress Asia's high savings rate and its strong attachment to education; they believe that financial restructuring will produce prosperity.

Name	Role	Date	Name	Role	Date	Name	Role	Date
Abdul, Paula	musician, dancer	6/19/62	Bossy, Mike	athlete	1/22/57	Close, Glenn	actor	3/19/47
Abdul-Jabbar, Kareem	athlete	4/16/47	Boucher, Rick	representative	8/1/46	Coen, Ethan	director	9/21/57
Abraham, Spencer	senator	6/12/52	Bourque, Ray	athlete	12/28/60	Coen, Joel	director	11/29/54
Adams, Scott	cartoonist	6/8/57	Bowden, Terry	athlete	2/24/56	Coffey, Paul	athlete	6/1/61
Alexander, Jason	actor	9/23/59	Bowie, David	musician	1/8/47	Cole, Gary	actor	9/20/57
Allen, Debbie	choreographer	1/16/50	Boy George	musician	6/14/61	Cole, Natalie	musician	2/6/50
Allen, Joan	actor	8/20/56	Bradley, Pat	athlete	3/24/51	Collins, Phil	musician	1/30/51
Allen, Karen	actor	10/5/51	Bradshaw, Terry	athlete	9/2/48	Collins, Susan	senator	12/7/52
Allen, Tim	actor, comedian	6/13/53	Branagh, Kenneth	actor, director	12/10/60	Comenici, Nadia	athlete	11/12/61
Alley, Kirstie	actor	1/12/51	Braugher, Andre	actor	7/1/62	Conners, Jimmy	athlete	9/2/52
Allison, Davey	athlete	2/25/61	Breathed, Berkeley	cartoonist	6/21/57	Conrad, Kent	senator	3/12/48
Allman, Duane	musician	11/20/46-10/29/71	Brett, George	athlete	5/15/53	Cooper, Alice	musician	2/4/48
Allman, Greg	musician	12/7/47	Bridges, Jeff	actor	12/4/49	Copperfield, David	magician	9/16/56
Amos, Tori	musician	8/22/64	Brinkley, Christie	model	2/2/54	Costas, Bob	TV anchor	3/22/52
Anderson, Harry	actor	10/14/49	Brisco-Hooks, Valerie	athlete	7/6/60	Costello, Elvis	musician	8/25/54
Anderson, Kevin	actor	1/13/59	Broderick, Matthhew	actor	3/21/62	Costner, Kevin	actor, director	1/18/55
Anderson, Loni	actor	8/5/46	Brooks, Albert	actor	7/22/47	Coupland, Douglas	author	12/30/61
Anderson, Lynn	musician	9/26/47	Brooks, Garth	musician	2/7/62	Couples, Fred	athlete	10/3/59
Anderson, Melissa Sue	actor	9/26/62	Brosnan, Pierce	actor	5/16/53	Couric, Katie	TV anchor	1/7/57
Anderson, Richard Dean	actor	1/23/50	Brown, Blair	actor	4/23/48	Crapo, Mike	senator	5/20/51
Andretti, Michael	athlete	10/5/62	Brownback, Sam	senator	9/12/56	Crenshaw, Ben	athlete	1/11/52
Archer, Anne	actor	8/25/47	Browne, Jackson	composer, musician	10/9/48	Crow, Sheryl	musician	2/11/62
Arkin, Adam	actor	8/19/57	Browner, Carl	EPA head	12/16/55	Crowe, Cameron	director	7/13/57
Arnaz, Desi Jr.	actor, musician	1/19/53	Bryson, Peabo	musician	4/13/51	Crowell, Rodney	musician	8/17/50
Arnaz, Lucie	actor	7/17/51	Buckingham, Lindsey	musician	10/3/47	Cruise, Tom	actor	7/3/62
Arnold, Tom	actor	3/6/59	Buckley, Betty	actor, singer	7/3/47	Crystal, Billy	actor, comedian	3/14/47
Ashford, Evelyn	athlete	4/15/57	Buffett, Jimmy	musician	12/25/46	Csonka, Larry	athlete	12/25/46
Ashman, Howard	lyricist	1950-91	Burke, Delta	actor	7/30/56	Cuomo, Andrew	cabinet member	12/6/57
Assante, Armand	actor	10/4/49	Burton, LeVar	actor	2/16/57	Curry, Tim	actor	4/19/46
Austin, Patti	musician	8/10/48	Burton, Tim	director	8/25/58	Curtin, Jane	actor	9/6/47
Austin, Tracy	athlete	12/12/62	Buscemi, Steve	actor	12/13/57	Curtis, Jamie Lee	actor	11/22/58
Autry, Alan	actor	7/31/52	Busfield, Timothy	actor	6/12/57	Cusack, Joan	actor	10/11/62
Aykroyd, Dan	actor, comedian	7/1/52	Bush, George W.	governor	7/6/46	Cyrus, Billy Ray	musician	8/25/61
Azinger, Paul	athlete	1/6/60	Bush, Jeb	governor	2/11/53	Dafoe, Willem	actor	7/22/55
Babyface	musician	4/10/59	Butcher, Susan	athlete	12/26/56	Daley, William M.	cabinet member	8/9/48
Bacon, Kevin	actor	7/8/58	Butler, Brett	actor, comedian	1/30/58	D'Angelo, Beverly	actor, musician, producer	11/15/54
Baker, Anita	musician	1/26/58	Byrne, David	musician	5/14/52	Daniels, Jeff	actor	2/19/55
Baker, Kathy	actor	6/8/50	Byrne, Gabriel	actor	5/12/50	Danson, Ted	actor	12/29/47
Bakula, Scott	actor	10/9/55	Cage, Nicholas	actor	1/7/64	Danza, Tony	actor	4/21/50
Baldwin, Alec	actor	4/3/58	Cameron, James	director	8/16/54	Daschle, Thomas	senator	12/9/47
Baldwin, Daniel	actor	10/5/60	Campbell, Bruce	actor	6/22/58	David, Larry	writer, director	1947
Baldwin, William	actor	2/21/63	Campbell, Earl	athlete	3/29/55	Davis, Geena	actor	1/21/57
Banderas, Antonio	actor	8/10/60	Campbell, John	athlete	4/8/55	Davis, Judy	actor	4/23/55
Barkin, Ellen	actor	4/16/55	Campion, Jane	director	4/30/54	Day-Lewis, Daniel	actor	4/29/57
Barkley, Charles	athlete	2/20/63	Canseco, Jose	athlete	7/2/64	Dean, Howard, M.D.	governor	11/17/48
Barnes, Roy	governor	3/11/48	Capshaw, Kate	actor	11/3/53	DeFrantz, Anita	athlete, attorney	10/4/52
Barrett, Syd	musician	1/6/46	Carey, Drew	actor, comedian	5/23/58	DeGeneres, Ellen	actor, comedian	1/26/58
Barry, Dave	columnist	7/3/47	Carmen, Eric	composer, musician	8/11/49	DeLay, Tom D.	representative	4/8/47
Baryshnikov, Mikhail	dancer, choreographer	1/28/48	Carpenter, John	musician	1/16/48	Depardieu, Gerard	actor	12/27/48
Basinger, Kim	actor	12/8/53	Carpenter, Mary Chapin	musician	2/21/58	Depp, Johnny	actor	6/9/63
Bassett, Angela	actor	8/16/58	Carper, Thomas R.	governor	1/23/47	Derek, Bo	actor	11/20/56
Bates, Kathy	actor	6/26/48	Carradine, Keith	actor	8/8/49	de Varona, Donna	athlete	4/26/47
Battle, Kathleen	singer	8/13/48	Carreras, Jose	singer	12/5/46	Devers, Gail	athlete	11/19/66
Baxter, Meredith	actor	6/21/47	Carrey, Jim	actor, comedian	1/17/62	DeWine, Mike	senator	1/5/47
Bayh, Evan	senator	12/26/56	Carter, Lynda	actor	7/24/51	Dickerson, Eric	athlete	9/2/60
Beamon, Bob	athlete	8/29/46	Carter, Nell	actor	9/13/48	Dillon, Matt	actor	2/18/64
Beattie, Ann	writer	9/7/47	Case, Steve	industrialist	8/21/58	Dionne, Marcel	athlete	8/3/51
Becker, Walter	musician	2/20/50	Cash, Rosanne	musician	5/24/55	D'Onofrio, Vincent	actor	6/30/59
Belushi, Jim	comedian, actor	6/15/54	Cassidy, David	musician	4/12/50	Donovan (Leitch)	musician	5/10/46
Benatar, Pat	musician	1/10/53	Caulkins, Tracy	athlete	1/11/63	Dorsett, Tony	athlete	4/7/54
Bench, Johnny	athlete	12/7/47	Cauthen, Steve	athlete	5/1/60	Douglas, James (Buster)	athlete	4/7/60
Bening, Annette	actor	5/29/58	Cawley, Evonne Goolagong	athlete	7/31/51	Dove, Rita	poet, writer	8/28/52
Benson, Robby	actor	1/21/56	Cellucci, Argeo Paul	governor	4/24/48	Down, Lesley-Ann	TV journalist	3/17/54
Berenger, Tom	actor	5/31/50	Chan, Jackie	actor, martial arts expert	4/7/54	Dreier, David	representative	7/5/52
Bergen, Candice	actor	5/9/46	Chapman, Tracy	musician	3/30/64	Drescher, Fran	actor, producer	9/30/57
Berman, Chris	sportscaster	5/10/55	Charo	actor, musician	1/15/51	Dreyfuss, Richard	actor	10/29/47
Bernard, Crystal	actor	9/30/64	Chast, Roz	cartoonist	11/26/54	Dryden, Ken	athlete	8/8/47
Bernhard, Sandra	actor, comedian	6/6/55	Chavez, Julio Cesar	athlete	7/12/62	Dryer, Fred	actor, athlete	7/6/46
Bernsen, Corbin	actor	9/7/54	Cher	actor, musician	5/20/46	Duke, Patty	actor	12/14/46
Bettman, Gary	athlete	6/2/52	Chow Yun-Fat	actor	5/18/55	Duncan, Sandy	actor, singer	2/20/46
Bird, Larry	athlete	12/7/56	Christie, Linford	athlete	4/2/60	Dunne, Griffin	actor	6/8/55
Black, Clint	musician	2/4/62	Chuck D	musician	8/2/60	Duran, Roberto	athlete	6/16/51
Blades, Ruben	actor, musician, composer	7/16/48	Chung, Connie	TV anchor	8/20/46	Dutton, Charles S.	actor	1/30/51
Blair, Linda	actor	1/22/59	Cisneros, Henry	politician	6/11/47	Duvall, Shelley	actor	7/7/49
Boggs, Wade	athlete	6/15/68	Clancy, Tom	writer	4/12/47	Earnhardt, Dale	athlete	4/29/52
Bogosian, Eric	author, actor	4/24/53	Clarke, Bobby	athlete	8/13/49	Easton, Sheena	musician	4/27/59
Bolton, Michael	musician	2/26/53	Clarke, Marcia	lawyer	8/31/53	Ebersol, Dick	sportscaster	7/28/47
Bonds, Barry	athlete	7/24/64	Clay, Andrew Dice	comedian	9/29/58	Eckersley, Dennis	athlete	10/3/54
Bonilla, Henry	representative	1/2/54	Clemens, Roger	athlete	8/4/62	Edwards, Anthony	actor	7/19/63
Bono	musician	5/10/60	Clinton, Bill	politician	8/19/46	Edwards, John	senator	6/10/53
Bono, Mary	representative	10/24/61	Clinton, Hillary Rodham	politician	10/26/47	Eichhorn, Lisa	actor	2/4/52
Boone, Debbie	singer	9/22/56	Clooney, George	actor	5/6/61	Elliot, Bill	athlete	10/8/55

Elliott, Chris	actor	5/31/60	
Ellroy, James	writer	3/4/48	
Elvira	actor	9/17/51	
Elway, John	athlete	6/28/60	
Engler, John	governor	10/12/48	
Enya	musician	5/17/61	
Erdich, Louise	writer	7/6/54	
Erving, Julius	athlete	2/22/50	
Estefan, Gloria	musician	9/1/57	
Estevez, Emilio	actor	5/12/62	
Estrada, Erik	actor	3/16/49	
Etheridge, Melissa	musician	5/29/61	
Evans, Lee	athlete	2/25/47	
Everett, Rupert	actor	5/29/59	
Evert, Chris	athlete	12/21/54	
Evigan, Greg	actor	10/14/53	
Ewing, Patrick	athlete	8/5/62	
Fabio	model	3/15/61	
Fagan, Donald	musician	1/10/48	
Fairchild, Morgan	actor	2/3/50	
Falana, Lola	actor	9/11/46	
Fallows, James	journalist	8/2/49	
Fawcett, Farrah	actor	2/2/47	
Feingold, Russell	senator	3/2/53	
Feinstein, Michael	singer	9/7/56	
Field, Sally	actor	11/6/46	
Fielder, Cecil	athlete	9/21/63	
Fingers, Rollie	athlete	8/25/46	
Fiorentino, Linda	actor	3/9/60	
Firth, Colin	actor	9/10/60	
Firth, Peter	actor	10/27/53	
Fishburne, Laurence	actor	7/30/61	
Fisher, Carrie	actor, writer	10/21/56	
Fisk, Carlton	athlete	12/26/47	
Fitzgerald, Peter	senator	10/20/60	
Fleming, Peggy	athlete	7/27/48	
Flockhart, Calista	actor	11/11/64	
Flutie, Doug	athlete	10/23/62	
Fogelberg, Dan	musician	8/13/51	
Foley, Dave	actor, comedian	1/4/63	
Fonda, Bridget	actor	1/27/64	
Forbes, Malcom "Steve" Jr.	politician	7/18/47	
Ford, Faith	actor	9/14/64	
Foreman, George	athlete	1/10/49	
Fosbury, Dick	athlete	3/6/47	
Foster, Jodie	actor, director	11/19/62	
Fox, Michael J.	actor	6/9/61	
Fox, Vivica A.	actor	7/30/64	
Foxworthy, Jeff	actor, comedian	9/6/57	
Frampton, Peter	musician	4/22/50	
Franken, Al	actor	5/21/51	
Freeh, Louis	FBI director	1/6/50	
Frey, Glen	musician	11/6/48	
Frist, William	senator	2/22/52	
Gable, Dan	athlete	10/25/48	
Gabriel, Peter	musician	2/13/50	
Galas, Diamanda	performance artist	1952	
Garcia, Andy	actor	4/12/56	
Garofalo, Janeane	actor, comedian	9/28/64	
Gates, Bill	industrialist	10/28/55	
Gates, Henry Louis, Jr	author, scholar	9/16/50	
Gatlin, Larry	musician, actor	5/2/48	
Gaultier, Jean-Paul	designer	4/24/52	
Gayle, Crystal	musician	1/9/51	
Geary, Anthony	actor	5/29/47	
Gere, Richard	actor	8/31/49	
Gervin, George	athlete	4/27/52	
Gibb, Barry	musician	9/1/46	
Gibb, Maurice	musician	12/22/49	
Gibb, Robin	musician	12/22/49	
Gibbons, Leeza	TV anchor	3/26/57	
Gibson, Kirk	athlete	5/28/57	
Gibson, Mel	actor	1/3/56	
Gibson, Thomas	actor	7/3/62	
Gibson, William	author	3/17/48	
Gifford, Kathie Lee	TV anchor	8/16/53	
Gilbert, Melissa	actor	5/8/64	
Gill, Vince	musician	4/12/57	
Gilmore, James S., III	governor	10/6/49	
Givens, Robin	actor	11/27/64	
Glover, Danny	actor	7/22/47	
Goldberg, Whoopi	actor, comedian	11/13/49	

Goldblum, Jeff	actor	10/22/52	
Goldin, Nan	photographer	1953	
Goldthwait, Bobcat	comedian	5/1/62	
Goldwyn, Tony	actor	5/20/60	
Goodenow, Bob	athlete	10/29/52	
Goodlatte, Bob	representative	9/22/52	
Goodman, John	actor	6/20/52	
Gordon, Mary	author	12/8/49	
Gore, Al	politician	3/31/48	
Gore, Tipper	politician	8/19/48	
Gossage, Goose	athlete	7/5/51	
Grammer, Kelsey	actor	2/20/55	
Grams, Rod	senator	2/4/48	
Grant, Amy	musician	12/25/60	
Grant, Hugh	actor	9/9/60	
Graves, Bill	governor	1/9/53	
Green, Al	musician	4/13/46	
Greene, Joe	athlete	9/24/46	
Greenwood, Bruce	actor	8/12/56	
Gregg, Judd	senator	2/14/47	
Gregory, Cynthia	dancer	7/8/46	
Gretzky, Wayne	athlete	1/26/61	
Grey, Jennifer	actor	3/22/60	
Grier, David Alan	actor	6/30/55	
Grier, Pam	actor	5/26/49	
Griffin, Archie	athlete	8/21/54	
Griffith, Melanie	actor	8/9/57	
Grisham, John	author	2/8/55	
Groening, Matt	cartoonist	2/15/54	
Guest, Christopher	actor, writer	2/5/48	
Guisewhite, Cathy	cartoonist	1950	
Gumbel, Bryant	TV anchor	9/29/48	
Gumbel, Greg	TV anchor	5/3/46	
Guthrie, Arlo	musician	7/10/47	
Gwynn, Tony	athlete	5/9/60	
Hagel, Chuck	senator	10/4/46	
Hagler, Marvin	athlete	5/23/54	
Hall, Arsenio	comedian	2/12/55	
Hall, Daryl	musician	10/11/48	
Hamill, Dorothy	athlete	7/26/56	
Hamill, Mark	actor	9/25/51	
Hamilton, Linda	actor	9/26/56	
Hamilton, Scott	athlete	8/28/58	
Hamlin, Harry	actor	10/30/51	
Hammer	musician	3/29/63	
Hanks, Tom	actor	7/9/56	
Hannah, Daryl	actor	12/3/60	
Harewood, Dorian	actor	8/6/51	
Harper, Tess	actor	8/15/50	
Harrelson, Woody	actor	7/23/61	
Harris, Ed	actor	11/28/50	
Harris, Emmylou	musician	4/2/47	
Harris, Franco	athlete	3/7/50	
Harrison, Gregory	actor	5/31/50	
Hart, Mary	actor	11/8/51	
Hartley, Hal	film director	11/3/59	
Hartman, Phil	comedian	9/24/48-5/28/98	
Hasselhoff, David	actor	7/17/52	
Hearns, Thomas	athlete	10/18/58	
Heiden, Eric	athlete	6/14/58	
Helprin, Mark	author	6/28/47	
Hemingway, Mariel	actor	11/21/61	
Henderson, Ricky	athlete	12/25/58	
Henley, Don	musician	7/22/47	
Herman, Alexis	cabinet member	7/16/47	
Herman, Pee-Wee	actor	8/27/52	
Hershey, Barbara	actor	2/5/48	
Hill, Anita	legal scholar	7/10/56	
Hines, Gregory	choreographer, dancer, actor	2/14/46	
Hinton, S.E.	author	7/28/48	
Hodges, Jim	governor	11/19/56	
Holmes, Larry	athlete	11/3/49	
Holyfield, Evander	athlete	10/19/62	
hooks, bell	author, feminist	9/25/52	
Hooks, Jan	actor, comedian	4/23/57	
Hornsby, Bruce	musician	11/23/54	
Houston, Whitney	musician	8/9/63	
Howard, Ron	actor, director	3/1/54	
Huckabee, Mike	governor	8/24/51	
Hulce, Tom	actor	12/6/53	
Hull, Brett	athlete	8/9/64	
Hunt, Helen	actor	6/15/63	

Hunter, Holly	actor	3/20/58	
Hunter, Jim (Catfish)	athlete	4/8/46	
Hurt, Mary Beth	actor	9/26/46	
Hurt, William	actor	3/20/50	
Huston, Angelica	actor	7/8/51	
Huston, Whitney	musician	8/9/63	
Hutchinson, Tim	senator	8/11/49	
Hutton, Timothy	actor	8/16/60	
Hyman, Flo	athlete	7/31/54-1/24/86	
Ian, Janis	musician	4/7/51	
Ice-T	musician, actor	2/16/58	
Idol, Billy	musician	11/30/55	
Iman	model	7/25/55	
Ingram, James	musician	2/16/56	
Ireland, Kathy	model, fashion designer	3/8/63	
Irons, Jeremy	actor	9/19/48	
Irving, Amy	actor	9/10/53	
Ito, Lance	judge	8/2/50	
Jackson, Bo	athlete	11/30/62	
Jackson, Jermaine	musician	12/11/54	
Jackson, Kate	actor	10/29/48	
Jackson, Michael	musician, dancer	8/29/58	
Jackson, Reggie	athlete	5/18/46	
Jackson, Samuel L.	actor	12/21/48	
James, Rick	musician	2/1/48	
Jarmusch, Jim	film director	1/22/53	
Jenner, Bruce	athlete	10/28/49	
Jett, Joan	musician	9/22/60	
Jillian, Ann	actor	1/29/50	
Jobs, Steve	industrialist	2/24/55	
Joel, Billy	musician	5/9/49	
Johanns, Mike	governor	6/18/50	
John, Elton	musician	3/25/47	
Johnson, Ben	athlete	12/30/61	
Johnson, Beverly	model	10/13/52	
Johnson, Don	actor	12/15/49	
Johnson, Earvin (Magic)	athlete	8/14/59	
Johnson, Gary E.	governor	1/1/53	
Johnson, Tim	senator	12/28/46	
Johnston, Lynn	cartoonist	5/28/47	
Jones, Grace	musician, actor	5/19/52	
Jones, Rickie Lee	musician	11/8/54	
Jones, Tommy Lee	actor	9/15/46	
Jordan, Michael	athlete	2/17/63	
Joyner, Florence Griffith	athlete	12/21/59-9/21/98	
Joyner-Kersee, Jackie	athlete	3/3/62	
Judd, Naomi	musician	1/11/46	
Judd, Wynonna	musician	5/3/64	
Judge, Mike	cartoonist	10/17/62	
Kanaly, Steve	actor	3/14/46	
Kane, Carol	actor	6/18/52	
Karan, Donna	fashion designer	10/2/48	
Kasich, John	representative	5/13/52	
Katzenberg, Jeffrey	film producer	1950	
Keaton, Diane	actor	1/5/46	
Keaton, Michael	actor	9/9/51	
Keenan, Mike	athlete	10/21/49	
Kelley, Jim	athlete	2/14/60	
Kempthorne, Dirk	governor	10/29/51	
Kennedy, Caroline	scholar, author	11/27/57	
Kennedy, John, Jr.	magazine editor	11/25/60-7/16/99	
Kenny G	musician	6/5/56	
Kerns, Joanna	actor	2/12/53	
Keyes, Alan	politician	8/7/50	
Khan, Chaka	musician	3/23/53	
Kidder, Margot	actor	10/17/48	
King, Betsy	athlete	8/13/55	
King, Stephen	author	9/21/47	
Kingsolver, Barbara	author	4/8/55	
Kinnear, Greg	actor	6/17/63	
Kinski, Nastassja	actor	1/24/60	
Kinsley, Michael	columnist	3/9/51	
Kiraly, Karch	athlete	11/3/60	
Kirby, Bruno	actor	4/28/49	
Kirkland, Gelsey	dancer	12/29/53	
Kite, Tom	athlete	12/9/49	
Kitzhaber, John A.	governor	3/5/47	
Kline, Kevin	actor	10/24/47	
Knight, Wayne	actor	8/7/55	
Koch, Bill	athlete	6/7/55	
Kristol, William	columnist	12/23/52	
Krone, Julie	athlete	7/24/63	

Krzyzewski, Mike	athlete	2/13/47	
Kulwicki, Alan	athlete	12/14/54	
Ladd, Cheryl	actor	7/12/51	
Lafleur, Guy	athlete	9/20/51	
Lambert, Jack	athlete	7/8/52	
Landis, John	director	8/3/50	
Landrieu, Mary	senator	11/23/55	
Lane, Nathan	actor	2/3/56	
lang, k.d.	musician	11/2/61	
Lang, Stephen	actor	7/11/52	
Lange, Jessica	actor	4/20/49	
LaPaglia, Anthony	actor	1/31/59	
Largent, Steve	athlete	9/28/54	
Larroquette, John	actor, comedian	11/25/47	
Larson, Gary	cartoonist	8/14/50	
LaTourette, Steven	representative	7/22/54	
Lauer, Matt	TV anchor	12/30/57	
Lauper, Cyndi	musician	6/20/53	
Lawrence, Vicki	actor	3/26/49	
Leavitt, Michael O.	governor	2/11/51	
Leary, Denis	comedian, actor	8/18/57	
Lee, Ang	film director	10/23/54	
Lee, Spike	director	3/20/57	
Leguizamo, John	actor	7/22/65	
Leigh, Jennifer Jason	actor	2/5/62	
Lennox, Annie	musician	12/25/54	
Leno, Jay	comedian, TV host	4/28/50	
Leonard, Sugar Ray	athlete	5/17/56	
Letterman, David	comedian, TV host	4/12/47	
Levy, Eugene	comedian	12/17/46	
Lewis, Carl	athlete	7/1/61	
Lewis, Huey	musician	7/5/51	
Leyner, Mark	author	1/4/56	
Lewis, Richard	actor, comedian	6/29/47	
Lieberman-Cline, Nancy	athlete	7/1/58	
Limbaugh, Rush	columnist	1/12/51	
Lin, Maya	architect	10/5/59	
Lincoln, Blanche	senator	9/30/60	
Liotta, Ray	actor	12/18/55	
Locke, Gary	governor	1/21/50	
Locke, Sondra	actor	5/28/47	
Locklear, Heather	actor	9/25/61	
Loggins, Kenny	musician	1/17/47	
Long, Shelley	actor	8/23/49	
Lopez, Nancy	athlete	1/6/57	
Lopiano, Donna	athlete	9/11/46	
Louganis, Greg	athlete	1/29/60	
Louis-Dreyfus, Julia	actor	1/13/61	
Love, Courtney	musician	7/9/64	
Loveless, Patty	musician	1/4/57	
Lovett, Lyle	actor	11/1/57	
Lovitz, Jon	actor, comedian	7/21/57	
Lowe, Rob	actor	3/17/64	
Lucci, Susan	actor	12/23/48	
Lunden, Joan	TV anchor	9/19/50	
LuPone, Patti	actor	4/21/49	
Lydon, John ("Johnny Rotten")	musician	1/31/56	
Lynch, David	film director	1/20/46	
Ma, Yo Yo	musician	10/7/55	
MacDowell, Andie	actor	4/21/58	
MacLachlan, Kyle	actor	2/22/59	
MacNelly, Jeff	cartoonist	9/17/47	
MacPhail, Andy	athlete	4/5/53	
MacPherson, Elle	model, actor	3/29/64	
Macy, William H.	actor	3/13/50	
Madigan, Amy	actor	9/11/51	
Madonna (Ciccone)	musician, actor, producer	8/16/58	
Maher, Bill	comedian	1/20/56	
Mahre, Phil	athlete	5/10/57	
Malkovich, John	actor	12/9/53	
Malone, Karl	athlete	7/24/63	
Malone, Moses	athlete	3/23/55	
Maloney, Carolyn	representative	2/19/48	
Maloney, James	representative	9/17/48	
Mamet, David	playwright	11/30/47	
Manchester, Melissa	musician	2/15/51	
Mandel, Howie	comedian	11/29/55	
Mandrell, Barbara	musician	12/25/48	
Manilow, Barry	musician	6/17/46	
Manoff, Dinah	actor, director, writer	1/25/58	
Mantegna, Joe	actor	11/13/47	
Mapplethorpe, Robert	photographer	11/4/46-3/9/89	
Maravich, Pete	athlete	6/27/47-1/5/88	
Marin, Cheech	actor, comedian	7/13/46	
Marinaro, Ed	actor	3/31/50	
Marino, Dan	athlete	9/15/61	
Markey, Edward	representative	7/11/46	
Marlette, Doug	cartoonist	12/6/49	
Marsalis, Branford	musician	8/26/60	
Marsalis, Wynton	musician	10/18/61	
Martins, Peter	choreographer, dancer	10/27/46	
Maslin, Janet	critic	8/12/49	
Matalin, Mary	commentator	8/19/53	
Mathers, Jerry	actor	6/2/48	
Matheson, Tim	actor, director	12/31/47	
Mattingly, Don	athlete	4/20/61	
McAdoo, Bob	athlete	9/25/51	
McArdle, Andrea	actor	11/5/63	
McCurry, Michael	commentator	10/27/54	
McDonnell, Mary	actor	4/28/52	
McDormand, Frances	actor	6/23/57	
McEnroe, John	athlete	2/16/59	
McEntire, Reba	musician	3/28/55	
McFerrin, Bobby	musician	3/11/50	
McGwire, Mark	athlete	10/1/63	
McInerney, Jay	author	1/13/55	
McKean, Michael	actor	10/17/47	
McKinney, Tamara	athlete	10/16/62	
Mears, Rick	athlete	12/3/51	
Meat Loaf	musician	9/27/47	
Mellencamp, John	musician	10/7/51	
Menendez, Robert	representative	1/1/54	
Menken, Alan	composer	7/22/49	
Merchant, Natalie	musician	10/26/63	
Mercury, Freddie	musician	9/5/46-11/24/1991	
Messier, Mark	athlete	1/18/61	
Meyers, Anne	athlete	3/26/55	
Mfume, Kweisi	politician	10/24/48	
Michael, George	musician	6/26/63	
Miller, Cheryl	athlete	1/3/64	
Miller, Dennis	actor, comedian	11/3/53	
Minelli, Liza	actor, singer	3/12/46	
Minghella, Anthony	director	1/6/54	
Mirren, Helen	actor	7/2/46	
Modine, Matthew	actor	3/22/59	
Molinari, Susan	politician	3/27/58	
Molitor, Paul	athlete	8/22/56	
Montana, Joe	athlete	6/11/56	
Moon, Warren	athlete	11/18/56	
Moore, Demi	actor	11/11/62	
Moranis, Rick	actor	4/18/53	
Morial, Marc	politician	1/3/58	
Morrissey	musician	5/22/59	
Moseley-Braun, Carol	politician	8/16/47	
Moses, Edwin	athlete	8/31/55	
Moses, William	actor	11/17/59	
Mosley, Walter	author	1/12/52	
Mr. T	actor	5/21/52	
Mulgrew, Kate	actor	4/29/55	
Murphy, Calvin	athlete	5/9/48	
Murphy, Dale	athlete	3/12/56	
Murphy, Eddie	actor, comedian	4/3/61	
Murray, Bill	actor, comedian	9/21/50	
Murray, Eddie	athlete	2/24/56	
Murray, Patty	senator	10/10/50	
Myers, Dee Dee	commentator	9/1/61	
Myers, Mike	actor, comedian	5/23/63	
Naber, John	athlete	1/20/56	
Nadler, Jerrold	representative	6/13/47	
Naughton, James	actor	7/6/46	
Navratilova, Martina	athlete	10/18/56	
Neeson, Liam	actor	6/7/52	
Neill, Sam	actor	9/14/47	
Nelligan, Kate	actor	3/16/51	
Newton-John, Olivia	actor, musician	9/26/47	
Nickles, Don	senator	12/6/48	
Nicks, Stevie	musician	5/26/48	
Noone, Peter	musician	11/5/47	
Nugent, Ted	musician	12/13/48	
Oates, John	musician	4/7/48	
O'Brien, Conan	comedian	4/18/63	
O'Brien, Tim	author	10/1/46	
Ocean, Billy	musician	1/21/50	
O'Donnell, Rosie	TV host, actor	3/21/62	
Olajuwon, Hakeem	athlete	1/21/63	
Oldman, Gary	actor	3/21/58	
Olmos, Edward James	actor	2/24/47	
O'Neal, Tatum	actor	11/5/63	
O'Neil, Ed	actor	4/12/46	
Ontkean, Michael	actor	1/24/46	
O'Rourke, P.J.	columnist	11/14/47	
Orr, Bobby	athlete	3/20/48	
Osbourne, Ozzy	musician	12/3/48	
Osmond, Donny	musician	12/9/57	
Osmond, Marie	musician	10/13/59	
Ovitz, Michael	agent	12/14/46	
Owens, Bill	governor	10/22/50	
Paglia, Camille	scholar, author	4/2/47	
Palmer, Robert	musician	1/19/49	
Palminteri, Chazz	actor, writer	5/15/51	
Parsons, Gram	musician	11/5/46-9/19/73	
Parton, Dolly	musician, actor	1/19/46	
Patinkin, Mandy	actor	11/30/52	
Patrick, Craig	athlete	5/20/46	
Pauley, Jane	TV anchor	10/31/50	
Paxton, Bill	actor	5/17/55	
Payton, Walter	athlete	7/25/54	
Pena, Federico F.	cabinet member	3/15/47	
Pendergrass, Teddy	musician	3/26/50	
Penn, Sean	actor, director	8/17/60	
Penny, Joe	actor	9/14/56	
Perez, Rosie	actor	9/6/64	
Perlman, Rhea	actor	3/31/48	
Perlman, Ron	actor	4/13/50	
Peters, Bernadette	actor	2/28/48	
Petty, Tom	musician	10/20/53	
Pfeiffer, Michelle	actor	4/29/57	
Phillips, Mackenzie	actor	11/10/59	
Pickering, Charles	representative	8/10/63	
Pincay, Laffit, Jr.	athlete	12/29/46	
Pirner, David	musician	4/16/64	
Piscopo, Joe	actor, comedian	6/17/51	
Pitino, Rick	coach	9/18/52	
Pitt, Brad	actor	12/18/64	
Plant, Robert	musician	8/20/48	
Plummer, Amanda	actor	3/23/57	
Plunkett, Jim	athlete	12/5/47	
Pop, Iggy	musician	4/21/47	
Posey, Parker	actor	11/8/64	
Potvin, Denis	athlete	10/29/53	
Powell, Mike	athlete	11/10/63	
Prefontaine, Steve	athlete	1/25/51-6/1/75	
Presley, Priscilla	actor	5/24/46	
Preston, Billy	musician	9/9/46	
Prince (The Artist)	musician	6/7/58	
Puckett, Kirby	athlete	3/14/61	
Pullman, Bill	actor	12/17/54	
Quaid, Dennis	actor	4/9/54	
Quaid, Randy	actor	10/1/50	
Quindlen, Anna	author	7/8/53	
Quinn, Aidan	actor	3/8/59	
Racicot, Marc	governor	7/24/48	
Radner, Gilda	actor, comedian	6/28/46-5/20/89	
Raffi	musician	7/8/48	
Rahal, Bobby	athlete	1/10/53	
Raimi, Sam	film director	1959	
Raitt, Bonnie	musician	11/8/49	
Ramone, Dee Dee	musician	9/18/52	
Ramone, Joey	musician	5/19/51	
Ramone, Johnny	musician	10/8/51	
Ramone, Tommy	musician	1/29/52	
Rashad, Phylicia	actor	6/17/48	
Ratzenberger, John	actor	4/6/47	
Reed, Jack	senator	11/11/49	
Reed, Ralph	political activist	6/21/61	
Reeve, Christopher	actor	9/25/52	
Reeves, Keanu	actor	9/2/64	
Regalbuto, Joe	actor	8/24/49	
Reich, Robert	politician	6/24/46	
Reinking, Ann	actor, dancer, singer	11/10/49	
Reiser, Paul	actor, comedian	3/30/57	
Reitman, Ivan	director	10/27/46	
Reynolds, Butch	athlete	6/8/64	
Rhames, Ving	actor	5/12/61	
Rice, Jerry	athlete	10/13/62	

Name	Profession	Date
Rich, Frank	columnist	6/2/49
Richards, Michael	actor	7/21/49
Richardson, Miranda	actor	3/3/58
Richardson, Natasha	actor	5/11/63
Richardson, Patricia	actor	2/23/51
Richie, Lionel	musician	6/20/50
Rickman, Alan	actor, director	2/21/46
Ride, Sally K.	astronaut	5/26/51
Riegert, Peter	actor	4/11/47
Ripken, Carl Jr.	athlete	8/24/60
Ritter, John	actor	9/17/48
Ritts, Herb	photographer	1952
Robbins, Tim	actor, director	10/16/58
Rodgers, Bill	athlete	12/23/47
Rodgers, Nile	musician	9/29/52
Rodman, Dennis	athlete	5/13/61
Rodriguez, Johnny	musician	12/10/51
Roemer, Tim	representative	10/30/56
Rohrabacher, Dana	representative	6/21/47
Romano, Ray	comedian	12/21/57
Ronstadt, Linda	musician	7/15/46
Rose, Axel	musician	2/6/62
Roseanne	comedian, TV host	11/3/52
Rossellini, Isabella	actor	6/18/52
Roth, David Lee	musician	10/10/54
Roth, Mark	athlete	4/10/51
Roth, Tim	actor	5/14/61
Rourke, Mickey	actor	7/16/53
Rowland, John G.	governor	5/24/57
Rudner, Rita	actor, comedian	9/17/56
Ruehl, Mercedes	actor	2/28/48
Rundgren, Todd	musician	6/22/48
Rush, Geoffrey	actor	7/6/51
Russell, Kurt	actor	3/17/51
Russert, Tim	TV journalist	5/7/50
Russo, Rene	actor	2/17/54
Ryan, Meg	actor	11/19/61
Ryan, Nolan	athlete	1/31/47
Sade	musician	1/16/59
Saget, Bob	actor, comedian	5/17/56
Sajak, Pat	game show host	10/26/47
Salazar, Alberto	athlete	8/7/58
Samms, Emma	actor	8/28/60
Samuelson, Joan Benoit	athlete	5/16/57
Santorum, Rick	senator	5/10/58
Sarandon, Susan	actor	10/4/46
Sartain, Gailard	actor, writer, visual artist	9/18/46
Sayles, John	director, writer	9/28/50
Scalia, Jack	actor	11/10/51
Schafer, Edward T.	governor	8/8/46
Schmidt, Mike	athlete	9/27/49
Schnabel, Julian	artist	10/26/51
Schollander, Don	athlete	4/30/46
Schumer, Charles	senator	11/23/50
Schwarzenegger, Arnold	actor, athlete	7/30/47
Scott Thomas, Kristin	actor	5/24/60
Seagal, Steven	actor	4/10/51
Seagren, Bob	athlete	10/17/46
Seidelman, Susan	director	12/11/52
Seinfeld, Jerry	actor, comedian	4/29/55
Sellecca, Connie	actor	5/25/55
Sessions, Jeff	senator	12/24/46
Sessions, Pete	representative	3/22/55
Seymour, Jane	actor	2/15/51
Shackelford, Ted	actor	6/23/46
Shaffer, Paul	musician	11/28/49
Shaheen, Jeanne	governor	1/28/47
Shandling, Gary	actor, comedian	11/29/49
Sheehan, Patty	athlete	10/27/56
Shepard, Cybill	actor	2/18/49
Shire, Talia	actor	4/25/46
Short, Martin	actor, comedian	3/26/50
Shorter, Frank	athlete	10/31/47
Shriver, Maria	TV anchor	11/6/55
Siegelman, Don	governor	2/24/46
Silkwood, Karen	activist	2/19/46-11/13/74
Simmons, Gene	musician	8/25/49
Simmons, Richard	fitness guru	7/12/48
Simpson, O.J.	athlete, actor	7/9/47
Sinbad	comedian	11/10/56
Sinise, Gary	actor	3/7/55
Siskel, Gene	film critic	1/26/46-2/20/99
Slaney, Mary Decker	athlete	8/4/58
Slater, Helen	actor	12/14/63
Slater, Rodney	cabinet member	2/23/55
Sliwa, Curtis	activist	3/26/54
Smiley, Jane	author	9/26/49
Smirnoff, Yakov	actor, comedian	1/24/51
Smith, Billy	athlete	12/12/50
Smith, Gordon	senator	5/25/52
Smith, Harry	TV anchor	8/21/51
Smith, Jaclyn	actor, fashion designer	10/26/47
Smith, Lee	athlete	12/4/57
Smith, Ozzie	athlete	12/26/54
Smith, Patti	musician, poet	12/30/46
Smitts, Jimmy	actor	7/9/55
Snowe, Olympia	senator	2/21/47
Snipes, Wesley	actor	7/31/63
Sorbo, Kevin	actor	9/24/58
Sorvino, Paul	actor	2/17/54
Souder, Mark	representative	7/18/50
Spacek, Sissy	actor	12/25/49
Spacey, Kevin	actor	7/26/59
Spader, James	actor	2/7/60
Spiegelman, Art	cartoonist	2/15/48
Spielberg, Steven	director	12/18/47
Spinks, Leon	athlete	7/11/53
Spitz, Mark	athlete	2/10/50
Springfield, Rick	musician	8/23/49
Springsteen, Bruce	musician	9/23/49
Stallone, Sylvester	actor	7/6/46
Stanley, Paul	musician	1/20/50
Starr, Kenneth	lawyer, judge	7/21/46
Steel, Danielle	author	8/14/47
Steele, Shelby	scholar, critic	1/1/46
Steenburgen, Mary	actor	2/8/53
Stephanopoulous, George	commentator	2/10/61
Stern, Howard	radio personality	1/12/54
Stevens, Cat	musician	7/21/47
Stewart,Jon	comedian	11/28/62
Sting	musician, actor	10/2/51
Stipe, Michael	musician	1/4/60
Stockton, John	athlete	3/26/62
Stoltz, Eric	actor	9/30/61
Stone, Oliver	director	9/15/46
Stone, Sharon	actor	3/10/58
Stones, Dwight	athlete	12/6/53
Strange, Curtis	athlete	1/30/55
Streep, Meryl	actor	6/22/49
Strummer, Joe	musician	8/21/52
Struthers, Sally	actor	7/28/48
Studi, Wes	Actor	12/17/47
Sulzberger, Arthur Ochs, Jr	publisher	9/22/51
Summer, Donna	musician	12/31/48
Summitt, Pat	athlete	6/4/52
Sununu, John	representative	9/10/64
Swann, Lynn	athlete	3/7/52
Tan, Amy	author	2/19/52
Tarantino, Quentin	actor, director, writer	3/27/63
Tartikoff, Brandon	producer	1/13/49-8/27/97
Taylor, James	musician	3/12/48
Taylor, Lawrence	athlete	2/4/59
Taymor, Julie	director	12/15/52
Tenet, George	politician	1/5/53
Thomas, Clarence	Supreme Court justice	6/23/48
Thomas, Isiah	athlete	4/30/61
Thomas, Richard	actor	6/13/51
Thompson, Daley	athlete	7/30/58
Thompson, Emma	actor, writer	4/15/59
Thornton, Billy Bob	actor, director, writer	8/4/55
Tiegs, Cheryl	actor, model	9/25/47
Tomei, Marisa	actor	12/4/64
Torricelli, Robert	senator	8/26/51
Townsend, Robert	director, actor	2/6/57
Travis, Randy	musician	5/4/59
Travolta, John	actor	2/18/54
Tritt, Travis	musician	2/9/63
Trottier, Bryan	athlete	7/17/56
Trudeau, Gary	cartoonist	7/21/48
Trump, Donald	industrialist	6/14/46
Tucci, Stanley	actor, director	1/11/60
Tucker, Tanya	musician	10/10/58
Turner, Kathleen	actor	6/19/54
Turow, Scott F	author	4/12/49
Turturro, John	actor	2/28/57
Twiggy	actor	9/19/46
Tyler, Steven	musician	3/26/48
Udall, Mark	representative	7/18/50
Udall, Tom	representative	5/18/48
Ullman, Tracy	actor, comedian	12/30/59
Unser, Al Jr.	athlete	4/19/62
Urich, Robert	actor	12/19/47
Valvano, Jim	coach	3/10/46-4/28/93
Van Halen, Eddie	musician	1/26/57
Van Peebles, Mario	actor	1/15/57
Van Sant, Gus	director, writer	7/24/52
Vandross, Luther	musician	4/20/51
Ventura, Jesse	governor	7/15/51
Vereen, Ben	entertainer	10/10/46
Versace, Gianni	fashion designer	12/02/46-7/15/97
Vicious, Sid	musician	5/10/57-2/2/79
Vilsack, Tom	governor	12/13/50
Wadkins, Lanny	athlete	12/5/49
Wagner, Lindsay	actor	6/22/49
Wagner, Lisa	athlete	5/19/61
Waits, Tom	musician	12/7/49
Walker, Herschel	athlete	3/3/62
Wallace, Rusty	athlete	8/14/56
Walsh, Joe	musician	11/20/47
Walton, Bill	athlete	11/5/52
Washington, Denzel	actor	12/28/54
Wasserstein, Wendy	author	10/10/50
Waters, John	director	4/22/46
Watson, Tom	athlete	9/4/49
Watterson, Bill	cartoonist	1958
Watts, Andre	musician	6/20/46
Watts, J.C.	politician	11/18/57
Wayans, Damon	actor, comedian	9/4/60
Wayans, Keenan Ivory	actor, comedian	6/8/58
Weathers, Carl	actor	1/14/48
Weaver, Sigourney	actor	10/8/49
Weber, Andrew Lloyd	composer	3/22/48
Wenner, Jann	publisher	1/7/46
West, Cornel	scholar, critic	6/2/53
Whitaker, Forest	actor, director	7/15/61
Whitaker, Pernell	athlete	1/2/64
White, Reggie	athlete	12/19/61
White, Vanna	TV personality	2/18/57
Whitman, Christine Todd	governor	9/26/46
Wiest, Dianne	actor	3/28/48
Wilkins, Dominique	athlete	1/12/60
Wilkinson, Signe	cartoonist	1950
Williams, Hank, Jr.	musician	5/26/49
Williams, Jody	activist	10/9/50
Williams, Montel	talk-show host	7/3/56
Williams, Robin	actor, comedian	7/21/52
Williams, Vanessa	actor, musician	3/18/63
Williams, Walter Ray, Jr.	athlete	10/6/59
Willis, Bruce	actor	3/19/55
Wilson, Cassandra	musician	12/04/55
Winfield, Dave	athlete	10/3/51
Winfrey, Oprah	talk-show host, actor	1/29/54
Winger, Debra	actor	5/16/55
Winningham, Mare	actor	5/6/59
Winwood, Steve	musician	5/12/48
Wonder, Stevie	musician	5/13/50
Woo, John	director	5/1/46
Woodard, Alfre	actor	11/2/53
Woods, James	actor	4/18/47
Wright, Steven	actor	12/6/55
Wyden, Ron	senator	5/3/49
Yankovic,Weird Al	musician, comedian	10/23/59
Yanni	musician	11/4/54
Yearwood, Trisha	musician	9/19/64
Yoakam, Dwight	musician	10/23/56
Young, Sean	actor	11/20/59
Young, Sheila	athlete	10/14/50
Young, Steve	athlete	10/11/61
Yount, Robert	athlete	9/16/55
Zahn, Paula	TV anchor	2/24/56
Zemeckis, Robert	director	5/14/51
Zukerman, Pinchas	musician	7/16/48

Note: Individuals are either American or have careers of significance in the United States.

POPULATION

(in thousands)	
1940	132,594
1941	133,894
1942	135,361
1943	137,250
1944	138,916
1945	140,468
1946	141,936
1947	144,698
1948	147,208
1949	149,767

Percent increase in population from 1930 to 1940: 7.2

BIRTHS AND DEATH

(in thousands)	Births	Deaths
1940	2,360	1,417
1941	2,513	1,398
1942	2,809	1,385
1943	2,935	1,451
1944	2,795	1,411
1945	2,735	1,402
1946	3,289	1,396
1947	3,700	1,445
1948	3,535	1,444
1949	3,581	1,446

MARRIAGE AND DIVORCE

(in thousands)	Marriages	Divorces
1940	1,596	264
1941	1,696	293
1942	1,772	321
1943	1,577	359
1944	1,452	400
1945	1,613	485
1946	2,292	610
1947	1,992	474
1948	1,811	408
1949	1,585	386

MEDIAN MONEY INCOME OF PERSONS WITH INCOME IN 1947

Males	$2,406
Females	$1,372

GROSS DOMESTIC PRODUCT

	Gross domestic product	Percentage change from previous year
1940	$101.2	10.1
1941	$126.7	25.2
1942	$161.6	27.6
1943	$198.3	22.7
1944	$219.7	10.8
1945	$223.2	1.6
1946	$222.6	-.3
1947	$244.6	9.9
1948	$269.7	10.3
1949	$267.8	-.7

Note: In billions; current U.S. dollars.

HOUSEHOLD CHARACTERISTICS

	Number of households[1]	Median size of household
1940	34,949	3.77
1941	35,850	3.67
1942	46,450	3.59
1943	36,875	3.46
1944	37,500	3.41
1945	37,500	3.40
1946	38,183	3.61
1947	39,138	3.63
1948	40,720	3.56
1949	42,107	3.50

[1] In thousands.

LABOR

(in thousands)

	Total labor force age 14 and over (including armed forces)	Total civilian labor force	Number of males in civilian labor force	Number of females in civilian labor force	Civilian labor force: number employed	Civilian labor force: number unemployed
1940	56,030	55,640	41,480	14,160	47,530	8,120
1941	57,380	55,910	41,270	14,640	50,350	5,560
1942	60,230	56,410	40,300	16,110	53,750	2,660
1943	64,410	55,540	36,840	18,700	54,470	1,070
1944	65,890	54,630	35,460	19,170	53,960	670
1945	65,140	53,860	34,830	19,030	52,820	1,040
1946	60,820	57,520	40,740	16,780	55,250	2,270
1947	61,608	60,168	43,272	16,896	58,027	2,142
1948	62,748	61,442	43,858	17,583	59,378	2,064
1949	63,571	62,105	44,075	18,030	58,710	3,395

EDUCATION

	Percent of 5-17 year olds enrolled in public elementary and secondary schools	Number of teachers in public elementary and secondary schools	Average annual salary of instructional staff in public elementary and secondary schools	Expenditures for public elementary and secondary schools (per capita)	Number of high school graduates (public and private)	Number of college graduates (public and private)
1940	85.5	875,477	$1,441	$91.64	1,221,475	186,500
1942	84.2	858,888	$1,507	$94.21	1,242,375	185,346
1944	80.4	827,990	$1,728	$105.04	1,019,233	125,875
1946	80.6	831,026	$1,995	$145.88	1,080,033	136,174
1948	79.4	860,678	$2,639	$204.86	1,189,909	271,019

AGE AND SEX

(in thousands)

	1940	1941	1942	1943	1944	1945	1946	1947	1948	1949
TOTAL Males	66,062	n.a.	n.a.	n.a.	69,047	69,695	70,380	n.a.	72,965	74,243
0 to 4 years	5,355	n.a.	n.a.	n.a.	6,438	6,702	6,840	n.a.	7,712	8,069
5 to 9 years	5,419	n.a.	n.a.	n.a.	5,683	5,777	5,922	n.a.	6,577	6,865
10 to 14 years	5,952	n.a.	n.a.	n.a.	5,448	5,399	5,390	n.a.	5,527	5,676
15 to 19 years	6,180	n.a.	n.a.	n.a.	5,997	5,895	5,814	n.a.	5,558	5,440
20 to 24 years	5,692	n.a.	n.a.	n.a.	6,076	6,035	6,028	n.a.	5,993	5,950
25 to 29 years	5,451	n.a.	n.a.	n.a.	5,575	5,590	5,652	n.a.	5,878	5,974
30 to 34 years	5,070	n.a.	n.a.	n.a.	5,346	5,385	5,403	n.a.	5,453	5,505
35 to 39 years	4,746	n.a.	n.a.	n.a.	4,947	5,014	5,078	n.a.	5,230	5,307
40 to 44 years	4,419	n.a.	n.a.	n.a.	4,599	4,661	4,713	n.a.	4,825	4,892
45 to 49 years	4,209	n.a.	n.a.	n.a.	4,242	4,275	4,313	n.a.	4,426	4,495
50 to 54 years	3,753	n.a.	n.a.	n.a.	3,949	3,977	3,995	n.a.	4,022	4,050
55 to 59 years	3,011	n.a.	n.a.	n.a.	3,382	3,455	3,515	n.a.	3,620	3,659
60 to 64 years	2,398	n.a.	n.a.	n.a.	2,611	2,677	2,754	n.a.	2,932	3,017
65 to 69 years	1,896	n.a.	n.a.	n.a.	1,976	2,006	2,043	n.a.	2,134	2,190
70 to 74 years	1,271	n.a.	n.a.	n.a.	1,398	1,423	1,449	n.a.	1,499	1,524
75 years and over	1,239	n.a.	n.a.	n.a.	1,380	1,422	1,470	n.a.	1,578	1,630
TOTAL Females	65,608	n.a.	n.a.	n.a.	69,054	69,926	70,849	n.a.	73,607	74,973
0 to 4 years	5,187	n.a.	n.a.	n.a.	6,206	6,445	6,576	n.a.	7,394	7,737
5 to 9 years	5,266	n.a.	n.a.	n.a.	5,485	5,570	5,711	n.a.	6,316	6,588
10 to 14 years	5,794	n.a.	n.a.	n.a.	5,301	5,250	5,232	n.a.	5,353	5,485
15 to 19 years	6,153	n.a.	n.a.	n.a.	5,859	5,756	5,667	n.a.	5,424	5,311
20 to 24 years	5,895	n.a.	n.a.	n.a.	6,120	6,122	6,126	n.a.	6,021	5,934
25 to 29 years	5,646	n.a.	n.a.	n.a.	5,825	5,880	5,956	n.a.	6,122	6,182
30 to 34 years	5,172	n.a.	n.a.	n.a.	5,547	5,621	5,686	n.a.	5,787	5,844
35 to 39 years	4,800	n.a.	n.a.	n.a.	5,059	5,137	5,228	n.a.	5,435	5,536
40 to 44 years	4,369	n.a.	n.a.	n.a.	4,668	4,739	4,811	n.a.	4,940	5,020
45 to 49 years	4,046	n.a.	n.a.	n.a.	4,221	4,277	4,345	n.a.	4,509	4,598
50 to 54 years	3,504	n.a.	n.a.	n.a.	3,846	3,907	3,961	n.a.	4,050	4,105
55 to 59 years	2,833	n.a.	n.a.	n.a.	3,239	3,334	3,425	n.a.	3,602	3,682
60 to 64 years	2,331	n.a.	n.a.	n.a.	2,556	2,629	2,714	n.a.	2,918	3,026
65 to 69 years	1,911	n.a.	n.a.	n.a.	2,027	2,065	2,107	n.a.	2,213	2,281
70 to 74 years	1,299	n.a.	n.a.	n.a.	1,497	1,539	1,578	n.a.	1,647	1,686
75 years and over	1,404	n.a.	n.a.	n.a.	1,598	1,655	1,726	n.a.	1,878	1,959

RACE

(in thousands)

	White[1]	Black	Indian	Chinese	Japanese	All other[2]
1940	118,215	12,866	334	78	127	50
1941	n.a.	n.a.	n.a.	n.a.	n.a.	n.a.
1942	n.a.	n.a.	n.a.	n.a.	n.a.	n.a.
1943	n.a.	n.a.	n.a.	n.a.	n.a.	n.a.
1944	123,791			14,310		
1945	125,053			14,568		
1946	126,423			14,806		
1947	n.a.			n.a		
1948	131,127			15,445		
1949	133,446			15,770		

[1] White population includes Mexicans for all years.
[2] Comprises Filipinos, Hindus, Koreans, Hawaiians, Malays, Siamese, Samoans, and Maoris.

IMMIGRATION

	Total number of immigrants admitted	Naturalization certificates issued
1940	70,756	235,260
1941	51,776	277,294
1942	28,781	270,364
1943	23,725	318,933
1944	28,551	441,979
1945	38,119	231,402
1946	108,721	150,062
1947	147,292	93,901
1948	170,570	70,150
1949	188,317	66,954

Note: Structure of data may change from year to year due to changes in collection and reporting procedures of the data providers.

POPULATION

(in thousands)

1950	152,271
1951	154,878
1952	157,553
1953	160,184
1954	163,026
1955	165,931
1956	168,903
1957	171,984
1958	174,882
1959	177,830

Percent increase in population from 1940 to 1950: 14.5

BIRTHS AND DEATHS

(in thousands)

	Births	Deaths
1950	3,544	1,452
1951	3,751	1,482
1952	3,824	1,494
1953	3,902	1,518
1954	4,017	1,481
1955	4,047	1,529
1956	4,163	1,564
1957	4,255	1,633
1958	4,204	1,648
1959	4,249	1,660

MARRIAGE AND DIVORCE

(in thousands)

	Marriages	Divorces
1950	1,667	385
1951	1,595	381
1952	1,563	388
1953	1,546	390
1954	1,490	379
1955	1,531	377
1956	1,585	382
1957	1,518	381
1958	1,451	368
1959	1,494	396

MEDIAN MONEY INCOME OF PERSONS WITH INCOME IN 1950

Males	$2,831
Females	$1,559

MEDIAN MONEY INCOME OF PERSONS WITH INCOME IN 1955

Males	$3,797
Females	$1,926

GROSS DOMESTIC PRODUCT

	Gross domestic product	Percentage change from previous year
1950	$294.6	10.0
1951	$339.7	15.3
1952	$358.6	5.5
1953	$379.7	5.9
1954	$381.3	1.4
1955	$415.1	8.9
1956	$438.0	5.5
1957	$461.0	5.3
1958	$467.3	1.4
1959	$507.2	8.5

Note: In billions; current U.S. dollars.

HOUSEHOLD CHARACTERISTICS

	Number of households[1]	Median size of household
1950	43,554	3.47
1951	44,656	3.44
1952	45,504	3.44
1953	46,334	3.43
1954	46,893	3.45
1955	47,788	3.45
1956	48,785	3.43
1957	49,543	3.44
1958	50,402	3.44
1959	51,302	3.42

[1] In thousands.

LABOR

(in thousands)

	Total labor force age 14 and over (including armed forces)	Total civilian labor force	Number of males in civilian labor force	Number females in civilian labor force	Civilian labor force: number employed	Civilian labor force: number unemployed
1950	64,749	63,099	44,442	18,657	59,748	3,351
1951	65,983	62,884	43,612	19,272	60,784	2,099
1952	66,560	62,966	43,454	19,513	61,035	1,932
1953	67,362	63,815	44,194	19,621	61,945	1,870
1954	67,818	64,468	44,537	19,931	60,890	3,578
1955	68,896	65,848	45,041	20,806	62,944	2,904
1956	70,397	67,530	45,756	21,774	64,708	2,822
1957	70,744	67,946	45,882	22,064	65,011	2,939
1958	71,284	68,647	46,197	22,451	63,966	4,681
1959	71,946	69,394	46,562	22,832	65,581	3,813

EDUCATION

	Percent of 5-17 year olds enrolled in public elementary and secondary schools	Number of teachers in public elementary and secondary schools	Average annual salary of instructional staff in public elementary and secondary schools	Expenditures for public elementary and secondary schools (per capita)	Number of high school graduates (public and private)	Number of college graduates (public and private)
1950	83.2	914,000	$3,010	$208.83	1,199,700	432,058
1952	84.7	962,864	$3,450	$312.68	1,196,500	329,986
1954	83.5	1,042,000	$3,825	$264.76	1,276,100	290,825
1956	83.6	1,149,000	$4,156	$294.22	1,414,800	308,812
1958	83.5	1,261,000	$4,702	$341.14	1,505,900	308,812

AGE AND SEX

(in thousands)

	1950	1951	1952	1953	1954	1955	1956	1957	1958	1959
TOTAL Males	74,833	n.a.	78,104	73,337	80,696	82,001	83,355	84,858	86,206	87,651
0 to 4 years	8,236	n.a.	n.a.	n.a.	9,072	9,323	9,517	9,752	9,936	n.a.
5 to 9 years	6,715	n.a.	n.a.	n.a.	8,351	8,764	9,223	9,190	9,339	n.a.
10 to 14 years	5,660	n.a.	n.a.	n.a.	6,553	6,785	6,984	7,643	7,969	n.a.
15 to 19 years	5,311	n.a.	n.a.	n.a.	5,616	5,682	5,796	6,005	6,340	n.a.
20 to 24 years	5,606	n.a.	n.a.	n.a.	5,488	5,399	5,376	5,399	5,495	n.a.
25 to 29 years	5,972	n.a.	n.a.	n.a.	5,867	5,807	5,766	5,711	5,612	n.a.
30 to 34 years	5,625	n.a.	n.a.	n.a.	6,054	6,071	6,057	6,021	5,953	n.a.
35 to 39 years	5,518	n.a.	n.a.	n.a.	5,637	5,686	5,770	5,880	5,980	n.a.
40 to 44 years	5,070	n.a.	n.a.	n.a.	5,451	5,496	5,531	5,550	5,555	n.a.
45 to 49 years	4,526	n.a.	n.a.	n.a.	4,899	4,988	5,082	5,180	5,262	n.a.
50 to 54 years	4,129	n.a.	n.a.	n.a.	4,289	4,348	4,422	4,512	4,600	n.a.
55 to 59 years	3,630	n.a.	n.a.	n.a.	3,804	3,837	3,879	3,913	3,947	n.a.
60 to 64 years	3,038	n.a.	n.a.	n.a.	3,220	3,257	3,293	3,334	3,365	n.a.
65 to 69 years	2,425	n.a.	n.a.	n.a.	2,552	2,587	2,611	2,643	2,669	n.a.
70 to 74 years	1,629	n.a.	n.a.	n.a.	1,850	1,896	1,918	1,939	1,948	n.a.
75 years and over	1,744	n.a.	n.a.	n.a.	1,994	2,076	2,130	2,187	2,236	n.a.
TOTAL Females	75,864	n.a.	78,923	80,299	81,718	83,245	84,737	86,371	87,858	89,452
0 to 4 years	7,927	n.a.	n.a.	n.a.	8,735	8,982	9,163	9,392	9,569	n.a.
5 to 9 years	6,485	n.a.	n.a.	n.a.	7,996	8,384	8,830	8,803	8,948	n.a.
10 to 14 years	5,459	n.a.	n.a.	n.a.	6,333	6,555	6,731	7,345	7,645	n.a.
15 to 19 years	5,305	n.a.	n.a.	n.a.	5,439	5,504	5,626	5,826	6,149	n.a.
20 to 24 years	5,876	n.a.	n.a.	n.a.	5,411	5,367	5,335	5,355	5,425	n.a.
25 to 29 years	6,270	n.a.	n.a.	n.a.	6,033	5,937	5,851	5,758	5,635	n.a.
30 to 34 years	5,892	n.a.	n.a.	n.a.	6,289	6,321	6,315	6,277	6,196	n.a.
35 to 39 years	5,729	n.a.	n.a.	n.a.	5,858	5,914	6,003	6,119	6,227	n.a.
40 to 44 years	5,134	n.a.	n.a.	n.a.	5,640	5,713	5,763	5,791	5,803	n.a.
45 to 49 years	4,544	n.a.	n.a.	n.a.	4,985	5,103	5,228	5,361	5,480	n.a.
50 to 54 years	4,144	n.a.	n.a.	n.a.	4,385	4,461	4,551	4,658	4,765	n.a.
55 to 59 years	3,605	n.a.	n.a.	n.a.	3,939	4,002	4,065	4,119	4,170	n.a.
60 to 64 years	3,022	n.a.	n.a.	n.a.	3,355	3,433	3,509	3,587	3,657	n.a.
65 to 69 years	2,578	n.a.	n.a.	n.a.	2,708	2,766	2,828	2,899	2,972	n.a.
70 to 74 years	1,783	n.a.	n.a.	n.a.	2,123	2,183	2,222	2,256	2,280	n.a.
75 years and over	2,111	n.a.	n.a.	n.a.	2,488	2,619	2,716	2,826	2,935	n.a.

RACE

(in thousands)

	White	Black	Indian	Chinese	Japanese	All other[1]
1950	134,942	15,042	343	118	142	110
1951	138,120			16,241		
1952	140,412			16,616		
1953	142,633			17,003		
1954	144,995			17,423		
1955	147,406			17,864		
1956	149,853			18,323		
1957	152,388			18,810		
1958	154,771			19,283		
1959	157,290			19,813		

[1] *Comprises Filipinos, Hindus, Koreans, Hawaiians, Malays, Siamese, Samoans, and Maoris.*

IMMIGRATION

	Total number of immigrants admitted	Naturalization certificates issued
1950	249,187	66,346
1951	205,717	54,716
1952	265,520	88,655
1953	170,434	92,051
1954	208,177	117,831
1955	237,790	209,526
1956	321,625	145,885
1957	326,867	138,043
1958	253,265	119,866
1959	260,686	103,931

Note: Structure of data may change from year to year due to changes in collection and reporting procedures of the data providers.

POPULATION

(in thousands)

1960	180,684
1961	183,756
1962	186,656
1963	189,417
1964	192,120
1965	194,592
1966	196,907
1967	199,119
1968	201,177
1969	203,213

Percent increase in population from 1950 to 1960: 18.4

BIRTHS AND DEATHS

(in thousands)

	Births	Deaths
1960	4,258	1,712
1961	4,268	1,702
1962	4,167	1,757
1963	4,098	1,814
1964	4,027	1,798
1965	3,760	1,828
1966	3,606	1,863
1967	3,521	1,851
1968	3,502	1,923
1969	3,571	1,916

MARRIAGE AND DIVORCE

(in thousands)

	Marriages	Divorces
1960	1,523	393
1961	1,548	414
1962	1,577	413
1963	1,654	428
1964	1,725	450
1965	1,800	479
1966	1,857	499
1967	1,927	523
1968	2,059	582
1969	2,146	660

MEDIAN MONEY INCOME OF PERSONS WITH INCOME IN 1960

Males	$4,822
Females	$2,348

SELECTED PER CAPITA INCOME

1960	$2,277
1965	$2,869

GROSS DOMESTIC PRODUCT

	Gross domestic product	Percentage change from previous year
1960	$526.6	3.8
1961	$544.8	3.5
1962	$585.2	7.4
1963	$617.4	5.5
1964	$663.0	7.4
1965	$719.1	8.5
1966	$787.8	9.5
1967	$833.6	5.8
1968	$910.6	9.2
1969	$982.2	7.9

Note: In billions; current U.S. dollars.

HOUSEHOLD CHARACTERISTICS

	Number of households[1]	Median size of household
1960	52,799	3.33
1961	53,291	n.a.
1962	54,652	3.31
1963	55,189	n.a
1964	55,996	3.33
1965	57,251	3.31
1966	58,092	3.3
1967	58,845	3.28
1968	60,444	3.23
1969	61,805	3.19

[1] In thousands.

LABOR

(in thousands)

	Total labor force age 14 and over (including armed forces)	Total civilian labor force	Number of males in civilian labor force	Number of females in civilian labor force	Civilian labor force: number employed	Civilian labor force: number unemployed
1960	72,142	69,628	46,388	23,240	65,778	3,852
1961	74,175	71,603	47,378	24,225	66,796	4,806
1962	74,681	71,854	47,380	24,474	67,846	4,007
1963	74,571	71,833	47,129	24,704	67,762	4,070
1964	75,830	73,091	47,679	25,412	69,305	3,786
1965	77,178	74,455	48,255	26,200	71,088	3,366
1966	78,893	75,770	48,471	27,299	72,895	2,875
1967	80,793	77,347	48,987	28,360	74,372	2,975
1968	82,272	78,737	49,533	29,204	75,920	2,817
1969	84,239	80,733	50,221	30,512	77,902	2,831

EDUCATION

	Percent of 5-17 year olds enrolled in public elementary and secondary schools	Number of teachers in public elementary and secondary schools	Average annual salary of instructional staff in public elementary and secondary schools	Expenditures for public elementary and secondary schools (per capita)	Number of high school graduates (public and private)	Number of college graduates (public and private)
1960	82.2	1,387,000	$5,174	$375	1,864,000	392,000
1962	n.a.	n.a.	n.a.	n.a.	1,925,000	417,000
1964	85.5	1,625,000	$6,240	$460	2,290,000	498,000
1966	85.7	1,786,000	$6,935	$537	2,672,000	556,000
1968	86.7	1,962,000	$7,883	$659	2,702,000	672,000

AGE AND SEX

(in thousands)

	1960	1961	1962	1963[1]	1964[1]	1965	1966	1967[1]	1968[1]	1969[1]
TOTAL Males	88,331	90,736	92,117	92,626	93,935	95,875	95,920	96,694	97,569	98,482
0 to 4 years	10,330	10,487	10,559	10,554	10,532	10,432	10,135	9,795	9,452	9,164
5 to 9 years	9,504	9,748	10,010	10,171	10,304	10,426	10,580	10,642	10,655	10,622
10 to 14 years	8,524	9,075	8,997	9,153	9,351	9,635	9,861	10,101	10,277	10,425
15 to 19 years	6,634	6,958	7,576	7,748	8,133	8,655	8,950	8,909	9,129	9,294
20 to 24 years	5,272	5,734	5,945	6,023	6,303	6,872	6,625	7,042	7,242	7,607
25 to 29 years	5,333	5,409	5,391	5,336	5,441	11,091	5,632	5,875	6,243	6,485
30 to 34 years	5,846	5,805	5,727	5,537	5,441		5,326	5,323	5,392	5,494
35 to 39 years	6,080	11,994	12,012	11,942	11,942	11,961	11,738	11,601	11,452	11,294
40 to 44 years	5,676									
45 to 49 years	5,358	10,273	10,401	10,495	10,619	10,741	10,822	10,936	11,045	11,172
50 to 54 years	4,735									
55 to 59 years	4,127	7,659	7,775	7,891	8,020	8,130	8,131	8,370	8,491	8,630
60 to 64 years	3,409									
65 to 69 years	2,931	2,918	2,895	2,866	2,855	2,870		5,194	5,225	5,288
70 to 74 years	2,185						7,931			
75 to 79 years		4,727	4,828	4,911	4,993	5,061		2,461	2,497	2,517
80 to 84 years	2,387									
85 years and over								446	469	490
TOTAL Females	90,992	92,907	94,473	95,905	97,399	98,704	99,937	101,169	102,291	103,439
0 to 4 years	9,991	10,122	10,187	10,168	10,126	10,002	9,715	9,391	9,069	8,795
5 to 9 years	9,187	9,424	9,686	9,841	9,973	10,092	10,226	10,268	10,263	10,205
10 to 14 years	8,249	8,784	8,691	8,848	9,043	9,321	9,542	9,784	9,954	10,093
15 to 19 years	6,586	6,781	7,389	7,663	8,030	8,395	8,806	8,784	8,949	9,144
20 to 24 years	5,528	5,725	5,929	6,284	6,550	6,794	6,981	7,530	7,809	8,169
25 to 29 years	5,536	5,489	5,463	5,522	5,633	5,697	5,840	6,083	6,443	6,694
30 to 34 years	6,103	5,965	5,874	5,760	5,654	5,570	5,527	5,538	5,607	5,717
35 to 39 years	6,402	12,439	12,524	12,560	12,558	12,469	12,359	12,237	12,060	11,882
40 to 44 years	5,924									
45 to 49 years	5,522	10,617	10,801	10,970	11,146	11,303	11,476	11,652	11,814	11,981
50 to 54 years	4,871									
55 to 59 years	4,303	8,194	8,344	8,501	8,672	8,835	9,013	9,201	9,387	9,583
60 to 64 years	3,733									
65 to 69 years	3,327	3,363	3,373	3,376	3,391	3,427	3,476	6,484	6,560	6,667
70 to 74 years	2,554						2,929			
75 to 79 years		6,002	6,212	6,414	6,621	6,797	2,124	3,484	3,607	3,709
80 to 84 years	3,179						1,230			
85 years and over							694	727	769	799

[1] Excludes armed forces overseas.

RACE

(in thousands)

	White	Black	Indian	Chinese	Japanese	Filipino	All Other[1]
1960[2]	158,832	18,872	524	237	464	176	218
1961	162,488			21,154			
1962	164,930			21,660			
1963	166,454			22,078			
1964	168,754			22,580			
1965[2]	170,737	21,147		1,931			
1966[2]	172,416	21,519		2,001			
1967[2]	173,899	21,869		2,090			
1968[2]	175,475	22,210		2,161			
1969[2]	177,082	22,596		2,243			

[1] Comprises Asian Indians, Koreans, Polynesians, Indonesians, Hawaiians, Aleuts, Eskimos, and other races. [2] Excludes armed forces overseas.

IMMIGRATION

	Total number of immigrants admitted	Naturalization certificates issued
1960	265,099	119,442
1961	271,000	132,450
1962	284,000	127,307
1963	306,000	124,178
1964	292,000	112,234
1965	297,000	104,299
1966	323,000	103,059
1967	362,000	104,902
1968	454,000	102,726
1969	359,000	98,709

Note: Structure of data may change from year to year due to changes in collection and reporting procedures of the data providers.

POPULATION

(in thousands)	
1970	205,052
1971	207,661
1972	209,896
1973	211,909
1974	213,854
1975	215,973
1976	218,035
1977	220,239
1978	225,585
1979	225,055

Percent increase in population from
1960 to 1970: 13.4

BIRTHS AND DEATHS

(in thousands)

	Births	Deaths
1970	3,731	1,921
1971	3,556	1,928
1972	3,258	1,964
1973	3,137	1,973
1974	3,160	1,934
1975	3,144	1,893
1976	3,168	1,909
1977	3,327	1,900
1978	3,333	1,928
1979	3,473	1,906

MARRIAGE AND DIVORCE

(in thousands)

	Marriages	Divorces
1970	2,159	708
1971	2,190	773
1972	2,282	845
1973	2,284	915
1974	2,230	977
1975	2,153	1,036
1976	2,155	1,083
1977	2,178	1,091
1978	2,282	1,130
1979	2,359	1,170

SELECTED PER CAPITA INCOME

1970	$4,077
1975	$6,091

GROSS DOMESTIC PRODUCT

	Gross domestic product	Percentage change from previous year
1970	$1,035.6	5.4
1971	$1,125.4	8.7
1972	$1,237.3	9.9
1973	$1,382.6	11.7
1974	$1,496.9	8.3
1975	$1,630.6	8.9
1976	$1,819.0	11.5
1977	$2,026.9	11.4
1978	$2,291.4	13.0
1979	$2,557.5	11.6

Note: In billions; current U.S. dollars.

HOUSEHOLD CHARACTERISTICS

	Number of households[1]	Median size of household
1970	63,401	3.14
1971	64,374	3.14
1972	66,676	3.06
1973	68,251	3.07
1974	69,859	2.97
1975	71,120	2.94
1976	72,867	2.89
1977	74,142	2.91
1978	76,030	2.81
1979	77,330	2.78

[1] In thousands.

LABOR

(in thousands)

	Total labor force age 14 and over (including armed forces)	Total civilian labor force	Number of males in civilian labor force	Number females in civilian labor force	Civilian labor force: number employed	Civilian labor force: number unemployed
1970	85,903	82,715	51,195	31,520	78,627	4,088
1971	86,929	84,113	52,021	32,091	79,120	4,993
1972	88,991	86,542	53,265	33,277	81,702	4,840
1973	91,040	88,714	54,203	34,510	84,409	4,304
1974	93,240	91,011	55,186	35,825	85,936	5,076
1975	94,793	92,613	55,615	36,998	84,783	7,830
1976	96,917	94,773	56,359	38,414	87,485	7,288
1977	99,534	97,401	57,449	39,452	90,546	6,855
1978	102,537	100,420	58,542	41,878	94,373	6,047
1979	104,996	102,908	59,517	43,391	96,945	5,963

EDUCATION

	Percent of 5-17 year olds enrolled in public elementary and secondary schools	Number of teachers in public elementary and secondary schools	Average annual salary of instructional staff in public elementary and secondary schools	Expenditures for public elementary and secondary schools (per capita)	Number of high school graduates (public and private)	Number of college graduates (public and private)
1970	86.9	2,023,000	$8,840	$1,732	2,896,000	792,000
1972	88.1	2,070,000	$10,100	$1,878	3,043,000	921,000
1974	88.2	2,155,000	$11,185	$2,004	3,081,000	946,000
1976	88.9	2,196,000	$12,448	$2,097	3,154,000	926,000
1978	89.2	2,208,000	$14,244	$2,200	3,147,000	921,000

AGE AND SEX

(in thousands)

	1970	1971	1972	1973	1974	1975	1976	1977	1978	1979
TOTAL Males	100,269	101,253	102,051	102,800	103,454	104,202	104,927	105,699	106,502	107,006
0-4 years	8,742	8,821	8,803	8,500	8,329	8,115	7,840	7,790	7,855	8,003
5-13 years	18,667	18,365	17,998	17,700	17,375	17,047	16,811	16,438	16,005	15,643
14-17 years	8,101	8,270	8,397	8,500	8,595	8,624	8,605	8,555	8,486	8,298
18-21 years	7,437	5,739	5,867	6,100	8,149	8,343	8,490	8,585	8,651	8,541
22-24 years	5,000	7,267	7,268	7,200	5,396	5,567	5,703	5,826	5,934	5,989
25-34 years	12,521	12,788	13,562	14,200	14,770	15,348	15,912	16,464	16,862	17,252
35-44 years	11,316	11,230	11,142	11,200	11,158	11,149	11,272	11,496	11,909	12,213
45-54 years	11,251	11,303	11,355	11,500	11,505	11,490	11,436	11,326	11,239	11,137
55-64 years	8,828	8,908	8,990	9,100	9,211	9,344	9,488	9,650	9,782	9,915
65 years and over	8,407	8,562	8,671	8,900	8,966	9,176	9,371	9,569	9,778	10,017
TOTAL Females	104,609	105,796	106,786	107,600	108,455	109,338	110,215	111,119	112,046	113,093
0-4 years	8,406	8,468	8,439	8,200	7,976	7,767	7,503	7,446	7,507	7,646
5-13 years	17,968	17,680	17,333	17,000	16,708	16,391	16,151	15,789	15,373	15,004
14-17 years	7,809	7,974	8,093	8,200	8,283	8,310	8,288	8,228	8,153	7,977
18-21 years	7,270	5,595	5,695	5,900	7,958	8,140	8,277	8,372	8,434	8,451
22-24 years	4,980	7,180	7,174	7,200	5,404	5,553	5,693	5,819	5,925	6,049
25-34 years	12,772	13,030	13,792	14,400	15,000	15,570	16,138	16,684	17,074	17,611
35-44 years	11,826	11,730	11,632	11,700	11,665	11,666	11,808	12,047	12,474	12,862
45-54 years	12,059	12,157	12,236	12,300	12,315	12,279	12,204	12,063	11,945	11,814
55-64 years	9,838	8,908	10,113	10,200	10,296	10,431	10,576	10,746	10,886	11,037
65 years and over	11,681	12,005	12,278	12,600	12,849	13,228	13,576	13,925	14,276	14,641

RACE

(in thousands)

	White	Black	Indian	Chinese	Japanese	Filipino	All Other[1]
1970	177,749	22,580	793	435	591	343	721
1971	180,411	23,084			2,725		
1972	181,894	23,465			2,875		
1973	183,032	23,796			3,031		
1974	184,083	24,113			3,193		
1975	185,158	24,436			3,457		
1976	186,241	24,767			3,672		
1977	187,409	25,118			3,874		
1978	188,657	25,487			4,083		
1979	189,968	25,863			4,268		

[1] Comprises Asian Indians, Koreans, Polynesians, Indonesians, Hawaiians, Aleuts, Eskimos, and other races. *Note: Excludes armed forces overseas.*

IMMIGRATION

	Total number of immigrants admitted	Naturalization certificates issued
1970	373,000	110,000
1971	370,000	108,000
1972	385,000	116,000
1973	400,000	121,000
1974	395,000	132,000
1975	386,000	142,000
1976	399,000	143,000
1977	462,000	160,000
1978	601,000	174,000
1979	460,000	164,000

Note: Structure of data may change from year to year due to changes in collection and reporting procedures of the data providers.

POPULATION

(in thousands)

1980	227,757
1981	230,138
1982	232,520
1983	234,799
1984	237,001
1985	239,279
1986	241,625
1987	243,934
1988	246,329
1989	248,777

BIRTHS AND DEATHS

(in thousands)

	Births	Deaths
1980	3,612	1,990
1981	3,629	1,978
1982	3,681	1,975
1983	3,639	2,019
1984	3,669	2,039
1985	3,761	2,086
1986	3,757	2,105
1987	3,809	2,123
1988	3,910	2,168
1989	4,021	2,155

MARRIAGE AND DIVORCE

(in thousands)

	Marriages	Divorces
1980	2,390	1,189
1981	2,422	1,213
1982	2,456	1,170
1983	2,446	1,158
1984	2,477	1,169
1985	2,413	1,190
1986	2,407	1,178
1987	2,421	1,157
1988	2,389	1,183
1989	2,404	1,163

SELECTED PER CAPITA INCOME

1980	$10,037
1985	$14,464

GROSS DOMESTIC PRODUCT

	Gross domestic product	Percentage change from previous year
1980	$2,784.2	8.9
1981	$3,115.9	11.9
1982	$3,242.1	4.1
1983	$3,514.5	8.4
1984	$3,902.4	11.0
1985	$4,180.7	7.1
1986	$4,422.2	5.8
1987	$4,692.3	6.1
1988	$5,049.6	7.6
1989	$5,438.7	7.7

Note: In billions; current U.S. dollars.

HOUSEHOLD CHARACTERISTICS

	Number of households[1]	Median size of household
1980	80,776	2.76
1981	82,368	2.73
1982	83,527	2.72
1983	83,918	2.73
1984	85,407	2.71
1985	86,789	2.69
1986	88,458	2.67
1987	89,479	2.66
1988	91,066	2.64
1989	92,830	2.62

[1] In thousands.

LABOR

(in thousands)

	Total labor force age 14 and over (including armed forces)	Total civilian labor force	Number of males in civilian labor force	Number of females in civilian labor force	Civilian labor force: number employed	Civilian labor force: number unemployed
1980	108,544	106,940	61,453	45,487	99,303	7,637
1981	110,315	108,670	61,974	46,696	100,397	8,273
1982	111,872	110,204	62,450	47,755	99,526	10,678
1983	113,226	111,550	63,047	48,503	100,834	10,717
1984	115,241	113,544	63,835	49,709	105,005	8,539
1985	117,167	115,461	64,411	51,050	107,150	8,312
1986	119,540	117,834	65,422	52,413	109,597	8,237
1987	121,602	119,865	66,207	53,658	112,440	7,425
1988	123,378	121,669	66,927	54,742	114,968	6,701
1989	125,557	123,869	67,800	56,000	117,342	6,528

EDUCATION

	Percent of 5-17 year olds enrolled in public elementary and secondary schools	Number of teachers in public elementary and secondary schools	Average annual salary of instructional staff in public elementary and secondary schools	Expenditures for public elementary and secondary schools (per capita in average daily attendance)	Number of high school graduates (public)	Number of bachelor's degrees conferred
1980	87.0	2,211,000	$16,715	$2,230	2,762,000	929,417
1982	86.6	2,158,000	$20,327	$2,753	2,711,000	935,000
1984	87.3	2,142,000	$22,994	$3,185	2,503,000	969,510
1986	87.9	2,213,000	$26,322	$3,768	2,388,000	987,823
1988	88.6	2,283,000	$29,177	$4,257	2,464,000	994,829

AGE AND SEX

(in thousands)

	1980	1981	1982	1983	1984	1985	1986	1987	1988	1989
TOTAL Males	110,888	111,423	112,498	113,714	114,765	116,648	117,360	118,987	120,203	121,445
0 to 4 years	8,417	8,667	8,886	9,121	9,115	9,213	9,274	9,341	9,446	9,598
5 to 9ears	8,495	8,204	8,161	8,174	8,367	8,609	8,851	9,037	9,226	9,321
10 to 14 years	9,314	9,321	9,214	9,091	8,994	8,762	8,487	8,450	8,525	8,689
15 to 19 years	10,776	10,363	10,084	9,767	9,551	9,478	9,483	9,446	9,322	9,123
20 to 24 years	10,882	10,914	10,906	10,933	10,684	10,707	10,232	10,083	9,773	9,529
25 to 29 years	9,897	9,995	10,298	10,539	10,615	11,006	11,026	11,119	11,064	10,979
30 to 34 years	8,845	9,273	9,234	9,445	9,715	10,166	10,367	10,727	10,973	11,151
35 to 39 years	6,964	7,087	7,701	8,012	8,278	8,793	9,256	9,321	9,530	9,782
40 to 44 years	5,756	5,896	6,095	6,453	6,784	6,910	7,030	7,662	7,939	8,319
45 to 49 years	5,376	5,342	5,367	5,443	5,570	5,684	5,817	6,031	6,365	6,608
50 to 54 years	5,619	5,546	5,453	5,367	5,319	5,284	5,260	5,286	5,394	5,511
55 to 59 years	5,480	5,474	5,429	5,410	5,412	5,383	5,359	5,298	5,195	5,121
60 to 64 years	4,700	4,782	4,892	4,969	5,062	5,188	5,097	5,068	5,096	5,079
65 to 74 years	6,791	6,892	7,003	7,105	7,317	7,475	7,645	7,824	7,945	8,095
75 years and over	3,575	3,668	3,775	3,887	3,982	4,062	4,178	4,295	4,409	4,541
TOTAL Females	116,869	117,884	119,035	120,267	121,393	122,631	123,718	124,928	126,126	127,317
0 to 4 years	8,040	8,272	8,486	8,705	8,702	8,792	8,854	8,910	9,009	9,155
5 to 9 years	8,114	7,841	7,796	7,807	7,984	8,214	8,440	8,625	8,802	8,891
10 to 14 years	8,923	8,921	8,811	8,690	8,573	8,339	8,077	8,035	8,102	8,260
15 to 19 years	10,382	10,015	9,708	9,404	9,216	9,109	9,128	9,051	8,926	8,725
20 to 24 years	10,702	10,818	10,810	10,780	10,626	10,507	10,185	9,901	9,600	9,356
25 to 29 years	9,906	10,072	10,359	10,562	10,694	10,886	10,984	10,989	10,943	10,851
30 to 34 years	8,977	9,463	9,410	9,600	9,887	10,179	10,407	10,683	10,905	11,068
35 to 39 years	7,160	7,320	7,937	8,243	8,535	8,969	9,467	9,469	9,664	9,894
40 to 44 years	5,988	6,147	6,346	6,716	7,052	7,167	7,316	7,929	8,210	8,589
45 to 49 years	5,677	5,643	5,676	5,741	5,847	5,968	6,110	6,326	6,668	6,921
50 to 54 years	6,080	5,999	5,877	5,785	5,694	5,661	5,627	5,641	5,744	5,866
55 to 59 years	6,136	6,126	6,092	6,064	6,037	5,960	5,909	5,823	5,701	5,605
60 to 64 years	5,446	5,553	5,681	5,777	5,805	5,877	5,865	5,831	5,837	5,788
65 to 74 years	8,862	9,000	9,131	9,257	9,429	9,534	9,681	9,844	9,953	10,087
75 years and over	6,476	6,693	6,915	7,135	7,312	7,469	7,669	7,873	8,061	8,261

RACE

(in thousands)

	Total	Hispanic origin	Not of Hispanic origin — White	Black	American Indian, Eskimo, Aleut	Asian, Pacific Islander
1980 (April)	226,546	14,609	180,906	26,142	1,326	3,563
1981	229,466	15,560	181,974	26,532	1,377	4,022
1982	233,792	16,240	182,782	26,856	1,420	4,367
1983	235,825	16,935	183,561	27,159	1,466	4,671
1984	237,924	17,640	184,243	27,444	1,512	4,986
1985	240,133	18,368	184,945	27,738	1,558	5,315
1986	242,289	19,154	185,678	28,040	1,606	5,655
1987	244,499	19,946	186,353	28,351	1,654	5,985
1988	246,819	20,786	187,012	28,669	1,703	6,329
1989	248,765	21,648	187,713	29,005	1,755	6,698

Note: Excludes armed forces overseas.

IMMIGRATION

	Total number of immigrants[1] (in thousands)
1980	531,000
1981	597,000
1982	594,000
1983	560,000
1984	544,000
1985	570,000
1986	602,000
1987	602,000
1988	643,000
1989	1,090,000

[1] *Includes persons granted permanent residence under the legalization program of the Immigration Reform and Control Act (IRCA) of 1986.*

Note: Structure of data may change from year to year due to changes in collection and reporting procedures of the data providers.

POPULATION

(in thousands)

1990	249,949
1991	252,636
1992	255,382
1993	258,089
1994	260,602
1995	263,039
1996	265,453
1997	267,901
1998	268,922

Percent increase in population from 1980 to 1990: 9.8

BIRTHS AND DEATHS

(in thousands)

	Births	Deaths
1990	4,158	2,148
1991	4,111	2,170
1992	4,065	2,176
1993	4,000	2,269
1994	3,979	2,286
1995	3,900	2,312
1996	3,915	2,322
1997	3,882[1]	2,294

[1] *Preliminary estimates.*

MARRIAGE AND DIVORCE

(in thousands)

	Marriages	Divorces
1990	2,443	1,182
1991	2,371	1,187
1992	2,362	1,215
1993	2,334	1,187
1994	2,362	1,191
1995	2,336	1,169
1996	2,344	1,150
1997	2,384	1,163

SELECTED PER CAPITA INCOME

1990	$19,220
1995	$23,370A

GROSS DOMESTIC PRODUCT

	Gross domestic product	Percentage change from previous year
1990	$5,743.8	5.6
1991	$5,916.7	3.0
1992	$6,244.4	5.5
1993	$6,558.1	5.0
1994	$6,947.0	5.9
1995	$7,269.6	4.6
1996	$7,661.6	5.4
1997	$8,110.9	5.9
1998	$8,511.0	

Note: In billions; current U.S. dollars.

HOUSEHOLD CHARACTERISTICS

	Number of households[1]	Median size of household
1990	93,347	2.63
1991	94,312	2.63
1992	95,669	2.62
1993	96,391	2.63
1994	97,107	2.67
1995	98,990	2.65
1996	99,627	2.65
1997	101,018	2.64

[1] *In thousands.*

LABOR

(in thousands)

	Total civilian labor force	Number of males in civilian labor force	Number females in civilian labor force	Civilian labor force: number employed	Civilian labor force: number unemployed
1990	124,800	68,200	56,600	118,793	7,047
1991	126,346	68,400	56,900	117,718	8,628
1992	128,105	69,200	57,800	118,492	9,613
1993	129,200	68,200	56,600	120,259	8,940
1994	131,056	70,800	60,200	123,060	7,996
1995	132,304	71,400	60,900	124,900	7,404
1996	133,943	72,100	61,900	126,708	7,236
1997	136,297	73,300	63,000	129,558	6,739

EDUCATION

	Percent of 5-17 year olds enrolled in public elementary and secondary schools	Number of teachers in public elementary and secondary schools	Average annual salary of instructional staff in public elementary and secondary schools	Expenditures for public elementary and secondary schools (per capita of enrollment)	Number of high school graduates (public)
1990	90.2	2,362,000	$32,638	$4,604	2,320,300
1992	91.4	2,428,000	$35,552	$4,966	2,211,900
1994	91.5	2,512,000	$37,446	$5,333	2,227,000
1996	91.3	2,606,000	$39,465	$5,695	2,283,000
1997	91.2	2,668,000	$40,562	$5,911	2,336,000

AGE AND SEX

(in thousands)

	1990	1991	1992	1993	1994	1995	1996	1997
TOTAL Males	121,239	122,979	124,493	125,921	127,076	128,314	129,810	131,018
0 to 4 years	9,599	9,836	9,986	n.a.	10,094	10,025	9,868	9,801
5 to 9 years	9,232	9,337	9,396	n.a.	9,657	9,843	9,954	10,104
10 to 14 years	8,739	9,051	9,271	n.a.	9,602	9,685	9,727	9,757
15 to 19 years	9,173	8,834	8,762	n.a.	9,036	9,265	9,619	9,827
20 to 24 years	9,743	9,775	9,706	n.a.	9,311	9,087	8,999	8,979
25 to 29 years	10,702	10,393	10,140	n.a.	9,619	9,530	9,538	9,470
30 to 34 years	10,862	11,034	11,107	n.a.	11,058	10,902	10,653	10,340
35 to 39 years	9,833	10,174	10,481	n.a.	10,920	11,071	11,259	11,286
40 to 44 years	8,676	9,258	9,287	n.a.	9,728	9,990	10,310	10,596
45 to 49 years	6,739	6,907	7,541	n.a.	8,181	8,560	9,060	9,074
50 to 54 years	5,493	5,656	5,858	n.a.	6,410	6,622	6,776	7,383
55 to 59 years	5,008	4,987	5,022	n.a.	5,244	5,317	5,455	5,646
60 to 64 years	4,947	4,945	4,891	n.a.	4,740	4,727	4,711	4,745
65 to 74 years	7,907	8,022	8,126	n.a.	8,290	8,342	8,325	8,268
75 to 84 years	4,586	4,769	4,010	n.a.	4,206	4,330	4,486	4,628
85 years and over			909	n.a.	980	1,017	1,070	1,112
TOTAL Females	127,470	129,198	130,589	132,006	133,265	134,441	135,474	136,618
0 to 4 years	9,159	9,386	9,526	n.a.	9,633	9,566	9,418	9,349
5 to 9 years	8,803	8,900	8,954	n.a.	9,201	9,377	9,487	9,634
10 to 14 years	8,322	8,620	8,829	n.a.	9,150	9,229	9,254	9,283
15 to 19 years	8,709	8,371	8,312	n.a.	8,580	8,799	9,043	9,241
20 to 24 years	9,389	9,419	9,345	n.a.	9,015	8,795	8,561	8,532
25 to 29 years	10,625	10,325	10,049	n.a.	9,558	9,476	9,469	9,399
30 to 34 years	10,971	11,125	11,166	n.a.	11,119	10,966	10,708	10,401
35 to 39 years	10,013	10,344	10,618	n.a.	11,040	11,178	11,318	11,338
40 to 44 years	8,913	9,496	9,518	n.a.	9,970	10,228	10,506	10,777
45 to 49 years	7,004	7,188	7,820	n.a.	8,498	8,889	9,376	9,396
50 to 54 years	5,820	5,989	6,198	n.a.	6,781	7,008	7,157	7,780
55 to 59 years	5,479	5,436	5,464	n.a.	5,692	5,767	5,907	6,111
60 to 64 years	5,679	5,637	5,550	n.a.	5,342	5,320	5,288	5,311
65 to 74 years	10,139	10,258	10,336	n.a.	10,422	10,417	10,345	10,230
75 to 84 years	8,447	8,705	6,555	n.a.	6,719	6,815	6,944	7,077
85 years and over			2,349	n.a.	2,542	2,611	2,692	2,759

[1] *Excludes armed forces overseas.*

RACE

(in thousands)

	Total	Hispanic origin	White	Black	American Indian, Eskimo, Aleut	Asian, Pacific Islander
			Not of Hispanic origin			
1990 (April)	248,765	22,372	188,307	29,299	1,796	6,992
1991	252,124	23,432	189,590	29,849	1,829	7,425
1992	255,002	24,361	190,657	30,333	1,856	7,794
1993	257,753	25,334	191,606	30,778	1,882	8,153
1994	260,292	26,302	192,426	31,189	1,906	8,469
1995	262,761	27,274	193,198	31,566	1,929	8,794
1996	265,179	28,305	193,875	31,927	1,952	9,120
1997	267,636	29,348	194,571	32,298	1,976	9,443

Note: Excludes armed forces overseas.

IMMIGRATION

	Total number of immigrants[1] (in thousands)
1990	1,536,000
1991	1,827,000
1992	974,000
1993	904,000
1994	804,000
1995	720,000
1996	916,000

[1] *Includes persons granted permanent residence under the legalization program of the Immigration Reform and Control Act (IRCA) of 1986.*

Note: Structure of data may change from year to year due to changes in collection and reporting procedures of the data providers.

Bibliography

The following list has been organized into nine sections: a general list, for broad references and texts that apply to more than one decade covered by this book; and one list for each of the eight chapters, for references that are specific to a particular period. Sources used by the authors and additional suggestions for further research are included. Research for this volume was completed in September 1999; Internet sites are accurate as of that point.

General

Ambrose, Stephen. *Rise to Globalism: American Foreign Policy Since 1938*. 8th ed. New York: Penguin Books, 1997.

Arkin, William M., and Robert S. Norris. *"The Internet and the Bomb: A Research Guide to Policy and Information about Nuclear Weapons."* May 1997. http://www.nrdc.org/nrdcpro/nuguide/guinx.html.

Baldassare, Mark. *Trouble in Paradise: The Suburban Transformation in America*. New York: Columbia University Press, 1986.

Barson, Michael, and Steven Heller. *Teenage Confidential: An Illustrated History of the American Teen*. San Francisco: Chronicle Books, 1998.

Brooks, Tim, and Earle Marsh, eds. *The Complete Directory to Prime Time Network and Cable TV Shows 1946–Present*. New York: Ballantine Books, 1995.

"The Bureau of Atomic Tourism." April 19, 1999. http://www.oz.net/~chrisp/atomic.html.

Chafe, William H. *The Unfinished Journey: America Since World War II*. 4th ed. New York: Oxford University Press, 1999.

Collins, Philip. *The Golden Age of Television*. Los Angeles: R. R. Donnelley & Sons, 1997

Daniel, Clifton, ed. *Chronicle of America*. New York: DK Publishing, 1997.

Daniel, Clifton, ed. *Chronicle of the Twentieth Century*. New York: DK Publishing, 1995.

Diggins, John Patrick. *The Proud Decades: America in War and in Peace, 1941–1960*. New York: W. W. Norton, 1989.

Douvan, Elizabeth. "The Age of Narcissism, 1963-1982." In *American Childhood: A Research Guide and Historical Handbook*, edited by Joseph M. Hawes and N. Ray Hiner. Wesport, Conn.: Greenwood Press, 1985.

Federation of American Scientists. "The High Energy Weapons Archive." 1999. http://www.fas.org/nuke/hew.

George, Nelson. *The Death of Rhythm and Blues*. New York: Penguin, 1988.

Goldman, Eric F. *The Crucial Decade—And After: America, 1945-1960*. New York, Vintage Books, 1960.

Hodgson, Godfrey. *America In Our Time*. New York: Vintage Books, 1976.

———. *The World Turned Right Side Up: A History of the Conservative Ascendancy in America*. Boston: Houghton Mifflin, 1996.

Internet Movie Database. 1999. http://us.imdb.com.

Isaacs, Jeremy, and Taylor Downing. *Cold War: An Illustrated History, 1945-1991*. Boston: Little, Brown, 1998.

Jennings, Peter, and Todd Brewster. *The Century*. New York: Doubleday, 1998.

Johnson, Richard A. *American Fads*. New York: Beech Tree Books, 1985.

Jones, Landon Y. *Great Expectations: America and the Baby Boom Generation*. New York: Ballantine Books, 1980.

Juno, Andrea, and V. Vale, eds. *Incredibly Strange Music*. Vol. 1. San Francisco: Re/Search Publications, 1993.

———. *Incredibly Strange Music*. Vol. 2. San Francisco: Re/Search Publications, 1994.

Kisseloff, Jeff. *The Box: An Oral History of Television 1920-1961*. New York: Penguin Books, 1995.

Lanning, Michael Lee. *The African-American Soldier: From Crispus Attucks to Colin Powell*. Secaucus, N.J.: Birch Lane Press, 1997.

Lawson, Steven F. *Running for Freedom: Civil Rights and Black Politics in America Since 1941*. New York: McGraw-Hill, 1991.

May, Elaine Tyler. *Homeward Bound: American Families in the Cold War Era*. New York: Basic Books, 1988.

Meredith, Geoffrey, and Charles Schewe. "The Power of Cohorts." *American Demographics* (December 1994): 22–27+.

Mitchell, Susan. "The Next Baby Boom." *American Demographics* (October 1995): 22–27+.

Palladino, Grace. *Teenagers: An American History*. New York: Basic Books, 1996.

Patterson, James T. *Grand Expectations: The United States, 1945-1974*. New York: Oxford University Press, 1996.

Potter, David M. *People of Plenty: Economic Abundance and the American Character*. Chicago: University of Chicago Press, 1954.

Poulos, Stacy, and Demetra Smith Nightingale. "The Aging Baby Boom: Implications for Employment and Training Programs." The Urban Institute. 1999. http://www.urban.org/aging/abb/agingbaby.html.

Powell, Polly, and Lucy Peel. *'50s & '60s Style*. London: Apple, 1988.

Price, David. "Cold War Hot Links." May 4, 1998. http://www.stmartin.edu/~dprice/cold.war.html.

Ravitch, Diane. *The Troubled Crusade: American Education, 1945-1980*. New York: Basic Books, 1983.

Rosenberg, Norman L., and Emily S. Rosenberg. *In Our Times: America Since World War II*. Englewood Cliffs, N.J.: Prentice Hall, 1995.

Ross, Loretta J. "Anti-abortionists and White Supremacists Make Common Cause." *The Progressive* (October 1994): 24+.

Russell, Cheryl. *The Master Trend: How the Baby Boom Generation Is Remaking America*. New York: Plenum Press, 1994.

Stark, Steven D. *Glued to the Set*. New York: Bantam Doubleday Dell Publishing Group, Inc., 1997.

Strickland, Charles E., and Andrew M. Ambrose. "The Baby Boom, Prosperity, and the Changing Worlds of Children, 1945-1963." In *American Childhood: A Research Guide and Historical Handbook*, edited by Joseph M. Hawes and N. Ray Hiner. Westport, Conn.: Greenwood Press, 1985.

Susman, Warren. *Culture as History: The Transformation of American Society in the Twentieth Century*. New York: Pantheon Books, 1984.

Trager, James. *The People's Chronology*. New York: Henry Holt, 1992.

U.S. Bureau of the Census. *Historical Statistics of the United States: Colonial Times to 1970*. 2 vols. Washington, D.C., 1975.

———. *Statistical Abstract of the United States*. Various vols. Washington, D.C.

U.S. Department of Health and Human Services. National Center for Health Statistics Home Page. June 10, 1999. http://www.cdc.gov/nchswww.

Wetterau, Bruce. *The New York Public Library Book of Chronologies*. New York: Prentice Hall Press, 1990.

Winkler, Allan M. *Life Under A Cloud: American Anxiety About the Atom*. New York: Oxford University Press, 1993.

Wolfe, Tom. *The Right Stuff*. New York: Farrar, Straus & Giroux, 1979.

Zinn, Howard. *A People's History of the United States*. New York: New Press, 1997.

Chapter One: The War Years

All-American Girls Baseball League, 1943–1954: Homepage. October 12, 1998. http://www.dlcwest.com/~smudge/enhanced.html.

Alperovitz, Gar. *The Decision to Use the Atomic Bomb and the Architecture of an American Myth*. New York: Knopf, 1995.

"America from the Depression to World War II: Black-and-White Photographs from the FSA-OWI 1935–1945." Library of Congress Online Exhibit. http://memory.loc.gov/ammem/fsahtml/fahome.html.

Berlage, Gai Ingham. *Women in Baseball: The Forgotten History*. Westport, Conn: Praeger Publishers, 1994.

Biondi, Victor, ed. *American Decades: 1940-1949*. Detroit, Mich.: Gale Research, 1995.

Garver, Thomas. *Just Before the War*. Balboa, Calif.: Newport Harbor Art Museum, 1968.

Groves, Leslie R. *Now It Can Be Told: The Story of the Manhattan Project*. New York: Da Capo Press, Inc., 1983.

Harris, Mark Jonathan, et al. *The Homefront: America During World War II*. New York: G. P. Putnam's Sons, 1984.

Hoopes, Roy. *Americans Remember the Home Front*. New York: Hawthorne Books, Inc., 1977.

Johnson, Susan E. *When Women Played Hardball*. Seattle, Wash.: Seal Press, 1994.

O'Neill, William L. *A Democracy at War*. New York: Macmillan, 1993.

Rhodes, Richard. *The Making of the Atomic Bomb*. New York: Touchstone, 1986.

Roosevelt, Eleanor. *On My Own*. New York: Harper & Brothers, 1958.

———. *This I Remember*. New York: Harper & Brothers, 1949.

Roosevelt, Franklin D. *The Public Papers and Addresses of Franklin D. Roosevelt: 1941*. New York: Harper & Brothers, 1941.

"Rutgers Oral History of World War II: Web Archive." September 17, 1999. http://history.rutgers.edu/oralhistory/orlhom.htm

Szasz, Ferenc Morton. *The Day the Sun Rose Twice: The Story of the Trinity Site Nuclear Explosion, July 16, 1945*. Albuquerque: University of New Mexico Press, 1995.

"Women Come to the Front: Journalists, Photographers, and Broadcasters During World War II." Library of Congress Online Exhibit. February 25, 1999. http://lcweb.loc.gov/exhibits/wcf/wcf0001.html.

Chapter Two: The Late 1940s

Associated Press. "Dr. Kinsey Is Dead; Sex Researcher, 62" *New York Times*. 26 August 1956.

http://www.english.upenn.edu/~afilreis/50s/kinsey.html.

Bergman, Ingrid, and Alan Burgess. *Ingrid Bergman: My Story.* New York: Dell Publishing, 1980.

"Buckminster Fuller: Thinking Out Loud." American Masters. wNetStation. 1999. http://www.pbs.org/wnet/bucky.cgi.

Cheney, Glenn Alan. *They Never Knew: The Victims of Atomic Testing.* Danbury, Conn.: Franklin Watts, 1996.

Dmytryk, Edward. *Odd Man Out: A Memoir of the Hollywood Ten.* Carbondale: Southern Illinois University Press, 1995.

"ENIAC 50th Anniversary Celebration: The Birth of the Information Age." University of Pennsylvania. April 1, 1997.
http://homepage.seas.upenn.edu/~museum/index.html.

"Faster Than Sound." NOVA Online. WGBH Science Unit. October 1997. http://www.pbs.org/wgbh/nova/barrier.

Fearnley, Christopher J. "The R. Buckminster Fuller FAQ." May 10, 1999. http://www.CJFearnley.com/fuller-faq.html.

Fischer, G. "Nobel Prize in Physiology or Medicine 1948." *Nobel Lectures: Physiology or Medicine 1942–62.* Amsterdam: Elsevier Publishing Company, 1963. The Electronic Nobel Museum Project. July 8, 1998.
http://www.nobel.se/laureates/medicine-1948-press.html.

"For European Recovery: The Fiftieth Anniversary of the Marshall Plan." Library of Congress. April 22, 1999.
http://lcweb.loc.gov/exhibits/marshall.

Fried, Albert, ed. *McCarthyism: The Great American Red Scare.* New York and Oxford: Oxford University Press, 1996.

"General Chuck Yeager: First Man to Break the Sound Barrier." The Hall of Science and Exploration. http://www.achievement.org/autodoc/page/yea0int-1.

"Living Under a Mushroom Cloud: Fear and Hope in the Atomic Age." State Historical Society of Wisconsin. September 8, 1998.
http://www.shsw.wisc.edu/atomic/intro.htm.

McLemee, Scott. "The Man Who Took Sex Out of the Closet." *Salon* (5 November 1997):

Muuss, Mike. "History of Computing Information." U.S. Army Research Lab. http://ftp.arl.mil/~mike/comphist.

Pace, Eric. "Benjamin Spock, World's Pediatrician, Dies at 94," *New York Times,* 17 March 1998.

"Presper Eckert Interview." National Museum of American History/Smithsonian Institution. February 2, 1988.
http://www.si.edu/resource/tours/comphist/eckert.htm.

"Resolving the DDT Dilemma." World Wildlife Fund Canada and World Wildlife Fund USA, 1998.
http://www.wwf.org/toxics/progareas/pop/ddt.htm.

Shelton, Harry. *The Invention of Television.* Sugar Land, Tex.: Bell Towne Publishers, 1988.

Silverman, Steve. "Zippers and Velcro." Useless Information. http://home.nycap.rr.com/useless/zippers/zippers.html.

Spock, Benjamin, and Mary Morgan. *Spock on Spock: A Memoir of Growing Up With the Century.* New York: Pantheon Books, 1989.

"Timeline: DDT." U.S. Army Center for Health Promotion and Preventative Medicine, Entomological Sciences Program. January 7, 1999.
http://chppm-www.apgea.army.mil/ento/timefram/DDT.htm.

"Velcro FAQ." The Velcro Companies.
http://www.velcro.com/htm/loop/invent.htm.

"Welcome to the George C. Marshall Foundation." George C. Marshall Foundation. September 27, 1999.
http://www.gcmarshallfdn.org/.

"What's New." The Atomic Veterans History Project. 1997.
http://www.aracnet.com/~pdxavets/index.shtml.

Chapter Three: The 1950s

Allen, Maury. *Where Have You Gone, Joe DiMaggio: The Story of America's Last Hero.* New York: Dutton, 1975.

American Fabrics and Fashions Magazine. *Encyclopedia of Textiles.* Englewood Cliffs, N.J.: Prentice-Hall, 1980.

Asbell, Bernard. *The Pill: A Biography of the Drug That Changed the World.* New York: Random House, 1995.

The Astounding B Monster.
http://www.bmonster.com/index.html.

Atomic Archive. March 18, 1999.
http://www.atomicarchive.com.

The Atomic Café. 88 min. New York The Archives Project, 1982.

Berliner, Michael, ed. *Letters of Ayn Rand.* New York: Dutton, 1995.

Berry, Chuck. *Chuck Berry: The Autobiography.* New York: Harmony Books, 1987.

Boas, Maxwell, and Steve Chain. *Big Mac: The Unauthorized Story of McDonald's.* New York: Dutton, 1976.

"Booknotes Transcript with Porter McKeever, author of *Adlai Stevenson: His Life and Legacy.*" C-Span Booknotes. Air date: August 6, 1989. 1997.
http://www.booknotes.org/transcripts/10047.htm.

"B.O.S.C.H. B-Movie Guide."
http://huizen.dds.nl/~penquin/index_frame.html.

Branch, Taylor. *Parting the Waters: America in the King Years, 1954–63.* New York: Simon & Schuster, 1988.

Branden, Barbara. *The Passion of Ayn Rand.* New York: Doubleday & Company, 1986.

Cecelski, David S. *Along Freedom Road: Hyde County, North Carolina and the Fate of Black Schools in the South.* Chapel Hill: University of North Carolina Press, 1994.

Chambers, Jack. *Milestones: The Music and Times of Miles Davis.* New York: Quill–William Morrow, 1983, 1985.

"Chuck Berry." Rock and Roll Hall of Fame and Museum.
http://www.rockhall.com/induct/berrchuc.html.

Davis, Miles, with Quincy Troupe. *Miles: The Autobiography.* New York: Simon and Schuster, 1989.

"Fifty Years of the Transistor." Lucent Technologies.
http://www.lucent.com/ideas2/heritage/transistor/index.html.

Filreis, Alan. "The Literature & Culture of the American 1950s." December 1998.
http://www.english.upenn.edu/~afilreis/50s/home.html.

Halberstam, David. *The Fifties.* New York: Villard Books, 1993.

Herman, Jan, "Taking a Shine to Ayn Rand," *Los Angeles Times,* 20 March 1998.

The Horror Movie Database. 1998.
http://www.drcasey.com/cgibin/template?page=main-movie.

Hughes, Langston. *Fight for Freedom: The Story of the NAACP.* New York: W. W. Norton, 1962.

"ICMA Quick Card Facts." The International Card Manufacturers Association.
http://www.icma.com/icmahome.htm.

Jackson, Kenneth T. *Crabgrass Frontier: The Suburbanization of the United States.* New York: Oxford University Press, 1985.

Jacobs, Frank. *The Mad World of William Gaines.* Secaucus, N.J.: Lyle Stuart, 1972.

"Joe DiMaggio: Career Statistics." CNN/ Sports Illustrated. 1997.
http://cgi.cnnsi.com/baseball/mlb/ml/players/Joe.Dimaggio.101.

Kelly, Barbara M. *Expanding the American Dream: Building and Rebuilding Levittown.* Albany: State University of New York Press, 1993.

Klingaman, William K. *Encyclopedia of the McCarthy Era.* New York: Facts On File, 1996.

Layman, Richard, ed. *American Decades: 1950–1959.* Detroit, Mich.: Gale Research, 1994.

"MAD Magazine Time Line." MAD. 1999. No longer posted at http://www.dccomics.com/mad.

Mandell, Lewis. *The Credit Card Industry: A History.* Boston: Twayne Publishers, 1990.

Mariani, John F. *The Dictionary of American Food and Drink.* New York: Hearst Books, 1994.

Martin, John Barlow. *Adlai Stevenson and the World: The Life of Adlai E. Stevenson.* Garden City, N.Y.: Doubleday, 1977.

"Oh, the Humanity: The Worst Movies on Earth." Oh, the Humanity. http://www.ohthehumanity.com.

Pearce, Christopher. *Fifties Source Book.* London: Virgin, 1990.

Rudberg, E. G. "Nobel Prize in Physics 1956." *Nobel Lectures: Physics 1942-62.* Amsterdam: Elsevier Publishing Company, 1963. The Electronic Nobel Museum Project. 8 July 1998.
http://www.nobel.se/laureates/physics-1956-press.html.

Steinberg, Shelia, and Kate Dooner. *Fabulous Fifties: Designs for Modern Living.* Atglen, Pa.: Schiffer Publishing, 1993.

Summers, Harry G., Jr. *Vietnam War Almanac.* Novato, Calif.: Presidio Press, 1999.

Sumsion, Michael, "Chuck Berry." *The Rough Guide to Rock,* edited by Mark Ellingham. New York: Viking Penguin, 1996.

Talbott, Strobe, trans. and ed. *Khrushchev Remembers.* Boston: Little, Brown, 1970.

U. S. Dept. of Transportation, Federal Highway Administration. *America's Highways, 1776–1976: A History of the Federal-aid Program.* Washington, D.C.: 1977.

"The Vietnam War: 1961–1970." Multieducator.
http://www.multied.com/vietnam.

Wasserman, Harvey, and Norman Solomon. *Killing Our Own.* New York: Delacorte Press, 1982

Williams, Juan. *Eyes on the Prize: America's Civil Rights Years, 1954-1965.* New York: Viking, 1987.

Chapter Four: The 1960s

Albert, Judith Clavir, and Stewart Edward Albert, eds. *The Sixties Papers: Documents of a Rebellious Decade.* Westport, Conn.: Praeger Publishers, 1984.

Allen, Robert L. "The Port Chicago Disaster and Its Aftermath." *The Black Scholar* (Spring 1982): 3–29.

Anderson, Terry H. *The Movement and the Sixties.* New York: Oxford University Press, 1995.

"Battlefield: Vietnam." Public Broadcasting System.
http://www.pbs.org/battlefieldvietnam/index.html.

Buckingham, William A., Jr. "Operation Ranch Hand:

Herbicides in Southeast Asia, 1961-1971." 1997.
http://cpcug.org/user/billb/ranchhand/ranchhand.html.

Caldwell, Anne E. *Origins of Psychopharmacology from CPZ to LSD*. Springfield, Ill.: Thomas, 1970.

Collins, Michael. *Carrying the Fire: An Astronaut's Journey*. New York: Farrar, Straus, & Giroux, 1974.

Cortright, Edgar, ed. "Apollo Expeditions to the Moon." NASA SP-350, 1975. February 9, 1999. http://www.hq.nasa.gov/office/pao/History/SP-350/cover. html.

Cott, Jonathan, and Christine Doudna. *The Ballad of John and Yoko*. Garden City, N.Y.: Dolphin Books, 1982.

"The Cuban Missile Crisis: Fourteen Days in October." The Crisis Center. 1997. http://hyperion.advanced.org/11046/days/index.html.

DeLeon, David, ed. *Leaders from the 1960s: A Biographical Sourcebook of American Activism*. Westport, Conn: Greenwood Press, 1994.

Dvorkin, Connie. "The Suburban Scene." *Sisterhood is Powerful: An Anthology of Writings from the Women's Liberation Movement*, edited by Robin Morgan. New York: Vintage, 1970, pp. 407-411.

Edelman, Bernard, ed. *Dear America: Letters Home from Vietnam*. New York: W. W. Norton, 1985.

Edlen, B. "Nobel Prize in Physics 1964." *Nobel Lectures: Physics 1963-70*. Amsterdam: Elsevier Publishing Company, 1970. The Electronic Nobel Museum Project. July 8, 1998. http://www.nobel.se/laureates/physics-1964-press.html.

Ferriss, Susan, and Ricardo Sandoval. *The Fight in the Fields: Cesar Chavez and the Farmworkers' Movement*. New York: Harcourt Brace, 1997.

Finklestein, Norman. *Thirteen Days/Ninety Miles: The Cuban Missile Crisis*. New York. Simon & Schuster, 1994.

Fraser, Ronald, et al. *1968: A Student Generation in Revolt*. New York: Pantheon Books, 1988.

"The Free Speech Movement Archives." April 8, 1999. http://www.fsm-a.org/index.html.

Gitlin, Todd. *The Sixties: Years of Hope, Days of Rage*. New York: Bantam Books, 1989.

Griswold del Castillo, Richard, and Richard A. Garcia. *Cesar Chavez: A Triump of Spirit*. Norman: University of Oklahoma Press, 1995.

Gurley Brown, Helen. *Having it All*. New York: Simon & Schuster/Linden Press, 1982.

———. *The Late Show: A Semiwild but Practical Survival Plan for Women Over 50*. New York: William Morrow & Company, 1993.

———. *Sex and the Single Girl*. New York: B. Geis Associates, 1962.

Hamilton, Neil A. *The ABC-CLIO Companion to the 1960s Counterculture in America*. Santa Barbara, Calif.: ABC-CLIO, 1997.

Hauser, Thomas. *Muhammad Ali: His Life and Times*. New York: Simon & Schuster, 1991.

Hersh, Seymour M. "Ex-GI Tells of Killing Civilians at Pinkville," *St. Louis Post-Dispatch*, 25 November 1969. In *Reporting Vietnam*. New York: Library of America, 1998.

———. "Hamlet Attack Called Point-blank Murder," *St. Louis Post-Dispatch*, 20 November 1969. In *Reporting Vietnam*. New York: Library of America, 1998.

———. "Lieutenant Accused of Murdering 109 Civilians," *St. Louis Post-Dispatch*, 16 September 1969. In *Reporting*

Vietnam. New York: Library of America, 1998.

Hirschman, Charles, Samuel Preston, and Vu Manh Loi. "Vietnamese Casualties During the American War: A New Estimate." *Population and Development Review* 21 (December 1995): 783–812.

"Instant Karma!: the John and Yoko Magazine Since 1981." July 8, 1999. http://www.instantkarma.com/index.html.

"The Invention of the LASER at Bell Laboratories: 1958-1998." Bell Labs. 1998. http://www.bell-labs.com/history/laser.

"Inventor of non-stick cookware." T-Fal. http://www.t-fal.com/insidetfal/nonstick/invent.html.

Katz, Donald. "The Triumph of Swoosh." *Sports Illustrated* (August 1993): 54–73.

Kelsey, Frances O. "Historical Perspective." Remarks given at the workshop "Thalidomide: Potential Benefits and Risks." U.S. Food and Drug Administration, National Institutes of Health, and the Centers for Disease Control and Prevention. September 9, 1997. http://www.fda.gov/oashi/patrep/nih99.html.

Knox, William E. "Close-up of Khrushchev During a Crisis." *New York Times Magazine*, 18 November 1962.

Layman, Richard, ed. *American Decades: 1960-1969*. New York: Gale Research, 1995.

Lenz, W. "The History of Thalidomide." Lecture given at the 1992 UNITH Conference. London, Ontario. June 28, 1999. http://www.thalidomide.ca/history.html.

McLuhan, Marshall, and Quentin Fiore. *The Medium Is the Message*. New York: Random House, 1967.

———. *Understanding Media: The Extensions of Man*. New York: McGraw-Hill, 1964.

Mailer, Norman. *Of a Fire on the Moon*. Boston: Little, Brown, 1970.

Maraniss, David. "Ali's Amazing Grace: Still Preaching, Now He Contemplates His 'House in Heaven,' " *Washington Post*, 8 June 1997: A01.

Marchand, Philip. *Marshall McLuhan: The Medium and the Messenger*. New York: Ticknor & Fields, 1989.

Marshall, Kathryn. *In the Combat Zone: An Oral History of American Women in Vietnam, 1966–1975*. Boston: Little, Brown, 1987.

The Marshall McLuhan Center on Global Communications. July 1997. http://www.mcluhanmedia.com.

Matthiessen, Peter. *Sal Si Puedes: Cesar Chavez and the New American Revolution*. New York: Random House, 1969.

"May 4, 1970: General Information." http://www.kent.edu/ksuMay4/welcome.htm.

Miller, James. *"Democracy Is in the Streets": From Port Huron to The Siege of Chicago*. New York: Simon & Schuster, 1987.

Morgan, Robin, ed. *Sisterhood Is Powerful: An Anthology of Writings from the Women's Liberation Movement*. New York: Vintage Books, 1970.

"Named Campaigns: Vietnam." http://www2.army.mil/cmh-pg/reference/vncmp.htm.

"No Room in the Cemetery," *Afro-American*, 4 June 1966. In *Reporting Vietnam*. New York: Library of America, 1998.

"The Playboy Interview: Marshall McLuhan, *Playboy Magazine*, March 1969. " The Marshall McLuhan Center on Global Communications. 1996. http://www.mcluhanmedia.com/mmclpb01.html.

"Press Kit: Apollo 11 Lunar Landing Mission." National

Aeronautics and Space Administration. http://www-lib.ksc.nasa.gov/lib/archives/apollo/elaine/1A PPLLM/AP11PT1.pdf and http://www-lib.ksc.nasa.gov/lib/archives/apollo/elaine/1A PPLLM/AP11PT2.pdf

Rükl, Antonín. *Atlas of the Moon*. Edited by Dr. T. W. Rackham. Translated by Jana Hajnovicová. Waukesha, Wis.: Kalmbach Publishing Company, 1996.

"The San Francisco Diggers (1966–1968) and Beyond . . . " The Digger Archives. May 11, 1999. http://www.diggers.org.

Santos, Gonzalo. "Cesar Chavez's Funeral." April 30, 1993. gopher://csf.colorado.edu:70/0R6047-11646-/psn/psn-arch ives/cesar.chavez.

Shepard, Alan, and Deke Slayton. *Moon Shot: The Inside Story of America's Race to the Moon*. Atlanta, Ga.: Turner Publishing, 1994.

Strasser, J. B., and Laurie Becklund. *Swoosh: the Unauthorized Story of Nike and the Men Who Played There*. New York: HarperBusiness, 1993.

Summers, Harry G., Jr. *Vietnam War Almanac*. New York: Facts On File, 1985.

Tanner, Leslie B., ed. *Voices from Women's Liberation*. New York: New American Library, 1970.

"Teflon History." DuPont. 1999. http://www.dupont.com/teflon/history.html.

Ture, Kwame (formerly Stokely Carmichael), and Charles V. Hamilton. *Black Power: The Politics of Liberation in America*. New York: Vintage, 1992.

"Veterans and Agent Orange: Update 1996." Institute of Medicine. 1996. http://www.nap.edu/readingroom/books/veterans/index.h tml.

"Vietnam: Table of Contents." http://intellit.muskingum.edu/intellsite/vietnam_folder/viet namtoc.html.

"The Vietnam War." MultiEDUCATOR. http://www.multied.com/vietnam.

Viorst, Milton. *Fire in the Streets: America in the 1960s*. New York: Simon & Schuster, 1979.

"We Remember Marc Gregoire." All Things Considered, National Public Radio. 12 January 1996. http://www.real.com/contentp/npr/nc6j12.html.

Wilford, John Noble. "NASA at 40." The New York Times on the Web. http://www.nytimes.com/library/national/science/nasa/in dex.html.

Williams, David R. "Lunar Exploration." National Space Science Data Center (NASA). June 22, 1999. http://nssdc.gsfc.nasa.gov/planetary/lunar/apollo_25th.ht ml.

Wilson, Thomas C. "Vietnam-Era Military Service: A Test of the Class-Bias Thesis." *Armed Forces & Society* (Spring 1995): 461–471.

Witchel, Alex. "ON TOUR WITH: Helen Gurley Brown; Go Ahead, Say It: Sex and the Senior Woman." *New York Times*, 1 April 1993.

Woodstock 69. 1996. http://www.woodstock69.com.

Chapter Five: The 1970s

Adams, Russ. "Bar Code History Page." April 6, 1999. http://www.adams1.com/pub/russadam/history.html.

Alexander, Ron. "Mary Tyler Moore: A Late-Night Cult." *New*

York Times, 9 April 1984.

American Indian Movement Grand Governing Council. http://www.aimovement.org/index.html.

"The American Radicalism Collection." Michigan State University Libraries Special Collections. May 11, 1999. http://www.lib.msu.edu/spc/digital/radicalism.

Bernstein, Carl, and Bob Woodward. All the President's Men. 2nd ed. New York: Touchstone Books, 1994.

Biondi, Victor, ed. American Decades: 1970-1979. Detroit, Mich.: Gale Research, 1995.

Bluestone, Barry, and Bennett Harrison. The Deindustrialization of America: Plant Closings, Community Abandonment, and the Dismantling of Basic Industry. New York: Basic Books, 1982.

Centers for Disease Control and Prevention, the American Society for Reproductive Medicine, the Society for Assisted Reproductive Technology, and RESOLVE. 1996 Assisted Reproductive Technology Success Rates. Atlanta: Centers for Disease Control and Prevention, 1998.

Commission on Population Growth and the American Future. Population Growth and America's Future. Washington, D.C., 1971.

Crowley, Monica. Nixon Off the Record. New York; Random House, 1996.

Davis, Angela. Angela Davis: An Autobiography. New York: Random House, 1974.

Dorn, Jonathan. "Polartec: Building a Better Sheep." Backpacker. (April 1998). http://www.polartec.com/01_malden_mills/01_02_articles/01_02_polartec.html.

Emery, Fred. Watergate: The Corruption of American Politics and the Fall of Richard Nixon. Reprint ed. New York: Touchstone Books, 1995.

Farnsworth, Malcolm. "Watergate." VCEpolitics.com. http://vcepolitics.com/wgate.htm.

Finch, Christopher. Jim Henson: The Works. New York: Random House, 1993.

Formisano, Ronald P. Boston Against Busing: Race, Class, and Ethnicity in the 1960s and 1970s. Chapel Hill: University of North Carolina Press, 1991.

Gallup, George H. The Gallup Poll: Public Opinion, 1935-1971. Volume 3: 1959-1971. New York: Random House, 1972.

Givens, Ron. "Music to Our Ears." Newsweek (7 August 1989): 68.

Haffner, Katie. "The Epic Saga of the WELL." Wired. May 1997. http://www.wired.com/wired/archive/5.05/ff_well.html.

Heath, G. Louis, ed. Vandals in the Bomb Factory: The History & Literature of the Students for a Democratic Society. Lanham, Md.: Scarecrow Press, Inc., 1976.

Hersh, Seymour. The Price of Power: Kissinger in the Nixon White House. New York: Summit Books, 1983.

Isaacson, Walter. Kissinger: A Biography. New York: Simon & Schuster, 1992.

Karlen, N. "Mary Never Slept Here: Life in a Sitcom Shrine." New York Times, 12 January 1995.

Kent, Steven, Jer Horwitz, and Joe Fieldler. "History of Video Games." 1999. http://www.videogames.com/features/universal/hov/index.html.

Kissinger, Henry. Years of Upheaval. Boston: Little, Brown & Co., 1982.

Kleinfield, Sonny. A Machine Called Indomitable. New York: Times Books, 1985.

Kutler, Stanley I. Abuse of Power: The New Nixon Tapes. New York: Free Press, 1997.

———. The Wars of Watergate: The Last Crisis of Richard Nixon. New York: W. W. Norton, 1990.

Levy, Steven. Insanely Great: The Life and Times of Macintosh, the Computer That Changed Everything. New York: Viking, 1994.

Matthiessen, Peter. In the Spirit of Crazy Horse. New York: Viking, 1991.

Means, Russell, and Marvin J. Wolf. Where White Men Fear to Tread: the Autobiography of Russell Means. New York: St. Martin's Press, 1995.

Moore, Mary Tyler. After All. New York: Dell, 1996.

Neus, Elizabeth, "As First 'Test-Tube' Baby Turns 20, Fertility Debate Still Rages," Salt Lake City Tribune, 23 July 1998. http://www.sltrib.com/1998/jul/07231998/Science/44335.htm.

"The 1979 Nobel Prize in Physiology or Medicine," October 11, 1979. The Electronic Nobel Museum Project. September 22, 1988. http://www.nobel.se/laureates/medicine-1979-press.html.

"The Occupation of Wounded Knee." The Web Environment at U-M. http://www-personal.umich.edu/~jamarcus/wknee.htm.

O'Connor, John J, "'Mary Tyler Moore': Breezy, Inane, and Pleasant," New York Times, 21 April 1971.

O'Regan, Tom. "From Piracy to Sovereignty: International VCR Trends." Continuum: The Australian Journal of Media and Culture 4, 2 (1991). March 5, 1996. http://kali.murdoch.edu.au/~cntinuum/4.2/oregan.html.

Portney, Kent E. Siting Hazardous Waste Treatment Facilities: The Nimby Syndrome. Westport, Conn.: Auburn House, 1991.

"Production of Walkmans Hits the 50-Million Mark," Asian Wall Street Journal Weekly, 10 July 1989.

Reitman, Judith. "VCRs: the Saga Continues." Marketing & Media Decisions 20 (September 1985): 83+.

Rheingold, Howard. "The Virtual Community: Homesteading on the Electronic Frontier." Rheingold's Brainstorms. September 9, 1999. http://www.rheingold.com/vc/book/intro.html

"Russell Means." American Indian Movement. http://www.russellmeans.com/aim.html.

Sanford, Glen. "History." April 12, 1999. http://www.apple-history.com/history.html.

Schell, Jonathan. The Fate of the Earth. New York: Knopf, 1982.

———. The Time of Illusion. New York: Vintage Books, 1975.

Schneider, David. "Raymond V. Damadian: Scanning the Horizon," Scientific American (June 1997). http://www.sciam.com/0697issue/0697profile.html.

Schwartz, Robert. "Frankenstein's Footsteps." New England Journal of Medicine 340, 3 (January 21, 1999): 243+.

Seymour, Martin Lipset, and William Schneider. The Confidence Gap: Business, Labor, and Government in the Public Mind. rev. ed. Baltimore, Md.: The Johns Hopkins University Press, 1987.

Shapiro, Walter. "Walkpeople Invade." Washington Post Magazine, 7 February 1982.

Smith, Charles. "Revisiting Solar Power's Past." Technology Review (July 1995). http://www.techreview.com/articles/july95/Smith.html.

Smith, Paul Chaat, and Robert Allen Warrior. Like a Hurricane: The Indian Movement from Alcatraz to Wounded Knee. New York: The New Press, 1996.

Smith, Steven. "The Fertility Race, Part 7: Twenty Years of Test-Tube Babies." Minnesota Public Radio. 23 July 1998. http://www.news.mpr.org/features/199711/20_smiths_fertility/part7.

Staten, Vince. Can You Trust a Tomato in January? New York: Simon & Schuster, 1993.

Stern, Kenneth S. Loud Hawk: The United States versus the American Indian Movement. Norman: University of Oklahoma Press, 1994.

"The Triumph of the Nerds: The Television Program Transcripts." PBS Online. 1999. http://www.pbs.org/nerds/transcript.html.

"A VCR Surge That Defies the Recession." Business Week (1 September 1980): 28E.

"Videotopia: The Exhibit of the True History of Video Games." The Electronics Conservancy, Inc. June 15, 1999. http://www.videotopia.com.

"Watergate 25." The Washington Post Company. 1997. http://www.washingtonpost.com/wp-srv/national/longterm/watergate/front.htm.

"Watergate: the 25th Anniversary." MSNBC's Time and Again 2000. http://www.msnbc.com/onair/msnbc/timeandagain/archive/watergate/timeline.asp.

Woz Org. http://www.woz.org.

Chapter Six: The 1980s

Adler, Bill. The Cosby Wit: His Life and Humor. New York: Carroll & Graf, 1986.

Andersen, Christopher P. Citizen Jane: The Tubulent Life of Jane Fonda. New York: H. Holt, 1990.

Arbel, Avner, and Albert E. Kaff. Crash: Ten Days in October—Will It Strike Again? Chicago, Ill.: Longman Financial Services, 1989.

Berry, Dawn Bradley. The 50 Most Influential Women in American Law. Chicago: Contemporary Books, 1997.

Biondi, Victor, ed. American Decades: 1980-1989. Detroit, Mich.: Gale Research, 1995.

Bloom, Allan. The Closing of the American Mind: How Higher Education Has Failed Democracy and Impoverished the Souls of Today's Students. New York: Simon & Schuster, 1987.

Bosanko, Deobrah. "Abortion's Slow Decline." American Demographics (September 1995): 20+.

Bowen, Ezra. "Flunking Grade in Math." Time (20 June 1988): 79.

Brower, Montgomery, et al. "From Prison, Anti-abortion Leader Randall Terry Says that God, Not the Law, Is His Judge." Time (November 20, 1989): 109+.

Cannon, Carl. "Sandra Day O'Connor: 1981, The First Woman Justice on the U.S. Supreme Court." Working Woman (Nov.–Dec. 1996): 54+.

Fingerman, Dan. "The Cosby Show Episode Guide." http://www.fortunecity.com/lavendar/pulpfiction/515/guides/CosbyShowThe_episodeguide.df.

Frady, Marshall. Jesse: The Life and Pilgrimage of Jesse Jackson. New York: Random House, 1996.

Gates, David. "He Didn't Need A Weatherman." Newsweek

(12 December 1994).

"The Gates Operating System," *Time* (13 January 1997).

Gorbachev, Mikhail. *Memoirs.* New York: Doubleday, 1995.

"The HIV Daily Briefing." AEGIS (AIDS Education Global Information System). http://www.aegis.com.

Hochschild, Arlie. *The Second Shift.* New York: Avon Books, 1989.

Isaacson, Walter. "The Battle Over Abortion." *Time* (6 April 1981): 20+.

"Jerry Rubin, 1960's Radical and Yippie Leader, Dies at 56." *New York Times,* 29 November 1994.

Lacayo, Richard. "The Shifting Politics of Abortion." *Time* (23 October 1989): 35+.

Lewis, Michael M. *Liar's Poker: Rising Through the Wreckage on Wall Street.* New York: Norton, 1989.

"Major U.S. Supreme Court Rulings on Reproductive Health and Rights." Planned Parenthood. 23 May 1997. www.plannedparenthood.org/ABOUT/NARRHISTORY/court.html.

Manes, Stephen, and Paul Andrews. *Gates: How Microsoft's Mogul Reinvented an Industry and Made Himself the Richest Man in America.* New York: Simon & Schuster, 1994.

Marsh, Dave. *Glory Days: Bruce Springsteen in the 1980s.* New York: Pantheon Books, 1987.

National Commission on Excellence in Education. *A Nation at Risk: The Full Account.* Portland, Ore.: USA Research, 1984.

Natural Resources Defense Council, Inc. "The NRDC Nuclear Program: Nuclear Data, Table of USSR / Russian Nuclear Warheads: 1949–70 and 1971–96." 1997. http://www.nrdc.org/nrdcpro/nudb/datab9.html.

O'Hare, William. "A New Look at Asian Americans." *American Demographics* (October 1990): 26+.

Ride, Sally, with Susan Okie. *To Space and Back.* New York: Lothrop, Lee & Shepard, 1986.

Risen, James, and Judy L. Thomas. *Wrath of Angels: The American Abortion War.* New York: Basic Books, 1998.

Shilts, Randy. *And the Band Played On.* New York: St. Martin's Press, 1987.

"Supreme Court Decisions Concerning Reproductive Rights: A Chronology 1965–1998." NARAL. December 1998. www.naral.org/publications/facts/sup.html.

Terry, Randall. "Operation Rescue." *Policy Review* (Winter 1989): 82+.

"Trends in the HIV and AIDS Epidemic 1998." Centers for Disease Control and Prevention. 1998. http://www.cdc.gov/nchstp/od/Trends.htm.

Wickenden, Dorothy. "What NOW? The Women's Movement Looks Beyond 'Equality.'" *New Republic* (5 May 1986): 19+.

Chapter Seven: The 1990s

American Almanac, 1996-1997: Statistical Abstract of the United States. Austin, Tex.: Hoover's, 1996.

"Atomic Bomb Chronology: 1980-1998." Tokyo Physicians for Elimination of Nuclear Weapons. http://www.ask.ne.jp/~hankaku/english/np11y.html.

Beaucchamp, Tom L. and Leroy Walters, eds. *Contemporary Issues in Bioethics.* Belmont, Calif.: Wadsworth Publishing Company, 1999.

Becker, Elizabeth. "Clinton Adviser Says North Korea Is Advancing Its Nuclear Program," *New York Times,* 12
March 1999.

Bell, Terrel H. "Reflections One Decade After 'A Nation at Risk.'" *Phi Delta Kappan* (April 1993): 592+.

Berners-Lee, Tim, and Robert Cailliau. "WorldWideWeb: Proposal for a Hypertext Project." (12 November 1990). http://www.w3.org/Proposal.

Bly, Robert. *Iron John: A Book About Men.* Reading, Mass.: Addison-Wesley Publishing Company, 1990.

Braus, Patricia. "Sorry, Boys—Donna Reed Is Still Dead." *American Demographics* (September 1995): 13+.

Broad, William J., "Experts Say Pakistan Test Was Either Small or a Failure," *New York Times,* 31 May 1998.

———. "Explosion Is Detected By U.S. Scientists," *New York Times,* 29 May 1998.

Brock, David. *The Seduction of Hillary Rodham.* New York: Free Press, 1996.

Burns, John F. "India Detonated a Hydrogen Bomb, Experts Confirm." *New York Times,* 18 May 1998.

———. "Pakistan, Answering India, Carries Out Nuclear Tests; Clinton's Appeal Rejected." *New York Times,* 29 May 1998.

Carter, Ashton, et al. "Catastrophic Terrorism." *Foreign Affairs* (November/December 1998): 80+.

Castro, Janice, ed. "Slouching Towards Creation." Time.com. March 1997. http://cgi.pathfinder.com/time/cloning/index.html.

"A CERN Invention You are Familiar With: The World Wide Web." European Laboratory for Particle Physics (CERN). March 30, 1998. http://www.cern.ch/Public/ACHIEVEMENTS/web.html.

"Cloning: In Our Own Image," *Los Angeles Times,* 27 April-1 May 1997. http://www.latimes.com/HOME/NEWS/SCIENCE/REPORTS/CLONING.

Consumer Guide. *Great Cars of the Fifties.* Skokie, Ill.: Publications International, 1985.

Davis, William V., ed. *Critical Essays on Robert Bly.* New York: G. K. Hall, 1992.

Eastland, Terry. "Is Affirmative Action on the Way Out?" *Commentary* (March 1998): 25+.

Edmondson, Brad. "Motherhood: Squeezed in the Middle." *American Demographics* (June 1997).

"The Next Baby Boom." *American Demographics* (September 1995): 2.

———. "No More Baby Booms." *American Demographics* (September 1997).

Edwards, Clifford H., and Wallace E. Allred, "More on 'A Nation at Risk.'" *The Clearing House* (November/December 1993): 85+.

Encyclopedia of American Cars, 1930-1980: 50 Years of Automobile History. New York: Beekman House, 1984.

Fein, Esther B., "Nada, Nada, Nada; Has the End of 'Seinfeld' Ruined Festivus for the Rest of Us?," *New York Times,* 27 December 1997. http://www.nytimes.com/specials/seinfeld/sein1227.html.

Feldman, Gayle. "Making Book on Oprah." *New York Times,* 2 February 1997.

Gates, Jeff. "Twenty-first Century Capitalism." *The Humanist* (July 17, 1998): 9+.

Genetics & IVF Institute Homepage. 1995–1999. http://www.givf.com/givfhome.html.

Greenspan, Alan. "Our Economy Has Remained Strong." *Vital Speeches of the Day* (1 July 1998): 546+.

Gromov, Gregory R. "History of the Internet and WWW:
The Roads and Crossroads of Internet History." 1995–1998. http://www.internetvalley.com/intvalweb.html.

Hamilton, Neil A. *Militias in America.* Santa Barbara, Calif.: ABC-CLIO, 1996.

Harris, John. *Clones, Genes, and Immortality: Ethics and the Genetic Revolution.* New York and Oxford: Oxford University Press, 1998.

Hilin, Hank. *Al Gore, Jr.: His Life and Career.* Secaucus, N.J.: Carol Publishing Group, 1992.

Holtz, Geoffrey T. *Welcome to the Jungle: The Why Behind "Generation X."* New York: St. Martin's Press, 1995.

Howe, Neil, and Bill Strauss. *13th Gen.* New York: Vintage Books, 1993.

Jacobs, A. J. "Mr. Seinfeld's Neighborhood." *Entertainment Weekly.*

Kifner, John. "Pakistan Sets Off Atom Test Again, But Urges 'Peace'." *New York Times,* 31 May 1998.

King, Norman. *Everybody Loves Oprah!: Her Remarkable Life Story.* New York: Morrow, 1988.

Krepinevich, Andrew F., and Steven M. Kosiak. "Smarter Bombs, Fewer Nukes." *Bulletin of the Atomic Scientists* (1 November 1998): 26+.

Lacayo, Richard. "The Two Americas." Time (18 May 1992): 28+.

Langworth, Richard. *Fifty Years of American Automobiles.* New York: Beekman House, 1989.

Lerner, Jacqueline V. *Working Women and Their Families.* Thousand Oaks, Calif.: Sage Publications, 1994.

Ludvigsen, Karl. *The Encyclopedia of the American Automobile.* New York: Exeter Books, 1982.

"MAADA: American Automobile Industry Turns 100." Metro Atlanta Automobile Dealers Association. http://www.maada.com/museum/exhibit.html.

Maraniss, David. *First in His Class: A Biography of Bill Clinton.* New York: Simon & Schuster, 1995.

Meyers, Carole Terwilliger. "Kramer's Reality Tour of NYC's Upper West Side." Carousel Press. 1999. http://www.carousel-press.com/kramer.html.

Miller, Berna. "The Echo Bust Continues." *American Demographics* (November 1997).

Moschovitis, Christos, Hilary Poole, Tami Schuyler, and Theresa Senft. *History of the Internet: A Chronology, 1843 to the Present.* Santa Barbara, Calif.: ABC-CLIO, 1999.

Newman, Katherine S. *Declining Fortunes: The Withering of the American Dream.* New York: Basic Books, 1993.

"The Older-Mom Birth Bonanza?" *American Demographics* (September 1996).

Peterson, Peter, G. "Will America Grow Up Before It Grows Old?" *The Atlantic Monthly* (May 1998).

Pilat, Joseph F., and Walter L. Kirchner. "The Technological Promise of Counter-proliferation." *Washington Quarterly* (Winter 1995): 153+.

Polson, Gary, and Lora Polson. "The Virtual Pet Home Page." May 24, 1999. http://www.virtualpet.com/vp.

"Preparatory Commission for the Comprehensive Nuclear-Test-Ban Treaty Organization (CTBTO PrepCom), Vienna." CTBTO PrepCom Open Web Site. June 14, 1999. http://www.ctbto.org/ctbto/index.shtml.

Russell, Cheryl. "Boomers May Go Bust." *American Demographics* (August 1998): 14+.

———. "Why Teen Births Boom." *American Demographics* (September 1995).

Samp, Jef. "Critical Thoughts About Tamagotchi."
http://www.sims.berkeley.edu/courses/is296a-3/s97/Focus
/Identity/FINAL.

Sanger, David E. "N. Korea Consents to U.S. Inspection of a
Suspect Site." *New York Times*, 17 March 1999.

Seinfeld, Jerry. *The Seinfeld Scripts: The First & Second
Seasons*. New York: HarperPerennial, 1998.

Shenon, Philip. "Suspected North Korean Atom Site Is
Empty, U.S. Finds." *New York Times*, 28 May 1999.

Stern, Kenneth S. *A Force Upon the Plain: The American
Militia Movement and the Politics of Hate*. New York:
Simon & Schuster, 1996.

Sublette, Carrey. "Nuclear Weapon Nations and Arsenals."
February 20, 1999.
http://www.fas.org/nuke/hew/Nwfaq/Nfaq7.html.

Thau, Richard D., and Jay S. Heflin, eds. *Generations Apart:
Xers vs. Boomers vs. the Elderly*. Amherst, N.Y.:
Prometheus Books, 1997.

Tracy, Kathleen. *Jerry Seinfeld: The Entire Domain*.
Seacaucus, N.J.: Birch Lane Press Book, Carol Publishing
Group, 1998.

"Treaties." U.S. Arms Control and Disarmament Agency.
http://www.acda.gov/treaties.htm.

Weber, Joseph, and Amy Barrett. "Viagra: The New Era of
Lifestyle Drugs." *Business Week* (May 11, 1998).

Whitman, David. "The Shifting State of Black Ghettos." *U.S.
News & World Report* (January 18, 1993): 33+.

Wild, David. *Seinfeld: The Totally Unauthorized Tribute (not
that there's anything wrong with that)*. New York: Three
Rivers Press, 1998.

"Will Boomers Finally Start Saving?" *American
Demographics* (June 1996).

Wood, Jonathan. *Great American Cars*. New York: Gallery
Books, 1985.

Chapter Eight: The Future

Coley, Richard J. "Computers and Classrooms: The Status of
Technology in U.S. Schools." Educational Testing Center.
1999. http://www.ets.org/research/pic/compclass.html.

Crispell, Diane. "Generations to 2025." *American
Demographics* (January 1995).

Dychtwald, Kenneth, and Joe Flower. *Age Wave: How the
Most Important Trend of Our Time Will Change Our
Future*. New York: Bantam Doubleday Dell Publishing,
1990.

Edmondson, Brad. "Children in 2001." *American
Demographics* (March 1997): 14+.

"The Minority Majority in 2001." *American Demographics*
(October 1996).

"Falling Through the Net: Americans and the Digital Divide."
National Telecommunications and Information
Administration; U.S. Department of Commerce. 1999.
http://www.ntia.doc.gov/ntiahome/fttn99/

Heilbroner, Richard L. *An Inquiry Into the Human Prospect*.
New York: W. W. Norton, 1975.

Karlen, Neal. "And the Meek Shall Inherit Nothing." *New
York Times*, 29 July 1999. F1+.

Manning, Robert. "The Nuclear Age: The Next Chapter."
Foreign Policy (December 22, 1997): 70+.

National Center for Education Statistics. "Advanced
Telecommunications in U.S. Public Elementary and
Secondary Schools, Fall 1996." U.S. Department of
Education, 1997.

"New Studies Show Children As Caregivers for Aging
Parents." *Elder Law Issues* 4, 40. 1993–1999.
http://www.elder-law.com/elder/1997/issue440.html

President's Committee of Advisors on Science and
Technology. "Report to the President on the Use of

Technology to Strengthen K-12 Education in the United
States." March 1997.
http://www.whitehouse.gov/WH/EOP/OSTP/NSTC/PCAS
T/k-12ed.html.

Reich, Robert B. *The Work of Nations: Preparing Ourselves
for 21st-Century Capitalism*. New York: Knopf, 1991.

Russell, Cheryl. *The Baby Boom: Americans Aged 35 to 64*.
Ithaca, N.Y.: New Strategist Publications, 1999.

Appendix I and II

Brown, Gerry, and Mike Morrison. *The 2000 ESPN
Information Please Sports Almanac*. New York:
Hyperion, 1999.

Brunner, Borgna, ed. *1998 Information Please Almanac*.
New York: Houghton Mifflin Co., 1998.

Congress.Org. Home Page. http://congress.org.

"The Governors, Political Affiliations, and Terms of Office,
1999." NGA Online.
http://www.nga.org/Governor/GovMasterList.htm.

Internet Movie Database at Internet Movie Database.
1999. http://us.imdb.com.

"Profiles of Clinton Cabinet Members." Facts On File
News Services. May 1, 1997.
http://www.facts.com/wnd/cabinet.htm.

"Senators of the 106th Congress." United States Senate.
http://www.senate.gov/senators/index.cfm.

U.S. Bureau of the Census. *Statistical Abstract of the
United States*. Washington, D.C., various volumes.

The U.S. House of Representatives Member Office Web
Services. House Information Resources.
http://www.house.gov/house/MemberWWW.html.

Chart and Map Sources

Chapter One: The War Years

The Home Front
Map (p. 9): Berlage, Gai Ingham. *Women in Baseball: The Forgotten History.* Westport, Conn.: Praeger Publishers, 1994.

Johnson, Susan E. *When Women Played Hardball.* Seattle, Wash.: Seal Press, 1994.

Trinity
Map (p. 13): "Map of A-bomb Damage." Hiroshima Peace Museum.
http://www.city.hiroshima.jp/image/ABombDamage/damage-map.gif.

Chapter Two: The Late 1940s

Population and Family
Chart (p. 18): Federal Security Agency, Public Health Service, National Office of Vital Statistics. *Vital Statistics–Special reports 34, 1.*

Map (pp. 18–19): Federal Security Agency, Public Health Service, National Office of Vital Statistics.

Education
Map (pp. 20–21): Department of Veterans Affairs. Washington, D.C.

Economics
Map (p. 23): U.S. Bureau of the Census. U.S. Census of Business. Washington, D.C.

Cultural Currents
Chart (p. 24): Department of Agriculture. Annual Report of Bureau of Agricultural Economics and Federal Power Commission. Washington, D.C.

The Bomb: The Iron Curtain
Map (p. 31): "Welcome to the George C. Marshall Foundation." George C. Marshall Foundation. September 27, 1999. http://www.gcmarshallfdn.org/.

The Protest: The Civil Rights Movement
Chart (p. 33): Martin Luther King, Jr., National Historic Site. January 5, 1998.
www.nps.gov/malu/documents/jim_crow_laws.htm.

The Tube: On the Air
Chart (p. 34): U.S. Government Printing Office. *Historical Statistics of the United States: Colonial Times to 1970,* Series R 93-105. Washington, D.C., 1976.

Chapter Three: The 1950s

Population and Family
Map (pp. 42–43): U.S. Bureau of the Census. U.S. Census of the Population. Washington, D.C.

Education
Map (p. 44): U.S. Bureau of the Census. *Statistical Abstract of the United States.* Washington, D.C., various volumes.

Economics
Map (pp. 46–47): U.S. Bureau of the Census. Income of Families and Persons in the United States. Washington, D.C.

Cultural Currents
Map (p. 48): Department of Commerce, Bureau of Public Roads and Highway Statistics. *Statistics Summary to 1945* and subsequent annual reports. Washington, D.C.

The Bomb: Cold War Politics
Map (pp. 54–55): Atomic Archive. http://www.atomicarchive.com.

Wasserman, Harvey, and Norman Solomon. *Killing Our Own.* New York: Delacorte Press, 1982.

The Bomb: Cold War Culture
Chart (p. 57): "The Astounding B Monster: A Movie

History and the People Who Made It." The Astounding B Monster. http://www.bmonster.com/index.html.

B.O.S.C.H. B-Movie Guide.
http://huizen.dds.nl/~penquin/index_frame.html.

Internet Movie Database at Internet Movie Database. 1999. http://us.imdb.com.

"Leonard Maltin Summary." Internet Movie Database. 1999. http://us.imdb.com.

The Horror Movie Database. 1998.
http://www.drcasey.com/cgi-bin/template?page=main-movie.

"Oh, the Humanity: The Worst Movies on Earth."
http://www.ohthehumanity.com.

The Protest: Desegregation
Chart (p. 59): (A.) Alabama Department of Archives and History. Code of the City of Montgomery, Alabama. Charlottesville: Michie City Publishing Co., 1952.
(B.) and (C.) Alabama Department of Archives and History. Inez Jessie Baskin Papers. Montgomery, Alabama.

The Tube: "Rilly Big Shews"
Map (p. 61): U.S. Bureau of the Census. *Statistical Abstract of the United States.* Washington, D.C., various volumes.

The Tube: Hollywood Strikes Back
Chart (p. 62): U.S. Bureau of the Census. *Statistical Abstract of the United States.* Washington, D.C., various volumes.

Map (pp. 62–63): U.S. Bureau of the Census. Statistical Abstract of the United States. Washington, D.C., various volumes.

Attack of the Suburb!
Map (pp. 64–65): U.S. Bureau of the Census. *Statistical Abstract of the United States.* Washington, D.C., various volumes.

Chapter Four: The 1960s

Population and Family
Chart (p. 76): U.S. Bureau of the Census. *Statistical Abstract of the United States.* Washington, D.C., various volumes.

Chart (p. 77): Department of Labor, Bureau of Labor Statistics: monthly reports, "Employment and Earnings." Washington, D.C.

Education
Map (pp. 78–79): Fraser, Ronald, et al. *1968: A Student Generation in Revolt.* New York: Pantheon Books, 1988.

Miller, James. *"Democracy Is in the Streets": From Port Huron to the Siege of Chicago.* New York: Simon & Schuster, 1987.

Economics
Map (pp. 80–81): Executive Office of the President, Office of Economic Opportunity. unpublished data.

Cultural Currents
Map (p. 83): Department of Justice, Federal Bureau of Investigation. *Uniform Crime Reports for the United States,* Washington, D.C.

The Bomb: The Cuban Missile Crisis
Map (p. 89): This map is an interpretation of a diagram used during the Cuban Missile Crisis. Original diagram located at the "The Cuban Missile Crisis: Washington Journal Feature, 35 Years Later."
http://www.c-span.org/guide/society/cuba/.

The Protest: From Civil Rights to Black Power
Map (p. 90): Williams, Juan. *Eyes on the Prize: America's Civil Rights Years, 1954–1965.* New York: Penguin USA, 1988.

Hampton, Henry, ed. *Voices of Freedom: An Oral History of the Civil Rights Movement From the 1950s Through the 1980s.* Reissue edition. New York: Bantam Books, 1991.

The Protest: War Is Over ... If You Want It
Chart (p. 93): Fraser, Ronald, et al. *1968: A Student Generation in Revolt.* New York: Pantheon Books, 1988.

Miller, James. *"Democracy Is in the Streets": From Port Huron to the Siege of Chicago.* New York: Simon & Schuster, 1987.

The Protest: R-E-S-P-E-C-T
Charts (p. 94–95): Gallup, George H. *The Gallup Poll: Public Opinion,* 1935–1971, Vol. 3. New York: Random House, 1972.

Vietnam War
Map (p. 99): "Battlefield: Vietnam." Public Broadcasting System.
http://www.pbs.org/battlefieldvietnam/index.html.

Summers, Harry G., Jr. *Vietnam War Almanac.* New York: Facts On File, 1985.

"The Vietnam War: 1961–1970." MultiEDUCATOR.
http://www.multied.com/vietnam.

Vietnam Soldiers
Map (pp. 100–101): U.S. Bureau of the Census. *Statistical Abstract of the United States.* Washington, D.C., various volumes.

What a Long, Strange Trip
Map (pp. 102–103): Artist's rendering based on setlists located at "Grateful Dead Tour By Tour Project."
http://www.math.ukans.edu/tbt/.

If You're Going to San Francisco ...
Map (p. 105): Gaskin, Stephen. *Haight Ashbury Flashbacks.* Berkeley, Calif: Ronin Publishing, 1998.

Hoskins, Barney. *Beneath the Diamond Sky: Haight-Ashbury 1965-1970.* New York: Simon & Schuster, 1997.

Perry, Charles. *The Haight Ashbury: A History.* New York: Random House, Inc., 1985.

Technology: To the Moon
Map (p. 108): Rükl, Antonín. *Atlas of the Moon.* Edited by Dr. T. W. Rackham. Translated by Jana Hajnovicová. Waukesha, Wis. Kalmbach Publishing Company, 1996.

Chapter Five: The 1970s

Population and Family
Map (pp. 116–17): U.S. National Center for Health Statistics, *Vital Statistics of the United States,* annual, and *Monthly Vital Statistics Report.* Washington, D.C.

Chart (p. 117): Bureau of the Census. *Historical Statistics of the United States: Colonial Times to 1970.* Washington, D.C.

Education
Chart (p. 118): *National College Bound Seniors,* annual. New York: College Entrance Examination Board, annual.

Map (p. 119): Formisano, Ronald P. *Boston Against Busing: Race, Class, Ethnicity in the 1960s and 1970s.* Chapel Hill and London: University of North Carolina Press, 1991.

Economics
Chart (p. 120): U.S. Employment and Training Administration, *Manpower Report of the President,* Washington, D.C. annual.

Map (pp. 120–21): U.S. Employment and Training Administration, *Manpower Report of the President,* Washington, D.C., annual.

Cultural Currents
Chart (p. 122 and p. 123): Seymour, Martin Lipset, and William Schneider. *The Confidence Gap: Business, Labor,*

and Government in the Public Mind. Rev. ed. Baltimore, Md.: The Johns Hopkins University Press, 1987.

The Bomb: The Arms Race

Chart (pp. 128 and p. 129): "The NRDC Nuclear Program: Nuclear Data." Natural Resources Defense Council. 1997.
http://www.nrdc.org/nrdcpro/nudb/datab10.html.

The Protest: Militancy Grows

Map (pp. 130–31): American Indian Movement Grand Governing Council.
http://www.aimovement.org/index.html.
Means, Russell, and Marvin J. Wolf. *Where White Men Fear to Tread: The Autobiography of Russell Means.* New York: St. Martin's Press, 1995.
"The Occupation of Wounded Knee." The Web Environment at U-M. http://www-personal.umich.edu/~jamarcus/wknee.htm.
"Russell Means." American Indian Movment.
http://www.russellmeans.com/aim.html.
Smith, Paul Chaat, and Robert Allen Warrior. *Like A Hurricane: The Indian Movement from Alcatraz to Wounded Knee.* New York: The New Press, 1996.
Stern, Kenneth S. *Loud Hawk: The United States versus the American Indian Movement.* Norman and London: University of Oklahoma Press, 1994.

Protest: Environmentalism

Map (pp. 132–33): Container Recycling Institute. August 18, 1999. http://www.container-recycling.org.
Earthday Network Home. http://www.earthday.org.
"Earth Day 1970 & 1990: Historical Precedents." Earth Day Network.
http://www.cco.caltech.edu/~cetfers/unused/eday.history.html.
"EDF Wins Injunction in Tellico Case." Environmental Defense Fund. 1973. http://www.edf.org/pubs/EDF-Letter/1973/Jan/c_tellico.html.
Environmental Disaster Timeline. Earthbase, Inc. 1996.
http://www.earthbase.org/home/timeline/indexa.html.
"Federal Historic Preservation Case Law, 1966-1996, Case 13." Advisory Council on Historic Preservation.
http://www.achp.gov/book/case13.html.
"Historical Overview of the Exxon Valdez Oil Spill." Official Exxon Valdez Oil Spill Restoration Web Site. 1997. http://www.oilspill.state.ak.us/nwhistory.html.
"Love Canal @ 20." University at Buffalo. 1998, 1999.
http://ublib.buffalo.edu/libraries/units/sel/exhibits/love-canal.html.
"Meltdown at Three Mile Island." PBS Online. 1999.
http://www.pbs.org/wgbh/pages/amex/three.
"Santa Barbara's Oil Disaster." Santa Barbara Wildlife Care Network. January 28, 1998.
http://ourworld.compuserve.com/homepages/sbwcn/spill.htm.
"Spill Profiles." U.S. Environment Protection Agency. March 1, 1999.
http://www.epa.gov/oerrpage/oilspill/oilprofs.htm.
"Three Mile Island 2 Accident." U.S. Nuclear Regulatory Commission. http://www.nrc.gov/OPA/gmo/tip/tmi.htm.
"The Trans Alaska Pipeline System (TAPS)." The Dalton Management Unit. December 16, 1998.
http://www.ndo.ak.blm.gov/dalton/pipe1.htm.

Watergate

Map (p. 137): Farnsworth, Malcolm. "Watergate." VCEpolitics.com. 1999. http://vcepolitics.com/wgate.htm.
"Watergate 25." The Washington Post Company. 1997.

http://www.washingtonpost.com/wp-srv/national/longterm/watergate/front.htm.
"Watergate: the 25th Anniversary." MSNBC's Time and Again 2000. http://www.msnbc.com/onair/msnbc/time-andagain/archive/watergate/timeline.asp.

Chapter Six: The 1980s

Population and Family

Chart (p. 146): U.S. National Center for Health Statistics. *Vital Statistics of the United States,* annual; Monthly Vital Statistics Report; and unpublished data. Washington D.C.
Map (p. 146–47): Immigration and Naturalization Service. *Statistical Yearbook.* Washington, D.C., 1982, 1988.
Chart (p. 147): Immigration and Naturalization Service. *Statistical Yearbook.* Washington, D.C., 1982, 1988.

Education

Chart (p. 148): *The Digest of Education Statistics: 1996.* National Center for Education Statistics. National Education Association: Washington, D.C., unpublished data.
The Northwester Lindquiest-Endicott Report. Evanston, Ill.: Northwester University Placement Center.
Chart (p. 149): The Annual Gallup Poll of the Public's Attitudes Toward the Public Schools. *Phi Delta Kappan* (various years).

Economics

Chart (p. 150): U.S. Bureau of the Census, *Current Population Reports.* Bureau of the Census. Washington, D.C.

Cultural Currents

Chart (p. 153): U.S. Bureau of the Census. *Current Population Reports,* series P-20, No. 440 and earlier reports. Bureau of the Census: Washington, D.C.
U.S. Bureau of the Census. *Statistical Abstract of the United States.* Bureau of the Census: Washington, D.C., various volumes.
Map (p. 153): U.S. Bureau of the Census, Statistical Abstract of the United States. Bureau of the Census. Washington, D.C., various volumes.

The Bomb: The Arms Race

Map (p. 158-59): U.S. Bureau of the Census. Statistical Abstract of the United States. Bureau of the Census, Washington, D.C., various volumes.

The Protest: Matters of Life and Death

Map (p. 160-61): "Major U.S. Supreme Court Rulings on Reproductive Health and Rights." Planned Parenthood. May 23, 1997.
www.plannedparenthood.org/ABOUT/NARRHISTORY/court.html.
"Supreme Court Decisions Concerning Reproductive Rights: A Chronology 1965–1998." NARAL. December 1998. http://www.naral.org/publications/facts/sup.html.

Chapter Seven: The 1990s

Population and Family

Charts (p. 174): "Selected Social Characteristics of Baby Boomers 26 to 44 years old: 1990." U.S. Bureau of Census. February 1996.
http://www.census.gov/population/censusdata/cph-l-160s.txt.
Map (p. 174-75): "Selected Social Characteristics of Baby Boomers 26 to 44 years old: 1990." U.S. Bureau of Census. February 1996.
http://www.census.gov/population/censusdata/

cph-l-160s.txt.

Education

Map and Chart (p. 177): U.S. Bureau of the Census. *Statistical Abstract of the United States.* Washington, D.C., various volumes.

Economics

Charts (p. 178 and p. 179): "Selected Social Characteristics of Baby Boomers 26 to 44 years old: 1990." U.S. Bureau of Census. February 1996.
http://www.census.gov/population/censusdata/cph-l-160s.txt.

Cultural Currents

Chart (p. 181): *The Gallup Poll Monthly* (October 1995).

The Bomb: After the Cold War... What?

Map (pp. 186–87): Sublette, Carey. "Nuclear Weapons Frequently Asked Questions: Nuclear Weapon Nations and Arsenals." High Energy Weapons Archive. February 20, 1999.
http://www.fas.org/nuke/hew/Nwfaq/Nfaq7.html.

The Protest: The Left and the Right

Map (pp. 188–89): Hamilton, Neil A. *Militias in America.* Santa Barbara, Calif.: ABC-CLIO, 1996.

Tube: An Era of Choice

Map (p. 191): Jacobs, A. J. "Mr. Seinfeld's Neighborhood." *Entertainment Weekly.*
Meyers, Carole Terwilliger. "Kramer's Reality Tour Of NYC's Upper West Side." Carousel Press. 1999.
http://www.carousel-press.com/kramer.html.
Seinfeld, Jerry. *The Seinfeld Scripts: The First & Second Seasons.* New York: HarperPerennial, 1998.
Tracy, Kathleen. *Jerry Seinfeld: The Entire Domain.* Secaucus, N.J.: Birch Lane Press Book; Carol Publishing Group, 1998.
Wild, David. *Seinfeld: The Totally Unauthorized Tribute (not that there's anything wrong with that).* New York: Three Rivers Press, 1998.

Family and Faith Revisited

Chart (p. 196): U.S. Bureau of the Census. *Statistical Abstract of the United States.* Washington, D.C., various volumes.
Chart (p. 197): U.S. Bureau of the Census. *Statistical Abstract of the United States.* Washington, D.C., various volumes.

Chapter Eight: The Future

Population and Family

Map (p. 206-207): U.S. Bureau of the Census. *Statistical Abstract of the United States.* Washington, D.C., various volumes.

Education

Map and Charts (pp. 208–209): Coley, Richard J. "Computers and Classrooms: The Status of Technology in U.S. Schools." Policy Information Testing Center, Educational Testing Service, 1999.
http://www.ets.org/research/pic/compclass.html.

Economics

Charts (p. 210 and p. 211): Poulos, Stacy, and Demetra Smith Nightingale. *The Aging Baby Boom: Implications for Employment and Training Programs.* Washington, D.C.: The Urban Institute, 1999.

Contributors

Neil A. Hamilton holds a master's degree from the University of Miami in Coral Gables, Florida, and a doctorate from the University of Tennessee–Knoxville. He is a professor of history at Spring Hill College in Mobile, Alabama, and has written articles and books on history and popular culture, including *The ABC-CLIO Companion to the 1960s Counterculture in America.* He lives in Fairhope, Alabama.

Jon Keith Brunelle is a writer and performer living in New York City. He is the author of various short theater pieces and two full-length solo works: *Sunday Afternoon in the Unisphere,* commissioned by Franklin Furnace for their cybercast series, and *Tales from the Dancing Egg,* which enjoyed a run at Manhattan's 13th Street Repertory Theatre.

Beth Scully is a comedy writer. A former political consultant, she lives in Brooklyn, New York, with her television set and her partner.

Rebecca Sherman is member of the National Writers Union. She writes about cultural issues, human rights, and public health from her home outside Boston, Massachusetts.